Genealogical Abstracts from
The Democratic Mirror
and
The Mirror
1857-1879
Loudoun County Virginia

Patricia B. Duncan

HERITAGE BOOKS
2008

HERITAGE BOOKS
AN IMPRINT OF HERITAGE BOOKS, INC.

Books, CDs, and more—Worldwide

For our listing of thousands of titles see our website
at
www.HeritageBooks.com

Published 2008 by
HERITAGE BOOKS, INC.
Publishing Division
100 Railroad Ave. #104
Westminster, Maryland 21157

Copyright © 2008 Patricia B. Duncan

All rights reserved. No part of this book may be reproduced or transmitted in any form or by any means, electronic or mechanical, including photocopying, recording or by any information storage and retrieval system without written permission from the author, except for the inclusion of brief quotations in a review.

International Standard Book Numbers
Paperbound: 978-0-7884-4577-4
Clothbound: 978-0-7884-7658-7

INTRODUCTION

This book provides abstracts of articles containing genealogical or other historical information from The *Democratic Mirror and The Mirror* newspapers of Loudoun County, Virginia. The *Democratic Mirror* newspapers were published 1857-1861, with later issues titled *The Mirror*.

Microfilms of the following Loudoun County newspapers are available through the Interlibrary Loan service of the Library of Virginia.

    The Democratic Mirror and *The Mirror* newspapers:
    (Library of Virginia Reel Series 284)

        17 Jun 1857 - 4 Dec 1861
        14 Jun 1865 - 31 Dec 1874
        12 Jul 1865 – 31 Oct 1878
        7 Jan 1875 - 25 Feb 1879
        6 Feb 1879 - 15 Nov 1883
        1 Jan 1880 - 27 Dec 1883
        24 Jan 1884 - 27 Dec 1888
        3 Jan 1889 - 31 Dec 1891
        7 Jan 1892 - 20 Dec 1894
        3 Jan 1895 - 16 Dec 1897
        6 Jan 1898 - 27 Dec 1900
        3 Jan 1884 - 31 Oct 1901
        1 Jan 1901 - 7 Aug 1902
        4 Jun 1908 - 24 Dec 1919
        4 Jul 1913 - 22 Dec 1916

    The Loudoun Telephone newspapers:
    (Library of Virginia Reel Series 363)

        7 Jan 1881 - 26 Dec 1884
        2 Jan 1885 - 21 Dec 1888
        4 Jan 1889 - 25 Dec 1891
        1 Jan 1892 - 28 Apr 1893
        4 May 1894 - 11 Sep 1896

Some of the above reels show overlapping dates. Although some issues appeared on both reels, most reels contain mainly issues that do not appear in the other reels. There are also a number of missing issues in each series.

The front page of each issue usually consisted of business cards and general entertainment articles. Subsequent pages contained advertisements and legal notices, local general and personal news, obituaries, marriage announcements, and some national and international news.

Although some entries in this book are the complete article, many are shortened abstracts. Marriage announcements and obituaries were sometimes long and flowery, and parts have been omitted here.

Abbreviations may have been used in these abstracts. Administrator/Administratrix may be abbreviated as Admr. and Executor/Executrix as Exor. Ages are often shortened to year month day (y m d.) Months are sometimes abbreviated and dau. might be used as an abbreviation for daughter.

As with any transcription of records, it is advisable to obtain a copy of the original document to verify the accuracy. Although every effort is made to transcribe accurately, mistakes are inevitable.

Special thanks to the Library of Virginia and the Special Collections Library of Albuquerque, New Mexico.

The Democratic Mirror
Wednesday, 17 June 1857   Vol. II, No. 41

The Democratic Mirror
Published at Leesburg, Loudoun County, Virginia
Editor Josiah B. TAYLOR
Publisher Benjamin F. SHEETZ

Wednesday, 17 June 1857   Vol. II, No. 41

The Alexandria *Sentinel*, the death of Col. Wm. R. SMITH, of Fauquier, father of the editor of that paper.

[MISSING ISSUES]

Wednesday, 15 September 1858   Vol. IV, No. 1

Married: On Wednesday evening, the 8th inst., by Rev. H. R. SMITH, Stephen H. GIBBONS and Sarah E. McKIM, all of Leesburg.

Married: On the 5th instant, at the Parsonage, by Rev. Thomas SEWELL, James V. B. PILCHER, of Baltimore, formerly of Harper's Ferry, to Miss Margaret Jane WORFORD, youngest daughter of Elizabeth and Abraham WORFORD, Esq. of Loudoun.

Died: In Washington City, on the morning of the 2d instant, William B., son of Landon W. and Louisa WORTHINGTON, in his 29th year.

Died: In Washington City, on Tuesday the 7th inst., Mrs. Louisa WORTHINGTON, wife of L. W. WORTHINGTON, in her 48th year.

Died: In this town, on Monday evening last, Carlene B., daughter of Geo. D. and Annie WILLIAMSON, aged 2y 6m 16d.

Died: In this town, on Sunday evening last, Virginia B., infant daughter of Dr. E. S. and Roena E. CASTLE, aged 14 months.

Died: In Leesburg, on the 30th ultimo, Owen Chapman, infant son of James and Ann Eliza MUSE, aged 2m 1d.

Died: In this town, on Sunday week, Charles HOUGH, son of L. W. S. and Sarah HOUGH, aged 3y 3m 16d.

Wednesday, 22 September 1858   Vol. IV, No. 2

Married: In Hillsboro, at the Parsonage, on the 13th instant, by the Rev. Wm. S. BAIRD, Mr. Geo. Henry ALLEN and Miss Martha JONES, both of Loudoun.

Married: On the 5th instant, by Rev. Wm. S. HAMMOND, Mr. Partick [Patrick] CARROLL and Miss Mary Jane SNOOTS, daughter of Mr. John SNOOTS, of Loudoun.

Died: In Union, Loudoun Co., on Saturday morning the 11th inst., of croup, William Hirst, son of Rev. A. and Martha E. ROBEY, aged 3y 10m 6d.

Died: On the 15th August last at his residence in this county, Thomas GREGG, in the 79th year of his age.

Wednesday, 39 [29] September 1858 Vol. IV, No. 3

Hon. Henry BEDINGER – minister to Copenhagen, arrived in this county on Tuesday last, after an abscence of five years.

Married: On Thursday morning, 16th inst., at the residence of the bride's father in Fauquier, by Rev. J. H. WAUGH, E. B. MANTOR, Esq., of Clarke and Miss Hattie N. OREAR, daughter of Enock OREAR.

Wednesday, 6 October 1858 Vol. IV, No. 4

Married: In Leesburg, on Wednesday, 29th ult, by Rev. Saml. GOVER, Benjamin D. RIDGEWAY to Miss Elizabeth T. SHELL, all of Loudoun.

Married: On the 30th, in Leesburg by Rev. S. GOVER, Mr. William T. DICKEY, to Miss Eliza A. CUMMINGS, all of Loudoun.

Died: On the 25th inst., at the residence of their grandfather, Mr. John S. KNOX, of Fauquier Co, William G., aged 7 years, son of Wm. G. and M. C. SOMMERVILLE. Also later on the same day, James, aged 13, eldest son of the same parents. Thus in less than ten days four children have been taken from this afflicted family.

Wednesday, 13 October 1858 Vol. IV, No. 5

Married: At "Chantilly," Fairfax Co, on Thursday morning, the 7th instant, by the Right Rev. Bishop JOHNS of Virginia, Mr. Kersey JOHNS, son of Bishop JOHNS, of Maryland, and Miss Laura STUART, daughter of the late C. C. STUART, Esq. of Fairfax Co.

Married: In Washington on the 5th instant, by the Rev. Andrew G. CAROTHERS, Mr. John T. MILLER, of Washington, to Miss Catharine K. SHEID, of Loudoun Co.

Married: On the 5th inst. at Morrisonville, by Rev. J. T. EAKIN, Mr. Joseph GORMAN, of Jefferson, formerly of Clarke Co, to Miss Mary C. LYNN, of Loudoun Co.

Married: On the 4th inst., by Rev. S. V. BLAKE, Chas. HAYMAKER and Miss Margaret CLARKE, dau. of Wm. C. CLARKE, all of Jefferson.

Married: On the 28th ult, by the same, Wm. GRUBBS, of Clarke Co, and Mary C. FOREMAN, of Frederick Co.

Died: On the 24th ult, Mrs. Virginia SOWERS, consort of Daniel H. SOWERS Esq., of Clarke Co.

Died: On the 29th ult, near Hard Scrabble, Berkeley Co, Miss Susan MYERS, aged about 30 years.

Died: On Friday week, in Charlestown, after a severe illness, Irianna Kearney, second child of Mr. Wm. L. HEDGES, in her 7th year.

Died: At Harpers Ferry, on the 28th ult., of an acute and suffering illness, arising from a fearful fall, whereby his arm was terribly broken, Geo. S. FORTNEY, son of G. W. and Mary E. FORTNEY, aged 8y 11m.

Died: On the 13th of Aug, at his residence in Green Co, Ohio, where he had resided since 1833, Samuel HOWELL, formerly of Charlestown, VA, in the 96th year of his age.

Died: On Sunday the 26th ult, after a short illness, Mr. Alfred TAYLOR, of Harpers Ferry, aged about 50 years.

Wednesday, 20 October 1858   Vol. IV, No. 6

Mr. Wm. H. SAUNDERS, formerly of Leesburg, has been appointed Constable for the District of Columbia.

Married: In Leesburg on Tuesday evening, Oct. 12th by the Rev. O. A. KINSOLVING, Alexander H. ROGERS, and Julia, only daughter of Dr. Thomas H. CLAGGETT, all of Loudoun Co.

Married: At Woodville, Fairfax Co, by Rev. Mr. BROWN, on the morning of the 7th inst., Geo. OTTWUNDER, formerly of Shenandoah Co, to Miss Annie M., dau. of the late Wm. COCKRELL, Esqr.

Married: On Thursday evening, the 14th of Oct, by Rev. And. ROBEY, Mr. Andrew J. LLOYD, to Miss Sarah J. STICKLES, both of Clark Co, Va.

Departed this life on the 29th of September, at her residence in Richmond Co, Va, after a protracted illness, Mrs. Elizabeth McAdam BEACHAM, in the 69th year of her age. For upwards of 48 years she was a member of the Baptist Church.

Died: Near Clarksburg, in this state, on the 24th of Sept, Arrean Elizabeth, youngest dau. of Benjamin and Nancy E. FRANKS, in the 3d year of her age.

Wednesday, 27 November [October] 1858   Vol. IV, No. 7

Married: In Leesburg, on the 21st instant, by Rev. S. GOVER, M. John H. THOMAS to Miss Margaret FARE, all of Loudoun.

Married: On the 14th inst., by Rev. W. S. BAIRD, Mr. Burr W. SIMPSON to Miss Elizabeth S. GROSS, both of Loudoun.

Married: At the house of Charles WILLIAMS, on Tuesday evening, the 12th inst., by Rev. Elder FURR, Mr. George M. FRY to Miss Elenor STOUT, dau. of John L. STOUT, all of Loudoun.

Married: On Monday, the 18th inst., by Rev. Thomas WARE, Mr. Eli CARTER to Miss Martha E. LUMM, all of Loudoun.

Married: At Winchester, on the 12th inst., by the Rev. James R. GRAHAM, George M. GORDON, of Washington, to Miss Virginia, dau. of Col. James P. , of the former place.

Wednesday, 3 November 1858   Vol. IV, No. 8

In Circuit Ct 24 Nov 1858 – Samuel PURSEL Jr., Exor and Amanda C. OSBURN, Ex. of Nicholas OSBURN dec'd against Daniel SHREVE in his own right and as Admr. wwa of Charles SHREVE dec'd, William SHREVE, Benjamin F. SHREVE, Charles W. SHREVE, Thomas J. SHREVE, Mary E. SHREVE, Ann O. SHREVE, Arthur B.

SHREVE, the four latter being infant children of Benjamin SHREVE and Ann Maria MINOR infant child of Ann E. MINOR and others.

Married: On the 21st Oct at Decoverly Hall, Montgomery Co Md., by Rev. Daniel MOTZER, Aurelius COE, Esq. of Loudoun Co, to Miss Maria Louis BELT, of the former place.

Married: In Winchester on Wednesday, the 20th inst., by the Rev. W. G. EGGLESTON, William H. BAKER, Esq., editor of the Berkeley Springs, *Constitution*, to Mrs. Emma CLARK, dau. of the late Col. Robert GUSTIN, all of Morgan Co, Va.

Married: At Edwards Ferry, by Rev. S. V. HOYLE, Oct. 21st, J. W. MORAN, Esq., and Margaret A. HOUSER, all of Loudoun.

Married: On Tuesday, the 26th of Oct, in Leesburg, by Rev. Samuel GOVER, Thadeus W. HANES and Catherine A. TORRISON, all of Loudoun.

Died: At the residence of her father, near Leesburg, Oct. 4th, Martha A. E. STEVENS, dau., of John and Roxanna STEVENS in the 10th year of her age.

Died: At the residence of John P. SMART, in this town, on Sunday morning last, Francis Ludwell, infant son of L. Henry and Henrietta LUCKETT.

Wednesday, 10 November 1858   Vol. IV, No. 9

Tom, a negro man belonging to Mrs. Leah HUTCHISON, of this county, killed a free negro, Reuben HURLEY, on Friday evening last, near Aldie.

Marietta, a slave belonging to Mr. John FRANCIS of this county, charged with infanticide, was tried before the County Court on Tuesday, found guilty and ordered to be transported.

Married: In St. Louis, on the 27th of Oct, in St. George's Church, by the Rev. E. BERKLEY, Benjamin GRAYSON, of Iowa, to Nannie S. RHODES, second daughter of H. H. RHODES, of Va, and grand daughter of the late Chas. Landon CARTER Esqr., of Fauquier Co.

Married: In Philadelphia, on the 2nd inst., by the Rev. W. R. DEWITT, D.D., Hon. John W. GEARY, Ex-Gov of Kansas, to Mrs. HENDERSON, of Cumberland, Pa.

Married: At Harmony, on Tuesday evening Nov 2d, by Rev. S. H. ROGERS, Mr. James W. GOODWIN to Miss Jane V. CUMMINS, of Loudoun.

Married: At the M. E. Church, on Thursday, 28th, ultimo at 6 o'clock, by the Rev. Mr. BROWN, John G. BEACH, to Miss Willie M. BARKER, both of Alexandria.

Married: On Wednesday evening, the 27th ultimo in Rockville, Md., by Rev. Mr. DOUGHERTY, Mr. William KILGOUR, of Cumberland, Md., to Miss Rose QUEEN of the former place.

Married: In the Presbyterian Church in Charlestown, on Thursday evening, 27th ult, by Rev. W. B. DUTTON, David HUMPHREYS,

Esq., to Miss Mary E. CAMERON, dau. of the late Samuel CAMERON, of this county.

Married: On the 3d instant, by the Rev. Dr. HARRISON at Parnwillallice, the residence of her father, Major William D. NUTT, Mr. Peter WISE, of Alexandria, and Miss Alice E. NUTT, of Alexandria Co.

Married: On the 3d instant, at St. Paul's Church by the Rev. James T. JOHNSTON, Mr. Baker W. JOHNSON, of Florida, to Sarah J. RAND, of Alexandria, Va.

Married: In Warrenton, on Tuesday morning, 2d inst., by Rev. R. R. GURLEY, Rev. John W. PUGH, Pastor of the Presbyterian Church of Warrenton, and Miss Ada C., dau. of William H. JENNINGS, Esq., Clerk of the County Court of Fauquier.

Married: On the 28th ultimo, by the Rev. D. B. EWING, Dr. Waller L. HOLLADAY to Miss Mary Bell HENDERSON, all of Orange Co, Va.

Married: In Clarke Co, on the 12th of October, 1858, by the Rev. G. W. WILLIAMS, J. Randolph GRIGSBY, Esq., formerly of Fairfax Co, to Miss Bettie M. ALEXANDER, all of Clarke Co, Va.

Married: On Sunday, the 31st Oct, by the Rev. C. CAST, Mr. Ludwig Henry STAUB, of Cumberland, formerly of Martinsburg, and Miss Catharine GRAZIER, of Martinsburg.

Wednesday, 17 November 1858   Vol. IV, No. 10

Negro Tom tried for murder of Reuben HURLEY – found guilty of murder in the Second Degree.

Died: At the residence, near the Rehoboth Church in the German Settlement, on Friday morning the 5th inst., after a protracted illness of several months, Peter COMPHER Sr., aged 81y 2m 12d.

Married: At Oakley, Fauquier Co, the residence of Henry S. DULANY, Esq. on Tuesday morning, the 2nd instant, by the Rev. O. A. KINSOLVING, Dr. Augustine S. MASON, of Falmouth, Va, to Mary M. ELIASON.

Married: On the 10th inst., by Rev. Chas. WHITE, Mr. John M. GIBSON, of Loudoun, and Miss Lydia K. SMITH, of Berryville.

Married: On Tuesday, 2d inst., in the Lutheran Church near Lovettsville, by Rev. J. B. ANTHONY, Mr. Blanco W. BRAMHALL, to Miss Rebecca Jane, dau. of John GRUBB, Esq.

Married: On Thursday, 4th inst., by the same, Mr. John LYND, to Miss Elizabeth BOREN, both of Loudoun.

Wednesday, 24 November 1858   Vol. IV, No. 11

Died: At the residence of his father in New Orleans, La, on the 26th of Aug, 1858, Erville Edwin, eldest son of James W. and Arthelia KEENE, aged 3y 3m.

Died: Near Waterford, on the 19th of Oct, Mary Eliza, the daughter of C. Means and Sarah J. VANDEVENTER, in her 7th year.

Married: In Leesburg, on Thursday, the 28th Oct, by the Rev. S. GOVER, James T. FLINN and Adeline V. WILEY, all of Loudoun.

Married: On the 14th inst., at the residence of Mr. James DAVIS, by Elder KIDWELL, Mr. R. S. DAVIS to Miss Ann FAIRFAX, and Mr. J. R. DAVIS to Miss Roxey GOSSUM; also Mr. L. DAVIS to Miss Harriet DAVIS, all of Prince William Co. Va.

Married: On Thursday, the 11th inst., at the Meadows, the residence of the bride's grandmother, in Louisa Co., John M. PATTON Jr., Esq. of Richmond, and Miss Sallie L. TAYLOR, dau. of Alexander TAYLOR, Esq.

Married: At the residence of the bride's father, in Highland, Howard Co, Mo, on the 31st ultimo, by the Rev. Green CAREY, Mr. John S. ROBINSON, of Boone Co, Mo, and Miss Parmelia M., dau. of Samuel PULLER, Esq., late of Fauquier Co Va.

Wednesday, 1 December 1858   Vol. IV, No. 12

Hon. Henry BEDINGER, our late minister to Denmark, died at Shepherdstown, Jefferson Co., on Friday morning last. On Tuesday previous he was attacked with pneumonia and died the succeeding Friday. He was a native of Jefferson Co. ...

Death of David CALDWELL at his residence in this town on Thursday morning last, in the 43d year of his age. On Friday morning at 7 o'clock, his remains were taken to the Episcopal Church, services by Rev. Mr. KINSOLVING, of Middleburg, and Rev. Dr. McCABE, of Baltimore. Body was taken to Richmond city for interment.

Married: In Emanuel Church, Baltimore, on Tuesday morning, the 22d of Nov. 1858, by Rev. Henry V. D. JOHNS, M. D., Arthur Lee ROGERS, of Leesburg, and Charlotte, daughter of the late Gen. George RUST of Loudoun Co.

Married: At the residence of the bride's father, on the evening of the 25th inst., by Rev. A. COMPTON, Mr. Albert G. SMITH and Miss Elizabeth C. BLACKWELL, eldest dau. of Mr. Jas. BLACKWELL, all of Fauquier Co.

Married: In Middleburg, on the 24th inst., Marietta F., dau. of Col. H. B. POWELL, to Richard C. HOLLYDAY, of Talbot Co., Md.

Married: In Washington, on Tuesday last, by the Rev. W. W. BENNETT, Rev. J. C. GRANBERRY, of the M. E. Church South, to Miss Virginia MASSEY, of Petersburg.

Married: Near Harpers Ferry on the 4th ultimo, by the Rev. Wm. S. BAIRD, Mr. Joseph YOUNG and Miss Mary Jane FOX, both of Loudoun.

Married: In Leesburg, on Thursday, the 11th ultimo, by Rev. Mr. DALBY, James W. DOWNS and Mary Ann THOMAS, all of Loudoun Co.

Died: In Washington on the 26th inst., suddenly, Mrs. Mary S. EDWARDS, consort of Alpheus L. EDWARDS, of the First Comptroller's Officer, formerly of Loudoun Co. On Wednesday last, as Mr. EDWARDS and his wife were walking in their garden, near the Northern Market House, She was so frightened by a ferocious dog springing against the fence in the attempt to seize her, that she died on Friday from the effects of the shock to her nervous system.

In Chancery, 23 Oct 1858 – John BRADFIELD & wife Ann, Oliver P. COLLIER & wife Jane Ann, Franklin BRADFIELD, George J. BLACK & wife Sarah M., Nathan BRADFIELD, John William BRADFIELD, Thomas W. CARROLL & wife Miriam E., Abraham N. BRADFIELD, Thomas D. BRADFIELD and Bushrod O. BRADFIELD against George H. ALLDER, Admr. dbn cta of Nathan NICHOLS dec'd and in his own right, Abraham ALLDER, John E. ALLDER, George F. ALLDER, Jane A. ALLDER, Rosannah ALLDER and Nathan ALLDER, A. H. ROGERS appointed his guardian ad litem – for interest in share of infant Nathan ALLDER.

Wednesday, 8 December 1858   Vol. IV, No. 13

Married: On the 30th ult., by Rev. Saml. GOVER, Joseph W. BROWN and Malinda P. WARNER, all of Loudoun.

Married: In Leesburg, on the same day, by the same, Alexander P. BRECKINRIDGE and Mrs. Susan B. SEEDERS, all of this place.

Married: On the 17th of Nov, at the Lutheran Parsonage at Harper's Ferry, by Rev. Mr. SMELTZER, Daniel LINK and Miss Maria B. OSBURNE, both of Jefferson Co.

Died: At the residence of his brother, B. P. NOLAND, Esq., in Middleburg, on the 29th ult., Noble B. NOLAND, son of Col. Lloyd NOLAND, in the 21st year of his age.

Wednesday, 15 December 1858   Vol. IV, No. 14

Married: In Waterford, on the 8th inst., by Rev. Sam. GOVER, Mr. William S. KEYES and Miss Virginia RINKER, all of Loudoun.

Married: On the 7th inst., at the residence of the bride's father, by Rev. O. A. KINSOLVING, Benj. S. WHITE, of Maryland and Mary Elizabeth, dau. of Joseph MEADE, of Loudoun Co.

Married: In Leesburg, on the 30th ult., at the M. E. Parsonage, by Rev. E. D. OWEN, Daniel L. SMITH and Mary G. MOORE.

Married: At the same time and place by the same, Jacob WORKING and Leanna C. MOORE, all of this county.

Married: On the 2nd inst., by the Rev. C. WALKER, Dr. G. F. MASON, on Charlestown, to Miss Margaret B. HOLLIDAY, dau. of Dr. R. J. McKim HOLLIDAY, of Winchester.

Married: At the residence of the bride's uncle, Mr. T. ROE, Muskingum Valley, Ohio, on the 8th inst., by Rev. Dr. JENNINGS, Mr. Levi WHITE of Loudoun co, to Miss Cynthia Annie TALLMAN, formerly of Ottawa, Illinois.

Died: In Washington, on the 8th inst., Mary Ann WALL, aged 63 years, a member of the Society of Friends, and mother of Wm. WALL of the firm of Wall, Stephens & Co, and of Capt. Nicholas WALL, of St. Louis, Mo.

Died: On Wednesday last, after a lingering illness, Mrs. Courtney S. STONE, wife of Samuel STONE Esq., of Charlestown, aged 56 years. She was a member of the Presbyterian Church.

Died: On Wednesday morning last, after a brief illness, Miss Ann R. CRAIG, of Charlestown, aged about 75 years. She was a member of the Methodist Episcopal Church for more than 30 years.

Wednesday, 22 December 1858   Vol. IV, No. 15

Married: On the morning of the 14th inst., by Rev. B. GRIMSLEY, Jos. F. RYAN, Sheriff of Clarke and Miss Ann J., and at the same time, by same, Jos. B. LINDSEY and Miss Mary E., daughters of Ottoway McCORMICK, Esq., all of Clarke Co.

Wednesday, 29 December 1858   Vol. IV, No. 16

Married: In Washington city, on Tuesday evening, 21st instant, by Rev. Mr. NADAL, Mr. Edwin DRISH, of Leesburg, and Miss S. Indiana POWELL, dau. of Grafton POWELL, Esq. of Washington.

Married: On fourth day, the 22nd by Friends ceremony, Robert M. STABLER, of Montgomery Co, Md., and Hannah B. TAYLOR, of Loudoun.

Married: At the residence of Capt. SKILMAN in this Co, on the 21st, James A. MOXLEY to Mary C. HALL, all of Loudoun.

Died: In Washington city, on Tuesday, 21st instant, at 11 p.m., Mrs. Mary A. SCRIVENER, mother-in-law of Grafton POWELL Esq. in the 82d year of her age.

Died: On Monday, the 19th of December, near Belmont, Loudoun Co, Mrs. Mary E. FOWLER, aged 41 years.

Wednesday, 5 January 1859   Vol. IV, No. 17

Married: In Leesburg, Dec. 30, 1858, by the Rev. Samuel GOVER, John C. MOCKE to Elizabeth MONDAY, all of Loudoun.

Married: On the 16th ult. at the residence of the bride's father, in Adams Co, Ohio, by Rev. Mr. HILE, Samuel C. ALLEN, of Decator, Illinois, to Jane E., dau. of Enos and Sarah GORE, formerly of Loudoun Co.

Died: On the 24th of Dec at the residence of Mr. B. P. NOLAND of Middleburg, Miss Lavinia P. ANDERSON, in the 56th year of her age.

Died: At Grassland, the residence of her husband on Thursday morning, the 23d inst., Mrs. Hannah TEBBS, wife of Col. Samuel J. TEBBS, aged about 50 years.

Died: Mrs. Amanda O. FOX, wife of Dr. Joseph B. FOX of Sangamon Co., Illinois, died at his residence Dec. the 8th 1858, aged 54y 3m 18d. Born and raised in Loudoun. Member of the M. E. Church for upwards of 30 years.

Wednesday, 12 January 1859   Vol. IV, No. 18

Co. Court – Mr. Joel OSBURN charged with mal-treating his servant, a negro man, causing his death.

Death of Gen. HENDERSON – born in 1783 in Dumfries, Va and entered the service of his county in 1806, when 23 years of age. ... He was a brother of the late Richard HENDERSON, of Leesburg.

Died: Suddenly in this town, on Monday night last, Mrs. Elizabeth Jane HIRST, wife of Mr. S. N. HIRST, of Wetzel Co. Va, and daughter of Mr. S. M. BOSS, of Leesburg, in about the 24th year of her age.

Died: At the residence near Silcott's Spring, on the 25th ultimo, Stacy Malon NICHOLS, in the 35th year of his age.

Wednesday, 19 January 1859   Vol. IV, No. 19

At the residence of Major Wilson C. SANDERS of this county, have died since the 1st of December 1858, three colored persons: Sandy BERRY aged 80 years, Hannah CARTER aged 90 years, and Jim CARTER aged 108 years. Jim served his master through the Rev. War. He was also in the war of 1812. He attained 108th year on the 1st of January. On the 3d of this month he followed to the grave the remains of his fourth wife, Hannah, named above, on which occasion he contracted pneumonia, which resulted in his death on the 11th inst.

Married: On the 25th Nov at the bride's residence by Rev. Wm. S. BAIRD, Mr. Amos T. HUNT and Mary Ann VIRTZ, all of Loudoun.

Married: In Waterford, on the 1st ult., by the same, Mr. Charles J. TOWNER and Miss Fanny A. HOUGH, all of Loudoun.

Married: On Thursday, 8th inst., by the same, Mr. Geo. W. RILEY, and Miss Hannah A. COOPER, all of Loudoun.

Died: In this town, on the 10th inst., suddenly, while on a visit to her parents and friends, Elizabeth Jane HIRST, wife of Samuel N. HIRST, of Milo, Wetzel Co. Va, dau. of S. M. and Elizabeth F. BOSS, of this town. Member of the M. E. Church, South, for 9 years.

Wednesday, 27 January 1859   Vol. IV, No. 20

Married: On Thursday, the 30th Dec 1858, near Neersville, by Rev. J. B. ANTHONY, Mr. John B. EVERHART, to Miss Susan A. NEER, all of Loudoun.

Married: On the 20th inst., in the German Ref. Ch., near Lovettsville, by Rev. G. H. MARTIN, Mr. Samuel D. DARR and Miss Emeline A. WENNER, both of Loudoun.

Died: At the Marine Barracks, Washington, Wednesday 19th inst., Anne Maria Cazenove, wife of the late Brevet Brigadier General Archibald HENDERSON. At half past 4 o'clock, on Sunday morning, the 15th inst., at Walnut Hill, his residence near Middleburg, Loudoun, after a protracted illness of eight weeks, Mr. James CRAIN, in his 68th year.

Wednesday, 2 February 1859   Vol. IV, No. 21

Thomas P. BEALL, one of the editors of the Charlestown Spirit of Jefferson, died on Wednesday morning, in his 25th year, after a lingering illness of 18 months or more. Member of the M. E. Church.

Married: At the residence of the bride's mother, near Gainsville, on the morning on the 18th ult., by Rev. A. COMPTON, Mr. Bryon L. GALLEHER, of Prince William and Miss Annie E., daughter of the late Thos. B. GAINES, of Prince William Co.

Married: On the 6th ult., at the residence of the bride's father, by Elder T. W. NEWMAN, Mr. Martin Van Buren DAVIS, of Prince William Co and Miss Nancy Ann WOODYARD, of Fairfax Co.

Married: On the 13th ult., by the Rev. Wm. S. BAIRD, Mr. Lewis TAYLOR and Mrs. Elizabeth R. LOVE, both of Loudoun.

Married: At the Legation of the U.S., in the city of Brussels on the 5th inst., the Rev. W. BRURY, Episcopal Chaplain and Mr. VERBOUTSRAETEN, the Deacon of St. Gudule Cathedral, officiating, Miss STROTHER, daughter of the late Hon. J. F. STROTHER, former member of Congress from Virginia, to Baron Philip Fahnenberg de BURGHEIM.

Married: In Alexandria, on the 27th ult, by Rev. D. P. WILLS, Robt. G. ALLNUTT and Miss Martha S. ASH, both of Loudoun.

Died: At the residence of James W. HAMILTON, Berlin, Frederick Co Md., on Friday evening, the 14th ult., of pneumonia, after a short sickness, Mr. George W. HOUSEHOLDER, youngest son of the late Gideon HOUSEHOLDER, of Loudoun Co, in his 18th year of age.

Died: In Lovettsville, Jan. 18th 1859, after a protracted illness, Flora Virginia, infant daughter and only child of J. C. and Charlotte STONEBURNER, aged 9m 4d.

Wednesday, 9 February 1859   Vol. IV, No. 22

Married: On the 19th ult., by the Rev. James A. M. La TOURRETTE, Frank G. ROBBINS, of Louisville, to Miss Fannie C. CLAGETT, of Chicago.

Married: On the 27th inst., by Rev. Wm. S. HAMMOND, Mr. Wm. H. B. HAYS to Miss Lydia A. PEACHER, all of Jefferson Co.

Married: At Harpers Ferry, on the 25th ult., by Rev. Mr. DEALE, Mr. Robert H. BREWER, and Miss Jane E., dau. of Meshick KIRBY, Esq., all of said place.

Married: In Leesburg, Feb 2nd, by Rev. Joseph A. PROCTOR, Mr. Alfred WYNKOOP to Miss Leah Elizabeth WHITE, all of Loudoun.

Died: Near Wheatland, on the 25th ult., of scarlett fever, Nancy Catharine, eldest dau. of Noble B. and Licinda PEACOCK, aged 7 years.

Died: On the 9th of Dec. 1858, at Springfield, Ill., Mrs. Pleasants HOUGH, consort of Jno. HOUGH, formerly of Hillsborough, in the 68th year of her age.

Wednesday, 16 February 1859   Vol. IV, No. 23

We report the death of Dr. Decatur HEATON.

Married: At the Church of the Epiphany, Washington, DC, on the 3d inst., by the Rev. Charles H. HAL, Frederick SCHLEY, Esq. Editor of "*The Frederick Examiner*," to Miss Florence WASHINGTON, eldest daughter of R. C. WASHINGTON, of the former city.

Married: On Jan 27th, by Elder T. W. NEWMAN, Mr. Charles Murphy ELGIN, of Loudoun, and Miss Sarah BEACH, of Fairfax Co.

Married: At Orange Court House, on Thursday evening, the 3d inst., by the Rev. D. B. ERVING, Mr. Jno. S. PAYNE, editor of the "Southern Chronicle," to Miss Mary V. THRIFT, both of Orange.

Died, of consumption, on the 2d instant, at Greenwood, the residence of his father in Loudoun Co, Charles Isaac, third son of Mason and Deuana CHAMBLIN, aged 25 years.

Wednesday, 23 February 1859   Vol. IV, No. 24

Married: Near Waterford, Feb. 15th, by Rev. T. A. WARE, Mr. Charles W. MYERS to Miss Sally Ann VIRTS, all of Loudoun.

Married: At the residence of the bride's brother, Josiah B. TAYLOR, in Hillsborough, Feb 17th, by the same, Robt. J. T. WHITE Esq., to Miss Mary Louisa TAYLOR, both of the above place.

Married: In Washington, on the 15th instant, by the Rev. Andrew G. CAROTHERS, Lt. Henry B. TYLER, U.S. Marines, to Miss Mary M. EDWARDS, both of that city.

Died: At her residence in Leesburg, on Tuesday morning, Miss Eva TOWNER, in the 78th year of her age.

Died: Near Wheatland, on Tuesday the 15th inst., of scarlet fever, Winfield Scott, third son of Noble B. and Lucinda PEACOCK, in the 10th year of age.

Died: Dr. James Decatur HEATON departed this life on the 15th of Feb 1859, at half past 1 o'clock in the morning, in the 43d year of his age. ... Wife and children mourn.

Wednesday, 2 March 1859   Vol. IV, No. 25

Married: On the 22nd instant, at the residence of the bride's father, by the Rev. A. J. MYERS, Mr. Robert C. McGINN, of Middleburg, to Lizzie, dau. of Robert WRIGHT Esq., Pleasant Shade, Baltimore Co. Md.

Married: On the 15th instant, at the bride's residence, by Rev. Wm. S. BAIRD, Mr. John P. DERRY and Miss Jane Eliza EDWARDS, both of Loudoun.

Died: On Wednesday night of 23d inst., Francis Ann, second dau. of Aaron and Hannah DAILEY, in the 19th year of her age.

Died: On the 16th instant, at his residence, near Purcellville, Richard COPELAND, in the 97th year of his age.

Died: Mrs. Kate M. STEWART was born of respectable parentage in Loudoun in 1816, and some few years afterwards, having lost her parents, she and an only sister were taken to the Western Co. by an aged Aunt and Uncle, who emigrated there and with whom they lived until they were married, and in a brief space of time after her marriage, her beloved companion was removed from her by death, after which she remained with her brother-in-law until she was removed on the 3d of Feb 1859, at the house of her brother-in-law, Mr. Thos. SNELL, in Clinton, Dewitt Co, Illinois. She leaves behind her an only sister.

Wednesday, 9 March 1859   Vol. IV, No. 26

Married: On Saturday morning, the 20th ultimo, at Falley Seminary, Oswego Co, New York, by the Rev. Mr. ___, Mr. Thomas C. MORALLEE, of Leesburg, and Miss Gertrude E. WILLARD, of Newport, New York.

Died: At La Grange, Georgia, on the 7th of February, 1859, in his 48th year, Dr. Joseph Addison BRADEN, a native of Loudoun Co and recently a citizen of Florida.

Died: At the residence of his son, Thomas LITTLETON, in Leesburg, on Sunday, 27th of Feb, Mr. John LITTLETON, in his 78th year. Member of the Methodist Episcopal Church for upwards of half a century.

Died: Near Wheatland, on Tuesday, the 8th ultimo, Mrs. Mary BEANS, wife of Uriah BEANS.

Died: In Mt. Gilead, Morrow Co, Ohio, Feb. 17th after a lingering illness, Georgianna, dau. of Edward and Eliza HART, in her 23rd year.

Wednesday, 16 March 1859   Vol. IV, No. 27

Died: At her residence near this town, on the 10th inst., Mrs. Mary SAUNDERS, relict of the late Thomas SAUNDERS, in her 62d year.

Died: In Charlestown, on Wednesday morning 9th instant, Mrs. Jane C. CAMPBELL, wife of James W. CAMPBELL Esq., Sheriff of this County, and daughter of Thomas A. MOORE Esq., in her 26th year.

Wednesday, 23 March 1859   Vol. IV, No. 28

Died: In Woodville, Rappahannock, Co, on Sunday night the 13th inst., Miss Amelia THOMAS, aged about 75 years. She was the oldest sister of George T. THOMAS, of Culpeper Co, and Aunt of the late Mrs. Maria E. HENDERSON. Member of the Methodist Episcopal Church, South.

Wednesday, 30 March 1859   Vol. IV, No. 29
No marriages or deaths.

Wednesday, 6 April 1859   Vol. IV, No. 30
Died at the residence of her husband, Washington JARVIS, in Leesburg, Mrs. Louisa JARVIS, in her 33d year. Member of the Methodist Episcopal Church for many years.

Died suddenly on the 26th of Feb, at Locust Bottom, Prince William Co, Thos. W. GALLEHER, in his 57th year. Native of Loudoun, and a member of the M. E. Church since age 15. A widow and nine children are left to mourn.

Died: In this town, on Monday, the 4th instant, Annie Sophia, youngest child of Thomas W. and Susan BIRKBY, aged 14 months.

Wednesday, 13 April 1859   Vol. IV, No. 31
Death of Col. H. B. POWELL suddenly in Middleburg, on Wednesday morning last.

Poem – dedicated to Annie S., infant dau. of Thomas W. and Susan BIRKBY, who departed this life on the 4th instant.

Wednesday, 20 April 1859   Vol. IV, No. 32
Married: On Wednesday, the 13th instant, by the Rev. Samuel GOVER, Joseph F. HOUGH, of Loudoun, to Mary E. TIMS, of Washington City.

Married: On Thursday evening, the 14th of April, by Rev. Andrew ROBEY, Mr. James W. BROWN to Miss Eliza A. STILLIONS, all of Loudoun.

Died: At his residence, in this town, on Thursday night last, after an illness of several months, Benjamin D. RATHIE, in the ___ year of age. Leaves a wife and six helpless children. Buried on Saturday.

Died: On the 5th instant at Cloverdale, Frederick Co, Mrs. Mary Elizabeth LUPTON, in the 31st year of her age, wife of Jonah J. LUPTON and daughter of Stacy J. and Pleasant TAVENNER, leaving a husband and two children. She suffered for two years.

Wednesday, 27 April 1859   Vol. IV, No. 33
Married: On the morning of the 19th inst., at the residence of the brides' mother near Goose Creek Meeting House, by Friends ceremony, Samuel N. BROWN to Mary Ann NICHOLS, daughter of the late Joshua NICHOLS of this county.

Married: At "The Manse" in Leesburg, on Tuesday morning the 19th inst., by Rev. H. R. SMITH, Daniel T. WOOD, of Frederick Co. and Mariam G. NICHOLS, of Loudoun.

Died: At the residence of R. A. WEAVER Esq., near Warrenton Va, on the 11th inst., Mrs. Margaret Henderson WALLACE, widow of the

late Michael WALLACE, on Madison Co, aged about 72 years. She was the last survivor of the children of Alexander HENDERSON, of Dumfries, and sister of the late Richard H. HENDERSON.
Died: On the 15th instant, in Jeffersonton, Culpeper Co, at the residence of her father, Theodore N. DAVISSON, Mrs. Julia E. HENING, consort of Dr. Wm. H. HENING, of Powhatan Co, in her 23rd year.

Wednesday, 4 May 1859   Vol. IV, No. 34

John JONES Jr. and wife and others against Ezekiel POTTS, Maranda BOWEN & wife Martha C., Mary BELL, Ann BELL, Matilda BELL and Harriet BELL and others – partition of 9a lot No. 3 allotted to heirs of Jonas POTTS dec'd in division of estate of David POTTS dec'd..

Wednesday, 11 May 1859   Vol. IV, No. 35

Died: At the residence of Mr. Robert ELGIN, in this county, on Saturday, 7th inst., Mrs. Pamelia C. LINN, in the 67th year of her age. She was a member of the Old School Baptist Church.

Wednesday, 18 May 1859   Vol. IV, No. 36

Married: Near Upperville, May the 10th, by the Rev. T. A. WARE, Dr. Aurelius P. BROWN, of Front Royal, to Miss Mary C. LITTLETON, of Loudoun Co.
Married: At Eudora, on the morning of the 12th inst., by the same, Henry E. PEYTON, of Fauquier Co, to Miss Mary Elizabeth, daughter of Noble S. BRADEN, Esq., of Loudoun County.
Married: At Goresville, Loudoun Co., on the 12th inst., by Rev. Jos. A. PROCTOR, Mr. E. Grey CAUFMAN, to Susan Virginia, only daughter of Tilghman GORE, Esq.
Died: At "Orksey," his father's residence, in Madison Parish, Louisiana, on the 24th ult., in the 23rd year of his age, Dr. Daniel H. BUCKNER, son of Dr. B. H. BUCKNER, and grandson of the late Ariss BUCKNER, of Loudoun County.
Died: On the 4th instant, at Springfield, Stafford Co., in her 43rd year, Mrs. Marion L. TALIAFERRO, wife of Col. J. M. TALIAFERRO, daughter of the late George GRYMES, of King George.

Wednesday, 25 May 1859   Vol. IV, No. 37

Died: On Monday morning the 16th inst., an infant child, son of John W. PATTON, aged 3 months.
Chancery Ct., 4 May 1859 – Moses P. WATSON and Henry MILHOLLEN, creditors of Joseph P. MEGEATH dec'd against Fenton FURR, an Admr., and Burr H. RICHARDS, other Admr. of Joseph P. MEGEATH dec'd, Elizabeth MEGEATH widow, James G. MEGEATH, Marrietta MEGEATH, Virginia MEGEATH, Burr H.

RICHARDS & wife Josephine, Samuel MEGEATH, Stephen D. MEGEATH, and Joseph M. MEGEATH, Martha E. MEGEATH, Tholemiah MEGEATH, and Elizabeth MEGEATH, infant children of Joseph P. MEGEATH by David HIXSON, their guardian ad litem – debts.

Wednesday, 1 June 1859   Vol. IV, No. 38

Died: At his residence, in Fairfax Co, on Friday, the 25th of March 1859, Mr. Benjamin BURKE, in his 78th year, and on Tuesday, the 24th of May 1859, after a protracted illness, Mrs. Mildred BURKE, relict of the late Benjamin BURKE, in the 86th year of his age.

Died: In Snickersville, on the 7th inst., John Keen, infant son of F. M. and Elizabeth BRADFIELD. At the same place, on the 11th inst., Elizabeth, wife of Francis M. BRADFIELD, aged 29y? 1m 16d.

Died: Near Neersville, on the 8th day of May 1856, Dr. William CALHOUN. He was by profession a cancer doctor.

Died: Suddenly at his residence on the 15th of May 1859, Mr. Nicholas ROPP, aged 74y 8m 1d.

Died: On the 14th of April, at the residence of his father, Isaac N. F. EATON, in the 21st year of his age, eldest son of Dr. Isaac and Malinda EATON.

Wednesday, 8 June 1859   Vol. IV, No. 39

No marriages or deaths.

Wednesday, 15 June 1859   Vol. IV, No. 40

Married: At Mt. Ephraim, Fauquier Co., the residence of the bride's mother, on Tuesday the 7th inst., by the Rev. John Wm. McMURRAN, Rev. Robert L. McMURRAN and Miss Mary Archer, eldest daughter of the Rev. J. J. ROYALL, dec'd.

Married: On the 6th inst., by the Rev. H. SUTER, Dr. J. Conway BROUN, of Middleburg, to Miss Ann Rebecca McCORMICK, of Clarke.

Married: At New Orleans, on the 18th of May 1859, at the residence of Mr. Charles PRIDE, by the Right Rev. Leonidas POLK, Mr. Thomas S. POWELL, of Washington City, to Miss Hannah F. ROWLAND, of the former place.

Died: Suddenly in Clarke Co., on the 6th of June 1859, of paralysis (second attack), Catherine Elizabeth HOOE, third daughter of Henry D. and Mary A. HOOE, aged 29y 17d.

Wednesday, 22 June 1859   Vol. IV, No. 41

Married: In Carlisle, Pa, on the morning of the 7th inst. at the residence of E. BEATTY Esq., by the Rev. Dr. WING, John J. WHITE, of Loudoun, to Mary C., dau. of Col. A. M. PIPER, of the former place.

Married: At the residence of the bride's father, on Thursday, the 16th instant, by the Rev. S. V. HOYLE, Peter C. MYERS, Esq., and Sarah E. HANES, all of Loudoun.

Married: On the 7th inst., in the Presbyterian Church, at Harpers Ferry, by the Rev. Charles WHITE, James H. BURTON, chief Engineer of the Royal Small Arms Manufactory, at Enfield Lock, Middlesex, England, and Eugenia Harper, daughter of Geo. MAUZY.

Married: On the 14th instant, by the Rev. Father BOYLE, Mr. Howard H. YOUNG, of Fairfax Co, to Miss Florence E. DARRELL, daughter of William S. DARRELL, Esq., of Washington.

Died: In this town, on Monday morning last, Annie Brown, daughter of Dr. E. S. and Roena CASTLE, aged 6y 10m. On the same morning, in the same hour, and within a few steps of the above, Kate, only daughter of Mrs. Mary E. STROTHER, aged 5 years. At 9 o'clock on Tuesday morning, both little coffins were placed side by side in the same hearse and followed to the M. E. Church South, services by Rev. Jos. A. PROCTOR. Burial in Union Cemetery.

Died: Near Germania, Harrison Co., Ohio, on the 29th ult., Christopher ABEL, formerly of Loudoun Co. aged 74y 2m 23d.

Died: In Iowa, on the 15th of April, Geo. ABEL, son of the late Christopher ABEL, of Ohio.

Died: At his residence near Waterford, in this county, on Wednesday, the 13th of April, of pulmonary disease, Mr. Jonas S. VIRTS, aged 35y 2m 2d.

Wednesday, 29 June 1859   Vol. IV, No. 42

Died: At his residence near Philomont, Friday, the 24th inst., Jonathan TAVENNER, in the __ year of his age.

Died: In Washington on Wednesday, the 15th inst., Jilson J. DOVE, formerly of Loudoun Co, in the 39th year of his age.

Died: On the 1st inst., at the residence of his brother-in-law, Dr. G. B. WOOD, near Kansas City, Missouri, Dr. A. M. BONHAM, formerly of Clarke Co.

Wednesday, 6 July 1859   Vol. IV, No. 43

Married: In Leesburg, on the 4th inst., by Rev. Samuel GOVER, Mr. Elias HOLE and Miss Mary MONDAY, all of Loudoun.

Died: Suddenly, on the 13th of June, near the Short Hill Mountain, in this county, Mrs. Malinda JOHNSON, wife of Robert JOHNSON, in the 70th year of her age.

Died: In Darnestown, Md., on Tuesday evening, June 28th, Mrs. Mary BERRY, in the __ year of her age.

Wednesday, 13 July 1859   Vol. IV, No. 44

Married: On Monday morning, July 4th, by Rev. John LANDSTREET, Mr. James E. HESSER to Miss Adelia DISHMAN, all of this county.

Miss Elizabeth D. BINNS died on the evening of Tuesday, July 5th, in the 66th year of her age, and the 32nd of her Christian pilgrimage.
Cornelius S. TAYLOR died in Middleburg, July 2nd, in his 27th year.

Wednesday, 20 July 1859   Vol. IV, No. 45

Married: On Wednesday, July 6th, by the Rev. O. A. KINSOLVING, Mr. Thomas W. DUDLEY Jr., of Richmond, to Miss Fanny B., daughter of Dr. Wm. B. COCHRAN, of Middleburg.

Died: In this town, on Wednesday evening last, after a life of much suffering, Mr. William NEWTON, in the __ year of his age. He was in the war of 1812-13.

Died: In this county, on Friday morning, 15th inst., Elizabeth DANIEL, consort of David DANIEL, in the 66th year of his age.

Died: Near Morrisonville, on the 29th ultimo, Mr. James MERCHANT, in the 71st year of his age.

Wednesday, 27 July 1859   Vol. IV, No. 46

A monument has been erected during the past week in the Sharon Cemetery over the remains of Noble B., son of Col. Lloyd NOLAND. Born March 3, 1838, died Nov. 28th 1858.

Died: At Washington DC, on the evening of 12th of July 1859, Helen Adgate, eldest child of W. C. and M. J. C. LIPSCOMB, in the 9th year of her age.

Died: In Paris, Fauquier Co, on Saturday evening, 16th inst., H. L. Eby, son of the Rev. James H. and Laura A. MARCH, of the Baltimore Con., aged 3y 2m 3d.

Died: On Thursday evening last, in Charlestown, after a protracted illness, Mrs. Sarah E. HALEY, aged 35y, wife of Mr. Franklin HALEY, and dau. of the late John AVIS Sr.

Wednesday, 3 August 1859   Vol. IV, No. 47

[*Alexandria Gazette* of Saturday] Col. Wm. MINOR, of this county, died at his residence yesterday. He was in the war of 1812. (Col. MINOR was the father of Col. John W. MINOR, of Loudoun)

Died: On the 6th ult., at his residence in this county, Mr. Benj. BROWN, in the 78th year of his age.

Died: At his residence in Zanesville, Ohio, on Thursday, July 14th, 1859, of consumption, after an illness of about nine months, Norval CHAMBLIN, in the 56th year of his age.

Died: On Monday, July 11th, at Bay, St. Louis, Mississippi, Alfred Sidney, only son of J. W. and Arthelia KEENE, aged 1y 4m 21d.

Died: On Wednesday, the 20th of July, at the residence of Edmund WINSTON, in the county of Hanover, Lucy Peachy POWELL, youngest child of D. Lee and Maria L. POWELL, aged 1y 1m 20d.

Died: At his residence of Circleville in this county, on Saturday, the 23d inst., of typhoid fever, Mr. Troy BALLENGER, in 36th year of his age.

Died: In Falmouth, Va, on the 17th inst., of billious dysentery, William, son of William and Mary HEAD, in the 5th year of his age.

Wednesday, 10 August 1859   Vol. IV, No. 48

A man named FILLER, living a few miles from Waterford, was on Saturday last found lying dead in his stable. A slight bruise on his breast led to the conclusion that his death was by a kick from a colt.

Married: In Petis Co, Missouri, on the __ ult., by Rev. Mr. SCRUGG, Mr. James W. ROWLETT, formerly of Kentucky, to Miss Margaret, youngest dau. of Humphrey SHEPHERD, formerly of Loudoun Co.

Married: On the 9th instant, in Leesburg, by the Rev. Samuel GOVER, Mr. Charles GANT to Miss Elizabeth BRAWNER, all of Loudoun.

Married: On Thursday morning last, by the Rev. Charles E. AMBLER, at the residence of the bride's father, near Charlestown, Henry SPEARS, of Paris, Ky, to Miss Maria C., dau. of Edward E. COOKE, Esq. of Jefferson Co.

Died: William Fitzhugh RANDOLPH, of Chillowee, Cumberland Co, Va, died at his late residence, in Millwood, Clarke Co, Va, on the 16th of July 1859, in the 64th year of his age.

Wednesday, 17 August 1859   Vol. IV, No. 49

Albert EASTER, a few Negro boy, about 14 years old, was found guilty of stealing chickens and sentenced to 30 days in jail, with 15 stripes as a passport to admission, and 15 more upon coming out as a certificate of merit.

Married: On Tuesday morning, Aug 9th in Emmanuel Church, Middleburg, by Rev. Wm. SPARROW, D.D., the Rev. O. A. KINSOLVING (Rector of the Church) to Lucy Lee, eldest daughter of Gen. Asa ROGERS, of Loudoun.

Married: At Annapolis, Md., on Tuesday evening, the 9th instant, James Buchanan HENRY Esq., of New York, and Mary H. NICHOLSON, daughter of Col. Joseph H. NICHOLSON, of the former place

Died: On the evening of the 30th of July, at the residence of her husband, in Fauquier Co., Mrs. Catharine HOOE, wife of Mowison [Howison] HOOE.

Died: On Monday, June 27th, near Mt. Gilead in this county, John, son of John W. and Mary PATTON, aged 3y 27d.

Died: Mr. Jonathan HART, on Wednesday, the third of Aug 1859, after a lingering illness, departed this life, aged 72y 10m 17d.

Wednesday, 24 August 1859   Vol. IV, No. 50

Married: On the 28th of July, by Rev. F. H. RICHEY, Mr. Eli C. H. HOUSE to Mary J. PIERPOINT.

Married: On the 7th instant, by the same, Thos. B. MARCHE, formerly of Washington City, to Frances E. MORRISON, of this county.

Married: In Washington City, at the Church of the Ascension, on Tuesday, the 9th instant, by the Rev. Dr. PINCKNEY, Mr. Townsend D. SEATON, of Loudoun County, to Mrs. Mary Peyton JOHNSON, of Washington City.

Married: On the 11th inst., at the Howard House, Baltimore, Md., by the Rev. J. P. SMELTZER, Mr. Henry FLATHER of New York City, to Miss Sarah S. HOCKENSMITH, of Bolivar, Jefferson Co. Va.

Died: Suddenly, at Lovettsville, on Monday, the 15th instant, Mr. Thomas BENTLEY, in the 68th year of his age.

Died: On Tuesday afternoon, the 16th instant, at the residence of her husband, near Lovettsville, after three days sickness, Mrs. Catharine HOUSEHOLDER, wife of Jacob HOUSEHOLDER, and eldest dau. of the late Peter COMPHER.

Wednesday, 31 August 1859   Vol. IV, No. 51

At the farm of Mr. E. C. BROUN, near Middleburg, on Friday night last. Two negro men, 16 and 18 years, were found dead with a double-barrelled shot gun, empty, laying close by their side. One belonged to Mr. J. M. MORAN and the other to James T. SKINNER.

Married: On Thursday, Aug 18th, by Rev. Jos. A. PROCTOR, Mr. Michael COCHLAND, to Miss Mary Elizabeth NEWTON.

Died: On the 21st instant, at his residence in Winchester, Col. James P. RIELY, in the 51st year of his age. He was Clerk of County Court of Frederick Co.

Died: At his residence near Mountsville, Aug. 9th, 1859, of dropsy, Mr. John FRANCIS, in his 59th year. Member of the M. E. Church.

Died: In Baltimore, on the 19th of Aug. 1859, Georgietta, daughter of Coleman and M. Virginia YELLOTT, aged 2y 20d.

Wednesday, 7 September 1859   Vol. IV, No. 52

Negroes Edgar (property of Jno. Marshal LUCK) and Charles (property of Miss Elizabeth MORAN) who were servants of Mr. Benj. F. SKINNER – Charles fired what he thought was an empty gun at Edgar, killing him. Charles then shot himself.

Married: On the 30th inst., in the German Reformed Church, by the Rev. G. H. MARTIN, Mr. Peter S. VIRTS, to Miss M. C. BOOTH, both of Loudoun County.

Married: On Wednesday, August 17th at St. Mary's Church, Beechwood, New York, by the Rev. William CREIGHTON, D.D., Capt. J. G. BENTON, U.S. Army, to Miss C. Louisa, daughter of Gen. J. Watson WEBB.

Married: On the 25th ult. by Rev. J. E. JOYNER, Rev. George F. DOGGETT, of the Virginia Annual Conference, to Mrs. Virginia S. F. HUGHES, of Prince George Co. Va.

Married: In Washington City, August 25th 1859, by Rev. C. M. BUTLER, Capt. Henry T. HARRIS, of Culpeper Co, and Miss Abebella [Arebella?] SUDDITH, of Charlestown, Jefferson Co Va.

Died: On the 1st inst., in Alexandria, Washington T. HARPER, in the 57th year of his age.

Died: On Wednesday, the 24th of August, Mr. John J. LALEY, of Bolivar, Jefferson Co, aged 62 years.

Wednesday, 14 September 1859   Vol. V, No. 1

Married: On the Potomac River, on the morning of the 8th inst., by Rev. C. H. NOURSE, Mr. Fayette OSBURN, to Miss Sarah WORTHINGTON, all of Loudoun.

Married: Near Allenton, St. Louis Co, Mo, July 26, 1859, by Rev. Mr. DOWNING, Mr. Wm. Adolphus JACOBS, formerly of Loudoun Co, to Miss Mary Elizabeth, dau. of Joseph POTTERFIELD, of the former place.

Married: Aug. 25th, at the house of the bride's father, in Tankerville neighborhood, by the Rev. J. B. ANTHONY, Mr. S. Lewis GRUBB, to Miss Margaret Ann FRY, all of Loudoun.

Died: In San Francisco, Ca, on the 2d ult, Margaret M., wife of M. E. GREENWELLE, U. S. Coast Survey and daughter of Mrs. E. MANNING, of Washington City.

Died: At half past 1 a.m. on Tuesday, September 7th, Mr. Wm. H. JACOBS, in the 62d year of his age.

Chancery Ct., July 12: William FAWLEY & wife Elizabeth, William SPRING & wife Lydia Ann, John BARTLETT & wife Sarah, Peter STONEBURNER & wife Catharine, William KERN & wife Margaret KERN, John COMPHER & wife Susan against Elizabeth COMPHER, Samuel COMPHER & wife Hannah Ann, Joseph COMPHER & wife Susan, Jonas COMPHER & wife Mary C., Elizabeth Ann COMPHER now TRITAPOE & husband George C. TRITAPOE, John H. W. COMPHER, Marietta COMPHER, Sarah C. COMPHER, Jonas C. COMPHER and Wm. F. COMPHER by Isaac H. ROBBINS, their Guardian ad litem – debts of estate of Mary C. COMPHER dec'd.

Wednesday, 21 September 1859   Vol. V, No. 2

Married: On Thursday the 1st of September at the residence of the bride's father, by Rev. E. G. SHIP, Mr. Edmund B. HUGHES, of Orange, to Miss Mildred A., second dau. of James SHIFFET of Madison Co.

Married: In Christ Church, Shepherdstown, on the 15th inst., by Rev. C. W. ANDREWS, Lt. William LEE, U.S.A., to Miss Lillie PARRAN, dau. of the late Dr. Richard PARRAN.

Married: On the 14th inst., at "Woodley," the residence of Daniel W. SOWERS, Esq., in Clarke Co, by Rev. H. W. DODGE, Mr. Edward T. GRADY, of Loudoun, to Miss Lucy E. SOWERS.

Died: In Leesburg, on the 12th of September, Cecelia Ann, dau. of John F. MILBOURN, in the 7th year of her age.

Died: At his residence near Philomont, September 9th, 1859, Mr. Jacob MARSHALL, in the 86th year of his age.

Died: In Lynchburg, on Saturday morning, September 2d, Maggie CARTER, daughter of Rev. George W. CARTER, aged 2 years.

Died: In Owingsville, Kentucky, Sept. 1st, at 10 p.m., Mrs. Elizabeth FADELEY, wife of Thomas FADELEY, formerly of Charlottsville, Va.

Died: In Louisville, Kentucky, of consumption, on the 30th of July, at the residence of her husband, Mrs. M. A. B. RONALD, wife of F. S. RONALD, and dau. of the late M. T. THOMPSON, of Loudoun Co.

Died: August 10th 1859, at her residence near the Stone Church, Lovettsville District, of puerperal convulsions, Mrs. Catherine HOUSEHOLDER, wife of Jacob HOUSEHOLDER, and daughter of the late Peter COMPHER, aged 42y 2d.

Died: In Spring Valley, Greene Co., Ohio, on Tuesday, 6th inst., Mary Jane MARCH, mother of the Rev. James H. MARCH, of the Baltimore Conference, in the 47th year of her age.

Died: In Charlestown, September 8th, Henry Clay, youngest son of Wm. A. and Amelia SUDDITH, aged 31 years.

Wednesday, 28 September 1859   Vol. V, No. 3

Married: On the 21st inst., by Rev. Saml. GOVER, Samuel G. STONEBURNER, to Miss Martha V. G. NIXON, all of Loudoun.

Married: On Thursday, September 21st, at the Valley Farm near Union, by the Rev. A. ROBEY, Mr. John SWENEY, to Miss Margaret A. LEG, all of Loudoun.

Married: At Harper's Ferry, on the 20th inst. by the Rev. Norval WILSON, Thomas W. POTTS to Miss Mary CHAMBLIN.

Died: At Lewensville, Fairfax Co, on the morning of the 5th August, of brain fever, Mary Mitchell, only dau. of Frank H. and Emily JANNEY, aged 4m 10d.

Died: At his residence in Leesburg, on Wednesday evening, the 21st inst., William L. BOGUE, in the 46th year of his age.

Wednesday, 5 October 1859   Vol. V, No. 4

A negro man was sold on the block, in Warrenton, for $2050, Wm. B. BRAWNER purchaser. A boy about 12 years old, to a citizen of the county, for $1110. Another, about 15 or 16, to Mr. Richard H. FOOTE, for $1,310.

Married: On the 31st July, by the Rev. Dr. John McCRON, Lewis W. BLACK to Miss Nora E. PEREGOY, all of Baltimore, Md.

Married: On the 22d inst., at the residence of the bride's father, Col. Samuel J. TEBBS, by the Rev. E. D. OWEN, Dr. Lucien Spence DUVAL, of Florida, to Miss Cornelia C. TEBBS, of Fauquier.

Married: On Tuesday last, by Rev. Mr. ___, William J. STEPHENS Esq. of Harper's Ferry, to Miss Elizabeth THOMAS, of Carroll's Manor, Frederick Co. Md.

Married: At Prospect Hill, Fauquier, on the 17th of September, by Rev. C. H. SHIELD, C. Marshall BARTON, of Frederick Co, to Miss Ellen H. MARSHALL, of Fauquier, daughter of the late Dr. Jaquline A. MARSHALL.

Died: On the 28th inst., near Harmony in this county, of consumption, Rev. Saml. H. ROGERS, in the 29th year of his age, after a lingering illness.

Died: On Wednesday night, the 28th of September, Mrs. Nelly S. NEWTON, in the 64th year of her age.

Died: At her residence in Fairfax Co, on Thursday, the 22d ult., after a protracted illness, Mrs. Catherine BORCHFORD, in the 54th year of her age.

Departed this life, suddenly, on Thursday evening, 22d, at the residence of his mother-in-law, Mrs. Eliza R. MUSE, in Frederick Co., Rev. John T. TRONE, of the Baltimore Annual Conference, in the 25th year of his age.

To Charles H. HEATH, Abel JAMES & wife Sally, William HEATH, Shelton HEATH, John HEATH, Gustavus HEATH, Frances Ann HEATH, Catherine HAWLEY, Richard HAWLEY, Artemus HAWLEY, James P. POPKINS, Roseline HAWLEY, Lamech HAWLEY, Andrew HAWLEY, Samuel CHURCH, ___ BARKER son of Louise BARKER formerly Louise HAWLEY, the widow and children of Richard HEATH, the widow and children of Alfred HEATH, David HIXSON, Guardian ad litem of Richard POPKINS, Thomas POPKINS and George W. POPKINS, infants, William H. HOLLADAY & wife Patsey L., Thomas R. THROCKMORTON & Lucinda, ___ & wife Mary late Mary McKIM, ___ & wife Elizabeth late Elizabeth McKIM, heirs of Jane late Jane McKIM, Samuel H. McKIM, Robert W. McKIM, William A. McKIM, Joseph M. McKIM, the heirs of William M. McKIM, William A. McKIM and the heirs of John McKIM – notice to take depositions on 12 Oct 1859 at house of S. H. McKIM in Canton, Missouri for case in chancery.

Wm. G. MARLOW as Admr. dbn wwa of Thomas MARLOW dec'd and in his own right, Mary E. DURBURROW, Draco MARLOW, Tuisce MARLOW, Parmenio MARLOW, John S. MARLOW, Thomas J. MARLOW and Sarah MARLOW, Seldon M. GIBSON, Guardian ad litem of Robert MARLOW, Olivia MARLOW and Louisa MARLOW, A. T. M. FILLER, J. P. SCHOOLEY, trustee, Lydia M. FILLER and Charles B. TEBBS, trustee for Lydia M. FILLER – on Thursday 13

Oct 1859 will take depositions at hotel of John SNOOTS in Lovettsville for chancery suit .

Wednesday, 12 October 1859   Vol. V, No. 5

J. M. CHILTON, lawyer of New Orleans, and a native of Loudoun Co, died on the 30th ult.

Married: On Sunday, 9th instant, by the Rev. John LANDSTREET, Mr. John W. B. PARKER of this place, to Miss Sarah F. FLOWERS, formerly of Washington DC.

Married: On Thursday, 6th instant, by the Rev. Mr. HUETT, at Trinity Church, Baltimore Co, George T. RUST, of this County to Rebecca C., eldest daughter of John YELLETT, Esq. of Maryland.

Married: In Shepherdstown, on Tuesday evening week, by Rev. Dr. EDWARDS, of Hagerstown, Dr. Chas. W. MAGILL, of Hagerstown, Md., to Miss Louisa T., eldest daughter of John H. McENDREE, Esq. of Shepherdstown.

Died: In Newton Co, Missouri, on the 18th of September, Abraham, youngest son of Abraham and Isabella HEWITT, aged 3y 26d.

Died: On the 7th of August 1859, in Ashland Co, Ohio, John BAKER, aged 69y 1m 9d, formerly a resident of this county.

Died: Near Morrisonville, on the 28th of September 1859, Mr. Thomas F. SCOTT, aged 25y 10m 18d.

Wednesday, 19 October 1859   Vol. V, No. 6

Married: On Tuesday, the 11th inst., at the "Vineyard" near Millwood, Clarke Co, Va, by the Rev. Mr. JONES, Andrew E. KENNEDY Esq. of Jefferson Co, and Maria Pendleton, second dau. of the late Philip P. COOKE.

Married: on Tuesday evening, 11th instant, by the Rev. Dr. DUTTON, Dr. William WALLACE of Fredericksburg to Miss Jennie A. HURST, dau. of William HURST Esq. of Jefferson Co.

Married: On the evening of the 8th instant, near Lovettsville, by Rev. G. H. MARTIN, Mr. J. VIRTZ, to Miss Sarah Jane LONG, all of Loudoun.

Wednesday, 26 October 1859   Vol. V, No. 7

Married: In Leesburg, on the 19th by Rev. S. GOVER, William H. JOHNSON and Miss Frances C. DENNIS, all of Loudoun.

Married: On Monday, the 24th instant, by the Rev. Samuel S. GOVER, Mr. Herod FEASTER and Miss Georgeanna GEASLAN, all of Loudoun.

Married: On the 17th inst., by Friends Ceremony, at the residence of Reuben HAINES, Carroll Co., Md, Thos. R. SMITH of Loudoun to Ellen HAINES, of Carroll.

Married: At the same time and place, by the same Ceremony, Wm. J. SMITH, of Loudoun, and Portia, dau. of Nathan HAINES, of Carroll.

Married: On the 18th inst., by Friends Ceremony, at the residence of Aquilla JANNEY, Samuel T. NICHOLS to Cornelia G. JANNEY, all of Loudoun.

Married: In Warrenton, on the evening of the 11th inst., by the Rev. Wm. E. JUDKINS, Mr. Addison W. UTTERBACK, and Miss Virginia TONGUE, all of Warrenton.

Married: On the 27th of September, by Rev. T. J. BAYTON, at the residence of W. SMITH Esq., Mr. R. DORSEY Warfield, of Georgetown DC, and Miss Martha GUNNEL, of Fairfax Co.

Died: Near Purcelville, on the 12th inst., at the residence of Mary TAYLOR, Mrs. Mariah BARNEY, in the 57th year of her age.

Died: Near Morrisonville on Wednesday evening, the 12th inst., at the residence of his brother, after a protracted sickness of four months, Thos. Janney HAMILTON, son of the late John HAMILTON of this county, aged 28 years.

Wednesday, 2 November 1859   Vol. V, No. 8

Chancery Ct. 10 Oct: William GILL in his own right and as Admr. of Levi WILLIAMS dec'd, Armistead F. OSBURNE, Theodoric LEITH, Ulysses M. MONROE, George KEENE, William F. HAMPTON, William A. LUNCEFORD, Fenton FURR and Marshall CARPENTER and Milton CARPENTER, partners under the name and firm of M. & M. CARPENTER and Andrew ROBEY against John WILLIAMS and all other heirs of said Levi WILLIAMS dec'd and all persons interested in his real estate – debts.

Chancery Ct. 10 Oct: John FRY and Barbara E. B. FRY, Mary CRIDER w/o John H. CRIDER dec'd, son of Frederick CRIDER Sr. dec'd, Sarah J. McCLANAHAN d/o said J. H. CRIDER, Wm. H. McKILRICK & wife Mary, dau. of J. H. CRIDER, Charles STONEBURNER & wife Emily F., dau. of J. H. CRIDER, Matilda A. CRIDER and Charles A. CRIDER, children of J. H. CRIDER and M. C. McCLANAHAN a grandson of J. H. CRIDER dec'd against Frederick CRIDER Jr., Lemuel CRIDER and Elizabeth SIDEBOTTOM – interest in estate of late Frederick CRIDER Sr. and estate of William H. CRIDER dec'd and in portion in which the mother of said William is entitled.

Wednesday, 9 November 1859   Vol. V, No. 9

Chancery Ct. 14 Sep: Thomas B. MARCHE & wife Frances formerly Frances M. MORRISON against Joseph E. MORRISON, __ MORRISON an infant child of Joseph E. MORRISON, John S. MANN & wife Charity, Joseph Edward MANN and Wm. MANN, infant children of said Charity, Joseph S. HART & wife Rachel A., Eliza Jane MORRISON and Edward Hart MORRISON infant children of complainant Frances E. MARCHE formerly MORRISON, and Joseph P. GRUBB as Exor. of Edward MORRISON dec'd and

George K. FOX Jr. guardian of said infants – dower of estate of Edward MORRISON dec'd.

Wednesday, 16 November 1859   Vol. V, No. 10

Married: ON the 10th inst., in St. James' Church, Leesburg, by Rev. Walter W. WILLIAMS, Frank F. JONES, Esq., and Miss Marion Steuart, daughter of W. A. POWELL Esq. of Loudoun.

Married: At Montpelier, the residence of the bride's father, on the 9th inst., by the Rev. Mr. WARE, Peregrine A. FITZHUGH, of Washington city, to Sallie J., second dau. of Ludwell LUCKETT Esq. of Loudoun.

Married: On the 30th of October at the residence of the bride's father, Wm. Gillmore CORDER, by the Rev. Wm. GILLMORE, Wm. STRATHER to Miss Mary J. CORDER, all of Warren Co. Va.

Wednesday, 23 November 1859   Vol. V, No. 11

Died: In this town on Friday, the 18th inst. after a protracted illness of typhoid fever, Alcinda SIMPSON, in the 11th year of her age.

Wednesday, 30 November 1859   Vol. V, No. 12

Married: On Tuesday evening, the 22nd inst. by Rev. H. R. SMITH, James L. GARDNER and Miss Susan E. MUSE, all of Loudoun.

Married: By Rev. Elder J. HERNDON, on the 17th inst. Geo. W. WYNKOOP and Jane BURCH.

Married: On Wednesday, the 24th inst., by Rev. John LANDSTREET, Geo. H. WORTMAN to Miss Martha Ann THOMAS, all of this county.

Died: On Sunday the 13th inst., near Peugh's Mill, Mrs. SHERZER, wife of John SHERZER, in the 32nd year of her age.

Died: In this town, on Thursday, 17th inst., Mr. William TORRISON, in the 57th year of his age.

Wednesday, 7 December 1859   Vol. V, No. 13

Married: On Thursday Nov 22d at the residence of the bride's father, by Rev. Mr. DOUGHERTY, W. H. ADAMS to Miss M. Kate BEALE, all of Frederick Co. Md.

Wednesday, 14 December 1859   Vol. V, No. 14

Married: At "Woodgrove" by Rev. H. R. SMITH, on Wednesday morning, 7th inst., Lewis BEARD of Washington to Miss Eliza R. HEATON of Loudoun.

Married: On Tuesday the 22d ultimo, in Loudoun Co, by the Rev. Wm. G. COE, Benjamin F. MORGAN, Esq. of Fairfax to Miss Hattie E. DAILEY, of Loudoun.

Died: On Friday night, the 9th inst., at his father's residence near Waterford, Madison HOPE, in the 19th year of his age.

Died: After a short illness, at the residence of his father in this county, on Thursday the 24th inst., Payton W. CHAMBLIN, in the 34th year of his age. Member of the Baptist Church.

Died: On the 17th ult., in the German Settlement, Mrs. Elizabeth GRUBB, aged 78y 8m 20d.

Died: On Saturday, the 26th ult, near Woodgrove, Mrs. Marcia A., wife of Harman LODGE.

Wednesday, 21 December 1859   Vol. V, No. 15

Married: On the 13th of December near Taylortown, by the Rev. G. H. MARTIN, James W. SPRING to Miss Mary L. DAVIS, both of Loudoun.

Married: On Thursday morning, the 15th inst., at the residence of J. Mortimer DIVINE, in Hillsboro, by the Rev. S. S. ROSZELL, Dr. Wm. A. BAKER to Miss Mary Cornelia A. BIRKIT, all of Loudoun.

Married: On the 11th inst., in All Saint's Church, in Frederick city Md, by the Rev. Chas. SEYMOUR, Josias Henry CLAPHAM, to Lydia Ellen GRUBB, both of Virginia.

Died: On Saturday morning, the 10th inst., near Purcelville, Johnny, infant son of James and Mary J. ALDER, aged 2y 9m.

Died: On the 14th inst. at the residence of her father in Hillsborough, Lucie, second daughter of Silas MARMADUKE Esq. at the early age of 19. About two years ago she was the picture of health. She was a member of the Methodist Church.

Died: At the residence of her brother-in-law, John ROBINSON, Esq. in Boone Co, Mo, on Friday the 9th of December, Rebecca J. PULLER, dau. of Samuel and Sarah PULLER, late of Fauquier co Va in the 17 year of age.

Wednesday, 28 December 1859   Vol. V, No. 16

No marriages or deaths.

Wednesday, 4 January 1860   Vol. V, No. 17

Married: Dec 22, 1859, by the Rev. John LANDSTREET, Manly W. RUSK to Miss Anne M. NIXON, all of Loudoun.

Married: In Leesburg, on the 22d ultimo, by Rev. W. W. WILLIAMS, Mr. William FULTON, formerly of England, to Miss Mary J. ELGIN, of Ohio.

Married: On Thursday evening, the 29th of December, by Rev. Andrew ROBEY, George J. MORELAND to Miss Hannah V. ORR, all of Loudoun.

Died: On Friday morning, December 30th, 1859, Willis Briant, son of J. W. and V. A. GALLEHER, of this town, aged 4y 8m 21d.

Wednesday, 11 January 1860   Vol. V, No. 18

Married: January 5th 1860, by Rev. John LANDSTREET, John T. DANIELS, to Miss Harriet Ann MOFFATT, all of this county.

Died: In this county, near Gumspring, on the 14th of December 1859, of consumption, Mrs. Alice LEE, consort of A. D. LEE Esq., in the 53d year of her age.

Died: On the 10th of December near Purcelville, John Isaac, aged 2y 9m, and the 17th, Sally, in the 8th year of her age, children of James and Mary Jane ALDER.

Wednesday, 18 January 1860   Vol. V, No. 19

Married: At the residence of the bride's father, Cedar Grove, Mason Co, Ky, on Monday the 3d instant, by the Rev. J. A. SHACKELFORD, Mr. Philip T. KAIGHN to Miss Anne E. KIRK.

Died: On Thursday, the 15th instant, Henry A. Wise, infant son of James H. and Francis A. JONES.

Died: In Alexandria, on Sunday, the 8th instant, William FOWLE, Esq. in 77th year of her age.

Died: At Chattanooga, Tennessee, on the 3d inst., Dr. Samuel M. EDWARDS, aged 30 years, sixth son of Gen. Samuel M. EDWARDS of Washington.

Wednesday, 25 January 1860   Vol. V, No. 20

Married: On Thursday evening, the 12th of January by Rev. Andrew ROBEY, Mr. Henry BELL to Miss Jane E. MARLOW, both of Clarke Co.

Married: On Wednesday morning the 18th of January by the same, Mr. Lewellen LANKAM to Miss Sophia STICKLE, both of Clarke Co.

Married: On Thursday evening, the 19th of January, at "Wedding Valley," in this county, by the same, Mr. Daniel T. GRIMES to Miss Sarah E. RUTTER, all of Loudoun.

Married: On Wednesday, the 4th inst., by Rev. F. H. RICHEY, Mr. Laban L. HILL to Miss Margaret V. WEADON.

Married: In Leesburg, on the 24th inst., by the Rev. S. GOVER, John W. PIERPOINT and Miss Mary E. SHRIGLEY.

Married: In Leesburg, on the 24th inst., by the Rev. S. GOVER, Samuel SHRYOCKE and Miss Lizabeth MILLS, all of Loudoun.

Married: On Wednesday morning last at "Aspin Hill" in Jefferson Co, by Rev. Dr. DUTTON, Mr. Joshua G. WYATT, of Baltimore, to Miss Kate D. HURST, daughter of Capt. James G. HURST.

Married: On the 10th inst., by the Rev. D. ZACHARIAS, D.D., at the Central Hotel in Frederick City, Mr. John O. WEANING, of Martinsburg, Va to Miss Eliza SOUDER, of Loudoun County.

Died: At his residents in

Pleasants Co. Va, on the 30th December 1859, Mr. Giles HAMMATT, formerly of Leesburg, in his 64th year.

Wednesday, 1 February 1860   Vol. V, No. 21

Married: On Thursday evening, the 26th of January, at 1½ o'clock p.m., by Rev. Andrew ROBEY, Mr. Thomas FINSSELL [TRUSSELL] to Miss Jemima PETTET, all of Loudoun County.

Married: The same evening at 2½ o'clock by the same, Mr. Albert THOMPSON to Miss Nancy WILEY, both of Clarke County.

Married: the same evening at 3½ o'clock by the same, Mr. Thomas H. DUKE to Miss Portia SHAFER, both of Clarke County.

Married: On Sunday morning the 15th inst., near Hoysville, by Rev. J. P. ETCHISON, Mr. Tilghman EVERHART to Miss Elizabeth SNOOTS, both of Loudoun.

Married: On Sunday morning, the 22d inst., in the German Reformed Church, Lovettsville, by Rev. G. H. MARTIN, William WENNER Jr., to Miss Louisa VINCEL, both of Loudoun.

Married: On Thursday the 19th inst., by Rev. Wm. GILMORE, Mr. Garret A. E. WYNKOOP, to Miss Margaret J. HARDING, all of Loudoun.

Married: On the 12th instant, at the residence of the bride's father, near Mountsville, by the Rev. T. HERNDON, Mr. Bushrod E. WILKINSON to Miss Mary E. WYNKOOP.

Died: At the residence of her husband, on the 20th of January, Mrs. Sarah McKINNEY, in the 4th [43 per tombstone] year of her age.

Died: At his residence, near Snickersville, the 25th of December, Mr. Samuel LODGE, in the 71st year of his age.

Died: On Thursday morning the 26th ult. of scarlet fever, Mary Virginia, second dau. of Richard E. and Octavia FURR, in the 4th year of her age.

Wednesday, 8 February 1860   Vol. V, No. 22

Married: On the 2d inst., by the Rev. Samuel GOVER, Mr. William H. McNELEA and Miss Susan M. WILEY, all of Loudoun.

Married: On the 31st of January, near Lovettsville, by the Rev. G. H. MARTIN, Mr. John W. DEMORY to Miss Jane P. VIRTS, both of this county.

Married: In this town, on Tuesday last, by Rev. S. GOVER, Mr. George M. SHUGARS to Miss Julia Ann TAYLOR, all of Loudoun.

Married: At Frankville, on Thursday the 26th ult. by Rev. H. R. SMITH, Mr. Columbus WALTER, of Montgomery Co, Md, to Miss Julia A. REAVES, of Loudoun.

Married: On the 3rd ult, at the residence of the bride's father, by the Rev. E. D. OWEN, Mr. Alex M. HOLTZCLAW, of Pr. William, to Miss Maria F. RECTOR, of Fauquier.

Married: On the 22d ult. at Morrisonville, Va, by Elder A. H. SPILMAN, Joseph C. GEE, of Culpeper to Miss Ellen C. COLBERT, of Fauquier.

Died: On Saturday week, after a short but severe illness, Mr. Jonathan COCKRILL, of Jefferson Co., formerly of Loudoun, aged about 30 years. He leaves an aged mother, sisters and brothers.

Died: A Soldier of 1812, departed this life at his residence in Leesburg on the 11th of January 1860, Richard JONES, in the 74th year of his age. He was a member of the M. E. Church.

Died: In this county on the 30th ult., at the residence of her son-in-law, A. H. BEANS, Mrs. Mary HILL, in the 60th year of age.

Died: In this town, on Saturday evening last, of consumption, James William FOX, in the 22d year of age. Member of the M. E. Church, South.

Wednesday, 15 February 1860   Vol. V, No. 23

Married: In Leesburg, on the 8th instant, by the Rev. Samuel GOVER, Mr. Thomas S. COCKERELLE and Lauria [Laura] E. LACEY, all of Loudoun.

Wednesday, 22 February 1860   Vol. V, No. 24

Married: At "Oakham" near Middleburg, on Thursday 9th inst., by Rev. O. A. KINSOLVING, Mr. Alex. K. PHILIPS, of Fredericksburg, to Miss Anne D. ROGERS, dau. of Col. Hamilton ROGERS, of Loudoun.

Married: On Wednesday evening, the 15th of February, at Pleasant Valley, Clarke Co. Va, by the Rev. Andrew ROBEY, Mr. Charles M. LITTLETON of Loudoun County to Miss Sarah J. CARTER of Clarke County Va.

Died: At "Strawberry Vale," Fairfax Co, on Thursday the 9th inst., Mrs. Anna Beall GANTT, wife of John F. GANTT Esq. and dau. of Mrs. Charlotte WILSON, of Leesburg, in the 36th year of her age.

Died: Suddenly in Baltimore city on Friday evening last, Daniel E. STANSLURY [STANSBURY?] in the 40th year of his age.

Died: In Alexandria on the 14th inst., Thomas CLOWES, son of Thomas and Martha CLOWES, aged 7y 10m.

Wednesday, 29 February 1860   Vol. V, No. 25

Married: On the 21st inst., by Rev. Saml. GOVER, Mr. George W. HARRISON to Miss Mary Jane HENSEY, all of Loudoun.

Died: At the residence of her husband, in Jefferson Co, on Wednesday last, Mrs. Mary CASTLEMAN, wife of Henry W. CASTLEMAN and dau. of Jas. SINCLAIR, of this town, in her 36th year. Corpse was brought to Leesburg on Saturday afternoon, services in Episcopal Church from Rev. Mr. LEAVELL, interment in Union Cemetery.

Died: On the 20th inst., Emily Virginia, youngest child of Samuel and Nancy BRECKENRIDGE, aged 13m 27d.

Wednesday, 7 March 1860   Vol. V, No. 26

Married: In the Presbyterian Church in this town, on Tuesday morning the 6th inst., by Rev. H. R. SMITH, Christian NISEWANNER and Miss Albina A. McDANIEL, all of Loudoun.

Married: On the 1st inst., by the same, Phillip D. MARTIN and Miss Margaret E. WILLIAMS, all of Loudoun.

Married: On the 23d February by Rev. J. P. ETCHISON, Mr. John W. BARTLETT to Miss Elizabeth H. KERN, both of Loudoun.

Died: Suddenly at his residence near Leesburg, on the 22d February, John CAMPBELL, in his 80th year, leaving an aged wife and a large number of children and grand and great grand children.

Died: In Butler Co Ohio, on the 10th of February 1860, Martha J., wife of Maj. CRAIG, in the 33d year of her age.

[*Charlestown Free Press*] Died: On the 22d February 1860, after a painful sickness of about 4 weeks, Mrs. Mary E. CASTLEMAN, dau. of Jas. SINCLAIR Esq. of Leesburg, and wife of Henry W. CASTLEMAN Esq. of Jefferson Co Va in the 25th year of her age.

Wednesday, 14 March 1860   Vol. V, No. 27

Married: In Memphis, Tenn, on the 16th of Feb, Dr. Charles McCORMICK, son of Province McCORMICK Esq. of Clarke Co, and Miss Laura AYRES, only daughter of T. S. AYRES, of Memphis.

Died: Of consumption on the 15th of February at the residence of her brother, Wm. W. WENNER, near Lovettsville, Lydia J., consort of Henry A. JOHNSON, of Md, in the 27th year of her age.

Died: Of Scarlet Fever in Waterford, February 23d, Samuel Wetherill, son of S. W. and Catharine LIGGETT, in the 4th year of his age.

Wednesday, 21 March 1860   Vol. V, No. 28

Married: By the Rev. Wm. Conner BLUNT, in the Southern Methodist Church in Washington City, 13th of March, Mr. Alfred KIDWELL to Miss Sarah E. GRAY, all of Alexandria, Va.

Married: On Sunday, March 11th, at Washington DC, by the Rev. B. SUNDERLAND, D.D., John H. DUFFEY Esq. to Miss Susannah SCHAFER, both of Alexandria.

Married: On the 15th instant, by the Rev. Geo. W. HARRIS, Samuel R. SEATON to Miss Ensebia E. GIBSON, both of Loudoun.

Married: On Thursday the 15th inst., by the Rev. William GILLMORE, Mr. George W. BARR and Miss Amelia THOMAS, all of Loudoun.

Died: Near Leesburg on Thursday the 8th inst., of consumption, Mrs. Ann PEACOCK, in the 38th year of her age.

Wednesday, 28 March 1860   Vol. V, No. 29

Married: Near Taylortown on the 15th of March by Rev. G. H. MARTIN, John H. W. COMPHER to Miss Margaret Ann SPRING, both of Loudoun.

Married: On the 20th inst., near the same place, by the same, Charles W. GOODHART to Miss Mary C. HICKMAN, both of this county.

Married: On Thursday morning last, at the residence of the bride's mother, in Winchester, by Rev. C. C. WALKER, J. Smith GILKESON to Miss Virginia Lee CABELL, all of Winchester.

Married: In the Presbyterian Church, in Charlestown, on Thursday morning last, by the Rev. Dr. DUTTON, Mr. Lewis DINKLE, of Frederick Co. to Miss Maggie A. KELLEY, of the former place.

Died: On the 6th of March 1860, at the residence of his brother-in-law, Mr. Samuel JENKINS, of this county, Mr. George W. MISKEL, in the 41st year of his age.

Wednesday, 4 April 1860   Vol. V, No. 30

Moses HORNER, the fugitive slave of Charles T. BUTLER Esq. of Jefferson Co Va, whose trial in Philadelphia caused such an excitement, was returned to jail at Charlestown. He had escaped in August 1859.

Married: On Wednesday, March 28th, at the residence of the bride's father, by the Rev. Robert W. WATTS, Mr. Wm. H. HIBBS to Miss Sarah E. WALKER, both of Loudoun.

Married: On the 9th of March, in the German Reformed Church at Lovettsville, by the Rev. G. H. MARTIN, Mr. Thomas J. BROWN to Miss Matilda Jane COOPER, both of Loudoun.

Departed this life, on Saturday, March 17th, 1860, in the 67th year of her age, Mary, wife of Charles WILLIAMS, Esq. of this county.

Died: At the residence of Mr. John T. BRONAUGH, near Warrenton, Va, on Sunday evening, April 1st, Mrs. Emily E. CROSS, consort of Rev. Wm. G. CROSS, of the Virginia Annual Conference of the M. E. Church, South.

Wednesday, 11 April 1860   Vol. V, No. 31

From Warrenton, Mr. PHILIPS charged with the murder of Mr. C. R. AYRES last year at Rectortown, verdict of manslaughter and given three year sentence.

Died: At Prospect Hill, Fairfax Co, on Saturday afternoon, March 31st, Florence Jones, dau. of J. D. and Lucinda BURKE, aged 22 months.

Wednesday, 18 April 1860   Vol. V, No. 32

Married: In this town, on Tuesday morning, by Rev John LANDSTREET, James H. MUSE and Mary E. HOOK, all of Leesburg.

Married: On the 31st of March, by the Rev. G. A. NIXDORFF, Mr. Joseph L. DAVIS, of the vicinity of Leesburg, to Miss Juliann BUXTON, of Petersville district, Md.

Died: In Washington city on Sunday evening last, Frank Pierce, youngest child of Maj. Jas. F. DIVINE. The remains were brought to this town on Tuesday and interred in the Union Cemetery.

Wednesday, 25 April 1860   Vol. V, No. 33

Mr. Gustavus B. WILLIAMS killed himself on Monday evening week, near Fairfax Court House.

Married: On Tuesday evening, 17th of April, by Rev. Andrew ROBEY, Mr. James W. STEADMAN to Miss Sarah E. KLINE, both of Jefferson Co. Va.

Died: In this town, on Friday, the 20th inst., Mrs. Caroline M., wife of Dr. Thomas F. TEBBS, and daughter of Stuart THORNTON, of Norfolk, in the 33d year of her age.

Departed this life, at Unison, on the night of the 20th March, Mrs. Amanda, wife of John KEEN, Esq. and daughter of Rev. Wm. F. BRODDUS, D.D., of Fredericksburg, aged 28 years.

Died: On the 17th inst., at Monmouth, Illinois, of consumption, William H. GARDINER, formerly of Fairfax Co, in the 50th year of his age.

Died: On the 7th of March, at the residence of her son-in-law, Mr. Samuel P. THOMPSON, near Hillsborough, Mrs. Jane HOUGH, wife of Mr. William HOUGH dec'd.

Died: In this city, on the 15th instant, after a painful and protracted illness, Frank Pierce, aged 7y 6m 5d, youngest son of Maj. James F. and H. Elizabeth DIVINE, late of Va.

Wednesday, 2 May 1860   Vol. V, No. 34

Married: At the residence of Charles M. CASTLEMAN, Esq., in Alexandria, on the 25th instant, by the Rev. Thomas E. CARSON, Miss Minnie FRANCIS to Mr. James W. JOHNSTON, all of Loudoun Co.

Died: In Leesburg, on Monday, April 30th, 1860, Jane Hamilton, dau. of John W. and Anna S. WILDMAN in the 8th year of her age. Her funeral will take place this evening (Wednesday) at 3 o'clock from the residence of Mrs. Jane D. WILDMAN.

Died: In Henry Co, Iowa, on the 14th of April, after a short illness, Emily, wife of Jonathan SCHOOLEY, formerly of Loudoun County, aged about 36 years.

Wednesday, 9 May 1860   Vol. V, No. 35

Married: At the bride's father's residence in Rhea Co, Tenn., on the 12th of April 1860, by Rev. Mr. PHILLIPS, Mr. Burton LIEUTY, Merchant of Sulpher Springs, Tenn., to Miss Virginia McPHERSON, formerly of this place.

Married: On the 5th of April, near Berry's Ferry, by Rev. Jesse PORTER, James W. LLOYD to Miss Catherine E. RUTTER, both of Clarke Co.
Died: In this town on Tuesday, the 8th inst., Mr. Robert W. GOVER, in the 78th year of his age.

Wednesday, 16 May 1860   Vol. V, No. 36

Married: May 15, 1860, by Rev. Jno. LANDSTREET, John L. BURCH to Miss Mary M. McCLANAHAM, all of this county.
Married: On Thursday, the 3d inst., at the residence of the bride's father, by the Rev. Wm. GILMORE, Mr. Philip F. VANSICKLER, and Miss Sarah P. DAVIS, all of Loudoun.
Died: At the residence of W. Y. McFARLAND, Esq., in Bealton, Bell Co, Texas, on the 24th of April 1860, John SURGHNOR, in the 68th year of age. He left our town but a few months since with hopes of improving his health.
Died: In Hillsborough, Highland Co Ohio, on the 10th inst., Charles W. JACOBS, in the 46th year of age, formerly of this county.
Died: At Harper's Ferry on Monday, the 7th inst., Charles Anthony CLOWE, in the 20th year of his age, eldest son of Henry W. CLOWE, Esq., formerly of Loudoun.

Wednesday, 23 May 1860   Vol. V, No. 37

A little son of Mr. Peter VIRTS, aged about 14 years, was thrown from a colt a few miles from Leesburg on Sunday last, it is thought death must ensue. [see next issue]
Died: Suddenly, on Thursday evening, 10th inst., near Charlestown, Jefferson Co Va, Mrs. Uphemia MANNING, of Washington, formerly of Loudoun Co.

Wednesday, 30 May 1860   Vol. V, No. 38

Married: On Wednesday evening, May 23d, by Rev. Andrew ROBEY, Mr. Turner H. GALLEHER to Miss Jane D. JACOBS, eldest dau. of Capt. R. P. JACOBS, all of Loudoun.
Married: On the 14th of May, by Rev. Wm. GILMORE, Archibald F. SNAUFFER to Rebecca D. ALLNUMT [ALLNUT], of Frederick Co. Md.
Died: Near Leesburg, on Friday morning last, 25th inst., George W. VIRTS, son of Martha and Peter VIRTS, in the 14th year of his age.

Wednesday, 6 June 1860   Vol. V, No. 38 [should be 39]

Married: On the evening of the 30th May, by Elder John CLARK, William A. JACKSON, of Westmoreland Co Va to Miss Lucetta J. W., dau. of Thomas WEEDON, Esq., of Fauquier Co.
Married: Also by the same on the morning of the 31st of May, John R. LUCKETT, to Miss Mary M., dau. of Thos. WEEDON.

Died: In this place, on Saturday the 2d of June, 1860, Mary E., wife of J. Edwin YOUNG, Esq.

Died: At his father's residence in Leesburg, on the evening of the 2nd inst., George H. SAUNDERS, in the 20th year of age.

Died: On Thursday last, the 31st inst., at the residence of her brother, Richard H. SUMMERS, Miss Rebecca SUMMERS, in the 68th year of age. Member of the M. E. Church.

Wednesday, 13 June 1860 Vol. V, No. 39

Married: At Crawfordis, near Charlestown, on Wednesday, June 6th, by the Rev. N. G. NORTH, Joseph C. BARTLETT Esq., of Frederick Co, Va to Miss Eleanor A. WORTHINGTON, daughter of late Robert WORTHINGTON.

Married: Near Providence chapel, on the 27th day of May 1860, by the Rev. Jesse PORTER, James MUGANT of Jefferson Co to Miss Eliza KELLY of Clark Co Va.

Wednesday, 20 June 1860 Vol. V, No. 40

Married: At Trap, Loudoun Co, on the 14th inst., by Rev. R. W. WATTS, Mr. T. Sherman LAKE, of Upperville, to Miss Martha J. LITTLETON.

Married: In Berryville, on Tuesday morning last, by the Rev. Mr. WHITE, Mr. Wm. H. MOORE, to Mrs. Amelia H. BEARD, daughter of the late Dr. Alexander STRAITH, all of Jefferson Co.

Married: At the residence of her mother, in the county of Brunswick, on Wednesday, the 13th inst., by the Rev. J. C. BAILY, Rev. E. S. TAYLOR, of Loudoun Co., to Miss Margaret E. BASS, of Brunswick Co. Va

Died: At his son's residence in Washington City, June 6th 1860, Mr. Samuel DAILY, in the 70th year of age.

Wednesday, 27 June 1860 Vol. V, No. 41

Died: At the residence of R. M. BENTLY, Esq., on Saturday last, J. H. Tegmeyer, infant son of John H. and Bettie P. STAUB, aged 6m 9d.

Wednesday, 4 July 1860 Vol. V, No. 42

Married: On Tuesday, the 19th inst., by Rev. X. J. RICHARDSON, Mr. Rynord JACOBS to Miss Sally FRITZ, all of this county.

Married: In Middleburg on Wednesday, 27th June, by the Rev. O. A. KINSOLVING, George LEE, Esq. of Nashville, Tenn and Laura F., youngest daughter of Gen. Asa ROGERS, of Loudoun County.

Died: In Charlestown Wednesday morning last, after a long illness, Mrs. Margaret SHEETZ, relict of the late Michael SHEETZ, aged 73 years.

Died: In this town, on the 26th June 1860, Leven, infant son of L. W. S. and Sarah HOUGH, aged 8m 15d.

Died: At her residence near Leesburg, the 17th of June 1860, Mrs. Magdalena WILLIAMS, in the 78th year of age, wife of the late Ellis WILLIAMS.

Wednesday, 11 July 1860   Vol. V, No. 43

Died: In Leesburg, on the 9th inst., Miss Lucy Ellen, daughter of the late Col. William ELLZEY.

Wednesday, 18 July 1860   Vol. V, No. 44

Died: At his residence near Lovettsville, on Tuesday morning, the 3rd inst., of cholera morbus, after a short sickness, Mr. John GEORGE Sr. aged 82y 4m 24d.

Died: At his residence near Hoyesville on Monday morning, the 2d inst., after a short sickness, Mr. Henry FAWLEY, in his 77th year.

Wednesday, 25 July 1860   Vol. V, No. 45

Married: On Thursday evening, July 5th, near Halifax Court House, Va, by the Rev. Mr. BUTLER, Jno. Henry POWELL, of Loudoun, to Rebecca, only daughter of Thos. LEIGH Esq., of Halifax Co Va.

Died: At West End, Fairfax Co, on the 17th instant, after a brief illness, Lydia Virginia HEATON [HAMILTON?], aged 34 years, the consort of E. J. HAMILTON, who with four children survives. She was a native of Loudoun Co.

Died: In Snickersville, on the 16th instant, Mrs. Phebe HOFFMAN, aged 81y 2m 13d. She was a member of the Baptist Church for many years and the last of the CLAYTON family, who was amongst the first settlers of the village.

Wednesday, 1 August 1860   Vol. V, No. 46

Died: At his residence near this place, on Saturday 21st inst., Gustavus ELGIN, in the 70th year of his age.

Died: At Mt. Gilead, at the residence of his grandfather, on Sunday morning, July 22nd 1860, Wm. Benjamin, only son of G. W. and E. LICKEY, aged 2m 22d.

Died: In Knoxville, Tenn., on Wednesday morning, July 25th, Lewis Klein, infant son of Geo. W. and M. E. BRADFIELD, aged 10m 14d.

Wednesday, 8 August 1860   Vol. V, No. 47

Married: On Tuesday evening, the 31st July, by Rev. Andrew ROBEY, Mr. Henry G. SAMPSELL to Mrs. Lucinda UTTERBACK, all of Loudoun.

Married: At Castle Point, on Thursday, July 26th, by the Rt. Rev. W. H. ODENHEIMER, Hon. M. R. H. GARNETT, of Va, to Mary P. daughter of E. A. STEVENS, of Hoboken.

Died: In Leesburg, on Monday evening, 6th inst., of typhoid fever, Mr. Ewell ATTWELL, in the 42d years of his age.

Died: At Waterford, on Monday night, 6th instant, of paralysis, Mrs. MOUNT, wife of Mr. John MOUNT, of that place.

Died: At her residence in this county on the 20th ult., Mrs. Albinah CRAVEN, wife of Joel CRAVEN Sr., in the 71st year of her age. She leaves a husband and large family of children.

Wednesday, 15 August 1860   Vol. V, No. 48

Married: At Eastern View, Fauquier Co, the residence of the bride's father, on the morning of the 26th ultimo, by Rev. Mr. WARD, of the Va Conference, T. L. GALLEHER, Esq., of Richmond, to Miss Emma Walton, second daughter of George BROUN, Esq.

Married: On Tuesday evening week, in Charlestown, by the Rev. Wm. J. PERRY, Mr. John A. BLAKE, of Rippon, Jefferson Co, to Miss Maggie A. RUST, of Charlestown.

Died: Of typhoid fever, on Saturday morning, the 12th inst., in his 16th year, John Armistead, second son of R. C. BRADEN, Esq.

Died: In Leesburg, Aug. 10th, Theodore I.?, eldest child of John T. and Mary PERRY, in the 18th year of his age, and the third year of his Christian Pilgrimage.

Wednesday, 22 August 1860   Vol. V, No. 49

Married: At the Parsonage in Warrenton, on Thursday, the 16th inst., by the Rev. E. D. OWEN, Mr. James H. SWART and Miss Elizabeth F., dau. of Mr. John SMALE, all of Leesburg.

Died: At Woodburn, near Leesburg, on Thursday, August 16th, Thomas Clagett, infant son of Alexandria H. and Julia H. ROGERS, aged 11m 28d.

Died: In Leesburg, on Sunday, August 19th, at 1 p.m., of congestion of the brain, Herbert Adolphe, infant son of Horatio N. and Mary L. EGGLESTON, aged 7m 18d.

Died: On the 15th August, at the residence of Mr. Franklin CARTER, Loudoun Co, Henry Braden, infant son of Henry E. and Mary E. PEYTON, aged 5m 21d.

Died: In Washington on Friday, the 17th instant, Mrs. Jane CASTLEMAN, wife of Stephen D. CASTLEMAN, and daughter of Thomas COOKENDORFER, in the 41st year of her age.

Died: At Fairfax C. H., on Sunday morning 19th inst., Kate S., infant daughter of Henry W. and J. M. THOMAS, aged 5 months.

Died: In the village of Hamilton, July 31st, Martha, wife of John HUGHES, aged 46 years.

Died: On Tuesday, August 14th at Oakley his residence in Nelson Co Va, William T. HELM, formerly of Clarke Co in his 65th year.

Died: At Capon Springs, on Monday 12th instant, A. J. O'BANNON, Fourth Auditor of the U. S. Treasury, aged 45. ...

Wednesday, 29 August 1860   Vol. V, No. 50

Mahlon TAVENNER charged with counterfeiting coin. [later issue states found not guilty]

Died: In Philadelphia, on Thursday last, after a protracted illness, Anne Harriotte, daughter of Henry T. HARRISON Esq., of this town, in the 19th year of age.

Died: At his residence near Gum Spring, on Thursday, 16th inst., Lewis N. BRADSHAW, in the 31st year of his age.

Wednesday, 5 September 1860   Vol. V, No. 51

Died: In Middleburg, on Wednesday, August 29th, of typhoid fever, Dr. Scott B. SMITH, son of Hugh SMITH, in his 26th year.

Died: On Sunday night last, after a lingering illness of consumption, Judge Robert Baldwin SHERRARD, of Marysville, California, son of Joseph H. SHERRARD Esq. of Winchester, aged 33 years.

Wednesday, 12 September 1860   Vol. V, No. 52

Mr. George ISLER, of Jefferson Co, died on Friday evening last, in the 69th year of his age. He left an estate worth from $40,000 – $50,000, including 15 or 20 servants, which he liberated by his will. Sister, Mrs. Susan LINDSEY, of Nashville, Illinois, formerly of this town, children of brother Mr. Abraham ISLER.

Married: At the residence of the bride's father, H. KEYES Esq., of Charlestown, on the 5th of September 1860, by Rev. Walter W. WILLIAMS, of Leesburg, Rev. Charles E. AMBLER, of Charlestown, to Miss Susan W. KEYES.

Married: On the 20th ult., at the M. E. Parsonage, Harper's Ferry, by the Rev. G. G. BROOKS, Nathan H. COPELAND and Sarah C. DUNCAN, of Jefferson.

Married: On the 5th instant, by Rev. Thaddeus HERNDON, John E. FRANCIS, of Miss., to Miss Mary E. HOGE, of Loudoun.

Married: On Sunday the 2d inst., by Rev. Goheen HAMMOND, Mr. Braden E. HUMMER to Miss Laura T. WHALEY, all of Loudoun.

Died: On the 29th of July, ultimo, in Knox Co, Missouri, Mrs. Jane FULTON, wife of John FULTON, Esq., formerly of this county, in her 54th year. About a year ago a cancer appeared on her breast.

Died: In Leesburg, on the 30th Aug 1850 [60], Marie Cooper CHANDLER, dau. of Catharine and William CHANDLER, Commander U. S. Navy, aged 23m 1d.

Wednesday, 19 September 1860   Vol. VI, No. 1

Married: At the M. E. Church, Smithfield, Jefferson Co, Va, by Rev. J. H. WAUGH, Joseph A. RAUM Esq. of Charlestown, to Miss Lizzie G. BARNES, of the former place.

Died: In Charlestown, On Thursday morning last, Mrs. Idela TUTWILER, wife of Jacob TUTWILER, aged 58 years.

Wednesday, 26 September 1860   Vol. VI, No. 2

Married: At "Bedford" near Shepherdstown, Va, on Wednesday morning the 19th inst., by Rev. Chas. W. ANDREWS, D.D., Col. Armistead T. M. RUST, of Loudoun, and Miss Ida LEE, daughter of Edmund I. LEE, Esq., of Jefferson Co Virginia.

Married: At "Ellerslie" in Jefferson Co, on Thursday evening last, by Rev. Dr. W. B. DUTTON, Mr. John HILLERY, of Maryland, to Miss Jennett S. HENDERSON, dau. of the late Richard HENDERSON, of Jefferson County.

Married: In Washington, on Saturday afternoon, 16th instant, by the Rev. Mr. HAMILTON, Charles M. MILLER, of Shepherdstown, Jefferson Co, to Miss Levinia FLOWERS, of that city.

Died: On the 26th of August, Mrs. Mary E. CARTER, wife of James L. CARTER, of Clarke Co, and daughter of Mrs. Elizabeth CONRAD, of Loudoun Co, aged 31 years. Also on the 13th of September, her little son Lewis Conrad CARTER, aged 2w 4d.

Died: On the 28th of August last at St. Louis, Mo, Mrs. Elvira McLEAN, wife of Hector D. McLEAN of that city, daughter of the late Charles G. WINTERSMITH, of Harper's Ferry.

Died: On Sunday morning last after a brief illness, Mrs. Sarah Warden ISLER, wife of Mr. Abraham ISLER of Jefferson Co, aged 63 years.

Died: On the 6th, Fleet, youngest son of Maria and Fleet G. RUST, Esq., Carrington, Upper Fauquier, aged 8y 6m.

Died: At his residence in Culpeper County, on Friday last, Hon. James French STROTHER. At one time represented the Loudoun district in the Congress of the U.S.

Died: On Thursday, 20th inst., Roland Belt, only son of Bushrod L. and Virginia FOX, aged 1y 4m.

Died: On the 20th inst., Vincent MOSS Esq. of Loudoun, aged 92 years.

Died: Mrs. Mary Cecilia WHITE, consort of John R. WHITE Esq., of "Locust Thicket," near Hillsborough, departed this life on Saturday, 15th inst. She was born May 1814 and in the summer of 1829 converted to the M. E. Church.

Wednesday, 3 October 1860   Vol. VI, No. 3

Married: In this town, on Wednesday morning, September 26th 1860, by Rev. John LANDSTREET, Mr. Christian DEBOW, of Baltimore and Miss Elizabeth A. LOTT, of Leesburg.

Married: In Trinity Church, Shepherdstown, on the 20th inst., by Rev. Dr. ANDREWS, Rev. Jos. R. JONES, Rector of the Episcopal Church at Millwood, in Clarke Co, and Miss Courtney B., dau. of John W. BYRD, of that county.

Married: On the 30th ult., by Rev. S. GOVER, Daniel H. KEYES and Angelina RINKER, all of Loudoun.

Married: On the 26th instant, at Fountain Rock, the residence of the bride's father, in Jefferson Co, Va by the Rev. Charles W. ANDREWS, D.D, Henry A. DIDIER, of Baltimore, and Angelica, second daughter of Hon. Alexander R. BOTELER.

Died: On Sunday the 9th inst., at Hughesville, blind Alice, daughter of Benjamin F. TAYLOR, in the 17th year of her age.

Died: At home in Princeton, Mercer Co Va, on the 18th of August 1860. Mrs. Elizabeth A. ASHWORTH, aged 29y 7m 11d, of consumption. She was the daughter of Solomon and Charity VANVACTOR, formerly of Loudoun, where she was born and raised. On the 13th of September 1852 she married Mr. Granville H. ASHWORTH, of Mercer Co. Va. Member of the Methodist Church.

Wednesday, 10 October 1860   Vol. VI, No. 4

Married: At the Parsonage of the German Reformed Church, near Lovettsville, on Thursday, the 27th of Sept., by the Rev. George H. MARTIN, Mr. Robert BOOTH to Elizabeth FRITTS, both of Loudoun.

Married: At the residence of Andrew SEITZ, Esq. near Hoyesville, on Wednesday evening, the 26th inst., by Rev. George H. MARTIN, Mr. Thomas J. COST, of Wheatland, to Miss Jane Amelia YAKEY, only dau. of the late Martin YAKEY.

Died: Dr. Frank T. GRADY on the morning of Tuesday, 18th September after an illness of seven months.

Died: In Rectortown, Fauquier, Saturday evening, August 25th, 1860, Sarah M. SAMPSELL, wife of A. J. SAMPSELL, in less than an hour of illness.

Died: At "Temple Hall," Loudoun Co. on 26th Sept., Henrietta, infant dau. of Henry A. and Elizabeth BALL, aged 18 months.

Wednesday, 17 October 1860   Vol. VI, No. 5

Married: At "Fontanville," Fairfax Co, the residence of the bride's father, on Tuesday evening, 9th Oct., by the Rev. Henry C. CHEATHAM, Dr. Robt. I. SIMPSON, formerly of Loudoun Co, and Miss Mary Randolph, youngest dau. of Capt. Chas. F. FORD, all of Fairfax Co.

Married: On the 2d inst. in the 3d Reformed Church, Baltimore, by Rev. S. S. FOULK, Anthony S. CHAMBERS, formerly of Martinsburg, to Miss Mary E. MIDDLEKAUF, of Baltimore.

Married: On the 9th inst., by the Rev. S. H. M. LEMON, Mr. Wm. H. TIPPETT, of Loudoun Co, to Miss Emma ARNOLD, of Washington.

Died: At her father's residence in Clarke Co, on the 5th inst., Mrs. Emma NELSON, the wife of Philip NELSON, and daughter of Mr. John E. PAGE, at the age of 28 years.

Died: Very suddenly, on October 9th, at Waveland, the residence of her husband, in Fauquier co, Eleanor Love, aged 36, the wife of John Augustus WASHINGTON.

Died: At his residence at Oatland, on Tuesday, the 4th inst., Hugh H. DOWNS, aged 35y 9m 24d.

Died: On Sabbath, the 7th inst., at the residence of Maj. George PETER, from injuries sustained by a fall from his horse, Jas. Henderson PETER, third son of the late Jno. P. C. PETER, Esq. of Montgomery Co Md. He was nearly 20 years of age.

Wednesday, 24 October 1860   Vol. VI, No. 6

Died: On September 16, 1860, at the residence of her father, in Loudoun County, Lanea, youngest daughter of Fielding and Hannah TAVENNER, in the 6th year of her age.

Married: At Oxford, Md, on the 10th inst., by the Rev. G. W. KENNEDY, John H. B. LEWIS, Esq. of Jefferson Co, Va. to Miss Mary Ellen KENNEDY, dau. of the officiating clergyman.

Married: On Thursday evening, the 11th instant, at the residence of the bride's father near Fairfax Court House, by the Rev. W. G. COE, Mr. William W. SKINNER, of Washington, Co, Va, and Miss Gertrude, eldest dau. of Mr. John W. GRAHAM, of Fairfax Co.

Wednesday, 31 October 1860   Vol. VI, No. 7

Died: In Leesburg, on Saturday night last, after a protracted illness of much suffering, Mrs. Harriet DRISH, wife of Mr. William D. DRISH, in the 61st year of her age.

Died: Near Middleburg, on the morning of the 16th inst., of consumption, Miss Sarah Richardson McCARTY, daughter of the late Geo. Washington McCARTY, in the 33d year of her age.

Died: In this town, on Wednesday, the 24th inst., Charles, infant son of Geo. T. and Ellen LAMDEN, aged 2m 18d.

Died: In Baltimore on the 27th instant of consumption, George ISETT, formerly of Leesburg, in the 30th year of his age.

Married: In the Parsonage of the Ger. Ref. Church, near Lovettsville, on the 16th instant, by the Rev. G. H. MARTIN, Mr. John W. CRIM and Miss Catharine M. CARN, both of Loudoun.

Married: On Tuesday, the 23d instant at the residence of the bride's father, near Hamilton, by Rev. Samuel GOVER, Charles G. WARNER, to Caroline V. TAVENNER, of Loudoun.

Married: On Wednesday, 16th inst., in the Chapel of William and Mary College, by Rev. R. T. BROWN, M. Dulany BALL, Esq. of Fairfax Co, to Miss Sallie U. WRIGHT, of Williamsburg.

Wednesday, 7 November 1860   Vol. VI, No. 8

In Warrenton, last week, a young man named McCLANAHAN, attacked a son of Inman H. SUDDITH, of that place, for alledged slander of him. SUDDITH defended himself with a knife, severing McCLANAHAN's femoral artery, causing his death in a few moments.

Married: In Leesburg, on Tuesday evening, the 30th ultimo, by Rev. H. R. SMITH, John McKIMMY and Sarah J., only dau. of James GARRISON Esq.

Married: On the 21st of October, by the Rev. Geo. W. HARRIS, Robert E. RUSSEL, Esq. and Miss Ellen FURR, daughter of Wm. FURR, Esq., both of Loudoun County.

Married: At Oakwood, Fauquier Co, on Thursday, November 1st 1860, by the Rev. A. D. POLLOCK, James Henry RIVES and Eliza Gordon SCOTT, eldest daughter of Robert E. SCOTT, Esq.

Married: On Thursday, the 1st inst., by the Rev. O. A. KINSOLVING, William CARMICHAEL Esq. of Maryland and Harriet H., eldest daughter of Dr. F. W. POWELL, of Middleburg.

Died: On board steamer Planet, near Vicksburg on Saturday, 20th inst., H. H. RHODES, of Virginia, aged 58 years.

Died: Near Danville, Montgomery Co Missouri, Oct 23d, 1860, Mortimer McILHANY, in the 60th year of his age.

Wednesday, 14 November 1860   Vol. VI, No. 9

Married: On Thursday morning, November 1st by the Rev. S. S. ROSZEL, Harvie Sheffield DUVAL, of the U.S. Coast Survey, and Mary Louisa, dau. of the late Rev. Stephen Asbury ROSZEL.

Married: On Tuesday evening, the 30th ultimo, at Grape Hill, in Nelson Co, Va, by the Rev. George W. NULLEY, Alpheus L. EDWARDS Esq. of Washington city, DC, and Matilda C. SMILEY, the gifted bard of the former place.

Married: On Thursday evening, the 1st instant by Rev. H. R. SMITH, James B. ELGIN of Montgomery Co Md and Miss Sarah, daughter of B. F. TAYLOR Esq. of Loudoun.

Married: At Exeter on the 25th of Oct 1860, Sallie, infant daughter of Abner C. and Lizzie A. TRUNDLE, aged 10m 9d.

Married: On the 9th inst., by Rev. George WOODBRIDGE, D.D., Rev. Henry A. WISE, Rector of the Church of our Saviour, Philadelphia, to Hattie, daughter of H. Barton HAXALL Esq. of Richmond, Va.

Married: On the 22d of Oct., by Rev. A. BROADDUS, at the residence of the bride's father, in Caroline Co, Mr. John G. SHIRLEY, of Jefferson Co, to Miss Mary Ellen GARRETT, of Caroline Co, Va.

Married: At Clover Lea, Hanover Co, Va, on the 6th inst. by Rev. Mr.. CORRAWAY, Col. Lewis W. WASHINGTON, of Beall Air, Jefferson Co. Va, to Ella M., daughter of Geo. W. BASSETT, Esq. The groom is the great grandson of two brothers of Gen. WASHINGTON, and the bride the great grandmother [dau.] of the only sister of Gen. WASHINGTON, and also great-granddau. of the sister of Mrs. Geo. WASHINGTON.

Married: On the 7th instant by the Rev. George W. HARRIS, Isaac FLETCHER, Esq., of Fauquier, to Miss Mary E. CASTLEMAN, eldest dau. of Alfred CASTLEMAN, Esq., of Clarke Co.

Wednesday, 21 November 1860   Vol. VI, No. 10

No marriages or deaths.

Wednesday, 28 November 1860   Vol. VI, No. 11

Married: On the 14th inst., in Dinwiddie, by the Rev. Nelson HEAD, Chas. O. KENT, to Miss Mary Nelson HEAD, daughter of the officiating minister, both of that place.

Married: On the 21st inst., at the residence of Mr. Isaac GEORGE, in Alexandria, by Rev. N. S. GREENAWAY, Mr. Daniel J. HOGE, to Miss Sarah E. TAYLOR, both of Loudoun County.

Married: On the 21st inst., in Christ Church, by the Right Rev. Bishop JOHNS, Wm. Elzey GRAY of Loudoun Co, to Rachel, daughter of the late Dr. Sidney W. SMITH, of Alexandria, Va.

Married: At Hill and Dale, the residence of the bride's father, on Wednesday, 21st instant, by Rev. H. SUTER, Mr. C. VANDEVENTER, of Loudoun, and Miss Cecelia MORGAN, daughter of Col. Benj. MORGAN, of Clarke Co.

Wednesday, 5 December 1860   Vol. VI, No. 12

Married: At the residence of the bride's mother, Mrs. STEWART, November 27th 1860, by the Rev. Henry C. CHEATHAM, Mr. John F. SIMPSON, of Loudoun County and Miss Fannie A. STEWART, of Fairfax County.

Died: In Leesburg, on Sunday morning, the 2d of December, at 5 o'clock, Mrs. Henrietta GASSAWAY, widow of the late Thomas GASSAWAY, in the 71st year of her age.

[From *White Hall (Ill.) Sentinel*] Died in White Hall, on the 21st inst. of pulmonary consumption, Wilson J. DRISH, M. D. Aged 55 years. He was a native of Leesburg, Va, but removed to this place several years ago.

Died: In Washington city, on the 16th ult., Hattie C., infant dau. of William and Sallie C. BURKE.

Wednesday, 12 December 1860   Vol. VI, No. 13

Married: On Thursday the 6th inst., by Rev. H. R. SMITH, William H. FAIR and Miss Betsey GREGG, all of Loudoun.

Died: On Saturday, the 1st of December at his residence in Hillsborough, Dr. Samuel TURNER, in the 62d year of his age. He located in Hillsborough in 1821.

Wednesday, 19 December 1860   Vol. VI, No. 14

Married: In Washington DC, on Tuesday, the 11th inst., by the Rev. Mr. McCAULEY, John H. KELCHNER, formerly of Pa, to Miss Martha E. GARNER, of Leesburg, Va.

Died: At "Potomac Furnace" on Wednesday the 13th inst., Mrs. Jane MULLEN, wife of Michael MULLEN Esq. in the 57th year of her age.

Died: On the 26th of November, at the residence of his sister-in-law, in this county (Mrs. C. L. DOWNS), Samuel G. HANCOCK, in the 79th year of his age, after a short but painful illness.

Died: At the residence of her father, on the 11th of December, Kate, daughter of George HICKMAN, of Loudoun, in her 3d year.

Died: In Leesburg, on Monday, the 10th inst., of typhoid fever, Miss Eleanor SEIBER, in the 17th year of her age.

Chancery Ct. Oct 16th 1860: Conway ROBINSON, William LEIGH and Raleigh T. COLSTON against Fielding LITTLETON, late Sheriff of Loudoun Co, Admr. of Josiah MURRAY dec'd, David HIXSON Sheriff of Loudoun, Admr. dbn of Josiah MURRAY dec'd, Harriet MURRAY, widow, Ralph MURRAY, John MURRAY and the unknown descendants of Samuel MURRAY dec'd – debts.

Wednesday, 26 December 1860   Vol. VI, No. 15

Married: In Warren Co, on Tuesday the 4th inst., by Rev. W. GILMORE, Vincent R. RUST, of Kanawha, and Miss Anna M. HICKS, of Warren Co.

Married: On Thursday, the 6th inst. by the same, Charles E. POWELL and Miss Elizabeth SKILLMAN, all of Loudoun.

Married: On the same day, by the same, Burr W. GARRET and Miss Lucinda FRANCIS, all of Loudoun.

Died: At the Pickett House Leesburg on Wednesday last, Benj. MAULSBY, in the 71st year of his age.

Died: In Leesburg, on Tuesday morning, the 18th instant, Mrs. Dorcas ADAMS, in the 48th year of her age.

Departed this life, October 28th, 1860, Mary J. NICHOLS, dau. of William and Catharine NICHOLS, in the 21st year of her age.

Wednesday, 2 January 1861   Vol. VI, No. 16

Married: In Leesburg, on Monday, the 30th inst., by the Rev. S. GOVER, Mr. George MONDAY and Miss Mary WILS, both of Loudoun.

Married: In Georgetown DC, on the 24th inst., by the Rev. H. C. KEMIE, Mr. Edward S. WRIGHT to Miss Mary A. DIVIND [DIVINE], both of Loudoun.

Married: On the 11th inst., on Great Ca-capon [Capon?], Morgan Co, Va. by Rev Wm. CHAMPION, Rev. G. L. TORREYSON, of Baltimore Annual Conference M. E. S. to Emma F., second daughter of N. N. CLABAUGH.

Married: Near Gum Spring, Loudoun Co, on the 14th ultimo, by Rev. W. G. HAMMOND, Mr. G. W. F. MANKIN and Miss Mary C. HU[T]CHINSON, both of Loudoun.

Died: At the "Beveridge House," in Middleburg, on Monday, Dec. 24th, John W. STEVENS, in the 32d year of his age.

Wednesday, 9 January 1861   Vol. VI, No. 17

Married: In Lewistown, Frederick Co Md, on Tuesday, January 1st, by Rev. L. D. HERRON, on the East Balt. Con, M. E. C., Mr. James W. N. SMITH to Miss Annie E. CURRY, both of Loudoun Co.

Married: On the 1st inst., by Rev. A. H. SPILLMAN, Mr. Alfred HALL to Miss Amanda Virginia SQUIRES, all of Fauquier.

Died: In Middleburg, on Sunday, 16th Dec, Mrs. Tingey Ann, wife of Henry G. SMITH, and daughter of Daniel F. DULANY Esq., of Fairfax Co, aged 26 years. Leaves a husband and two little boys.

Died: On Thursday, December 27th, near Mt. Gilead, Thomas, fifth son of David L. and Margaret F. HUGHES, aged 2y 2m 28d.

Died: At her residence in Hamilton on second day, the 24th of 12th month, Sarah SANDS, in the 77th year of her age.

Wednesday, 16 January 1861   Vol. VI, No. 18

Married: On the 13th Dec, by Rev. Jesse PORTER, Mr. Albert CARLISLE, of Loudoun, and Miss Cornelia KNIGHT, of Clarke co.

Married: By the same, on the 24th December, Mr. Wm. BRABHAM and Miss Sarah Jane JENKINS, all of Loudoun.

Married: by the same, on the 27th December, Craven SHELL and Miss Lucinda BELL, both of Clarke Co.

Died: At Harper's Ferry, on the 24th of November, Mrs. Martha Ellen AVIS, aged 37 years, wife of William AVIS, and daughter of Thomas and Ellen MARLOW, of Frederick Co Md.

Wednesday, 23 January 1861   Vol. VI, No. 19

Married: On Wednesday evening, the 16th instant, by the Rev H. R. SMITH, Mr. William A. DENNIS and Miss Mary E. KELLY, all of Loudoun.

Wednesday, 30 January 1861   Vol. VI, No. 20

Married: On Thursday, January 10th 1861, by Rev. S. S. ROSZEL, James E. KIDWELL and Miss Mary E. MYERS, both of Loudoun.

Married: On Sunday, the 20th of Jan, by the Rev. Andrew ROBEY, Mr. Ephraim FURR, to Miss Amanda FULLER, both of Clarke Co.

Died: On the morning of the 19th instant, while on a visit to her Aunt in Washington City, Miss Virginia Clay, daughter of James H. MUSE, of Leesburg, in the 17th year of her age.

Wednesday, 6 February 1861   Vol. VI, No. 21

Married: On Thursday, the 24th ultimo, at the residence of David CARR, Esq., by Rev. F. H. RICHEY, Mr. Jonathan GORE to Miss Susan C. TAYLOR, both of Loudoun.

Married: On Thursday, 24th ultimo, by Friends Ceremony, in Waterford, Lewis W. STEER to Elizabeth M. HOUGH, dau. of Amosa and Ann E. HOUGH.

Died: Near Dranesville, Fairfax Co, Va on Wednesday evening, the 23d ult., after a painful illness of 8 days, of bilious pneumonia, Major James COLEMAN, in the 63d year of his age, leaving a wife and large family of children.

Chancery Ct., 4 Feb 1861: Julia HOUSHOLDER against James W. HAMILTON Exor. of Gideon HOUSHOLDER dec'd, James W. HAMILTON as Exor of John HAMILTON dec'd, James W. HAMILTON and Edward F. HAMILTON Admrs. dbn of Hamilton HOUSHOLDER dec'd, James W. HAMILTON individually, Columbus HOUSHOLDER and Columbus SPECHER & wife Martha and others – settlement of estate of Gideon HOUSHOLDER dec'd.

Wednesday, 13 February 1861   Vol. VI, No. 22

Married: On Thursday, the 7th inst., at the residence of Mr. Benjamin SAUNDERS, near Leesburg, by Rev. R. W. WATTS, Mr. George W. WYNKOOP, to Miss Susan A. SAUNDERS, all of Loudoun.

Married: On the 5th of February, at Gumspring, by Rev. A. ROBEY, Mr. Albert DAVIS to Miss Susan E. AMBLER, all of Loudoun Co.

Died: Near Leesburg, on Wednesday, the 9th ult, James William, eldest son of Samuel and Matilda LACOCK, in the 22nd year of his age.

Wednesday, 20 February 1861   Vol. VI, No. 23

Married: By the Rev. H. SHAULL, at the residence of the bride's father, near Smithfield, on the 5th inst., J. W. McGINNIS, Esq. to Miss Rosanna E., third dau. of Bartholomew and Sally SHAULL, all of Jefferson Co.

Married: On the morning of the 13th inst., at the parsonage, Duffield's, Jefferson Co, Va, by Rev. Silas BILLINGS, George W. NEILL, Esq., of Jefferson Co, to Miss Elizabeth W. SHEPARD, formerly of Rochester, NY.

Married: On the 30th of Jan, by the Rev. G. W. HARRIS, Mr. Richard C. CHAMBLIN and Miss Sarah E. ATWELL, both of this county.

Married: On Tuesday, the 12th instant, by the Rev. H. R. SMITH, Wm. A. HAVENNER and Lydia D. EDWARDS, all of Loudoun.

Died: At his residence near Aldie, in this county, on the 5th of December 1860, Mr. William A. DENNIS, in the 86th year of age.

Died: In Waterford, on the 4th instant, Mrs. Cornelia J. McKINNEY, in the 30th year of her age, wife of James H. McKINNEY.

Wednesday, 6 March 1861   Vol. VI, No. 25

Married: At the residence of Thomas NICHOLS, on the 20th of 2d months, by Friends Ceremony, Wm. G. SMITH to Elizabeth NICHOLS, all of Loudoun.

Married: On Thursday, 21st instant, at the Charles Street Church, Baltimore, by Rev. John S. MARTIN, Rev. Wm. J. PERRY, of the Baltimore Conference, to Miss Hattie R., daughter of the officiating minister.

Died: In this county, on Saturday morning, of consumption, Mr. Harvey O. MILLS, formerly of Alexandria, in the 26th year of his age.

Died: In this town, on Saturday last, Mrs. Margaret JOHNSON in the __ year of her age.

Died: At her residence in Rectortown, Fauquier Co, Harriet WEADON, wife of Capt. John WEADON, in the 52d year of her age.

Wednesday, 13 March 1861   Vol. VI, No. 26

Died: In this town, on Wednesday last, Mr. Jabez T. WOODWARD, in the 75th year of his age.

Died: At Beauford, Mo, on Friday, March 1st, 1861, Mr. Michael HAVENER, formerly of this county, in the 51st year of his age.

Died: In St. Louis, Missouri, at the residence of her son, Steuart CARTER, Friday evening, at 10½ p.m. of pneumonia, Mrs. Judith A. CARTER, aged 57 years.

Departed this life on the 5th of February, Dr. Caleb B. R. KENNERLY, of Clarke Co.

Died: Near Brimfield, Peoria Co, Illinois, on Thursday, 21st February, 1861, after a protracted and excruciating disease of cancer, Capt. Elam JACOBS, formerly of Loudoun Co, in his 66th year.

Died: On the 2d instant after a lingering illness of consumption, Miss Mary, second daughter of Dr. Randolph KOWNSLAR, of Berryville, aged 22 years.

Married: On the 25th of Feb in Snickersville, by Rev. Jesse PORTER, George CALLAHAN to Miss Margaret KENT, both of Loudoun Co.

Married: On the 28th, by the same, in Clarke Co, David F. WOOD to Miss Mary E. FLOYD, both of that county.

Married: On the 21st ult., by Rev. J. H. WAUGH, John T. HARRIS and Miss Sarah BACKHOUSE, dau. of George BACKHOUSE, Esq., all of Jefferson County.

Wednesday, 20 March 1861   Vol. VI, No. 27

Married: At Wm. H. KIDWELL's, on the 17th ult., by Elder Lloyd KIDWELL, Mr. Daniel W. BLUNDELL, of the County of Loudoun, and Miss Eliza KIDWELL, of Fairfax Co.

Wednesday, 27 March 1861   Vol. VI, No. 28
Married: At Sailor's Rest, on Thursday, the 21st inst., by Rev. S. GOVER, Mr. Adam F. LOY and Miss Hannah A. FRY, all of Loudoun.
Died: After a protracted illness of consumption, on the 19th inst., Mrs. Rebecca CHINN, daughter of the late Walter ELGIN, in the 54th year of her age.

Wednesday, 3 April 1861   Vol. VI, No. 29
Married: On Thursday, the 14th instant, by the Rev. X. J. RICHARDSON, Mr. John D. FRY and Miss Mary C. MANN, all of this county.
Married: At the Presbyterian Mance, on Thursday morning, the 28th inst., by Rev. H. R. SMITH, Mr. George W. MATTHEW and Miss Mary A. JAMES, all of Loudoun.

Wednesday, 10 April 1861   Vol. VI, No. 30
Married: On the 19th of March, by Rev. Whiteford SMITH, D. D. of South Carolina Conference, Rev. W. W. DUNCAN, of the Virginia Conference, and Miss Medora RICE, of Union District, South Carolina.
Married: In Charlestown, on the 19th ultimo, by Rev. Mr. SHARP, David J. COE, of Loudoun, and Miss Mary J., daughter of Adam BARR, of Jefferson Co Virginia.

Wednesday, 17 April 1861   Vol. VI, No. 31
Married: On Tuesday evening, the 9th of April, in the M. E. Church, South, in Hillsborough, by Rev. John F. POULTON, Dr. James W. TAYLOR and Miss Sophie A., daughter of Dr. Frederick A. DAVISSON, both of the above place.
Married: On the morning of the 10th instant, at the residence of Dr. Wm. H. McVEIGH, Fairfax co, by Elder Thaddeus HERNDON, Elder Thomas B. SHEPHERD, of Clarke Co, to Miss Ella V., second daughter of the late Thomas ROGERS, of Loudoun.
Died: On Monday, the 8th instant, at Red Hill near Gumspring, Mrs. Martha ALLEN, in the 74th year of her age.
Died: In Jefferson, Frederick Co Md, on the 7th inst., of consumption, Miss Eliza H. LYNCH, in the 38th year of her age.
Died: In Leesburg, on Tuesday the 2d of April, Mrs. Margaret H. HANES, in the 56th year of her age.

Wednesday, 24 April 1861   Vol. VI, No. 32
Died: On Thursday, the 4th of April, at his residence in Loudoun Co, Mr. William EWERS, in the 60th year of his age.

Wednesday, 1 May 1861   Vol. VI, No. 33

No marriages or deaths. Part of paper is missing.

Wednesday, 8 May 1861   Vol. VI, No. 34

Married: On the 23d inst., by the Rev. Geo. W. HARRIS, Mr. B. Fenelon TAYLOR, of Wilmington, Del., to Miss Eliza R., daughter of Col. T. TAYLOR of Loudoun.

Departed this life in Baltimore, Md, on Sunday evening, April 21st, Bettie P. STAUB, aged 28 years, wife of John F. STAUB.

Died: At his residence in Loudoun Co., on the 22d of April 1861, Joshua PANCOAST, in the 77th year of his age.

Died: On Monday, the 30th of April, Miss Catharine SAUNDERS, in the 37th year of her age.

Died: In this County, near Hillsborough, on Monday the 6th inst., Capt. Peter DERRY, in the 62d year of his age.

Wednesday, 15 May 1861   Vol. VI, No. 35

Married: On the 8th of May, by the Rev. Walter W. WILLIAMS, Dr. S. L. INGRAM, of Richmond, to Miss Eliza SMART, daughter of Mr. John P. SMART, of Leesburg.

Married: At his residence near Hoyesville, on Monday evening, the 29th ultimo, after a protracted sickness of 7 months, Mr. Jno. YAKEY, aged 53y 2m 27d.

Married: At Cross Keeys, Macon county, Alabama, by the Rev. A. S. M. HARDY, J. L. MORAN to M. E. daughter of James MOUNT Esq.

Wednesday, 22 May 1861   Vol. VI, No. 36

Married: In Leesburg, May 10th, by Rev. Jos. A. PROCTOR, the Rev. Wm. G. CROSS of the Va. Annual Conference M. E. Church, South, to Miss Emily A. SAUNDERS, of Leesburg.

Married: In Washington, on the 7th inst., by the Rev. Dr. SUNDERLAND, Dr. W. F. ALEXANDER, of Jefferson, to Miss Mary C. SHERMAN, of New Jersey.

Married: At "Risteau's Fancy," the residence of the bride, on Thursday evening, 2d inst., by the Rev. John Edwin AMOS, Dr. Samuel KEPLER Jr., to Miss Kate V. RISTEAU, all of Baltimore Co, Md.

Married: On Tuesday evening the 14th instant, at the residence of the bride's father, by Rev. H. R. SMITH, John CAMPBELL, M.D., of Adams Co, Ohio, and Bettie Jane, dau. of Amos WHITACRE, Esq. of this county.

Died: Of apoplexy in Waterford, May 8th, Mrs. Catharine FLOWERS, in the 71st year of her age.

Departed this life on the 30th of April, Miss Catharine SAUNDERS after a painful and protracted illness. Before she died she requested her aged father to promised to meet her in Heaven when he died.

Wednesday, 29 May 1861   Vol. VI, No. 37

No marriages or deaths. From here to end of printing in early 1862, paper was only two pages long.

Wednesday, 5 June 1861   Vol. VI, No. 38

No marriages or deaths.

Wednesday, 12 June 1861   Vol. VI, No. 39

A. M. BALL Esq. died very suddenly at Harper's Ferry, on Saturday morning last, of apoplexy. He was to manage the Rifle Factory about to be established at Fayettesville, N. C., and his family had already gone.

Married: At Waterford, on the 23d of May by the Rev. John PICKETT, Richard M. JOHNSON, Esq. to Mrs. E. J. W. PIDGSON, all of Loudoun County.

Wednesday, 19 June 1861   Vol. VI, No. 40

Married: At the Loudoun Female Collegiate Institute, Leesburg, on Thursday, the 13th inst., by Rev. C. H. NOURSE, Mr. Chas. H. McMURRAN, of Alexandria, Va to Miss Jane PETER, third dau. of the late J. P. C. PETER Esq. of Montgomery Co Md.

Wednesday, 26 June 1861   Vol. VI, No. 41

No marriages or death, only ads and war news.

Wednesday, 3 July 1861   Vol. VI, No. 42

Married: On Thursday, June 20th, by the Rev. Samuel CORNELIUS Jr., Mr. Samuel W. SNEDEKER to Miss Cath. BEACH.

Died: At Belton, Texas, on the 21st June, after a lingering and painful illness, Mrs. Mary E. McFARLAND, consort of Wilson E. McFARLAND Esq. and dau. of the late Dr. Samuel SUMMERS, of Leesburg.

Wednesday, 10 July 1861   Vol. VI, No. 43

No marriage or deaths.

[MISSING ISSUES]

Wednesday, 23 July 1861   Vol. VI, No. 46

No marriages or deaths, only ads and war news.

Wednesday, 30 July 1861   Vol. VI, No. 47

Died: On Thursday morning the 25th inst., Burr Chamblin, infant son of W. B. and Laura R. LYNCH, aged 1y 7m.

Wednesday, 8 August 1861   Vol. VI, No. 48

Died: Suddenly at the Limestone Mill, Mr. Aaron R. SAUNDERS.

Wednesday, 14 August 1861   Vol. VI, No. 49

Tribute of Respect from the Loudoun Cavalry held at Camp Mason on the 12th of Aug 1861, for the death of Cumberland Geo. ORRISON.

Died: On the 24th of July, in her 62d year, Mrs. Kernon H. McVEIGH, wife of Townsend McVEIGH, Esqr. of this county. She was a member of the Presbyterian Church.

Died on the 5th ult, at the Pt. of Rocks while engaged in the service of his country, from a musket ball at the hands of the Federal troops, Mr. George ORRISON, in the 26th year of his age.

Died: At "Aron" Fairfax Co., Wednesday the 7th, Alice, daughter of Richard H. and Martha COCKERILLE, in the 6th year of her age.

Died: In this town, on the 4th inst., Rebecca Jane, infant daughter of James H. and Mary E. MUSE.

Died: On Sunday, Aug. 4th, Mary, infant daughter of Christophe[r] and Elizabeth DeBOW.

Wednesday, 21 August 1861   Vol. VI, No. 50

Died: Charles N. NORRIS, 17 years old, shot. Left parents, brothers and sisters.

Wednesday, 28 August 1861   Vol. VI, No. 51

Married: On the 13th of Aug, by Rev. R. W. WATTS, Mr. James FINDLAY of Maryland to Miss S. Roberta, eldest daughter of Franklin CARTER Esq. of Loudoun Co.

Married: On the 22d inst., in the M. E. Church, in Leesburg, by S. GOVER, Charles E. ROLLINS, and Amey Ann MYERS, all of Loudoun.

Married: On Thursday the 15th instant, by Rev. Joseph HELM, Mr. Harrison BROWNER to Miss Annie C. WYNKOOP, all of Loudoun.

Died: On Saturday evening, July 10th near Woodgrove, in this county, Amanda, eldest daughter of Ashford WEADON, aged 22 years.

Died: At Culpeper C. H., Va, on Monday the 12th inst., George N. MYERS, of Charlestown, in the 20th year of his age. He was a member of the "Jefferson Guard," and was engaged in the grand battle of the 21st July, at Bull Run, where he received a musket ball through the thigh, which resulted in his death.

Died: At the residence of his father in this county, on Thursday last, Mr. James CORNELL, in the __ year of his age. He was a member of

Roger's Loudoun Artillery, and passed through the terrible ordeal of the 21st July to thus early fall a victim to ruthless disease.

Wednesday, 4 September 1861   Vol. VI, No. 52

Tribute of respect at the meeting held at Camp Johnson, August 25th 1861, by the Potomac Greys on the death of George W. STEWART.

Wednesday, 11 September 1861   Vol. VII, No. 1

We regret to learn that intelligence was brought to Gen. EVANS, in this town on Saturday last, of the sudden death of his mother which occurred at her home in South Carolina a few days previous.

Tribute of respect at a meeting of the Loudoun Artillery at Mason's Hill (5 miles from Arlington Heights) on Sunday Sept. 1st 1861 for deaths at their homes in Loudoun of fellow soldiers John W. HOWSER and James CORNELL, the former from the effects of a wound received in the battle of Manassas and the latter from disease contracted in our camp at Fairfax Courthouse.

Wednesday, 18 September 1861   Vol. VII, No. 2

Lt. Col. LACKLAND of the 2nd Reg. of Va Volunteers, died at his home near Charlestown, on Wednesday morning last, in the 31st year of his age.

Leonard SADLER, one of the oldest citizens of Charlestown died at his residence in that place on Tuesday last, in the 68th year of his age.

Tribute of respect at a meeting of Mt. Gilead Rifle Co. held at Camp Johnson, 4th of September 1861 for Edward TILLETT, a soldier. Jas. E. SIMPSON chairman, W. E. GARRETT, Secretery.

Wednesday, 25 September 1861   Vol. VII, No. 3

Died: In Leesburg on Friday evening, the 20th instant, Mrs. Jane ADAMS, wife of James ADAMS, aged 48 years.

Died: At Occoquon Mills, Prince William Co., on Sunday, the 15th instant, Mrs. Sarah GASKINS.

Died: At Sunnyside, Loudoun Co, Augst. 23d?, Lizzie, second dau. of Joshua and Ellen FLETCHER, of typhoid fever.

[MISSING ISSUES]

Wednesday, 16 October 1861   Vol. VII, No. 6

Died: At his residence, Cedar Grove, Montgomery Co Md, Sept. 25, of apoplexy, Col. Benjamin SHREVE, formerly of Loudoun Co.

Mr. Henry VIRTS, son of Jacob VIRTS dec'd, died September the 29th 1861, aged 39y 1m 3d. He has left a wife and seven children.

[MISSING ISSUE]

Wednesday, 30 October 1861   Vol. VII, No. 8
Died: Near Oxford, Miss. on Sunday morning 6th of October, Nettie, only child of Henry C. and Lizzie G. GIST, formerly of this county, aged 2 years.

Wednesday, 6 November 1861   Vol. VII, No. 9
Died: At Springfield, Fauquier Co, on Friday morning, 1st November, Farley Carrin, dau. of Major John D. and Parke F. R??ers [ROGERS?, blank spaces], in the 6th year of her age.
Died: On the 22d ult., of a wound received in the battle of Leesburg, on the morning of the 21st, Flavius OSBURN, son of Joel and Emily OSBURN, of Snickersville, in the 21st year of his age.

[MISSING ISSUES]

Wednesday, 20 November 1861   Vol. VII, No. 15
[note: this page is located after undated page below on microfilm]
Died: In Leesburg, at the residence of his brother-in-law, Mr. John BIRD, November the 13th, 1861, Mr. Job P. McINTOSH, of Washington DC, in the 39th year of his age.

Wednesday, 25 December 1861   Vol. VII, No. 20
Married: Near Dranesville on Thursday the 28th November by Rev. H. R. SMITH, Alfred D. KEEN, Merchant at ?? to Mrs. Catharine ROSSEAU.
Married: On Thursday the 18th inst., by the same, Alfred G. DAYMUDE and Julia A. WILEY, all of Loudoun.

Wednesday, 1 January 1862   Vol. VII, No. 21
Married: At Mt. Gilead, December 19th, by Elder John W. JONES, Mr. George ISH and Mrs. Ann D. TROUNCER, all of Loudoun.
Married: In Berryville, on the 14th inst., by Rev. C. WHITE, Presley MARMADUKE, of Western Virginia (formerly of Jefferson) and Miss Kate V. MARMADUKE of Shepherdstown, Jefferson Co.
Died: On Sunday the 8th of Dec. in Leesburg of typhoid fever, Charles William, son of Charles D. and Mary E. BIRD, aged 7y 3d.
Died: In Williamsburg, Va on Monday 23d of Sept. 1861, Isabella Sophia, consort of Rev. John C. McCABE D.D. Chaplain C. S. Army.

Wednesday, 15 January 1862   Vol. VII, No. 23
Married: At Great Bridge, Va, on Thursday, the 8th inst., by the Rev. C. B. RIDDICK, Rev. J. A. PROCTOR of the Va Conference and Miss Kate M. FOREMAN, of Norfolk Co.

Wednesday, No date on page

Married: At the residence of the bride's father, in this town, on the 13th instant, by the Rev. John COSBY, Chaplain of 30th Va Regiment, Wm. Robert HENDRICK, Esq. of Mecklenburg Co Va and Hattie, daughter of Robt. W. GRAY, Esq.

Died: On Monday the 11th of October 1861, near Wheatland, Archibald McDANIEL, aged 65y 2m 12d.

Died: At Guilford Station, in this county, on the 1st of November, Mr. Isaac H. ROBBINS, in the 53d year of his age.

Died: At his residence in this place, on Saturday morning, 16th inst., after a most sudden illness, Mr. John SIEBER, in the 57th year of his age.

The Mirror
Published at Leesburg, Loudoun County, Virginia

Wednesday, 14 June 1865   Vol. X, No. 1

Married: In this town on Thursday evening last, by the Rev. H. R. SMITH, Mr. John E. BRENNER, of Alexandria, and Miss Fannie C. CRISSEY, of Leesburg.

Wednesday, 21 June 1865   Vol. X, No. 2

Charles McDONOUGH, late of Moseby's Command, was killed near Middleburg on Saturday last, by a party of Federal soldiers. Since the disbandment of his command, McDONOUGH has had one or two difficulties in that neighborhood, and on the day mentioned being surprised by the party alluded to, attempted to make his escape, when he was fired upon and killed almost instantly.

Jim BROOKENS, a well known free negro of this town, was also arrested on Saturday last, and taken to Harpers Ferry.

Married: At the Lutheran Parsonage, in Frederick city, Md, on Tuesday evening, 13th inst., by Rev. Mr. DIEHL, Mr. Thomas B. NORRIS and Miss Amanda V. L. CARR, both of Loudoun county.

Married: At the same time and place, by the same, Mr. Fielding BROWN and Miss Sallie CARR, both of Loudoun.

Married: On Tuesday, June 13th, near Knoxville, by the Rev. Henry NICE, Mr. William Fenton STOUTZENBERGER and Miss Julia Ann RHODERICK, all of Loudoun county, Va.

Married: In Leesburg, on Tuesday evening, April 11th 1865, by Rev. W. W. WILLIAMS, Capt. Alfred GLASSCOCK of Fauquier county, and Hattie, daughter of C. Fenton FADELEY, of this town.

Wednesday, 29 June 1865   Vol. X, No. 3

The site and name of the Post Office at Hoysville, Loudoun county, has been changed to Taylortown, and Samuel W. SLATER, appointed Postmaster, vice J. W. PAXSON.

Married: On the evening of the 14th inst., at the Dill House, by the Rev. Dr. ZACHARIAS, Will C. AMES, of Clearfield county, Pa, to Miss C. DEMORY, of Loudoun county, Va.

Wednesday, 5 July 1865   Vol. X, No. 4

Married: In Frederick city, Md, on the 27th ult, by the Rev. George DIEHL, Mr. Isaac DUST to Mrs. Susan SUTHRON, both of Jefferson county, Va.

Wednesday, 12 July 1865   Vol. X, No. 5

Court: Will of Ezra BOLEN admitted to probate.

Death of Gen. Robert L. WRIGHT –death occurred at his residence in this county, on Saturday last. Mr. W. represented Loudoun in the Legislature f few years ago.

Married: On the 26th ultimo, by the Rev. G. DEIHL, at the City Hotel, Dr. Henry H. SMITH of Richmond, Va, to Miss Sarah E. LAKE, of Fauquier county, Va.

Died: In Leesburg, Va on Wednesday July 5th 1865, Mrs. Eliza Ann, wife of William HALL, in the 54th year of her age.

Died: On Sunday, the 18th instant, Mrs. Sophia S., wife of Mr. David W. KYLE, of Bedford co, Va, and daughter of John M. and Mary E. FORBES of Fauquier co Va, in her 19th year.

Died: On the 8th of July, Washington HUMMER, in the 69th year of his age. Formerly a Justice of the Peace for many years, but had for some time past been living in privacy at his residence in the lower end of the County.

Died at Wheatland, in the county of Loudoun on the 8th of July, Gen. Robert L. WRIGHT, aged about 56 years.

Wednesday, 19 July 1865   Vol. X, No. 6

Joseph LITTLE, an aged citizen of Jefferson county, Va, died suddenly in Jefferson, Md, last week, whither he had been on business.

Tribute of Respect of Olive Branch Lodge, No. 114 of Free and Accepted Masons for Gen. Robert L. WRIGHT.

At a meeting of the members of the Vestry of St. James Church, held 17th July 1865, whereas John P. SMART has departed this life, given tribute of respect.

Died: At his residence near Leesburg, on Saturday last, Mr. Horace LUCKETT, in the 70th year of his age.

Died: In this town, on Monday last, Miss Mary POWELL, daughter of Wm. A. POWELL, Esqr.

John P. SMART died at his residence in Leesburg, on Monday morning, in his 68th year. In this town, on the 12th inst.,

Died: Mary Elizabeth, daughter of John E. and Henrietta WRIGHT, aged six years, six months and six days. Near Middletown, Md., on the 30th ult.,

Died: Albert J. MOORE, formerly of Loudoun Co., Va, aged 40 years, 4 months and 16 days.

Wednesday, 26 July 1865   Vol. X, No. 7

Married: In Frederick City, Md., by the Rev. Mr. ___, Mr. Henry HOUGH to Miss Georgianna HARDY, both of Loudoun.

In memoriam: Miss Mary POWELL.

Wednesday, 2 August 1865   Vol. X, No. 8

Married: On July 22d, at the residence of Mrs. Mary ADIE, in Leesburg, Va, by the Rev. W. W. WILLIAMS, Miss Kate KERCHEVAL, of Fauquier county, Va to Jas. A. LOWNDS, of Baltimore MD.

Married: At the First Baptist Church in Richmond, on the 19th ultimo, by Rev. F. McCARTHY, Mr. Wm. F. ADAMS to Miss B. A. MONCASTLE, all of Richmond.

Wednesday, 9 August 1865   Vol. X, No. 9

George K. FOX, Jr., Esq. late Clerk of the County Court of Loudoun, reached home on Friday night last, direct from the "Devil's Kitchen," with the Records of the County, which were removed more than three years ago by order of the Court. They were returned in good condition, without the loss of a single paper or even so much as the rubbing of the binding on the books. The office is now open and in good running order except a few minor papers which were left behind, and which have been more or less injured.

Married: On July 25th at Mt. Gilead, Loudoun county, Va, by Rev. Mr. HERNDON, L. J. DENHAM to Carrie C. FRERE.

Died: In Leesburg, on Monday evening, July 31st, 1865, William Washington, infant son of Wm. H. and Francis E. JOHNSON, aged 1y, 10m and 16d.

Died: At his residence near Leesburg, on Saturday, the 5th inst., Mr. James HIGDON, aged about 72 years.

Died: In Leesburg, on the 4th inst., George H., infant son of Edmund C. CHAYTOR of this town, formerly of Georgetown, aged 10 months.

Died: On Wednesday, 2nd inst., Matilda, daughter of Elder Richard E. FURR, of Loudoun aged 2y 8m.

Died: In Omaha city, Nebraska, on the 10th of July 1865, Mr. Franklin D. WELSH, of Loudoun county, aged about 35 years. He had gone to Nebraska on business, where he was attacked with measles from which he died. Through the kindness of a former country man, Mr. S. D. MEGEATH, his remains were carefully encased and forwarded to his friends in Virginia, where they arrived on the 22d and were interred in the South Fork burying ground.

Died: In Petersburg, Va, on the 23d of July 1865, in the 27th year of his age, John H. MATTHEWS, recently Captain of Co. K. 6th

Va Cavalry, C.S.A., of wounds received on the 31st of March last, near Dinwiddie Court House, second son of the late Col. John MATTHEWS of this county.

Wednesday, 16 August 1865   Vol. X, No. 10

August Ct.: Henry TAYLOR qualified as Admr. of Mary TAVENNER, Chas. L. MANKIN of Lewis F. MANKIN; Thos. E. CARR, of Joseph CARR; Jacob COST of Mary Ann COST; Wm. GRUBB of Mary E. GRUBB; Margaret F. HUGHES, of David L. HUGHES; Dr. M. H. BALDWIN, of John? VANSICKLER; Mary J. SKINNER of Alex. G. SKINNER; John J. DILLON and Thos. J. NICHOLS of Anne DILLON; Richard JAMES of John BOYE; Rich. James of Phillip BOYER. Wm. H. FRANCIS, qualified as Executor of Independence C. FRANCIS; F. M. UPDYKE of Albina WHITE; R. L. BAKER and A. M. T. VANDEVANTER, of Robt. L. WRIGHT; Henry SAUNDERS of R. G. SAUNDERS; ___ LICKEY of Wm. LICKEY; Samuel C. LUCKETT and J. P. SCHOOLEY, of Benj. GRUBB; Elizabeth WHITE of T. W. WHITE; Samuel R. ADAMS of Richard ADAMS; F. M. CARTER of Elizabeth CARTER; B. F. TAYLOR of Euphema TAYLOR; B. F. TAYLOR of Wm. MYERS; James E. POLAND of Alexander POLAND; W. H. EIDSON of Joseph EIDSON and Benj. BIRDSALL of Elizabeth BIRDSALL.

Married: On Tuesday, August the 8th by Rev. S. GOVER, Mr. Thomas D. WINE to Miss Margaret SHACKELFORD, all of Loudoun.

Died: In Middleburg, Loudoun county, Va, July the 27th 1865, Mrs. J. E. BARTLETT, in the 69th year of her age.

Died: In this county, July 30th 1865, Annie Jennet, daughter of Robert and Margaret A. POWER, aged 13m 12d.

Died: Hector PEARCE was born April 1st 1799 and died at his residence near Snickersville July 27, 1865. The partner of his bosom died in 1861, they sleep side by side in Ketoctin Cemetery. Two daughters and one son remain.

Wednesday, 23 August 1865   Vol. X, No. 11

Two negroes, Alfred and his wife Clara, who were living with their former master, John BAKER, Esq., near Salem, Fauquier county, Va, were killed, it is said, by the notorious Nick CARTER, about two o'clock last Sunday morning. The negroes, it is said, had given information concerning his whereabouts to the Government troops some time since, and he killed them to prevent against being informed upon.

The mother of the late General Turner ASHBY, of the Confederate army, died on the 27th ult., in Virginia.

Married: At Edwards' Ferry, on Monday, August 16, by Rev. C. H. NOURSE, Stephen HEFFNER of Montgomery county, Md, to Miss Annie, daughter of George RHODES, of Loudoun county, Va.

Married: On the 7th instant, East Patrick street, Frederick, by the Rev. B. C. FLOWERS, Mr. Zachary Tayloe COLCLAZER, of Frederick county Md, to Miss Sarah E. COLCLAZER, of Loudoun county, Va.

Married: In Baltimore on the 14th inst., by Rev. Father CLARK, Michael CAMPBELL and Rebecca WOODY.

Died: At the Loudoun Hotel in Leesburg on the 12th inst., Earnest Lynnwood, son of Phillip & Ann E. BROOKS, aged 5 months.

Thursday, 31 August 1865   Vol. X, No. 12

By the commissioner of the Bureau of Refugees, Freedmen and Abandoned Lands, the following tracts are confiscated: that tract of land formerly owned by W. M. SAFFER near Aldie 500 acres; by Robt. A. ISH near Aldie; by Chas. F. SIBBS [TIBBS?] near Aldie 300 acres; by Burr P. NOLAND near Aldie; by John F. SIMPSON near Aldie 200 acres; by John W. FAIRFAX ½ W of President Monroe Manson 150 acres; house and lot known as the "Old President Monroe Mansion"; formerly owned by John W. FAIRFAX; old post office building and lot in Aldie formerly owned by John STOVER; land formerly owned by Wm. N. BERKELEY 600 acres; tract of timber formerly owned by Sanford I. RAMEY near Stumptown 30 acres; land formerly owned by Sand I. RAMEY 2 miles NW from Waterford 30 acres; house and lot formerly owned by Sanford I. RAMEY situated in Leesburg; land formerly owned by Sanford I. RAMEY near Waterford of 300 acres; land formerly owned by Sanford I. RAMEY near Luckett's store of 330 acres; by Josiah WHITE and Thomas WHITE of 300 acres; by Turner McDANIEL near Wheatland; by James WHITMAN and Joseph WHITMAN near Morrisonville of 40 acres; by Samuel CRANBECKER of 120 acres; by Jas. SMITH near Wheatland 150 acres; by John ELDRIDGE near Waterford 400 acres; by Matthew HARRISON adjoining Leesburg; by Arthur L. RODGERS on the N side of Leesburg 111 acres; land called "Big Spring Farm" formerly owned by George W. BALL 1,000 acres; by John M. ORR 1 mile N of Leesburg of 5 acres; house and lot formerly owned by John M. ORR in Leesburg 1 acre; house and lot formerly owned by John M. ORR in Leesburg 1 acre; house and lot formerly owned by John M. ORR in Leesburg; by Edwin R. ONLY near Leesburg of 4 acres. by Thomas W. EDWARDS 1 mile from Leesburg of 500 acres; by George R. HEAD on the corner of King and Loudoun sts.

Leesburg; dwelling house and lot formerly owned by George R. HEAD on Loudoun st., Leesburg; store and lot formerly owned by George R. HEAD on King st. Leesburg; by Henry C. CLEGGETT in Leesburg; house and lot by A. R. MOTT in Leesburg; house and lot by A. R. MOTT in Leesburg; house and lot formerly owned by A. R. MOTT in Leesburg as a drug store; dwelling house and lot formerly owned by A. R. MOTT; house and lot formerly owned by Charles T. TIBBS; house and lot by William B. LYNCH in Leesburg adjoining the Valley Bank; house and lot by William B. LYNCH in Leesburg adjoining Jas. M. WALLACE; house and lot by James ADAMS in Leesburg; land formerly owned by James ADAMS ½ mile east of Leesburg 3 acres; by Armistead T. RUST 400 acres; by Armistead T. RUST of 10 acres; by John W. MINOR of 300 acres near Goresville; of George RUST near Waterford 75 acres; by George RUST on the Point of Rocks road of 300 acres; by George RUST on Point of Rocks road 250 acres; house and lot in Waterford formerly owned by Thomas F. TIBBS; land formerly owned by Daniel SCHRIVES 250 acres; by Charles DAWSON and Nicholas DAWSON 500 acres; by Charles and Nicholas DAWSON 300 acres; by Arthur L. CHICHESTER 400 acres; by William H. GRAY 300 acres; by Francis MASON 1,000 acres; by Francis MASON 400 acres; by Francis MASON 400 acres; by Francis MASON 1,000 acres; by Richard MARLOW; by Richard MARLOW and John MARLOW; by James WHITEMAN 100 acres; by John GEORGE 200 acres; by ___ THOMPSON and M. C. PAXSON 150 acres; house and lot formerly owned by J. W. BERNAUGH in Lovettsville; land formerly owned by Jacob H. MANNING 200 acres; by Nathan GREGG; by Joseph SUGAR 10 acres; by Robert Gilmore BOWIE 150 acres; by Archibald CLARK and Isaac CLARK 175 acres; by Archibald CLARK and Isaac CLARK called the "Westly Farm," 150 acres; tract called "Braden Farm" formerly owned by Oscar BRADEN 300 acres; by William BEANS 100 acres; by Joseph HURT 75 acres; by John BOLAND and William BOLAND 500 acres; by John BOLAND 1,000 acres; by Samuel COOPER 8 acres; by Charles J. GIDDINGS 230 acres; by Sanderson THRIFT; by Charles F. BERKELEY; tract called "Woorull" formerly owned by Charles F. TURLEY 500 acres; by William P. HUTCHISON; tract formerly owned by Benjamin F. SAFFER 150 acres.

Married: At the Presbyterian Manse, on Thursday, 24th instant, by Rev. H. R. SMITH, Mr. J. Thomas SPINKS and Miss Mary MATHERS, all of Loudoun.

Died: In this town, on Monday evening last, of paralysis, Mr. Parkinson L. LOTT, in the 56th year of his age. At the residence of his aunt, Mary WATERS, near Middleburg, Va on the 26th of June last, James T., son of Thomas and the late H. Isabella HOUGH, in the 21st year of his age.

Died: On the 3rd of August, in the 3d year of her age, Matilda Ashby, third daughter of Richard E. FURR.

Died: Near Megeath's Mill, in this county, of typhoid phneumonia, Mrs. Jane GIBBONS, in the 63d year of her age.

Thursday, 7 September 1865   Vol. X, No. 13

George W. BALL, Thomas W. EDWARDS and Sanderson THRIFT, of Loudoun, during the past week received the pardon of President JOHNSON. With it carries a restoration to their rights of property.

Death of Burr W. HARRISON, Esqr. – at his residence in Leesburg on Tuesday afternoon, after a protracted suffering which for several years had confined him to his room. He was a lawyer of high standing. He was in the 73d year of his age.

Charles G. ESKRIDGE, Esq. for many years Clerk of the County Court of Loudoun, died recently at his residence at Fairfax C. H.

Thursday, 14 September 1865   Vol. X, No. 14

George W. SAPPINGTON was murdered near Glade Spring depot, on the Virginia and Tennessee Railroad, last Sunday night, by some unknown person. For some time previous to the close of the war he was a lieutenant of the Provost Guard in Lynchburg. Leaves a family, who reside in Jefferson Co., Va.

Married: At Cottage Hill, Loudoun county, Va, August 23, 1865, by Rev. Andrew ROBEY, Mr. Addison FRANKS to Miss Eliza BOUGHIE, all of the above named county.

Thursday, 21 September 1865   Vol. X, No. 15

Married: Near Berlin, by the Rev. G. H. MARTIN, on the 12th inst., Richard JAMES Esq. to Mrs. Mary Catharine ARNOLD, both of Loudoun. On the 14th, at the same place and by the same, Mr. John Thomas MYERS to Miss Virginia Ellen LAYCOCK, all of Loudoun.

Died: At the residence of Isaac CARR, on the morning of the 30th of August, Mrs. Nancy KETTLE, in the 89th year of her age.

Thursday, 28 September 1865   Vol. X, No. 16

Married: Near Taylortown, on the 14th inst. by the Rev. X. J. RICHARDSON, Mr. Sydney BENNETT, Deputy Sheriff of Loudoun, and Miss Mary Elizabeth, daughter of Jonas P. SCHOOLEY Esq., all of this county.

The Mirror 61

Married: Near Lovettsville, on the 19th inst., by the same, Mr. William SNOOTS and Miss Margaret Ann MUNDY, all of this county

Married: At the residence of the bride's father, on the 20th inst., by the Rev. J. A. HAYNES, Mr. Ctthbert [Cuthbert] B. ROGERS, and Miss Annie, daughter of Beverly HUTCHISON Esqr., all of this county.

Married: In Leesburg, on Thursday, the 21st inst., by Rev. H. R. SMITH, Bushrod UNDERWOOD and Miss Susan H. DAVIS, all of Loudoun.

Married: On the 12th instant, by Rev. W. HARRISON, Maj. T. B. HUTCHISON, and Miss Annie KINCHELOE, all of Fauquier county.

Married: On the 18th inst., in Frederick, Md., by Rev. Dr. ZACHERIAS, Mr. James T. POTTS and Miss Eliza BASCUE, both of Loudoun county.

Died: Jonah PURSEL died at his residence in Snickersville, on Wednesday morning, Sept. 20, 1865, in his 73rd year.

Died: At her residence in Poolesville, Md., Mrs. Annie McINTOSH, aged thirty years, eldest daughter of Mrs. Clara SMITH, of this place.

Thursday, 5 October 1865   Vol. X, No. 17

The farm belong to the heirs of the late Peter COST containing 211 acres was sold on Thursday last for $20 per acre. Purchaser, Mr. Thos. POWELL.

Married: In Leesburg, on Tuesday morning October 3d, by Rev. S. GOVER, Mr. John SMALE and Miss Hattie WHITMORE, all in Loudoun.

Married: On the 19th September, by Rev. Jos. HELM, Mr. Benj. DAVIS and Miss Annie E. COCKERILLE, all of Loudoun.

Married: In this county, on the 28th ult., by the same, Charles W. WHITE and Miss Sarah E., daughter of David BALES, all of Loudoun.

Married: In the Grove Church, in this county, on the same day, by the same, Mr. George W. WHITE and Miss Hannah E., daughter of Mortimore BALES, all of Loudoun.

Married: On the 12th ult., at the residence of the bride's father, John H. SETTLE, by Rev. Robert BELL, Mr. Marshall W. CARPENTER, of Loudoun, and Miss Kate M. SETTLE, of Rappahannock county.

Died: Of consumption, at the residence of Edward L. RUSE, in Jefferson county, on the 19th of July 1864, Miss Martha J. ARNOLD, formerly of Loudoun county, Va, in her 25 year.

Died: At Unionville, Jefferson county, of scarlet fever and diptheria, November 3d, 1862, Frank McKendree RUSE, aged 2y 3m

22d; of the same disease Nov. 18th 1862, Agnes J. RUSE, aged 4y 2m 17d, children of Edward L. RUSE.

Thursday, 12 October 1865   Vol. X, No. 18

Oct. Ct.: Wm. BRISLINE, a native of Ireland, who more than two years ago appeared before the court and declared his intention of becoming a citizen of the U.S., again appeared and having taken the necessary oaths, was declared a citizen accordingly.

Married: At the residence of the officiating minister, in Leesburg, on Thursday, October 5th, by the Rev. S. GOVER, Mr. John W. KELLY and Miss Sarah E. STEADMAN, all of Loudoun.

Died: Near Woodgrove, on the morning of the 14th of September, Mrs. Elizabeth BEANS, wife of Isaiah B. BEANS, and daughter of the late Thomas MOSS, in the 73rd years of her age.

Thursday, 19 October 1865   Vol. X, No. 19

Married: On Thursday, the 28th of September 1865, at the residence of the bride's father, near Hillsboro, Va, by Rev. S. S. ROSZEL, Marshall M. BIGHAM, formerly of Chambersburg, Pa but for the last ten years a resident of Baltimore, to Miss Carrie L. CALDWELL, of Virginia.

Died: On Friday the 6th instant, near Farmwell, in this county, after a short illness, John R. ELLMORE, in the 25th year of his age. He was a kind and dutiful son and an affectionate brother. On Monday the 11th of September 1865 in Rochester, Sangemon county, Illinois, Dr. R. F. PRICE, a native of Loudoun county, Va. On Friday the 6th of October at the residence of her father in Middleburg, Mrs. Fanny B. DUDLEY, the wife of Mr. Thomas U. DUDLEY Jr., and daughter of Dr. Wm. B. COCHRAN, in the 27th year of her age.

Thursday, 26 October 1865   Vol. X, No. 20

Married: Near Paxson's Store, on the 19th at the bride's father, by the Rev. S. GOVER, Mr. Joseph FRY and Miss Mary C. VIRTS, all of Loudoun.

Married: At St. James' Church, Richmond, Va, on the evening of the 17th by the bride's father, Mr. J. Van Leu McCREERY and Miss Nannie, daughter of the Rev. H. S. KEPLER, all of Richmond.

Married: In Frederick County on the 26th ult., by the Rev. R. T. BERRY, Mr. Thomas W. TIMBERLAKE of Warren county, and Miss Fanny J. GRIGGS, daughter of the late James GRIGGS of Jefferson county.

Married: At Poplar Hill, Prince George county, Md, on 17th October, by Rev. P. C. COLL, John S. BARBOUR, of Virginia, to Susan S., daughter of Henry DANGERFIELD, Esqr.

Married: At the residence of Rev. Samuel ROSZELL, Oakland, Loudoun county, Va on the 18th inst., by the Rev. Dr. WAUGH, Nannie, only daughter of Col. Daniel F. DULANY, to J. P. DeBUTTS, Esqr.

Married: At Edge Hill, near Paris, Fauquier county, Va, on the 4th instant, by the Rev. Mr. LANDSTREET, Mr. Douglass GIBSON to Miss Helen J., daughter of W. W. ROGERS, Esq.

Died: On Tuesday the 11th of October, at his residence near Hillsborough, Mr. Nathan NEER, in the 72d year of his age.

Thursday, 2 November 1865   Vol. X, No. 21

Died: In this town, on Friday evening last, of croup, Edwin, youngest child of James M. WALLACE, aged 4y 5m 11d.

Thursday, 9 November 1865   Vol. X, No. 22

Married: On Thursday, the 26th of October 1865, at the residence of Mr. John GAINES, by the Rev. John WOOLF, Mr. Francis E. ROBEY and Miss Martha E. GAINES, all of Loudoun.

Married: At the Loudoun Hotel, in Leesburg, on Tuesday 2d November, by the Rev. Samuel GOVER, Mr. Wm. H. OTLEY and Miss Mary E. CONNER, all of Loudoun.

Married: At the Loudoun Hotel, in Leesburg, on the 2d inst., by the Rev. S. GOVER, Mr. Gunnell SMITH and Mrs. Mary A. WILKENSON, all of Loudoun.

Married: October 31st, at the residence of the bride's mother, by the Rev. John LANDSTREET, Joseph T. JANNEY and Miss Edith HUNTER, all of Alexandria.

Married: At the residence of Levi NIXON, in this county on Wednesday the 31st ult., by Rev. Joseph HELM, Mr. Wm. F. McKNEW, of Washington city, and Miss Laura P. MAJOR, of Loudoun.

Married: At Elkhart city, Logan county, Illinois, on the 26th of September last, by Rev. Mr. SMITH, Mr. Balis LAKE, of Menard county, Illinois to Miss Sallie McENDREE, formerly of Loudoun county, Va.

Married: At Falling Waters Church, Berkeley county, on the 12th ult., by Rev. L. F. WILSON, Mr. Robert G. HARPER, of Baltimore, formerly of Shepherdstown, to Miss Ophelia F. WILSON, daughter of the officiating clergyman.

Died: On the 19th October, after a protracted illness of consumption, Mrs. Adaline M. SHEETZ, wife of Mr. Daniel M. SHEETZ, of this town, aged 39 years. *Charlestown Free Press.*

Died: At Marrianna, Florida on the 25th of July last, aged 37 years, Charles A. HENDERSON, eldest son of the late Gen. Arch'd. HENDERSON, U. S. Marine Corps.

Died: In Alexandria, on Sunday 28th ult., Mr. Wm. F. SIMPSON, printer, formerly of Leesburg, but for several years a resident of the former place.

Lines on the death of Sergeant John Major BIRKBY of Marshall's Battery who fell near Petersburg, June 18th 1864 in the 30th year of his age. Poem by Lyda LYTTON Richmond, June 27, 1864.

In Memoriam – Henry C. BIRKBY of the Seventeenth Virginia Regiment who died at Fort Delaware, July 17th 1864 in the 27th year of his age. Poem by Lyda LYTTON.

Thursday, 16 November 1865   Vol. X, No. 23

Married: On the 17th of October, at the residence of the bride's mother, near Upperville, by the Rev. Mr. RITCHIE, M. S. PEACH, formerly of Alexandria to Miss Tacie G. FLETCHER, of Loudoun county.

Married: On Wednesday Nov. 1st at St. Mark's Lutheran Church, by the Rev. Dr. STORK, Captain Wm. L. STORK and Clintonia W., dau. of the late James H. WARNER, both of Baltimore.

Married: On Wednesday, the 1st instant, at the U. S. Hotel, Frederick city, Md., by the Rev. B. C. FLEWERS, Mr. Joseph MYERS, of Jefferson county, Va, and Miss Lucinda THOMPSON of Loudoun county, Va.

Died: At his residence near Leesburg, on Saturday, the 4th inst., Robert CURRY, aged 67 years.

Died: Of diptheria, on Monday the 30th ultimo, Ada Lee, aged 1y 6m and on Monday the 6th inst., Alice Catherine, aged 4y 9m, children of Bushrod W. and Virginia FOX.

Died: On the 22d August 1864 suddenly of dysentery, Thomas E., youngest son of George W. and Ruth Hannah NOLAND, aged 3y 3m 2d.

Thursday, 23 November 1865   Vol. X, No. 24

Married: At St. Charles Hotel, Point of Rocks on the 14th of November by the Rev. G. H. MARTIN, Mr. Isreal W. WILLIAMS, formerly of Loudoun, now a resident of the Point of Rocks, to Miss Emma Jane BERRY, daughter of George BERRY, Esq.

Married: On the 16th inst., near the Point of Rocks, by the same, Mr. Robert H. COOPER to Miss Margaret Ann COOPER, both of Loudoun.

Married: On the 9th inst., by Elder T. HERNDON, Mr. Wm. PEARSON and Emily ANDERSON, all of Fauquier county.

Married: On the same day by the same John H. BUTLER and Miss Susan F. PICKETT, of Prince William county.

Married: On the 28th of September in Georgetown DC, by the Rev. Dr. SAMSON, Mr. Thomas Benton JAMES and Miss Eliza P. BLAKELEY, all of Loudoun

Married: On Tuesday the 7th of Nov., at Spring Hill, Fauquier county, at the residence of the bride's mother, by the Rev. Mr. LANDSTREET, George SLATER Esq. of Baltimore Md to Ellen, the eldest daughter of the late George GLASCOCK and granddaughter of Aquilla GLASCOCK, Esq.

Died: Near Lovettsville on Saturday last, Mr. Adam HOUSEHOLDER, aged 92 years.

Died: In Leesville, Carrol County, Ohio, Mrs. Martena K. BENEDUM, wife of Charles E. BENEDUM, in the 40th year of age; third daughter of S. M. and Elizabeth BOSS, of this town.

Thursday, 30 November 1865   Vol. X, No. 25

Married: In Leesburg, at the residence of the bride's mother, on Wednesday morning, the 22d instant, by Rev. Walter W. WILLIAMS, Captain Wm. B. LYNCH, Editor of the *Washingtonian*, to Miss Jane D. WILDMAN.

Married: On the 22d instant, at the residence of the bride's father, by Rev. Mr. BARTEN, Miss Rose SKINNER to Mr. Beverly TURNER, all of Fauquier county.

Married: In the Baptist Church at Warrenton, Va., by Rev. Mr. BITTINGS, Dr. R. SOWERS, of Clarke county, Virginia to Miss Mary Francis SMITH, of Fauquier county.

Died: On the 14th of 10th month (October) at the residence of his brother, David BROWN, in this county, Wm. BROWN, in the 62d year of his age.

Died: In Leesburg, Saturday, the 18th instant, of croup, Henry, son of Richard H. and Anne E. TURNER, aged 16 months and was interred in the Sharon Cemetery at Middleburg, on the 20th.

Thursday, 7 December 1865   Vol. X, No. 26

Married: On the 30th of November in Leesburg by Rev. S. GOVER, Mr. John M. SHIPMAN and Miss Ellen Lewis SHIPMAN, all of Loudoun.

Wednesday, 13 December 1865   Vol. X, No. 27

Married: On the 28th ultimo, at the residence of the bride's mother, by Rev. John WOLF, Mr. Wm. S. GRIFFITH to Miss Margaret A. GOODING, all of Loudoun.

Married: On Thursday, Nov. 30th 1865 at the residence of Mr. John DEMARY, by Rev. X. J. RICHARDS[ON], Mr. George W. BAKER and Miss Elizabeth VIRTS, all of Loudoun.

Married: On the same day, at the Parsonage of the New Jerusalem Church, by the same, Mr. John ALLENDER to Miss Susan VICKERS, of the same vicinity.

Married: At the residence of the bride's father near Leesburg, by the Rev. H. R. SMITH on Wednesday morning the 6th inst., Mr. John V. TAVENNER, of Frederick county, to Miss Margaret E., second daughter of James THOMAS Esqr.

Died: On Sunday the 3d instant, at the residence of Mr. S. C. LUCKETT, Mr. Crawford K. WHITE, aged thirty-eight years.

Died: At his residence near Leesburg, on Tuesday, the 5th of December 1865 in his 58th year, Wm. D. HAVENNER.

Wednesday, 20 December 1865   Vol. X, No. 28

Married: at Easternview, Fauquier county, Va the residence of the bride's father, on the 14th inst. by the Rev. Mr. POLLOCK, Mr. T. L. GALLEHER to Miss Fannie A. BROWN, daughter of Geo. BROWN, Esq.

Married: On the 12th inst. in Alexandria in the Second Presbyterian Church by Rev. J. T. LEFTWICH, Mr. Thomas CLOWES, of Alexandria to Mrs. Henrietta SWANN, daughter of the late Cook FITZHUGH, of Fairfax county.

Married: Near Farmwell by Rev. H. R. SMITH on Thursday the 14th inst., Mr. Peter A. DRANE and Miss Harriet R. HOWSER.

Married: At the same time by the same, Mr. George M. ELLMORE and Miss Mary E. HOWSER, all of Loudoun.

Married: On the 6th inst. in Frederick city, Md by Rev. Dr. ZACHARIAS, Mr. Thomas H. HUTCHINSON to Miss Mary KIMMA, both of Leesburg.

Married: On the 7th instant, by Rev. George DIEHL, at the U. S. Hotel, Mr. W. B. EASTON of Georgetown DC to Miss Eliza V. LOCKER of Loudoun county.

Married: On Tuesday September 17th by Rev. J. Hoffman WAUGH, J. W. DANIEL and Sarah J. COPELAND, all of Loudoun.

Married: On Thursday September 21st by the same, Theophilus BELL and C. Elizabeth ARNETT, both of Loudoun.

Married: On Tuesday, October 17th by the same, Wm. R. JONES and Bettie A. GREGG, both of Loudoun.

Married: On Thursday October 19th, James W. McDANIEL and Maria REED, both of Loudoun by the same.

Married: On Wednesday, October 25th by the same, John T. SIMPSON, of Jefferson county, and Rosanna A. ALDER, of Loudoun.

Married: On Tuesday, November 7th by the same Nathan N. ALDER and Elizabeth ALDER, both of Loudoun.

Married: On Tuesday November 7th by the same, James DORRELL and Mrs. FLEMING, both of Loudoun.
Married: On Wednesday November 22d, by the same, Henry MOORE and Mary Elizabeth POTTS, both of Loudoun.
Married: On Tuesday December 5th by the same, William Flavius DOWDELL and Sarah Ann LESLIE, both of Loudoun.
Married: On Thursday, December 7th by the same, James M. TRASSELL, of Jefferson county, and Louisa Ann WEADON, of Loudoun.

Wednesday, 27 December 1865   Vol. X, No. 29

Jas. D. GIBSON Esq. an esteemed citizen of Jefferson county, died suddenly at his residence last week from appoplexy.
We regret to learn that in a difficulty at Guilford Station, in this county, on Saturday last, between John W. SEXTON and Mr. James McDANIEL, with regard to some mules, the former was shot by the latter. Mr. S. leaves a wife and several children.
Married: At a residence of the bride's father in this county, on Thursday the 7th inst., by Rev. Joseph HELM, Mr. Richard H. ROGERS and Miss Annie CARR, daughter of Mr. Josephus CARR, all of Loudoun.
Married: By Elder John W. JONES, December 19th at the residence of the bride's mother, Mr. Bushrod OXLEY to Miss Althea, daughter of the late Lemuel DANIEL, of this county.

Wednesday, 3 January 1866   Vol. X, No. 30

Capt. Otho THOMAS, a Lieutenant in the war of 1812, died recently at his residence near Point of Rocks, Md. in the 77th year of his age.
Married: In Leesburg on the 28th of Dec. by the Rev. S. GOVER, Mr. Isaac F. HAWS and Miss Mary B. BEACH, all of Loudoun.
Married: At the residence of Wm. OTLEY on the 25th of December by the Rev. Thadeus HERNDON, John Thomas CONNER and Miss Mary Helen BROWN, all of Loudoun.
Married: At the residence of the bride's father on the 19th of December by the same, Mr. John J. OTLEY and Miss Maria TAVENNER, daughter of Lott TAVENNER, all of Loudoun.
Married: Near Hamilton on the 28th of December by the Rev. J. HOFFMAN, George W. LOWE and Franceria HAINES, all of Loudoun county.
Died: On the 13th of December, Charles Thomas, son of Wm. H. MOFFETT, aged 17m 5d.

Wednesday, 10 January 1866   Vol. X, No. 31

Married: By the Rev. G. H. NORTON at St. Paul's Church, Alexandria on the 22d ultimo, Wm. H. CROCKFORD, of Orange, to Hattie TEBBS of Fauquier.

Married: In Warrenton Va on the 21st December by Rev. J. W. PUGH, Mr. Edward L. FISHER and Miss Sue Ida SOWERS, daughter of the late David A. SOWERS, all of Fauquier.

Married: On the morning of the 23d November 1865 by Rev. Mr. CUTTER at the bride's residence in Louisa county, Mr. Mahlon G. HATCHER of Loudoun to Miss Bettie LIPSCOMB.

Married: On 26 December, 1865 by Rev. Jos. HELM, Mr. Thomas M. WEADON to Miss Frances A. BALLENGER, all of Loudoun.

Wednesday, 17 January 1866   Vol. X, No. 32

Married: On the 10th of January by the Rev. Andrew ROBEY, Mr. Charles W. BARTON to Mrs. Sallie Ann MOORE, all of Loudoun county, Va.

Married: On Thursday January 11th at the residence of the bride's father by Rev. Samuel RODGERS, Mr. John T. GRIMES to Miss Mary J. AULT, all of Loudoun.

Married: On the 21st of December by Rev. Samuel RODGERS, Mr. Philip W. CARPER to Miss Georgeanna AUSTIN, all of Loudoun.

Married: On Tuesday evening the 9th instant at Hill and Dale by Rev. H. SUTER, Joseph H. SHEPHERD and Miss Mattie E., daughter of Colonel Benj. MORGAN, all of Clarke county.

Died: In Gonzales, Texas on the 28th of November last, of affection of the heart, Clement Kenady TEBBS, aged 20 years, son of A. Sidney TEBBS, formerly of this place.

Wednesday, 24 January 1866   Vol. X, No. 33

Married: On Thursday morning, the 18th inst., by the Rev. H. R. SMITH, at the residence of the bride's father, near Hamilton, Mr. James T. ROBINSON of Warren county, to Miss Lizzie A., eldest daughter of Mr. Samuel CROCKETT.

Married: On Thursday evening by the same, Mr. David GENTLE to Miss Margaret SEWELL, all of Loudoun.

Married: Near Seiglin, on the 16th of January by the Rev. S. GOVER, Mr. Duane M. TURNER of Fairfax and Miss Georgianne FISHER, of Loudoun.

Wednesday, 31 January 1866   Vol. X, No. 34

Married: By Rev. Hoffman WAUGH, near Snickersville on the 17th inst., Joseph R. HILL and Sarah Elizabeth LODGE, all of Loudoun.

Married: By the same near Hillsborough, on the 25th inst., Joseph PRICE and Mary Ann OSBOURN, all of Loudoun.

Wednesday, 7 February 1866   Vol. X, No. 35

Died: At his residence in this county, on the 16th ult., Mr. Jesse McINTOSH in the 65th year of his year.

Died: At his residence in this county on Monday January 23d, Miss Elizabeth MORAN in her 68th years.

Wednesday, 14 February 1866   Vol. X, No. 36

On Tuesday last, about one o'clock near Rippon, in this county. Mrs. Jane Amanda BURNS, wife of Mr. Caleb BURNS, and daughter of the late William F. LOCK, Esq. of this town, was so severely burned by her clothes taking fire as to result in her death five hours afterwards. She was sitting upon the floor amusing her twin babes when her dress came in contact with the stove. Mrs. BURNS was in her 33rd year. She leaves four little children, the youngest twins eight months old.
Charlestown Free Press.

Married: On the 31st ultimo, at the Dill House by the Rev. Dr. Geo. DIEHL, Mr. James H. GATTON to Miss Susan E. POLAND, of Loudoun.

Married: In Washington City, on the 4th of January by the Rev. James N. DAVIS, James W. McDONOUGH, of Leesburg to Miss Mary J. CARTER of Dumfree, Prince William county, Va.

Married: In Leesburg on Tuesday the 7th of February by Rev. Samuel GOVER, Mr. James W. RYAN and Miss Mary R. LEE, all of Loudoun.

Died: At "Arcadia," in this county on New Year's day, Mrs. Mary E. HEMPSTONE, wife of Cephas HEMPSTONE, Esqr. in the fifty second year of her age.

Died: On the 27th January 1866 at his residence in Frederick county, Va, Stacy J. TAVENNER, in the 63rd year of his age, formerly a resident of Loudoun.

Wednesday, 21 February 1866   Vol. X, No. 37

Peter COST died in 1850 providing that his wife shall have all his real and personal estate during her life and at her death it should be sold and distributed to his brother and sisters or their descendants. Mrs. COST died in 1865 and the Deputy Commissioner states the personal property was all consumed long ago.

Married: At the residence of Mrs. Ann E. McCORMICK, Muscatine, Iowa, on the 30th of January 1866 by the Rev. J. ARMSTRONG, Mr. James WOODALL, of Baltimore Md, to Miss Lizzie RATHIE, formerly of Leesburg.

Married: In Georgetown DC on Thursday the 8th instant by Rev. Mr. TILLINGHAST, John W. HEAD of Leesburg and Lizzie A. JOHNSON, of the former place.

Married: In Leesburg on Thursday the 15th of February 1866 by Rev. Samuel GOVER, Mr. George W. HARPER to Miss Ellen MONDAY, all of Loudoun.

Married: In St. James Church, Leesburg on Tuesday morning the 13th instant by the Rev. Walter WILLIAMS, John P. SELLMAN of Montgomery county Md, to Anna M., daughter of Christian HEMPSTON, Loudoun county.

Married: In Leesburg on Tuesday the 13th by Rev. Samuel GOVER, Mr. John L. TOWNER and Miss Emily WILDMAN, all of Loudoun.

Married: Thursday February 1st 1866 at the residence of the bride's mother, in Sperryville, Rappahannock county, Va, by Rev. Mr. BOON, J. W. BEACH, of Loudoun county, to Miss Lucy E. TOTTEN, of Sperryville.

Died: At the "Pickett House," in Leesburg on Monday night February 19th of paralysis, Mrs. Ann DOUGLAS, consort of Col. Charles DOUGLAS, aged about 65 years.

Died: At Eudora, in this county, on the 17th day of January, Mrs. Mary Ann BRADEN, wife of Noble S. BRADEN Esqr.

Died: At the residence of his mother, in Fairfax, on Thursday night February last, James M., son of the late Wm. and Leah H. WRENN, in the 23rd year of his age.

Wednesday, 28 February 1866   Vol. X, No. 37

Married: On the 15th inst. at the residence of the bride's aunt by the Rev. Mr. HANES, Mr. John E. CARRUTHERS to Miss Victoria V. WRIGHT, all of Loudoun.

Married: On the 22nd inst. at the residence of the bride's mother, Mrs. Hannah WHITE, by the Rev. Jos. HELM, Mr. Mason LOVELESS to Mrs. Catharine E. BEALES, all of Loudoun.

Married: At the same time and place by the same Mr. Thos. N. CARRUTHERS to Miss Virginia Elen WHITE, all of Loudoun.

Married: On Thursday morning February 22nd by Rev. J. H. MARCH, Mr. William C. CARRELL of Monticello, Florida, formerly of Charlestown to Miss Sue R. LOCK, daughter of the late William F. LOCK Esqr. of Charlestown.

Married: In Baltimore on the 12th of February 1866 by Rev. Dr. J. J. BULLOCK, Septimus H. STEWART, formerly of Charlestown and Carrie, daughter of Isaac SOLOMON Esq. of Baltimore.

Departed this life on the morning of Feb. 20th in the 66th year of her age, Ann Bartlet DOUGLASS, consort of Col. Charles DOUGLASS and daughter of Dr. Asher WATERMAN of revolutionary memory.

Wednesday, 7 March 1866   Vol. X, No. 38
No marriages or deaths.

Wednesday, 14 March 1866   Vol. X, No. 39
Married: On the 9th inst., by the Rev. S. GOVER, Mr. Thomas J. STEADMAN and Mrs. Elizabeth MATTHEWS, all of Loudoun.

Married: At Hamilton on the 6th inst. by Rev. Jos. HELM, Mr. John W. COCKERILLE and Miss Mary E. BELL, all of Loudoun.

Married: In Alexandria Va March 6th at the residence of the bride's father, J. N. HARPER Esqr. by the Rev. Robert H. ANDREWS, of Richmond, Albert T. SKINNER of New York to Miss Mary L. HARPER, of this city.

Married: On the 20th ultimo, near Silcott's Spring, by Rev. Thaddeus HERNDON, Mr. William YOUNG to Elizabeth, daughter of Sampson LICKEY, Esq., all of Loudoun county.

Married: On Wednesday, March 7th by Rev. Samuel RODGERS, Mr. J. Rice SMITH and Miss Virginia A. RHODES, all of Loudoun.

Married: On Tuesday, February 27th by Rev. H. WISLER, Mr. Mark M. RODEFFER of Shenandoah county, to Miss Mary Kate SOUDER, of Loudoun county.

Died: In Culpeper, at the residence of her son-in-law, James M. MOREHEAD, on Tuesday the 6th inst., of pneumonia, Mrs. Elizabeth M. HUNTON, widow of the late Eppa HUNTON, of Fauquier county, aged seventy-three.

Died: On Sunday the 4th of February after a short illness at the Plains, Fauquier Co, Mrs. Mary Ann FOSTER, the beloved wife of Major Thomas FOSTER.

Died: On the 10th of February 1866, at the residence of Mr. Thomas MOSS, after seventeen days of painful suffering, Mr. James WILDMAN, aged 78y 11m 5d, another soldier of the war of 1812 gone.

Died: On the 28th of February in Charlestown at the residence of her mother, Mrs. Rachel LOCK, Mrs. Mary Catharine LINE, wife of John D. LINE, aged 36 years.

Died: On Tuesday 29th ult. of diptheria, Lizzie Marian, second daughter of John M. and Bettie C. LOCKE, aged 8y 5m 27d.

Died: At "Cassilis" in Jeff. county on the 26th ult., William, infant daughter [son?] of Andrew E. KENNEDY.

Died March 1865, Walter JANNEY, son of the late Dr. JANNEY of Clarke county, Va.

Departed this life in Washington city, on the 7th inst., Sallie M., wife of Anon [?] H. BRADLEY.

Wednesday, 21 March 1866   Vol. X, No. 40

Died: In Washington city, on the 14th instant, Sarah S. SEEDERS in the 68th year of her age, widow of Wm. SEEDERS of Leesburg, Va.

Wednesday, 28 March 1866   Vol. X, No. 41

Married: On the 22nd inst., at the Lutheran Church, near Lovettsville, by Rev. X. J. RICHARDSON, Mr. Tilghman COOPER to Miss Ann C. WRIGHT, all of Loudoun.

Married: On Thursday 22nd inst., by Rev. Samuel RODGERS, Mr. John N. FOLLIN to Miss Mary E. FRENCH, all of Loudoun.

Married: At the Presbyterian Manse, in Leesburg on Tuesday morning the 20th inst., by Rev. H. R. SMITH, Mr. James W. NICHOLS and Miss Hannah HOWELL, all of Loudoun.

Married: Near Goresville on Tuesday the 13th inst., by Rev. Walter W. WILLIAMS, Mr. Lee M. DADE of Montgomery county, Md. to Miss Medora L. SANDERS, daughter of Major Wilson C. SANDERS, of Loudoun.

Died: In this town on Monday morning March 16th, Mrs. Ruth SOWERS, in the 77th year of her age, widow of the late Brooks SOWERS, for many years editor of the *Genius of Liberty*, formerly published in this town.

Died: On the 14th day of March at the residence of Mr. Alfred DULIN, in this county, Miss Maria O'HARRO, aged about 62 years.

Wednesday, 4 April 1866   Vol. X, No. 42

The death of S. B. T. CALDWELL took place at the residence of Mr. Bernard HOUGH, in this county, on Wednesday night last, of paralysis, in his 76th year. He came to Loudoun in 1815 and established in Leesburg, the "*Genius of Liberty*" newspaper which he edited for several years. On Friday his remains were interred in the Presbyterian burying ground of this place.

Yesterday, a man named John B. McGINN was found dead in his room at his boarding house in Washington. He is represented to have been a teacher in Centreville, Va, in 1857, and at Middleburg in 1860. After the war commenced he was a scout for the Federal army in this section of Virginia and it is said knew nearly all of Mosby's men.

Married: Near Philomont on the 28th of March by the Rev. Thaddeus HERNDON, Mr. John G. HERNDON of Fauquier and Miss Parmelia A. LOGAN of Loudoun.

Wednesday, 11 April 1866   Vol. X, No. 43

No marriages or deaths.

Wednesday, 18 April 1866   Vol. X, No. 44

Mr. Henry S. TAYLOR of this county died on Thursday of last week in the 67th year of his age.

A shooting affair took place in Lang's Tavern, D.C., on last Sunday week, which resulted in the serious wounding of Samuel S. GASKINS, by Benj. F. HOUGH, formerly of Leesburg.

Died: In Leesburg on Thursday the 12th of April 1866 of paralysis, Miss Elizabeth A. CLAGETT, daughter of the late Dr. Henry CLAGETT, in the 57th year of her age.

Died: On Sunday morning the 11th of March after a long and painful affliction, Christiana M., consort of Mr. James W. MANKIN, in the 49th year of her age.

Died: In Middleburg, January 21st 1866, Norman, second son of the late Dr. Wm. H. and H. R. McVEIGH.

Wednesday, 25 April 1866   Vol. X, No. 45

Mr. Daniel WHITE, died very suddenly on Monday last, at his residence in Maryland, near White's Ferry, of spotted fever. He was in Leesburg on Saturday where he remained until near sundown, he was taken with the fever on Sunday and died Monday.

Married: In Montgomery county, Md, on Tuesday, the 13th inst., by the Rev. Mr. TRAPNELL, Col. C. W. PAXSON, of Loudoun county, and Miss Sarah Frances TRUNDLE, of Maryland.

Married: In Leesburg on the 23d inst., by Rev. Samuel GOVER, Mr. Joseph MYERS and Miss Martha E. PIERPOINT, both of Loudoun.

Died: In Washington on the 17th instant, Mr. James H. SLACK in the 29th year of his age. He leaves a wife and three children.

Died: Suddenly on Wednesday the 11th inst. at his residence, Sharon, Fairfax county, Va. in the 42nd year of his age, Lieut. Commander M. Patterson JONES, U. S. Navy, eldest son of the late Commodore Thomas Ap. Catesby JONES, U.S. Navy.

Died: In Palmyrs, Missouri, March 26th 1866, Ada Lee, youngest daughter of Jno. H. HUGES and adopted daughter of Mr. and Mrs. KELBER, of that place, aged 14 years.

Died: In the vicinity of Lovettsville on the 2nd of April, Mrs. Catharine WENNER consort of Mr. Emanuel WENNER in the 49th year of her age.

Died: On Thursday the 8th of April, in this county, James F. CRAVEN in the 77th year of his age, he was in the war of 1812.

Died: On the 7th inst. at his residence, near Warrenton, Nathaniel E. GRAY in the 47th year of his age.

Died: In Fauquier county on the 1st instant, Wm. F. PAYNE in the 80th year of his age.

Died: At his residence near Philomont, on the 10th instant, 1866, Mr. Enoch GARRETT in the 64th year of his age. He departed, leaving a large family of children (though nearly all grown.)

Wednesday, 2 May 1866   Vol. X, No. 46

Married: On the 25th ult. in Trinity Church, Shepherdstown by the Rev. Charles W. ANDREWS, D.D., Capt. Dudley D. PENDLETON and Helen M., daughter of the Hon. Alexander R. BOTELER, all of Jefferson County.

Married: In Leesburg on the 25th of April by Rev. S. GOVER, Mr. William W. LEE and Miss Nancy C. NELSON, all of Loudoun.

Minister: In Leesburg on the 1st day of May, by Rev. S. GOVER, Mr. Lewis ARTHER and Miss Margaret A. BALL, all of Loudoun.

Died: Near Leesburg, on Thursday, the 26th of April at the residence of his father, Mr. John H. THOMAS, William Edgar, in the 18th year of his age.

Wednesday, 9 May 1866   Vol. X, No. 47

The remains of B. S. WHITE and Dolphin T. RAWLINS, of the 2nd Va infantry, Stonewall Brigade, and G. Upshur MANNING and Charles Hector ISLER, of Co. B, 12th Va Cavalry, were brought to Charlestown on last Tuesday week and interred. The first two were killed at the battle of Chancellorsville on the 3rd of May 1863 and the other two at Brandy Station on the 9th of June 1863.

The remains of Maj. James THOMSON son of John A. THOMSON Esq. of Jefferson county have also been brought from the field on which he fell. He was killed on the 6th of April 1865 near the High Bridge, whilst leading in the last charge of the Cavalry of the Army of Northern Virginia. – *Free Press*.

Married: On the 25th of April by Rev. W. C. MEREDITH, Dr. John B. WORTHAM, of Alabama and Miss Sarah Roberta, daughter of Col. R. L. BAKER, of Frederick county.

Married: On the 26th of April at Spring Dale, Frederick county, by the same, Dr. Cornelius BALDWIN, of Winchester, and Miss Anna M., daughter of the late C. Marshall JONES, of New Orleans, La.

Married: On Thursday morning the 26th of April, in Winchester, by Rev. J. B. AVIRETT, John J. BROWN, of Upperville and Miss Harriet A. CHRISMAN, of Newtown.

Married: On the evening of the 26th of April at Winchester, Va. by Rev. J. R. GRAHAM, Dr. A. M. FAUNTLEROY of Staunton and Miss Sallie H. CONRAD, daughter of the Hon. R. Y. CONRAD of Winchester.

The Mirror
Wednesday, 16 May 1866   Vol. X, No. 48

Married: On Wednesday morning, the 2nd inst. in Jefferson county, at the residence of Col. R. W. BAYLOR, by Rev. Charles WHITE, Mr. Edward AISQUITH of Charlestown, to Mrs. Kate Knox BAYLOR, of Jefferson county, daughter of the late Thomas J. LIKENS, of Mississippi.

Died: In this town on Thursday the 26th of April, Mr. Thomas Jefferson EDWARDS, in the 62nd year of his age.

Died: At the residence of her son, near Aldie, in this county, on the 20th of April, Mrs. Mary AYRES, in the 75th year of her age.

Among the noble sacrifices to the lost cause of Confederate Independence we number Lewis ADIE, of Leesburg. As a member of Company 'D' 43rd Battalion, P. R. He was sadly missed. After the capture of a portion of SHERIDAN's supply train, near Berryville, Clarke County, in that action he fell after two of the enemy had met their doom through him. He has bequeathed to his widowed mother his unknown grave, to his sisters and brothers a wide spare in the family circle.

Wednesday, 16 May 1866   Vol. X, No. 48

Liquor licenses were granted: Henry C. HARDING, William SRY, Robert E. DIVINE, Lorenzo D. ROBERTS, James W. WALLACE, Chancellor & Bro.,. C. W. PAXSON, Samuel ORRISON, William S. KEYES, George H. HUTCHISON, Charles E. LLOYD, Eli DUVAL, John B. LOCKHART and John F. WAESCHE.

Licence to keep ordinaries were granted to Philip BROOKS, William S. PICKETT and James W. RUSSELL. Licence to keep house of private entertainment were granted to James H. WHALEY, Matthew P. LEE and Susan SAFFER.

Married: On the 10th inst., at the Lutheran Church near Lovettsville by Rev. X. J. RICHARDSON, Mr. David E. FRY to Miss Sarah E. FRY, all of this county.

Married: On Thursday, 10th instant, at the residence of the bride's father, Mr. W. H. UTTERBACK, of Fairfax co., and Miss Cecilia L. PALMER, of Loudoun co.

Died: Near Hoysville, March 10th, Mrs. Mary M. YEAKY, wife of John W. YEAKY, in the 23d year of her age.

Died: In Frederick county, Md, on Sunday the 29th of April at "Otterbourne," the residence of her father, Col. Henry DUNLOP, Helen, wife of Mr. Thomas CLAGETT Jr., of Prince George county, aged 22 years.

Wednesday, 23 May 1866   Vol. X, No. 49

Married: On Tuesday morning, May 8th by the Rev. Mr. CURTIS, Dr. J. J. HENSHAW of Lovettsville, and Miss Maggie

ROUSER, eldest daughter of Henry ROUSER Esq., of Mechanicstown, Md.

Married: On Tuesday May 15th at the residence of her father, Mr. Wm. B. JACKSON, by Elder Joseph FURR, Mr. John F. ELGIN and Miss Anna JACKSON, all of Loudoun.

Died: At the Baltimore Infirmary on the 14th instant, Garah HARDING, of Loudoun county, and late of the Confederate army. His remains were interred on the 15th instant, in the Baltimore Cemetery, with Masonic honors.

Died: On the 16th of May at Oakwood, near Warrenton, Fauquier county, after a brief illness, Mrs. Margaret G. LEE, widow of Robert Eden LEE, and daughter of Judge John SCOTT deceased.

Died: On the 10th inst., after a short illness, in the 49th year of her age, Mrs. Mary Winifred, wife of Rev. E. P. PHELPS, of the Baltimore Conference M. E. Church.

Died: On the 9th of May in Strasburg, Shenandoah county, Mrs. Ann WOODWARD, aged 47y 3m 5d, wife of William H. WOODWARD. She leave eight children.

Wednesday, 30 May 1866   Vol. X, No. 50

Married: On Tuesday the 22d inst. at the residence of the bride's father, near Hamilton, by the Rev. Joseph HELM, Lt. Lewis SHUMATE and Miss Mary T., daughter of the officiating clergyman, all of Loudoun.

Married: On Thursday the 24th of May at Forrest Mills, the residence of the bride's father, by Friend's Ceremony, William BROWN Jr. and Lydia N., daughter of Asa M. JANNEY, all of Loudoun.

Married: On Thursday the 17th instant, in Frederick City Md, by Rev. Dr. ZACHARIAS, Dr. Thomas J. DUNOTT to Miss Lizzie, daughter of the officiating clergyman.

Died: At her residence, "Mountain Home" May 26th 1866 of typhoid fever, Mrs. Margaret BROWN, widow of the late Joseph BROWN, in the 78th year of her age.

Died: At the residence of her daughter, Mrs. M. A. DAVIS, in Baltimore on the 20th inst., Mrs. Mary KEPLER, in the 89th year of her age.

Wednesday, 6 June 1866   Vol. X, No. 51

Married: On the 31st of May, at the bride's father, by Rev. S. GOVER, Mr. William H. AYRES, and Miss Virginia E. VIRTS, all of Loudoun.

Died: At the residence, after a brief but severe illness of only a few weeks, on the 10th day of May, Mr. Wm. H. H. BEANS, aged twenty-seven years and two months.

Wednesday, 13 June 1866   Vol. X, No. 52

The remains of Capt. Chas. H. BALL, of the Loudoun cavalry, who was killed at the battle of Spottsylvania, were brought to this town on Friday last, and interred in the Union Cemetery.

The case of Benj. F. HOUGH, of Georgetown, indicted for the murder of Samuel A. GASKINS, resulted in a verdict of manslaughter. The jury was out but fifteen minutes.

Died: Near Leesburg, on the 8th instant after a short illness, Robert J. DRANE, of Drainesville, Va, aged 39 years.

Wednesday, 20 June 1866   Vol. XI, No. 1

Mr. Charles T. CHAMBLIN, at the time he was wounded, a Lieut. in the 8th Virginia regiment, coughed from his throat a few days since, a minnie ball that had been lodged there for more than four years. He was shot at "Seven Pines," June 1, 1862, the ball entering the side of the nose just below the left eye. It was probed four inches and found to have passed near perpendicularly in scarcely missing the brain. It disabled him for duty and has ever since caused much pain in damp weather. When coughed up on Tuesday evening last, it seemed to have come from just below the right ear, under the jaw bone, and caused but little pain and was followed by no blood. It is an ounce minnie.

Married: On Tuesday morning, the 12th inst. by Rev. H. R. SMITH, Col. John LESLIE, of Loudoun, and Julia B. PATTERSON, of Montgomery county Md.

Died: At his residence, in this county, on Tuesday the 12th of May, Mr. David DANIEL in the 79th year of his age.

Died: In Baltimore, 7th inst., after a protracted illness, Amanda Elizabeth, daughter of Jno. W. and Mary A. WOODDY, formerly of Virginia, in the 25th year of her age.

Wednesday, 27 June 1866   Vol. XI, No. 2

Married: In Georgetown, DC, June 12, by Rev. A. A. TAYLOR, John F. BLUNDON to Fannie F. NOLAND, of Loudoun county.

Died: In Winchester on Tuesday night, June 19th, after a brief illness, Mrs. Arabella LUCKETT, widow of the late Robert

LUCKETT of Loudoun county, and daughter of the late Robert WHITE of Winchester.

Wednesday, 4 July 1866   Vol. XI, No. 3

Section of page where marriages and death probably listed was torn out.

Wednesday, 11 July 1866   Vol. XI, No. 4

In the death of Mr. Asa JACKSON, which occurred in this town on Friday morning last, this community has lost a most useful citizen. On Saturday evening his remains were interred in the Union Cemetery, followed to the grave by the Masonic and Odd Fellow Fraternities.

Mr. Henry G. SMITH, one of the Deputy Sheriffs for Loudoun county, died on Saturday last of consumption.

Married: At Glenn Welby, the residence of the bride's parents on the evening of the 3d inst., by the Rev. J. D. BLACKWELL, Col. R. Welby CARTER, of Loudoun County, to Miss Sophia D. CARTER, of Fauquier county.

Married: On the morning of the 3d inst., in the Protestant Episcopal Church, by the Rev. J. R. HUBARD, Col. M. D. WICKERSHAM, of Mobile to Miss Eugenia D. FRISTOLE, of Rappahannock county.

Married: On the 24th of May inst. at the residence of the bride's father, by Rev. A. MAXWELL, Mr. William E. MAXWELL, of Frederick county, to Miss Susan SLAYMAN, of Loudoun county.

Died: In this town, on Friday evening, July 6, 1866, Mr. Asa JACKSON, in the 69th year of his age.

Died: Upon the premises of his father, deceased, known as Mountain Farm, on the 7th inst., of consumption, Henry G. SMITH, aged 35 years.

Died: On the morning of the 30th of June, of consumption, Mrs. Pleasant TAVENER, widow of Stacy J. TAVENER, deceased. She was born in Loudoun county, March 16th, 1806. Her husband proceeded her to the grave on the 27th of January 1866. He was born in the same county, May 9th 1893, and died of the same disease.

Wednesday, 18 July 1866   Vol. XI, No. 5

Married: On Tuesday morning, 3d instant, at Laurel Hill the residence of the bride's father, by the Rev. Mr. HUGHES, Capt. Frederick DABER, of Charlestown, and Miss Virginia, daughter of Thomas G. FLAGG, Esqr. of Berkeley county.

Married: On Tuesday, the 3rd July 1866, at St. Paul's Church, Richmond, by the Rev. Dr. MINNIGERODE, Capt. J. Frank

RANSON, late C.S.A. of Jefferson county, West Virginia to Helen F., daughter of Ambrose CARLTON, of Richmond city.
Married: In the village of Hamilton, on the 10th inst., by Rev. H. R. SMITH, Asbury JANNEY to Miss Annie, daughter of Thomas NICHOLS, all of this county.
Married: In Newton county, Missouri, June 2d, 1864, Mr. PARKER to Miss Maria HEWETT, formerly of Leesburg.
Married: In the same county, September 7th 1865, Mr. MORROW, of Missouri, to Miss Judith HEWETT, formerly of Leesburg.
Married: In the same county, December 4th 1864, Mr. ???SON [page creased] to Miss Lydia HEWETT, formerly of Leesburg.
Died: On Monday night, the 9th instant, in the city of Baltimore, Thomas J. E. FOX, leaving a widow and a daughter, an only child. Mr. FOX was born in Leesburg in the year 1834.

Wednesday, 25 July 1866   Vol. XI, No. 6

Our obituary column this morning contains the announcement of the death of Mr. Tarlton V. B. OSBURN. He died of paralysis in the 53d year of his age.
Mr. Wm. D. DRISH, for many years a prominent grocery merchant of this town, died on Sunday night last, in his 73d year.
Married: On Thursday evening the 19th inst. at Belmont, the residence of the bride's father, by Rev. Samuel RODGERS, Mr. Washington MERCER to Miss Martha KEPHART.
Married: On Wednesday evening, 11th instant, by Rev. Dr. Wm. B. EDWARDS, Mr. Charles T. PECK, formerly of Loudoun, to Miss Annie E. BREMERMAN, of Georgetown.
Died: July 14, at the residence of his father in Waterford, after a lingering illness from consumption, John T. MOUNT, eldest son of Wm. T. and Bettie MOUNT, aged 17 years.
Died: In this town, on the 3d instant, Stonewall Jackson, son of C. TURNER, in the 4th year of his age.
Died: At the residence of his brother, Bushrod OSBURN, near Hillsboro, on the 16th of July 1866, of paralysis, Tarleton V. B. OSBURN, aged 53 years.
Died: In Frederick county, Va, on the 23d of June, William CARSON, in the 10th year of his age, only surviving child of Gen. James H. and Catharine CARSON.

Wednesday, 1 August 1866   Vol. XI, No. 7

Married: By Rev. H. R. SMITH, on Thursday evening the 26th of July, James Albert JOHNSON and Lucinda C. HAVENNER, all of Loudoun.

Wednesday, 8 August 1866   Vol. XI, No. 8

Married: On the 2nd inst. in Leesburg, by Rev. Samuel GOVER, Mr. James HUNT and Miss Sarah J. COMET, all of Loudoun.

Married: By Rev. H. R. SMITH on Thursday evening, the 2d inst., Mr. W. Flavius BEANS and Miss Annie R., eldest daughter of Mrs. Virginia VIRTS, all of Loudoun.

Married: On the 31st of July, at the Potomac Furnace, by Rev. X. J. RICHARDSON, Mr. Joseph H. FRY to Miss Sophia APPELL, all of Loudoun.

Married: On the 31st of July, in Leesburg by the Rev. Samuel GOVER, Mr. Samuel P. LOVE and Miss Eliza M. ARNETT, all of Loudoun.

Died: In this county on Friday, the 27th of July, 1866, Mrs. Margaret THOMAS, wife of Mr. John W. THOMAS, in the 29th year of her age. She leaves several small children.

Wednesday, 15 August 1866   Vol. XI, No. 9

Married: On the 12th of June at the Potomac Furnace, by Rev. X. J. RICHARDSON, Mr. Richard HEATER to Miss Matilda A. APPELL, all of Loudoun.

Married: Tuesday morning the 7th inst., by the Rev. Samuel RINGGOLD at the Episcopal Church in Clarksville, Tenn., W. F. KEPHART of Louisiana, formerly of Loudoun, to Miss Sallie E. TRUNDLE, eldest daughter of H. L. TRUNDLE, Esq., formerly of Lafayette county, Missouri.

Married: On the 19th of July by Rev. F. H. RICHEY, Mr. Joseph CONNER and Miss Amanda KAMSEY. [RAMSEY]

Married: On the 24th of July, by the same, Mr. Samuel D. HARDING and Miss Sallie JENKINS.

Married: On the 7th of August, by the same, Jr. Wm. H. MOORE and Miss Mary P. UNDERWOOD, all of Loudoun county.

Died: After a long and painful illness, Mrs. Henry A. BALL, on Thursday 9th of August, 1866 in the 52nd year of her age.

Wednesday, 26 August 1866   Vol. XI, No. 10

Died: Of cholera, at St. Louis, Mo. on Monday, August 13th, Miss Amelia ROSS, aged 17 years, eldest daughter of John A. and Emiline A. ROSS, of Georgetown, DC.

Died: At the residence of E. L. BENTLEY, in this town on Friday, 17th inst., Julia Carter, daughter of Hugh and Rose NELSON, aged 7 months.

Wednesday, 29 August 1866 Vol. XI, No. 11

Died: In Hanaball, Missouri, on the 7th instant, Mr. James McDANIEL, formerly of Leesburg, aged about 65 years. Tribute of respect by the Knight Templars of Missouri.

Wednesday, 5 September 1866 Vol. XI, No. 12

Married: On Wednesday evening 15th inst., at the residence of the bride's father by Rev. H. SUTER, Major Paul JONES of Alabama, to Miss Lucy THOMPSON, daughter of John A. THOMPSON Esq., of Jefferson county.

Married: In Leesburg, on the 28th of August by Rev. Samuel GOVER, Mr. George W. ORRISON and Miss Sarah R. MILLS, all of Loudoun.

Died: On the 7th instant at his late residence in this county, Mr. John MORGAN, in the 73d year of his age. He desired to depart.

Died: August 15th of typhoid fever, Miss Caroline R. HICKMAN, daughter of George HICKMAN, in the 23rd year of her age.

Died: At his residence near Lovettsville August 27th of typhoid fever, George HICKMAN in the 50th year of his age, one of the most active and zealous supporters of the Lutheran Church of which for many years he was a member.

Died: In St. Louis, Mo. August 17, 1866 after a short illness, Mrs. Hannah A. BENNETT aged about 50 years, wife of the late John H. BENNETT, formerly of Loudoun county. Also in the same city August 16, 1866, Sydnor BENNETT, youngest son of the above, aged about 15 years.

Died: July 25, 1866 at Perry Farm, St. Charles county, Missouri, Sallie E., second daughter of Charles R. and Elizabeth KEEN, aged 3y 6m 13d.

Died: Near Hillsborough on the 18th instant, George, only son of George and Elizabeth RECTOR, aged 9y 15d.

Wednesday, 12 September 1866 Vol. XI, No. 13

Married: On the 23d ult. in Loudoun county by Rev. Dr. HAYNES, Mr. Wm. A. O'BANNON, of Charlestown, to Miss Mattie D. JEFFRIES, of Loudoun.

Married: In Shepherdstown, on the 27th ult., by Rev. J. F. CAMPBELL, at the residence of Mrs. CROWL, Mr. W. H. VANDEVENTER, of Mercer county, Pa to Miss Elizabeth V. McDONALD, of Shepherdstown.

Married: In Martinsburg, on Monday, 27th ult., by Rev. ___, Mr. Wm. H. LYNN, to Miss Annie FURR, daughter of Mr. Wm. G. FURR, both of Loudoun county.

Married: Near Farmwell Station, August 30th 1866 by Elder John W. JONES, Mr. Johnathan W. NIXON, and Mrs. Mary Francis LEFEVER, all of Loudoun.

Died: (From the Adams Pa *Sentinel*) On the 29th of August, in Gettysburg, P., of pulmonery consumption, Charles C. MASON Esq. of Leesburg, Va.

Departed this life on the 7th of June, Dolly, eldest child of John W. and Mary A. WOODDY, formerly of Virginia, in the 25th year of her age. On her death bed she asked her parents to allow her to receive the services of a Catholic priest. After careful instruction she was baptized.

Wednesday, 19 September 1866   Vol. XI, No. 14

Married: On the 7th inst., by Rev. Geo. W. HARRIS, Mr. Edward WILLIAMS and Mrs. Sarah T. GRIMES, both of Loudoun county.

Married: On Thursday, the 7th instant, by the Rev. Wm. EGGLESTON, Jas. T. MURPHY, of Jefferson county, to Miss Mary V. BARTON, of Loudoun.

Married: By Rev. H. R. SMITH, on Tuesday the 11th inst., Mr. John M. ADRAIN, and Miss Mary E. GREENLEASE, all of Loudoun.

Died: Near Hamilton, in this county, on the 8th of August of typhoid fever, Annie, dau. of William N. EVERHART, in her 23d year.

Wednesday, 26 September 1866   Vol. XI, No. 15

Married: On the 4th instant at the Lutheran Parsonage, by the Rev. G. DIEHL, Mr. James M. MULL, of Loudoun county, to Miss Cornelia C. WHIP, of Fairview, Frederick county, Md.

Married: On Tuesday September 18th at the residence of the bride's father by Rev. Samuel RODGERS, Mr. John F. REEVES to Miss Mary J. DAILEY, all of Loudoun.

Married: On the 18th at the residence of her brother, in Washington, by the Rev. Mr. Geo. G. MARKHAM, Albert O. BROWN to Miss Eliza L. MOCK, both of Loudoun county.

Died: At the residence of Francis MARKELL in Frederick City, Maryland on Friday the 14th inst., Mrs. Charlotte MAULSBY, relict of the late Benjamin MAULSBY of Leesburg Va, in the 72nd year of her age.

Wednesday, 3 October 1866   Vol. XI, No. 16

(From the Omaha Nebraska *Herald*)   James G. MEGEATH – Mr. MEGEATH has reason to be proud of the position he occupied before the Democratic Convention as a candidate for the nomination as Delegate to Congress. He was not only the choice of his own county, but also of almost entire North Platte.

Wednesday, 10 October 1866   Vol. XI, No. 17

Married: On Wednesday the 26th instant, at the residence of the bride's father near Waterford by Rev. Saml. GOVER, Mr. John W. VIRTS and Miss Henrietta HOUGH, all of Loudoun.

Died: In this town on Friday evening last of typhoid fever, Mr. John W. KELLY, aged 28 years. Mr. K. was a member of the Loudoun Guard and served faithfully as a private soldier in that command throughout the late war.

Died: In Baltimore Jun 13th Jane MEAD, aged 11m 24d, on the 29th of August, at the residence of her grandfather, Joseph MEAD, Fannie MEAD, in the 6th year of her age – only children of B. S. and Mary E. WHITE.

Wednesday, 10 October 1866   Vol. XI, No. 17

Married: On the 24 instant, at Rockland, Loudoun county by Rev. E. T. PERKINS, Henry T. MICHIE, of Staunton, Va to Virginia, only daughter of the late Hon. Henry BEDINGER.

Married: In this county on Thursday the 4th inst., by Rev. Jos. HELM, Mr. Cicero DOWNS and Miss Martha BALLENGER, all of Loudoun.

Died: On the 27th ult in Loudoun county at the residence of his brother-in-law, Samuel JANNEY, Joseph JANNEY, in the 66th year of his age.

Died: In Leesburg on Tuesday, October the 2d, of typhoid fever, Willy, only son of John W. and Susan BIRD, in his 6th year.

Died: At Mount Airy near Middleburg, Va on 20th of August, after a severe illness of a week duration, Lloyd Grafton, third son of David Alexander and Angeline D. ELGIN aged 1y 5m 12d.

Wednesday, 17 October 1866   Vol. XI, No. 18

Warrenton Sentinel, Oct. 11 – We regret to announce that on last Monday afternoon, a difficulty occurred at Oak Hill, in the upper part of this county, which resulted in the killing of one of our most worthy citizens. Mr. James F. JONES, formerly one of the justices of the county, by Mr. M Buckner BAYLY, commonly known as "Buck" BAYLY, a merchant at the above named place. We understand the difficulty grew out of a charge on the part of Mr. JONES that Mr. BAYLY had been disloyal to the South and had piloted the Yankees to Mr. JONES' house. Mr. BAYLY retreated into his store, returned with a pistol and fired upon Mr. JONES, the ball entered his neck ranged downwards and lodged in his lungs, of which he died in a few hours. Mr. JONES leaves a wife and nine small children. Mr. BAYLY is also a married man

Married: In Leesburg on the 10th inst., by the Rev. Samuel RODGERS, Mr. John R. BEUCHLER and Miss Mary V., daughter of Mr. John L. RINKER, all of Leesburg.

Died: In Norfolk, Va, October 5th, Walter Bradley, only child of Theodrick and Gertrude WILLIAMS, aged 7m 19d.

Wednesday, 24 October 1866   Vol. XI, No. 19

Married: On Monday the 15th instant at Farmwell Church by Rev. J. C. HUMMER, Mr. John R. McNELEA, of Loudoun county, and Miss Martha S. STROTHER, of Fairfax county.

Married: On Tuesday evening the 16th instant at the residence of the bride's father by Rev. Samuel RODGERS, Mr. James H. RYAN and Miss Margaret A. BURGESS, all of Loudoun.

Married: At the same time and place by the same, Mr. Elisha GREGG and Miss Mary C. STEVENS, all of Loudoun.

Married: On the 18th instant by the Rev. J. C. HUMMER, Mr. R. H. EDWARDS and Miss Martha J. FRANKLIN, all of Loudoun.

Married: On the 18th instant by Rev. Geo. W. HARRIS, Mr. Charles H. MILLARD and Miss Maggie A. JONES.

Married: On the 18th of October by Rev. Samuel GOVER, Mr. William MATHERS and Miss Martha C. AYRES, all of Loudoun.

Died: In Alexandria on Saturday October 13th after a lingering illness, Rebecca STABLER, daughter of Edward and Mary STABLER deceased.

Died: In Alexandria October 17, Benedict W. ATHEY in the 24th year of his age.

Died: At Idle Wilde in Amherst county, Va at the residence of her father, on the 7th of October, Miss Victoria C. MOSBY, eldest daughter of Mr. Alfred D. MOSBY and the beloved sister of Colonel John S. MOSBY.

Died: On the cars between Jackson, Miss. and New Orleans on Saturday Sept. 29th 1866, Miss Sallie J., eldest daughter of Capt. S. H. SUMMERS, of Washington county, aged 18 years. She was on her way from Tennessee, with the family of Judge CALDWELL of Grimes county, to visit her father and died after a brief illness.

Wednesday, 31 October 1866   Vol. XI, No. 20

We chronicle the death of Major Charles H. STEWART of Charlestown, Jefferson county, Va, who died near Baltimore on Friday the 19th inst. in the 37th? year of his age. Major STEWART was the founder and Editor of the *Loudoun Democrat* published in this town. As a Lt. and afterwards a commander of the celebrated 2d Va regiment of the Stonewall Brigade until the final surrender of the armies of the Confederacy. His remains were brought here on Saturday night last and on yesterday morning were emtombed in Edge Hill Cemetery.

Married: On the 18th inst. at the residence of the bride's father by Rev. Geo. W. HARRIS, Mr. Chas. H. MILLARD of Md and Miss Maggie A. JONES of Loudoun.

Married: On the 23d inst. at the residence of the bride's father at Neersville, by Rev. Francis H. RICHEY, Charles F. GALLOWAY and Susannah J., daughter of John GRUBB Jr., all of Loudoun.

Married: On the 25th inst., by Rev. Francis H. RICHEY, William T. JONES and Rachel A. POMEROY, all of Loudoun.

Married: In Martinsburg, West Va. on Thursday the 24th of October by Rev. H. C. McDANIEL, Mr. George W. SURVICK, of Leesburg to Miss Alice M. CHARLTON, of the former place.

Died: At the residence of her mother, Mrs. RICH, in Washington city on Wednesday evening 24th inst., Mrs. Isabella M. HALL, formerly of Leesburg, in the 25th year of her age.

Wednesday, 7 November 1866   Vol. XI, No. 21

Married: In Middleburg on the 20th of September by the Rev. John LANDSTREET, Mr. John T. CLINE and Miss M. M. BARKER, all of Loudoun.

Married: On Tuesday the 23d of October by Elder Joseph FURR, Mr. James WEADON to Miss Mary J. JONES, all of Loudoun.

Died: On the 30th of October 1866 at home in Wood Grove, Mrs. Harriet BLAKEY, wife of Dr. R. O. BLAKEY, aged 53 years.

Wednesday, 14 November 1866   Vol. XI, No. 22

Mr. Samuel FRY fell dead at the Point of Rocks Md, on Tuesday the 6th inst. He had crossed the Ferry and was walking up towards the canal bridge, apparently in good health when it is supposed he died from heart disease.

Married: November 1st by Rev. R. W. WATTS at the residence of the bride's father, Mr. Edward A. SMITH, of Loudoun to Miss Mary S. RURTON [BURTON??], of Albemarle.

Married: On Tuesday Nov. 6 by Rev. Dr. PINKNEY, Stirling MURRAY, of Baltimore county Md to Anna THORNTON, daughter of Dr. Thomas MILLER of Washington, DC.

Married: On Tuesday Nov. 6 at the residence of Mr. E. S. LEADBEATER by the Rev. J. T. LEFTWICH, Harry C. SLAYMAKER to Miss Anna LEADBEATER, all of Alexandria.

Married: On the 8th inst., near Waterford by Rev. S. GOVER, Mr. George PUSSEY, and Mrs. Veline TAVENNER, all of Loudoun.

Died: Near Bloomfield in this county on Sunday the 4th of November 1866, Mrs. Mary A. THOMAS, wife of Herod THOMAS in the 66th year of her age.

Wednesday, 21 November 1866   Vol. XI, No. 23

Married: On the 8th of November at the residence of the bride's father by the Rev. John LANDSTREET, Theodorick B. LEITH to Anna A, daughter of Gibson GREGG Esq., all of Loudoun.

Married: On the 8th inst. by the Rev. George W. HARRIS, Dr. Edward WOOTTEN, of Montgomery county, Md and Miss Bettie OREAR, youngest daughter of Enoch OREAR, Esq. of Fauquier county.

Married: On Thursday the 8th day of November 1866, at the residence of Mr. William HILL by Rev. F. H. RICHEY, Franklin PURSELL and Mary S. HILL, all of Loudoun.

Married: On the 25 of October at the residence of Mr. George MATHERS by the Rev. X. J. RICHARDSON, Mr. James FRIBBY [TRIBBY] to Miss Sarah C. CRIM, all of Loudoun.

Married: On the 8th inst. at Taylortown by the same, Mr. John W. COMPHER to Miss Isabelle BOWERS, all of Loudoun.

Married: On the 15th inst. at Berlin Ferry by the same, Mr. George H. SNOOTS to Miss Sarah R. COOPER, all of Loudoun.

Died: On the 3d inst. at the late residence of her father, Valeria, daughter of the late Jacob HOUSEHOLDER, in the 12th year of her age. Thus a father and daughter passed into eternity within a few hours of each other.

Died: On the 10th instant, Mr. George E. SLATER, of the German Settlement in the 72nd year of his age.

Died: Of dyptheria on Monday morning the 12th inst., Miss Martha A. CUMMINS, aged 17 years.

Died: At Selma near Leesburg on the 10th inst., Colonel William BEVERLY, of Blanfield, Essex county, Va, aged 72 years. His remains were deposited in the cemetery at Leesburg for the present. The death of Col. B. will be regretted by a large number of friends in DC, Va, and Alabama.

Died: On the 6th inst., at Point of Rocks, suddenly of heart disease, Mr. Samuel FRY, in the 58th year of his age.

Died: At his residence near Lovettsville on the 2d last, Jacob HOUSEHOLDER in the 55th year of his age. In the death of the aged men above, they were consistent members of the Ev. Lutheran church.

Died: On the 17th inst. of inflammatory rheumatism, Silas Clayson, son of Samuel L. COMES, in the 11th year of his age.

Wednesday, 28 November 1866   Vol. XI, No. 24

Married: On the 8th inst. at the residence of the bride's father by the Rev. P. W. YATES, Mr. A. F. MENEFEE to Miss Lucy C. HEATON, all of Rappahannock.

Married: In Parish, Va, on the 15th inst. at the residence of Mrs. Susan MARSHALL by the Rev. Thaddeus HERNDON, Mr.

Wm. D. SOWERS, of Loudoun to Miss Maria V. ADAMS, daughter of B. F. ADAMS, Esq. of Fauquier county.

Married: At Hopewell, Frederick county, Nov. 14th, according to the order of the Society of Friends, Lewis N. HOGE, of Loudoun to Susan B. JOLLIFE, of Frederick county, Va.

Married: At St. Paul's Church on Thursday the 15th of November by the Rev. Chas. MINNEGERODE, J. Pendleton ROGERS, to Miss Ellen, daughter of Thomas W. McCANCE, all of the city of Richmond.

Wednesday, 5 December 1866   Vol. XI, No. 25

Married: On Tuesday evening 27th ult. by Rev. Samuel RODGERS, Mr. John P. EVANS to Mrs. Rowena CASTLE, all of Leesburg.

Married: On the 28th of November in Leesburg at the residence of the bride's mother by Rev. Samuel GOVER, Mr. John C. BAKER, of New York and Sarah V. SMITH, of Leesburg.

Married: On the 29th of November near Taylortown by the Rev. X. J. RICHARDSON, Mr. Samuel W. GEORGE to Miss Virginia YEAKY, daughter of John YEAKY deceased, all of Loudoun.

Married: On the same day by the same at the New Jerusalem Ev. Lutheran Parsonage, Mr. Samuel SLATER Sr. to Miss Julia Ann FRY, all of Loudoun.

Married: On the same day by the same at New Jerusalem Ev. Lutheran Church, Mr. Adam COOPER to Mrs. Mary Elizabeth FILLER, all of Loudoun.

Married: On Thursday 22d of November by the Rev. Samuel RODGERS, Mr. James W. MYERS to Miss Mary E. HAFENNER [HAVENNER], all of Loudoun.

Married: On the 20th of November by Rev John WOOLF, at the residence of Moses WILSON, Esq., Mr. John E. BRAWNER to Miss Mary F. DENNIS, all of Loudoun.

Married: On the 11th of November by Elder Thaddeus HERNDON, Mr. James W. BELL to Miss Susannah F. SMITH, all of Prince William county.

Married: On the 20th of November by the same, Mr. Guilford G. CRAVEN to Miss Julia A. LICKEY, all of Loudoun.

Married: On Tuesday evening the 26th of November at the residence of the bride's father by Rev. T. W. DOSH, of Winchester, Rev. Joseph A. SNYDER and Miss Virginia, daughter of Mr. Israel ALLEN, living near Mt. Jackson, Va.

Died: Of diptheria on Saturday 17th of November at residence of Mrs. Lavinia MEAD, Miss Sallie BALENGER, in her 20th year.

Died: On the 23d of November of typhoid fever, Mrs. Sarah C., wife of Jacob HOUSEHOLDER, recently died, in her 33d year. For many years a worthy member of the M. E. Church.

Died: On the 27th of November of typhoid fever, Miss Virginia C., daughter of Jacob HOUSEHOLDER, recently died, in the 23d year of her age. For more than six years she was a member of the Lutheran Church.

Died: In Waynesville, Warren county, Ohio, on the 11th of November, Gideon DAVIS, a native of Loudoun county, in the 84th year of his age.

Died: At his residence near Lovettsville in this county on Sunday morning December 2d of cancer of the stomach, Mr. Emanuel WALTMAN.

Wednesday, 12 December 1866   Vol. XI, No. 26

Married: At the residence of the bride's father on the 5th inst., by the Rev. Geo. HARRIS, Samuel D. LESLIE Jr. and Martha Ann, daughter of Edward D. POTTS, all of Loudoun.

Married: On the 6th of December by Rev. Jos. HELM, Mr. Nimrod TAVENNER and Miss Rebecma [Rebecca] Jane WHITE, all of Loudoun county.

Married: November 29th by Rev. John LANDSTREET, William A. REEDER to Lucelia E., daughter of Samuel TORREYSON Esq., all of Loudoun county.

Wednesday, 19 December 1866   Vol. XI, No. 27

On Wednesday last the remains of Lt. Wm. THRIFT were brought to this town for final interment. He was an office in the Loudoun Cavalry, and his death occurred in the skirmish near the Fauquier Springs in 1862.

Married: On 13th December by Rev. John LANDSTREET, Mr. V. B. WALTMAN to Hannah C., daughter of Fenton FURR, Esq., all of Loudoun.

Married: On the 20th of November 1866, by the Rev. F. H. RICHEY, Mr. Johnathan MATTHEWS to Miss Mary J. BEANS, all of Loudoun.

Married: In New York, on Thursday the 15th of November, by the Rev. Mr. SCOTT, of Pensacola, Florida, Colonel Harry GILMOR, of Maryland, to Mentorian, daughter of the late Colonel Jasper STRONG, formerly of the U. S. Army.

Married: At the Presbyterian Manse, on Tuesday the 11th inst., by Rev. H. R. SMITH, Mr. Charles T. JENKINS and Mrs. Elizabeth DODD, all of Loudoun.

Married: Near Belmont, on Thursday morning the 13th inst., by the Rev. H. R. SMITH, Mr. Charles R. ELGIN and Miss Susan Alice, eldest dau. of Luther THRASHER, Esq., all of Loudoun.

Died: In Leesburg on the 11th instant, of brain fever, Charles W., son of Charles E. and Airy A. ROLLINS, aged 2y 11m.

Wednesday, 26 December 1866   Vol. XI, No. 28

Married: On Tuesday evening the 18th inst. at ???land, near Leesburg the residence of the bride's father, by the Rev. E. T. PERKINS, William E. HARRISON to Lizzie, only daughter of Thomas W. EDWARDS, Esq.

Married: On Thursday the 20th inst. at the Loudoun Hotel, Leesburg, by the Rev. J. C. HUMMER, Burr W. PRESGRAVES to Rosa Ellen HAVENNER, all of Loudoun.

Married: In Frederick City, Maryland on the 17th instant, by Rev. James CURNS, Mr. John RUSE Jr. and Miss Olevia E. GEORGE, both of Loudoun.

Married: Near Belmont by Rev. H. R. SMITH on Tuesday evening the 18th inst., Mr. Joseph R. HAVENNER and Miss Emily T. HAVENNER, all of Loudoun.

Died: Near Morrisonville in this county on Thursday morning the 13th of December, Nathaniel M., son of Jacob CRUSON, aged 23 years.

Died: In this town on Sunday morning last, after a brief illness of a few days, Mr. John W. HEAD, of Washington, aged about 23 years.

Wednesday, 2 January 1867   Vol. XI, No. 29

Married: In Leesburg by Rev. H. R. SMITH on Wednesday evening the 26th instant, Mr. Daniel G. ALEXANDER, of Massachusetts to Miss Almeda WALLACE, of this town.

Married: On Thursday the 20th instant by Rev. Samuel GOVER at the residence of the bride's parents, Philip B. TRITIPOE and Sarah E. SHRY, all of Loudoun.

Married: By Elder T. HERNDON on the 18th inst., Jno. W. CABLE to Mary J. CARTER, all of Fauquier.

Married: By the same on the 20th instant, Wm. F. SKILLMAN to Sarah E. HAMPTON, all of Loudoun.

Married: On the 6th inst. at the residence of Abner CONRAD, by Rev. X. J. RICHARDSON, Mr. William WOLF to Miss Elizabeth SEXTON, all of Loudoun.

Married: On the 13th inst. at the New Jerusalem Ev. Lutheran Church by the same, Mr. Job M. MILLER, of Knoxville Md, to Miss Sarah V, daughter of Mr. John MANN, of Loudoun.

Married: On the 18th inst. at the same place, by the same, Mr. William O. HOUSHOLDER, to Miss Mary C., daughter of Mr. William RICHARD, all of Loudoun.

Married: On the 19th inst., at the same place by the same, Mr. Henry H. HOUGH to Miss Fanny E., daughter of Mr. Thomas JOHNSON, all of Loudoun.

Married: On the 20th inst., at the residence of the bride's mother by the same, Mr. John W. FRY to Miss Susan, daughter of Mrs. Charlotte DAVIS, all of Loudoun.

Married: On the same day, at the residence of the bride's father by the same, Mr. Daniel J. H. FRY to Miss Sarah C. E., daughter of Mr. Samuel COMPHER, all of Loudoun.

Married: On the same day at the residence of the bride's father by the same, Mr. Chester C. GAVER to Miss Amelia F., daughter of Mr. David SHRIVER, all of Loudoun.

Wednesday, 9 January 1867 Vol. XI, No. 30

Mr. William VANDEVANTER, formerly of Loudoun county, but who has been residing in Monroe county, Missouri for the last twenty five years, was brutally murdered at his house in that state on the night of the 29th of December, by two negro men, who shot him through a window, the ball passing entirely through the head. The negroes then rushed into the house and fired upon his wife, the ball striking her in the right temple and coming out under the chin. Mr. V. died instantly, his wife was living the next morning. Money was the object of the murderers and it is known that they secured $500 in gold.

Married on the 27th December near Warrenton, Eugene CALLAHAN, white, late soldier of the U. S. Army and a native of Lowell, Mass., to Roberta HUNDELL [HUDNELL], colored, formerly the slave of T. B. STEWART of Fauquier. – *Warrenton Index*.

Married: At the Church near Sunny Side in Waterford, on the 27th day of the 12th month, 1866, John W. HUTCHINSON, of the city of New York, to Emma Eliza, daughter of John B. DUTTON, of the former place.

Married: On Thursday, the 13th of December at the residence of the bride's mother, by the Rev. T. R. SHEPHERD, Mr. Burr P. FRED to Miss Rebecca J. ROGERS, all of Loudoun.

Married: On the 20th ult. at the Dill House, Frederick, Md. by Rev. Dr. ZACHARIAS, Henry C. HILLERY to Miss Sophia C. LOCKER, both of Loudoun county.

Married: In Bedford county, Va on Wednesday the 2d of January at the residence of the bride's mother by Rev. Mr. BROWN, Capt. William MEADE, of Loudoun, and Miss Cornelia F. MEADE, of Bedford.

Died: On Friday the 29th of December, 1866, of pneumonia, Mrs. Mary, wife of Benjamin SAUNDERS, in her 60th year.

Died: Near Mt. Gilead, Loudoun county, on Saturday morning 22nd of December of diptheria, Howard Franklin, only child of James E. and Mary J. TAVENER, aged one year and ten months.

Died: At his residence near Belmont on Tuesday the 1st instant, Aquilla BAUCKMAN, aged 49 years.

Died: On Thursday morning last, 27th ult. in Charlestown, Mrs. Orra Moore BUSKIRK, relict of the late Wm. Van BUSKIRK, of Cumberland, Md, and daughter of the late John DIXON, Esq., of that place in the 62nd year of her age.

Wednesday, 16 January 1867   Vol. XI, No. 31

Married: On Thursday the 3d instant, by the Rev. John WOOLF, Mr. Samuel T. WYNKOOP and Miss Catherine E., daughter of Mr. Richard WYNKOOP, all of Loudoun.

Married: In Leesburg, on the 10th of January by Rev. Samuel GOVER, Mr. George H. LOY and Miss Henrietta CORDELL, all of Loudoun.

Married: On the 2nd inst., at the New Jerusalem Ev. Lutheran Parsonage by the Rev. X. J. RICHARDSON, Mr. Jacob E. WOODS to Miss Mary E., daughter of Mr. John HUMMER, all of Loudoun.

Married: On the 2d inst., at the residence of Mr. John MANCHE, Mr. William A. HESKELL, of Jefferson County, W Va, to Miss Sarah E., daughter of Mr. Peter COLE, of Loudoun.

Married: On the same day at the residence of the bride's father, Mr. Samuel R. SAGLE to Miss Sallie A., daughter of Mr. John FRITTS, all of Loudoun.

Married: On the 10th inst., at the residence of the bride's father, Mr. Abner EDWARDS, to Miss Mary B. M., daughter of Mr. Abner CONARD, all of Loudoun.

Wednesday, 23 January 1867   Vol. XI, No. 32

Married: On Thursday morning the 10th inst. in the Methodist Church in Charlestown, by Rev. Robert SMITH, Mr. George W. NOLAND, of Baltimore, formerly of Jefferson county, to Miss Cornelia A. RILEY, of Charlestown.

Married: On the evening of the same day, by the same, at the residence of Mrs. BEALL, near Flowing Spring, Mr. Samuel C. NOLAND to Miss Lydia E., daughter of Mr. Jacob H. MOLER, all of Jefferson county.

Married: On Tuesday last, in Frederick county, Md. by Rev. Joseph TRAPNALL, Mr. John S. EASTERDAY, of Charlestown, to Miss Rachael A., daughter of Judge Joseph EASTERDAY, of the former county.

Married: At Sherwood Forest the residence of the bride's parents on Tuesday the 8th instant, by the Rev. Henry WALL, John TAYLOE Jr., son of Col. John TAYLOE, of King George to Jane E. FITZHUGH, daughter of Henry FITZHUGH, Esq., of Stafford, Va.

Married: On the 8th instant at the Fourth Presbyterian Church, Washington by Rev. J. C. SMITH, D.D., pastor, Mr. Phineas JANNEY of Loudoun county to Miss Clara CONNELLY, daughter of Thos. C. CONNELLY, Esq., of Washington.

Married: On December 27th 1866, by Elder T. W. NEWMAN, Mr. Appa H. CREAL and Rachel FLINN, all of Fauquier county.

Married: By the same, January 2d 1867, Mr. Albert BALL, of Prince William county, and Miss Narcissa THARPE, of Fauquier county.

Married: By the same, January 3, 1867, Mr. Lucien M. MANUEL, of Jefferson county, and Miss Mary Susan MANUEL, of Prince William county.

Died: Near Leesburg on Thursday the 17th inst., Mrs. Mahala J. SLACK, in the 43d year of her age.

Wednesday, 30 January 1867   Vol. XI, No. 33

Married: Near Landmark, Fauquier county on the 20th instant, by Rev. T. J. McVEIGH, Mr. Benj. F. HURST and Miss Malinda FLINN, all of Fauquier.

Married: On the 18th instant, at West Alexander, Pa by the Rev. Josias STEPHENSON, R. P. H. STAUB, Esqr. of Martinsburg, W Va., to Delia A. GOSHORN, daughter of Wm. A. GOSHORN, of Wheeling, W Va.

Married: On the 10th inst. at the Lutheran Church, Middletown, by Rev. Dr. STROBLE, Mr. Jacob E. BOYER to Miss Malinda B. JOHNSON, both of the vicinity of Lovettsville.

Married: At the residence of Samuel GREGG, Fauquier county, on the 10th of January by Rev. T. J. McVEIGH, Mr. George B. SINCLAIR Jr. and Miss Lydia A. E. MITCHELL, all of Fauquier.

Married: On the 11th inst. by Rev. Samuel RODGERS, Mr. Henry HIBBS to Miss Fannie A. GULICK, all of Loudoun.

Died: In Leesburg on Tuesday the 22d of January 1867, William T., infant son of Wm. J. and M. F. COCKRAN, aged 10m 15d.

Died: On the 7th inst., at Philomont, Loudoun county, Alice RADCLIFF, in the 14th year of her age, only daughter of William and Emily RADCLIFF.

Wednesday, 6 February 1867   Vol. XI, No. 34

Married: Thursday January 31st at the residence of the bride's father, by Rev. Samuel RODGERS, Mr. G. H. M. BEAVERS to Miss Margaret M. DONOHOE, all of Loudoun.

Died: Near Leesburg on Wednesday the 30th of January 1867, Mr. Christopher HOWSER, in the 92d year of his age.

Departed this life at Soldier's Rest on the evening of January 19th 1867, Mrs. Evelina THOMAS, wife of Wm. P. THOMAS and daughter of the late Minor FURR, after a long and distressing illness.

Died: On the 28th of January near Leesburg, Miss Mary McFARLAND in the 25th year of her age.

Wednesday, 13 February 1867   Vol. XI, No. 35

Married: On the 17th of January at the New Jerusalem Ev. Lutheran Church by Rev. X. J. RICHARDSON, Mr. James M. SLATER and Miss Mary DARR, all of Loudoun.

Married: On the 5th instant at the same place by the same, Mr. William H. VIRTS to Miss Marietta, daughter of Mr. Robert S. ORME, all of Loudoun.

Married: By Rev. H. R. SMITH on Thursday evening, the 7th inst., Mr. George R. ELGIN and Mrs. Sarah E. DOWNS, all of Loudoun.

Wednesday, 20 February 1867   Vol. XI, No. 36

On Sunday night, Mr. George RHODES, one of the oldest citizens of Loudoun, departed this life at his residence near Leesburg in the 91st year of his age. Mr. R. was born in this town when Leesburg was in its infancy, and his long life was passed almost within its suburbs. There are now but four building standing in the town, the erection of which was beyond his recollection. He had for a very long time been a member of the Methodist Church, having at the disruption of that body, sided with the Church South.

Died: At his residence in Prince William county Va, near Evergreen, on the 14th of December 1866, of brain fever, Presley G. GARDNER, aged 63 years. He was originally from Fairfax county.

Wednesday, 27 February 1867   Vol. XI, No. 37

Married: On the 19th instant, by Rev. Geo. W. HARRIS at the residence of the bride's father, Dr. Wm. M. LUPTON, of Hamilton and Miss Josephine KERFOOT, daughter of Daniel S. KERFOOT, Esq. of Fauquier county.

Married: On Thursday, January 17th 1867 by Rev. J. C. HUMMER, Mr. Jno. W. ORRISON and Miss Prudence V. PRESGRAVE, all of Loudoun.

Married: On Thursday, January 24th by the same, Mr. Chas. C. WALKER and Miss Annie E. DARNE, all of Loudoun.

Married: On the 24th of January last, by Elder Joseph FURR, Mr. James R. STALLINGS, of Maryland, to Miss Hannah B. ORRISON, of Loudoun.

Married: On the 14th inst., by the same, Mr. Albert SILCOTT to Deboram [Deborah] M. YOUNG, all of Loudoun.

Married: In Middleburg, Tuesday the 12th instant, by Rev. O. A. KINSOLVING, Capt. Virginius DABNEY to Anna W., eldest daughter of Maj. B. P. NOLAND.

Married: On February 12th at the residence of Harry? BITZER, Esq., by Rev. Jno. LANDSTREET, Samuel L. COX to Miss Mary D. HESSER, both of Loudoun county.

Married: At "Killmane," Montgomery county, Md. at the residence of the bride's uncle, Mr. David YOUNG by Rev. Mr. SHIPLEY, Dr. Thos. H. SCHAEFFER, at Leesburg, Loudoun county and Miss Bettie YOUNG, of the former place.

Died: On Tuesday February the 12th near Morrisonville, of consumption, Mr. Samuel C. E. RAMSEY. He leaves a wife and four children.

Died: In Middleburg on Friday night February 15th 1867, Lewis Chamberlayne, only son of Dr. George BAGBY, aged 15m.

Died: In Leesburg on Thursday the 21st instant, Thomas Wheeler, infant son of William W. and Isabella ATHEY, aged 1m 4d.

Wednesday, 6 March 1867   Vol. XI, No. 38

Married: In Leesburg at the Loudoun Hotel, on Tuesday evening February the 26th 1867, by Rev. Father MAGUIRE, J. Monroe HEISKELL to Essie Fairfax, daughter of Col. John W. MINOR of Loudoun.

Married: At Lexington Va on Wednesday, February 20th by the Rev. Wm. D. JONES, George W. NORRIS, Esq., of Baltimore Co., Md. and Mrs. Jane Powell GRADY, formerly of Loudoun.

Married: On the 26th inst., at New Jerusalem Ev. Lutheran Church by X. J. RICHARDSON, Mr. Jacob FRY to Miss Mary Catherine RHODES, all of Loudoun.

Married: On the 28th of February in Waterford by the Rev. Samuel GOVER, William T. SCHOOLEY and Julia Ann DIVINE, all of Loudoun.

Died: On Thursday morning, February 21st, Pauline, daughter of Charles F. and Ann Eliza ELGIN, aged 3y 5m.

Died: At Philadelphia on the 22nd ult., Mary S., wife of Arthur MILLER, in the 27th year of her age.

Wednesday, 13 March 1867   Vol. XI, No. 39

Mr. Larkin N. Sanddrs [SANDERS], living near the Plaines Station, in Fauquier county, died on the 14th of January last, in the 97th year of his age, and in fourteen days therefore, he was followed to the grave by his wife, Fanny, who was in the 87th year of her age. They had been united for 57 years.

Married: At the residence of the bride's father in this county on the 28th of February by Rev. Dr. HAINES, Mr. John HUTCHINSON and Miss Margaret E., daughter of Richard L. ROGERS.

Married: By Rev. H. R. SMITH, at "The Manse" on Thursday evening the 7th inst., Mr. Charles W. WYNKOOP and Miss Florence M. BURCH, all of Loudoun.

Married: On the 26th of February by the Rev. John WOOF, at the residence of Mr. J. WILDMAN, Mr. Edward HENRY to Mrs. Sarah HAMILTON, all of Loudoun.

Died: At the residence of his father in this county on the 28th of February, after a short but painful illness, Samuel C., son of Samuel C. and the late Mary B. LUCKETT, in the 16th year of his age – the youngest child and only son of a fond father.

Wednesday, 20 March 1867   Vol. XI, No. 40

Married: On the 21st of February by Rev. J. E. ARMSTRONG, Tiphen W. ALLEN, of Shenandoah county, and Mrs. Mary B. PATTERSON, of Augusta.

Married: By Rev. H. R. SMITH, on the morning of the 17th inst., Mr. James T. MERCHANT and Miss Sarah C. McDANIEL, all of Loudoun.

Married: On the 7th inst. near Taylortown, by Rev. X. J. RICHARDSON, Mr. Peter C. MYERS to Miss Mary M. COMPHER, all of Loudoun.

Married: On the 28th of February at the E. M. Parsonage, Middleburg, by Rev. John LANDSTREET, Lawson E. JOHNSON, of Fairfax, to Lydia A. SUMMERS, of Loudoun.

Wednesday, 27 March 1867   Vol. XI, No. 41

Married: On the 18th inst., at Werford [Waterford] by Rev. T. T. PERKINS, S. E. CHAMBERLIN (Capt. U.S.A.) and Edith D. MATTHEWS, daughter of Edward Y. and Sarah J. MATTHEWS, of Loudoun county.

Married: In Leesburg on the 21st instant, by Rev. Samuel GOVER, James W. STEADMAN and Miss Sallie MORELAND, all of Loudoun.

Married: On the 7th inst., near Taylortown, by Rev. X. J. RICHARDSON, Mr. Peter C. MYERS and Miss Mary M. COMPHER, all of Loudoun.

Married: On the 14th instant, by the Rev. John WOLF, in Snickersville, Mr. James H. MONROE to Miss Julia MILEY, all of Loudoun.

Died: On the 15th inst., in Prince William county, at the residence of his daughter, Mrs. Virginia HUTCHINSON, John BAYLY Sr., in the 88th year of his age.

Wednesday, 3 April 1867   Vol. XI, No. 42

Married: On the 14th ult. by Rev. X. J. RICHARDSON, Mr. William H. HARPER to Miss Susannah MUNDAY, all of Loudoun.

Married: On the 28th of March, by Rev. J. A. HAYNES, Richard C. McCARTY Jr. and Miss Martha Eleanor MEGEATH, all of Loudoun.

Married: On the same day by the same, John T. LAWS and Miss Laura J., daughter of Johnathan W. NIXON, all of Loudoun.

Married: On Tuesday 28th of August 1866, by Rev. W. H. HARRISON, D.D., assisted by Rev. Dr. DEIHL, of Frederick Md, Rev. P. L. HARRISON, of Clearfield, Pa and Miss Fannie M. BANTZ, of Morrisonville, Loudoun county.

Died: On Sunday, the 24th of March, at the residence of her father, Luudwell [Ludwell] LAKE, near Rector's Cross Roads, Fauquier county, in the 19th year of her age, Mary Agnes, the wife of Andrew J. BARBER.

Wednesday, 10 April 1867   Vol. XI, No. 43

Married: On Tuesday April 2d by Rev. Samuel RODGERS, John H. HOWSER and Malinda A. MILBOURN, all of Loudoun.

Married: On the 26th ultimo, at the German Reformed Church, near Lovettsville, by the Rev. H. WISSLAR, Mr. Charles W. FRY to Miss Annie A. SMITH.

Married: At the residence of Mr. Geo. P. HUNTER on the 4th inst., by Rev. X. J. RICHARDSON, Mr. Michael L. HUNTER to Miss Ruth H. ROBERTS, all of Loudoun.

Died: In Burlington, Vermont, April 2d, Capt. George A. THACHER [THATCHER?] formerly member of Caledonia County bar, and more recently of the Loudoun County bar in Virginia, aged 28y 5m.

Wednesday, 17 April 1867   Vol. XI, No. 44

Died: On the 18th of October 1866 at the residence of James ODELL, Esq., in Carroll county, Indiana of congestion of the brain, Mrs. Euphemia A. ODELL, eldest daughter of Maj. Geo. W. and Ruth H. NOLAND, of Loudoun county, and consort of John C. ODELL, Esq., of the former state, at the early age of 28 years.

Married: In Leesburg, on the 15th inst., by Rev. Jas. McDONOUGH, Mr. Junius RICHARDSON and Miss Bridgett MURPHY, all of Loudoun.

Wednesday, 24 April 1867   Vol. XI, No. 45

Died: On Saturday the 13th of April 1867 at the residence of her sister-in-law, Mrs. Virginia REED, near Broad Run, Loudoun county, of consumption, Gertrude REED, youngest daughter of John and Laura REED, in the 16th year of her age. Her remains were buried in the Churchyard at Hamilton, Va.

Died: On the 31st ultimo, Mrs. Catherine Frances BITZER, consort of Mr. Harmon BITZER, aged about 49 years. Bereavement to her weeping husband, daughter and sons.

Wednesday, 1 May 1867   Vol. XI, No. 46

The grand jury was again in session on Monday in hearing the testimony relative to the murder of Wm. McCREA, a negro man found dead near his home in September 1865, and John TAYLOR, another negro who was murdered in his own house in September 1866. Wife and daughter of TAYLOR examined.

Married: In Winchester Va on the 18th of April, by the Rev. N. WILSON, W. W. B. GALLEHER, Junior Editor of the "*Virginia Free Press*" of Charlestown, Jefferson county, and Miss Belle WILSON, daughter of the officiating clergyman.

Married: On the 16th April at the bride's mother, by Rev. T. MAXWELL, Richard Henry GRIMES and Martha M. LEE, all of Loudoun.

Married: In Baltimore on Tuesday the 22nd instant, by the Rev. Dr. MAHAN, at the residence of the bride's father, Thomas B. FERGUSON, of South Carolina, to Jennie B. daughter of Governor Thomas SWANN.

Died: On Monday evening, April 15th, the burns received in the morning, Edward Burton, youngest child of James B. and Sarah ELGIN, in the 16th month of his age.

Wednesday, 8 May 1867   Vol. XI, No. 47

No marriages or deaths.

Wednesday, 15 May 1867   Vol. XI, No. 48

Married: On the 30th ult. at the residence of the bride's father, by Rev. Mr. HARRIS, Mr. John D. KERFOOT, of Clarke county, to Miss Mary E. CARR, daughter of John CARR, Esq., of Fauquier county.

Wednesday, 22 May 1867   Vol. XI, No. 49

Married: On the 9th ult. on Beaver Creek, by Rev. G. W. STEVENSON, Mr. J. W. BELL, formerly of Loudoun county, and Miss Mary E. MINNICK, of Rockingham county, Va.

Wednesday, 29 May 1867   Vol. XI, No. 50

Married: In the M. E. Church, South, Leesburg, on Sunday evening, May 26th 1867, by Rev. Samuel H. RODGERS, Mr. Frederick C. SHAW, of Washington city, to Miss Kate M., daughter of Mr. James F. DIVINE, of this town.

Married: At Selma, the residence of Mr. William BEVERLY, on the 22d inst. by Rev. E. T. PERKINS, John V. BROWN, of Baltimore, Md, to Minnie V., daughter of the late Dr. Joseph GRAY, of Loudoun county.

Married: On the 15th inst. at "Valley View," the residence of J. D. BUDD, Esq., by the Rev. T. J. McVEIGH, Mr. William V. MOSS, and Miss K. Blanche McVEIGH, youngest daughter of Townsend McVEIGH, Esq., all of Loudoun.

Married: On the 16th instant, by Rev. J. F. POULTON, at the residence of the bride's father, in Prince William county, Joseph M. DAVIS, of King George county, Va, and Miss Sallie E. GLASCOCK.

Married: On Thursday, the 16th inst., at the residence of the bride's father, by Rev. Jos. HELM, Mr. Joseph C. OSBURN and Miss Elizabeth H., daughter of Ellwood HATCHER, all of Loudoun.

Married: On Tuesday, 14th of May, at the residence of James V. BROOK, Esq., by Rev. John W. PUGH, Wm. Edmond HURXTHALL, Esq., to Miss Jeannie Brooke, only daughter of the late Hon. Samuel CHILTON, all of Fauquier.

Married: May 20th by Rev. John LANDSTREET, Thomas E. CARR to Annie, youngest daughter of Wm. CHAMBLIN, Esq., all of Loudoun.

Wednesday, 5 June 1867   Vol. XI, No. 51

Married: On the 29th of May 1867 at the residence of the bride's mother, by the Rev. John LANDSTREET, Wm. E. FORD, of Fairfax county, to Miss Ketmah, daughter of the late Thomas O. HUMPHREY, of this county.

Married: On the 28th of May at the parsonage of the Foundery M. E. Church, Washington City, by Rev. Mr. BROWN, Geo. WRIGHT of New Jersey to Miss Victoria TOWNER, of Leesburg.

Married: At the residence of the officiating clergyman on the 16th by Elder Joseph FURR, Mr. Samuel B. PAXSON, of Boonsborough, Md. to Miss Sarah E. WILLIAMS, of Loudoun.

Married: At the residence of Mr. Joseph FRY, Loudoun county, on Tuesday morning, May 28th 1867, by Elder J. A. HAYNES, Mr. Wm. L. LAWSON, of Maryland to Miss Annie E. LAWSON, of Fauquier Co.

Married: By the same, on the 17th day of January at the house of the bride's mother, Mr. Maalon [Mahlon] T. TAVENNER and Miss Lucie T. MURRAY, all of Loudoun.

Married: By the same on the 14th of May 1867, Samuel TRIPLETT, Esq. to Mrs. Amanda RICHARDS, all of Loudoun.

Married: On the 23d of May at the house of Mr. Austin O. ASHBY, near Bloomfield, Loudoun county by Jesse PORTER, James F. WILEY to Nancy W. HESS.

Married: On the 30th of May at New Jerusalem Church by Rev. X. J. RICHARDSON, Mr. Samuel MICHAEL, of Washington county, Md, to Miss Mary S. HICKMAN, daughter of Geo. S. HICKMAN dec'd., of Loudoun.

Died: At Uniontown, Pa May 14th 1867, William STONE, aged 74y 10m. Mr. S. was born in Westmoreland county, Va in 1792. He moved from Loudoun county, Va to Uniontown, Pa in 1832 where he lived until he died.

Wednesday, 12 June 1867   Vol. XI, No. 52

George K. FOX Sr., for many years Commissioner of the Revenue of Loudoun county, died in Leesburg on Friday last, in the 72nd year of his age. Mr. F. had lived out threescore years and ten in this town.

Married: On the 4th of June by Rev. John LANDSTREET, Ludwell HUTCHINSON to Miss Fanny R. SKINNER, all of Loudoun county.

Married: On the 6th of June, at the bride's father's by Rev. Samuel GOVER, Peter W. FRY and Mary E. LOY, all of Loudoun.

Married: On the 5th inst. at Trinity Church, Staunton Va by Rev. James A. LATANE, Hugh L. POWELL, Esq., of New York (formerly of Leesburg) to Ellen M., daughter of Dr. Francis T. STRIBLING.

Married: By elder J. H. HAYNES, May 30th 1867, at Mr. Samuel GREGG's in Fauquier county, Mr. John Wm. BICKSLER, of Loudoun, to Miss Susan Rebecca MITCHEL, of Fauquier.

Died: Near Woodgrove, on the 14th of May, at the residence of his uncle, Isaiah B. BEANS, Dr. R. Albert BEANS, aged 32 years.

[MISSING ISSUES]

Wednesday, 25 December 1867   Vol. XII, No. 28

James ROPER, the largest land holder and wealthiest man in Jefferson county, Va is dead. ROPER was a colored man, the natural son of an eccentric Englishman, who bequeathed most of his property to the recently deceased.

Married: On the 10th instant, by the Rev. John WOOLF, at the residence of the bride father, Mr. Jos. G. BROWN and Miss Virginia MONDAY, all of Loudoun.

Married: On the 12th inst., by the same, at the residence of the bride's father, Mr. Joel F. CAUFMAN and Miss Matilda CARLISLE, all of Loudoun.

Married: By the same, on the 16th instant, at the residence of the bride's mother, Enoch C. WILSON and Miss Alice L. COCKS, all of Loudoun.

Married: At the residence of the bride's mother, near Philomont, on the 5th inst., by Elder Paul YATES, Albert T. GARRETT and Miss Emma F., daughter of William and Eliza EWERS.

Married: On the 12th ultimo, at Chelsea, Fauquier county, the residence of the bride's father, by the Rev. Mr. BLACKWELL, Lucie D., daughter of Mr. William SMITH, and Channing M. SMITH, of the same county.

Married: By the Rev. James McDONOUGH, Dec. 18th, 1867, Mr. Samuel P. WRIGHT to Miss Margaret Ann America FAWLEY, all of Loudoun.

Married: On the 19th inst., at New Jerusalem Ev. Lutheran Parsonage, by X. J. RICHARDSON, Mr. William F. TRIBBY to Miss Emma Jane MOCK, all of Loudoun.

Married: On the 19th December, at Philomont, by the Rev. John LANDSTREET, Joseph S. WELSH, to Miss Mary E., daughter of John W. MARTIN, Esq.

Married: On the 19th of December, at Aldie, by the same, John W. BELT to Miss Virginia T., daughter of Geo. H. BOZZAL.

Married: On the 19th instant, near Goresville, by Rev. S. GOVER, David W. FRY and Nancy C. HOUGH, all of Loudoun.

Departed this life on the 8th inst., at his residence near Goose Creek, in this county, Mr. Joel CRAVEN Sr., in the 79th year of his age.

Wednesday, 8 January 1868   Vol. XII, No. 29

Mr. Daniel T. WINE Jr. whose marriage on the 24th ult. we published last week, was buried on Saturday, he having died the preceding Friday from the effects of injuries received a few days after his marriage.

Casper SPRING, a thrifty citizen of this county, died at his residence near Hoyesville, last week, in his 80th year.

Married: On the 10th of November at the house of the bride's mother, by Dr. J. A. HAYNES, Mr. B. F. VANHORN and Miss Betty UNDERWOOD, both of Loudoun.

Married: By the same at the house of the bride's father, December 19th, Mr. C. F. FRANKS and Miss Margaret NALLS, both of Loudoun.

Married: At the same, near Landmark, December 26, Mr. Evan O. LUNSFORD and Mrs. Catharine LOVETT, both of Fauquier.

Married: Thursday, January 2d, by Rev. Samuel RODGERS, Mr. Wm. C. HOWSER and Miss Linnie E. HAVENNER, all of Loudoun.

Married: At the Central Hotel, in Frederick city, Md, on the 24th ult., by Rev. Dr. ZACHARIAS, Mr. Charles L. NICHOLS to Miss Harriet A. GATTON, both of Point of Rocks.
Married: At the same place, by the same, Mr. Thomas INGIN to Miss Annie FRENCH, both of Point of Rocks.
Married: On the 26th ult. at Berlin Ferry, by Rev. X. J. RICHARDSON, Mr. Charles R. RINKER to Miss Anna HANVEY, all of Loudoun.
Died: December 25th, Mason B. BEACH, in his 29th year.
Died: On Tuesday, 31st of December 1867, at his late residence, 4 miles south of Leesburg, Francis ELGIN, in his 62d year.
Died: On the 22nd December 1867, at St. Bernard, Fauquier county, after a painful and lingering illness, Mrs. Eliza Ariss, wife of B. Frank GALLAHER, of Washington city, and daughter of the late Richard Bernard BUCKNER, aged 34y 2m 20d, leaving a husband, mother, brothers, sisters and a daughter.

Wednesday, 15 January 1868   Vol. XII, No. 30

Married: January 2d, 1868, in Norfolk county, by the Rev. P. A. PETERSON, Rev. Oscar LITTLETON, of the Virginia Conference, M. E. Church, South, and Alice M. BERNARD.
Married: On the 1st of January, by Rev. Father ROYLE, Wm. A. SOLLERS, of Washington, and Miss Cora TOWNER, of Leesburg.
Married: On the 7th January, 1868, in Leesburg, at the Loudoun Hotel, by Rev. Samuel GOVER, Mr. John T. BLINCOE and Miss Martha J. HAVENNER, all of Loudoun.
Married: January 7, 1868, by the Rev. John LANDSTREET, Henry B. LINKINS, of Annapolis, Md to Carrie, daughter of John DAVIS, of this county.
Married: In Leesburg, on the 7th of November 1867, by Elder J. O. WILSON, of Baltimore city, John B. SANTMYERS, Esq. to Louisa C., daughter of Wm. ARNETT, all of Loudoun.
Died: In Baltimore, on the 9th inst., Mrs. Marie Beverley CLARKE, relict of the late Dr. George CLARKE, of Georgetown, DC, and daughter of the late Robert BEVERLEY, Esqr. of Blandfield, Essex county, Va, aged 76 years.
Died: At his residence at Gum Spring, on the 3rd of January, of pneumonia, Walter R. BRADSHAW, in the 36th year of his age.

Wednesday, 26 February 1868   Vol. XII, No. 36

Married: On the 11th inst. by the Rev. John WOOLF, at the residence of the bride's father, Mr. Jno. T. POPKINS and Miss Martha F. McINTOSH, all of Loudoun.
Married: January 21st 1868 by Elder T. W. NEWMAN, Mr. Charles E. REED and Miss Pattie B. NELSON, all of Loudoun.

Married: By the same, January 23d 1868, Mr. Newman T. FOX to Margaret E. CUNNINGHAM, all of Loudoun.

Married: On the 14th inst. in Martinsburg, by the Rev. J. J. KAIN, Mr. Anson B. VINCEL of Loudoun county, to Miss Elizabeth R. BLONDEL, of Martinsburg.

[MISSING ISSUES]

Wednesday, 20 May 1868   Vol. XII, No. 48

Married: On the 14th instant, at the residence of the bride's father, by Rev. X. J. RICHARDSON, Mr. Gabriel V. WARNER to Miss Sarah J. STOCKS, all of Loudoun.

Died: At his residence near Hamilton in this county on Friday the 1st of May, after a short but painful illness, Elijah HOLMES, in the 72d year of his age.

[MISSING ISSUES]

Wednesday, 10 June 1868   Vol. XII, No. 51

Married: Tuesday morning, 5th of May 1868, by Elder T. W. NEWMAN, Mr. George F. JENKINS, of Fauquier county, to Miss Lucy C. BALL, of Prince William county.

[one entry cut out of paper]

Married: June the 8th in Leesburg, by Rev. Mr. SHOAFF, Mr. Charles J. SWARTZ, and Miss Edmonia DANIEL, both of Loudoun county.

Married: In Leesburg, on the 4th of June, 1868, by the Rev. Mr. SHOAFF, Cyrus G. SAUNDERS, of San Francisco, California, to Miss Martha SAUNDERS, daughter of the late Thomas SAUNDERS, of Loudoun County.

[MISSING ISSUES]

Wednesday, 15 July 1868   Vol. XIII, No. 4

From the *Alexandria Gazette* of Monday evening – Mr. Lyttleton TYLER, in this city, unexpectedly died about 8 o'clock this morning at his room in the City Hotel. Mr. TYLER was the youngest son of the late Judge John Webb TYLER, of Fauquier county.

Col. A. M. ASHBY, late C.S.A. was shot and killed at Knoxville, Tenn, on Friday, by one E. C. CAMP. Col. ASHBY was a Virginian, and a cousin of the celebrated Colonel Turner M. ASHBY, of cavalry fame, who was killed in the Valley in the early part of the war.

Died: At the residence of her husband, near Morrisonville, on Thursday night last, Mrs. Hannah MARTIN, wife of Mr. Wm. A. MARTIN.

Wednesday, 22 July 1868   Vol. XIII, No. 5

Died: On Monday, July 6th 1868, Nancy A. McPHERSON, wife of W. S. McPHERSON, in the 78th year of her age.

Died: In Leesburg, on Monday the 29th instant, Thomas Munsey, son of Wm. D. and Mary E. EASTERDAY, aged 7m 11d.

Died: In Leesburg, on Monday, 20th instant, at 10 o'clock p.m., Mary Elizabeth, daughter of William P. and Ann Virginia SMITH, aged 7y 6m 5d.

[MISSING ISSUES]

Wednesday, 23 June 1869   Vol. XIV, No. 1

Married: In Leesburg, on Monday evening, June 21st, by Rev. Mr. MITCHELL, Mr. H. Clay WALLACE and Miss Henrietta FORSYTH, all of this town.

Married: May 20th by Rev. David SHOAFF, Mr. Joseph T. WHITTINGTON and Miss Alberta WHITTINGTON, both of Fauquier Co.

Married: June 15th, at the residence of the bride's father, by the same, Dr. William J. WILLIAMS, of Rappahannock Co., and Miss Adeline CHAPPELEAR, of Fauquier, Va.

[MISSING ISSUE]

Wednesday, 7 July 1869   Vol. XIV, No. 3

Married: On the 22nd of June, at the Point of Rocks, by Rev. J. W. SMITH, George H. C. HICKMAN to Miss Mary E. RITCHIE, both of Loudoun Co.

Died: In Leesburg, on Thursday, July 1st, 1869, Sarah Elizabeth, daughter of John T. and Mary E. GRIMES, aged 11m.

[MISSING ISSUES]

The following appeared in the Friday, 21 August 1919 issue: Fifty Years Ago 25 August 1869: On the 20th inst., at the home of her son, Mr. Samuel ORRISON, Mrs. Laney ORRISON, at age of 96 years.

The following appeared in the Friday 28 August 1919 issue: Fifty Years Ago 1 September 1869: Died at her residence near Goresville, on Monday evening, August 23, Mrs. Phoebe GRAY, in her 73rd year. Died on the 15th inst., of typhoid fever, at the residence of her father near Hamilton, Miss Susannah LOVE, in the 25th year of her age.

The following appeared in the Friday 18 September 1919 isuse: Fifty Years Ago 22 September 1869: Died near Goresville, on the 13th inst., James M., son of Catharine and William MATHEWS, aged 1y 8m. Man named DAVIS was stabbed in Warrenton on Saturday night by John EDD and it is thought he will die from the effects.

The following appears in the Friday 25 September 1919 issue: Fifty Years Ago 29 September 1869: Married at St. James Episcopal Church on Thursday morning 23 September 1869, by Rev. R. T. DAVIS, Powell HARRISON Esq. and Miss Janet KNOX, daughter of Col. Chas. M. FAUNTLEROY. On the 23rd inst. in the Methodist Church at Mountsville, by Rev. L. H. CRENSHAW, Mr. D. Fauntleroy NEILL, to Miss Mary A. FRANNIE, both of Loudoun Co. Died in Aldie, on 19 Sept, of consumption, Mrs. Sarah WHITLOCK, in the 12th year of her age. Died on the 12th inst. after a protracted illness, Mrs. Elizabeth RAMEY, wife of John RAMEY, of Jefferson Co. and daughter of the late Hyland CROW, Esq. of Loudoun, aged 65 years. Died at Hamilton, on September 22, of consumption, Mr. Henry OFFATT, in the 31st year of his age.

The following appeared in the 1 October 1919 issue: Fifty Years Ago 6 October 1869: Died in Leesburg on Saturday October 2, 1869, William Bernard, infant son of William and Martha DIVINE? [page torn]

The following appeared in the 8 October 1919 issue: Fifty Years Ago 13 October 1869: Married at Mt. Sharon, the residence of Mrs. TALIAFERRO, in Orange Co. Va, on Thursday October 7, 1869, by the Rev. Theodore CARSON, Rev. Richard T. DAVIS, rector of St. James Episcopal Church, Leesburg, to Miss Louise T. FROST, of Orange Co. Va. Died at Tranquility, Loudoun Co., on Wednesday Oct. 7, Mrs. Sallie BRONAUGH, in her 86th year. Died in Washington DC on Tuesday, Oct. 5, 1869, John A. DIVINE, son of Major Jas. F. and Elizabeth DIVINE, of Leesburg, aged 26 years. He was a member of the Loudoun Guard 17th Va regiment.

The following appeared in the 15 October 1919 issue: Fifty Years Ago 20 October 1869: Married in the Leesburg M. E. church, South, on Tuesday morning, Oct. 19, 1869, by Rev. Dr. Nelson HEAD, Mr. E. G. MARLOW, of Md, and Miss Annie M. FOX, daughter of the late Geo. K. FOX, of Leesburg. Married on the

30th of Sept., by Friends ceremony, at the residence of the mayor of the city of Philadelphia, Eli J. NICHOLS, of Loudoun Co to Lydia E. HAWES, of Chester co Pa. Married in Georgetown DC on Wed., Oct. 6, 1869, by Rev. J. WILSON, Mr. Thos. W. BEAVERS, of Loudoun, and Miss Anna SKILLMAN. Died at the residence of Mrs. Eugene HOUGH, in Leesburg, on Oct. 18th, Mrs. Catherine GASSAWAY, widow of the late Charles GASSAWAY, in her 79th year. Died at her residence in Baltimore, on the 14th inst., Josephine H., wife of Lewis W. HOPKINS and daughter of Rachel W. and Isaac HOGE, of Loudoun. Died at her residence near Unison, Loudoun Co., on Oct 5, Mr. Michael PLASTER, in his 83rd year.

Wednesday, 27 October 1869   Vol. XIV, No. 19

Married: In Philadelphia, on Tuesday evening, September 28, 1869, by the Rev. Joseph E. SMITH, Lewis H. SAUNDERS, formerly of Leesburg, Va, to Miss Anna Eliza, daughter of the late John G. WILL, all of Philadelphia.

Married: At the Presbyterian Church, Culpeper C. H., Va, on the afternoon of October 21st by the Rev. Charles H. NURSE, Dr. Otho M. MUNCASTER, of Washington, DC, to Miss Mary R. NURSE, daughter of the officiating clergyman.

Married: October 20th in the M. E. Church, South, in Middleburg, by Rev. D. SHOAFF, William J. LUCK, M.D., of Loudoun, and Miss Bettie RECTOR, of Fauquier county.

Married: Also, at the same time and place, by the same, Mr. Howard RECTOR, of Fauquier county, and Miss Mary F. LEITH, of Loudoun county.

Married: On the 12th inst., at "Media" near Charlestown, Va, by the Rev. W. T. LEAVELL, assisted by the Rev. J. E. POINDEXTER, Miss Julia Yates LEAVELL and Major Edward H. McDONALD, of Louisville, Ky, formerly of Virginia.

Married: On Tuesday, 12th inst., in Winchester, by Rev. Dr. FINLEY, Edmund Pendleton SWARTZ, of Berkeley county, and Miss Laura B. CLOWE, dau. of Col. Henry W. CLOWE, formerly Superintendent of the Harper's Ferry Armory.

Died: On the 6th of September, 1869, Lillie Bell, only child of Mary and James W. WHALEY, aged 1y 6d.

The following appeared in the 5 November 1919 issue: Fifty Years ago 3 November 1869: Married on the 19th inst., at Leillich's Hotel, in Frederick city, by Rev. Dr. DIEHL, Richard CHAMBLIN to Miss Mary E. ADAMS, both of Loudoun Co. Married at Lincoln, on Tuesday morning, Nov. 2, 1869, by Rev. Dr. HEAD, Mr. Summerfield BOLYN, sheriff of Loudoun, to Miss Sarah, dau. of Mr. William HOLMES, all of this county.

Married in Leesburg on 2 Nov., by Rev. Samuel GOVER, James W. SEATON and Susan HAWES, all of Loudoun. Married in Washington City, on Tuesday afternoon, Oct. 19, at the residence of Rev. B. Peyton BROWN, Mr. Daniel SHAFER to Miss Sarah E. BROWN, daughter of the late Richard BROWN, all of Loudoun. Married on 21st inst., by Elder B. P. DULIN, Mr. Francis E. THRIFT to Miss Lydia J. BRADFORD, both of Loudoun. Died at the residence of her daughter, near White's Ferry, in Maryland, on Sunday, October 30th 1869, Mrs. Mary W. MARLOW, consort of the late George MARLOW, of this county, in her 63rd year. Died in this town, 21 October 1869, Francis B., 3rd son of Francis E. and Minerva A. SHREVE, aged 19y 10m 18d.

The following appeared in the 12 November 1919 issue: Fifty years ago 10 November 1869: Married 4 Nov. 1869 by Rev. John LANDSTREET, Prof. James W. GRUBB and Miss Carrie B., daughter of the late Nathan WHITE, all of this county. Married on 2nd inst., by Rev. Dr. HAYNES, of Middleburg, this county, at the residence of the bride's father in Staunton, Dr. G. H. EYSTER and Miss Inez Josephine, daughter of Rev. J. A. ENGLISH. Died on the 2nd inst., at the residence of his parents, Philadelphia, William H. CANBY, aged 28 years. Departed this life on the 22nd October, Mrs. Elizabeth COE, in her 75th year. Died in Alexandria, on 29th ultimo, Mrs. Winifred A. HAYES, wife of Mr. Nathaniel HAYES, in her 38th year. Died near Morrisonville on 29th of October, after a lingering and painful illness, Mrs. Margaret MERCHANT, wife of Landon O. MERCHANT.

The following appeared in the 19 November 1919 issue: Fifty years ago 17 November 1869: Married 10 Nov at the Cross roads, by the Rev. David SHOAFF, Mr. James W. RAWLINGS and Miss Mary F. RECTOR, both of Fauquier Co. Married on the same day, near Landmark, by the same, Mr. Asa Hamilton RECTOR and Miss Ann F. RECTOR, both of Fauquier Co. Married 4 Nov. 1869 in the Methodist church, at Rectortown, by Rev. L. H. CRENSHAW, Mr. William E. PAYNE and Miss Ella C. McCARTY, both of Rectortown Fauquier Co. Married on 27th ult., at the residence of Mr. Alfred CLEVENGER, at Winchester, by Rev. W. C. EGGLESTON, Mr. Hugh Sidwell JANNEY to Miss Margaret Ellen RILEY, both of this county. Married on 11th inst., at the residence of Mrs. Wm. THOMPSON, in Washington DC, by Rev Jas. H. WOOLF, Mr. George W. LEE to Miss Leah F. PALMER, both of this county.

[MISSING ISSUE]

The following appeared in the 3 December 1919 issue: Fifty years ago 24 November 1869: Married on November 18, in Leesburg, by Rev. J. W. LUPTON, Mr. Peter C. MYERS and Miss Mary Virginia CRIDLER, all of Loudoun.

The following appeared in the issue: Fifty years ago 22 December 1869: Married: On 15th of Dec., in Leesburg, by S. GOVER, John WIGGINTON and Mary HOLE, both of Loudoun; December 15th at the M. E. C. S. parsonage, in Middleburg, by Rev. D. SHOAFF, Mr. Wm. D. HUTCHISON and Miss Mary V. HUTCHISON, all of Loudoun Co.; December 15, by Rev. John LANDSTREET, L. Dow HESS to Miss Annie K., daughter of the late Alexander McFARLAND. Died at his residence in this county on 8th of November, of cancer of the stomach, Mr. Robt. JAMES in his 54th year. Died at Warrenton on the 13th inst., after a brief illness in her 35th year, Mrs. Rose D. POULTON, wife of Rev. J. F. POULTON, and daughter of the late Dr. DAVISSON, of Hillsborough.

[MISSING ISSUES]

The following appeared in the 24 December 1919 issue: Fifty years ago 22 December 1869: Married: On 15th of Dec., in Leesburg, by S. GOVER, John WIGGINTON and Mary HOLE, both of Loudoun; December 15th at the M. E. C. S. parsonage, in Middleburg, by Rev. D. SHOAFF, Mr. Wm. D. HUTCHISON and Miss Mary V. HUTCHISON, all of Loudoun Co.; December 15, by Rev. John LANDSTREET, L. Dow HESS to Miss Annie K., daughter of the late Alexander McFARLAND. Died at his residence in this county on 8th of November, of cancer of the stomach, Mr. Robt. JAMES in his 54th year. Died at Warrenton on the 13th inst., after a brief illness in her 35th year, Mrs. Rose D. POULTON, wife of Rev. J. F. POULTON, and daughter of the late Dr. DAVISSON, of Hillsborough.

Wednesday, 29 December 1869   Vol. XIV, No. 28

Married: On the 16th inst. at the residence of the bride's mother, by X. J. RICHARDSON, Mr. John W. LOY to Miss Jane E. BEST, all of Loudoun.

Married: By Rev. J. A. HAYNES, at Middleburg, on the 22nd inst., Mr. John T. BALL and Miss Catharine E. LIGHTFOOT, both of Loudoun Co.

Married: On the 20th inst. in Middleburg, by Rev. J. A. HAYNES, Mr. W. LIGHTFOOT and Miss Josephine A. DAVIS, both of Loudoun Co.

Married: On the 21st inst. by the Rev. Jas. H. WOLFF, at the residence of the bride's parents, Mr. Samuel ELLMORE of Loudoun to Miss Mary E. COCKEREL, of Fairfax county.

Married: on the 23d inst. by Rev. Jas. H. WOLFF, at the residence of the bride's parents, Mr. Samuel JENKINGS Jr. to Miss Mary C. BICKSLER, all of Loudoun.

Died: Suddenly, in Washington, on the 24th inst., at 6½ o'clock, Mrs. Rachel WAUGH, widow of the late A. P. WAUGH, of Georgetown, DC, aged 69.

[MISSING ISSUES]

Wednesday, 18 January 1871   Vol. XV, No. 31

Married: January 10th in Upperville by Rev. D. SHOAFF, Mr. Robt. W. FULWILER, of Columbia Tennessee, and Miss Dora W. HAINES, of Fauquier Co.

Married: On Tuesday evening, December 27th, at the residence of the bride's father, by Rev. Andrew ROBEY, Mr. James BELL to Miss Susan F. SHELTON, all of Stafford Co. Va

Married: On Thursday morning, the 5th of January, by the same, Mr. Charles W. CLOE to Miss Mary M., daughter of Capt. RANDALL, all of Stafford Co. Va.

Married: On the evening of the same day, by the same, at Mt. Pisga, Mr. Charles A. BRYAN, Deputy Clerk of the Circuit and County Courts of Stafford, to Miss Margaret N., daughter of the late James MORTON and of Mrs. Lucy H. MORTON, all of Stafford Co.

Married: At Hamilton, January 11th, by the Rev. Jno. LANDSTREET, Jno. Z. SHUGART to Miss Maggie J., daughter of Samuel THOMPSON Esq.

Married: January 12th, by the same, George S. WATERS to Miss Emily R. MOBBERLY.

Wednesday, 25 January 1871   Vol. XV, No. 32

Married: On Thursday morning, January 18, at the residence of Col. D. Lee POWELL, by Rev. J. D. POWELL, Mr. William BROOKE, of Alexandria, Va, to Miss Florence POWELL, of Richmond, Va.

Married: At Hamilton, on Thursday morning, January 19th by Rev. Mr. MANN, Mr. Townsend H. VANDEVANTER and Miss Nannie, daughter of Mr. Geo. W. JANNEY, all of Loudoun.

Married: At Hamilton, on Thursday evening, by Rev. Mr. LUPTON, Mr. Edward TAVENNER and Miss Katie, daughter of Mr. Hiram TAVENNER, all of Loudoun.

Married: January 19, by Rev. Jno. LANDSTREET, John W. MOSSBURY to Miss Ann C. WYNKOOP, all of this county.

Married: On Tuesday, the 17th inst., at the residence of the bride's father, by the Rev. John WOOLF, Mr. Charles E. HOWELL, of Washington, DC, to Miss Mattie JEFFRIES, of Loudoun Co.

[MISSING ISSUES]

Wednesday, 21 June 1871   Vol. XVI, No. 1

Married: In Washington DC by Rev. W. V. TUDOR, on the 26th of May, at the Mount Vernon M. E. Church, Mr. Edward S. ROWE, of Richmond Va to Miss M. Virginia STEPHENS, of Loudoun county.

Died: At her residence near Snickersville in this county, on the 15th inst., Mrs. Elizabeth HILL, in the 90th year of her age.

Wednesday, 28 June 1871   Vol. XVI, No. 2

Married: On the 8th of June, in Lexington, Va by Rev. J. W. PRATT, Dr. Wm. P. McGUIRE, of Winchester to Nannie Holmes, daughter of J. Randolph TUCKER, of the Washington Lee University, Lexington, Va.

Died: On the 24th inst., at the Hamilton Depot, Mattie, daughter of J. B. and Eliza FRANKLIN, aged 2 years.

Death of Jonah HOOD – This gentleman, at one time Justice of the Peace of Loudoun, and at the time of his death postmaster at Aldie, died at his residence near that place on Tuesday last, in the 76th year of his age.

Wednesday, 5 July 1871   Vol. XVI, No. 3

Married: In the M. E. Church, South, on Wednesday morning, the 28th inst. by Rev. J. W. LUPTON, Mr. David CONRAD and Annie B. SULLIVAN, all of Loudoun.

Died: In Leesburg on Monday evening, July 3d, 1871 after a protracted illness of much suffering; Mrs. Frances SMALE, wife of Mr. John SMALE, aged 58 years.

Died: In Charlestown, Jefferson county, W Va. on Sunday morning last, in the 73d year of his age, David HOWELL Sr. Mr. H. was the oldest native citizen.

Died: In Warrenton on the 25th inst. at the residence of his brother-in-law, Mr. S. Gustavus F. PHILLIPS of Stafford, in his 82nd year. The deceased was a brother of the late Col. Wm. F. PHILLIPS, for many years clerk of Fauquier Circuit Court.

The Mirror
Wednesday, 12 July 1871   Vol. XVI, No. 4

Died: Near Hillsborough on Friday June 30th 1871 at 11 o'clock a.m., Thomas William, son of Josiah T. and Mary J. WHITE, aged 11 years and six days.

Wednesday, 12 July 1871   Vol. XVI, No. 4

Married: On the 5th inst., at Wood Grove, by the Rev. H. W. DOGE, Mr. E. R. PURCELL to Miss Harriet M. HEATON, all of Loudoun.

Died: At his residence near Lovettsville, on the evening of the 24th of June 1871, Mr. Jacob BOGER, aged 72y 4m 14d.

Died: Near Waterford on Monday June 26th 1871, Edgar, son of Elisha and Samantha COCKERILL, aged 9y 8m.

Just as we were going to press on Tuesday afternoon, this town was visited by a severe storm of rain. We regret to state that the lightening struck the new building of Mr. PAXSON, in course of erection a short distance from town, by which Mr. Thomas NORRIS had his leg badly burned and Charles SLACK was instantly killed.

County Ct: J. W. FOSTER qualified as Admr. wwa of Mort. C. LOVETTE, dec'd. Noble B. PEACOCK Admr. of Geo. W. LEOPOLD dec'd. Jas. PEUGH Admr. of Leonidas PEUGH dec'd. The will of Jacob BOGER was admitted to probate. Frank M. MYERS qualified as Notary Public for Loudoun. Estate of E. J. REYNOLDS dec'd. committed to the Sheriff. John H. LYNN Executor of Elizabeth LYNN dec'd. gave new bond. John S. MANN's application for ordinary licence at Lovettsville was refused.

Mr. Richard TREHEARN, recently of this town, died at Hamilton on Monday night last. A few weeks ago Mr. T. injured himself in lifting a piece of heavy timber, paralysis of the entire lower portion of the body soon followed.

We understand that a youth named TRENARY, living near Lincoln in this county, and aged about 14 years, last week swallowed a quantity of corrosive sublimate. Result, death in 48 hours.

Attempted rape - $20 reward. A negro man named Enoch CORUM, attempted to commit an outrage upon a white lady in Loudoun county. He is almost black in colour, 5' 10" or 11" in height, between 21 and 22 years of age, heavy set with a full face, his hands and wrists are considerably scarred. He has been shot at several times, one of which shots went through his face near his mouth, going in one side and coming out the other. ... Enoch CORUM delivered into the custody of Mr. TYLER, and upon affadavit of his father was found guilty.

Wednesday, 19 July 1871   Vol. XVI, No. 5

Died: At Oakland, Prince William county, on Wednesday morning, July 12, 1871, Mrs. Sinah Ann Newton, wife of Geo. P. WISE, Esq. and youngest daughter of the late Wm. NEWTON, Esq. of Alexandria, Va, in the 64th year of her age.

Died: At her residence near Leesburg on the 11th inst., Mrs. Mary Jane FAIRFAX, wife of Col. John W. FAIRFAX, of Loudoun.

Died: At her residence in Hillsboro on Sunday the 16th inst., Mrs. Elizabeth R. WHITE, in about the 65th year of her age.

Died: In Charlestown, on the 8th inst., in the 57th year of her age, Miss Catharine C. SHEETZ, daughter of the late Michael SHEETZ of that town.

Died: At his residence near Aldie, on the 28th of June 1871, Squire MATTHEWS, in the 69th year of his age.

Wednesday, 26 July 1871   Vol. XVI, No. 6

Death of Noble S. BRADEN, who has been in declining health for many months. For many years a magistrate of this county, and presiding justice of the County Court. In May 1855 he was elected to the Senate of Virginia. He attained the venerable age of seventy-two years.

Death of Col. D. Lee POWELL – We learn from sources in Richmond that this gentleman, son of the late W. A. POWELL of this town, and Principal of the Richmond Female Institute, died suddenly in that city on Monday night.

Sudden death yesterday morning of Mr. Charles H. McCURDY, of this county, for some time past sojourning at the "Carter House" in this town. He was found dead in his bed on Friday morning, having expired from suffocation superinduced by epilepsy, to which he was subject. He was for one session a member of the Legislature of this state. *Free Press*

Married: On Thursday evening the 13th of July 1871 by Rev. Andrew ROBEY, Mr. G. T. S. HUNNICUTT, Associate Editor of the Greenville Conservative, N.C. to Miss Hannah LOWRY, youngest daughter of the late Peter LOWRY of Stafford County, Va.

Married: On the 29th of June, at Flushing, L. I., John F. B. MITCHELL, of Flushing, to Mary, daughter of the late Hon. Henry BEDINGER, of Jefferson county.

Died: Near Hamilton, on the 5th inst., Miss Laura L. GARNER, in the 28th year of her age. Her health had been evidently declining for about 18 months.

Wednesday, 2 August 1871   Vol. XVI, No. 7

Isaac B. MYERS, a native of Harper's Ferry, but who had resided in Richmond since 1862, fell from the third story window of his boarding house in Louisville, KY, one night last week and was so fatally injured that he died in a few hours. Married:

Married: On the 25th inst. by the Rev. H. WISSLER of Lovettsville, Mr. Joseph M. RIDGEWAY to Miss Sarah Jane BAKER, all of Loudoun county.

Married: On the 16th instant at the Lutheran Church, Frederick City, Md. by the Rev. Dr. DIEHL, Jonas S. SPRING to Miss Catharine BRADY, all of Loudoun county.

Died: In Leesburg on the 1st instant, India, only daughter of J. H. and C. E. MANNING, aged 4y 2m. The funeral will take place from her father's residence at 2¼ p.m. today (Wednesday).

Died: Mrs. Martha L. SMITH – death came suddenly, but found her upon her knees, like a wise servant, waiting the coming of her Master. The morning of the 11th of July was a sad one to Geo. D. SMITH. In less than three short hours, the wife and mother slept sweetly in death.

Wednesday, 9 August 1871   Vol. XVI, No. 8

Married: June 15th 1871 in Darnestown Presbyterian Church, by Rev. C. H. NOURSE, assisted by Rev. Chas. BEACH, Dr. Chas. H. NOURSE to Alice, eldest daughter of Upton DARBY, Esq., all of Montgomery county, Md.

Died: Aug. 4th at the residence of her son-in-law, Harmon REID, Esq., Mrs. Mary BIRKIT, relict of the late John BIRKIT, of Hillsborough, in the 71st year of her age.

Died: On the 4th of August 1871, at the residence of her son-in-law, Rev. J. S. HEBRON, in Loudoun county, Mrs. Selina POWELL, wife of Chas. L. POWELL, of Alexandria.

On Sunday afternoon, a daughter of Mr. Thos. CLARKSON, living in "The Neck" about three miles east of Leesburg had shot and killed her sister during the afternoon of that day. Mrs. BEAVERS, Mrs. GRIMES, near neighbors, and Geo. CLARKSON, a brother of the parties said they found the injured sister lying upstairs, dead, and the other sister apparently very much distressed who informed them that her and her sister intended to go to Sunday School, her sister had gone up stairs to dress herself. Verdict – we examined the body of Carolline CLARKSON dec'd. and she came to her death by reason of a gun shot wound inflicted by her sister, Mary CLARKSON, believed to have been accidental.

Wednesday, 16 August 1871   Vol. XVI, No. 9

Died: In Leesburg, Wednesday morning, August 9th at the residence of Mr. William DIVINE Sr., Eveline, infant daughter of Sallie and Henro [Henry?] MORGAN, of Washington, D.C.

August Ct.: will of Lemuel MARSHALL admitted to record with W. B. MARSHALL as Executor. Letters of Administration granted Geo. C. DULIN on the estate of Samuel G. DULIN dec'd. W. C. SHAWEN qualified as Executor of Noble S. BRADEN dec'd. Josiah T. WHITE qualified as Admr. of Elizabeth R. WHITE dec'd.

Enoch CORUM, negro found guilty of attempted rape, punishment affixed two years in the pententiary.

Occurrence at Paris, Bourbon county, Ky on the night of the 6th inst. Mr. HIBLER who resided in Leesburg for a year or two just after the close of the war and married a lady of this county ... Last Monday night about half past ten o'clock a personal difficulty occurred between Geo. M. HIBLER, Circuit Clerk of this county and Noah S. ALEXANDER, son of Charlton ALEXANDER of this city, which resulted in almost instant death of the latter. Mr. HIBLER was acquitted.

Wednesday, 23 August 1871   Vol. XVI, No. 10

Mr. Hanson ELLIOTT a native and for many years a citizen of Loudoun, died at the residence of his son, near Castleman's Ferry, in Clarke county, on Saturday night, the 12th inst. in his 87th year. Member of the masonic fraternity for over sixty years, by which order he was buried in Berryville on the 13th.

Married: On Tuesday the 15th of August, at Blakeley, the residence of Richard B. WASHINGTON, in Jefferson county, W Va. by Rev. William H. MEADE, Col. R. P. CHEW, formerly of the C.S.A to Miss Louisa F., daughter of the late Col. John A. WASHINGTON, of Mount Vernon.

Died: In Leesburg, at 5½ o'clock on Monday morning, August 21st 1871, Mrs. Emma S. MITCHELL, wife of Rev. James MITCHELL, and daughter of Bishop SCOTT, of the M. E. Church in the 33d year of her age.

Mr. Robt. WHITE, an old citizen of Georgetown upwards of eighty years old, who had visited Loudoun to be present at an old fashioned Methodist Camp-meeting at the home of his early life. He was in the altar attending the morning love-feast, at the conclusion of his remarks he took his seat, and in five minutes was a corpse. For many years he was a successful merchant in Georgetown, at different periods Mayor of the City and Collector of the Port.

On Friday last a young man named SMITH, son of Mr. Job SMITH, living near Morrisonville, in this county was thrown from a horse against a fence and died in a few hours.

County Ct: J. C. DONOHOE qualified as Admr. of Wesley McPHERSON dec'd. Estate of late Wm. CARLISLE, was admitted to the hands of the sheriff. L. W. DERRY qualified

Exor. of Peter DERRY dec'd. R. D. HALEY qualified as Exor. of John REED dec'd.

Wednesday, 30 August 1871   Vol. XVI, No. 11

Married: In Washington on the 21st instant by Rev. J. L. ROBERTS, Mr. J. W. JEFFRIES, of Alexandria, to Miss Jennie ELMORE, of Loudoun county.

Died: On the 14th instant, at his residence near Fairfax C. H., Va., after a long illness, Mr. James Oscar WRENN, aged 60 years.

Died: At Woodland, Loudoun county, on the 11th of August, Edward L. CARTER.

Wednesday, 6 September 1871   Vol. XVI, No. 12

Married: In Frederick City, Md, August 24th by Rev. Osburn ENGLE, of the Episcopal Church, Mr. W. S. ERWIN, of San Francisco, California, to Miss Sallie A. FOX, daughter of Mr. Geo. W. FOX, of Jefferson county.

Died: At "Springsbury" Clarke county, August 10th, William Taylor TUCKER, youngest son of Dr. Alfred B. and Eliza T. TUCKER, aged 12y 6m.

Wednesday, 13 September 1871   Vol. XVI, No. 13

Married: In Alexandria, Va on Monday evening, the 11th of inst. at the residence of the bride's father by Rev. Andrew ROBEY, Mr. John T. BURRAGE to Miss Constace BOYER, both of the above named place.

Married: On the 3d of September by Rev. L. T. WIDEMAN, Mr. John A. RYAN and Miss Alice GHANT.

Died: Suddenly, Sept. 5, 1871, aged 60, John HARDING, late of Baltimore Md, but for several years past a citizen of Fauquier Co. Mr. HARDING was a native of Leesburg, but engaged in business in Fauquier as late as 1837.

County Ct: Estate of S. H. EDWARDS was committed to Andrew SEITZ as Admr. Mahlon STOCKS qualified as committee of Wm. STOCKS. Licence to retail spiritous liquors was granted Volney PURCELL, at Snickersville.

Peter SMITH, the body servant and foster brother of the late Charles Fenton MERCER, died at Aldie, on Sunday, the 3d instant, and was buried on Monday. He was a month or two older than his master, and was for a long time his body servant. He was about 97 years of age. To the day of his death the old man claimed an interest in the MERCER estate and was buried, as he requested in the burying ground near the home of his early youth.

Wednesday, 20 September 1871   Vol. XVI, No. 14

Death of Maj. Arthur L. ROGERS, which took place at his residence in Middleburg, on Wednesday morning last, the 13th inst., in the 38th year of his age. He was a son of Gen. Asa ROGERS, a graduate of the University of Virginia, a practising lawyer of this county at the time of his death.. ... Major ROGERS was a gallant artillery officer during the war, and being badly wounded just before its close was brought to the residence of Dr. WELLFORD, in this city.

Robt. Isaac HALLINGSWORTH [HOLLINGSWORTH?] for many years a successful instructor of youth in this county, died at his residence in Waterford on Sunday last, in about his 50th year.

Wednesday, 27 September 1871   Vol. XVI, No. 15

Married: On Wednesday last, September 20th 1871, in the Southern M. E. Church, by Rev. Dr. Nelson HEAD, Mr. John W. GOODWIN, of Washington D.C., and Ratie [Katie?] J. ATTWELL, of Leesburg. Sept. 19 by Rev. Jno. LANDSTREET, James W. DIXON of Baltimore Md, to Mrs. Mary M. BRADFIELD of Loudoun.

Married: On the 12th inst., at the Glade Parsonage, by Rev. A. R. KREMER, Mr. William F. LUCKETT, to Miss Emma SELSAM, both of Lewistown, in Frederick County, Md.

Wednesday, 4 October 1871   Vol. XVI, No. 16

Married: September 19th by Rev. John LANDSTREET, James W. DIXON, of Baltimore to Mrs. Mary M. BRADFIELD, of Loudoun county.

Married: In Christ Church, Washington DC, on Thursday evening, Sept. 28th 1871, by Rev. Mr. McGUIRE, Mr. F. Alonzo DIVINE, of Virginia, and Miss Wilhimah M., daughter of Mr. Wm. H. LUSBY, of Washington

Married: In Jefferson county, on Tuesday evening, 26th September 1871 at the residence of the parents of the bride, by Rev. H. E. MISKIMON, Mr. John J. BANEY and Miss Rebecca FEAGANS, daughter of C. H. FEAGANS.

Died: At his residence in Upperville Va, on Saturday the 23rd ult. George CALVERT, Esq. (elder brother of the late J. S. CALVERT, of Richmond) in the 77th year of his age.

On Sunday last, 1st instant, Col. Lewis W. WASHINGTON, died at his home in Jefferson county, W Va. after a few days illness in the 59th year of his age.

Wednesday, 11 October 1871   Vol. XVI, No. 16 [17]

Married: On the 4th instant, at "Cedar Grove," King George county Va by the Rev. E. R. McGUIRE, Col. W. F. M. HOLLIDAY, of Winchester to Caroline Calvert, daughter of Dr. Richard H. STUART.

Married: On the 5th inst. by Rev. J. W. LUPTON at the residence of the bride's father, Mr. Bushrod J. TAYLOR and Miss Sarah E. THRASHER.

Married: In Leesburg October 5th 1871, by Rev. James McDONOUGH, Mr. John W. RAWLINGS to Miss Elvira F. KINNER, all of Loudoun.

Married: Oct. 5th by Charles KING, Mr. Edward O. VANHORN and Miss Ann E. FRITTS, both of Loudoun county.

Died: Of diphtheria on Thursday September 28th 1871, Mollie Grubb, daughter of Thomas E. and Mary J. CAMP, aged 3y 2m 19d.

Died: On Tuesday evening the 3d inst. in Leesburg at the residence of John V. SCHLEIF, Maudie, youngest daughter of John and Emma FRIDELL, of Washington DC, aged 8 months.

Died: At Potomac Furnace in this County, on the 14th of September, Miss Mary A. APPEL, the eldest daughter of Thomas and Mary APPEL, aged 29 years and 3 months.

County Ct.: Wm. D. EASTERDAY qualified as Admr. of Susannah M. JACKSON dec'd. Estate of Jos. K. HAVENNER dec'd. committed to Sheriff. Geo. L. MOORE Admr. of Sarah MOORE dec'd. Andrew ROBEY Guardian of Ella Virginia BOGER. Chas. L. HOLLINGSWORTH Admr. of Robt. J. HOLLINGSWORTH. Maria E. MOORE's will partly proved and continued. Powers of Sarah E. BENEDUM Admr. of Jas. H. BENEDUM dec'd. revoked, estate committed to Sheriff.

General F. B. Van BUREN, a cousin of President Van BUREN, died at Herndon, Va on Thursday morning in the 81st year of his age. His remains have been taken to New York.

Wednesday, 18 October 1871   Vol. XVI, No. 17

No marriages or deaths.

Wednesday, 25 October 1871   Vol. XVI, No. 18

Married: In the M. E. Church, South, Leesburg, on Tuesday morning, Oct. 24th by Rev. Dr. HEAD, Mr. Geo. C. DULIN and Miss M. Lizzie, eldest daughter of John W. HAMMERLY, all of Loudoun.

Married: On Tuesday morning 17th instant in Leesburg by Rev. Dr. HEAD, Mr. Albert C. THOMAS, of Baltimore, and Miss Sarah J. SEIBER.

Married: On the 18th inst. at "The Shelter" Prince Wm. Co. by Rev. R. T. CROWN, William D. FITZHUGH, of Fauquier Co, and Bettie C. GRAYSON, daughter of the late Dr. John B. GRAYSON, formerly of Prince William County.

Died: In Leesburg on Saturday last, Charles, Infant son of Wm. B. and Jane D. LYNCH.

Wednesday, 1 November 1871   Vol. XVI, No. 19

Married: At the residence of Foxhall A. DAINGERFIELD in Harrisonburg, on Monday the 16th October, by Rev. A. W. WADDELL, Thomas N. LANGHORNE, of Lynchburg, to Orra H. GRAY, daughter of Algernon S. GRAY, of Harrisonburg, Va.

Marriage: October 26th 1871, in the M. E. Church South, at Mountsville, by Rev. L. H. CRENSHAW, Mr. John R. CASTLEMAN, of Clarke county, and Miss Laura FRANCIS, daughter of Wm. H. FRANCIS Esq., of Loudoun county.

Died: Of diphtheria on Friday October 13th 1871, Ada Blanch, daughter of Thomas E. and Mary J. CAMP, aged 5y 1m 1d.

Died: At Aldie on the morning of the 22d inst., Charles F. BERKELEY, in the 38th year of his age.

Died: At her residence in Fauquier county on the 1st day of October, Mrs. Eliza McCARTY, wife of the late Dennis McCARTY. She was born on the 24th day of Sept. 1814 and was a member of the Methodist church for many years.

Died: At his residence in Fairfield township on Thursday morning the 5th of October, Mr. Samuel CROOK, in the 76th year of his age. Born in Loudoun county but some 39 or 40 years ago emigrated to Columbiana County and settled upon the farm where he died, which was then almost a dense forest and by industry he cleared out a fine and productive farm.

Died: On Thursday evening, the 19th of October at his residence in Centre township, Benjamin LODGE in the 77th year of his age. He came to Columbiana county when it was almost a wilderness. In the fall of 1808, 63 years ago, His father came from Loudoun, bought some land and settled in the NE corner of Salem township, his son Benjamin then in his 14th year.

Died: Thomas Clarkson TAYLOR, minister of the Society of Friends and founder of Taylor & Jackson's Academy in this city. He was apparently in his usual health. At about 11 o'clock on Tuesday he suddenly bowed his head on his desk as if in pain, and shortly afterwards went over to Dr. S. W. MURPHY (Teacher of Ancient Languages in the Academy) and told him he was suffering terrible pain in the lower part of his abdomen and should have to go home. About half past 3 yesterday afternoon he breathed his last. In his 47th year and born in

Loudoun county, his parents being Jonathan and Lydia B. TAYLOR. *Wilmington Delaware paper 28th ult.*

Wednesday, 8 November 1871 Vol. XVI, No. 20

Died: In Richmond on Thursday afternoon, Nov. 2d at half past 1 o'clock, Annie M. DOGGETT, eldest daughter of Bishop D. N. S. and M. A. DOGGETT, in the 33d year of her age.

Died: On Tuesday morning Oct 31st 1871 of typhoid fever, Mrs. Mary Jane DARNE, wife of James T. DARNE, aged 43 years.

Married: On the 24th of October, Mr. Thomas M. SHALL, of Jefferson co., to Miss Nannie F. LITTLETON, of Loudoun co.

Married: On the 25th of October 1871, by Elder Joseph FURR, at his residence, Mr. Zachariah T. PIERCE, of Fauquier county, to Miss Annie A. DOWDELL, of Loudoun county.

Wednesday, 15 November 1871 Vol. XVI, No. 21

Married On Wednesday evening 1st November at the residence of Marshal PARKS, Esq., Mr. Robert W. TUCKER, of Norfolk, and Sophia, daughter of Dr. S. K. JACKSON, of Princess Anne county, Va.

Married: On the 2d instant at the residence of James H. JONES, Esqr. by Rev. C. C. MEADOR, William N. HUTCHISON and Martha R. THOMAS, both of Loudoun.

Died: At his residence in Waterford on the morning of the 12th instant, David MANSFIELD, aged about 50 years.

Died: At his residence near Middleburg, on Sunday, November 29th, Mr. Geo. L. BITZER, in the 71st year of his age.

Died: At the residence of her father, Fenton FURR on Sunday October 22d, Miss Mary I. FURR.

Wednesday, 22 November 1871 Vol. XVI, No. 22

Married: On the 2nd inst. in Leesburg by Rev. J. W. LUPTON, Mr. Charles L. MYERS and Miss Jennie WALLACE.

Married: On Tuesday November 14th at the residence of Harmon BITZER by the Rev. B. F. DULIN, George W. FOUCHE and Miss Mary M. FRANKLIN, all of Loudoun.

Married: On the 14th inst. in Winchester at the residence of the bride's father, Henry M. BAKER, Esqr., by the Rev. T. W. DOSH, Mr. Thomas S. CHAMBLIN, of Loudoun county, and Miss Beatrice BAKER of Frederick county.

Married: On the 14th inst., by Rev. J. W. LUPTON, Mr. Alonzo T. RYAN and Matha [Martha?] E. CAMPBELL, all of Loudoun county.

Married: On the 15th inst. by the same, Mr. Wm. B. CLEMENS and Miss Mary E. CAMPBELL, all of Loudoun.

Died: November 13th, Herewaldo Robert, eldest son of Captain WAKE, B. N. of Wikefield, Near Guilford, aged 20 years. His remains were interred in Union Cemetery in this town on Wednesday, his coffin shrouded with the flag of his native land.

Died: Near Hughesville on the 6th inst. at the residence of her father, Miss Henrietta HOGE, in about her 18th year, daughter of Mr. Jesse HOGE.

Died: After a lingering illness on the 12th inst. at the residence of her husband, Samuel N. BROWN, Mary Ann BROWN, in about the 35th year of her age.

Died: At "Exeter," near Leesburg, on Monday last, in the 11th year of her age, Lizzie, eldest daughter of Col. E. V. WHITE.

Died: In Leesburg on Tuesday last, Miss Dorcas A. OSBURN, in the 52d year of her age. Member of the Episcopal Church.

County Ct.: George L. BITZER's will was admitted to probate with John H. PRIEST as Exor.

Wednesday, 29 November 1871   Vol. XVI, No. 23

Married: At Waterford, November 16th by Rev. Charles KING, Miss Annie Elizabeth HICKS, of Cleveland Ohio and Mr. Robert FRITTS, of Hillsborough, Va.

Mr. Jacob WINE, for many years an efficient Constable in the Waterford District, died at his residence in that town on the 19th inst. in the 47th year of his age.

Death of John Berkely LEE – which occurred at his residence near Oatlands on the 18th inst. in about the 34th year of his age.

Mrs. CHINN, consort of the late Frank CHINN, died suddenly at her home in Aldie on Monday. Sitting in her chair knitting when she expired. She was in about the 60th year of her age.

On Wednesday last, Mr. Francis Lee SMITH, of Alexandria was married to Miss Jannie L. SUTHERLIN, only daughter of Major W. T. SUTHERLIN, of Danville, Va.

Wednesday, 6 December 1871   Vol. XVI, No. 24

Married: On the 28th November at the M. E. Church South, Leesburg, by Rev. Nelson HEAD, Mr. James H. GALLEHER and Emma E. DALTON, both of Leesburg.

Married: On the 28th inst. at the residence of the bride's father, Lovettsville, by Rev. X. J. RICHARDSON, Mr. Luther H. POTTERFIELD to Miss Kate E., daughter of Frederick EAMICH, Esq.

Married: On the 15th inst., at the Central Hotel, by Rev. A. J. PELCE?, Wm. A. JAMES to Miss Mary L. GRUBB, both of Loudoun county.

Married: On Thursday evening, Nov. 23, at the residence of the bride's father, by Geo. H. WILLIAMS, Mr. Richard KEENE, to Miss Julia ASHFORD, all of Fairfax county.

Married: By Rev. J. A. HAYNES, on the 28th ult. at the house of the bride's father, Jos. NALLS, Esq. and Miss Melinda Emma HIBBS, both of Fauquier.

Married: By the same on the 29th ult. at the house of the bride's mother, Charles E. TAYLOR, Esq. and Miss Annie L. TILLET, both of Loudoun.

Married: In Richmond, November 28th by the Rev. M. D. HOGE, Harvey McVEIGH, formerly of Alexandria, and Miss Mary RICHARDSON, of Richmond.

Died: At Cottage Grove in Loudoun county, Thursday noon Nov. 16, Elder James SMITH, aged 80, on the 5th of Oct 1871. He was born in Scotland, near the city of Glasgow. He came to the U.S. when he was 4 years old. On Monday the 18th inst. his body was taken to Falls Church for interment.

Died: On the 30th ult. after a long illness at the residence of R. McDUELL, near Knoxville Md, Ann Celinda STALEY, in the 31st year of her age.

Died: At her residence near Millsville, Loudoun Co., Mrs. Sarah BARTON, wife of Bailey R. BARTON, in the 64th year of her age. Her funeral was preached on the morning of the 30th by Rev. Dr. HAINES.

William BUTTS, Esq. died at his residence near Hillsborough on Friday morning, December 1st, in the 80th year of his age. Mr. BUTTS was born in Shepherdstown, West Va. He was a Lieutenant in Capt. Van BENNETT's company that marched from that place to Baltimore during the last war with England, and participated in the military operations in defence of that city. After his term of enlistment expired, he joined the artillery company of Capt. Robert WILSON, of Martinsburg, and went with that officer to Norfolk, Va, where he assisted in the defence of Crany Island against the British. He settled in Hillsborough and resided there ever since. He was buried on Sunday at Arnold Grove with military honors.

Wednesday, 13 December 1871   Vol. XVI, No. 25

Married: On the 6th inst. in Leesburg by Rev. J. W. LUPTON, Mr. John BIRCH of Georgetown, D.C. and Miss Mary J. GRIMES, of Loudoun.

Married: In Leesburg on the 7th of December 1871, by S. GOVER, George T. WRIGHT and Charlotte C. RAMSEY, all of Loudoun.

Married: At. St. James Episcopal Church, Leesburg on the 6th instant, by the Rev. R. T. DAVIS, Mr. Thomas Julian

DELANEY to Miss Evelyn Byrd, second daughter of the late Dr. George LEE.
Married: At the residence of the bride's father, December 6th 1871, by the Rev. Lorenzo D. NIXON, Mr. Thomas MOSS to Miss Matilda L. SMITH, all of Loudoun.
Married: On the same day by the same at the residence of Mr. John F. ALLEN, Esqr., Mr. James E. DANIELS, of Fairfax county, to Elizabeth H. GANT, of Loudoun.
Married: At the residence of the bride's uncle on Thursday the 30th of November, Mr. Jacob R. WALKER, of Waterford to Miss M. R. GELKINSON, of Staunton. Va.

Wednesday, 20 December 1871   Vol. XVI, No. 26

Married: At "Temple Hall," in this county, on Tuesday morning, Dec 19th 1871, by Rev. J. W. LUPTON, Mr. Samuel P. NELMS, of Baltimore and Miss Susan A., daughter of the late Henry A. BALL, of Loudoun.
Married: At the same time and place by Rev. Mr. HEPBRON, Mr. Charles C. MERCIER and Miss Kate E., daughter of the late Henry A. BALL, all of Loudoun.
Married: On Dec. 13 by Rev. Jno. LANDSTREET, P. W. SEATON of Fauquier Co. to Ann C., daughter of G. E. THOMAS, of Loudoun county.
Married: On Dec. 18 by the same, William BEST to Martha A., daughter of Sampson LICKY, all of Loudoun county.
Married: On the 4th instant, by the Rev. H. WISSLER, of Lovettsville, Mr. Geo. F. LONGBRAKE, of W. Va. to Miss Mollie S. SANBOWER, of this county.
Married: On the 5th of December, by Rev. T. HERNDON, James Philip SMITH and Annie Marshall FOLEY, all of Prince William county.
Married: On the 7th, by the same, Jacob W. SYMONS and Sarah E. ROBEY, all of Fauquier county.
Married: On the same day, by the same, Dodridge PICKETT, of Prince William county, to Mollie CALDWELL, of Fauquier Co.
Married: On the 14th instant, at Christ Church, in Alexandria, by Rev. Mr. McKIM, R. G. NEVITT, of Charles county, Md, to Mary G., dau. of the late Col. Dodridge C. LEE, of Fairfax co.

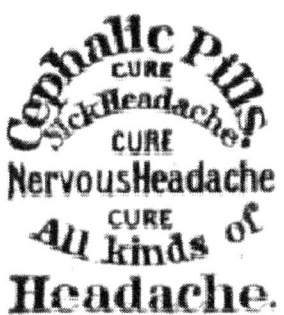

Wednesday, 27 December 1871   Vol. XVI, No. 27

Married: At the Presbyterian Parsonage in Leesburg on the 19th inst., by Rev. J. W. LUPTON, Mr. John T. PERRY Jr., and Miss Sarah M. WILLIAMS.

Married: At the residence of the bride's father, on the 14th of Dec. 1871, by the Rev. L. D. NIXSON, Mr. Beverly T. HAVENER; to Miss Rebecca Virginia DAILY, all of Loudoun county.

Married: On the 12th instant, in Mt. Hope Church, by the Rev. B. P. DULIN, Mr. Edward B. PAXSON and Miss Sarah C. ALEXANDER, second daughter of Rev. I. T. ALEXANDER, all of Loudoun.

Married: On the river at Edwards' Ferry, Wednesday, December 20th 1871 by the Rev. Lorenzo D. NIXON, Mr. John F. SHRYOCK, to Miss Annie JOHNSON, both of Loudoun Co.

Married: On Thursday, December 21st 1871, by the same, Mr. Richard H. PALMER to Miss Susan M., only daughter of Mr. George W. DORRELL, all of Loudoun Co.

Died: In this town on Saturday night, Dec. 23d 1871, of consumption, Mr. Charles T. CHAMBLIN, eldest son of Mr. Jas. H. CHAMBLIN, in the 29th year of his age.

Death of Mr. Charles T. CHAMBLIN – who died at the residence of his father, Mr. James H. CHAMBLIN in this town on Saturday ni8ght last, in the 29th year of his age. Mr. CHAMBLIN was a Lt. in the 8th Va Regiment during the war, and in one of the battles around Richmond received a severe wound in the face, which no doubt laid the foundation of the disease, consumption. His funeral took place on Christmas Day.

Wednesday, 3 January 1872   Vol. XVI, No. 28

Married: By Rev. T. HERNDON on the 31st of December, Mr. John J. OTLEY and Miss Henrietta YOUNG, all of Loudoun.

Married: December 28th by the same, Mr. John T. SLACK and Ann E. J. OSBORNE, of Paris, Fauquier county.

The Rev. Mr. BOYDEN, rector of the Episcopal church at Fairfax C. H. who has been ill for some time, died at the residence of his father, in Fauquier county on Friday, the 22d of December, in the 29th year of his age.

Wednesday, 10 January 1872   Vol. XVI, No. 29

The Death of John JANNEY occurred at his home in Leesburg at 11 o'clock on the night of Friday January 5, 1872. Mr. JANNEY was born in the city of Alexandria on the 8th of November, 1798 and was in the 74th year of his age. In about the 12th year of his age, he was removed by his father, Elisha JANNEY, to Hillsborough in this county. He removed to Leesburg and studied law in the office of R. H. HENDERSON and in 1822 was admitted to practice at the bar of this county. He was elected to the House of Delegates in 1836. ... His funeral took place at 12 o'clock, on Monday, conducted by Rev. A. D. POLLOCK. Grave in Union Cemetery.

Wednesday, 17 January 1872   Vol. XVI, No. 30

Married: In Georgetown on the 8th instant, by the Rev. John H. DESHIELD, at the residence of John M. ATHEY, Thomas COATES of Loudoun county, to Mollie A. ATHEY, daughter of J. M. ATHEY, of Georgetown DC.

Married: On the 11th of January 1872 at the residence of the bride's father by Rev. L. D. NIXON, Mr. James W. WILSON to Miss Mary C. HUTCHISON, all of Loudoun Co.

Married: Jan 11th near Waterford by Rev. Charles KING, Alfred SHELL and Mrs. Julia A. MOORE.

Married: December 27, by Rev. Jno. LANDSTREET, John T. VICKERS to Miss Rachel A. C. WADE, all of Loudoun Co.

Married: On the 4th inst. at the Reformed Parsonage near Lovettsville by Rev. H. WISSLER, Mr. John H. WILKLOW to Miss Susan WADE, all of Loudoun.

Married: On the 9th instant, at New Jerusalem Eve. Lutheran Church, by Rev. X. J. RICHARDSON, Mr. Samuel F. SWANK to Miss Rosanna SHORT, all of Loudoun.

Died: On the 25th of December at the residence of his son in this county, Thos. G. DOWDELL, in the 63d year of his age.

Rev. J. H. JONES, for 52 years a minister in the Baptist Church died near Richmond on the 30th of December in his 74th year.

Wednesday, 24 January 1872   Vol. XVI, No. 31

Married: January 16 by Rev. Jno. LANDSTREET, Frederick H. FRITTS to Mary B., daughter of G. W. MOORE, all of this county.

Married: At the Presbyterian Parsonage, in Leesburg, on the 18th inst. by Rev. J. W. LUPTON, Mr. David H. CURRY and Miss Sarah A. T. JACKSON, all of Loudoun.

Married: Near Warrenton on the 9th instant, by Rev. John L. CARROLL, Mr. William H. FOX, of Fairfax county and Miss Catharine JOHNSON, of Fauquier county.

Married: At Kosse?, Texas, December 40th? 1871, by Rev. J. W. PHILIPS, John D. ROBERTS, of Houston, to Miss Eliza B. HORNER, of Fauquier county.

Married: On the 9th instant, by Rev. J. S. HAYNES, at Mr. Wm. FLETCHER's Fauquier county, John G. ROBINSON, Esqr. and Miss Fannie M. SKINNER.

Married: Near Mavin's Mill, on Goose Creek, January 18th 1872 by Rev. L. D. NIXON, Mr. John T. SMOOT, to Mrs. Virginia F., eldest daughter of Mr. Henson HARDY, all of Loudoun county.

Last week Alexander LORMAN, of Baltimore died, leaving a princely fortune of about one million dollars, mostly personal property. [lists legatees] Under the latter clause of this will, Col. Lorman CHANCELLOR, of Middleburg, who is a relative of the deceased, comes in for about $75,000.

Wednesday, 31 January 1872   Vol. XVI, No. 32

Married: On the 24th inst. by Rev. J. C. CARROLL, Mr. James G. PRIEST and Miss Kate, daughter of John N. GRANT, Esq., all of Fauquier county.

Married: In Washington DC, on the 22nd last, by Rev. Mr. HOLMEAD, James H. GRANT of Fauquier co. to Miss Alice THORNE of the District of Columbia.

Married: Jan. 18th by Rev. H. E. JOHNSON, Mr. James CARVER to Miss Belle GLASSCOCK, all of Fauquier.

Married: By the Rev. E. H. HENRY, on the 18th of Jan., James H. BUSSEY and Alice J. MARTIN, of Liberty, Fauquier county.

Married: In Richmond, on Thursday, the 25th inst. at the residence of the bride's father by Rev. Dr. WOODBRIDGE, Henry COOK, of Alexandria and Jenneta, daughter of Colonel R. W. WITHERS.

Died: In Alexandria at midnight, January 26th, Mrs. Catharine POWELL, relict of the late Hon. Cuthbert POWELL, aged 93 years.

Wednesday, 7 February 1872   Vol. XVI, No. 33

Died: In Hernando, Miss. on the 13th of January 1872, John M. FADLEY, who was born in Leesburg, Va. July 28th 1819. He moved to Hernando in 1857, where he has continued to reside since that time. For several years Mayor of our town.

Married: On the 23d instant, at White's Ferry, Montgomery county, Md, by Rev. W. H. REED, George YOUNG to Mattie JONES, both of Loudoun county.

Married: In the Southern Methodist church, Winchester, on the 10th inst., by Rev. J. E. ARMSTRONG, Edward G. HOLLIS, of the Winchester times and Miss Virginia, daughter of W. D. BROWN, all of Winchester.

Married: On Thursday night last, at 8 p.m. in Trinity church, Staunton, by Rev. R. H. PHILIPS, assisted by the Rev. J. C. WHEAT, Captain Hugh M. McILHANY, of Baltimore, to Miss Mattie C. TROUT, third daughter of N. K. TROUT, Esq., of the city of Staunton.

Died: On Sunday, 28th of January, Albert Neer, son of A. J. and E. M. SINGLETON, aged 4m 12d.

Wednesday, 14 February 1872   Vol. XVI, No. 34

Married: On the Mt. Middleton farm, at the residence of Mr. Wm. A. DENNIS, Jan. 24th 1872, by Rev. L. D. NIXON, Mr. Randolph S. THOMPSON, to Miss Alice S. McFARLAND, all of Loudoun.

Married: On the 5th instant, by the Rev. H. WISSLER, at the Reformed Church near Lovettsville, Mr. Jeremiah FAWLEY to Miss Lizzie A. FILLER, all of Loudoun county.

Married: In the same neighborhood on the same day by the same, at the residence of the bride's father, Mr. Morris W. McFARLAND to Miss M. Annie SKINNER, all of Loudoun.

Married: At Frederick city, Md, Jan. 3rd by the Rev. A. ENGEL, Mr. George E. NORTHEY of Baltimore, to Miss Elizabeth C. APPEL, of Loudoun.

Married: On the 5th ult., at the residence of the bride's father, near Goresville, by the Rev. Samuel A. BALL, Mr. Edward L. TITUS to Miss Mary C. McKIMMY, all of this county.

Married: On the 30th January, by the Rev. E. B. HENRY, Wilford S. EMBREY and Sarah E., daughter of Staunton G. EMBREY, all of Fauquier county.

Married: On Wednesday, the 24th ult. on horseback in front of the Tavern House of Wm. J. McGLAUGHLIN in Pocahontas county, when the thermometer stood 8 degrees below zero, by the Rev. G. L. BROWN, Daniel McCARTY, Esq., a pensioner for services in the war of 1812, aged 78 years, to Miss Ann GABRET, aged 28 years, all of Pocohontas county.

Married: On the 7th inst., in Lynchburg, Va by Rev. H. E. JOHNSON, Mr. G. W. CHAPALEAR, of Fauquier, to Miss Nannie O. BARRETT, of Lynchburg.

Married: By Rev. J. A. HAYNES, on Wednesday, the 7th instant, Mr. Mahlon J. GLASSCOCK and Miss Isabel L. GULICK, both of Loudoun Co.

Died: In Charlestown, W. Va, on Monday morning, February 12th 1872, Daniel M. SHEETZ in about the 48th year of his age.

County Ct: Estate of Edgar JARVIS dec'd. committed to the Sheriff as curator. Wm. GREGG and Mrs. Elizabeth WILSON qualified as Exors. of the estate of the late Wm. WILSON, John W. GARRETT qualified as Admr. of Enoch GARRETT dec'd. Court appointed a committee to resign Charlotte A. ROGERS a homestead out of the estate of her deceased husband, A. L. ROGERS.

Edgar JARVIS, for several years mail contractor on the Point of Rocks route, died at the Reamer House in this town, on Thursday night, in the 48th year of his age, and was buried on

Saturday by Laurel Division of the Son of Temperance, of which he was a consistent member.

Wednesday, 21 February 1872   Vol. XVI, No. 35

Married: On the 15th inst., at the residence of John W. FINKS, Esq. by Rev. H. H. WYER, Mr. Albert FLETCHER to Miss Sallie A. WITHERS, all of Warrenton.

Married: On Tuesday morning the 13th at the residence of Dr. WADDELL by the Rev. J. W. PRATT, Mr. John CARMICHAEL, of Augusta, Georgia, to Miss Virginia Brooke TUCKER, daughter of Hon. J. Randolph TUCKER, of Lexington, Va.

Married: At the residence of the bride's father on Tuesday, February 8, by the Right Rev. Bishop JOHNS, of Virginia, Gerard C. BROWN, of Croton Falls, N. Y., to Carrie D., daughter of Dr. ? W. BANCROFT, of Fairfax Co.

Died: In Baltimore on the morning of the 13th instant, of inflammation of the brain, Ellen A., aged 13 years, youngest daughter of John W. and Mary WOODY.

Died: On the 31st of January, Stephen A. Douglass, son of John W. and Mary A. WOODY, formerly of Leesburg, Va, in the 21st year of his age.

Died: On Friday morning, the 9th inst. in Charlestown, after a lingering illness, Mildred Elizabeth, only daughter of John W. and Nancy DALGARN, aged 11 years and 12 days.

Died: At Farmwell, Jan. 18th, 1872, Mrs. Rosanna HOUSER, in her 92d year, relict of the late Christopher HOUSER of this county.

Died: At the Reamer House in Leesburg on Thursday night February 8th, Edgar J. JARVIS, eldest son of the late Washington and Louisa A. JARVIS, in the 48th year of his age, after a long and painful illness.

Died: At Farmwell in Loudoun county, February 13th 1872, of pneumonia, after a few weeks painful illness, Mrs. Honor ARUNDLE, consort of Mr. Joseph ARUNDLE, in her 59th year. Member of the Southern Methodist Church for several years.

Wednesday, 28 February 1872   Vol. XVI, No. 36

Married: At the Presbyterian Parsonage on the 21st inst., by Rev. J. W. LUPTON, Mr. Thomas D. MOFFETT and Miss Violinda H. RUSK.

Married: At the residence of the bride's father in Leesburg on the 21st instant, by the same, Mr. Thomas F. BURCH and Miss Helen A. HAMMERLY, daughter of Mr. Jno. W. HAMMERLY.

Married: On Tuesday last, 13th inst., in the Baptist Church at Berryville, Va, by Rev. T. B. SHEPHERD, Rev. J. C. HAMNER, of Miami, Saline county, Mo. to Mrs. Harriet N. SMITH, late of Charlestown.

Married: February 21st 1872, by Rev. J. A. HAYNES, Mr. Geo. W. CRAIG and Miss Emma A. V. DODD, both of Loudoun county.

Married: By the same on the 22d instant, Mr. Francis T. CRAIG and Miss Emily J. CRAIG, both of Loudoun county.

Married: February 22d by Rev. Jno. LANDSTREET, Albert J. WYNKOOP to Miss Nancy STONE, all of this county.

Died: In Richmond, on Wednesday morning, the 21st instant, Mrs. Maria E. GRETTER, wife of George W. GRETTER, in the 56th year of her age.

Died: On Friday evening the 16th inst., in Leesburg, after a brief illness, Annie, eldest daughter of the late Charles E. and Emily E. LLOYD, aged 5y 6m.

Died: On Tuesday night, February 15, 1872 in Jefferson County, Mrs. Emily R. HOWELL, aged 27y 5m, wife of Mr. John M. HOWELL.

Died: At White's Ferry on the 9th inst., Alferando, child of Samuel and Margaret MANSFIELD, aged 3y 20d.

Died: At the residence of her son-in-law, T. A. HAVENNOR, near Belmont, at 3 o'clock on Sunday morning Feb. 25th 1872, of paralysis, Mrs. Catharine B. MORAN, in her 75th year.

Died: At the house of her son-in-law, Mr. JORDAN near Hanibal, Mo. on the 21st of January 1872, Mrs. Barbary DARNES, aged 94y 7m 7d. Member of the Methodist Church. Mrs. DARNES was born in Loudoun County, Va in 1777.

Wednesday, 6 March 1872   Vol. XVI, No. 37

Married: On the 23d ult., in the M. F. Church, Harper's Ferry by Rev. H. F. MISXIMON assisted by Rev. A. J. BENDER, Dr. A. M. KESSLER to Miss Alice R. KNOONCE, daughter of George KNOONCE, Esq. all of Harper's Ferry.

Married: On the 27th inst., by elder J. FURR, at the Valley Meeting House, Mr. John MAGAHA to Miss Mary BALES, all of Loudoun county.

Died: In this town, on Friday night last, after a short illness, Miss Sallie GRIMES, dau. of the late Henry GRIMES, of Leesburg.

Died: In this town on Saturday night, after an illness of only a few days, Mr. Charles NEWTON, in the 64th year of his age.

Wednesday, 13 March 1872   Vol. XVI, No. 38

Married: In Williamsport, Maryland, on Wednesday morning the 6th instant, at the residence of the bride's father, by the Rev. G. G. SMITH, Wm. B. DOWNEY, of Leesburg, Va., to Kate MOODEY, of the former place.

Married: Near "Oatland Mills," at the residence of the bride's father, Feb. 28th 1872, by the Rev. L. D. NIXON, Mr. Joel CORRUTHERS to Miss Sarah T. THOMAS, all of Loudoun.

Married: At the residence of W. D. EASTERDAY near Leesburg on Tuesday morning, March 12th 1872, by Rev. J. W. LUPTON, Mr. James F. RINKER and Miss Susan J., daughter of the late Asa JACKSON, all of Leesburg.

Died: At the residence Jno. IDEN at Oatlands on Sunday night March 10th 1872 after a protracted illness, Miss Elizabeth STOVER, daughter of the late Edwin A. STOVER, of Aldie.

March Ct: David J. LEE qualified as Exor of the late Corbin F. HANCOCK. Eliza F. MATTHEWS qualified as executrix of Squire E. MATTHEWS dec'd. Mahlon TAVENER qualified as Admr. of Hannah TAVENER dec'd.

Wednesday, 20 March 1872 Vol. XVI, No. 39

Married: At "Exeter," the residence of the bride's father, on Wednesday morning, March 13th 1872, by Rev. R. T. DAVIS, Mr. Samuel DONOHOE and Miss Mary Alice, daughter of Mr. Thomas BURCH, all of Loudoun.

Married: At Mount Hope Church, March 12th 1872 by the Rev. B. P. DULIN, Mr. Wm. H. HAVENER, to Miss Emma HAWS, all of Loudoun.

Married: On the 13th inst., at the residence of the bride's father, by Rev. X. J. RICHARDSON, Mr. John H. BOWERS to Miss Mary E. STOCKS, all of Loudoun.

Died: In Leesburg on Tuesday night March 5th 1872, Virginia, youngest daughter of Sarah Y. GOVER and the late John W. GOVER, aged 17y 5m.

Died: At the residence of her husband in Middleburg on Sunday March 17th 1872, Mrs. Susan W. NOLAND, wife of Major Burr P. NOLAND of this county. In Leesburg on Thursday morning, March 14th 1872, Earnest Linwood, the youngest son of T. A. and Annie McCABE, aged 1y 10m 8d.

Died: Samuel B. BERKER, of Middleburg Va, on March 6th in his 65th year. For twenty-five years past an active member of the M. E. Church South. He leave a wife and children.

Mr. David CARLISLE died very suddenly on Saturday morning last, at his home near Snickersville of heart disease.

County Ct: John MEAD appointed Guardian of Rosa Belle VANSICKLER. William GIDDINGS qualified as Admr. of Eli L. SCHOOLEY. John LYNN qualified as Admr. of George FRY. Estate of Washington JARVIS dec'd. committed to Wm. F. BARRETT, Sheriff of this county. Harmon COPELAND appointed Guardian of James A. MORRISON and William W. MORRISON infants. William WHITE qualified as Admr. of Nathan WHITE dec'd. John H. WILLIAMS qualified as Admr. of Joseph PILES dec'd. Mrs. Alice S. JANNEY qualified as Ex. of John JANNEY dec'd. John F. WATERS qualified as Admr. of Levi WATERS dec'd.

Wednesday, 27 March 1872   Vol. XVI, No. 40

Married: In Leesburg on the 21st inst. by Rev. J. W. LUPTON, Mr. William M. LYNN and Miss Isabella S. HIXSON.

Died: In Hamilton on the night of the 23d inst., Mrs. Elizabeth V. JANNEY, wife of the late John JANNEY, in her 67th year.

Death of Col. Charles DOUGLAS – died at the "Reamer House," in this town about four o'clock on Saturday morning last, after a short illness of dropsy of the heart in his 75th year. On Sunday afternoon interred in the burying ground of the Episcopal Church. Left an estate of about $40,000 and died without a will. His brother, Mr. Arch. N. DOUGLAS, of Albemarle co, is his sole heir and proposes to make his future home in Loudoun.

James L. MARTIN was born in Fauquier county on the 10th of March 1787 and died at the house of his son in Jacksonville, Illinois on the 9th of March 1872, aged 75 years wanting one day. He was married to Sarah A. B. MURRAY in Leesburg in February 1821, in which town be permanently located and engaged in mercantile pursuits. He converted and joined the M. E. church in the year 1830.

A dispatch from Warrenton Va dated March 25 says Young Frank HELM shot himself last night through the temple and was found a corpse this morning.

Wednesday, 3 April 1872   Vol. XVI, No. 41

Married: On the 12th instant, at Chelsea, the residence of the bride's father, by Rev. H. E. JOHNSON, Wm. H. LEWIS to Miss Sue SMITH, daughter of William SMITH, Esq., both of Fauquier.

Died: In Leesburg, on Tuesday, March 26th, Martha Virginia, infant daughter of William P. and Ann Virginia SMITH, aged 1y 11m.

Died: March 18th 1872, Mrs. John COCHERELL, after an illness of several months. She was a member of the Baptist Church at Northfork for about fifteen years.

Died: At residence of his son-in-law, Wm. D. SOWERS, near Aldie on the 13th instant, Benjamin F. ADAMS, in his 72d year.

Wednesday, 10 April 1872   Vol. XVI, No. 42

Married: In Winchester on Thursday morning 28th of March at the residence of L. V. SHEARER, by the Rev. M. L. SHUFORD,

Mr. Samuel C. ODAIR, to Miss Louisa L. ESKRIDGE, formerly of Loudoun county.

Married: On Tuesday the 2d instant, by Rev. J. W. LUPTON at the residence of the bride's mother in Leesburg, Mr. John G. GORE of Adams co., Ohio and Mrs. Sarah A. BROWN, of Loudoun.

Died: At her residence in Waterford on the 5th instant, Susan WALKER, relict of the late Isaac WALKER, aged 78y 3m 21d.

Mr. __ STEVENS while engaged in digging a well on the farm of Mr. H. S. SMITH near Guilford on Saturday last was seriously injured by the falling of a rock. He has since died and was buried in this town on Tuesday.

April Ct: Will of S. B. BARKER admitted to probate with Rebecca A. BARKER as Executrix. Arch. N. DOUGLAS qualified as Admr. of Chas. DOUGLAS dec'd. Geo. P. SOUDOR qualified as Admr. of estate of Susan SOUDOR dec'd. Estate of W. G. HAWS dec'd. committed to Sheriff. Admr. of Harrison CROSS having had his powers revoked, the estate committed to the Sheriff. Jas. CARLISLE qualified as Admr. of David CARLISLE dec'd. John B. LEE Admr. of Sally BRONAUGH having died, estate committed to Sheriff. Will of Naylor SHOEMAKER proved and recorded. Will of Samuel THOMPSON (col.) admitted to record and Summerfield BOLYN qualified as Admr.

Wednesday, 17 April 1872   Vol. XVI, No. 43

Married: April 4th 1782 by the Rev. John WOOLF, Mr. George SPAULDING to Miss Mary V. KEEYS, all of Loudoun.

Died: In Leesburg on Thursday morning 11th last 1872, Lorenzo D. ROLLINS, son of Charles E. and Ary A. ROLLINS, aged 9 months.

Miss Emily Ludwell LEE of Loudoun, who was on a visit to this city and stopping at Mrs. DUVALS, died very suddenly last evening. Doctors are of the opinion she died of heart disease. *Rich. State Journal 11th inst.*

Wednesday, 24 April 1872   Vol. XVI, No. 44

Married: By Elder Joseph FURR at the house of C. F. DOWDELL on the 9th of April 1872, Mr. Wm. A. LUNSFORD to Miss Mary E. DOWDELL, all of Loudoun.

At Tyrone, Penn., April 11th by Rev. Daniel HARTMAN, of Central Penn. Conference, Rev. Wm. I. BAIN, of Virginia Conference, M. E. Church, to Miss Sadie B. BEYER, of Blain county, Penn.

Mr. Alexander ELGIN, residing near Middleburg left the neighborhood of Aldie about 9 o'clock on the night of Sunday April 14th for his home. Next morning he was found lying in the road a short distance from his house, speechless. He died on

Wednesday but never spoke. It is supposed that he was thrown from his horse. He was about 40 years of age, and leaves a wife and several children.

Wednesday, 1 May 1872   Vol. XVI, No. 45

Married: In Mobile, Ala., on the 16th inst. by the Rev. Dr. FULTON, Dr. Alfred H. POWELL, of Baltimore (formerly of Leesburg) to Cora H., daughter of Moses WARING, Esq., of that city.

Married: At the residence of Captain KERSEY, in Alexandria on Thursday April 25th by Rev. E. F. BUSEY, Mr. William A. HUTCHISON of Loudoun to Mrs. Martha A. WHARLEY, of Fairfax, formerly of Alexandria.

Married: On the 23d inst. by Rev. J. W. LUPTON, at the residence of the bride's father, Mr. Charles F. BURGESS and Miss Mary E. HENDERSON.

Married: Near the burnt bridge, on Goose Creek April 23d 1872, at the residence of the bride's mother by Rev. L. D. NIXON, Mr. Wm. DOVE to Miss Elizabeth MILLER, all of Loudoun.

Married: In St. Louis April 18th 1872 at the residence of the bride's father, by Rev. W. G. ELIOT, D.D., James Andrew STEPHENSON, formerly of Fauquier county, to Miss Georgie, daughter of John YOUNG, Esq.

Died: On the morning of the 20th instant, after a lingering illness of consumption, John W. WOODY, aged 54 years, formerly of Virginia.

Reed POULTON of this county died at his home a few miles from Leesburg on the ___ ult. in the 80th years of his age.

Wednesday, 8 May 1872   Vol. XVI, No. 46

Died: In Leesburg, on Tuesday evening, April 30th 1872 on pneumonia, Mr. Thomas J. STEADMAN, in his 61st year.

Wednesday, 15 May 1872   Vol. XVI, No. 47

Died: March 1st 1872, at the residence of her son-in-law near Axiline schoolhouse, Elizabeth WYNKOOP, the consort of Joseph WYNKOOP deceased in the 83rd year of her age.

Married: At Herndon, May 7th 1872, at the residence of the bride's father, by Rev. L. D. NIXON, Mr. Charles N. BURR, of Loudoun to Miss Annie G. CAYLOR, of Fairfax county.

Married: On May 8th 1872 at the residence of Mr. Jas. M. CATLETT, the bride's brother-in-law in Fauquier county by Rev. R. H. McKIM, Ethelbert MILBURN of Alexandria and Korenore A., daughter of the late S. A. MARSTELLER, of Prince William county.

Married: In Washington on Wednesday May 8th by Rev. D. B. JUTTEN, pastor of the E street Baptist Church, T. Richard

BAKER, of Middleburg and Miss M. Inez ENGLISH, of Alexandria, Va.

On Friday morning last, after an illness of but six days of pneumonia, Mr. James GARRISON a well known citizen of this town breathed his last, in the 81st year of his age. On Saturday evening his remains were interred in Union Cemetery attended by members of Olive Branch Lodge A. F. & A. Masons, he had been a member for 53 years, having been initiated in 1819.

May Ct.: Will of the late Reed POULTON was admitted to record. Will of the late Jas. GARRISON admitted to record and Mary Ann GARRISON qualified as Executrix. Will of Jas. W. GULICK admitted to record with John F. ALLEN as Exor. Martha V. HOLTZCLAW qualified as Admr. of Jas. HOLTZCLAW dec'd. Bushrod OSBURN declining to execute a new bond as Admr. of T. V. B. OSBURN dec'd., his powers as Admr. were revoked and Walter C. OSBURN substituted. Will of Susan WALKER dec'd. admitted to record, J. M. WALKER and J. Ed. WALKER qualifying as Executors. Will of Chas. F. BERKELEY dec'd. admitted to record and powers of Admr. granted to Edmund BERKELEY, revoked by the Court. Applications of A. R. SWEENEY at Unison for ordinary license and Volney PURSEL at Snickersville for merchants license to retail liquor refused.

Wednesday, 22 May 1872   Vol. XVI, No. 48

Married: At the residence of Mr. W. L. HEDGES, in Charlestown, on Tuesday evening, May 14th 1872, by Rev. W. A. WADE, Mr. B. F. LEWIS, of that place, to Miss Alice DIVINE, of Hillsboro, Loudoun county.

Married: On the 16th instant, at Bethany Chapel, Franklin square, by the Rev. John A. WILLIAMS, William G. BREWER, of Montgomery county Md and Ida, daughter of Major Ben. S. WHITE, of Baltimore.

Died: May 11th 1872, at Williamstown, West Va, Kenner STEPHENSON, son of John W. and Mary R. HAMMAT, in the 6th year of his age.

Death of R. M. BENTLEY, Agent of the W. & O. Railroad at this place, occurred at his residence in Leesburg on Saturday night last, in the 45th year of his age. For a number of years a Justice of the Peace in this county and twice a representative in the Legislature of Virginia and at the time of his death, Recorder of the Corporation of Leesburg. A few weeks ago Mr. BENTLY was chosen a Vestryman of the Church of which he was a consistent member, and his is the fourth death that has occurred in that body within the past eighteen months. On Monday morning his remains were borne to the Episcopal

Church, where the funeral services were read by Rev. Mr. HEPBRON, after which they were conveyed to Union Cemetery and deposited in their narrow vault.

Wednesday, 29 May 1872   Vol. XVI, No. 49

Married: April 11, by the Rev. Jno. LANDSTREET, William E. BURKET to Mrs. Margaret TAYLOR, all of this county.

Married: May 14, by the same, Rev. Jno. T. MAXWELL to Laura V., daughter of Nelson GIBSON of Fauquier Co.

Married: In Georgetown on the 21st instant, Joseph BAUMBACK to Martena W. BUSSARD, all of Georgetown, DC.

Married: On the 20th instant, at the M. E. Parsonage in Frederick city, Md. by Rev. J. A. PRICE, Jacob WILLIAMS to Miss Ann SAUNDERS, both of Loudoun county.

Died: In McDonaugh County, Illinois, on the 14th of April 1872, Col. John G. HUMPHREY, Col. H. was a native of Loudoun county, from whence he emigrated to Illinois in 1836, and where he still has many relatives and friends.

Died: At "The Cottage," Sabbath morning, May 19th 1872, Town[s]end McVeigh MOSS, second son of William V. and Blanche MOSS, in his third year.

Illness of C. F. FADELEY – At the date of this writing, one o'clock, Tuesday afternoon, Mr. C. F. FADELEY, is extremely ill. P.S. Our fears are realized, he died a few minutes before 4 o'clock.

Wednesday, 5 June 1872   Vol. XVI, No. 50

Married: Under a sycamore tree, near Middleburg, May 28th by the Rev. Robert R. S. HOUGH, Mr. Abner CORNWELL, of Fauquier, and Henrietta McDANIEL, of Warren.

Married: On the 28th of May in Leesburg by Rev. J. W. LUPTON, Geo. H. ALLEN and Hannah COLE.

Died: Mrs. Judie MEGEATH, widow of the late Saml. A. MEGEATH, died in this city on Thursday night at half-past 11 o'clock. of typhoid pneumonia. Born in Warrenton in 1833, came to the Territory of Nebraska with her sister, Mrs. James G. MEGEATH, in 1857 and married in 1859. *Omaha Herald*.

Death of Chas. F. FADELEY – at this home in Leesburg at 4 o'clock on Tuesday, May 28th 1872 in the 55th year of his age.

On Friday evening last, just before night, a difficulty occurred on Heater's Island about ten miles from Leesburg, between Mr. Mason APPELL and Mr. P. H. HEATER, which resulted fatally to both the combatants. An old quarrel had existed between them for some time. Both used ordinary pocket knives and neither seemed to have received more than one or two blows. APPELL was stabbed in the heart and died almost instantly. HEATER was stabbed severing two ribs, opening the stomach and touching the right lung. He lingered until about six o'clock Saturday morning. Both were buried on Sunday. HEATER leaves a wife and two little children. HEATER's brother who lives close by the bloody scene is the husband of APPELL's sister.

Mr. James GARRISON who died recently in this town was a member of the Masonic Mutual Benefit Association with headquarters at Shepherdstown, W Va.

Wednesday, 12 June 1872   Vol. XVI, No. 51

Married: On the 6th inst., at the residence of John R. MONDAY, by Rev. X. J. RICHARDSON, Mr. Nathanniel P. OREM, to Miss Mary TARLTON, all of Loudoun.

Married: By Elder J. A. HAYNES on Tuesday the 4th inst., at the residence of Mr. Jno. SIMPSON, Samuel L. SIMPSON, Esq. and Gustie STEWART, of Loudoun county.

Died: At the residence of his father, Dr. Thomas MILLER, in Washington, June 30th, George R. MILLER, M.D., in the 26th year of his age.

Died: In Washington on Monday June 3d, very suddenly of paralysis, Mrs. Catharine A. ROACH, widow of the late Ed. N. ROACH.

June Ct.: Virginia DABNEY qualified as Guardian of R. Heath DABNEY and A. R. JACOBS as Guardian of Louisa R. JACOBS and others. Letters of Administration granted John BROWN on estate of Martha S. BROWN; to Alfred GLASSCOCK and Chas. W. FADELY on estate of late Cha[r]les F. FADELY; to A. C. BYRNE on estate of Kimball G. HICKS Jr., and C. H. LEE on estate of late R. M. BENTLEY.

Wednesday, 19 June 1872   Vol. XVI, No. 52

Married: On Thursday 13th June, at Granby Street M. E. Church, Norfolk, by Rev. J. C. GRANBERRY, D.D., L. W. S. HOUGH, Esq. of Leesburg and Miss Mary Lou, eldest daughter of J. G. WATTS, of that city.

Married: On the 12th instant, by Rev. Douglas F. FORREST, James Marshall McCORMICK of Clarke County, Va and Rosalie Allen TAYLOR, daughter of Lawrence B. TAYLOR of Alexandria.

Died: In Bloomfield on the 13th of May last Miss Margaret JOHNSTON, at the ripe old age of ninety seven years. Her father emigrated from Pennsylvania to this State at an early period in the history of our county, she was born in Virginia in March 1775. For eighty years she was a communicant of the Methodist Episcopal Church.

Wednesday, 26 June 1872   Vol. XVII, No. 1

Married: On Wednesday, the 12th inst., at Grace Church, Berryville, by the Rev. T. F. MARTIN, Mr. John H. WHITE, of Sioux City, Iowa, to Miss Gettie, daughter of Wm. D. McGUIRE, of Clarke county.

Married: On Tuesday evening, the 11th inst., at the Presbyterian Church, Berryville, by Rev. W. S. PALMER, D.D., Rev. Wm. H. THOMPSON, to Miss Annie, daughter of Col. John R. WHITE, of Loudoun county.

Married: June 6th 1872, at the residence of the bride's father, by the Rev. John WOOLF, Mr. Joseph I. STEELE to Miss Mary E. HAWS, all of Loudoun.

Married: On the 2d instant, at the residence of Mrs. STORM by Rev. H. E. MISKIMON, John H. BAYLISS to Sarah POTTS, all of Bolivar, Jefferson county, W Va.

Died: In Hamilton on Saturday morning, July 22d 1872, Mrs. Malinda DOWELL, widow of the late Conrad R. DOWELL, in the 67th year of her age.

Died: In New York on the 10th instant, in the 69th year of her age, Mrs. Esther Ann, widow of Fairfax CATLETT, of Virginia, and daughter of the late Henry LARERTY.

Wednesday, 3 July 1872   Vol. XVII, No. 2

Died: In Snickersville on Monday the 24th of June, Benjamin Claude, infant son of Joshua C. and Maggie B. FLETCHER, aged 7m 12d.

Mr. Alfred BELT, an old citizen of this county, died at his residence a few miles from Leesburg, on Monday last, in his 87th year.

Wednesday, 10 July 1872   Vol. XVII, No. 3

Married: On the 13th day of May, at Howard-Woodgrove, Loudoun county, by the Rev. Armstead FURR, John R. BLANDHEIM, of Alexandria to Mary G., only daughter of Thomas W. and Phebe H. ALLMOND, of Philadelphia.

Married: On the boat between Alexandria and Washington, July 4th 1872, by Rev. E. P. PHELPS, Mr. Howard HARDY to Miss Maggie FORSYTH, both of Leesburg.

Died: Near Leesburg, on Sunday the 2nd of June, Charles I., second son of Thomas and Rachel SEWELL, aged 4y 9m, died with consumption.

Died: On Saturday July 6, 1872, in this town, Miss Florida R. COCKERILLE, sister of Judge R. H. COCKERILLE.

Died: At her residence near Hillsboro, on Monday July 1st, 1872, Mrs. Ruth CLENDENING, relict of the late William CLENDENING Sr., in the 87th year of her age.

Died: At the residence of her son-in-law, Mr. Richard ROGERS, near Middleburg, on Monday morning, July 8th 1872, Mrs. Elizabeth McVEIGH, relict of the late James McVEIGH, in the 83d year of her age.

Departed this life on the 26th day of June 1872, at the residence of Jno. T. LYNN, Esq., Mrs. Augusta LYNN, in her 38th year, second wife of Luther L. LYNN, of Prince William county.

Wednesday, 17 July 1872   Vol. XVII, No. 4

Married: Near Round Hill at the residence of the bride's father on the 21st of May 1872 by the Rev. P. B. SHEPHERD, Mr. J. W. SILCOTT, of Snickersville to Alice A., daughter of Harmon LODGE, Esq.

Died: At the residence of her sister, Mrs. Charles TEBBS on Saturday, July 6th 1872, Miss Florida R. COCKERILLE, youngest child of the late Richard Henry COCKERILLE, of Fairfax.

Died: On Wednesday, 11th July 1872, departed this life at the residence of her husband, Alex. G. SMITH, near Arcola, Loudoun county, Mrs. Margaret SMITH, in her 67th year.

Mr. Albert O. BROWN, citizen of Waterford, died very suddenly in that town on Wednesday, of Cramp Cholic. A comparatively young man, and leaves a wife and two or three small children.

Wednesday, 24 July 1872   Vol. XVII, No. 5

Died: July 6th, Clara M., infant daughter of Thomas H. and Lucinda JACKSON, aged 5m 8d.

Died: Near Waterford, July 11th, John M., infant son of Marshal G., and Lanie K. SHAW, aged 8m 17d.

Died: In Winchester on the 12th of July at 5 o'clock a.m., at the residence of her husband, Hon. Robert Y. CONRAD, Mrs. Betty Whiting CONRAD, in the 63d year of her age.

Died: On Sunday evening, June 23rd 1872, at the residence of her son, Thos. VINCENT, Esq. in Montgomery co, Md, Mrs. Ann E., relict of the late Dr. Wm. B. VINCENT, of this county, and daughter of the late Col. Townsend PEYTON of Oak Hill, Loudoun county, in the 64th year of her age.

Wednesday, 31 July 1872   Vol. XVII, No. 6

Death of Mrs. Elizabeth Whiting CONRAD, wife of Hon. R. Y. CONRAD. Mrs. CONRAD was a sister of the late Humphrey POWELL, of Loudoun county.

An affray occurred near Rectortown on last Tuesday, between Fred. GLASSCOCK, and Decatur and Frank VANHORN, in which GLASSCOCK shot Frank VANHORN just above the hip, wounding him so severely as to cause his death last Wednesday evening. – *Warrenton Index* of Saturday.

Died: On July 17th at the residence of her father, Virginia Pleasant, youngest daughter of James L. and Mary A. McFARLAND, aged 17y 7m 7d.

Wednesday, 7 August 1872   Vol. XVII, No. 7

Married: In Hillsborough at the residence of the bride's brother, Dr. J. W. Taylor, on Tuesday morning, August 6th, by Rev. S. S. HEPBRON, John WHITOCK, of Little Rock, Arkansas, and Miss Virginia TAYLOR.

Married: In Frederick city, Md, by Rev. Dr. ZACHARIAS, on the 23d of July, Thomas FISHER of Point of Rocks, to Miss Sallie LONG, of Loudoun county.

Died: At the residence of her son, Mr. A. M. CHICHESTER, near Loudoun on the 21st of July, at an advanced age, Mrs. Mary CHICHESTER, consort of the late Mason CHICHESTER, of this county

Wednesday, 14 August 1872   Vol. XVII, No. 8

Married: On Sunday night in this place at Leesburg M. E. Church by Rev. Wm. H. FORSYTH, Mr. John A. TRAVERS and Miss Sarah E. G. O. FORSYTH, both of Baltimore.

Died: On the evening of the 5th instant, Fannie Beverley, infant daughter of Capt. Wm. N. & Kate S. McDONALD, in the sixth month of her age.

Died: Of diptheria on the 30th of August, little Willie, youngest child of Charles F. and Laninia C. WENNER, aged 2y 3m.

Died: In Georgetown on Friday the 9th instant in her 21st year, Jennie, eldest daughter of Hugh and Eliza J. CAPERION.

Died: On Thursday the 25th day of July 1872, at the residence of her parents, Fairview, Montgomery county, Md, Miss Emma SHREVE, eldest daughter of Capt. Daniel T. and Margaret R. SHREVE.

Wednesday, 21 August 1872   Vol. XVII, No. 9

Married: Tuesday August 15th 1872 at the residence of the bride's father on Goose Creek near the Railroad bridge, by Rev. L. D. NIXON, Mr. Albert L. SAUNDERS to Miss Sarah LEFEVERS, all of Loudoun county.

Died: Near Philomont, July 26th 1872 Lilian, infant daughter of Chas. W. and Lizzie ORRISON, aged 3m 21d.

Died: At the residence of Christian NICEWANER, August 8th 1872, near Lovettsville in this county, after a short but severe illness, Miss Sarah Margaret TRILBY [TRIBBY?], aged 28y 10d.

Mattie E. BEALES, died July 16, 1872, aged 6y 2m.

Wednesday, 28 August 1872   Vol. XVII, No. 10

Died: At his residence in Snickersville on Tuesday, August 20th, Mr. Rhuel MARSHALL, in his 76th year. One of the oldest, most correct and highly respected citizens of that community.

Died: In Georgetown DC on the 22d of August 1872, Mr. Burr P. NICHOLS, a native of Loudoun county, aged 41y 9m 22d.

Died: In Washington DC, August 22d 1872, Robert William, infant son of F. Alonzo and Willie M. DIVINE, formerly of Leesburg.

Died: Fell asleep in Jesus after a brief and painful illness of six months, John J. ISETT, in the 37th year of his age.

Died: July 6th 1872 at the residence of her husband, John W. VIRTS, Mrs. Elizabeth VIRTS in the 41st year of her age.

Died: At his residence near Aldie on Saturday August 3d 1872 of dropsy, Mr. John T. LYNN, in the 48th year of his age.

Wednesday, 4 September 1872   Vol. XVII, No. 11

Married: On Sunday, August 25th 1872 in Farmwell Church by Rev. L. D. NIXON, Mr. Joseph ARUNDEL, Esq., Depot agent at Farmwell Station, W. & O RR, Loudoun county, to Mrs. M. A. HINDS, late of Washington city, DC.

Died: John H. MYERS on 14th August 1872, of dysentery, in the 78th year of his age.

[*From the Platte City, Mo. Landmark*] In Platte City, Mo, August 18th 1872, after a lingering illness, Col. A. Sidney TEBBS, in his 62nd year. A Virginian, not only by birth, but by noble qualities that distinguish the descendents of the original settlers of that State. He chose the profession of law. He retired in 1855. He emigrated with his family to Missouri and purchased a well improved farm in the vicinity of Platte City. When the war broke out he started south, where he remained until the close of the war. In 1872 he sold his Platte county farm and passed the remaining months of his life among his children in New York, Missouri and Kansas.

Mr. Robert BENTLEY Sr. died at the residence of his son-in-law, Dr. A. R. MOTT, on Monday morning last, in the 81st year of his age. Mr. BENTLEY was born in Leesburg in 1792 and had resided in this town throughout his life with the exception of two years of his early manhood spent in the office of the *Alexandria Gazette*. For many years he was a successful merchant, but abandoned his pursuit about 25 years ago, when he retired to his farm a few miles from town, where he continued to reside, until harrassed by the ravages of the soldiers in the late war, he sought rest and quiet among his children here and with whom he died as stated above. He had a large family of children, grandchildren and great-grandchildren – 52 direct descendants. A soldier in the war of 1812 and for many years a member of the Masonic Fraternity. His funeral took place at 4 o'clock Tuesday evening conducted by Rev. W. W. WILLIAMS. His remains were borne to their final resting place in Union Cemetery by three of his grandsons and three of his grand-sons-in-law.

Dr. Thos. M. BOYLE, an old physician of this county, died at his home in Aldie on Monday evening last. His remains will be interred in Sharon Cemetery, Middleburg this Wednesday morning at 10 o'clock.

Wednesday, 11 September 1872   Vol. XVII, No. 12

Married: Sept. 3d 1872 by Rev. L. A. MANN, Capt. H. L. COGSILL, of Muskingum county, Ohio, to Miss Alice L. VINCEL, of Loudoun county.

Died: Suddenly in Baltimore on the 6th of September 1872, of paralysis of the brain, Sarsfield James FOLEY, of that city, formerly of Leesburg, Loudoun county, Va, aged 61 years.

Died: On the 17th of August of cholera infantum, Minnie Bond, only daughter of Thomas N. and Julia A. FISHER, aged 11m 26d.

Died: Near Leesburg Aug. 27th 1872, Miss Mary E. KITTLE, in the 36th year of her age.

Sept. Ct.: Albert G. CHAMBLIN qualified as Admr. of the estate of the late John T. LYNN. Will of Dr. Thos. M. BOYLE dec'd. was admitted to record, with Snowden C. HALL as Executor. Will of Mrs. Mary ANDERSON admitted to record, with Joseph and Benj. C. LACEY as executors. Will of Mrs. Mary CHICHESTER dec'd. previously admitted to probate in the Orphan's Court of Montgomery county, Md was admitted to probate here. Will of Robt. BENTLEY dec'd. admitted to record, Dr. A. R. MOTT qualifying as Executor.

Wednesday, 18 September 1872   Vol. XVII, No. 13

Married: Sept. 10th 1872, in Washington, by Rev. S. W. HARISCOCK, at the Parsonage at the Union Chapel M. E. Church, Mr. Townsend ORRISON to Miss Sallie E. WRIGHT, both of Loudoun county.

Died: At Rosemont, the residence of her husband, near Goresville, on Monday, Sept. 16th after a few days illness, Mrs. Fannie Whiting, wife of Walter J. HARRISON, and daughter of the late Dr. Wm. L. POWELL, in the 27th year of her age.

Wednesday, 25 September 1872   Vol. XVII, No. 14

Died: Near Middleburg, September 9th 1872 of typhoid fever, Sarah Metta, dau. of R. S. and Sallie CHINN, in her 19th year.

Died: In Atlanta, Georgia, at her father's residence on the 9th of September of consumption, Emma, daughter of Thomas and Mary HOGE, formerly of Loudoun, aged twenty six years.

Mr. Charles HAWLING, son of Mr. Lewis HAWLING, of this county, who went to South America about a year ago to look after the estate of his uncle, the late Dr. HAWLING, which was devised to his relatives in Loudoun, returned home one day last week.

Wednesday, 2 October 1872   Vol. XVII, No. 15

Jacob JOLLY died at the residence of his son Bushrod, in Warrenton on Sunday the 22d ult. The *Index* says if he had lived till the 15th of next December he would have been by his own reckoning 101 years old. He was born in Fauquier and lived his entire life in that county.

Married: In the Parsonage at Farmwell on the 26th of September, by Rev. L. D. NIXON, Mr. Edgar Bentley HAVENER to Miss Ann E. SWEEDY, all of this county.

Married: In Alexandria, on Tuesday morning, Sept. 17th by Rev. Mr. BUSEY, Mr. William MURRAY and Miss Elizabeth M. ATHEY, all of that city.

Mrs. VANDEVENTER, a revolutionary pensioner, died at Marion, Indiana, recently at the age of 104 years. Her husband who was a soldier in 1776, died 20 years ago at the same age.

Wednesday, 9 October 1872   Vol. XVII, No. 16

Brentsville, Oct. 7 – Rhoda FEWELL who killed James F. CLARKE, was indicted by the Grand Jury of Prince William county and the trial postponed until the next term of the County court.

Frederick Md, Oct. 7 – In the case of Dr. Jacob D. THOMAS, charged with the murder of John Lloyd BELT, on the 2d of October 1871, at Adamstown in this county, the defense will urge a postponement of the trial.

Married: On the 3d of October 1872 by S. GOVER near Leesburg, W. H. ROLLISON and Harriet CLARKSON, all of Loudoun.

Married: In Washington DC, Sept. 26 by Rev. Mr. YORK of the M. E. Church, Mr. A. C. STAATS, of Fairfax County, and Miss Libbie, eldest daughter of J. B. BOWMAN, Esq. of Vienna, Fairfax county.

Married: August 27, 1872 by L. H. CRENSHAW, Mr. James O. WREEN [WRENN] and Miss Lulu WRENN, all of Fairfax county.

Married: September 1872 by Rev. L. H. CRENSHAW, Henderson SAUNDERS and Laurena FOLLIN, daughter of Samuel FOLLIN, all of Fairfax.

Married: In Baltimore, on Wednesday Sept. 25th by the Rev. Alfred AMES, Thomas F. SEXTON, of Loudoun county, to Mrs. Florence BUCHANAN, of Pennsylvania.

Married: At the City Hotel in Cumberland on the 26th ultimo, by Rev. S. V. LEECH, Mr. G. NICHOLS, of Leesburg to Miss Martha A. McDONALD, of Hampshire county.

Wednesday, 16 October 1872   Vol. XVII, No. 17

Married: On Tuesday morning, the 15th inst. at the residence of the bride's father, by the Rev. Dr. HEAD, Mr. P. F. SHROFF to Miss Sophia E., daughter of John NORRIS, Esq., all of Leesburg.

Married: On the 13th of October 1872 by S. GOVER near Leesburg, Henry C. STEADMAN and Miss M. E. PATTERSON.

Married: In Farmwell church at 2 o'clock p.m., Oct. 8th by Rev. L. D. NIXON, Mr. James W. PEACOCK to Miss Martha J. MORAN, both of Loudoun county.

Married: In the same place on the same day, by the same at 7 o'clock, p.m., Mr. Jno. W. ARUNDLE, to Mrs. Orlinda MORAN, all of this county.

Wednesday, 23 October 1872   Vol. XVII, No. 18

Died: In Cumberland Md on the night of the 16th, Mollie E., wife of G. W. COOPER, in the 25th year of her age.

Wednesday, 30 October 1872   Vol. XVII, No. 19

Married: On Thursday afternoon the 24th inst. at the residence of the bride's father by Elder Benj. BRIDGES, Mr. Benjamin B. KEENE, of Loudoun to Miss Annie, daughter of James JENKINS, of Fairfax Co.

Married: In the church of the Epiphany, Danville, Va on Thursday the 17th instant by Rev. Geo. W. DAME, assisted by Rev. William M. DAME, of Loudoun co., Miss Ellen Page DAME, youngest daughter of the officiating clergyman, to Mr. Robert BRYDO, late of Toronto, C. W.

Died: Near Morrisonville Sept. 12th 1872, Mrs. M. BROWN, in the 47th year of her age, beloved wife of Jno. BROWN.

Died: July 14th 1872, at the residence of her husband, near Zainesville, Ohio, Nancy STEPHENS, wife of Thomas STEPHENS, and daughters of the late Thomas PURCELL, of Loudoun.

Wednesday, 6 November 1872   Vol. XVII, No. 20

Wesley JENKINS died at the residence of his sons, near Leesburg, on Monday morning last at an advanced age. He was a soldier in the war of 1812.

Mr. Wm. F. TURNER, highly respected citizen of Rippon, Jefferson county W Va, died in Baltimore last week of heart disease.

Wednesday, 13 November 1872   Vol. XVII, No. 21

Married: At the residence of T. G. CRAIGHEDS, Jasper, Tenn., October 2d by Rev. W. B. LYDA, Mr. John W. SIMPSON, son of J. W. SIMPSON dec'd., formerly of Leesburg, to Miss Susie W. HICOTT, daughter of Wm. HICOTT Sr., dec'd. of Montgomery, Ohio.

Married: In Charlestown, Nov. 6, 1872, by Rev. A. C. HOPKINS, Mr. John W. REED, of Loudoun county, to Miss Lucy G. HEDGES, daughter of Wm. L. HEDGES, of that place.

Married: At the residence of the bride's mother, Nov. 5, 1872, by the Rev. W. H. MEADE, Mr. Wm. Opie NORRIS to Miss Mollie B. CHEW, dau. of the late Roger CHEW, all of Jefferson co.

Married: In Hamilton, at the M. E. C. S., on the 7th inst. by Rev. J. C. DICE, Mr. Amos BEANS and Miss Phebe E. HOUGH, all of Loudoun county.

Married: At the same time and place by the same, Lewis D. HOLLINGSWORTH and Miss Annie M. GREGG, all of Loudoun county.

Died: In Winchester on the morning of the 29th of October 1872, Mrs. Caroline C. HOLLIDAY, wife of Colonel F. W. D. HOLLIDAY, of Winchester and daughter of Dr. R. H. and Julia C. STUART, of Ceder Grove, King George county, Virginia, in the 28th year of her age.

Died: At his residence in Philadelphia on the afternoon of the 23d ultimo, Samuel T. CANBY, in the 63d year of his age. Many of his early years were passed in this County, though the prime of his life was spent in Philadelphia.

Wednesday, 20 November 1872   Vol. XVII, No. 22

Married: On the 13th inst., by Rev. Mr. Branch, at the residence of Mr. Robert HARPER, near Leesburg, Mr. Augustus J. HULSEY, of Atlanta, Ga, to Miss Alice E. HARPER, daughter of W. Walton HARPER, of New York.

Married: November 12th, 1872 at the residence of the bride's father, by Rt. Rev. Bishop GIBBONS, John B. PURCELL, of Richmond and Miss Olympa, daughter of Col. Thos. H. WILLIAMSON, of the Virginia Military Institute.

Married: On the 15th of October 1872, by Elder Jos. FURR, at the house of Charles F. DOWDELL, Mr. John F. LYNN to Miss Louisa P. DOWDELL, all of Loudoun county.

Married: on the 14th inst. at the Osburn House by the Rev. Wm. H. FORSYTH, Mr. Joseph F. UNGER and Miss Henrietta SPRING, all of Loudoun county.

Married: On the 5th of November at the bride's residence, Burkettsville, Md, by the Rev. W. C. WIRE, Mr. Charles W. FRY and Miss Kate M. WIRE, both of Loudoun county.

Married: On the 3d of November at Abner CONRAD's in Loudoun, by the Rev. W. C. WIRE, of Burkettsville, Mr. Thomas W. WEBB and Miss Margaret G. RILEY, both of Loudoun county.

Married: On the 30th ultimo, at the residence of the bride's father in Waterford by the Rev. Mr. FOSTER, Mr. Orlando F. MANINGLY and Miss Annie M. HOUGH, all of Loudoun co.

On the 30th ultimo at the Dill House, Frederick, Md, by the Rev. J. A. PRICE,. Mr. Samuel COMPHER of this county, and Miss Mary E. JAMES, of Frederick county, Md.

On Wednesday, the 13th instant, at the residence of the bride's father, by Father DOHERTY, Mr. Richard C. SCOTT, of Petersburg, to Miss Lizzie C., daughter of Maj. John SCOTT, of Fauquier county.

On the 12th instant, at Trinity Church, Staunton, by the Rev. Churchill J. GIBSON, the Rev. Robert A. GIBSON to Susan B., fourth daughter of the Hon. Alex. H. H. STUART.

Wednesday, 27 November 1872   Vol. XVII, No. 23

Married: In the 2d Presbyterian Church, Richmond, Nov. 12th by Rev. Dr. C. H. READ, Julian BENFORD, of Richmond, to Miss Ella M. CLOWES, of Loudoun.

Married: November 13th 1872, at the residence of Mr. Thomas SIMPSON, by the Rev. John WOLF, Mr. James CARLISLE to Miss Mollie COOPER, all of Loudoun.

Married: On Thursday afternoon, 24th of October 1872, at the residence of the bride's father, by Elder Benjamin BRIDGES, Benjamin B. KEENE, of Loudoun county, to Miss Annie, daughter of Jas. JENKINS, Esq., of Fauquier.

Wednesday, 4 December 1872   Vol. XVII, No. 24

Married: On Wednesday, the 27th instant, at the residence of the bride's father, by Rev. Dr. NORTON, Rector of St. Paul's Church, Mr. William E. STRONG, of New York, and Alice Corbyn, daughter of Francis L. SMITH, Esq., of Alexandria.

Married: In Washington, on the 27th instant, Dr. F. A. ASHFORD, formerly of the 17th of Virginia Infantry, to Miss Belle KELLEY, daughter of Moses KELLEY, Esq., Cashier of the National Metropolitan Bank of that city.

Married: Nov. 28th by Rev. John LANDSTREET, John R. WHITE, Esq., of Locust Thicket, to Mary L. BECKTOL, daughter of the late Dr. Wm. WICKS.

Married: In St. John's Church, Charleston, W Va., on the 19th instant at 3½ p.m., by Rev. C. M. CALLAWAY, rector, assisted by Rev. Edw. Valentine JONES (with two other clergymen in the chancel) Governeur MORRIS, Esq., of Huntington, to Miss Florence WALTON, ward of Hon. S. A. MILLER, and A. A. PRESTON, Esq., to Miss Lollie, eldest daughter of Major N. FITZHUGH, of Charleston, W. Va.

Married: In Leesburg, on Nov. 26th by Rev. Dr. Nelson HEAD, Chas. A. ENGLISH, of Alexandria, Va, to Katie A. COCKRELL, formerly of Winnsboro, South Carolina.

Married: On Thursday, at 12 m. Nov. the 26th at the residence of the bride's father, by Rev. Andrew ROBEY, Mr. J. Calhoun COLVIN, of Prince William, to Lizzie, only daughter of John McCOY, Esq., of Stafford county, Va.

Married: 17th of October, by the same in Washington city, DC, Mr. Andrew COATS to Mrs. Mollie J. BOYER, of Loudoun county.

Married: October 29th 1872, at the residence of the bride's mother, by the Rev. H. E. JOHNSON, Mr. Wm. FLETCHER of Loudoun, to Miss Annie GLASSCOCK, of Fauquier.

Married: November 19th at "Leeds" by same, Mr. Robert WHITACRE to Miss Frances McCARTY, all of Fauquier.

Died: At the residence of her sister, Mrs. Ann S. WOOD, on Friday morning, November 29th 1872, after a brief illness, Miss Catharine S. EDWARDS in the 71st year of her age.

Died: November 25th in Loudoun county, at "Dunbarton," the residence of Major C. H. LEE, Virginia ROSE, daughter of the late Capt. Henry Bassett ROSE, of Alexandria, Va, and wife of Robert J. DELONY, of Georgia.

Wednesday, 11 December 1872   Vol. XVII, No. 25

Died: At his residence in Prince William county, on Sunday, December 1st 1872, Mr. Luther LYNN, in his 52nd year.

County Ct.: Will of Mrs. Mary CHICHESTER proved, received and probate of the same granted to A. M. CHICHESTER, one of her Executors. Benj. NIXON qualified as Admr. of Asbury M. NIXON dec'd.

Wednesday, 18 December 1872   Vol. XVII, No. 26

Died: On the 7th instant, of pneumonia, Mrs. Anna B. MAVIN, in the 68th year of her age.

The Mirror
Wednesday, 25 December 1872   Vol. XVII, No. 27

Died: In Hamilton, on Sunday morning last, 8th instant, Mr. Rodney HATCHER.

Died: Near Hamilton on Thursday last, Mrs. Rebecca TAYLOR, wife of Bernard TAYLOR in the 69th year of her age.

Departed this life, on the 7th inst., at his home near Goresville, William C. LUCKETT, in the 69th year of his age.

Married: On Wednesday, 4th Dec. at St. James Church Leesburg, by the rector Rev. T. R. DAVIS, Miss Bertie M. PANCOAST and Mr. Maurice G. OSBURN, all of Loudoun.

Married: At St. Paul's Chapel, Thursday evening December 12th by Rev. E. T. PERKINS, D.D., Dr. Charles G. EDWARDS, of Leesburg and Isa A. PERKINS, of Louisville, daughter of the officiating minister.

Married: At the residence of the bride's father, 5th inst., by Rev. L. D. NIXON, Mr. John R. CRAVEN, Merchant at Guilford, to Miss Adelaide D. HUMMER, all of Loudoun.

Married: In Charlestown, on Thursday evening last, by Rev. Wm. H. MEADE, Mr. David S. BRISCOE, of Baltimore, to Miss Ella STRAITH, daughter of Dr. John J. H. STRAITH of that town.

Death of Geo. K. FOX, Jr., Clerk of the County Court of Loudoun – occurred at his home in Leesburg about noon on Saturday, Dec. 14, 1872. He entered the Circuit Court office as Deputy to the late Thos. P. KNOX in 1848, being then in the 15th year of his age. In 1862 he was ordered by the Courts to take charge of the Records and remove them to a place of safety. This he did by conveying them to Campbell County, and remaining with them until the close of hostilities in 1865. After the war, being disqualified, under the laws of Congress, from holding office, he resumed his position as Deputy Clerk under Mr. C. P. JANNEY until 1879, when he was again elected Clerk for four years, but has only lived to serve out about ½ of his term. Mr. Fox had just reached his 40th year. He leaves a wife and four young daughters. On Sunday interred in Union Cemetery, attended to their final home by the Masonic fraternity.

Louisville Commercial of 13th inst: The new St. Paul's Chapel was the scene of a wedding of the wedding of the Miss Ida, eldest daughter of Rev. Dr. PERKINS the Rector of the parish, as he gave her in marriage to Dr. Charles G. EDWARDS, of Leesburg Va. The bride was dressed in a full traveling suit of brown poplin. The happy pair left on the 10 o'clock O. & M. train for the east.

Wednesday, 25 December 1872   Vol. XVII, No. 27

Married: In Leesburg on Tuesday morning, Dec. 24, 1872, by Rev. Dr. HEAD, Mr. Silas W. WRIGHT and Miss Julia W., daughter of the late S. M. BOSS, all of this town.

Married: At the residence of the bride's father, on Thursday evening, Dec. 19, 1872, by Rev. J. A. HAYNES, Mr. Henry C. GIBSON and Miss Ellen, daughter of Mr. John ALDRIDGE, all of this county.

Married: On Thursday Dec. 12th at Centreville, Fairfax county, by Elder PURRINGTON, Mr. William SUMMERS to Miss Jennie PALMER, all of Fairfax county.

Married: On Wednesday the 18th instant, at St. Paul's Church, Richmond, Va, by Rev. Chas. MINNEGERODE. Mr. James M. MARSHALL of Fauquier to Miss Alice B. POINDEXTER, of Tennessee.

Married: At Dranesville, Va Dec. 19th 1872, by Rev. Wesley HAMMOND, Mr. William T. GREEN, of Loudoun, to Miss Sarah W. DAY, of Norfolk.

Married: Dec. 18th by Rev. John LANDSTREET, Jno. E. GRUBB Jr. to Margaretta, daughter of Geo. NEAR.

Married: December 19th by Rev. Jno. LANDSTREET, Edgar BALLENGER to Dorcas O., daughter of John THOMPSON.

Married: On the evening of the 18th of December 1872, at the residence of the bride's father, at Fairfax C. H., by Rev. John McGILL, Benjamin EGLIN, of Washington DC, and Miss Nannie THOMAS, eldest daughter of Judge H. W. THOMAS.

Wednesday, 1 January 1873   Vol. XVII, No. 28

Married: On Monday the 23d instant, by Rev. Dr. Jas. L. BRYAN, Frank A. WISE, of Nevada, to Emma P. STEWART, eldest daughter of John T. STEWART, Esq. of Cambridge, Md.

Married: On the 26th instant, at St. James Church, Leesburg by Rev. Mr. OLIN, Prof. Perry Benj. PIERCE, of Manlius, New York and Susan, eldest daughter of James M. WALKER, of Loudoun.

Married: By Rev. J. A. HAYNES, on the 18th inst., Mr. Josephus HOSPITAL, and Miss Mary C. COSTELLO, both of Loudoun.

Married: By the same on the 19th inst., Mr. Thos. Nelson GARRISON and Miss Susan JONES, both of Fauquier.

Married: On the 24th, in Leesburg, by Rev. Samuel GOVER, Aaron W. MONDAY and Josephene E. BALES, all of Loudoun.

Wednesday, 8 January 1873   Vol. XVII, No. 29

Died at "Aron," Dec. 25th Mary Bathurst, daughter of Judge R. H. COCKERILLE, aged 14 years.

Died: At the residence of her husband, near Sudly Mills, on Friday the 3d of January 1873, Mrs. Mary HUTCHISON, consort of Mr. Thos. HUTCHISON, in the 58th year of her age.

Died: On Sunday the 5th inst. in Baltimore, Frank Minor NOLAND, son of R. W. N. NOLAND, Esq., of Middleburg, Loudoun county, in the 19th year of his age.

Died: January 4, 1873 at 4 a.m., at Ayreshire, the residence of his son, Geo. S. AYRE, near Upperville, Fauquier county, Thos. AYRE, in his 80th year. Born in the county of Durham, England, April 23, 1793, emigrated to America, and landed in Baltimore in August 1819.

Wednesday, 15 January 1873   Vol. XVII, No. 30

Married: On the 14th inst. in Leesburg by Rev. S. GOVER, Richard COCKERELL and Sallie HAWS, all of Loudoun.

Died: Near Leesburg, on the 4th of January 1873, Mrs. Maria BELT in the 50th year of her age.

Died: Near Goresville in this county, on Thursday, Dec 26th 1873, Mrs. Nancy MONEY, wife of the late Nicholas MONEY in the 80th year of her age.

Jan. Ct.: Wm. McCRAY qualified as Admr. on estate of late R. G. HATCHER.

Wednesday, 22 January 1873   Vol. XVII, No. 31

Died: On the 21st December at the residence of Mr. Daniel W. HENDRICKS, near Unionville, Mr. Wm. NICHOLS aged about 82 years.

Departed this life in Saline county, Missouri, December 3d 1872, Miss Alcinda GARRET, aged 27 years, daughter of Joseph and Elizabeth GARRETT, formerly of this county.

Died: At Bloomfield, Montgomery co., Md on the 11th instant, Emeline B. JONES, wife of Richard H. JONES. She died in the faith of the Holy Catholic church.

Died: Near Purcellville on the 19th instant of pneumonia, Benjamin BIRDSALL, in the 70th year of his age.

Died: Mary A. MILLS departed this life on Wednesday, 15th inst., in the 72d year of her age. She lived nearly out her three score years and ten.

Married: At "Locust Grove," on Tuesday morning, January 21st 1873, by Rev. Henry BRANCH, William N. WISE, clerk of the circuit court of Loudoun, and Ella, daughter of Mr. Washington VANDEVANTER, all of Loudoun.

Married: On the 16th instant at the residence of the bride's father, by the Rev. Father KEANE, Mr. Frank H. GASSAWAY to Liss [Miss] Bessie, daughter of Judge Geo. W. PASCHAL, all of Washington city.

Married: On the 9th instant, at the Lutheran church near Lovettsville by the Rev. Samuel A. BALL, Mr. John W. MILLS to Miss Anna J. SWANK, both of Loudoun county.

Married: On the same day by the same at the residence of Mr.
Wm. H. VIRTS, near Waterford, Mr. Edward H. DAVIS to Miss
Sallie S. ORME, both of Loudoun county.

Married: On Thursday January 9th in Trinity church, Columbia, S.
C., by the Rev. P. J. SHAND Rector, the Rev. John R.
JOYNER of North California to Miss Carrie F. KNAPP, of Va.

Married: On Jan. 9th 1873, by Rev. John WOLF, at his residence,
Mr. Richard F. POLAND to Miss Eliza RUTTER, all of
Loudoun.

Married: On Thursday morning, January 16th, at the bride's
residence, by Rev. Andrew ROBEY, Mr. Thatcher S.
BRADSHAW, of Memphis, Tenn., to Mrs. Virginia E., widow of
the late Dr. MOORE, of Stafford county, Va.

Wednesday, 29 January 1873   Vol. XVII, No. 32

Married: On the 21st inst. at the residence of Mr. CRIM, Milltown,
Va, by the Rev. S. A. BALL, Mr. Armistead M. CRIM to Miss
Susanna SHOEMAKER, both of Loudoun.

Died: John Young ATWELL, only child of R. M. Johnson and
Carrie V. ATWELL, died in Bloomfield, Nov. 15th aged 1y 5m
11d.

Wednesday, 5 February 1873   Vol. XVII, No. 33

Married: January 23rd by Rev. John LANDSTREET, Robt. E.
BUGGY to Miss Catharine SAGLE, all of this county.

Married: On the 28th inst. by Elder J. FURR, Mr. Burr T. TITUS to
Miss Martha V. HOUSER, all of Loudoun.

Married: On Thursday evening, January 30th 1873, at the bride's
residence, by Rev. Andrew ROBEY, Mr. Asbury EVANS to
Mrs. Emma F. BRAMWELL, all of Stafford County, Va.

Married: On the same evening, by the same, Mr. Robert
KNOXVILL to Mrs. Margaret E. CARTER, all of Stafford
County, Va.

Died: In this town, on Monday evening, February 3, 1873, of
pneumonia, Mrs. Sarah E. SKINNER, wife of Mr. Thos.
SKINNER, in her 46th year. Two brief weeks ago the subject
removed with her husband to Leesburg from Alexandria.

Mr. Phineas OSBURN of this county died at his residence near
Snickersville on Friday last, after a severe illness of about six
weeks. He was in the 70th year of his age.

Wednesday, 12 February 1873   Vol. XVII, No. 34

Married: On the 21st instant, at the Lutheran Church near
Lovettsville, by the Rev. A. BUHRMAN, Mr. John BEATY to
Miss Annie ARNOLD, both of Loudoun county.

Married: On the 28th instant, at the residence of the bride's parents, by Rev. A. BUHRMAN, Mr. Jno. A. FRAZIER, of Illinois, to Miss Alcey V. VINSEL, of Loudoun county.

Married: On the 30th instant, at the residence of the bride's parents, by Rev. A. BUHRMAN, Mr. John L. SMITH to Miss Lizzie E. WIRE, both of Loudoun county.

Married: On the 30th inst. at the Lutheran Church near Lovettsville by the same, Mr. Henry S. SNOOTS to Miss Laura B. V. COLLINS, both of Loudoun county.

Married: On the 30th inst. at the Reformed Church, in Lovettsville by the same, Mr. Wm. E. DINGES to Miss Annabelle GEORGE, both of Loudoun county.

Married: In Warrenton Baptist church, on the 6th inst. by the Rev. J. L. CARROLL, Mr. T. N. FLETCHER, clerk of Fauquier county to Miss Georgia O., daughter of the Rev. Geo. W. LATHAM, late Chaplain of the U. S. Navy.

Died: Mrs. Hebe CHAMBLIN, wife of H. W. CHAMBLIN and last surviving child of Geo. W. GRAYSON, formerly of Warren County, died of consumption, at her residence in Loudoun on the evening of the 7th of January, aged 28 years.

Died: Suddenly of congestion of the heart at her residence in Unison on the 13th ultimo, Mrs. Elizabeth TAYLOR, in the 79th year of her age.

Died: Of consumption, in Illinois, on Saturday morning Jan. 19th, Mr. C. Osborn FOX, in the 48th year of his age.

Died: In Baltimore, on the 6th of February 1873, Alpheus Waters, son of Rev. Alpheus W. WILSON, aged about 5 months.

Died: At the residence of his father, near Hillsborough, on the 19th of January 1873, after a long and painful illness, Mr. Thompson POTTS, in about the 43d year of his age.

Dr. Thomas M. BOND died of pneumonia at his residence in Waterford on Friday night last, aged about 71 years.

Feb. Ct.: Geo. W. MONEY qualified as Admr. of Robt. MONDAY dec'd. Sally HEATER's will admitted to probate and Ebin HEATER qualified as Admr. wwa.

On Saturday morning last, the dead body of a white man, named Wm. D. SMITH, was found lying along the W. & O. Railroad about 4 miles above Leesburg, having been murdered by gunshot wounds. At a point on the railroad just beyond what is known as Bowie's cut and about 1 mile above Clarke's Station, we found the body of the murdered man, lying on its back. ... SMITH was a laboring man, about 40 years of age, and is said to have had a colored mistress, the wife of a negro man named BROOKS, who is now living at Hamilton. Testimony from Reuben JOHNSON (colored) lived on David CARR's farm near Hamilton; Harriet BROOKS (colored) the wife of David BROOKS, had lived for the last two months at Mr. McCOY's at

Hamilton Depot while her husband lives in Mr. Bush FOX's house. BROOKS was committed to jail. BROOKS is a large man, quite black and about 60 years of age. Wife Harriet is not more than 30 years old.

Wednesday, 19 February 1873   Vol. XVII, No. 35

Married: On February 6th by Rev. John LANDSTREET, Wm. D. Thompson to Rosana M., youngest daughter of Wm. GRUBB, all of this county.

Married: In Washington DC, January 22d 1873, by Rev. Thomas G. ADDISON, Mr. Edgar M. PARKER, of Staunton, Va, to Miss Nellie E. PARKER, of Leesburg.

Married: In Georgetown, on the 6th of February 1873, by Rev. Mr. VALIANT, Mr. Walter T. BEETLE, of Baltimore Md, to Miss Carrie E. DOVE, of Loudoun County.

Robt. JOHNSON and John EVERHEART, two old citizens of this county, residing in the Lovettsville neighborhood, died a few days ago at advanced ages, each of them not far from eighty.

Mr. __ DADE, the aged father-in-law of Mr. Christian HEMPSTONE, of this county, died at his residence in Montgomery county, Md, on Monday evening last, at the advance age of 81 years.

David BROOKS the negro man in jail charged with the murder of W. D. SMITH – on Saturday the body of SMITH was exhumed. On Sunday the remains of SMITH were reinterred in the public burying ground a short distance below Leesburg. Supposed that he had some relations living around Staunton Va.

Wednesday, 26 February 1873   Vol. XVII, No. 36

Capt. Geo. W. CHAMBERS, keeper of a restaurant at Harper's Ferry, had a difficulty with Patrick HAGAN on Monday week, the cause and result of which is thus stated: On Monday afternoon HAGAN went into CHAMBER's Liquor store and after words was forceably removed. CHAMBERS returned with a revolver and fired two shots into his head. HAGAN died in about five minutes. Capt. CHAMBERS is by birth a Marylander, though for a number of years a resident of Harper's Ferry. The funeral of the deceased man was held at the Catholic Church on Wednesday. He leaves a widow and several children, one a Priest in the Catholic Church.

Married: On Wednesday, February 5th 1873, at the residence of Mrs. Virginia LUCKETT, Lincoln, Loudoun county, by the Rev. S. A. BALL, Mr. Calvin BUTTS to Miss Margaret LUCKETT, both of Loudoun.

Married: At Markham station, Fauquier on the 20th instant, by Rev. Kinloch NELSON, General L. L. LOMAX and Miss Bettie W., eldest daughter of Dr. Alban S. PAYNE.

Married: At the residence of Nathaniel THOMAS, near Upperville, on Tuesday, Feb 25th 1873, by Rev. Henry BRANCH, Mr. Bushrod L. FOX, of Loudoun, to Miss Virginia, daughter of the late Dr. Wm. WERTENBAKER, of Maryland.

Died: Of consumption, at the residence of Armstead TAYLOR, Esq. on the 13th of February, Lawson G. BEARD, in the 31st year of his age.

Died: Feb. 24th 1873, at "Contest," Prince William county, Mr. Charles VERMILLION, aged 82 years and 10 days.

Death of Dr. W. P. WITHEROW – at his residence in Martinsburg W Va on Thursday last. Several months of each year spent in his professional duties in Leesburg.

Wednesday, 5 March 1873   Vol. XVII, No. 37

Married: On Wednesday evening, February 26th 1873, near Farmwell Station, at the residence of the bride's mother, by Rev. L. D. NIXON, Mr. Henry A. FEASTER, and Miss Susan A. BAUKMAN, all of Loudoun.

Married: At the residence of the bride's father, Feb. 25th 1873, by Rev. L. D. NIXON, Mr. James M. KETTLE to Miss Sarah Jane DONOHOE, all of Loudoun.

Married: By Elder J. A. HAYNES, on the 20th instant, K. B. COLE and Miss Sarah Jane HIXSON, both of Loudoun.

Married: On Thursday the 12th of December 1872, at "Mt. Prominent," near Aldie, the residence of the bride's mother, by the Rev. Dr. HOUGH, Edgar ISH, formerly of Texas, to Permelia Currell, eldest daughter of Capt. John LYNN, dec'd.

Died: At his residence in Loudoun, of pneumonia, on the 15th of February 1873, Mr. Gibson GREGG, in his 68th year of age.

Died: In Washington, on Friday morning, February 28th, Mamie, wife of James S. DAVIS, and daughter of F. A. LUTZ, in the 23d year of her age.

Died: At his residence in LaFayette county, Missouri, on Friday morning, the 21st of February 1873, Major James BEST, formerly of Loudoun county, aged 66 years.

Wednesday, 12 March 1873   Vol. XVII, No. 38

Married: By Rev. John LANDSTREET, March 4th, Mr. John LODGE, of Ohio, to Miss Kate M., eldest daughter of Mr. Benjamin LESLIE, of Hillsboro.

Married: On the 29th of February at the residence of the bride's father, near Darnestown, Md, by Rev. James S.

HENDERSON, Mr. Edgar D. VINSON to Miss Mary V., daughter of Mr. Wm. H. RICE, all of Maryland.

Died: At the residence of Mrs. DAUGHTRY, in Monroe, La, on the 25th of February 1873, of Meningitis, Mr. Robt. D. HOUGH, son of Mrs. E. T. HOUGH of Leesburg, in the 23d year of his age.

Died: At the residence of his sister, Mrs. S. L. DELANY, at "Oak Hill," near Leesburg, on the 6th instant, Dr. Thos. J. VILLARD, a native of Georgetown, DC, in the 48th year of his age.

Died: At his father's residence on the 14th of February 1873, Mr. Charles A. RITICOR, in the 32d year of his age.

Died: At the residence of her parents, three miles south of Leesburg, on Thursday the 6th of March 1873, Miss Rebecca HENDERSON, daughter of Mr. Charles HENDERSON, in the 20th year of her age.

County Ct: Will of Lawson G. BEARD dec'd. admitted to probate. Eli W. and Wm. G. BIRDSALL qualified as Admr. of Benj. BIRDSALL. Chas. W. JOHNSON qualified as Admr. of Robt. JOHNSON dec'd. Jas. F. RINKER qualified as Admr. of Jos. HOUGH dec'd. W. H. BOYER qualified as Admr. of John BOYER dec'd. H. F. SAFFER qualified as Admr. of Jas. H. WHALEY dec'd. Elizabeth C. THOMPSON qualified as Admx. of Saml. P. THOMPSON dec'd. James W. COX qualified as Admr. of Samuel COX dec'd. Wm. SMITH qualified as Admr. of John EVERHART dec'd. John F. WATERS qualified as Admr. of Peter CRIM dec'd.

Death of N. Carrol MASON – at his boarding house in Alexandria, on Saturday morning last, after nine days illness of pneumonia. Mr. M. was a native of Loudoun and son of the late Temple MASON. He was a lawyer by profession. About five years ago he lost his eyesight. His remains were brought to Leesburg on Monday morning and interred in Union Cemetery.

Mr. Wm. B. DOWNEY, for several years immediately succeeding the war, commonwealth attorney for Loudoun county, and more recently Editor of the *Loudoun Republican*, published in Leesburg, died at the residence of his father, in this county, on Sunday morning last, of consumption, in about his 30th year.

On Monday last, David BROOKS, negro, charged with the murder of Wm. D. SMITH, a white man, on 15th of February 1873, found no true bill and prisoner was discharged.

Wednesday, 19 March 1873   Vol. XVII, No. 39

Married: On the 13th instant, at the M. E. Church in Leesburg, by Rev. W. H. FORSYTH, Mr. Wm. H. BROOKS, to Miss Rosa B. STEADMAN, all of Loudoun county.

Married: By Rev. Mr. BRANCH, Wednesday, March 12th, Mr. T. H. GORE to Miss Mollie S. JANNEY, daughter of the late Dr. N. H. JANNEY, all of Loudoun county.

Married: On Tuesday, March 11th 1873, by the Rev. E. J. WILLIS, Mr. John G. AYERS, of Loudoun county, and Miss Ann Virginia CATHER, of Back Creek, Frederick county.

Married: On the morning of 17th at the St. James Hotel, in Washington, by the Rev. Dr. ADDISON, Solomon HOGE, late of Fauquier co. to Miss Sallie BASHAW, of the same county.

Died: At his residence in Fredericktown, Knox county, Ohio, on January 13th, 1873, L. G. EWERS, in the 72d year of his age, formerly a resident of Loudoun county.

Died: Near Leesburg, On Thursday, March the 6th 1873, of catarrh fever, George L., youngest children of George and Elizabeth JACOBS, aged 1y 8m 28d.

Died: At 332 North Eutaw street, Baltimore, on Saturday, March 8th, Mary Oden, wife of Wm. D. BOWIE, of Prince Georges county, Md.

Mr. Geo. KEENE, of this county, died at his son's residence near Unison, on Friday March 7th 1873, in the 84th year of his age.

Wednesday, 26 March 1873   Vol. XVII, No. 40

The Charlestown Free Press – Miss Mary V. ROBERTS, of Middleway, in this county, was burned to death on Monday night last. The theory is that Miss ROBERTS attempted to retire, and whilst passing through the hall fainted and fell, causing the explosion of the coal oil lamp.

Died: Near Haymarket, Prince William County, on Wednesday the 5th of March, 1873, Mrs. Elizabeth PICKETT, wife of Mr. Sanford W. PICKETT.

Died: In Baltimore on the 21st instant, Alfred POOR in the 45th? year of his age.

Death of Wm. E. HARRISON died at "Fruitland" near Leesburg, the residence of his father-in-law, Mr. Thos. W. EDWARDS, on Saturday evening last in the 40th year of his age, leaving a young wife and four little children.

Wednesday, 2 April 1873   Vol. XVII, No. 41

Married: On Thursday morning, Feb. 27th at the residence of the bride, by Rev. Andrew ROBY, Mr. John W. COOPER, to Mrs. Bettie A. COOPER, all of Stafford county.

Wednesday, 9 April 1873   Vol. XVII, No. 42

Died: In Baltimore on Saturday, the 5th instant, Juliet Leef, aged 17 years, daughter of James S. ROGERS.

Died: At the residence of her brother (Mr. George LICKEY's) near Round Hill, on the 30th of March, Mrs. Margaret VANSICKLER, wife of Emanuel VANSICKLER. She leaves an only child, a daughter.

Wednesday, 16 April 1873   Vol. XVII, No. 43

Married: By Rev. J. A. HAYNES, on the 8th instant, Jno. W. CROUCH, Esq., and Miss Sarah C. THOMPSON.

Married: On the 8th of April 1873, by Rev. J. B. LAKE, Mr. John T. DOWELL and Miss Lavenia ORRISON, both of Loudoun county.

Died: At his residence near Guilford Station, on Sunday morning, March 30, 1873, of pneumonia, Mr. Geo. M. WOODS in the 51st year of his age. Mr. W. had just returned from a visit to his friends in Pennsylvania, where he was seized with disease, and died after a few days illness.

Died: Near Philomont, at the residence of his brother, F. J. NICHOLS, 29th March 1873, Mr. Samuel NICHOLS, in the 66th year of his age.

Died: Mrs. Ary Ann, wife of Chas. ROLLINS, departed this life, April 5th 1873, at her residence in Leesburg, of brain fever.

April Ct.: Alex. McKENZIE, a native of Scotland, declared his intention to become a citizen of the U.S. Will of Rebecca K. WILLIAMS dec'd. admitted to probate with Chas. P. JANNEY as Admr. wwa Jos. B. NORTH was licensed to celebrate the rites of matrimony. Licenses to keep ordinaries were granted to Pamela JACKSON, Jacob E. BOUYER, James REAMER and James SWART.

Adam G. RICKETTS of Frederick County Md tried for the murder of his wife found guilty of murder in the second degree.

Wednesday, 23 April 1873   Vol. XVII, No. 44

No marriages or deaths.

Wednesday, 30 April 1873   Vol. XVII, No. 45

Died: In Leesburg, April 12th 1873, Annie L., daughter of Hezekiah and Amanda M. GARNER, in the 9th year of her age.

Mr. Elisha HOLMES died at his residence near Hughesville, on the 28th inst., in the 63d year of his age.

Wednesday, 7 May 1873   Vol. XVII, No. 46

Married: In Winchester, on Thursday morning, May 1st by Rev. Mr. ___, Mr. Julian A. HUTCHISON (of the firm of Edwards & Hutchison) of Leesburg, and Miss Jennie A., daughter of Mr. G. W. GINN, of Winchester.

Married: At the residence of the bride's brother, Dr. J. W. TAYLOR, in Hillsborough, on Tuesday, April 29th by Rev. Mr. DOLLEY, Dr. Bailey PRICE, of Md, and Miss Laura TAYLOR, daughter of the late Dr. Geo. W. TAYLOR, of Clarke.

Married: On Tuesday, at Rehoboth Church, by the Rev. J. C. DICE, Mr. Geo. W. ADAMS and Miss Orra, daughter of Joseph MOCK, Esq., all of Loudoun.

Died: At the residence of his father, L. M. HUMMER, near Leesburg, on the 21st of April, Richard Ezra, aged 1y 1m.

Died: Near Gum Spring, in Loudoun county, May 2nd, George SAUNDERS, aged 88y 2m. Soldier of the war of 1812.

Died: At the residence of her son A. J. KALB, in Quincy, Illinois, on the 15th of April 1873, Mrs. Susannah KALB, widow of the late Absalom KALB, formerly of Loudoun county, in the 75th year of her age. Her remains were conveyed to Springfield, Illinois and laid beside those of her husband in Oakridge Cemetery.

Wednesday, 14 May 1873   Vol. XVII, No. 47

Married: On the 1st of May, 1873, by the Rev. A. BOURBMAN, Robert L. GEORGE to Miss Florence NEER, both of this county near Lovettsville.

Died: In Washington on Thursday morning, May 8th 1873, Alexander, son of John W. and Susan V. BIRD, aged 1y 8m 8d.

Death of Henry Stout WILLIAMS – died at his residence at Taylortown, on Saturday last, after a few weeks illness of pneumonia.

May Ct.: Margaret C. WOODS qualified as Admx. of Geo. M. WOOD dec'd. Estate of Wm. D. SMITH dec'd. committed to Sheriff. Jno. and Thos. J. NICHOLS qualified as Admr. of Samuel E. NICHOLS dec'd. Will of Elizabeth S. STONE dec'd. admitted to probate, Chas. L. HOLLINSWORTH qualified as Admr. wwa. Will of Eleanor H. WOOD dec'd. admitted to probate, Chas. L. HOLLINGSWORTH qualified as Executor. Will of Thos. AYRE dec'd. admitted to probate, Geo. S. AYRE, qualified as Admr. wwa. Will of Wm. W. POSTON dec'd. admitted to probate, Benj. F. POSTON qualified as executor. Licence granted to Samuel W. SLATER, W. L. BROWN and C. F. McCOY to keep ordinaries at their respective houses in this county.

Wednesday, 21 May 1873   Vol. XVII, No. 48

Married: On the morning of the 15th of May 1873, at the residence of the bride's father, James D. MADDOX, Esq., by Rev. J. Spilman PETTY, Capt. J. Byrd UPDIKE and Miss Alice G. MADDOX, all of Warren county.

Died: Venerable in years, and respected by all who knew her, Mrs. Catharine ORRISON, feel asleep in Jesus, at her home in this town, on Sunday morning last, in the 81st year of her age.

Mrs. B. C. MASON, of Colross, Va, died in Baltimore on the 8th inst.

An accident occurred at Point of Rocks. It appears that about 8 o'clock on Saturday night, Samuel NAGLE and John GRACE, both living in the neighborhood were standing on the track in front of the hotel, with their faces to the east; hearing a train approaching from the west they jumped onto the adjoining track only to come in contact with the westward bound express train. NAGLE had both legs entirely severed from the body and one arm nearly cut off, he died in about an hour after. John GRACE sustained severe injuries.

Wednesday, 28 May 1873   Vol. XVII, No. 49

Married: On the 20th of May at the residence of the bride's father, by Rev. S. S. HEPBRON, Mr. Wm. H. LUCKETT and Miss Sarah J., daughter of Samuel C. LUCKETT, Esq.

Married: In Snickersville at the residence of Dr. Geo. E. PLASTER, on Wednesday morning, May 21st, by the Rev. Mr. MARTIN, Mr. James CRANE, of Jefferson county, West Virginia, to Miss Nellie E. LEITH, of Loudoun.

Died: Of pneumonia, on Sunday morning, May 4, 1873, Ruth H., daughter of Owen and Cecelia H. THOMAS, aged nearly seventeen years.

Died: In this county, May 18th, James HAMILTON, in his eightieth year. He was a soldier in the war of 1812.

Wednesday, 4 June 1873   Vol. XVII, No. 50

Last night at 9:30 o'clock at Belmont, the residence of the bride's father, in Fairfax county, Mr. Cassius F. LEE Jr., of this city, was married by Rev. Mr. MEADE, of Jefferson county, to Miss Mary LLOYD, daughter of Richard LLOYD, Esq. *Alex. Sentinel of Fryday.*

Died: At the residence of Mr. Alfred CLINE, in this town, on Monday morning, June 2d 1873, Miss Annie CLINE, in the 84th year of her age.

Wednesday, 11 June 1873   Vol. XVII, No. 51

Married: On the 4th inst., by Rev. John S. LINDSEY, in St. James Church, Warrenton, Mr. Geo. Albert HURXTHAL, and Miss Nathalie HORNER, daughter of Joseph HORNER, Esq., all of Warrenton.

Married: By the same on the 5th inst., at "Huntley," Fauquier Co, Mr. Thomas SMITH and Miss Elizabeth Eyre SKINNER, daughter of Mr. Jas. K. SKINNER, all of Fauquier Co.

Married: On the 25th inst. at the residence of Mr. STIMMEL, near Monococy Junction, Frederick County, Md, by Rev. Dr. DIEHL, Anton SCHELHORN, of Leesburg, to Miss Joana STIMMEL.

Married: On Tuesday, the 3d inst., at the residence of the bride's parents, near Williamsport, Md. by Rev. Henry EDWARDS, Mr. Mahlon H. RUSSELL, of Hampshire county, W Va (formerly of Loudoun county) and Miss Arabella W. McGILL, elder daughter of Mr. Edward W. McGILL.

Married: In the Lutheran church at Unionville, on the 4th inst., by Rev. A. A. P. NEAL, Mr. Volney P. HILL, of Loudoun county, and Miss Julia A. TRUSSELL, of Jefferson County.

Died: On the 19th of May, at 2, Lifton place, Leeds, England, aged 6y 7m 28d, Virginia May, youngest daughter of James Henry and Eugenie H. BURTON, of Virginia, U.S.A.

Died: In Georgetown, on Monday morning, the 26th ult., Mrs. Eliza J. CAPERTON, wife of Hugh CAPERTON.

Died: In Snickersville, May 24th 1873, Gracie T. MYERS, in the 14th year of her age.

Died: In this city on the evening of Monday, the 2d instant, Mr. George MATHIOT, of the U.S. Coast Survey, in the 54th year of his age. Mr. MATHIOT had been attached to the Coast Survey for 25 years, having had in charge the division of electrotyping.

Died March 17th 1873, near the Grove Church, Mrs. Sarah E. BROWN, beloved wife of Mr. Benjamin BROWN, and daughter of Richard WHITE, Esq., in the 40th year of her age. Member of the M. E. Church South for many years, and husband, children, only surviving sister and her aged father will mourn her loss. Interred in the Grove burial ground.

The St. Louis papers announced the death in that city on the 2d of June of Miss Leo HUDSON, the equestrian actress, whose trained horse Black Bess recently fell with her while playing Mazeppa, injuring itself so badly that it had to be killed. It seems that at the time of the accident, May 10th, Miss HUDSON was more seriously injured than she permitted herself to believe. Born in Leesburg on 22d of March 1843, and was 30 years of age. Her real name was Julia V. HODSON. She was twice married, and was well known in Baltimore, where she owns a house. She died intestate, and her remains were to be brought to Baltimore for interment.

Wednesday, 18 June 1873   Vol. XVII, No. 52

Died: June 6th 1873, Frank Moreland, infant son of James W. and Sallie A. STEADMAN, aged one month.

A man named WATSON, of Jefferson county, W Va died at Lovettsville on Saturday from the kick of a mule. WATSON was engaged in gathering straw in Loudoun for the Halltown paper Mill. On Thursday he was kicked in the stomach and death ensured on Saturday.

Hillsboro, Ohio – Mr. Geo. H. AYRE, of Langolan, Loudoun county, Va carried off one of Hillsboro's fair daughters, Miss Sarah J. BROWN, daughter of Mr. James BROWN. They departed for the Old Dominion on last Wednesday.

Wednesday, 25 June 1873   Vol. XVIII, No. 1

Married: In Snickersville at the residence of Mr. T. M. OSBURN, June 17th 1873, by Rev. J. M. DICE, Dr. Geo. E. PLASTER, of Snickersville to Sally Meade, daughter of Col. James M. TALIAFERRO, of Stafford county, Va.

Died: Philip HOPKINS, of Loudoun county, in the 84th year of his age, departed this life the 15th of June in the town of Staunton, Va, leaving a number of children.

Wednesday, 2 July 1873   Vol. XVIII, No. 2

Married: On the 24th of April 1873, at Foundry M. E. Church by the Rev. H. A. CLEVELAND, Wm. T. SWEET, of Georgetown DC, to Miss Lucy A. WATKINS, near Anacostia, D.C.

Died: At his residence near Bloomfield in this county on Friday the 27th of June 1873, Mr. Herod THOMAS, in his 75th year.

Died: On Sunday morning June 8th 1873, near Goresville, Loudoun county, of consumption, Virginia M. GRAY, in the 25th year of her age.

Mr. William HUNT of this town died on Friday evening last, in about the 70th year of his age. His remains were interred in the Presbyterian burying ground on Sunday morning by Loudoun Lodge of Odd Fellows, of which he was a member.

Wednesday, 9 July 1873   Vol. XVIII, No. 3

Married: On Wednesday, the 25th ult. in the Episcopal Church at The Plains, Fauquier county, by Rev. R. H. McKIM, Rev. John McGILL to Virginia, third daughter of Robert BEVERLY, Esq. of Fauquier county.

Died: At Vienna, Fairfax county, on the 28th day of June 1873, America Independence CANTWELL, wife of Joseph T. CANTWELL, aged 29y 11m 24d.

William J. SMITH of this county, died at his residence near Circleville, on Thursday last, in the 46th year of his age, of consumption.

Wednesday, 16 July 1873   Vol. XVIII, No. 4

Married: At Endora Manse, the 9th of July 1873 by Rev. Henry BRANCH, Dwight RIPLEY, of New York, to Eliza McHatton, daughter of the late R. H. CHINN, of New Orleans.

Married: On the 8th inst., in St. James Church, Warrenton Va by Rev. Jno. S. LINDSAY, Hon. James KEITH, Judge of the Circuit Court of the 11th judicial District, and Miss Lilias Gordon MORSON, of Warrenton, daughter of the late Arthur A. MORSON, Esq. of Richmond Va.

Married: At Mount Vernon Place M. E. Church, South, Washington D.C., June 19, 1873 by Rev. J. W. BOTCLER, Jas. T. HAYNE, and Carrie, daughter of James L. McFARLAND, Esq. of Leesburg, Loudoun County.

Died: At "Raspberry Plains," near Leesburg on Monday morning, July 14th, Miss Sallie HOFFMAN.

Died: At her residence near Lincoln, on the 12th inst., Eliza T., wife of William HOLMES, in the 71st year of her age.

Died: At the residence of her husband, in Middleburg, on Saturday July 12th 1873, Mrs. Fannie C., wife of J. E. BRENNER and daughter of F. J. and Mary E. CRISSEY, of Leesburg in her 33d year. Leaves a devoted husband and three small children.

Died: IN Woodville, Rappahannock County, Va, on the morning of July 11th 1873, Miss Martha T. THOMAS, last surviving aunt of the late Mrs. Maria E. HENDERSON. For many years connected with the Methodist Episcopal Church, South.

Died: In Winchester, on Tuesday evening last, July 8th 1873, Eugenia Howland, aged 10m, daughter of Alice and Wm. G. RUSSELL Jr. and grand-daughter of Rev. Norval WILSON and in Charlestown, on Wednesday evening, July 9th 1873, Cornelia Adaline, aged 1y 11m 13d, daughter of W. W. B. and Belle W. GALLAHER, and granddaughter of Rev. Norval WILSON.

County Ct.: Powers of David J. LEE as Executor of C. F. HANCOCK dec'd. were revoked. Alex. H. LEE qualified as Admr. d.b.n.wwa. John T. ROSS and Joseph THOMAS qualified as Admrs. of Herod THOMAS. Sydnor BENNETT qualified as Admr. of Henry S. WILLIAMS. Will of Wm. J. SMITH admitted to probate with Edward J. SMITH and Henry R. RUSSELL as Exors.

Wednesday, 23 July 1873   Vol. XVIII, No. 5

Married: On the 2nd of July at St. John's Chapel, West End, by Rev. Wm. SPARROW, D.D., assisted by Rev. John AMBLER, Rev. Geo. A. GIBBONS, of Maryland to Miss Laura WHALEY, of Fairfax county.

Married: In Leesburg July 17, 1873, by Rev. S. GOVER, Mr. Wm. H. HUNT to Miss Mary E. BALLENGER, all of Loudoun.

Married: In the Parsonage at Farmwell station, Loudoun, July 15th 1873, by Rev. L. D. NIXON, Mr. John B. McDONALD, of Nova Scotia, to Miss Virginia C. LYON, of this county.

Married: On the 16th inst., at the Parsonage of the M. E. Church, Leesburg, by Rev. W. H. FORSYTH, Theodore RYON, to Miss Annabell CAMPBELL, all of Loudoun county.

Died: At her residence near Aldie, June 15, '73, Mrs. Emsey FURR, wife of Wm. FURR, aged 62, of typhoid fever.

Died: In Baltimore, on Friday, the 18th instant, at 4 p.m. of consumption, Esther Fairfax HEISKELL, wife of J. Monroe HEISKELL, and daughter of Colonel John W. and Louisa Fairfax MINOR, of Greenway, Loudoun Co., aged 25 years.

Wednesday, 30 July 1873   Vol. XVIII, No. 6

Married: At Mount Ida, Alexandria county, at two o'clock Tuesday, by Rev. R. H. McKIM, Rev. Harry M. Melville JACKSON, of Norfolk, Va, to Miss Rebecca LLOYD, daughter of the late John J. LLOYD, Esq.

Married: On the 22nd instant, at Zion Church, Charlestown, W Va. by Rev. Mr. LEAVELL, Rev. Beverley D. TUCKER, of Warsaw, Va to Anna Maria, daughter of the late Colonel John A. WASHINGTON, of Mount Vernon.

Married: At the residence of the bride's father, near Leesburg, July 28th 1873, by Rev. Wm. H. FORSYTH, Albert SHINER to Miss Catherine SHELLHORN.

Died: On the 7th inst., at "Bellmont" her residence in Fauquier county, Mrs. Martha E., wife of Wm. W. CARTER, in the 54th year of her age.

Died: Suddenly, of disease of the heart, at Florence, Italy, on the 16th day of June 1873, Mrs. Anna Maria HORNER, relict of the late Inman HORNER, Esqr., aged 78 years.

Died: June 25th at the residence of her daughter, Mrs. A. M. ROBINSON, in Louisville, Ky, Mrs. Ann Mason BONNYCASTLE, widow of Chas. BONNYCASTLE, late Professor of Mathematics in the University of Virginia.

Died: In Washington on the 23d inst., John Divine, infant son of F. C. and Kate M. SHAW, aged ten months.

Died: Mr. Chas. F. COST, son of Jacob COST died at the residence of his uncle, Mr. Joseph DAVIS, on Wednesday last, 23d instant, near Woodburn, in the 29th year of his age.

Wednesday, 6 August 1873   Vol. XVIII, No. 7

Married: On the 31st of July, by Rev. Wm. H. FORSYTH, Mr. James BROOKS to Miss Annie HAWS, all of Loudoun.

Died: In Omaha, Nebraska, July 22d, 1873, after a lingering illness, Nancy, wife of Mr. Jonathan EWERS, in her 51st year.

Died: In Philadelphia, July 30, Colonel Burgess Ball LONG, of Virginia, in the 78th year of age. Born in Leesburg.

Death of Rev. Wm. G. CROSS – a member of the Baltimore Conference of the M. E. Church, South, died very suddenly on Monday afternoon in about the 50th year of his age. The funeral will take place from the M. E. Church, South, in this town at 10 o'clock this Wednesday morning, attended by the brethren of the Masonic fraternity of which he was a member.

Wednesday, 13 August 1873   Vol. XVIII, No. 8

Married: At the residence of T. B. S. WATSON, near Cartersville, in Cumberland county, Va, on the 5th of August 1873, by Rev. Dr. MORRISON, Mr. Braden E. FOX, of Loudoun and Miss Helen M. CARRINGTON, of the former place.

Died: At the residence of Mrs. SAMPSON, near Culpeper C. H. on Saturday morning last, Burr W., infant son of Powell and Janet HARRISON, of this town, aged about 13 months.

Mr. Wm. G. LEITH of this county died at his residence near Unison, on the 26th of July, in the 60th year of his age.

Mr. Lewis VERMILLION, a native of Loudoun, but for several years a resident of Ohio, died at Aldie in this county, on Friday last. Mr. V. had returned on a visit to his old home, about ten days previously and died suddenly as stated.

Aug. Ct: Saml. S. HIRST and John T. HIRST qualified as Admrs. of Hester HIRST dec'd. Geo. W. HUMMER qualified as Exor. of Thos. N. THOMPSON dec'd. R. H. LEITH and H. N. RECTOR qualified as Admrs. of Wm. G. LEITH dec'd. Chas. A. SMITH qualified as Admr. wwa of John M. THOMPSON dec'd.

Wednesday, 20 August 1873   Vol. XVIII, No. 9

The case of Page McCARTY, charged with the killing of John B. MORDECAI, in a duel, continued from Thursday last, physician Dr. CULLEN was still unable to reason of his wounds to appear to answer, the case continued.

Married: Near Farmwell Station, at the residence of Mr. Jas. R. ELLMORE, August 13th 1873, by the Rev. L. D. NIXON, Mr. Charles E. FLING to Miss Sarah Alice, youngest daughter of Mr. Joseph ARUNDLE, Esq., all of this county.

Died: In Leesburg on Tuesday evening, August 12th 1873, Henry, infant son of Henry and Sallie MORGAN, of Washington city, aged 14 months.

Died: Suddenly in Leesburg, on Wednesday morning, August 18th in the 59th year of her age, Mrs. Mary A. FURLONG consort of Mr. John FURLONG, of Alexandria.

Died: On the 30th ulto. at the residence of her son, H. Lewis TRUNDLE in Little Rock, Arkansas, Mrs. Christiana TRUNDLE, consort of Hezekiah TRUNDLE, late of Montgomery county, Md, in the 79th year of age.

Died: At Willow Island, Pleasants county, W Va, on the 26th of July 1873, Mrs. Alice HAMMAT, wife of Giles HAMMAT, and mother of John W. HAMMAT, formerly of Leesburg.

Wednesday, 27 August 1873   Vol. XVIII, No. 10

Died: On Thursday morning, August 7th 1873, near Goresville, Willie SEWELL, in the 3d year of his age.

Died: At Leavenworth the residence of her daughter Mrs. John L. POWELL, after a painful illness of nearly four months, Mrs. Sarah GRADY, wife of the late Dr. E. B. GRADY, in the nineteenth year of her age.

The dead body of Elijah MARLOW, an old man 72 years of age, was found in the woods a short distance from Purcellville, on Wednesday evening last, Mr. M. left the house of a neighbor at one o'clock in the afternoon to return to Mrs. BIRDSALL's, where he made his home, and his body was found between 5 and 6 in the evening. Death from natural causes.

A young negro man named PARKINSON died in this town, on Friday, and was buried Saturday afternoon by the Order of Colored Sons of Temperance, of which he was a member.

Alfred MARTIN was found dead in the county road a few hundred yards from the house of Robert TOMPKINS in the neighborhood of Melrose Station on the night of the 20th inst. A bullet had entered his head above the right ear. The verdict of the jury was that he came to his death by a pistol in the hands of Charles McBLAIR. McBLAIR is the son of Adjutant General McBLAIR of Maryland.

Edward E. COOKE died suddenly Thursday last. He died in his sleep. *Charlestown Free Press, 23d.*

Wednesday, 3 September 1873   Vol. XVIII, No. 11

Died: At the residence of Wm. H. SCHOOLEY, on the 8th of August 1873, Stephen Sands STOCKS, in his 58th year.

Died: At Oakfield, Loudoun county, the residence of Jno. P. DeBUTTS, on the 30th of August 1873, John Pendleton DULANY, youngest son of Col. Dan. F. DULANY.

Death of Wm. H. FRANCIS – died at his residence near Middleburg of cancer of the stomach on the 20th of August in the 59th year of his age.

Wednesday, 10 September 1873   Vol. XVIII, No. 12

Married: August 14th 1873, by the Rev. J. C. DICE, Mr. Burr M. WILDMAN and Miss Lizzie LOVELESS, all of Loudoun Co.

Married: At "Avon View," the residence of the bride's father, in Jefferson county, on Thursday, August 28th 1878 by Rev. John LEE, Milton ROUSE to Miss Mary C. OSBURN, daughter of Logan OSBORN, Esq.

Died: At the residence of her husband, near Hamilton Station, W. & O. RR, after a lingering illness, Mrs. Alcinda WARNER, wife of George WARNER, Esq., aged sixty years.

Died: In Hamilton, on Friday, August 29th 1873, Winton, infant son of Mrs. Laura and Dr. J. D. HARMAN, aged one year.

Died: In Aldie, Friday morning Sept. 5th 1873, at the residence of her grandfather, Capt. John MOORE, Margaret Fleming, daughter of J. E. DOUGLASS, of Alexandria, aged 17y 8m.

Died: September 3d, in the 87th year of her age, at the residence of her son-in-law, Rev. Nicholas LEWEN, Mrs. Catharine A. MINOR, relict of the late col. Wm. MINOR, of Virginia and mother of Col. John W. MINOR, of this county.

Died: At his residence in this county, on the 31st of August, Mr. George W. HUNTER, aged 64y 8m.

Died: Sunday, August 31st, Mary Rust, aged seven months, infant daughter of William V. and Blanche MOSS, formerly of Loudoun. She had been sick only a short time and died last night about 12 o'clock, of spasms. *Hannibal (Mo.) Courier.*

County Ct.: Will of George W. HUNTER admitted to record. Will of Agnes TAYLOR admitted to probate with Maria L. POWELL as Admx. wwa. Estate of Martha J. LEWIS committed to Sheriff for settlement. Letters of Administration granted Maria L. POWELL on estate of Sarah GRADY dec'd. Charles A. SMITH qualified as Admr. of Orrel THOMSON dec'd.

Wednesday, 17 September 1873   Vol. XVIII, No. 13

Married: August 21st 1873, by Elder A. B. FRANCIS, John F. POSEY to Elizabeth A. POSEY, both of Prince William county.

Married: September 9th 1873, by the same, Benj. MIDDLETON, formerly of Yorkshire, England, now of Fairfax county, to Miss Sarah E. ROBEY, of Loudoun county.

Married: By the Rev. J. B. LAKE on the 11th inst., at the residence of Major G. W. NOLAND, Mr. Jno. C. ODELL, of Delphi, Indiana and Miss Lizzie R. NOLAND, of Loudoun county.

Married: At St. James Church, Leesburg, on Tuesday morning, the 16th of September 1873, by the Rev. R. T. DAVIS, Mr. Joseph C. MILLAN, of Jefferson, Texas, and Miss Annie Thomas, only daughter of Fenton M. HENDERSON, Esq. of the former place. At the conclusion of the services the friends of the bride repaired to the residence of her aunt, Mrs. Sally M. LEE for feasting.

Wednesday, 24 September 1873   Vol. XVIII, No. 14

Married: On the 10th of September, by the Rev. W. W. CAMPBELL of First Presbyterian Church of Gettysburg, Louis D. WINE, of Washington DC, to Miss Lucy, daughter of James McCREARY, Esq., of Gettysburg, Pa.

Died: At her residence near Leesburg, on the 20th instant, after a long and painful illness, Mrs. Mary E. WYNKOOP, relict of the late William C. WYNKOOP, leaving two daughters.

Died: Near Hillsboro, at the residence of his mother, Mrs. Eliza NEER, on the 2d inst. Edward H. NEER, in his 47th year.

Died: On the 5th instant, Jos. WILLIAMS, son of John H. WILLIAMS, of Loudoun co. aged 18 years.

Dr. Thomas MILLER physician of Washington, died of heart disease at his residence in that city on Saturday morning, Native of Virginia. and has many relatives living in this county.

Wednesday, 1 October 1873   Vol. XVIII, No. 15

Married: On the 30th of September by the Rev. Jas. M. FOLLANSBEE, Mr. George R. KIDWELL, of Washington DC, to Miss Annie F. LUCKETT, of Loudoun county.

Died: At the residence of her nephew, Jas. M. KILGOUR, Esq., near Hillsborough, on Sunday, Sept. 28th, Miss Charlotte KILGOUR, at an advanced age. Her remains were conveyed to Rockville, Md, to be laid away among her ancestors in the family burying ground.

Mr. Alexander P. BRECKENRIDGE Sr., of Loudoun, died at the residence of his daughter in Hamilton, on Saturday, in the 75th year of his age.

Dr. Thomas MILLER died in Washington city. He was born in Port Royal, Caroline county, Va on 18 February 1806, and was 67 years of age. He was the son of Major MILLER, who went with his family to Washington during the administration of Pres. Madison and was attached to the Navy Dept. ...His funeral took place at the Church of the Epiphany on Wednesday.

Edward HUGHES, aged about 20 years, employed by Mr. A. G. SMITH, was taken sick with typhoid fever and while delirious wandered off. Found in about three feet of water on Goose Creek. Buried in the graveyard adjoining the "Free" Church.

Wednesday, 8 October 1873   Vol. XVIII, No. 16

Married: At the residence of Col. Gabriel VANDEVANTER, the bride's father, on Thursday morning, October 2d, by Rev. Mr.

HEPBORN, Mr. T. D. MILTON and Miss Lillie VANDEVANTER.

Married: On the 22d ultimo, at the Lutheran Parsonage, in Frederick city, by the Rev. Dr. DIEHL, Jacob P. HESSER, of this county, to Miss Mollie E. MERCER, of Virginia.

Married: On the 25th ultimo, at the Lutheran Parsonage, in Frederick city, Md, by Dr. DIEHL, Franklin A. T. MERRIMAN, of Frederick co. Md to Miss Sarah E. BOOTH, of Loudoun county.

Died: At the residence of his grandmother, Mrs. Mary ATTWELL, in Leesburg, on Monday morning, Oct. 6th 1873, of croup, Willie E., only child of John H. and Rachel GOODWIN, of Washington city, aged nine months and five days.

Wednesday, 15 October 1873   Vol. XVIII, No. 17

Married: In the Parsonage at Farmwell Station, on Thursday October 9th 1873, by Rev. L. D. NIXON, Mr. James L. MILLS to Miss Amelia F. GARDNER, all of Loudoun co.

Married: At St. Peter's Church, Poolesville, Md, Oct. 1st by Rev. Dr. McCABE, Dr. W. O. OVERFIELD, of Prince George's county, Md to Miss Lillie TALBOTT, of Georgetown, DC.

Married: Near Belmont at 7 o'clock in the evening of the same day by the same at the residence of the bride's father, Mr. Charles P. GREEN, of Georgetown, DC, to Miss Mollie E., only daughter of Thomas W. and Nancy E. MUSE, of this county.

Died: At the residence on the 18th of September of dropsy of the chest, Jonas W. POTTS, son of Edward D. and Eliza POTTS in the 42d year of his age.

On Thursday, Mrs. Helen BENTLEY, wife of Mr. Edgar L. BENTLEY died suddenly. On Saturday her remains were borne to Union Cemetery.

Wednesday, 22 October 1873   Vol. XVIII, No. 18

Married: On the 14th of October, in Grace Church, Berryville, by the Rev. T. F. MARTIN, John O. CROWN, editor of the *Clark Courier*, and Sadie J. SMITH, granddaughter of the late Col. Treadwell SMITH, of Clarke county.

Married: At the parsonage of the M. E. Church, October 1st, by Rev. W. H. FORSYTH, John REEVES to Miss Lydia C. VIRTZ, both of Loudoun county.

Married: On the 15th inst., by the Rev. Jas. M. FOLLANSBEE, Mr. A. S. ADAMS, of Danville, Va., to Miss Hattie R. ATWELL, of Leesburg.

Married: On the 15th instant, in the Second Presbyterian Church, Alexandria, by the Rev. E. H. CUMPSTON, assisted by Rev. J. D. BULLOCK, D.D., Edward CUMPSTON Jr., of Washington DC, to Anna Bartleman, daughter of G. W. D. RAMSAY, Esq.

Married: On the 15th instant, at Trinity Church, Washington DC, by the Rev. Wm. McGUIRE, father of the bride, W. A. SMOOT, of Alexandria, to Bettie C. McGUIRE.

Died: At his residence in this county, on Thursday, the 21st of August 1878, Mr. Wm. STOCKS, in the 89th year of his age. Mr. S. was a soldier in the war of 1812.

Wednesday, 29 October 1873   Vol. XVIII, No. 15

Died: On the 7th and 8th of October, Geneva and Gennetta, infant twin daughters of Jos. W. and Amanda HOWELL, aged about six weeks.

Married: At Mt. Middleton, Loudoun county, October 8th 1873, by the Rev. R. T. DAVIS, John O. JORDAN, Esq. of Richmond to Alice, third daughter of Thomas ELLZEY, Esq.

Married: At the residence of the bride's father, near Philomont, on Tuesday, the 21st, Samuel N. BROWN to Miss Rebecca NICHOLS. Friends ceremony.

Married: At the residence of Guilford GREGG, on Tuesday evening at 3 p.m., by the Rev. Mr. LAKE, Cornelius C. SHAWEN to Miss Mary GREGG.

Married: In Hamilton, on the 15th inst., at the residence of the bride's father by the Rev. J. C. DICE, Mr. Joseph T. POWER and Miss Mary S., daughter of James H. MUSE.

Mr. George W. JANNEY died at his residence in Baltimore on Sunday evening. Mr. JANNEY was a native and until the past year or two a citizen of this county. He died of typhoid fever.

Wednesday, 5 November 1873   Vol. XVIII, No. 20

Married: On the 28th of October at the chapel of the theological Seminary, Fairfax county, by Bishop JOHNS, assisted by Rev. Arthur JOHNS, Nicholas DAWSON, of Baltimore, formerly of Loudoun county, to Virginia Mason, daughter of General Samuel COOPER, of Virginia.

Married: On Tuesday evening, in Washington, by Rev. T. G. ADDISON, rector of Trinity Church, D. S. GREGORY, of New York, to Lucy F. MAURY, daughter of the late John W. MAURY, of Washington.

Married: At the residence of Mr. James LEE, in the vicinity of Gum Spring, on the 29th of October, 1878, by Rev. L. D. NIXON, Mr. William TAYLOR, to Miss Gustavia Ellen, daughter of the late Richard Y. MORAN, Esq., all of this county.

Married: At Baltimore, Thursday, Oct. 30th by Rev. A. L. MANN, Dr. Townsend HEATON of Ishneming, Michigan, to Miss Florence JANNEY, daughter of the late G. W. JANNEY.

Married: At the Ebenezer Church, on Tuesday, Oct. 28, 1873, by Rev. Dr. HAINES, Rev. C. F. JAMES, of Buchanan, and Miss Alice CHAMBLIN, of Loudoun.

Died: At the residence of his father-in-law, Mr. John WHITEMAN, near Philadelphia, September 27th Hamilton T. McVEIGH, in the 49th year of his age, eldest son of Townsend McVEIGH, Esq. of Loudoun county.

Wednesday, 12 November 1873   Vol. XVIII, No. 21

Married: In Leesburg, on Tuesday morning, Nov. 11, 1873, by Rev. Dr. HEAD, Mr. Robert G. BURKE, of Baltimore, and Miss Hattie Brown JOHNSON, only daughter of Mr. Peter W. JOHNSON, of this town.

Married: In Emanuel Church, at Volcano, West Va., October 28 by Rev. S. T. TOMPKINS, John REID, Esq., of New York city, to Lillie E. MUDGE, dau. of D. C. MUDGE of the former place.

Died: In Washington on the 5th of November 1873, George W., son of the late Alexander and Margaret POLAND, aged 14y 1m.

Wednesday, 19 November 1873   Vol. XVIII, No. 22

Married: On the 11th inst., by Rev. C. T. STEARN, Wm. H. DEMORY, of Loudoun county, to Virginia APSEY, of Frederick city.

Married: Nov. 12th at Poolesville in the Presbyterian Church by the Rev. C. N. CAMPBELL, Mr. B. R. WHITE and Miss Ella F. MATTHEWS, eldest daughter of William MATTHEWS, Esq., all of Montgomery county, Md.

Married: On the 11th of November 1873, by Rev. G. H. WILLIAMS, Mr. John W. COX, of Loudoun, to Miss Annie POWELL, youngest daughter of E. O. POWELL, Esq., of Fairfax county.

Died: In Hillsboro, Va, October 28, 1873, Mrs. Jennie F. POTTS, wife of E. F. POTTS, Esq. and daughter of the late J. P. WINEGERD, of Georgetown, DC.

The remains of the late Gen. W. JANNEY, who died in Baltimore a few weeks ago, were brought to Leesburg on Friday last, and interred in Union Cemetery.

Wednesday, 26 November 1873   Vol. XVIII, No. 23

Married: On the 18th instant, by the Rev. James M. FOLLENSBEE, Mr. Wm. H. FRANKLIN to Miss Laura L. CAYLOR, both of Loudoun.

Married: At Lovettsville, November 6th 1873, by the Rev. A. BUHRMAN, Addison T. PAINTER to Lucretia N. WORKING, of Lovettsville.

Married: By the same at the Lutheran Church near Lovettsville, November 11th, Mr. George W. VIRTZ to Miss Virginia ORME, both of Loudoun.

Married: November 9th 1873, by the Rev. John WOOLF, at the residence of Mr. Carr KNOWLS, Mr. Jos. L. HIBBS to Miss Alverna D. RIDGEWAY, all of Loudoun.

Married: November 11th 1873, by the same at the residence of Mr. John C. PAXSON, Mr. William ARNETT to Miss Mollie BALTHIS, all of Loudoun.

Married: November 13th by the same, at the residence of the bride's father, Mr. Richard A. SPROUSE to Miss Susan J. O'BANNON, all of Loudoun.

Married: On the 18th inst., by the Rev. Dr. HEAD, at the residence of the bride's mother, Mrs. Chas. B. MATTHEWS to Miss Rosalia S. ELGIN, all of Loudoun.

Married: In St. James church, Richmond, November 19, 1873, by Bishop F. M. WHITTLE, Lucy P. WHITTLE, daughter of the officiating clergyman, and Dr. John N. UPSHUR.

Married: On Tuesday evening, Nov. 11th at the residence of the bride's brother, by Rev. Andrew ROBEY, Seth R. COMBS, Esq., of Stafford county, to Miss Elenora S. GORRELL, of Fauquier county, daughter of Reazina S. GORRELL, Esq., of Harford county, Md.

Died: Suddenly in Baltimore on the 23d of November of apoplexy, Mr. Thomas SPATES, aged 54 years.

Died: On Monday night the 10th of the month, at his residence three miles north of Hillsboro, in this county, Edward HARDING, in the 86th year of his age.

Died: At the residence of her father, near Leesburg, on Tuesday evening, Nov. 18th 1873, of consumption, Ellen, third daughter of Joseph and Mary A. RHODES.

Mr. Judson EMERSON, a veteran of the war of 1812, and for many years subsequent, a resident of this town, died at the residence of his son-in-law, Mr. John LIGHTFOOT, near Aldie, on the 20th inst., in the 85th year of his age.

Mr. Samuel CLENDENNING, of Hillsborough, died at his home in that place on Monday last, in the 87th of his age.

Wednesday, 3 December 1873   Vol. XVIII, No. 24

Married: Nov. 12th at St. Peter's Church, Poolesville, Md. by Rev. Dr. Jas. D. McCABE, Richard T. GOTT, M.D., to Allie, daughter of the late Dr. POOLE, all of Poolesville, Md.

Died: At the residence of this mother, near Aldie, on the 21st of November 1873, Henry H., son of Ann V. and James H. GULICK, aged 17y 14d.

Died: Friday, Nov. 28, 1873, in the 71st year of her age, Elizabeth COLEMAN, relict of the late John I. COLEMAN, of "Hayfield," Loudoun county. Member of the Methodist Church.

Wednesday, 10 December 1873   Vol. XVIII, No. 25

Died: At the residence of his father, near Leesburg, on the morning of the 31st of October 1873, William T., oldest son of John W. and Alcinda C. LOVELESS, aged 15y 6m 5d.

Married: Dec. 3d 1873 at the residence of the bride's father, by Rev. J. F. CANNON, Mr. Wm. T. FLING and Miss Ellen V. HENDERSON, both of Loudoun county.

Married: On the 4th inst., in Leesburg, by the Rev. J. M. FOLLANSBEE, Mr. James B. CLIPP, of Jefferson county, W Va, to Miss Virginia BASCUE of Loudoun.

Married: At Guilford, Loudoun county, on the evening of the 4th of December 1873, by the Rev. R. T. DAVIS, Mr. Geo. JOHNSON, of England, and Miss Mary E. CRAMP.

Married: At the Lutheran Church near Lovettsville, November 20th 1873, by the Rev. A. BUHRMAN, Mr. Philip H. SOUDER and Miss Setha HOUGH, all of this county.

County Ct: D. C. NEER qualified as Admr. of Edward H. NEER dec'd.

Wednesday, 17 December 1873   Vol. XVIII, No. 26

Died: On Saturday, November 29th 1873, at her home in Lexington, Ky, of consumption, Addie V. ROSZEL, wife of S. G. ROSZEL (formerly of this town), aged 24 years.

Died: on the 4th inst., at her home near Taylortown, Miss Laura FAWLEY, daughter of Wm. FAWLEY, aged 22y 6m.

Died: At Rolla, Mo, on the 26th of July 1873, Mary E. WADE, in the 54th year of her age.

Died: At the residence of Mrs. Daniel T. WHITE, in this town, on Tuesday morning, of membranous croup, Emma T., daughter of Geo. M. and Theresa R. HIBLER, of Paris, Bourbon county, Ky, aged 5 years.

Married: In Leesburg in the M. E. Church South, on Thursday last, by Father J. J. KAIN, Mr. James A. ALLNUTT OF Montgomery Co Md, and Miss Millie L. MARLOW, of Leesburg.

Married: On December 10th at the residence of Mr. Curtis GRUBB Sr., by Rev. S. S. HEPBRON, Mr. Geo. S. EASTON, of Georgetown, DC, and Miss Rebecca S. GRUBB.

Mr. Thomas GREGG of this county died at his residence near Purcellville on Friday last, in the 60th year of his age.

Wednesday, 24 December 1873   Vol. XVIII, No. 27

Married: On December the 11th at the Bethel Church by the Rev. A. BURHMAN [BUHRMAN], Mr. Wm. F. McKIMMEY and Miss Isabella BEAMER, all of this county.

Married: On the 11th inst., in Saint Stephens Church, Culpeper, Va by the Rev. John S. LINDSAY, Rector of Saint James church, Warrenton, Mr. Maurice W. LAMBERT, of Georgetown DC, and Miss Blanche ASHBY, daughter of Samuel T. ASHBY, Esq. of Culpeper county, Va.

Married: In Alexandria, December 18th 1873, by Rev. L. H. CRENSHAW, Mr. James. T. MAGEATH and Miss Olivia FRANCIS, daughter of Mr. Thomas FRANCIS, deceased, all of Loudoun county.

Married: At Graseland, Fauquier county, December 3, 1873, by Rev. Mr. NELSON, William B. CLAGETT, of Washington DC, and Miss Ella Louisa, daughter of James D. HALL, of Fauquier county.

Married: On the 18th instant, at the residence of Mr. T. T. CRITTENDEN, by Rev. Dr. Jos. BULLOCK, of Alexandria, Henry N. GASSAWAY, of Washington, and Sallie Lee COLEMAN, of Louisville, Ky.

Married: Dec. 18th by Rev. J. F. CANNON, Mr. Geo. M. CORNWELL and Miss Sarah W. KIDWELL, both of Loudoun county.

Died: On Wednesday, the 10th instant, at the residence of Benjamin LESLIE, Esq., Hillsboro, Mr. Simon ELGIN, a deaf and dumb man, from Prince William county, age unknown.

Wednesday, 31 December 1873   Vol. XVIII, No. 28

Married: In Blacksburg, Dec. 23d 1873, by the Rev. W. F. WILHELM, Charles A. SMITH, of Loudoun county, and Miss Allie M. PETERMAN, of Montgomery county.

Married: On the 30th of September, at Merion Mansion, near Haddington, by Friend's Ceremony, Nathan J. BIRDSALL, of Indiana, to B. Elma WORLEY, of Philadelphia, formerly of Waterford.

Married: On the 17th instant, at the residence of Miss KEPHART, in Baltimore city, by the Rev. Dabney BALL, William T. COOKSEY to Miss Lillie FOUT, both of Baltimore.

Married: On Thursday, December 18th at the residence of Mr. Charles W. BUTTS, by Rev. S. S. HEPBRON, Mr. John E. WEBB, and Miss Mary E. BUTTS, both of Loudoun.

Married: At residence of the bride's father, on Christmas Eve 1873, by Rev. J. A. DUNCAN, D.D., Rev. Frank A. STROTHER, of Fauquier county, to Cora F. WINN, of Ashland, Va.

Wednesday, 7 January 1874   Vol. XVIII, No. 29

Married: At the residence of the bride's father, Dec. 23d 1873, by Rev. J. F. POULTON, Alpheus W. STROTHER to Agnes C. SMITH, both of Fauquier county.

Died: Dec. 15th at the residence of her father, Miss Julia Belle THOMAS, youngest daughter of James THOMAS Esq., of this county. Member of the Presbyterian Church in this town.

Died: In Baltimore, on the 20th of December, Samuel McPHERSON, a member of the Society of Friends, formerly of Jefferson County W Va, in the 76th year of his age.

Died: December 3d 1873, Jacob SCHAFFER, aged 69 years. For many years a member of the Lutheran Church. His illness was of but a few hours duration.

Charles BUCHANAN, a negro boy in the employment of Mr. B. G. CARTER was shot and instantly killed on Christmas day by the accidental discharge of his gun. He was about 25 years old.

Wednesday, 7 January 1874   Vol. XVIII, No. 29

Married: At the residence of Oscar G. HEWITT, near Bloomington, Ill, December 24th 1873, by Rev. R. CONOVER, Mr. Charles A. HEWITT, of Elgin, Ill., and Miss Katie B. KNOTTS, eldest daughter of Mrs. Annie E. KNOTTS, of Leesburg.

Died: At the residence of his brother, T. H. H. CHAMBLIN, in Galesburg, Ill., on Dec. 11th 1873, of lung disease, Norval CHAMBLIN, in the 26th year of his age. He was a son of Norval and Sarah T. CHAMBLIN, formerly of Loudoun county.

Mr. Thos. L. ELLZEY died at his residence near Arcola, on Tuesday morning last, after a painful illness of ten days. For a number of years prior to the war he was a Justice of the Peace and at one time a member of the Va House of delegates. Mr. E was in about the 63d year of his age.

William BALES, a well known colored blacksmith of this town, died last week from dropsy. His funeral on Saturday afternoon was largely attended.

Wednesday, 14 January 1874   Vol. XVIII, No. 30

Married: At the residence of the bride's father, near Woodgrove, by the Rev. Mr. DOLLY, on Tuesday evening, Dec. 30th, Mr. Marshall OVERFIELD and Miss Pleasant, daughter of Thompson OSBURN, Esq.

Married: On the 8th instant, in Leesburg, by the Rev. Jas. M. FOLLANSBEE, Mr. John FREY, of Switzerland, to Mrs. Ann E. POTTS, of Loudoun.

Married: At Catoctin Church, on Tuesday, December the 2d, by Rev. H. BRANCH, Mr. Charles Edgar FULTON, to Miss C. Ellen HOPE, all of Loudoun.

Married: At. St. James' Church in Warrenton, Wednesday the 7th inst. by the Rev. J. S. LINDSAY, Dr. J. C. BAYLOR, of Norfolk, to Miss Pattie PEMBERTON, daughter of Gen. John C. PEMBERTON, of Warrenton.

Married: On Thursday, the 8th inst. by the Rev. H. H. WYER, at the residence of the bride's father, J. P. CARRAWAY of Prentiss county, Mississippi, to Miss Fannie F. FANT, daughter of Col. J. M. FANT of Fauquier.

County Ct.: Benj. BRIDGES qualified as Admr. of Elizabeth SHRYOCK dec'd. E. E. STRICKLY qualified as Admr. of Amos JANNEY dec'd. Will of Edward HARDING admitted to probate and that of Samuel CLENDENNING partly proved and continued. N. B. PEACOCK qualified as Admr. of Thos. GREGG dec'd. Ed. ISH appointed Guardian of Frances and Gertrude LYNN. C. P. JOHNSON as Admr. of Robt. W. JOHNSON executed new bond.

Wednesday, 21 January 1874   Vol. XVIII, No. 31

Married: At Pleasant Dale, January 6th by the Rev. J. C. DICE, Mr. Samuel A. LAYCOCK and Miss Ella, daughter of Benjamin BROWN, Esq.

Married: On the 13th inst. at "Way Side" by Rev. J. C. DICE, Mr. John M. COLBERT and Miss Lydia WEADON, of Loudoun county.

Married: On the same day by the same at "Fair View," Mr. William H. WYNKOOP and Miss Sarah M, daughter of Jesse COLBERT, Esq., of Loudoun.

Married: In Grace Church, Berryville, Dec. 23d 1873, by Rev. T. F. MARTIN, George C. SHEPHERD to Miss Ella C., daughter of Col. Benj. MORGAN, all of Clarke county.

Married: Near Leesburg at the residence of the bride's father, Jan 14th 1874 by the Rev. L. D. NIXON, Mr. John W. LAWSON, to Miss Susan R. MILLS, all of Loudoun Co.

Married: At the residence of the bride's parents, January 13, 1874, by Rev. B. P. DULIN, Mr. Albert B. OMEAR, of Loudoun county, to Miss Catharine A. KERNS, of Fairfax county.

Married: At the residence of the bride's parents, by Rev. John McGILL, on the 14th of January 1874, Mr. Wilson H. THOMPSON to Miss Frank A. THOMPSON, all of Fairfax.

Married: In the M. E. Church, South, in Charlestown, on Wednesday afternoon, January 14th 1874, by Rev. W. A. WADE, assisted by Rev. J. W. TONGUE, Mr. Charles G. SKINNER, of Loudoun county, to Miss Lucie M. LOCK, daughter of the late Wm. French LOCK, of Charlestown.

Died: In Pettis County, Mo., January 10th of typhoid pneumonia, Ellen, daughter of the late Patrick McINTYRE, of Leesburg and wife of Humphrey SHEPHERD.

The powers of Alex. SPINKS as Admr. of Jas. SPINKS dec'd. were revoked and the estate committed to the Sheriff.

Mr. Thomas GORE died at his residence near Hughesville, on Sunday morning last, in the 93rd year of his age. Mr. G. was a member of the Society of Friends.

Wednesday, 28 January 1874   Vol. XVIII, No. 32

Married: On the 18th instant, by the Rev. James H. WOLFF, Dr. K. TAYLOR, formerly of this county, to Miss Louisa H. RUNNELLS, of Hampshire.

Married: By Rev. Jas. F. BRANNIN, on the 15th inst., Wm. H. LEWIS of Spottsylvania, to Miss Eugenia L. McCONCHIE, of Fauquier.

Married: On the 3rd inst. by Rev. John TRONE, Wm. R. COLVIN to Miss Laura V. CARRICO, all of Fauquier.

Married: On the 14th inst., by Rev. H. H. WYER, Wm. B. MELVIN to Miss Sopha HACKLEY, all of Fauquier.

Death of Dr. Edgar L. SMITH – a son of Mr. George D. SMITH of this county, died in St. Louis, Mo last week of pneumonia. His remains reached his childhood home on Friday and on Saturday were interred in Union Cemetery, Leesburg.

Mr. John HEATER, a well known thrifty farmer of this county, died at his home opposite the Pt. of Rocks on Wednesday last, at an advanced age.

Mr. Hugh HAGON died at his residence near Farmwell on last Thursday week.

Wednesday, 4 February 1874   Vol. XVIII, No. 33

Married: On the 28th inst. by the Rev. R. T. DAVIS, at the residence of the bride's father, Mr. Thos. R. MOORE, of Petersburg, Va to Miss Helen, daughter of Jas. H. CHAMBLIN, of Leesburg.

Married: On the 3d inst., in Leesburg by the Rev. J. M. FOLLANSBEE, Mr. Ebenezer GRUBB to Miss Mary Alice MYERS, both of Loudoun.

Married: On Tuesday evening, January 27th at the M. E. Church Parsonage, by the Rev. Wm. H. FORSYTH, Vincent PITMAN, Esq. to Miss Amelia V. NEWTON, of Leesburg.

Married: At the residence of the bride's parents, Montgomery county, Md, on the 27th instant, by Elder Jos. FURR, Mr. Samuel C. WHITE and Miss Maggie CHISWELL.

Married: Near Aldie, on the 8th of January, at the residence of the bride's parents, Mr. Chas. SAUNDERS to Miss Mary J., daughter of Melvin JOHNSON, all of Loudoun.

Married: At the residence of the bride's father, on the 27th of January by Rev. J. A. HAYNES, Henry H. RATRIE, Esq. and Miss Alice S. FOLEY, both of Loudoun Co.

Married: At Woodlawn Baptist Church, Fairfax county, January 28th 1874, at six p.m. by Rev. C. H. RYLAND, Joseph W. DILLON and Fannie J. GREGG, all of Loudoun county.

Died: Near Waterford, January 25th, John BURGORYE, aged 64 years.

Departed this life, on Sunday, the 25th of January, at the residence of Wm. B. BRUCE, in Charlotte County, Va, Miss Elizabeth H. MAJOR, late of Cornwall, England, aged 60 years. Member of the Protestant Episcopal Church. Her remains were brought to Leesburg and interred in the Union Cemetery on Friday afternoon.

Died: At Purcellville, on the 29th inst. of pulmonary consumption, Mary S. GREGG, aged 17y 4m, only child of the widow of the late Thomas GREGG.

Died in St. Louis, Missouri, on Tuesday the 20th of Jan. 1874, Dr. Edgar L. SMITH, son of George D. SMITH, Esq. of Loudoun county. ... His remains were brought to his native state and by the side of his mother were laid in the cemetery at Leesburg.

Wednesday, 11 February 1874   Vol. XVIII, No. 34

Married: On Wednesday, January 28th, at Trinity Church, Elizabeth, N. J., by Rev. F. M. McALISTER, Wm. S. HOGE, formerly of Loudoun, to May B. STEARNS, daughter of the late Rev. John STEARNS, formerly of New York City.

Died: Near Hillsborough, of Monday, January 26th, Johnnie, son of Thomas E. and Mary J. CAMP, after a long and unusually severe illness

Died: On the 4th instant, at "Glen Owen," Loudoun county, the residence of Robert BENTLEY, in the 68th year of her age, Elizabeth C., relict of the late P. Henry CABELL, of Lynchburg, Va.

Died: On the 3d instant, in Frankville, Loudoun county, Willie Leandar, infant son of Charles and Mary E. BURGESS, aged 11m 7d.

Died at the residence of his son-in-law, Eli M. PIERCE, in Wayne township, on the night of the 16th inst., Mahlon SCHOOLEY in the 86th year of his age.

We announce the death of Josiah R. TAYLOR, Esq. which took place at the residence of his brother, Dr. J. W. TAYLOR in Hillsborough a little before 12 o'clock on the night of the 3d

inst. Mr. TAYLOR was the found. For several years editor of the *Mirror*. A lawyer by profession. Mr. TAYLOR was in the 48th year of his age. On Thursday his remains were interred by the side of his ancestors at Arnold Grove.
Court Ct.: Ella V. BOGER's Guardian ordered to execute new bond. Will of Saml. CLENDENNING Sr. admitted to probate, Jos. GRUBB and Samuel CLENDENNING Exors. Will of Jno. HEATER admitted to probate, Rich'd. HEATER Executor. Jno. M. CHAMBLIN qualified as Admr. of Hannah KEYS dec'd. Chas. T. BIRKBY qualified as Admr. of Eliz'h. H. MAJOR. Jno. W. SAUNDERS qualified as Admr. of Hugh HIGGINS. Will of Elizabeth HEFFNER admitted to probate, Geo. M. RITCHIE Executor. Samuel D. HARDING qualified as Admr. wwa of Edward HARDING dec'd. Will of Lucy N. FONTAINE dec'd. partly proved and continued.

Wednesday, 18 February 1874   Vol. XVIII, No. 35

Married: On the 5th of Feb. 1874, by Elder Joseph FURR, in the New Valley Meeting House, Loudoun county, Mr. Edgar F. BURCH to Miss Mary V. WYNKOOP, all of Loudoun.
Married: At the residence of the bride's parents near Rectortown, on the 29th of January, by the Rev. __ LINTHICUM, Mr. S. F. JACKSON, to Miss Carrie H. REVENCOMB, all of Fauquier.
Married: On the 10th inst., by Rev. J. L. CARROLL, Mr. James F. GRIFFITH and Miss Harriet A. LUNSFORD, all of Fauquier.
Married: On the same day, by the same, Mr. Sidney LIMERICK and Miss Mildred JACKSON, all of Fauquier.
Married: On the 12th inst., at the residence of the bride's mother, near Goresville, by the Rev. Mr. NORTH, J. Franklin COMPHER to Ann Virginia, daughter of the late Jas. SIMMONS.

Wednesday, 25 February 1874   Vol. XVIII, No. 36

Married: On the 18th instant at the residence of the bride's mother, in Newton, Frederick county, Va, by Rev. G. STEVENSON, C. W. PERRY to Miss Nannie E., daughter of the late Rev. D. SHOAFF, of Baltimore Conference, M. E. Church, South.
Married: At "Mary Hill" near Rappahannock Station, on the 19th inst., by Rev. H. H. WYER, Horace JOHNSON, Esq., and Mrs. Mary E. JENNINGS, all of Fauquier.
Married: On Tuesday, Feb. 17th at the residence of Washington MUNROE,

Esq., near Unison, Loudoun County, by Rev. H. H. KENNEDY, Mr. Joseph M. HOWELL to Miss Rosalie S. JACOBS, all of Loudoun County.

Married: On Thursday, Feb. 19th at the residence of the bride's father, near Dover, Loudoun county, by Rev. H. H. KENNEDY, Mr. Wm. S. TIFFANY to Miss Tracy H. HIXON, all of Loudoun.

Married: On the 3d of February 1874, at the Presbyterian Manse, Charlestown, by the Rev. A. C. HOPKINS, John POPE to Miss Mary E. WATKINS, all of Jefferson county, West Virginia.

Married: On January 26th at Rocky Mount, Louisiana, by Rev. A. R. BANKS, Robert W. NORTH, of Mt. Holly, Arkansas, formerly of Charlestown, to Miss M. Amanda MORTON, daughter of J. W. MORTON, Esq.

Married: On the Bridge at Harper's Ferry, January 1st, by Rev. J. A. McFADEN, Mr. Jas. HINDMAN, of Alabama, and Miss Ginnie MAUZY, of Loudoun county.

Married: At Austin, Ark., Feb. 12th 1873 by the Rev. Mr. WEBB, S. W. YOUNG, formerly of Loudoun county, to Miss Sallie J. CAYLE, of Austin, Ark.

Married: At Langley, on the 16th inst. by the Rev. D. O'KANE, Mr. Aaron T. BEANS to Miss Martha KERNS, all of Fairfax county.

Married: In Alexandria, Va on the 18th inst., by the Rev. Joseph L. PURINGTON, Mr. John N. KERNS to Miss Martha A. KENDRICK, all of Fairfax county.

Married: In Waco, Texas, at the residence of the bride's father, on the 8th inst., by the Rev. R. T. BROWN, Mr. M. L. DISMUKES to Miss Ada B., second daughter of Dr. W. P. GUNNELL, formerly of Fairfax C. H., Va.

Married: On the 12th inst., by Rev. Jno. LANDSTREET, at the residence of Jas. BROWN, Esq., Mr. Oscar F. PIERCE, late of Loudoun county, to Miss Maria E. BROWN, of Piedmont, Hampshire County, W. Va.

Died; Of bronchitis, January 30, 1874, at the residence of her son, near New Baltimore, Fauquier county, Mrs. Frances ALLISON, aged 69 years.

Died: At the residence of her son-in-law, Charles T. GREEN, in Warrenton, on Thursday the 19th of February 1874, Mrs. Susan M. YOUNG, in the 74th year of her age.

Died: In Shepherdstown, on 2d of February, Mrs. Eliza HARPER, widow of the late Col. Charles HARPER, aged 65 years.

Died: At his residence, Baxter Springs, Kansas, December 16th 1873, of consumption, Rodney C. HOWELL, son of Amy W. and Craven HOWELL, aged 35 years 23 days. He was formerly of Loudoun Co, but had been a residence of Baxter for nearly five years.

Mr. Humphrey SHEPHERD, formerly of this county, died at his home in Pettis county, Mo. on the 19th of January of disease of the heart. Nine days previous he lost his wife (nee Miss Ellen McINTYRE) of pneumonia.

Wednesday, 4 March 1874   Vol. XVIII, No. 37

Married: At the residence of the bride's sister, in Leesburg, on Thursday, February 26th 1874, by the Rev. R. T. DAVIS, Maj. Burr P. NOLAND, of Middleburg, and Corie C., daughter of the late Burr W. HARRISON, of this town.

Married: On the 26th instant, in Leesburg by Rev. J. M. FOLLINSBEE, Mr. Edward M. KESSLER, of Frederick County Md to Miss Alvina FEAGINS, of Loudoun.

Married: On Tuesday, February 17th at the residence of Washington MONROE, Esq. near Unison, Loudoun county, by Rev. H. H. KENNEDY, Mr. Joseph HOWELL to Miss Rosalie S. JACOBS, all of Loudoun county.

Married: On Thursday, Feb. 19th at the residence of the bride's father, near Dover, Loudoun county, by Rev. H. H. KENNEDY, Mr. Wm. S. TIFFANY to Miss Tracy H. HIXON, all of Loudoun.

Married: In the Baptist Church of Fredericksburg, on Tuesday, the 17th February 1874, by Rev. Thos. S. DUNAWAY, Mr. C. F. FORD of Fairfax county, Va, to Miss Sallie B. RICHERSON, of Caroline county, Va.

Married: At the residence of the bride's parents on the 26th of February 1874 by the Rev. Geo. H. WILLIAMS, John S. MARTIN, Esq. to Miss Sarah Ann WASHBURNE, all of Fairfax county.

Married: On Tuesday, February 24th 1874 at the residence of the bride's father, by Rev. L. C. MILLER, Charles Z. SEDWICK, Esq., of Washington, DC, to Miss Mary M., daughter of T. C. McLEAREN, Esq. of Warrenton, Va.

A little boy, some four or five years of age, son of Mr. Samuel McAUTHER, residing near Hillsborough, was killed one day last week by a kick from a horse.

Wednesday, 11 March 1874   Vol. XVIII, No. 38

Married: On the 10th of February, at the Bethel Church, near Lovettsville, by the Rev. A. BUHRMAN, Mr. Chas. L. COMPHER to Miss Mary A. SNOOTS, all of this county.

Married: By the same, February 24th, Mr. Jacob F. COMPHER to Miss Mollie J. MORGAN, all of this county.

Died on the 27th of February in Lovettsville, Mrs. Sophie GOODHART, wife of J. W. GOODHART, in her 57th year.

Died: At her residence near Hamilton, on Wednesday morning, the 25th day of February 1874, Mrs. Jane E. ROGERS, widow of the late Samuel ROGERS, in about the 62d year of her age.

Wednesday, 18 March 1874   Vol. XVIII, No. 39

Died: At the residence of her parents in Washington city, on Tuesday, the 3d of March 1874, Mrs. Anna SILCOTT, wife of James B. SILCOTT, in her 26th year. Born and reared in city of Washington and became a bride on 6th of August 1873, after which she with her husband came to Loudoun.

County Ct.: Will of Jane E. ROGERS dec'd. admitted to probate. Jas. H. JONES qualified as Guardian of Henrietta, John W. and Arthur Lee JONES. Jno. M. FRIDAY licensed to celebrate the rights of matrimony.

John MURPHY, a negro man about 30 years of age, and formerly belonging to the late John GOVER, attempted suicide on Monday evening last, in the upper room of Chas. ANDERSON's (col'd.) house in this town. He is still alive at the hour we go to press.

Robt. H. MILLER, Esq. an old citizen of Alexandria, died in that city on Monday night. He had a number of relatives in this county.

Wednesday, 18 March 1874   Vol. XVIII, No. 39

Married: On Wednesday, March 11, at the parsonage of the M. E. Church by the Rev. Wm. H. FORSYTH, Wm. W. REEVES, Esq. to Miss Mary R. FRY, both of this county.

Died: At her father's residence near Philomont, on the 7th of March, Kate MONROE, aged 17 years.

Died: Near Philomont on the 7th of March, Mrs. Hannah TAVENNER, wife of Fielden TAVENNER, in the 63d year of her age.

Wednesday, 25 March 1874   Vol. XVIII, No. 40

Married: At the residence of the bride's father, near Hamilton, on the 17th instant, by the Rev. J. C. DICE, Mr. Jas. McFARLAND to Miss Jennie EVERHART.

Died: At the residence of her son-in-law, Mr. John WALRAVEN, in Jefferson County, West Va. on Sunday the 15th inst., Mrs. Catharine M. BACKHOUSE, widow of the late George BACKHOUSE, in the 73d year of her age.

Mr. Francis E. THRIFT of this county died at his home near Ball's Mill, on Tuesday morning last, in about the 66th year of his age.

Wednesday, 1 April 1874   Vol. XVIII, No. 41

Married: On the 11th ulto. at the Dill House, by Rev. ___ LITTLETON, Nelson BEAMER, of Loudoun County, to Mrs. Carrie CLARK, granddaughter of the late Joseph M. PALMER, of Frederick city.

Married: In the Episcopal Church at Charlestown, on Thursday afternoon last, March 26th 1874, by Rev. C. E. AMBLER, assisted by Rev. W. H. MEAD, Mr. George W. LAMBRIGHT, of

Knoxville, Tenn, formerly of Charlestown, to Miss Annie H. KEARSLEY, eldest daughter of Maj. G. W. T. KEARSLEY, of that place.

Married: In the Episcopal Church at Charlestown, on Tuesday afternoon, March 24th 1874, by Rev. W. H. MEADE, Mr. John M. HOWELL and Miss Fannie S. LAFITTE, all of that place.

Wednesday, 8 April 1874   Vol. XVIII, No. 42

Florence, a little daughter of R. E. MADDOX, of Warrenton, a few days ago, pulled from the stove upon her person a pot of boiling coffee. After suffering intense pain for 36 hours, death came to her relief.

Died: At her residence in Hamilton, on Thursday evening, at 10 minutes past seven o'clock, Mrs. Elizabeth, wife of Hiram TAVENNER, aged 64y 1m 21d. Mrs. TAVENNER was born in Massachusetts and was a cousin of Wm. Cullen BRYANT.

Died: Near Goresville, Va on the 29th of March 1874 of paralysis, Mr. Adam LOY, in the 64th year of his age.

Died: In Baltimore at the residence of his father-in-law, Daniel RADCLIFFE, Esq., James Harvey McVEIGH Jr., aged 35 years.

Died: In Charlestown on Thursday, April 2d 1874, after a lingering illness, Mrs. Susan Mercy GORMAN, aged 44y 9m, wife of Mr. Patrick GORMAN and daughter of Mr. Lewis F. YOUNG.

Died: On Friday morning, April 3, 1874, in Charlestown, at the residence of Mr. Patrick GORMAN, Mr. Lewis F. YOUNG, aged 87 years. The burial of the above father and daughter took place on Sunday afternoon at 2 o'clock.

Died: On the 23d ult. at the residence of Mr. Wm. HOUGH, of G., near Waterford, Mrs. Hannah COX, in the 83d year of her age. She was a member of the M. E. Church, for 49 years.

Died: At her father's residence, near Philomont, Katie MONROE. On Saturday the 7th of March, 1874 she died in the seventeenth year of her age.

Wednesday, 15 April 1874   Vol. XVIII, No. 43

Died: At her residence, within four miles of Bealton, Fauquier county, on the night of the 7th inst., Mrs. Ann DULANY, wife of the late French DULANY, aged about 73 years.

Died: At the residence of her husband, at Purcellville, on Monday, the 13th of April 1874, of cancer, Mrs. Elizabeth HATCHER, wife of Mr. Elwood HATCHER, in about her 60th year.

Died: In Leesburg on Saturday, April 11th 1874, Rosie Lee, daughter of Philip and Annie E. BROOKS, aged 1m 21d.

Mr. Henry C. WILDER died at the residence of his son-in-law, Mr. J. S. WIARD, in this place, on Monday afternoon, in the 68th

year of his age. Mr. WILDER was born in Portsmouth, Virginia and came here many years ago, and was employed as a hatter by his relative, the late Jas. GARRISON. Mr. WILDER had lived in Baltimore, Harper's Ferry and Berryville. His funeral will take place this Wednesday morning at 10½ o'clock.

Jennie, an aged colored women formerly owned by the late Chas. BINNS, died in this town on Saturday night, at the advanced age of over 100y, supposed to be 105.

Wednesday, 22 April 1874   Vol. XVIII, No. 44

Married: On the 9th at the residence of the bride's father in Waterford, by Rev. Samuel A. BALL, Mr. John E. JAMES and Miss Roberta HOUGH, both of Loudoun County.

Married: In Leesburg on the 16th inst., by Rev. S. GOVER, James E. HAWES and Jane H. KERN, all of Loudoun.

Married: On the 16th inst., by Rev. W. H. H. POWERS, Dr. Norman deV. HOWARD of St. Louis, Mo., to Miss Anna H., daughter of James K. SKINKER, of Fauquier county.

Died: In Warrenton on the 5th inst. after a brief illness, Mrs. J. Betty WITHERS, wife of S. Melvin WITHERS, in her 33rd year.

Died: On the 14th of April 1874, at Fairfax Court House, Mrs. KIDWELL, relict of Henson KIDWELL, deceased at an advance age, about 70 years.

Died: On April 14th 1874, at his residence near Herndon, Fairfax Co., William ROBEY, at an advanced age, about 80 years.

Wednesday, 29 April 1874   Vol. XVIII, No. 45

Married: On the 16th inst., by the Rev. Aaron WOOD, at the residence of the bride's father, Dr. S. T. NOLAND and Miss Isabella LYON.

Died: On the 10th instant, Maggie Jackson, only daughter of Thomas and Sallie DOVE, aged 1y 7m 10d.

Wednesday, 6 May 1874   Vol. XVIII, No. 46

Married: At Trinity Church, Washington, DC, by the Rev. Dr. ADDISON, James M. LOVE, Esq., of Fairfax C. H., to Miss Maria WEAVER, daughter of Charles WEAVER, Esq., of Washington, and grand-niece of ex-President James BUCHANAN.

Died: At Mt. Gilead on Tuesday morning last, Mrs. Elizabeth FRERE, in the 80th year of her age.

The wife of Mr. Jno. JONES, formerly of this city, but now of Middleburg, died at the house of her sister, Mrs. Shep. HARRISON in Fairfax co., a day or two ago. Mrs. HARRISON was so much affected by the death that her mind was deranged. She wandered off from her home and was not found until next day, when she was discovered in the family burying ground, four miles away from her residence. *Alex. Gazette.*

Wednesday, 13 May 1874   Vol. XVIII, No. 47

Married: At Woodburn, April 16th by the Rev. J. C. DICE, Mr. Decatur WYNKOOP and Miss Maggie WYNKOOP, all of this county.

Married: In Washington DC on Thursday, April 30, by Rev. ___, James A. WELLS and Miss Milley TRAMMELL, all of Fairfax County.

Married: At the same time and place, Richard HONLEY and Miss Susan WELLS, all of Fairfax county.

Married: On the 28th ulto., by Rev. J. B. LAKE, Mr. Charles F. McCORMICK, of Clarke county, to Miss Eoline V. KENDELL, of Paris, Fauquier county.

Died: On Wednesday the 6th instant near Ash Grove, Fairfax county, Mrs. M. A. GIBSON, wife of the late Joshua GIBSON, formerly of Loudoun county.

Died: At the residence of her daughter, Mrs. Frances HUGHES, on Friday morning the 8th of May, Mrs. Elizabeth SIMPSON, aged 76 years.

County Ct.: Susan A. FLETCHER's will admitted to probate. Allison F. SKILLMAN Admr. of Lucinda SKILLMAN dec'd. executed new bond. Chas. W. JOHNSON Admr. of Robt. JOHNSON dec'd. executed new bond. Sydnor BENNET and S. A. HOUSEHOLDER Admrs. of J. P. SCHOOLEY dec'd. executed new bond. C. B. WILDMAN qualified as guardian of Fanny Lee, Oliver and John HUGHES.

Wednesday, 20 May 1874   Vol. XVIII, No. 48

Married: In Piacenza, Italy, at the residence of the bride's father on the 18th of April 1874, by civil and religious ceremony, in the presence of Henry W. TRIMBLE, Esq., U.S. Consular Agent at Milan, The Marquis Louis Taffinni D'ACCEGLIO, Lt. Col. 6th Artilery, aide-de-camp to his Majesty Victor EMANUEL, to Mary, daughter of Morris S. WICKERSHAM, Esq. of Philadelphia.

Died: At Woodburn, on Monday May 18, 1874, Willie Clagett, infant son of Alexander H. and Julia H. ROGERS, aged 6 months.

Died: In Philadelphia, May 2d, Sallie A. McVEIGH, daughter of the late H. T. McVEIGH, formerly of Loudoun co., aged 17 years.

Died: Suddenly, in Waterford, on Saturday morning, May 16th 1874, Mrs. Betsy DIVIVE [DIVINE], widow of the late Jacob DIVINE, in the 87th year of her age.

Died: At her residence near Mt. Gilead, on Sunday 10th day of May, Miss Mary J. SMITH, in the 53rd year of her age. Member of the Baptist church at North Fork.

Died: At the residence of his father, in Charlestown, on Saturday morning, May 16th 1874, of consumption, Samuel B. MYERS, aged 32y 10m 20d. Interred at Edge Hill Cemetery on Sabbath afternoon by the Masonic and Odd Fellow fraternities.

Mr. Giles E. TILLETT, formerly of this county, was killed in the Tunnel on the Metropolitan railroad at Point of Rocks, on Saturday morning last, by a passing train. Mr. TILLETT was in the 40th year of his age, and leaves five orphan children. Interred in the burying ground at Waterford on Sunday.

Wednesday, 27 May 1874   Vol. XVIII, No. 49

Married: On the 14th instant, at the M. E. Church, by Rev. W. H. FORSYTH, Rev. S. A. BALL, of the Virginia Conference M. E. Church, to Miss Alberta COOKSEY, of Loudoun county.

Married: On the 19th of May 1874, by Rev. Andrew ROBEY, of Harper's Ferry, Mr. John PIPER Jr. to Miss Mary E. ACLEBERGER, all of Jefferson county.

Died: On March 6th 1874 in Perry township, Muskingum county, Ohio, Armstead M. COX, in the 40th year of his age. He was formerly a citizen of Loudoun.

Died: Near Broad Run station, Fauquier county, on the 25th of March 1874, of dyptheria, Mary T., aged 1y 25d and on the 12th of May, of the same disease, Maggie A., aged 4y 6m, children of Benjamin F. and Sallie J. FOLEY.

Died: At the residence of her son-in-law, Mr. Mortimer THOMPSON, near Pursellville, on Friday morning, May 15th 1874, of dropsy, Mrs. Elizabeth N. WILSON, widow of the late Wm. WILSON, of this county, in the 76th year of her age.

A little child 18 months old, son of Jas. E. KIDWELL, of Red Hill, in this county, was choked to death with a bean, at the residence of its grandfather, Mr. Israel MYERS, on Monday evening the 18th inst.

Wednesday, 3 June 1874   Vol. XVIII, No. 50

Died: In Leesburg, on Monday morning, June 1st, after a brief illness, Mrs. Rosabel, wife of Mr. Wm. BROOKS, in about the 25th year of her age.

Died: In this town, on Saturday morning, June 30th 1874, after protracted illness and great suffering, Mrs. Julia JACKSON, wife of Mr. Wm. JACKSON.

Died: On the 29th of April 1874, at the residence of her father, in Loudoun county, of dropsy in the chest, Sarah Jane SHUGARTS, aged 45y 2m 17d.

Died: In Jacksonport, Arkansas, on the 25th inst., John Webb TEBBS, formerly of Loudoun county.

Died: At Woodbine, near Hamilton, the residence of her grandfather, Mr. Israel MYERS, May 18th, Bessie Virginia, daughter of James E. and Mary E. KIDWELL, Aged 16m 14d.

Wednesday, 10 June 1874   Vol. XVIII, No. 51

Died: In Shelby county, Illinois, on the 20th of April 1874, of brain fever, Rosalie A., eldest daughter of Jno. Wade and Mary C. BARRETT, formerly of this county, aged 19 years.

Died: In Jackson co. Mo., on the 4th of February 1874, while on a visit, Miss Rachel GRUBB, of Loudoun county, in her 73d year.

Died: At his residence near Hillsboro on the 15th of May 1874, Mr. William GRUBB, in the 72d year of his age.

Died: Near Union, May 15th 1874, Ira Irving, the first born and infant son of Wm. N. HUTCHINSON and Martha R., his wife, in the third month of his age.

Died: June 2d 1873, in Loudoun county, at the residence of his son, Lewin T. JONES, Philip Ap. Catesby JONES, in about the 86th year of his age. The deceased was a brother of General Roger JONES, late Adjutant General U.S. Army and Commodore Thomas Ap Catesby JONES of the Navy.

Mr. H. H. GREGG, of Columbiana county, and Mr. J. G. KEITH, of Starke county, Ohio were in our office last Saturday. both are natives of Loudoun, the former having left here in 1835 and the latter in 1833. Both have relatives still living in Loudoun.

June Ct.: R. S. CHINN qualified as Admr. of Caldwell HOLLIDAY. J. W. HANCOCK qualified as Admr. of Jane T. L. HANCOCK, Samuel R. SKINNER, surviving Exor. of Peter SKINNER dec'd. power revoked and estate committed to Sheriff.

Wednesday, 17 June 1874   Vol. XVIII, No. 52

Mr. John W. DALGERN, proprietor and publisher of the *Spirit of Jefferson*, died at his residence in Charlestown, Jefferson county, W Va, on Tuesday, June 9th, aged 56y 17d.

Married: At "Glen Welby," the residence of the bride's father, on the 10th inst., by Rev. W. H. H. POWERS, Mrs. Wm. BEVERLY and Miss Mary Welby CARTER, both of Fauquier county.

Married: On Thursday, June 4th at the residence of the bride's father, by Rev. D. M. GILBERT, assisted by Rev. G. L. LEYBURN, Dr. Hunter H. POWELL, of Cleveland, Ohio, to Miss Emma, daughter of Wm. B. BAKER, Esq., of Winchester.

Married: On the 4th instant, at St. Ann's Church, Annapolis, Md, by the Rev. Mr. SOUTHGATE, Mr. J. West ALDRIDGE, of Loudoun county, to Miss Kate G., daughter of Gen. L. GIDDINGS, of the above mentioned city.

Died: In Hamilton, on Sunday evening, the 7th instant, James N. McFARLAND, aged 27 years.

Died: At the residence of his son-in-law, in Shenandoah county, Va on the 3d inst., Fielding FINKS, father of the senior proprietor of the *Warrenton Index*, in the 86th year of his age.

Died: At his residence in Warrenton, on the 8th inst., John L. FANT, in the 86th year of his age.

Wednesday, 24 June 1874   Vol. XIX, No. 1

Edgar, a little son of Dr. A. C. SPEIDEN, of Salem, Fauquier county, was fatally injured on Saturday. He was holding a horse out to graze in the yard, and was mischievously switching it upon the legs, when the animal kicked him in the stomach, causing his death in a few minutes.

Married: At the Parsonage of the M. E. Church, June 17th by the Rev. Wm. H. FORSYTH, Mr. John SMALE to Miss Olevia Jane SLACK, both of Leesburg.

Married: June 16th 1874, by Rev. J. B. LAKE, Mr. Levi H. SMALL, of Berkeley county, West Virginia, and Miss Vernon D. WERTENBAKER, of Loudoun county, at the residence of Mr. N. THOMAS, near Upperville.

Married: On Thursday evening, the 18th inst., at Sandy Hook, Md, by Rev. Andrew ROBEY, Mr. Wm. H. SWAIN of Bolivar to Corushia Scott WILSON, late of Strasburg, Va.

Married: In Washington DC, on Tuesday, the 16th instant, by Rev. B. F. BITTENGER, Mr. Landon E. CARTER, of "Salisbury," Fairfax county, to Miss Rose M. CARTER, daughter of Geo. F. CARTER, Esq., also of Fairfax county.

Death of Col. John LESLIE – died at his home near Morrisonville in this county on Friday morning last. Col. L. was an active business man and successful farmer.

Mr. John WILLIAMS, another old citizen of this county, died at his residence near Goresville on Saturday night, after a protracted illness of much suffering. His remains were interred in the Presbyterian burying ground of this town on Monday.

Thursday, 2 July 1874   Vol. XIX, No. 2

Died: In Leesburg, on Tuesday night, June 30th 1874, Mrs. Elizabeth F. BOSS, widow of the late Samuel M. BOSS, in the 73d year of her age.

Died: In Georgetown, DC, on the 22d instant, Charles Ham. TAVENNER, aged about 55 years. The deceased was a native of Loudoun, but for many years a citizen of Fauquier county. At the time of his death he was lessee of the Cattle Scales at Drover's Rest, and proprietor of Montgomery House in Georgetown. Member of the Methodist Church.

Died: On the 25th inst., James KEITH, second son of Dr. J. W. McILHANY in the 5th year of his age.

Dr. W. R. WINCHESTER, of this town, received a telegram from home on Saturday morning, summoning him to the death bed of a brother in Maryland.

Thursday, 9 July 1874   Vol. XIX, No. 3

A bibliographical sketch of the Missouri Legislature shows that 15 members of that body are natives of Virginia, two of whom went from this county: John M. FILLER a native of Loudoun county is a Republican Senator from the Lawrence county district. He emigrated in 1846. Colonel Mortimer McILHANY, the Speaker of the House, is a native of Loudoun who emigrated 29 years ago. He served through the war as a Confederate Lt. Col.

Mr. Wm. FLOOD, of Charlestown, died very suddenly near White Post, in Clarke county, on Friday night. He was in his 71st year.

Died: On Sunday morning the 28th inst., at his residence near Aldie, Wm. T. McCARTY, aged about 68 years. He was born and reared in Loudoun county, but spent the greater part of his life in Fauquier.

Died: At her residence, "Oak Level," Loudoun county, June 29th 1874, after an illness of five days, Edmonia E. SMITH, wife of P. H. SMITH, in the 54th year of her age.

Died: Near Annapolis, Md, on the 28th of June, Mr. Jacob WINCHESTER (brother of Dr. W. R. WINCHESTER, of this town) in the 27th year of his age.

Died: In Loudoun county, on the 5th instant, Mrs. Violet ETHERINGTON, wife of Mr. E. H. ETHERINGTON.

Death of Joseph RHODES – died at his home near Leesburg, on Thursday evening, July 2, 1874, in the 59th year of his age. Sixteen years ago, Mr. R. sustained an injury which deprived him of the use of his lower limbs and rendered him a bed ridden invalid. Member of the M. E. Church, South. He was a husband and father.

Thursday, 16 July 1874   Vol. XIX, No. 4

Died: In Georgetown, on July 7th, Mrs. Sophia, widow of the late Daniel BOLAND, of Bolington, Loudoun county.

Mr. Cephas HEMPSTONE died at his home near Goresville, on Sunday morning, the 12th of July, in the 70th year of his age.

County Ct.: W. A. McFARLAND qualified as Admr. of Jas. M. McFARLAND dec'd. Will of the late Elizabeth F. BOSS admitted to probate, Wm. CLINE Executor. Will of Jos. RHODES admitted to probate, Mary A. and Jos. R. RHODES, executors. Will of John LESLIE admitted to probate, Noble B.

PEACOCK, Executor. Will of late Wm. GRUBB admitted to probate, James GRUBB, Executor.

Mr. Calvin SKINNER of Herndon died very suddenly last Friday night from a supposed attack of cholera morbus.

Buckner BAYLISS, Esq. one of the oldest citizens of Washington, died quite suddenly at the Metropolitan Hotel, on Thursday evening last. Mr. BAYLIS was born in Fauquier but lived in Washington for more than 40 years.

Thursday, 23 July 1874   Vol. XIX, No. 5

Died: In Erie City, Pennsylvania, on the 30th of June 1874, Mrs. Lydia H. STERRETT, formerly of Leesburg, aged 76 years.

Died: In Philadelphia, June 25th 1874, Ann Eliza, wife of Lewis H. SAUNDERS, formerly of Leesburg, in the 25th year of her age.

Mr. Latimer ALDER, who was born and lived for many years in Loudoun county, died suddenly at the residence of his daughter, Mrs. Archibald THRESHER, in Allen county, Kansas, on the 23d of June, at the advance age of 91y 1m 7d. He was a consistent member of the Presbyterian Church.

Thursday, 30 July 1874   Vol. XIX, No. 6

Died: At the residence of her father, near Harper's Ferry, in Loudoun county, July 10th 1874, Margaret E. DEMORY, infant child of John W. DEMORY, aged 13 months.

Died: On the 17th, Prestiss, infant son of Col. Jno. S. and Mrs. Pauline MOSBY, aged 11 months.

Died: At the residence of her father near Salem, on the 19th inst., Robert, fourth son of Thomas A. RECTOR, aged about 19 years.

Died: At Oak Hill, on the 20th inst., after a short illness, Lizzie, beloved wife of Charles N. KEFAUVRE.

Died: At "Eudora Manse" Loudoun county, July 18th 1874, Henry, infant son of Rev. Henry and Melissa M. BRANCH.

Married: In Washington DC, on the 21st instant, by Rev. C. C. MEADOR, Mr. James E. TRIMMER to Miss Fannie S. FEWELL, all of Manassas.

Thursday, 6 August 1874   Vol. XIX, No. 7

Married: On the 26th of July, at the M. E. Church, South, Parsonage in the town of Bolivar, Jefferson Co W Va, by Rev. Andrew ROBEY, Mr. Baily T. PHILIPS to Miss Mary J. LINFIELD, both of Martinsburg, W Va.

Married: On Thursday, July 23d, 1874, at the residence of the bride's parents, by Rev. Henry CLEMENTS, Mr. James CAMPBELL, and Miss Martha V. KIDWELL, all of Fairfax county.

Married: July 8th at Amissville, by Rev. W. W. REESE, J. B. PAYNE, of Fauquier Co. to Mary Lou, daughter of Dr. Jno. A. ADAMS, of Rappahannock county, Va.

Thursday, 13 August 1874   Vol. XIX, No. 8

Married: On the 6th inst., by Rev. Mr. BEALL, Mr. J. W. BROWN and Miss Sarah MARTIN, both of Fauquier county.

Married: On the 22nd July, by Elder A. M. GRIMSLEY, Mr. B. F. BURGESS and Miss Lillie L. GARRISON, both of Fauquier.

Died: At Tuscumbia, Alabama, on the 1st inst., Gordon Hindman, infant son of John T. and Sallie A. TRIBBEY, of Loudoun county. Aged 4m 4d.

Thursday, 20 August 1874   Vol. XIX, No. 9

F. P. HUTCHISON, a stone mason living near Sudley Mills, Prince William county, left home on Tuesday the 14th instant and has since that time been missing. The horse he rode away and returned riderless.

Married: At Warren Green hotel on the 13th inst., by Rev. Jno. S. LINDSAY, Mr. Ethelred FEWELL and Miss Ann E. WEAVER, both of Fauquier.

Died: August 1st, 1874 at his residence at Weaversville, Fauquier county, C. Cullin BRIGGS, aged 58 years.

Died: On the 12th of August 1874, at Barrymore, Fauquier county, the residence of his son, Henry DeButts NORRIS, in the 72d year of his age, George W. NORRIS.

Died: Near Unison in this county at the residence of Henry W. CHAMBLIN, Mr. George W. GREYSON, in the 63d year of his age.

Death of Rev. Thos. E. AYRE, lately Principal of the Leesburg Academy, occurred at the residence of his uncle, G. B. HANES, in Buckingham county, on Monday the 10th of August 1874. He leaves a wife and little boy.

Thursday, 27 August 1874   Vol. XIX, No. 10

Died: In Washington city, on Monday morning, Aug 24th 1874, after a brief illness, Mrs. A. S. ADAMS, daughter of Mrs. Mary ATTWELL, of this town, in the 25th year of her age. Less than a year ago she became a joyous bride. She leaves a husband and an infant child.

Died: At St. Mark's Rectory, Frederick county, Md, on the 18th instant, William TRAPNELL, son of Rev. Joseph TRAPNELL, D.D., aged 25 years.

John W. GOLDEN, now confined in the jail of this county charged with the killing of Jos. McFARLAND, on Sunday, the 16th of August, was arraigned at the Court House on Tuesday last.

Thursday, 3 September 1874   Vol. XIX, No. 11

Married: At the residence of the bride's parents, in Jefferson County, W Va, on Thursday morning, August 27th 1874, by Rev. John W. LEA, Logan OSBURN Jr. to Miss Mary E. CASTLEMAN, second daughter of Henry W. CASTLEMAN, Esq.

Married: On the 25th of August 1874, near Leesburg, by Rev. Samuel GOVER, Mr. Winter Winfried CRUMMITT and Miss Mary E. STERNWELL.

Died: At his residence in Fairfax county, Va, near Herndon Station, Tuesday, August 14th inst., Mr. Joseph ORRISON, in the 65th year of his age.

Died: On the 27th of July 1874, of cholera infantum, Edward Clinton, son of Jacob and Susan ALLEN, aged 7 months and 27 days.

Died: At the residence of Mr. Chas. P. JANNEY, in this town, on Monday morning, Aug. 31st, after a few hours illness of membranous croup, Bessie, the only child of Dr. Erasmus D. and Margaret Scott MOORE, of Memphis, Tenn. and grandchild of Rev. A. D. POLLOCK, aged 23 months, died one o'clock Sunday night.

Thursday, 10 September 1874   Vol. XIX, No. 12

Married: Tuesday, September 1st, 1874, at the residence of the bride's father, by Rev. L. C. MILLER, William E. SAUNDERS, of Bryan, Texas, formerly of Warrenton, to Miss Alice E. PATTIE, daughter of Wm. A. PATTIE, Esq. of Warrenton, Va.

Married: In Washington DC, September 1st, by Rev. Mr. WILSON of the M. E. Church, South, of that city, Mr. Isaiah KEYS, of Manassas, and Miss Sallie M. MOUNTJOY, daughter of Mr. John MOUNTJOY, of Salem, Fauquier county.

Died: August 31st 1874, near Warrenton, Miss J. Adeline KEMPER, aged 69y 4d.

Died: In Muskingum county, Ohio, on the 31st of July 1874, of cancer of the mouth, Mr. Jacob LACOCK, in the 85th year of his age. Mr. L. was a native of Loudoun county but emigrated to Ohio about sixty years ago. Member of the Baptist Church.

"Old John HARPER," of Kentucky, the well known turfsman and owner of Longfellow, whose death has already been announced, was born at Harper's Ferry now in West Va, in the year 1800 and was carried to Kentucky in early childhood. His heirs include nephew Frank HARPER.

Rev. Warren B. DUTTON D.D. died at his residence in Charlestown at 7½ o'clock on last Saturday evening. Dr.

DUTTON had been a resident of Charlestown for more than 30 years, 25 of which spent in the Presbyterian congregation.

Died in Warrenton, on the 2nd September, Col. Wm. Winter PAYNE, in the 69th year of his life. He was born at Granville, Fauquier county, in the year 1807, and moved to Tuscumbia, Alabama in 1825, where he married the daughter of Col. John J. WINSTON. Col. PAYNE represented Franklin county in the Legislature of Alabama for seven years, having been elected when 22 years of age. He then moved to Sumter and continued to represent Sumter District in Congress until 1849, when he returned to Fauquier.

Thursday, 17 September 1874   Vol. XIX, No. 13

Married: September 3, 1874, at the residence of the bride's parents, by the Rev. W. S. KERNS, assisted by Rev. S. M. ATHEY, Mr. S. M. Smith, of Middleburg, to Henrietta SUNDERLIN, of Stafford County.

Married: On the 26th of August near Harper's Ferry Bridge, Md, by Rev. Andrew ROBEY, Mr. Milton MOLER to Miss Frances MOLER, all of Jefferson county W Va.

Married: On the 7th of September, by the same, under the shade of the trees on the banks of the Shenandoah River, James HAMILTON to Miss Amanda JONES, all of Jefferson county, W Va.

Married: At the Central Presbyterian Church, Atlanta, Ga. on Wednesday afternoon, September 9, 1874, by Rev Joseph R. WILSON, D.D. of Columbia S.C., Addison C. FOX, M.D., of Leesburg, and Miss Lou S. ANSEEY [ANSLEY], daughter of Mr. J. A. ANSLEY.

Married: At the residence of the bride's father, Centreville, Fairfax county, September 2, by Rev. John McGILL, J. E. BRENNER, of Middleburg, to Miss Jennie M. DEAR.

Died at her late residence in Bryan, on the 22d ult., after a painful and protracted illness, Francis [Frances] Osburn, relict of the late Wm. McINTOSH, Esq. of that city, aged 47y 10m. She was a daughter of Joel and Massey OSBURN of Loudoun County. She was married May 12, 1852 and left for the far west in the fall of that year. They settled in Boonsville, Texas. Surviving children are Walter and Mary.

County Ct.: Emily A. CROSS qualified as guardian of Elizabeth W. CROSS. Estate of Saml. DODD, Ormemelia WILLIAMS, and John WILLIAMS committed to Sheriff for administration. A. T. M. RUST qualified as guardian of Rebecca L. RUST and as committee of Frederick G. RUST. Jno. F. RYAN qualified as Admr. of Jos. McFARLAND dec'd. Wm. A. HUTCHISON Admr. of Eli HUTCHISON dec'd. ruled to execute new bond. Will of

Philip DeCatesby JONES dec'd. admitted to probate, Lewin T. JONES Admr. wwa. Will of Dorcas A. OSBURN admitted to probate with Amanda C. OSBURN Admr. wwa.

Mr. James STEPHENSON of this county, a pension soldier of the war of 1812, died at the residence of his son, Mr. Wm. H. STEPHENSON, near Aldie, on the 2d of September, in the 87th year of his age.

Thursday, 24 September 1874   Vol. XIX, No. 14

Married: At Trinity Church, Towsontown, on the 1st instant, by Rev. A. T. PINDELL, assisted by Rev. Dr. HOFF, John CARTER, of Va, to Miss Emily YELLOTT, of this place, daughter of the late John YELLOTT, of Dulaney's valley.

Married: On Tuesday, September 8, 1874, at "The Elms," Kenton county, Ky, by the Rev. E. W. BEDINGER, assisted by the Rev. F. P. MULLALLY, Rev. J. H. MOORE, formerly of Charlestown, to Miss Virginia BEDINGER, daughter of the officiating clergyman, and granddaughter of Hon. Wm. LUCAS, of Jefferson county.

Died: On August 2nd 1874, Mrs. Aseneth CHAMBLIN, wife of William CHAMBLIN, Esq., of Loudoun County.

Died: September 3d 1874, at Mountain View, Fauquier Co., the residence of Thos. MARTIN, Wade N. CLARK, in the 51st year of his age, leaving a wife.

Died: In Waterford, on Saturday the 19th of September 1874, Mr. Adam MASON, in the 80th year of his age.

A little more than a year ago, Albert SHINER, a German Tobacconist, came to this town attended by a dwarfish looking little fellow called REILY. REILY had formerly resided in Leesburg, and it was reported that he was going to marry a daughter of thrifty German of this place, Godfrey SHELHORN. In a few days SHINER wooed and won the fair Catherine. SHINER, assisted by REILY, at once went to making cigars at the residence of his father-in-law, SHELHORN where he remained a couple of months, when he took a house on King Street belonging to SHELHORN, and opened a tobacco store under the same roof. In June SHINER and his wife visited New York and brought home with them a plump little German girl, some fourteen years old, as a sort of family help. On the 13th July this child, Louisa SPEGER and Wm. REILY, went to Point of Rocks and returned man and wife. On Friday night, the 24th of July REILY disappeared. SHINER and his wife broke up housekeeping and left, and SHELHORN, the father-in-law had a public sale of their effects. This took place two weeks ago. Justice W. D. HEMPSTONE visited the house of Godfrey SHELHORN, a short distance from town, where he found the wife of Antoine SHELHORN, Godfrey's son and her sister. They informed him that after the sale a lot of articles had been brought there, among them some clothing belonging to REILY and his wife and were forwarded to New York. A bloody shirt of REILY's was left behind. Godfrey SHELBORN and SHINER and his wife were arrested. [gives witnesses and their testamonies.] $50 reward authorized by Mr. SHRINER for the return of Wm. REILY (may now go by the name of William WEELAND).

Thursday, 1 October 1874   Vol. XIX, No. 15

Married: By the Rev. B. P. DULIN, Sept. 22d 1874, at the residence of Wm. AYRE, Esq., Fairfax county, Mr. J. N. BALLARD, of Richmond, Va. to Miss Lizzie THRIFT, daughter of the late Col. James THRIFT, of Fairfax county.

Died: In Leesburg on Thursday the 24th of September 1874, Mrs. Mary E. HARRISON, wife of Mr. Henry T. HARRISON, of this town. She was a daughter of the late Walter JONES of Washington city.

Died: In Washington, on the afternoon of Saturday, Sept. 26, Sarah J., wife of Geo. A. TAVENER, formerly of this town.

Died: In this town, on Sunday morning, Sept. 27, 1874, Charlie, infant son of Anthony and Agnes DIBBREL.

Sketch of Gen. Eppa HUNTON a Conservative candidate for Congress in Virginia: Born in Fauquier county September 23d, 1823 and is 51 years old. ... He entered the army as Colonel of the 8th Va Regiment of Infantry. ...

Thursday, 8 October 1874   Vol. XIX, No. 16

Married: September 27th at the residence of the bride's father, Jas. A. ROLLINS, of Rappahannock, to Miss Susan E. THOMPSON, of Fauquier.

Married: On the 1st inst., by Rev. John S. LINDSAY, at St. James Episcopal Church, Mr. J. Blodget BRITTON, of Philadelphia, to Miss Fanny B. HORNER, of Warrenton.

Died: In Baltimore on Saturday last, Oct. 3, 1874, Mrs. Charlotte F. WILSON, formerly of Leesburg and daughter of the late Capt. ROSE, of this town, in her 75th year, nearly fifty of which was in the M. E. Church. Her remains were brought to this town on Monday morning and laid in Union Cemetery beside her beloved daughter who died but a few months ago.

Died: At his residence near Mountsville, of heart disease, on the 28 September, in his 65th year, Mr. Robert BOWMAN.

Died: In Washington on October 1, 1874, at 11 o'clock a.m. after long and painful suffering, Sophie, beloved wife of Edwin DROOP, of the firm of Metzerott & Co.

Dr. John S. HAWLING – the remains of this gentleman, who died in the city of Cordoba, Argentine Republic in December 1872, reached this town on Friday last, and today rest in his native Virginia in Union Cemetery. The remains addressed to A. H. ROGERS, Leesburg, were shipped from Rosanio on the 28th July 1874, on board the American bark "Samuel Hall," by Thos. B. WOOD, U. S. Consul.

Capt. John HENDERSON, of Jefferson county, West Va., died in New Orleans on the 1st inst. He was a civil engineer by profession and before the war for a time professionally engaged in Cuba upon lines of railroad. Early in the late war he took command of a company of cavalry, and was wounded by a member of his command. He was about 48 years of age.

Thursday, 15 October 1874 Vol. XIX, No. 17

Died: At Roseville, Loudoun county, Sept. 25th 1874, Walter Richard, son of Romulus and Catharine FERGUSON, aged 9y 5m 20d.

Married: In Middleburg on Thursday the 8th of October 1874 by Rev. William M. DAME, assisted by the Rev. Magrude MAURY, Bolling W. HAXALL Jr., of Baltimore and Lena A., daughter of Maj. B. P. NOLAND, of Loudoun county.

Married: By the Rev. T. B. SHEPHERD, at the residence of the bride's father, on Thursday, October 1st 1874, John H. ALEXANDER, of Clarke County, and Miss Emma J. HUGHES, of Loudoun county.

County Ct.: Will of Robt. C. BOWMAN admitted to probate, Geo. W. ADAMS, Executor. Aaron E. ALFRED qualified as Guardian of Howard BRADFORD. Julia B. LESLIE qualified as guardian of Jno. A. Jr., Elizabeth and John Bernard LESLIE. Jno. F. NEWLON qualified as Admr. of Rebecca PIGGOTT. Jno. W. GARRETT qualified as Admr. of Isaac JACKSON. Thomas REED licensed to celebrate matrimony. Estates of Jno. WILLIAMS and Abraham WORFORD committed to Sheriff.

Geo. M. HIBLER died at his home in Paris, Ky on the 6th of October after an illness of four days, in the 32d year of his age. He was a member of Capt. Ed. F. SPEARS' company of the Second Kentucky regiment, Breckinridge's division. ...

Thursday, 22 October 1874 Vol. XIX, No. 18

Married: At "Meadow Hill," near Hillsborough, in this county, the residence of the bride's father, on Tuesday morning, Oct. 20th 1874, by Rev. R. T. DAVIS, assisted by Rev. Theo. REED, Mr. Henry BRADLEY Jr. of Montgomery county, Md, and Miss Eppie, daughter of James M. KILGOUR, Esq.

Married: At the same time and place by Rev. R. H. McKIM, Dr. Pembroke THOMPSON, of Jefferson county W Va, and Miss Lizzie, daughter of the late James McILLHANEY, of this county.

Died: On Monday, October 12th 1874 near Mill Creek, Berkeley County, Phoebe E. WHITMORE, wife of Samuel P. WHITMORE, of Berkeley County, in the 40th year of her age.

Died: Suddenly at his residence near Hamilton, on Monday, the 12th of October, Mr. Israel MYERS, in the 60th year of his age.

Capt. Daniel T. SHREVE, a former citizen of this county, died at his home in Montgomery county, Md, on Friday last, of paralysis.

Thursday, 29 October 1874   Vol. XIX, No. 19

Married: In Middleburg, on the 20th instant, by Rev. J. A. HAYNES, Mr. Richard BEALES and Miss Mary E. THOMPSON, both of Loudoun.

Married: On the 13th inst., by the Rev. A. BUHRMAN, at the Lutheran Church, Lovettsville, Mr. Winfield S. SEITZ to Miss Anna R. RUSE, all of Loudoun County.

Married: On Wednesday morning, Oct. 21st 1874, at the residence of the bride's mother, near Sycolin Church, by Rev. L. D. NIXON, Mr. Townsend BELT to Miss Annie THRIFT, all of Loudoun Co.

Married: On the 14th inst. at the residence of the bride, by Elder John CLARK, Thompson Mason HIRST Sr. and Mrs. Lavinia E. PAYNE, all of Fauquier county.

Died: In Canton, Mo. Saturday, Oct 10th 1874, Lydia Lyder, wife of Alfred POULTON, aged 70y 7m 8d. She was born in Loudoun county March 2nd 1804 and was married July 26th 1825 to Alfred POULTON, and with her husband removed to Columbiana county, Ohio in June 1826 and in 1857 removed to Palmyra, Mo, and again in 1868 removed to Canton, Mo. She had been an invalid for many years.

Thursday, 5 November 1874   Vol. XIX, No. 20

Married: On the 4th inst. at "Mountain View," the residence of the bride's father, by Friends Ceremony, James W. JANNEY (of the firm of Janney & Hoge, of Washington) and Lucy, youngest daughter of Joseph NICHOLS, of this county.

Married: In the Presbyterian Church in Charlestown, on Tuesday evening, October 13, 1874, by Rev. R. T. BERRY, father of the groom, Mr. Arthur Holmes BERRY to Miss Lucy Edrington MANNING, youngest daughter of N. W. MANNING, Esq., of that place.

Married: In Trinity Church, Georgetown, DC, on the 15th inst. by Rev. Father STONESTREET, John F. COX, of Washington DC, and Gertrude V. WELCH, daughter of James S. WELCH, Esq. of Georgetown, formerly of Harper's Ferry.

Married: At Poolesville Md in the M. E. Church (South) on Wednesday, the 28th inst. by the Rev. Mr. BALL, Mr. Charles GRIFFITH to Miss Lina HEMPSTONE, all of Montgomery County, Md.

Married: at Poolesville Md in the Presbyterian Church, on Wednesday the 28th inst., by the Rev. Mr. CAMPBELL, Mr. Humphrey CISSELL to Miss Julia GRIFFITH, all of Montgomery County, Md.

Married: On the 20th inst., by the Rev. A. BUHRMAN, at the Lutheran Church, near Lovettsville, Mr. C. K. HOUGH to Miss Mary E. COOPER, all of this county.

Married: In Washington, DC on Sunday the 25th instant, by Rev. Mr. BITTINGER, Henry A. SIMMONS and Miss Sarah J. BEACH, both of that city.

Married: On the 14th instant, at the residence of the bride, by Elder John CLARK, Thompson Mason HIRST Sr. and Mrs. Livinia E. PAYNE, all of Fauquier county.

Married: At the residence of the bride's mother, Hazle Hill, Culpeper county, on Thursday evening, October 22d by Rev. Silas BRUCE, Mr. Hugh M. SMITH, of Rappahannock to Miss Mollie E. O'BANNON, of Culpeper county.

Married: At the Parsonage of the M. E. Church, Oct. 28, by the Rev. Wm. H. FORSYTH, John J. GOODIN, Esq., to Miss Olivia J. DENNIS, both of this county.

Died: In Georgetown, on the 27th instant, at 2 p.m. of typhoid fever, Alice, the eldest daughter of John M. and Mary E. ATHEY.

Died: In Alexandria, in Saturday, Oct 31st, of typhoid pneumonia, Corrie, daughter of Eli and Cornelia JANNEY, aged 3y 5m 18d.

Sudden death of Mr. Jonathan NIXON, an old citizen of this county, at his residence near Mt. Zion Church, on Tuesday last, caused it is said by a stroke of paralysis.

Thursday, 12 November 1874   Vol. XIX, No. 21

Died: In Leesburg, October 29th 1874, Ernest Ellwood, only son of R. D. and Annie BEALES, aged 12 years.

Married: On the 29th ultimo, by the Rev. A. BURHMAN [BUHRMAN], at the Lutheran Church at Tankerfield, Mr. Geo. H. BAKES [BAKER] and Miss Mary M. SWANK, all of Loudoun.

Married: In Washington on the 3d instant, by the Right Rev. Wm. PINCKNEY, D.D., assisted by the Rev. Dr. ELLIOTT, Arthur

PENDALL, Esq. and Miss Sallie C. MILLER, both of Washington.
Married: October 19, at the residence of the bride's father, by the Rev. J. G. HENNING, Mr. J. T. GOODRICK, formerly of Fredericksburg, Va, and Miss Mary J. LANMAN, of Leesburg.
Nov. Ct.: Jno. W. PIGGOTT qualified as committee of Ruth H. PIGGOTT. Thos. J. COST qualified as Admr. of Jarod LOCKER. Wills of B. W. WELSH dec'd. and Cephas HEMPSTONE dec'd. admitted to probate.

Thursday, 19 November 1874   Vol. XIX, No. 22

Married: In Baltimore, at the Cathedral, on the 29th of October, by Rev. Father STARR, Chancellor of the Archdiocese, Geo. H. LYBRAND to Miss Theo. S. B. STANSBURY, of Baltimore.
Married: In Tuesday morning, Nov. 17th 1874 at the residence of Mr. John J. HOGELAND, near Sycolin Church, by Rev. L. D. NIXON, Mr. Elijah V. RITICOR to Miss Massie V. AYRES, all of Loudoun county.
Married: On the 4th instant, by Rev. T. HERNDON, Mr. George R. GRIGGS, of Staunton, to Miss Fannie E. FOLEY, of Loudoun county.
Died: At the residence of her grandfather, Justus KUHLMANN, on Sunday morning, October 25th 1874, Ruth Emma, daughter of Charles and Mary WEADON, aged 3y 3m 3d.
Died: In Leesburg, on November 12th 1874, Frank, son of A. D. and Ella R. ACHERS, aged 1y 10m.
Died: November 7th 1874, Ada Jannie, daughter of Edgar B. and Annie E. HAVENER, aged 2m 11d.
Died: Mrs. Hattie R. ADAMS, wife of Mr. Amos S. ADAMS, died August 24, 1874. Mrs. ADAMS was the daughter of Mrs. Mary ATTWELL, a member of the Methodist Episcopal Church, South, Leesburg. Her death occurred at the house of a sister in Washington DC. *Baltimore, Oct. 16.*
Mrs. Rachel HOGE of this county died at her residence near Hughesville, on Tuesday night last in the 78th year of her age.

Thursday, 26 November 1874   Vol. XIX, No. 23

Married: November 5th 1874, Rev. John WOOLF, Mr. Geo. ASHBY, of Loudoun, to Miss Mary WILEY, of Clarke.
Married: November 11th by the Rev. L. D. NIXON, Mr. John W. CARROLL to Miss Amelia Ann HOUGH.
Married: November 12th by the same, Mr. George SMALLWOOD, of Loudoun, to Miss Mary E. KNIGHT, of Clarke.
Married: November 11th 1874, at Snickersville, by Rev. J. H. LAKE, Mr. Mason THROCKMORTON and Miss Annie HUMPHREY.

Died: At her residence "Pleasant Valley" Loudoun county on the 17th instant, Rachel Neill HOGE, wife of Isaac HOGE, deceased, aged 61 years.

Departed this life on the 4th instant, of consumption, at his residence near Circleville, Loudoun county, Benjamin W. WELSH, in the 55th years of his age.

At the residence of Captain Joseph JAQUES, in Knoxville, on the 4th instant, Mr. John Y. JOHNSON, of Loudoun, to Miss Sue AYERS. At the conclusion of the ceremony, Caption JAQUES handed to the bride his check for $10,000.

Thursday, 3 December 1874   Vol. XIX, No. 24

Married: In St. Paul's Church, Louisville, Ky, on Tuesday, the 24th of November 1874, by Rev. E. T. PERKINS, Edgar LITTLETON, Esq. Clerk of the County Court of Loudoun, and Miss Antoinette Addison, daughter of Mr. Samuel CAMPBELL, formerly of Leesburg.

Married: On Wednesday, November 25, 1874, at the residence of the bride's parents, by the Rev. E. H. HENRY, Mr. Geo. F. LEARNED, of Washington D.C. to Miss Mary L. CHAPMAN, of Fairfax C. H. Va.

Married: On Tuesday, November 24, 1874 at the residence of Samuel KITSEN, Esq., Mr. John DEAN to Miss Frances HARROVER, all of Fairfax county.

Married: On Tuesday, November 16, 1874, at Germantown, by Rev. G. H. WILLIAMS, Mr. Luther L. POLAND, of Prince William county, to Miss Mary C. MORGAN, of Fairfax county.

Married: On Tuesday, November 24, 1874, at the residence of Mr. James OLIVER, by the same, Mr. Greenberry M. CRONK to Miss Sarah Jane THOMPSON, all of Fairfax county.

Married: In Leesburg, on Wednesday, 25th inst., at the residence of the bride's mother, by the Rev. R. T. DAVIS, Mr. James H. FORSYTH to Miss Mollie RYON, all of Leesburg.

Married: On the 19th inst., at the residence of the bride's father near Taylortown, by the Rev. S. A. BALL, Mr. Robert A. BRADY and Miss Mary J. WILLIAMS, both of Loudoun County.

Married: On the 17th inst., by Jas. F. FRAUNING, at "Clifton," near Bowensville, the residence of the bride's mother, Robert STRINGFELLOW, of Culpeper county, to Susan E. MOORE, of Fauquier.

Married: On the 18th ultimo, at the residence of the bride's parents, by the Rev. Dr. C. G. LINTHICUM, Thompson M. HURST to Miss Emma H. ALLEN, all of Fauquier.

Little more than one week ago, Mr. James M. STEER of Waterford was summoned to Back Creek, in Frederick County, to attend the funeral of his sister, Mrs. Lydia Ann ROBINSON. While there he was seized with pneumonia and died. His remains were brought to his home and interred in the Friends burying ground at Waterford on Tuesday.

Mr. Ebenezer GRUBB, of this county, died at his home near Waterford, on Tuesday morning last, of paralysis, in about the 82nd year of his age.

Mr. Charles TRIBBEY, a jeweler, committed suicide Tuesday morning in his shop, No. 120 Bridge street, about ten o'clock, by shooting himself through the head with a pistol. He leaves a wife and six children. Mr. TRIBBEY was a native of Loudoun, but has been living in the District for a number of years.

Mrs. B. A. LOCKWOOD has entered a suit for a divorce for Maria Bell WEIGLE against Albert J. WEIGLE. The Plaintiff's maiden name was STROTHER and she was raised in Loudoun County. She sets forth that they were married at St. Paul's church and they lived here until the following October, and then went to Cincinnati, where Nov. 6th following he deserted her, leaving her without means.

Thursday, 10 December 1874   Vol. XIX, No. 25

Died: In this town, on Monday evening last, from the effects of measles, Charles Gray, only child of Dr. Charles G. and Isa A. EDWARDS, aged 1y 16d.

Died: Near Purcellville, Nov. 10th 1874, Mrs. Mary Ann, wife of John W. SIMPSON, aged about 59 years.

Thursday, 17 December 1874   Vol. XIX, No. 26

Married: On the 5th ultimo, at the residence of the bride, in Georgetown, D.C., by Rev. Peyton BROWN, Alexander POLAND, formerly of Leesburg, to Miss Clara TITLOW, formerly of Middletown, in Frederick county, all of Georgetown, D.C.

Married: On Tuesday, Dec. 14, at the residence of the bride's mother, by Rev. Jos. HELM, Mr. Benj. BROWN, to Miss Mary E. LACOCK, all of Loudoun.

Married: On Tuesday morning, Dec. 15th 1874, by Rev. Theo. REED, assisted by Rev. S. HEPBRON, Mr. Edgar HEPBRON, of Maryland, to Miss Alice, youngest daughter of Wm. B. JACKSON, Esq. of this county.

Died: On the 21st of October, Laura T., wife of Braden E. HUMMER, in the 34th year of her age.

Dr. F. W. POWELL, a prominent physician, died at his residence in Queenstown, Queen Anne's County, Maryland, on Saturday last, of paralysis, in the 64th year of his age. Dr. POWELL was formerly a resident of Loudoun county.

Dec. Ct.: Jas. M. WALKER qualified as Admr. of the late Samuel M. STEER. Will of the late Robt. CUNNINGHAM admitted to record, Robert H. CUNNINGHAM qualified as Administrator. Wm. SMITH appointed a committee of Hugh C. HILLEARY, a person of unsound mind. Susan F. STEADMAN qualified as guardian of Carrie H. STEADMAN. Wm. H. VIRTS qualified as Administrator of John M. VIRTS dec'd.

Thursday, 24 December 1874   Vol. XIX, No. 27

Henry M. BAKER of Frederick county, died in Winchester last Friday week. Mr. B. had gone to town in the morning with his wife and daughter. In the afternoon he went to a restaurant and died in his seat. The disease pronounced by the doctor to be paralysis of the heart.

Married: On Thursday evening, Dec. 10th 1874, at the residence of the bride's mother, by Rev. A. BUHRMAN, Mr. Charles W. SCOTT and Miss Rachel Ann COOPER, all of Loudoun county.

Married: In the Episcopal Church, Poolesville, Md, at 10 a.m., Dec. 17th 1874, by the Rev. Mr. TOWELS, Mr. Nathaniel WHITE to Miss Alice OFFUTT, all of Montgomery County, Md

Married: At "Beverly," in Jefferson County, the residence of the bride's parents, on Wednesday, Dec. 16th 1874, by Rev. A. C. HOPKINS, Mr. Thomas FRAZIER, of Loudoun county, to Miss Nettie, daughter of John BURNS, Esq.

Married: In this town, Dec. 22d, by Rev. J. F. CANNON, Mr. Alphonzo PALMER and Miss Annie E. FLING, both of Loudoun Co.

Married: At the residence of the bride's parents, near Waterford, Dec. 22, by Rev. W. H. FORSYTH, Rodney C. HOUGH, Esq. and Ann M. SHIPMAN, both of this county.

Died: At his residence, near Hughesville, December 16th at 11 p.m., Mr. John H. BROWN, in the 64th year of his age.

Died: At his residence in Upper Fauquier, on the 12th inst., Albert BAYLY, in the 76th year of his age.

Died: On Friday, the 11th inst., in Lynchburg, Va, Emma, wife of Wm. H. PHILLIPS, late of Warrenton.

Died: Olive, wife of Charles A. SMITH, Esq. died at his residence in Middleburg, on the 16th of Dec. 1874 in her 31st year.

Thursday, 31 December 1874   Vol. XIX, No. 28

Married: At McGaheysville, on Wednesday morning, 16th inst. by the Rev. J. H. MARCH, Mr. Richard E. HOPKINS and Miss Sallie C. WOLFE, daughter of the late Dr. Alfred WOLFE, all of Rockingham Co. Va.

Died: At Dover, Loudoun County, the residence of her husband, December 12th 1874, Mrs. William ROGERS, in her 67th year.

Rev. J. N. COOMBS, pastor of the Western Presbyterian Church, committed suicide in Washington, on Sunday last, by cutting his throat with a razor. ... Mr. COOMBS has been a minister in this city for 20 years, Born in Maryland, was almost 45 years ago, and was married near Leesburg about 23 years since. The remains will be interred in Oak Hill Cemetery today. Mr. COOMBS married a young lady of this county 20 years ago. For several years past she has been with her mother, near Hamilton, Mr. C. visiting her frequently.

Thursday, 7 January 1875   Vol. XIX, No. 29

Married: Dec. 24, 1874, at the residence of the bride's father, in Hillsboro, by Rev. A. B. DOLLY, Mr. John T. GRUBB to Miss Sallie GRUBB, all of Loudoun.

Married: At the residence of Patrick GAYNOR Jr., near Hillsboro, Dec. 15th 1874 by Rev. Mr. DOLLY, Mr. John ELLMORE to Miss L. SHAFFER.

Married: On Tuesday, 29th inst., at the residence of the bride's parents, by Rev. E. H. HENRY, Mr. F. A. KERBY, of Alexandria, Va, to Miss Annie D. DAY, daughter of Dr. Wm. B. DAY, of Dranesville, Va.

Married: By Rev. J. A. HAYNES, Dec. 30, 1874, at the residence of the bride's mother, Dr. T. L. LAWS, of Aldie, to Miss Virginia T. POLAND, of Prince William county.

Thursday, 14 January 1875   Vol. XIX, No. 30

Married: On Thursday evening, Jan. 7th, 1875, at the residence of Mr. HEFFNER, near the Broad Run bridge, by Rev. L. D. NIXON, Mr. Owen JENKINS to Miss Sarah E. ODEN, all of Loudoun county.

Married: Dec. 24th, 1874, by Rev. John WOLF, Mr. Theodore J. ARNETT to Miss Margaret V. TAYLOR, all of Loudoun.

Married: At the residence of Mr. Charles ELLMORE, on Wednesday the 6th inst., by Elder J. FURR, Mr. William H. FLING to Miss Mary L. ELLMORE, of Loudoun Co.

Married: At the residence of the bride's sister, near Hughesville, on Tuesday, January 5th, by Elder YATES, Mr. J. Alpheus TAVENNER to Miss Emma TALLMAN.

Married: January 7th 1875, at the residence of Mr. Geo. MEAD by Rev. J. M. FRIDAY, Mr. Abner W. M. CONARD and Miss Laura B. HARTMAN, all of Loudoun County.

Married: Dec. 24th, 1874, at the Lutheran Parsonage, Harper's Ferry, by Rev. S. M. FRIDAY, Mr. Joseph E. B. PEYTON, of

Loudoun county, and Miss Elizabeth E. DERRY, of Jefferson County, W. Va.

Married: On Thursday evening, January 7th, 1875, at the residence of the bride's parents, by Elder D. BARTLEY, of Illinois, Mr. Andrew NORMAN, formerly of Prince William Co., and Miss Ida R. GULICK, dau. of Francis and Nancy GULICK, of Loudoun.

Died: On Thursday, the 24th of December, near Morrisonville, Carl, son of John S. and Sarah BAKER, aged 3y 3m 24d.

Died at his residence in King George Co. Jan. 8th 1875, Mr. Lewis CROSS, in the 66th year of his age.

Mrs. Ann MAGILL, sister of Hon. J. R. TUCKER, died last week. The deceased was known throughout the state as an educator, having at one period of her life been in charge of a large female seminary at Winchester. At the time of her death she was connected with the school of Miss Mary Julia BALDWIN in Staunton.

County Ct.: John D. HARMON executed new bonds as Admr. of C. R. DOWELL dec'd. Will of Ebenezer GRUBB dec'd. admitted to probate with John COMPHER, Executor. Will of Rev. Jno. N. COOMBS dec'd. admitted to probate with Wm. and Edgar McCRAY Admrs. wwa. John W. GARRETT qualified as Admr. of John H. BROWN. Mary Ann GARRISON's will admitted to probate, with Susannah M. STANLEY, Executrix. Lewis N. CARR qualified as Admr. d.b.n.w.w.a of Jas. GARRISON dec'd. Estate of Elizabeth SIMPSON dec'd. committed to W. F. BARRETT, Sheriff.

Thursday, 21 January 1875 Vol. XIX, No. 31

Married: In Warrenton by H. H. WYER, on Jan. 5th, 1875, Mr. John W. PATTEN of Prince William county and Miss Frances M. ROSE, of Fauquier county.

Married: At the Dunbarton street M. E. Church, by the Rev. B. Peyton BROWN, on the 14th inst. Mr. H. M. TALBOTT to Miss Cora E. WILSON, both of Georgetown, D.C.

Died: Suddenly at the residence of her husband in Montgomery county, Md, on the 13th of January 1875, Mrs. Anna H. LOUGHBOROUGH, wife of Mr. Nathan LOUGHBOROUGH, formerly of Fauquier county.

Mrs. Susan NELMNS, wife of Mr. Samuel NELMNS, of Baltimore, and daughter of the late Henry BALL of Loudoun, died in that city on Thursday, and was buried in Union Cemetery, Leesburg, on Saturday.

Thursday, 28 January 1875   Vol. XIX, No. 32

Death of Matthew HARRISON – announced on Tuesday morning. He was in the 53d year of his age and was the eldest son of the late Burr W. HARRISON. ... He was admitted to the bar of Loudoun on Tuesday the 28th of October 1845. [long article] He leave a widow (a daughter of the late Walter JONES) and two daughters and a son.

Married: On the 14th instant, at Berlin, Md, by Rev. S. A. BALL, Mr. Jas. CORBIN and Miss Rosa SHUMAKER, both of Loudoun.

Married: In Warrenton by H. H. WYER, of Jan. 5th 1875, Mr. John W. PATTEN, of Prince William county, and Miss Frances M. ROSE, of Fauquier.

Married: In Baltimore on Jan. 7, 1875, by Rev. Father BRANDSTETER, B. C. BIEBELHEISER, of Baltimore, to Jennie T. CULLEN, daughter of Thomas CULLEN, Esq. of Loudoun Co.

Married: At Joshua KIRKBY's, Fairfax, Va, January 19, by Rev. L. H. CRENSHAW, Mr. Andrew J. HALL and Miss Ann Virginia KIRBY, daughter of John KIRBY, Esq., all of Fairfax, Va.

Married: On Thursday, Dec. 17, 1874, at the Church in Aldie, by Rev. S. G. FERGUSON, Mr. B. W. HOUGH, of Washington DC, to Miss Roberta V. CRIDDER, of Loudoun county.

Married: on the 20th inst., by the Rev. Dr. C. G. LINTHICUM, at the residence of the bride, Arthur W. TRIPLETT, of Prince William county, to Miss Ella D. GASKINS, of Fauquier.

Died: At his father's residence near Hamilton on the 1?th of January, Frank, son of Samuel and Ann ARNETT, aged 27y 1m.

Thursday, 4 February 1875   Vol. XIX, No. 33

Married: At the Methodist Parsonage, Falls Church, Va, January 26, 1875, by Rev. L. H. CRENSHAW, Mr. James S. REED and Miss Florence J. VEALE, both of Dranesville, Fairfax county.

Married: On the 26th of January 1875, at Warrenton, by O. C. BEALL, L. W. SMALLWOOD, of Loudoun Co. to Laura BALLARD, of Fauquier county.

Married: On the same day, and at same place, by the same, John M. BALLARD to Mary F. SQUIRES, both of Fauquier co.

Married: On the 19th January 1875, by the Rev. John K. HILLDRUP, at the residence of the bride's father, Mr. D. M. PATTIE Jr., of Fauquier to Miss Clara H. WILLIS, of Madison county.

Mr. John S. DIVINE, a native of this county, died at his home in Monticello, Florida, on Saturday, the 16th of January, of paralysis, in his 65th year. Mr. D. left here about forty years ago, and was successfully engaged in mercantile pursuits in his new home. He has three brothers still living in this county.

Rev. Lorenzo Dow NIXON, pastor of the Farmwell and Sycolin congregations, M. E. Church, South, died at his residence near Farmwell on Friday morning, of paralysis, in the 64th year of his age. His remains were brought to the M. E. Church, South, in this town, on Sunday morning, were services were held by Rev. J. C. DICE, assisted by Rev. Dr. FOLLANSBEE, and Rev. Mr. FORSYTH. The body was conveyed to Union Cemetery and interred with Masonic honors of which order he was a member. He was a native of Loudoun county.

Death of Mrs. Eliza Matilda LOVE – at the residence of her son-in-law, Rev. Wm. JOHNSON, in Laclede county, Mo., on 22d January 1875, in the 84th year of her age. Mrs. LOVE was the daughter of the late Ludwell LEE, who will be remembered by the older residents of Loudoun, as the former proprietor of the "Belmont" estate in this county, where the family of President MADISON were entertained, when they fled from Washington on the burning of the capitol in 1814. Her father was Ludwell LEE, Esq., son of Richard Henry LEE. Her maternal grandfather was Phillip Ludwell LEE, of Stratford Hall. She was married in 1811 to Richard H. LOVE, a gentleman of family in Fairfax county. By the marriage she had six children. Of these Ludwell and Thomas died in infancy; Richard entered at an early age the U.S. Navy until his death in 1855; Cecelia, who married Maj. Lewis ARMISTEAD of the U.S. Army died in 1850. The surviving son is Gen. John LOVE, of Indiana, who was graduated at West Point and served in the U.S. Army for 20 years. The surviving daughter is Mrs. Flora Lee JOHNSON, wife of the Rev. William JOHNSON, Episcopal minister at Lebanon, Mo.

Thursday, 11 February 1875   Vol. XIX, No. 34

Died: In St. Charles county, Mo., on the 9th of January, 1875, Mrs. Elizabeth KEENE, wife of Charles F. KEENE, formerly of Loudoun county.

Died: On Tuesday, January 26, 1875, Robert BAYLY, of Loudoun county, in the 90th year of his age.

Died: At her home, near Mt. Gilead, on the 26th of January 1875, of pneumonia, Miss Mary JONES, in the 57th year of her age.

Died at Sunny Bank, near Middleburg, on the morning of the 3d February, Miss Jane H., daughter of Geo. W. HENDERSON, Esq. in the 24th year of her age. Two years ago she united with the M. E. Church, South.

Died, near Middleburg on the morning of the 4th of February, 1875, Emily, wife of Mr. Joseph LOWE. Member of the M. E. Church, South, she leaves a husband and five sons.

Feb. Ct.: Will of the late Rev. L. D. NIXON admitted to probate, with Eliza N. NIXON as Admx. Harriotte J. HARRISON qualified as Admx. of the late Matthew HARRISON. Ed. H. BEANS qualified as guardian of Emma J. and Lauck EWERS.

The wife of Rev. W. G. EGGLESTON died at her home in Frederick county, Va on Sunday last after two or three days illness of pneumonia.

Thursday, 18 February 1875   Vol. XIX, No. 35

Died: At his residence near Mt. Gilead, on the 13th of January 1875, Mr. Samuel TILLETT, in the 53d year of his age.

Died: At her home at Guilford Station, on Saturday evening, Feb. 13th Mrs. James E. WARNER, wife of Dr. Jas. E. WARNER, of that place.

Died: At his residence at Guilford Station, on Thursday evening, 11th inst., Mr. John R. CRAVEN, in about the 43d year of his age.

Died: Near Guilford Station on Thursday the 11th inst., Mr. Lafayette LENT, son of Samuel E. LENT, in about the 20th year of his age.

Died: On Tuesday, February 9th, at Goresville, William Thomas, son of Wm. H. and Rachel C. MORELAND, aged 22 months.

Died: At Snickersville on the 10th instant, Henry, infant son of Dr. Geo. E. and Sallie T. PLASTER, aged 10 months.

Died December 19th, 1874 at the residence of her husband, in Middleburg, Mrs. Olivia M. SMITH. Native of Blacksburg, Montgomery county, Va; baptized in the Presbyterian church. Married on 23 December 1873 to Charles A. SMITH, Esq. of Middleburg. She leaves a husband, an infant and sisters.

Thursday, 25 February 1875   Vol. XIX, No. 36

Married: Jan. 21, 1875, in Loudoun, by Rev. J. M. FRIDAY, Hiram C. WALDRON, of Jefferson Co. W Va, and Miss Mary J. COPELAND, of Loudoun Co.

Married: At the residence of the bride's father, near Hamilton, by Rev. H. BRANCH, Mr. Henry VANDEVANTER to Miss Eliza VANDEVANTER, daughter of Washington VANDEVANTER, Esq., all of Loudoun.

Married: On the 18th of February, 1875, by Rev. William DINWIDDIE, at the house of the bride's father, Mr. John H. PARROTT, of Alexandria, Mr. Robert HARPER, of Leesburg to Miss Roberta W. PARROTT, of Alexandria.

Married: February 12, by the Rev. J. S. BIRCH, of Md., Mr. Wm. JONES, of Montgomery county, Md, and Miss Alice FECHTIG, of Leesburg.

Married: At the residence of the bride's father, Feb. 17th, 1875, by the Rev. R. T. DAVIS, Mr. Sidney FOUCHE to Miss Ella SHAFER, both of Leesburg.

Died: At Columbus, Ohio, February 18, 1875, at 12 o'clock m., of paralysis, Mrs. Fanny WEADON, formerly of Loudoun county, aged 76 years, buried in Middleburg, Va February 21st.

Died: At his residence, near Mountsville, February 16th, 1875, Mr. James Toliver MEGEATH, in the 33d year of his age.

Died: Friday, the 19th instant, Lucy Lee, relict of the late Fred'k. LLOYD, of Alexandria, Va and daughter of the late Wm. A. POWELL, of Leesburg.

Died: On Tuesday, February 23, Mr. William J. HARRIS, formerly of Jefferson county, W. Va.

Died: Tuesday, February 9th, at Goresville, Wm. Thomas, son of Wm. H. and Rachel C. MORELAND, aged 22 months.

Died: At his residence in Essex County, Va, on the 9th inst., Henry T. BAYNE, formerly of Loudoun county, in his 77th year.

Died: February 1st, 1875, at Spring Hill, Loudoun Co., John Thomas, son of Giles and Sophonia JACKSON, in the 23d year of his age.

Mrs. Samuel P. NELMS died on the 14th ult.

Mr. Jas. HUNTON, brother of Gen. Eppa HUNTON, who has been ill for a long time past at his residence near Warrenton, with typhoid pneumonia, died Monday after being delirious for over four weeks.

Thursday, 4 March 1875   Vol. XIX, No. 37

Married: On Tuesday, the 16th ult. at Greenwich, in Prince William Co., the residence of the bride's father, George B. STONE, of Washington DC, to Miss Minnie Winston PAYNE, daughter of Dr. John D. PAYNE.

Married: On the 18th ult., by Rev. Dr. J. F. POULTON, at the residence of the bride's father, Mr. Jackson N. SHAW and Miss Josephine HACKLEY, all of Fauquier Co.

Married: On Thursday, February 18th, at the bride's mother's, by the Rev. Dr. A. E. GIBSON, P. Frank GRADY, of Sandy Spring, Maryland, to Maggie A., daughter of the late David BEALL, of Baltimore.

Married: On the 23d ult., in Warrenton, by Rev. J. F. POULTON, Mr. Alexander G. POINTS, of Staunton, Va and Miss Mary Josephine, second daughter of Joseph H. and Mary E. WATSON.

Married: On the 25th ultimo, in Belmont, Loudoun county, by Rev. J. M. FOLLANSBEE, Mr. Edward F. MYERS to Miss Laura J. BAUCKMAN, both of Loudoun county.

Died: At her residence near Unison, on the 16th Feb., Mrs. Mary BURSON, in her 77th years.

Died on the morning of 16th February at Grit Land Mill, Loudoun Co., J. T. MEGEATH. He was united with the M. E. Church, South. For twelve months past was a great sufferer from pulmonary disease.

Died: Of consumption, on the 20th of February, 1875, at the residence of his sisters, Middleburg, in the 40th year of his age, Richard H. TURNER. He was a native of Va., but years ago went to Cincinnati, Ohio. Two year ago, consumption commenced and he has now passed away.

On Saturday the 20th ulto., James DOUGHTY, a flagman on a gravel train on the Baltimore and Potomac Railroad was killed by falling under the wheels of the cars. ... The remains were taken to his home in Baltimore. He was about 33 years of age and leave a wife but no children. The deceased is a son-in-law of Mr. Wm. H. HITAFFER, living near Leesburg. Member of the Methodist Church.

Police office Jno. FORSYTH of the southern district lost his life on Wednesday night by falling through a hatchway in the large warehouse No. 88 Camden st. He was 52 years old and leaves a wife and five children. *Balt. Sun, Feb. 25th* The deceased was a brother of Rev. W. H. FORSYTH, of this place.

Thursday, 11 March 1875   Vol. XIX, No. 38

Married: In Washington, on the 2d instant, W. H. WRIGHT, of Bloomington, Ill. and Laura G. GEORGE, of Loudoun county.

March Ct.: Will of Geo. WARNER admitted to probate, S. B. MERCIER, Exor. Will of Mary JONES admitted to probate, Henson SIMPSON, Admr. wwa. Will of Elizabeth KEENE admitted to probate. Mahlon G. HATCHER qualified as guardian of Adalaide and Frank HATCHER. Lucinda GOODHART qualified as Admx. of John GOODHART dec'd. Will of Sarah RICHARDS admitted to probate, P. S. GOCHNAUER Exor. T. M. BOLYN qualified as Admr. of

Bushrod T. BOLYN dec'd. Geo. W. HUMMER qualified as Admr. of Jno. R. CRAVEN dec'd. T. W. HATCHER qualified as guardian of Lindley and Lucy HATCHER. Will of Frederick ROLLER dec'd. admitted to probate, J. P. M. CONARD Exor. Will of Wyatt ALLEN admitted to probate.

Thursday, 18 March 1875   Vol. XIX, No. 39

Died: On March 17th, 1875, at the residence of her mother, in Leesburg, in the 45th year of her age, Mrs. Orra Lee ORR, wife of John M. ORR and daughter of Dr. George and Mrs. S. M. LEE. Funeral on Friday at 11 a.m.

Died: At the residence of her father in Leesburg on Friday the 5th ult., Annie CURRY, age 5y 2m, daughter of John and Ann CURRY.

Died: Suddenly, at his residence near Taylortown, on Saturday evening, Feb. 28th 1875, of paralysis, John GOODHART, aged 62y 11d.

Died: On the morning of Feb. 20th at 2 o'clock, of pneumonia, Jennie, daughter of J. Lewis and Martha HAWLING.

Died: In Leesburg, Feb. 23d, 1875, of diptheria, Ella Josephine GANTT, youngest daughter of Mrs. Annie E. GANTT, aged 4y 1m 21d.

The funeral of the late Mrs. Orra Lee ORR will take place at 11 o'clock a.m. on Friday from the Episcopal Church.

Last wee Mr. R. Chichester McCARTY died at an advanced age, of pneumonia. He was in the employ of the L. & A. Turnpike Co. at Goose Creek Bridge and formerly served as constable.

Thursday, 25 March 1875   Vol. XIX, No. 40

Married: On the 10th inst., at "Darby's Delight," near New Market, by Rev. E. R. ESCHBACH, Thos. S. YAKEY, of Loudoun Co to Miss Eliza E. JAMES, daughter of Mahlon JAMES, Esq.

Married: On the 9th of March, 1875, by the Rev. A. BUHRMAN, at the residence of the bride, Mr. David A. MEGAHA and Miss Mary Ellen WENNER, all of this county.

Died: In Leesburg, on Tuesday evening, March 16th, 1875, David Willoughby STEADMAN, aged 4y 3m 16d.

Died: In Alexandria, on the 18th inst., Mr. Lizzie J. SLAYMAKER, wife of Amos B. SLAYMAKER, aged 36 years.

Thursday, 1 April 1875   Vol. XIX, No. 41

Married: On the 18th inst., at the Washington House, Hagerstown, by Rev. X. J. RICHARDSON, Mr. William S. HICKMAN to Miss Maggie M. KALB, both of Loudoun county.

Died: At his country home near Warrenton, on the 19th inst., Jourdan M. SAUNDERS, in the 79th year of his age.

Death of Mr. John GRUBB Sr. occurred at his residence near Lovettsville, on Monday last in the 85th year of his age. He represented this county in the Legislature at one time.

Thursday, 8 April 1875   Vol. XIX, No. 42

Married: On Thursday, March 18, 1875, in Berketsville, by the Rev. Ambrois M. MAN, Mr. Samuel FRY, of Bolington, to Miss Rachel RHOE, of Berketsville.

Married: On the 18th inst., at the Washington House, Hagerstown, by Rev. X. J. RICHARDSON, Mr. William S. HICKMAN to Miss Maggie M. KALB, both of Loudoun county.

Married: On the 16th inst. by Rev. D. H. RIDDLE, Mr. A. Morgan VANMETRE to Miss Sallie E. MILLER, youngest daughter of Jacob MILLER, Esq., all of Berkeley county.

Married: On the Potomac river, on Sunday morning, April 4, 1875, by Rev. J. H. FORSYTH, Mr. Edward THOMPSON and Miss Martha Jane NEWTON, all of Leesburg.

Married: On the 28th of March, at the bride's parents near Harper's Ferry by Rev. Andrew ROBEY, Mr. Thos. J. INGRAM, of Springfield, Ill., to Mrs. Sarah DEMORY, of Loudoun county.

Married: On Thursday, April 1st, on the bridge at Harper's Ferry, by the same, Mr. Jas. S. PAYNE to Miss Mary C. SHEPHERD, all of Jefferson County.

Died: At his residence in this county on the 29th of March, 1875, Mr. John GRUBB Sr., in the 86th year of his age.

Died: James E. STONESTREET died at his residence in Harrison county, West Virginia, March 3d, 1875, aged 68 years. He removed from Loudoun county to Harrison in 1849.

Thursday, 15 April 1875   Vol. XIX, No. 43

Married: In Leesburg, on Wednesday evening, 7th instant, by Rev. W. H. FORSYTH, Mr. Geo. W. GRIMES, of this place, and Miss Lizzie ROSS, of Baltimore City.

Married: On the 7th of April, at the residence of the bride's parents, by Rev. Dr. PACKARD, Mr. Lafayette PARKER, of Dover Mill, Loudoun co., and Miss Mary Elizabeth JAVINS, of Fairfax co.

Married: On Tuesday, April 6th at the residence of the bride's father, near Leesburg, by Elder Benj. BRIDGES, Mr. Naaman PEACOCK, of Fairfax county, to Miss Roberta HITAFFER, daughter of Wm. H. HITAFFER, of Loudoun.

Died: Near Aldie, on the 27th of February 1873, Lizzie F., infant daughter of C. B. and Rose MATTHEWS, aged 3m 10d.

Died: In Lafayette county, Mo., February 11th, 1875, of consumption, Mary F. GARRETT, daughter of Joseph and Elizabeth GARRETT, formerly of Loudoun county.

Died: In this county, near Oatland, at the residence of her daughter, Frances DANIELS, on Friday evening, 19th March, 1875, Mrs. Elizabeth J. GOECHNEUER, in her seventy-eighth year. Years ago she united with the North Fork church.

Sam. ASHBY and Jas. M. SMITH, two negro men in the employment of Mr. Henson SIMPSON, near Northfork, in this county, got into a difficulty on Tuesday afternoon which resulted in the death of the latter. SMITH was from Ohio, and had only been in Loudoun about two weeks.

Thursday, 22 April 1875   Vol. XIX, No. 44

The marriage of Dr. W. H. RADER and Mrs. LOGAN, niece of Admiral POWELL took place at the Admiral's residence, Thursday last, and they left the same evening for their home in Loudoun county. *Washington Chronicle* of the 19th.

Nimrod T. ASHBY, a worthy citizen of Fauquier county, died on the 9th inst., in the 65th year of his age.

Died: At her home in Waterford, in this county, on the 12th instant, Mary E. WILLIAMS, wife of William WILLIAMS and daughter of the late Isaac WALKER, in the 52d year of her age.

Mr. Daniel SUMMERS, brother of Mr. Richard H. SUMMERS, and father of W. S. SUMMERS, Deputy Sheriff of this county, died at his residence near Gum Spring on Saturday last in the 75th year of his age. Member of the M. E. Church for many years.

Thursday, 29 April 1875   Vol. XIX, No. 45

Married: On the 18th of April, at the Valley Meeting house, by Elder Joseph FURR, Mr. Geo. L. CROSS to Miss Lucy A. ATHEY, all of Loudoun county.

Married: On the 21st instant, in St. James' Church, Warrenton, by Rev. John S. LINDSAY, William M. SPILLMAN, Esq., and Miss Heningham Lyons SCOTT, daughter of the late Robert E. SCOTT, Esq., all of Fauquier county.

Married: On the 15th instant, at the Reformed Church, Lovettsville, by the Rev. Hy. St. J. RINKER, assisted by the Rev. J. M. SOUDER, Mr. Ashland C. GEORGE to Miss Ella C. JOHNSON, all of Loudoun county.

Died: At the residence of her grandfather, Capt. Jno. MOORE, in Aldie, on Wednesday, the 21st inst., Rosa L. DOUGLAS, daughter of J. E. DOUGLAS, of Alexandria, in her 15th year.

At her residence in Jasper County, Iowa, on the 13th inst., Florida S., wife of Thos. W. HOUGH, and daughter of the late Jonas P. SCHOOLEY of this county.

Died: In this county, near Round Hill, at the residence of Mr. Mason JAMES, Friday morning, 16th of April, 1875, Miss Sarah

NICHOLS, in her 83d year. Years ago she united with the Ketocton Baptist Church.

Died: Near Minerva, in Carroll county, Ohio, on the 12th of April, 1875, Edward TILLETT Sr., aged 69y 21d. The deceased was born on 22d of March, 1806, near Leesburg, was united in marriage August 28, 1828, to Elizabeth BEIMENDERFER, who still survives him. They removed to Stark County, Ohio, in the year 1833, and from thence to Carroll County in 1838, where they resided until his death. They were the parents of five sons and five daughters, two of the sons have gone before him. They were the Grandparents of 39 children, 32 of who survive him.

Thursday, 6 May 1875   Vol. XIX, No. 46

Married: At the residence of the bride's sister in Baltimore, on Wednesday the 21st of April, by the Rev. Mr. ROGERS, Mr. S. E. ROGERS to Miss Lizzie E. MEGEATH, all of Loudoun.

Married: In Warrenton Baptist Church, on the 28th of April, by Rev. John L. CARROL, Mr. Frank W. JENNINGS and Miss Martha L. SOWERS, both of Warrenton.

Married: On Tuesday evening, April 27, by the Rev. Dr. CARTEIR, Mr. R. N. McVEIGH, of New York, to Mrs. Sophie DUNBAR, daughter of the late Dr. Joseph MAURAN, of Providence, R.I.

Died: At the residence of her father, Mr. John L. JORDON, in Berlin, Md., on the 29th of March, after a protracted illness, Hattie Lee JORDON, in the 9th year of her age.

Died: At his residence, near Morrisonville, on Sunday, May 2d, 1875, of consumption, Mr. Edward F. HAMILTON, son of the late John HAMILTON.

On Wednesday of last week, a sad accident occurred at Mount Airy, above Snickersville, on the Snickersville and Winchester turnpike. A son of Mr. John HUMMER, living at that pace, was killed by the discharge of a loaded musket which he was endeavoring to take down from the cross beams of the meat house where it had been placed. About 12 years of age.

Thursday, 13 May 1875   Vol. XIX, No. 47

Married: On Thursday, April 29th, 1875, at the residence of the bride's mother, one mile west of Hillsboro, by Rev. A. B. DOLLY, Mr. Joshua O. POTTS to Miss Adelaide WHITE, all of Loudoun.

Married: May 5th, at the Southern Methodist Parsonage, Hamilton, Va, by Rev. L. H. CRENSHAW, Mr. Wm. D. HOSKINSON and Miss Sophia C. EVANS, both of Loudoun.

Married: At the residence of the bride's father, in Frederick City, Md, on the 27th of April, by Rev. Dr. DEIHL, Mr. Geo. W.

WRIGHT of Loudoun county, to Miss Isadora V., only daughter of Grafton FOUT, Esq.

Married: In Jeffersonton, Va, on the 13th ultimo, by the Rev. Mr. GRIMSLY, Mr. L. B. SEATON, of Hannibal, Mo., and Miss Emma E. BEATY, daughter of John BEATY, of Jeffersonton, the bride being 19 years of age and the bridegroom 65.

Died: On Tuesday morning, April 20th, 1875, near Goresville, Loudoun county, of consumption, Samuel J. GRAY, in the 33d year of his age.

Died: Near Wheatland, April 20th, Mr. Charles WOLFORD, aged 47y 2m 15d.

Dr. William CROSS died at his home in Leesburg on Sunday morning, last, in the 71st year of his age. He had been successful in this town for nearly forty years. His funeral took place on Tuesday morning from St. James Episcopal Church, Rev. Mr. DAVIS officiating.

Ct.: Bernard HOUGH, Executor of S. B. T. CALDWELL to appear next term to show why he should not execute new bond. J. W. GOODHART qualified as Admr. of Martha E. FRY dec'd. John W. WOLFORD qualified as Admr. of Chas. WOLFORD dec'd. Estate of Taylor WATSON dec'd. committed to the Sheriff. Estate of Edgar L. BENTLY dec'd. committed to the Sheriff, H. C. SELLMAN qualified as Guardian of the minor children of said BENTLY. Will of the late Nelson FERROL admitted to record.

Winchester News – death in that place on Wednesday last, of the Hon. Robt. Y. CONRAD, one of Virginia's most gifted sons. He had been in feeble health for some time past, but the immediate cause of his death was typhoid pneumonia. He had reached the 69th year of his age.

Thursday, 20 May 1875   Vol. XIX, No. 48

Married: May 18th at the residence of Jas. LEWIS, Esq., by Rev. J. F. CANNON, Thos. M. GILCHRIST, of Hazletown, Penn., and Miss Ellen J. LEWIS, of Loudoun county.

Married: On May 12th at "Aspen Hill," the residence of the bride's father, in Fauquier co, Mr. Wm. A. HUDSON, of Staunton, to Miss Ida Florence, third daughter of Samuel RECTOR, Esq.

Died: In Leesburg, on Tuesday evening, the 11th inst., Harry, youngest son of Capt. J. H. MANNING, aged 15 months.

Thursday, 27 May 1875   Vol. XIX, No. 49

Died: On Wednesday evening last, at the residence of her husband, Mr. Wm. T. TITUS, in Leesburg, Mrs. Susan O. TITUS, in the 25th year of her age.

Cards have been received in Staunton for the wedding, on the 26th inst., of Col. Bolivar CHRISTIAN, of Augusta, and Miss Margaret PAXTON, daughter of R. C. PAXTON, Esq., near Leesburg Va.

Thursday, 3 June 1875   Vol. XIX, No. 50

Married: By Rev. R. T. DAVIS, at Carlheim, the residence of Charles R. PAXTON, Esq., near Leesburg, on Wednesday evening, May 26th at 8½ o'clock, Col. Boliver CHRISTIAN, of Lexington, Va, to Miss Margarett PAXTON, daughter of Charles R. PAXTON, Esq., of Loudoun county.

Married: At the residence of Dr. Geo. D. PLASTER, in Snickersville, at 5 o'clock, on Saturday evening, May 29th, 1875, by Rev. T. B. LAKE, Mr. Walter C. OSBURN and Miss Mattie C. TALLIAFERRO, all of Loudoun County.

Death of Mason CHAMBLIN – died at his home near Snickersville, on Friday last, in the 79th year of his age. For 24 years he was a member of the Short Hill Baptist Church, in the burying ground of which his remains were deposited on Sunday morning last, Rev. Mr. LAKE preached.

Thursday, 10 June 1875   Vol. XIX, No. 51

Married: On Tuesday, June 1st, 1875, at Cameron, the home of the bride's father, in Jefferson county, W. Va, by Rev. W. H. MEADE, Mr. Dennis M. MATTHEWS, of Baltimore county, Md, to Miss Harriet West ALDRIDGE, eldest daughter of Andrew ALDRIDGE, Esq.

Married: On the 25th of May, 1875, by the Rev. Dr. C. G. LINTHICUM, Elisha D. KINCHELOE, to Miss Emily A. CHAPPELLEAR, all of Fauquier county.

Mr. Ludwell LUCKETT died at his residence, Montpelier, in this county, on Monday, the 17th of May, in the 80th year of his age.

Augustine FITZHUGH, father of Mrs. B. G. CARTER, of this county, died at his home in King George county, Va, on the 22nd of May, after a brief illness of pneumonia, at the ripe old age of 85 years.

Thursday, 17 June 1875   Vol. XIX, No. 52

Married: On 3d inst., by Rev. J. A. SCOTT of Warrenton, Broadus M. PHILLIPS, and Ceretta Jane BROWN, both of Fauquier Co.

Married: At the residence of the bride's mother, in Hamilton on Thursday, June 3d, by Rev. Mr. TRAPNELL, Mr. J. H. T. FRAZIER, of Berlin, Md, to Mrs. Jeannie E. VIRTS, of Loudoun county.

Married: On the 19th of May, 1875, according to the order of the Society of Friends, Charles C. WAY, of Blue Rapids, Marshall

County, Kansas, to L. Anna HOGE, daughter of Eli J. HOGE, of Mountain Dell, Loudoun County.

Died: At Salentium, Loudoun Co., 26th May, 1875, Mary Campbell, wife of Maj. John J. WHITE. For sixteen years she has been a wife and mother.

Died: Passed away in the 49th year of her age, at "Peachgrove," her residence on Thursday morning, June 3rd, 1875, at 6½ o'clock, after a few months illness of consumption, Margaret Elizabeth, relict of Robert ELGIN, and daughter of John and Pamelia CURRELL, deceased.

County Ct.: Ed. NICHOLS was substituted trustee in place of Isaac HOGE dec'd., and A. J. BRADFIELD was substituted trustee in place of Jno. LESLIE dec'd., who was trustee for Jane E. BYRNE and children. Powell HARRISON was substituted Executor of the late Burr HARRISON, in place of M. HARRISON, dec'd. Will of Ludwell LUCKETT dec'd. admitted to probate, with L. H. and C. D. LUCKETT as Executors. Will of Wm. CROSS admitted to probate Mrs. Mary CROSS Executor. Will of Mason CHAMBLIN admitted to probate, H. C. CHAMBLIN, Executor. Will of Nathaniel THOMAS admitted to probate, John T. ROSS, Admr. wwa. John GRUBB qualified as Admr. of Mary GRUBB dec'd. Jas. G. DOWDELL qualified as Admr. of Sarah DOWDELL dec'd. Estates of Francis LUCKETT, John R. BURR and R. C. McCARTY were committed to the Sheriff.

Thursday, 24 June 1875   Vol. XX, No. 1

Married: On April 12th, at the Dill House, in Frederick City, Md, by the Rev. George T. TYLER, Mr. Thomas E. HOUGH to Miss Agnes P. WHITE, both of Loudoun county.

Married: In Rehobeth Church, June 17th, by Rev. W. T. SCHOOLEY, assisted by Rev. J. B. NORTH, Mr. George W. WOLFORD to Miss Fannie JAMES, only daughter of Jos. and Mary JAMES, all of this county.

Thursday, 1 July 1875   Vol. XX, No. 2

Married: On the 22d instant, by Elder S. R. WHITE, Mr. John TILLETT to Miss Mollie RICE, both of Loudoun county.

Died: At his residence near Gainesville, Prince William county, on the 21st of June, 1875, of typhoid fever, George W. SAUNDERS, in the 44th year of his age.

Died: May 2d, 1875, at her residence near Bloomfield, Loudoun county, Mrs. Lucinda PALMER, widow of Wm. C. PALMER. Member of the Baptist Church more than 30 years.

Died: On the 17th of May, 1875, at the residence of her husband, Mrs. Mary Ann LAYCOCK, wife of Mr. Jas. LAYCOCK, aged 52y 1m.

Death of Rev. Samuel GOVER – occurred at his home in Leesburg on Saturday morning last, in his 82d year. He was born in Leesburg and had spent the greater portion of his four score years at the home of his birth. For more than half a century he was a member of the M. E. Church. On Sunday afternoon his remains were interred in the burying ground of the old Stone Church. Services by Rev. Mr. CLEMMENTS, of the M. E. Church, Rev. Mr. CANNON, of the Presbyterian Church, and Rev. Mr. GARDINER, of the M. E. Church, South.

Thursday, 8 July 1875   Vol. XX, No. 3

Married: In Poolesville, Md, on the 4th inst., by the Rev. W. A. WADE, Clarence G. HEAD, to Miss Maggie E. ROLLINS, both of Leesburg.

Died: At the residence of Mr. Joseph LOWE, near Middleburg, on the 20th of February, 1875, of pneumonia or heart disease, Mrs. Catharine RUSSELL, in the 76th year of her age, leaving six children and many grandchildren.

Insane – Mr. William BIRKETT of this county was committed to the jail in Leesburg on Tuesday, as a lunatic.

Thursday, 15 July 1875   Vol. XX, No. 4

Married: At the residence of the bride's father, in Lexington, Ky, on Tuesday evening, 29th of June, 1875, by Rev. Dr. REED, Mr. Stephen G. ROSZEL (formerly of Leesburg) to Miss Mary Alice DRAKE, both of Lexington, Ky.

Married: On the evening of the 29th of June, at the bride's home, near Mt. Pleasant, in Frederick county, Md, near Mt. Pleasant in Frederick county, Md, by Rev. X. J. RICHARDSON, Mr. W. Scott DOWNEY, of Loudoun county, and Miss Laura J. COLLINS, of Maryland.

Died: At her residence near Woodgrove on Sunday the 4th instant in the 70th year of her age, Mrs. Patsy OSBURN, relict of Richard OSBURN. Her large family of children and grandchildren gather about her open grave and mourned.

Died: In Middleburg at the residence of her son-in-law, Col. L. CHANCELLOR, on the 1st of July, Mrs. Elizabeth SMITH, wife of the late Hugh SMITH, in her 73d year.

Henson McKENZIE (colored) better known in this community as "Binn's Henson," was killed by a passing train of cars on the B. & O. Railroad at Flemington, W Va, about ten days ago. He was in the employment of Mr. Chas. POWELL. His mutilated remains were buried at Flemington. He has a wife and several children living in this county.

County Ct.: The estate of Samuel A. TILLETT committed to the Sheriff. Will of the late Samuel GOVER admitted to probate, Annie M. HEAD, Executor.

Thursday, 22 July 1875   Vol. XX, No. 5

Married: In this town, July 11th, Rev. J. F. CANNON, Mr. George W. HARRIS and Miss Alice C. CAMPBELL.

Died: At his residence in Lawrence, Kansas, on the 4th inst., William S. WOOD, formerly of Loudoun county, in his 59th year.

Died: On the morning of July 8th, in Alexandria, Lizzie J., wife of Thos. LEADBEATER, and daughter of A. H. SLAYMAKER.

Died: In Belmont county, Ohio, on Monday the 12th inst., Mary CONARD. She had recently left home in Loudoun to visit her friends in Ohio when after a short illness she died. The remains were brought to Loudoun and buried on Thursday last.

Mr. James LEWIS, of this county, died at his residence about three miles from Leesburg, from the effects of sun-stroke. Mr. LEWIS was taken on Monday and died Saturday morning in about the 59th year of his age. He was from Hazletown, in Pennsylvania. He purchased a farm in this county some 5 or 6 years ago, where he resided up to the time of his death. On Sunday afternoon his remains were buried in Union Cemetery.

Thursday, 29 July 1875   Vol. XX, No. 6

Died: In Blacksburg, Montgomery county, Thursday morning, July 22, Henry W. JACKSON, only child of Rebecca Lloyd and Rev. H. Melville JACKSON.

Mr. ___ MYERS, of Washington, but who for several years past has been spending most of his time at the Osburn House, in this town, died at the boarding house of Mrs. Mary CLINE, near Snickersville, one day last week. His remains were taken to Washington for interment.

Thursday, 5 August 1875   Vol. XX, No. 7

Married: July 22d at the residence of the bride's mother, near Goresville, by Rev. H. CLEMENT, William H. RYAN, of Loudoun, to Miss Virginia E. LOY, daughter of the late Adam LOY, Esq.

Married: On the 27th of June, 1875, at the residence of Thomas W. FLEMING, near Paris, Va, by Rev. T. HERNDON, James T. GRUBBS, of Fauquier county, to Miss Annie E. ANDERSON, formerly of Winchester.

Married: On the 6th of May, by Rev. G. STEVENSON, at Stone Bridge, Bushrod T. GORU to Miss Annie E., daughter of John FOLK, all of Clarke County.

Mrs. Susan LANE, of this town, widow of the late Dr. LANE, of Centreville, died in this town on Wednesday morning last, after a lingering illness in the 89th year of her age.

Thursday, 12 August 1875   Vol. XX, No. 8

Married: In this town, August 5th by Rev. J. F. CANNON, Mr. J. T. LAMAR, of Hancock county, Ky, and Miss Mary E. PRICE, of Loudoun county.

Married: At the residence of the bride's brother, in Snickersville on Wednesday the 23d of June, by Rev. Samuel BROWN, Mr. Ashford WEADON and Miss Mollie R. O'BANNON, all of Loudoun.

Died: At Groveton, residence of F. M. CARTER, Esq., July 31st, Margaret Anna, infant daughter of M. E. and John CARTER, aged five weeks.

Died: In Leesburg, on Wednesday morning, August 4th, after a protracted illness, Susan BARBOUR, relict of the late Dr. Benedict M. LANE, of Centreville. She was the last of her generation having survived 14 brothers and sisters.

County Ct.: Gilbert B. GIBSON qualified as Admr. of the late Nathaniel THOMAS in the place of John T. ROSS, who refused to execute a new bond. Ann LEWIS qualified as Admx. of Jas. LEWIS dec'd. Jas. W. GRUBB qualified as Admr. of H. C. HILLEARY dec'd. Eliza STOCKTON qualified as the guardian of Sallie Q., Cecelia S., Hannah T. and Isaac P. LYTH. Will of the late Mahlon BEANS admitted to probate, N. B. PEACOCK qualified as Executor. Estate of the late E. L. BENTLY committed to the hands of the Sheriff. T. R. WILSON qualified as Admr. of Sarah J. BOLEY dec'd. P. H. CARR qualified as Admr. of Margaret E. ELGIN dec'd. and also of Robt. ELGIN dec'd. Harrison OSBURN qualified as Admr. of Patsy OSBURN dec'd.

Thursday, 19 August 1875   Vol. XX, No. 9

Mr. John R. SKINNER, of this county, was killed by the fall of a horse, which occurred on the 17th of July, near the Horse Pen Run, on Mr. J. C. COLEMAN's farm. He died on the 20th ultimo. He was a youth.

Death of Lemuel WATSON – died at his home in Leesburg at 8 o'clock on Sunday morning last, in his 65th year. For nearly half a century he was a member of the M. E. Church. On Monday afternoon buried in Union Cemetery, Rev. Dr. HEAD officiating.

Thursday, 26 August 1875   Vol. XX, No. 10

Died: In this town, on Tuesday last, Thomas Foster, youngest child of J. T. and Sarah STEADMAN, aged 18 months.

Died: Mrs. Amelia E. LOCK, wife of Franck LOCK, departed this life, August 9th, at her residence of Clarke county, aged 34y 2m 12d. Member of the Methodist Church.

Clara, a colored girl living with the Misses RUSSELL, in this town retired about 9 o'clock on Monday night in her usual health, a half hour later she was seized with heart disease, and died in a few minutes.

An unfortunate difficulty occurred at the Camp Meeting in Benton's woods, near the Pot House, in this county, on Tuesday night last, which resulted in the death of a negro man named Edward JONES (inquest gives as Edward JAMES alias Edward JONES), from a pistol shot fired by a white man named Thos. BUNDLE. It appears that JONES, who lived about Middleburg, was arrested between 9-10 o'clock on the night in question by the police officer TAYLOR, charged with selling whiskey. BUNDLE was an assistant policeman and fired when JONES ran away.

Thursday, 2 September 1875   Vol. XX, No. 11

Died: In Leesburg, Aug. 14, 1875, Virginia Wise, infant daughter of M. B. and Emily STEADMAN, aged 10m 3d.

Died: At his residence, near Sudley Mills, on Friday, the 27th of August, 1875, Mr. Thomas HUTCHISON, in his 79th year.

Alexander POLAND, one of the conductors on the Washington and Georgetown railroad met with a sudden death near the east capitol gate Saturday night about 11 o'clock. The street car lunged throwing Mr. POLAND over the dashboard. He was a resident of Georgetown and leaves a family. He was a son of the late Alex. POLAND, of this town. His remains were brought to Leesburg on Tuesday and interred in Union Cemetery.

Thursday, 9 September 1875   Vol. XX, No. 12

Matthew LEE, of Prince Wm. Co., living near Manassas battlefield, drowned himself in Bull Run near his residence, on Saturday. His body was found about 1 o'clock. Some two weeks ago Mr. LEE's son was arrested on a charge of firing a neighbor's stack yard, by which several hundred bushels of grain were destroyed.

Married: In Washington on the 2d inst., by Rev. J. G. BUTLER, George T. BARBEE and Mary Virginia AYRE, both of Fauquier county.

Died: At his father's residence, Middleburg, Aug. 23, 1875, Carl, only son of Charles A. and Olive P. SMITH, aged 9m 23d.

Alfred WRIGHT, better known in this community as "Gilmore's Alfred," died in this town on Friday night last, in about the 70th year of his age. "Uncle Alfred," was for many years a preacher in the Old School Baptist Church. On Sunday he was buried by the colored benevolent society.

Thursday, 16 September 1875   Vol. XX, No. 13

Died: In Fairfax county, Elizabeth Haller, infant daughter of A. C. and S. V. THOMAS, of Baltimore, aged 4m 9d.

Died: At Mt. Easton, on the 31st inst., Alice, infant daughter of Arthur and Emma R. OTLEY, aged 9m 24d. She left Mary her twin sister to make happy sisters.

County Ct.: Geo. W. TAYLOR appointed committee of R. W. PARKER, Will of Susannah HESKETT proved, Samuel CLENDENNING qualified as Executor. Estates of Wm. S. GRAY, Amanda FLETCHER, Geo. K. FOX Sr., John HAMILTON and Wilson THOMAS were committed to the Sheriff. Charles W. BAKER qualified as Guardian of Sarah A. and Nancy T. MOORE. John H. DRISH was substituted trustee in place of John HAMMERLY, for Phebe A. DRISH.

Mr. Thomas RICH, of Washington, died in that city on 10 Sept., in his 55th year. He has relatives and friends in this county.

Thursday, 23 September 1875   Vol. XX, No. 14

Married: On the 15th inst., in St. James' Church, Warrenton, Va, by the Rev. John S. LINDSAY, John R. TODD, Esq. of Norfolk, Va., and Miss Lilly Winter PAYNE, daughter of the last Richards PAYNE, Esq. of Fauquier county.

Married: In Leesburg, September the 16th 1875, at the residence of the bride's mother, by Rev. J. S. GARDNER, Mr. Samuel E. MONDAY and Miss Carrie B. BALLENGER.

Married: On Monday evening, September 20, by Rev. D. F. SPRIGG, James W. ATKINSON and Maria S. EDELIN, all of Alexandria, Va.

Died: At the residence of Mr. Geo. H. WENNER, near Lovettsville, on Sunday last, Mr. Wm. SHORT, son of Mr. Jacob SHORT, in the 26th year of his age.

Died: At Morven, Fauquier county, on the 7th September 1875, Thomas AMBLER, aged 84 years.

Died: At the residence of his son, Wm. A. REEDER, near Snickersville, in this county, on the 4th inst., Gourley REEDER, aged 87y 8m 27d.

Thursday, 30 September 1875   Vol. XX, No. 15

Married: At Northfork Church on Tuesday morning, Sept. 28th, 1875, by Rev. L. H. CRENSHAW, Mr. Thos. H. JAMES, of Colorado county, Texas (formerly of Loudoun) and Miss Virginia F., daughter of the late French SIMPSON, of this county.

Married: At Rockland, the residence of the bride's father, on Thursday, September 23d, 1875, by the Rev. H. B. LEE, assisted by Rev. R. T. DAVIS, Edmund L. LEE Jr., of Shepherdstown, W. Va., to Rebecca, daughter of Col. A. T. M. RUST of Loudoun county.

Married: At the residence of the bride's father, Mr. Wm. SHREVE, near Falls Church, Fairfax Co., on Tuesday the 15th instant, by Rev. Wm. G. HAMMOND, of the M. E. Church South, Mr. Andrew MELVILLE, formerly of Scotland, but now of Washington DC to Miss Barbara SHREVE.

Mrs. Mary NEWTON, wife of Mr. Alexander NEWTON, died at her home near Leesburg, on Monday evening last in about the 80th year of her age.

Thursday, 7 October 1875   Vol. XX, No. 16

Married: September 23d, 1875, in Loudoun county, by Rev. J. M. FRIDAY, Robert T. POWELL, of Washington, DC, and Martha E. KESSLER, of Loudoun county.

Died: In this town, on Tuesday morning last, William WILDMAN, in the 85th year of his age.

Died: In Gumspring, Sept. 24th, 1875, Lee Jackson LAMBERT, in the 12th year of his age. He was the son of Dr. and Mary LAMBERT, of Gumspring, Arcola, Loudoun County.

An Englishman, names SELLMAN, who for several weeks had been in the employment of Capt. L. T. JONES, near Waterford, was found dead in Mr. JONES' barn on Saturday morning. Inquest rendered death from natural causes. SELLMAN had been on a big drunk the day before his body was found.

Thursday, 14 October 1875   Vol. XX, No. 17

Married: On the 30th of September at the residence of Mrs. HEATER, near Taylortown, by Rev. S. A. BALL, Mr. John Henry WILLIAMS and Miss Sarah Jane HEATER, both of Loudoun.

Died: On Tuesday, September 28th, 1875, Hattie W. ROLLINS, daughter of Lewis and Jane ROLLINS, aged eleven years and one ___.

Died: At the residence of Mrs. Robt. ISH, near Aldie, on Monday the 11th of October, Mrs. Mary PROSSER, daughter of the late Jacob ISH, in about the 80th year of her age.

County Ct.: Jas. H. DODD qualified as Executor of Amanda DODD dec'd. J. B. THROCKMORTON qualified as Admr. dbn wwa of Sarah M. C. THROCKMORTON dec'd. Jonah NIXON appointed committee of George NIXON, a person of unsound mind. C. C. GAVER qualified as Admr. of John FRITTS dec'd.

Thursday, 21 October 1875   Vol. XX, No. 18

Married: On the morning of the 14th at the residence of Mr. Frank WILT, by the Rev. S. A. BALL, Mr. John P. DARR and Miss Margaret Ann WILT, both of Loudoun.

Married: At the residence of the bride's mother, near Rockville, Md, on Wednesday morning, October 20th 1875, by Rev. Chas. KILGOUR, Mr. Chas. O. VANDEVANTER, of Loudoun, and Miss Gennie, daughter of the late Alexander KILGOUR, of Maryland.

Circuit Ct.: Dr. John CULLEN appointed trustee in the place of Geo. B. McCARTY under the will of Geo. W. McCARTY dec'd.

At the colored church in Hamilton, in this county, on Tuesday night last, a difficulty occurred between two negro men, Sam WILLIAMS and Presley ASHBY, which resulted in the death of the former. ASHBY struck WILLIAMS in the head with a rock and although he was still alive on Wednesday morning, there was no hope of his recovery. ASHBY was committed to jail. [paper of 4 Nov. states he will recover]

Thursday, 28 October 1875   Vol. XX, No. 19

Married: At the house of the bride's mother near Leesburg, October 20th, by the Rev. H. CLEMENT, Charles C. CRIDLER and Sallie L. LEE, both of Loudoun county.

Married: In St. Peter's Church, Poolesville, Md, on Thursday, the 14th of October, 1875, by Rev. John TOWLES, Mr. Vernon HEMPSTONE, formerly of Leesburg, and Miss Lizzie, only daughter of Thos. H. POOLE, of Md.

Married: At the residence of Mr. J. P. STEADMAN, Oct. 17, 1875, by Rev. J. H. HAMILTON, Mr. John A. STEADMAN, formerly of Leesburg, to Miss Laura E. RAMSEY, of McConnelville, Ohio.

Thursday, 4 November 1875   Vol. XX, No. 20

Married: On the 27th inst., at the residence of Chas. DOWNES, Esq., by Rev. Thos. E. CARSON, Mr. Milton ZIMMERMAN and Miss Aramanta ALLISON, both of Fauquier Co.

Married: On October 25, in Saint Barnabas' Church, Baltimore, by Rev. A. P. STRYKER, Rev. Chas. J. KILGOUR, of Virginia to Fannie Claiborne, youngest daughter of the late Captain Charles B. BEAUFORD, U. S. R. S.

Married: On the 26th inst. at St. James' church, Warrenton, by the Rev. John S. LINDSAY, Mr. Mellville C. SHUSTER, of Washington, DC and Miss Mary A. WARD, eldest daughter of Dr. John WARD, of Warrenton.

Married: On the same day, by Rev. Mr. LADD, at the residence of the bride, James P. MARSHALL, of Mason County, Ky, and Miss Hester M. MARSHALL, of Fauquier Co.

Married: On the same day, at the Methodist Church, in Warrenton, by Rev. J. F. POULTON, John T. GRAY and Miss Margaret R. ALLISON, both of Fauquier county.

Married: On the 19th inst., in the church of the Ascension, Washington DC, by Rev. Dr. ELLIOTT, Mr. James A. MENEFEE, of Warrenton, and Miss Laura LAWS, of Washington DC.

Married: In St. Paul's church, Alexandria, by Rev. Dr. NORTON on the 25th inst., Robert F. TURNER, of Fauquier and Miss Mary W. CORSE, daughter of Maj. W. D. CORSE.

Died: Gaither, son of Washington and Martha MERCIER, died at White's Ferry, Md, October 19th, 1875, aged 5y 10m.

Thursday, 11 November 1875 Vol. XX, No. 21

Married: On Nov. 2d, 1875, at the residence of the bride's father, by the Rev. L. H. CRENSHAW, Mr. Wm. G. BIRDSALL and Miss Maggie A. THOMAS, daughter of Mahlon THOMAS, Esq., all of Loudoun.

Married: At the residence of the bride's father in the valley of the Tennessee, near Rhea Springs, Rhea Co., Tenn, Nov. 4, 1875, by the Rev. Steven Mason McPHERSON, John L. BALL, Esq. of Loudoun Co., and Mary J., only daughter of Steven CAWOOD, Esq.

Died: At Spring Place, Murray Co., Georgia, with consumption, Nov. 5th, 1875, Rev. T. J. McVEIGH, formerly of Loudoun Co., son of T. McVEIGH.

Died: In Baltimore, on Sunday morning, Nov. 7th, 1875, at 10 o'clock, Mrs. A. E. SELLMAN, aged 52 years, wife of J. J. M. SELLMAN and daughter of the late Alfred BELT, of Loudoun.

Nov. Ct.: J. W. GARRETT qualified as Admr. of Jas. W. CONNER dec'd., John W. FRY qualified as Admr. of Joseph FRY dec'd. N. B. PEACOCK qualified as Admr. of Michael BEAMER dec'd.

Mr. William BALL, who resided near Langley, in Fairfax county, was found lying on the road between that place and Georgetown, early this morning, dead with his neck broken. He left Georgetown late yesterday evening and is supposed to have fallen out of his wagon. He was the son of the late Warring BALL, of Fairfax.

have fallen out of his wagon. He was the son of the late Warring BALL, of Fairfax.

The *Washington News*: The marriage of Mr. William TYLER, son of Dr. Grafton TYLER, of Georgetown, D.C. to Miss Addie M. LUTZ, of Loudoun county, will take place on the 18th inst.

Thursday, 18 November 1875   Vol. XX, No. 22

Married: At 8 p.m., Nov. 9th in the Free Church, at Waterford, by the Rev. Theodore REED, Dr. J. Hamilton MOORE to Miss Ella MOUNT, eldest daughter of Wm. T. MOUNT, all of Loudoun.

Married: At the residence of Mrs. M. A. GAY, Alexandria, on Thursday evening at 7 o'clock, by Rev. Leo. BAIER, Prof. Job G. McVEIGH, of Hannibal College, Mo. and Miss Virginia MacFARLANE.

Died: At the residence of her grandfather, Rev. E. T. PERKINS, in Louisville, Ky, on Saturday the 13th of November, 1875, of cerebro-spinal meningetis, Hattie Griswold, infant daughter of Dr. Chas. G. and Isa A. EDWARDS, aged 7 months.

Died: At his residence near North Fork, on Friday, the 22d of Oct., Mr. William CONNER, in the 33d year of his age.

Died: On Friday, 12th inst., near Vienna, Fairfax county, of consumption, Amanda C., wife of Julius L. PECK, in the 45th year of her age.

Mr. J. E. DOUGLASS died yesterday afternoon, at the residence of his uncle, A. J. FLEMING, Esq., of consumption. He had been ill for some time past and his death was not unexpected. Previous to his illness Mr. DOUGLASS was a well known merchant in this city and in Richmond.

Thursday, 25 November 1875   Vol. XX, No. 23

Married: At Buoenas Ayres, Roanoke County, Va, on Thursday, the 18th of November, 1875, by Rev. E. H. ENGLE, M. M. ROGERS, Esq., of Baltimore (formerly of this county) and Miss Virginia, daughter of Col. George P. TAYLOR, of Roanoke County.

Married: On November 18, at the residence of the bride's parents, in Baltimore, by the Rev. Father STARR, E. L. BENTLEY, formerly of Leesburg, to Mamie E. McABEE, both of that city.

Died: At her residence near Mt. Zion Church, in this county, on Monday, the 8th of November, 1875, Mrs. Elizabeth HUTCHISON, widow of the late Sampson HUTCHISON, in the 88th year of her age.

Died: Suddenly, at Middleburg on the 15th Nov. 1875, of congestion of the lungs, Lloyd NOLAND, eldest son of Major R. W. N. NOLAND, in the 31st year of his age. He long had been an exemplary member of the Episcopal Church.

Died: In Georgetown, on the 26th instant, Miss S. M. BRONAUGH, in the 61st year of the age.

Died: At her home in Middleburg, on Monday evening last, Mrs. Sallie A. LUCKETT, widow of the late Francis W. LUCKETT, in the 80th year of her age.

Mr. Chas. P. JANNEY detained in Baltimore. On Friday last Mr. JANNEY and his wife went to Baltimore, taking with them their oldest child to consult a physician for an affection of his throat, they left their two younger children behind, one of them a bright little girl of four years old with her grandparents in Hillsborough. The day after they arrived in Baltimore, Mr. JANNEY was prostrated with diphtheria and is still confined to his bed. On Monday, diphtheria developed on little Becky and she died on Tuesday evening. The mother reached home on Wednesday and the remains will on Thursday be interred in Union Cemetery.

Thursday, 2 December 1875   Vol. XX, No. 24

Married: On the 25th inst., at Christ Church, Georgetown, by Rev. W. W. WILLIAMS, Harold SNOWDEN, local editor of the *Alexandria Gazette*, and Leila Leigh, daughter of the late Robert J. LACKEY, all of Virginia.

Married: At the residence of Lt. Barber, on the 18th of November, 1875, by Rev. Thomas W. BRUN, assisted by Rev. H. E. JOHNSON, William I. BRADFIELD, of Loudoun county, and Miss Mollie NORRIS, of Baltimore Co.

Married: On Wednesday, the 24th inst., in New York Avenue Church, by the Rev. Dr. MITCHELL, Dr. Robert FARNHAM and Emma J. LOWRY, daughter of the late Wm. LOWRY, all of Washington, DC.

Married: In Leesburg, on Tuesday, 23d instant, by Rev. J. S. GARDNER, Mr. Franklin LENT and Miss Alverd BURR, all of Loudoun.

Died: At the residence of her sister in Leesburg on Sunday afternoon, Nov. 28th, 1875, of consumption, Mrs. Laura E. HARMON, wife of Dr. J. D. HARMON, of Hamilton and daughter of the late C. R. DOWELL, in the 28th year of her age.

Died: In Lake City, Florida, on the 9th of November, at the residence of her daughter, Mrs. Dr. Wm. BALES, Mrs. Sophia S. EWART, relict of the late David EWART, of Columbia, S.C., and daughter of Andrew Joseph and Sophia De Meaux VILLARD, of Westmoreland county, Va, in the 79th year of her age.

Died: On Wednesday, Nov. 17th, at Stony Point, Loudoun county, Mary Best, daughter of Josiah T. and Mary J. WHITE, aged 16m 21d.

A dispatch from Washington, dated Friday says a carpenter named George LITTLETON was killed about 7½ o'clock this morning, by falling down the elevator hatchway at the new dining rooms of the Marble saloon, corner of Pennsylvania avenue and Ninth street. Mr. LITTLETON was in the employ of W. H. JOHNSON. He was sent to the Providence Hospital and died there soon after nine o'clock. He leaves a wife and three young children. Mr. L. was a nephew of Mr. Thos. LITTLETON, of Leesburg.

Thursday, 9 December 1875   Vol. XX, No. 25

Married: On the 30th of November, 1875, by Rev. Mr. CLEMENT, at the residence of the bride's mother, near Leesburg, Mr. Chas. MULLEN and Miss Mollie MORIARTY, both of Loudoun.

Married: On the 30th ult., near Lovettsville, by the Rev. Hy. St. John RINKER, Mr. John W. BAKER to Miss Sarah C. FRY, all of Loudoun county.

Married: In Harmony Church, on Thursday evening the 25th ult., by the Rev. Mr. JONES, of Hillsboro circuit, Dr. Robert TAVENNER and Miss Estell HOUGH, daughter of Wm. HOUGH, Esq., all of Loudoun county.

Married: In Washington, DC, on Thursday, 25th of November, by the Rev. L. B. WYNN, Jno. T. HERBERT, of St. Mary's Co., Md, and Miss Amanda E. KIDWELL, formerly of Loudoun.

Died: Near Pleasant Prairie, Mo, October 29th, 1875, in the 5th year of her age, Nellie, daughter of George and Jane Ann GRUBB, formerly of Loudoun county.

Died: At the residence of Mr. Robert HOSKINSON in Hamilton, on Thursday night last, of pneumonia, Mr. Thos. L. HOSKINSON, in the 73d year of his age.

Died: Near Snickersville, on Thursday, the 25th of November after a short illness, Mrs. Anna MARTS, wife of Mr. Samuel MARTS, in the 47th year of her age.

Died: In Baltimore, at the Church Home, on Thursday, December 24, 1875, at 4 p.m., Mrs. Elizabeth Lee, wife of Geo. M. GRAYSON, of Loudoun and daughter of H. T. HARRISON of Leesburg.

Mr. John IDEN of this county died at his home near Ball's Mill, on Saturday night last, of apoplexy, at 8 o'clock that night. He was in about the 55th year of his age. His remains were interred in the Cemetery at Middleburg, on Monday morning.

Capt. John MOORE died at his residence on Dumbarton street last night, in the 88th year of his age. Born in Prince George's county, Md, in 1788. He lived in Loudoun county for over forty years where his children were born and reared, and in Georgetown for thirty two years. He served with distinction through the war of 1812-14. About fifty years ago he removed to Georgetown. He was extensively interested in the construction of the Chesapeake & Ohio Canal. The deceased was the father of Col. L. T. MOORE, of Winchester.

Thursday, 16 December 1875   Vol. XX, No. 26

Married: At the residence of Mr. Frank BRANHAN, on Thursday, the 9th of December, 1875, by Rev. Dr. HEAD, Mr. Chas. W. HOUSER and Miss Mary F. DAVIS, all of Loudoun.

Married: At Bloomfield Church, on the 8th inst., by Rev. Thos. E. CARSON, Henry H. TAYLOR and Miss Alcinda E. JACOBS.

Died: In Leesburg on the 20th November, at residence of her uncle, Anthony DIBBRELL, Mamie, youngest child of the last Dr. E. S. McARTHUR, of Chesterfield co., Va, aged about 3y 11m.

Died: Mrs. Agnes WHITE, wife of James B. WHITE, Esq., died at Salentum, her husband's residence near Hillsborough, on Saturday last, in the 68th year of her age.

Dec. Ct.: Virginia IDEN qualified as Admx. of John T. IDEN dec'd. Will of Elizabeth HUTCHISON admitted to probate, Wm. L. SANFORD, Executor. Will of Elizabeth OGDEN admitted to probate, W. C. SHAWEN, Executor. Will of Sarah S. LUCKETT admitted to probate, John C. BRONAUGH, Executor. Will of Jas. SILCOTT admitted to probate, Virginia C. SILCOTT, Admx. Will of Gustavia B. ADIE admitted to probate, Julia H. ADIE, Executrix. Jas. H. DODD Executor of Susan A. FLETCHER executed new bond. Estates of Albert BEATTY and Jesse SMITH committed to Sheriff.

A pleasant reminiscence – In the third day's fighting around Gettysburg, in July 1864, Alexander GRAYSON, of this county, Captain of Company F, 8th Virginia Regiment, was killed and nothing could be learned of his remains, if buried at all, his body fills to this day an unknown grave. Recently a Richmond paper published a letter from A. A. Gen. W. H. TAYLOR, of Albany to the A. A. Gen. of Virginia, saying that a friend of his, Mr. J. W. HARRIS, of New York city, had in his possession a sword and pistol, marked A. GRAYSON, which he had found upon the Gettysburg battlefield. This letter attracted the attention of Mr. Geo. M. GRAYSON, of this county, a brother of Captain A. GRAYSON. Items were returned to him a few days ago.

Thursday, 23 December 1875   Vol. XX, No. 27

Married: On the 14th of December, by Rev. B. P. DULIN, Mr. John W. BITZER and Laura M. MOFFETT, all of Loudoun county.

Married: On Wednesday evening, December 15th at Trinity Chapel, New York, by Rev. Dr. PEET, Courtland H. SMITH, of

Alexandria, and Charlotte E., daughter of the late Thomas P. ROSSITER, of New York City.

Married: On December 21st, 1875, at Pursellville, by Rev. L. H. CRENSHAW, Mr. Presley MOORE and Miss Mary J. REYNOLDS, both of Loudoun.

Died: At his residence in Waterford, Nov. 13th, 1875, of consumption, Mr. James SILCOTT, in the 55th year of his age. Member of the Presbyterian Church.

Thursday, 30 December 1875   Vol. XX, No. 28

Capt. James L. HENDERSON died in Charlestown, West Virginia, on Monday last, in the 62nd year of his age. Native of Fauquier county, and for many years surgeon in the U.S. Navy and grandson of Commodore TRUXTON. He entered the U.S. Navy when only 14 years old, and remained until the breaking out of the late civil war.

Married: At "Nesting," the residence of the bride's father, in Middlesex County, Va, on Thursday, the 16th of December, 1875, by Rev. J. D. HANK, Mr. S. Roszel DONOHOE, Editor of the *West Point Star*, and Miss C. H. EUBANK, daughter of Joseph C. EUBANK, Esq.

Married: At the residence of the bride's parents, near Warrenton, on Thursday, December 23, 1875, by the Rev. A. D. POLLOCK, Mr. Matthew GILMOUR, of Richmond, to Miss Roberta, youngest daughter of the officiating clergyman.

Died: At "Raspberry Plains," near Leesburg, on Saturday night, Dec. 25th, 1875, Miss Mary Elizabeth HOFFMAN, daughter of the late Jacob HOFFMAN of Alexandria.

Thursday, 6 January 1876   Vol. XX, No. 29

Married: December 7th, 1875, at Ketoctin Baptist Church, Loudoun county, by Rev. J. B. LAKE, Miss Mollie PURCELL to Mr. Otis EUBANK, of Amherst County, Va.

Married: December 16th, 1875, near Middleburg, by the same, Miss L. SMALLWOOD to Mr. John M. BRYNE.

Married: December 22d, 1875, at Upperville, Va, by the same, Miss L. V. BOWIE to Mr. James W. WYNKOOP.

Married: December 28th, 1875, near Bloomfield, Loudoun county, by the same, Miss Emma WHITTINGTON to Mr. Matthew KERICK.

Married: In Waterford, on Thursday evening, Dec. 23, by Rev. Mr. BALL, Mr. Jonathan MYERS to Miss Kate MOORE, all of Loudoun county.

Died: At Mountsville, on Tuesday, January 4th, 1876, Mr. James MOUNT, in the 86th year of his age.

Died: At the residence of his parents, near Bloomfield, "Robbie," youngest son of Thomas and Annie PALMER, aged 3 years. From birth he had been afflicted with disease of the spine.

Mr. James MOUNT died at his residence at Mountsville in this county on Tuesday, 4th of January 1876, in his 86th year.

Col. Joseph R. COCKERILLE, a native of Loudoun, recently died at his home in Adams county, Ohio. Born in Loudoun County 1st of January 1819, died in his 57th year. When 18 years of age, he came to Ohio and settled in Adams County. From the time he became of age until he was 25 he taught school. At age of twenty one, he was elected Surveyor of his county. [details his careers] He leaves behind him a widow and two children.

Thursday, 13 January 1876   Vol. XX, No. 30

Married: On Jan. 11, 1876, by Rev. L. H. CRENSHAW, Mr. George D. SAVAGE and Miss Martha E. BALLENGER, both of Loudoun Co.

Married: In Alexandria, on Monday morning, 10th inst., by Rev. Mr. DINWIDDIE, Dr. R. C. POWELL to Mary C., daughter of the late Wm. GREGORY, all of that city.

Married: On Thursday evening, 6th inst., at the residence of the bride's parents, near Goresville, by the Rev. Henry CLEMENT, Charles E. FOX to Amanrella V. SNOOTZ, all of Loudoun Co.

Married: In St. James Church, Leesburg, on Thursday, January 6th, 1876, by the Rev. Jos. TRAPNELL, D.D., assisted by the Rev. R. T. DAVIS, Rector of the Church, and the Rev. Mr. BRADDOCK, Dr. Richard TRAPNELL, of Maryland, to Miss Edmonia, daughter of the late George MARLOW of Loudoun.

Married: In Warrenton, on the 29th ult., by Rev. Jno. F. POULTON, Mr. Marcellus EDWARDS and Miss Lucy EDWARDS, all of Fauquier County.

Married: On the 6th inst., at the residence of the bride's father, by the Rev. Jno. S. LINDSAY, Mr. Jno. A. NICHOLS, of Rappahannock county, Va, and Miss Lucinda A. SHERMAN, daughter of Abram B. SHERMAN, of Fauquier County.

Married: In St. James' Church, Warrenton, on the 30th of December, 1875, by the Rev. Jno. S. LINDSAY, Mr. Murray FORBES, of Fauquier county, and Miss Emily K. NORTH, daughter of Captain Jas. H. NORTH, of Culpeper county, Va.

Died: In Manchester, January 8th, Mrs. Anne S. BRONAUGH, wife of Dr. J. W. BRONAUGH, in her 67th year.

County Ct.: Mrs. Frances RYON qualified as Executrix of the late John H. RYON.

Thursday, 20 January 1876   Vol. XX, No. 31
Married: On the 12th inst., by Rev. Thos. E. CARSON, Mr. Robt. C. L. CHAMBLIN, and Miss Mary E. MILHOLLEN, both of Loudoun.

An accident occurred at Aldie in this county, on Saturday morning last, resulting in the death of a little son of Mr. Thos. WYNKOOP. It seems that the father had arranged a barrel of boiling water for the purpose of scalding a hog, and during his temporary absence the child, aged about 8 years, fell into the barrel, and was so severely scalded that he died at 7 o'clock that evening. Every particle of skin from his neck to the soles of his feet, peeled off.

Thursday, 27 January 1876   Vol. XX, No. 32
Mr. Alfred WRIGHT of this town, having for a number of years been engaged in the grocery business, died on Monday morning last, of cancer, in about the 70th year of his age. His remains were taken to Northfork, on Tuesday, for burial.

Rev. Chas. E. AMBLER, of the Protestant Episcopal Church, died in Charlestown, W Va, on Friday last. He had for a long time been in bad health.

Married: On Wednesday, 19th inst., at the Lutheran Church, Tankersfield, by Rev. S. A. BALL, Mr. S. J. J. COMPHER, and Miss Elizabeth R. EBBUT, both of Loudoun Co.

Married: On the 4th of December, 1875, by Elder Joseph FURR, at the house of the bride's mother, Mr. Zechariah T. BRUBAKER, of Juniatts County, Pa., to Miss Luranah MADDEN, daughter of William MADDEN, Esq., dec'd. of Huntington county, Pa.

Married: On Thursday the 23d, by the same, Mr. Samuel E. NEWLON to Miss Rosalie S. NEWLON, all of Loudoun County.

Married: On the 18th of January, 1876, at the residence of the late Timothy TAYLOR, Loudoun Co. by Rev. J. B. LAKE, Miss Hannah TAYLOR to Mr. Guilford CRAVEN.

Married: IN Alexandria on the 11th inst., by Rev. Wm. M. DAME, Mr. L. A. MARSTELLER, of Prince William County, and Miss Charlotte MITCHELL, of Fauquier.

Married: On the 16th, by Rev. C. G. LINTHICUM, in the M. E. Church, South, at Rectortown, W. Decatur VANHORN and Miss Virginia GAINES, all of Fauquier.

Thursday, 3 February 1876   Vol. XX, No. 33
Married: At the residence of the bride's mother, January 20th, 1876, by Rev. L. H. CRENSHAW, Mr. Peyton H. DAVIS to Miss Sallie M. LACOCK, daughter of Samuel LACOCK dec'd., all of Loudoun Co.

Married: On the 18th January, by the Rev. Dr. C. G. LINTHICUM, Sanford J. WEEDEN, of Loudoun, to Victoria M. JONES, of King George County.

Married: At. St. Paul's Rectory, Baltimore, on the 26th of January, by Rev. Dr. HODGES, Judge John Blair HOGE, of Martinsburg, to Mrs. M. S. ALSTON, of North Carolina.

Married; Near Silcott's Spring, Feb. 1st, 1876, by Rev. L. H. CRENSHAW, Mr. James E. SILCOTT and Miss Mary C. SILCOTT, daughter of Mr. Albert SILCOTT, all of Loudoun.

Died: At "Welbourn," Loudoun county, December 20th, 1875, Mrs. Mary E. EVANS, daughter of the late Thomas CLAGETT, of Prince George's county, Md, and wife of the late David FORREST, of Washington, D.C.

At about 7 o'clock on Monday evening, Mr. Lewis HUNT, the oldest man in this community, died in the 91st year of his age. He was a soldier in the war of 1812 and a pensioner under the government of the U.S. at the time of his death.

At half past three this (Thursday) afternoon, a grand wedding will take place in Warrenton, Va, the parties being Miss Jenny BETHUNE, daughter of Gen. J. B. BETHUNE, and Dr. Cornelius BOYLE, well known as Provost Marshal General at Gordonsville during the war.

Thursday, 10 February 1876 Vol. XX, No. 34

No marriages or deaths.

Thursday, 17 February 1876 Vol. XX, No. 35

Married: Feb. 15th, 1876, at the residence of the bride's father, by Rev. L. H. CRENSHAW, Mr. Charles TAYLOR and Miss Laura SIMPSON, dau. of John W. SIMPSON, Esq., all of Loudoun.

Married: Near Snickersville, Loudoun County, on 27th of January, 1876, by Rev. T. B. SHEPHERD, B. M. CARTER, of Frederick county, Va, to Miss Mary G. CALDWELL, of Loudoun county.

Married: On Feb. 3rd at White's Ferry, in Frederick Co., Md, by the Rev. H. CLEMENT, Isaac W. FRY to Margaret E. BAKER, all of Loudoun.

Married: In Leesburg, February 10th, 1876, by the Rev. Mr. GARDNER, Geo. W. POOLE and Matilda DOVE, all of Loudoun.

Married: At the bride's parents, January 27th, 1876, by Elder Benjamin BRIDGES, Mr. Albert MONEY to Miss Nannie, daughter of Thomas J. and Angelina PEACOCK.

Married: At the same time and place by the same, Mr. Adolphus J. JENKINS to Miss Narcissa, youngest daughter of Thos. J. and Angelina PEACOCK, all of Fairfax county.

Married: On the 18th of January, by Rev. Dr. G. LINTHICUM, Sanford J. WEEDEN, of Loudoun, to Victoria M. JONES, of King George county.
Married: Near Waterloo, in Culpeper county, on the 9th inst., by Rev. John L. CARROLL, Mr. Henry HOLT and Miss Mary S. BURKE.
Married: On the 7th inst., by the Rev. H. H. WYER, Mr. M. M. CARTER, of Loudoun, to Miss Isabella GOUGH, of Fauquier. [See entry two lines below. Date of 9th of Feb on the Fauquier Marriage Register]
Married: On Wednesday, January 26th, 1876, near Delaplane, Fauquier county, by the Rev. Thaddeus HERNDON, Mr. John J. ASHBY and Miss Louisa A. HERNDON, daughter of the officiating clergyman.
Married: On the 9th inst., by Rev. H. H. WYER, Mr. M. M. CARTER, of Loudoun, to Miss Isabella GOUGH, of Fauquier
Married: In Leesburg, February 3d, 1876, by Rev. Mr. GARDNER, Miss Fannie FEASTER of Loudoun county, to Mr. B. R. CROSS, of Prince William county.
Died: Near Farmwell, on February 1st, Mabyl, infant daughter of H. C. and Nettie B. HARDING, aged 6m 14d.
Feb. Ct.: John E. MOUNT qualified as Admr. of James MOUNT dec'd. Jas. E. CARRUTHERS qualified as Guardian of Rosella V. VIRTS, Clara H. A. VIRTS, and Henry J. T. VIRTS. Milton SCHOOLEY qualified as committee of Wm. STEER. Will of Lewis HUNT admitted to probate with Henry HEATON, Executor. Will of Alfred WRIGHT admitted to probate with Powell HARRISON executor.

Thursday, 24 February 1876   Vol. XX, No. 36

Married: In Leesburg, at the residence of the groom's parents, Wednesday, February 6th, 1876, by Rev. J. S. GARDNER, Mr. Benj. D. SURVICK to Miss Sarah V. SLACK.
Married: February 15th, 1876, at the residence of the bride's father, by Rev. J. M. FRIDAY, Mr. Jas. R. REED and Miss Mary V. SMITH, daughter of Job SMITH, all of Loudoun county.
Married: At the M. E. Parsonage Leesburg, Feb. 16th by the Rev. H. CLEMENT, Mr. Thomas WILEY to Miss Mary L. MOORE, all of Loudoun Co.
Married: At the residence of the bride's mother, on Thursday evening, February 17th 1876, by Rev. Dr. HEAD, Mr. Wm. S. SUMMERS (Deputy Sheriff) and Miss Nannie, daughter of the late G. M. WOODS, all of this county.
Married: On February 17th by Rev. Thos. E. CARSON, Mr. James W. DISHMAN and Miss Emma Virgie BENTON, both of Loudoun county.

Married: At Alexandria, Va on February 15th by Right Rev. F. M. WHITTLE, D.D., Assistant Bishop of Virginia, William G. HOWARD of Baltimore to Lucy, daughter of the late Col. George William BRENT, of Va.

Died: On the 16th instant, at his residence in this county, Rice SMITH, aged about 36 years.

Died: At the residence of her father, in Hamilton, on Sunday night last, Eva HARMAN, only child of Dr. J. D. HARMAN, aged 1y 8m.

Died: On the 8th of February, Viva Hunter, infant daughter of Chas. W. and Flora WYNKOOP, of this county.

At 10 o'clock on Sunday night after painful suffering and several weeks of patient confinement to his bed, Maj. Henry SAUNDERS breathed his last at "Rock Spring," his home near Leesburg, in the 88th year of his age. Born and reared within a short distance of the scene of his last conflict, and was the only survivor of his immediate family. Maj. SAUNDERS was born in this county in Nov. 1788. In 1812 he entered the U.S. Army as second Lt. of infantry. ... In early life he married a daughter of the late Gen. Wm. NORTH, of the U.S. Army. Three children were born, all of whom died in infancy. ...

Thursday, 2 March 1876   Vol. XX, No. 37

Died: At her residence, near Bloomfield, in this county, on Friday, 18 February 1876, Mrs. Phoeba HUMPHREY, in her 72d year.

Died: Near Bloomfield, on Sunday, the 20th of February 1876, Mr. John ROSS Sr., a soldier of the war of 1812, in his 88th year.

Died: At the residence of Mr. E. G. CAUFMAN, near Goresville, on Friday evening, Feb. 18th 1876, Miss Mary SHRY, a most worthy old lady, in about the 80th year of her age.

Died: Mr. Wm. A. WILSON, died of pneumonia, at the residence of his brother-in-law, Maj. B. P. NOLAND, in Middleburg, Va. on Tuesday, Feb. 29, 1876, aged 28 years.

Died: In Alexandria, on Tuesday last, of scarlet, fever, Arthur, son of John and Josephine STANDIFORD, aged 4y 2m.

Married: In Zion Church, Charlestown, on Thursday evening, February 10th, 1876, by Rev. W. H. MEADE, Mr. Richard D. RUTHERFORD and Miss Elizabeth Dick, third daughter of Mrs. A. M. FORREST, all of that place.

Married: In Cartersville, Feb. 16th 1876, by Rev. Mr. WAGNER, Mr. Norvelle R. ROBERTSON, of Cumberland county, Va, and Miss Carrie B. ROBERTS, formerly of Loudon County.

Married: At residence of the bride's mother, near Taylortown, on Thursday, February 24th, 1876, by Rev. Mr. RINKER, Mr. Joseph P. TITUS and Miss Annie GOODHART, all of this co.

Married: February 29th, by Rev. J. F. CANNON, Mr. Silas W. BEACH and Miss Christie V. SPINKS, both of Loudoun county.

Death near Bloomfield, of two aged people of this county. Mrs. Phoebe HUMPHREY died on the 18th of February in her 72d year, and two days later, on Sunday, the 20th her neighbor and friend, Mr. John ROSS, father of Mr. John T. ROSS, followed her to the grave, in the 88th year of his age. Mr. ROSS was a soldier during the war of 1812. Miss Mary SHRY, aged about 80 years, also died near Goresville, on the 18th of February.

Thursday, 9 March 1876   Vol. XX, No. 38

Married: On the 22d of February, 1876, at Clifton Place, near Jefferson, Md, by the Rev. N. H. SKYLES, assisted by Rev. J. A. PETERS, James W. GEORGE, of Lovettsville, to Miss Flora L. GROSS, of the above place.

Married: February 24th 1876, at the residence of the bride's father, near Lovettsville, by Rev. E. H. VAUGHAN, Mr. Kertis HICKMAN to Miss Rosia M. CONARD.

Died: At the residence of her husband, near Mt. Hope Church, on Wednesday, March 1st, 1876, Mrs. Mary BURCH, wife of Mr. Lewis D. BURCH, in the 69th year of her age.

Died: Mrs. Charles BALL, daughter of the late Frank ADAMS, near Aldie, died in Philadelphia, on the 29th ult.

Died: Near Leesburg, on Friday, the 25th, Rodger M., youngest son of Samuel H. and Lydia MULLEN, aged 4y 6m.

Died: Mrs. Ann A. ASHTON, died Sunday Feb. 27th 1876, aged 79 years. For perhaps more than half a century she had been a member of the Presbyterian church in Warrenton.

Died: Hannah G. Beale GASKINS departed this life at the residence of her husband, Col. Wm. E. GASKINS, near Midland station, Fauquier county, on the 4th instant, in the 43d year of her age.

Died: In Warrenton, on the 24th of February, in the 48th year of her age, Miss Mary F. SMITH, daughter of Mr. William SMITH, of Fauquier.

Died: On the 5th of March, in Alexandria, after a painful illness, Samuel HEFLEBOWER, aged 66 years.

Died: At her residence in Loudoun county, on Saturday, March 4th at half-past one o'clock, Susan E. HARRISON, widow of the late Col. John M. HARRISON, in the 72d year of her age.

Thursday, 16 March 1876   Vol. XX, No. 39

Married: Tuesday evening, February 29th, at the house of the bride's mother, by Rev. C. STATZMAN, Mr. Luther W. HICKMAN and Miss Anna M. ARNOLD, all of this county.

Married: At the residence of Mrs. Jane E. PANCOAST, in Leesburg, on Wednesday evening, March 8th, 1876, by Rev. R. T. DAVIS, Mr. H. Clay PORTER, of Danville, Va, and Miss Jennie E., dau. of the late Col. C. R. DOWELL, of Loudoun Co.

Married: On February 27th 1876, at the bride's residence in the town of Bolivar, by Rev. Andrew ROBEY, Mr. Edward LANDERS to Mrs. Maria Dora STORM, all of Jefferson county, W Va.

Died: At the residence of their brother, Billington McCARTY, near Mountsville, Mrs. Susan F. SMARR, on March 1st 1876, and on March 3rd, Miss Margaret Elizabeth McCARTY.

Died: In Alexandria, on Monday morning last, Mrs. Eliza DOUGLAS, wife of the late James DOUGLAS, and the venerable mother of Mr. R. Stuart DOUGLAS of Leesburg, in the 85th year of her age.

March Ct.: Ed. L. BROWN qualified as Admr. of Rev. F. C. TEBBS dec'd. Geo. W. BROWN qualified as Admr. of Wm. BROWN dec'd. Wills of John ROSS and the late Maj. Henry SAUNDERS admitted to probate. Estate of Jas. R. COLEMAN dec'd. committed to the Sheriff.

Thursday, 23 March 1876   Vol. XX, No. 40

Died: At Glebeland, Loudoun county, March 15, at midnight, Mary Ellen, wife of John ALDRIDGE, in the 56th year of her age.

Died: At her residence, near Dranesville, on Friday, March 17th 1876, Mrs. Ellen CARPER, in the 72d year of her age.

Died: Near Poolesville, Md, on the 27th ultimo, Mrs. B. A. ALLNUTT, wife of late James N. ALLNUTT, in her 64th year.

Died: In Washington city, on Tuesday night, March 21st 1876, of congestion of the brain, Miss Annie FREEMEN, of this county. Her remains were brought to Leesburg on the evening train, Wednesday, and will be interred in the Cemetery at this place today, Thursday.

Died: At her residence in Snickersville, February 10th 1876, Mrs. Mary C. HUMPHREY, widow of Abner G. HUMPHREY, in the 48th year of her age.

Died: At Windsor, in Loudoun county, after a week's illness, of pneumonia, Mrs. Susan E. HARRISON, widow of the late Col. John M. HARRISON, in the 72d year of her age.

Married: In Leesburg at the Presbyterian Church, on Wednesday, March 15th 1876, by the Rev. J. F. CANNON, Mr. George W. BROOKS to Miss Bettie A. BAILY, both of Loudoun.

Married: March 16, 1876, near Leesburg, by Rev. J. F. CANNON, Mr. Jas. D. BEACH and Miss Massie A. PRESTON, both of Loudoun Co.

Married: March 9th 1876, in Loudoun county, by Rev. J. M. FRIDAY, of Harper's Ferry, W. Va, Mr. George V. LAGLE, and Miss Martha A. DERRY, all of Loudoun county.

Married: By the Rev. Thad. HERNDON, at the bride's residence, near The Plains, Fauquier county, on the 9th day of March 1876, William E. BALL, Esq. to Mrs. Harriet Baynton TILLETT.

Married: Tuesday 14th inst., by Rev. J. F. POULTON, at the residence of the bride's parents, Mr. Peyton E. WILLIS and Miss Elizabeth KANE, all of Fauquier county.

Married: On the 16th inst., by the same, at the residence of the bride's mother, Mr. P. H. MARA, of Culpeper county, and Miss Louisa HEFLIN, of Fauquier County.

On Wednesday night last, Mrs. Mary E. ALDRIDGE, wife of Mr. John ALDRIDGE, died at Glebeland, near Mt. Gilead, in the 56th year of her age. And on Friday morning, Mrs. Ellen CARPER, aunt of Mrs. A., died at her home near Dranesville, in the 72d year of her age. Their remains were interred in Union Cemetery in this town.

Bethel Lodge, No. 76, I.O.G.T. Feb. 26th 1876, tribute of respect to John W. VIRTS.

Thursday, 30 March 1876   Vol. XX, No. 41

Married: On Thursday evening, March 23, 1876, at the residence of Mr. Thomas HARRISON, North of Waterford, by Rev. S. A. BALL, Mr. Geo. Samuel WRIGHT and Miss Mary L. C. HARRISON, both of Loudoun county.

Married: On the 16th inst., at the Lutheran Church, near Lovettsville, by Rev. Hy. St. J. RINKER, Mr. Charles T. WILLIAMS to Miss Sallie A. SEITZ, all of Loudoun county.

Married: In Charlestown, March 15th, Rev. T. B. SHEPHERD, Rev. E. J. WILLIS, Pres. Broadus Female College, Clarksburg, West Va. to Miss Mollie M. ROGERS, daughter of the late Thomas ROGERS of Loudoun Co.

Married: Wednesday evening, March 22d, 1876, at the residence of the bride's mother, Mrs. Jane E. ORRISON, by Elder Beal BRIDGES, Mr. Braden E. HUMMER, of Loudoun, to Miss Ellen E., daughter of the late Joseph ORRISON, of Fairfax county.

Died: In this town on Friday night last of paralysis, Mrs. Mary Ellen RATHIE, wife of Mr. Jos. L. RATHIE, in her 54th year.

Died: Near Round Hill, in this county, March 18, Col. E. T. BEST, in the 72nd year of his age. He was not united with any church. He leave a wife and four children.

Died: In Charlestown, W. Va, on Wednesday, 22nd of March, at the residence of her daughter, Mrs. WOODY, Mrs. Elizabeth SMALE, widow of the late Simon SMALE, of this town, in the 98th year of her age.

Died: Mrs. M. M. DIXON, wife of J. W. DIXON, died on the 20th and was buried at Short Hill on the 22d.

Died: In Washington city, on the 22d of March, 1876, of congestion of the brain, Miss Annie E. FREEMAN, formerly of this county. She was a member of the Presbyterian church.

Mrs. Mary Ellen RATHIE, wife of Mr. Jos. L. RATHIE, of this town, was stricken with paralysis about six o'clock on Friday evening, and died before daylight next morning. Member of the Presbyterian Church. Her remains were interred Sunday.

Mrs. Betsy SMALE nee LOTT, died in this place on Wednesday last, at the residence of her son-in-law, Samuel H. WOODY, aged 98 years. She has for many years been a member of the Protestant Episcopal Church. *Charlestown Free Press.*

Thursday, 6 April 1876 Vol. XX, No. 42

Married: In Washington city, on Thursday, March 30th 1876, by Rev. Mr. ATHENS, Mr. Edgar JANNEY, formerly of Loudoun county, and Miss Mary McPHERSON, of Washington.

Married: At the residence of Mrs. LONG, Frederick Co., Md, by the Rev. Mr. ___, Mr. John WASHINGTON to Miss Florence CRIM, all of Loudoun.

Died: At Grape Hill, Nelson county, Va, on Sunday, April 23, 1876, after a brief illness, Mrs. Matilda EDWARDS, wife of Rev. Alpheus L. EDWARDS.

Died: In Gum Springs, on Monday, March 20th, of pneumonia, Jacob F. NEWMAN, aged 19y 4d.

Died: Levi BEANS, was born on the 24th of May, 1783, in Loudoun County, and was married in 1805, moved to Ohio in 1806, and settled in Columbiana county about six miles west of New Lisbon in the woods. In 1818 he removed with his family to Belmont county, and settled in Goshen township near what was then Wrightstown, now Belmont, from which place he moved to a farm 1½ miles east of Morristown, on the National road, where he spent nearly all the remaining years of his life. The last two years he spent in Morristown, where he closed his life November 3d, 1875, in the 93d year of his age.

Mr. John SOUDER died very suddenly of paralysis, at his residence in the German settlement, on Monday, the 27th of March, 1876.

Thursday, 13 April 1876 Vol. XX, No. 43

Married: At "Clarenton," the residence of the bride's father, on Thursday morning last, by the Rev. J. F. CANNON, Maj. Wm. F. BARRETT, Sheriff of Loudoun county, and Miss Elizabeth A. BENNETT, daughter of Mr. Sydnor BENNETT, all of Loudoun county.

Died: Near Vienna, Fairfax Co., April 2d, Norman, infant son of Aurelius and Maria L. COE, aged 9m 27d, after a short but painful illness.

April Ct.: Will of Richard JAMES partially proved and continued. Estate of Mary E. McFARLAND committed to the Sheriff. P. H. CARR qualified as guardian of John F. ELGIN, an infant under 14 years of age.

As we indicated last week, Maj. Wm. F. BARRETT, High Sheriff of Loudoun, was on Thursday morning married Miss Lizzie A. BENNETT, daughter of My Sydnor BENNETT, of this county. [also lists those present and gifts they gave]

We are sorry to announce the death of Mr. Richard JAMES which occurred at his residence on Monday last. Mr. JAMES had reached about the 60th year of his age.

Thursday, 20 April 1876 Vol. XX, No. 44

Married: In the M. E. Church, South, Leesburg, on Wednesday morning, April 19, 1876, by Rev. Dr. HEAD, Mr. Jas. E. SMITH, of Maryland, and Miss Mattie A. BEACH, of Loudoun.

Married: At Port Republic, in the buggy of the groom in front of the Parsonage of the M. E. Church, South, on Thursday morning, April 6th, 1876, by Rev. Andrew ROBEY, Mr. Samuel H. KAYLOR, of Augusta, to Miss Mary R. BAKER, of Rockingham county, Va.

Married: In Danville, Ky, on the 6th of April, by Rev. Wm. F. JUNKIN, D.D., Mr. Lawrence RUST to Miss Evelyn, eldest daughter of the officiating clergyman.

Died: In this town on Tuesday morning, April 4th of water on the brain, Harvey, infant son of Geo. and Kate E. JACOBS, aged 4 days and 6 hours.

Died: At the residence of her brother, A. G. SMITH, near Gum Spring, on the 23d of February, 1876, Mrs. Harriet SHAFFNER, in the 79th year of her age.

Died: March 25th, Willie Annie, youngest child of William H. and Annie M. TAYLOR, aged three years and six months.

Died: At the residence of her son, T. T. WITHERS, Washington, D.C. on the evening of the 10th of April, 1876, Margaret H. WITHERS, in the 67th year of her age, consort of the late James O. WITHERS, of Warrenton.

Died: April 10, 1876, at his residence, Glen Burnie, near Delaplane station, Fauquier county, Dr. Robert L. McGUIRE, son of the late Rev. Edward McGUIRE, D.D., of Fredericksburg, in his 54th year.

Died: Near Unison, on the 28th of March, 1876, Rosalie Beatrice, infant daughter of Turner H. and Jane D. GALLEHER, aged 1y 11d.

Mr. John PURSELL, a native of Hillsborough in this county, died at his residence near Winchester, on the 29th of March, in the 98th year of his age.

Mrs. Tenie WRIGHT, died recently at the residence of her daughter, near Round Hill, in this county at a very advanced age, supposed to have been over 100 years.

Mr. Samuel MEGEATH of this county died at his home near Philomont, one day last week, of pneumonia, in about the 70th year of his age.

Thursday, 27 April 1876   Vol. XX, No. 45

Married: At Bethesda, Montgomery County, Md, by Rev. Parke P. FLOURNEY, March 30th 1876, Mr. Richard F. LOY and Miss Lydia R. BEST, both of Loudoun County.

Married: On the 19th instant, at Christ Church, near Chantilly, by Rev. Mr. McGILL, Richard M. CHICHESTER, and Miss Nannie, daughter of Hon. R. H. COCKERILLE, all of Fairfax county.

Married: At the residence of the bride's mother, in Leesburg, on Tuesday morning, April 25th 1876, by Rev. Dr. Nelson HEAD, Mr. C. Boyd BARRETT (firm of Biedler & Barrett, of Washington city) and Miss Mollie D., youngest daughter of the late Charles F. FADELY, of this place.

Died: At the residence of Daniel WHITE, on Friday, the 14th inst., of pneumonia, Mrs. Nancy VERMILLION, in her 61st year.

Died: March 26th, at "The Elms," Kenton county, Ky, Virginia, wife of Rev. J. H. MOORE, pastor of Washington church, Ky, eldest daughter of Rev. E. W. BEDINGER and granddaughter of Hon. Wm. LUCAS, of Jefferson co. W. Va.

Died: At the residence of her son-in-law, Dr. S. T. SHUMAN, in Middleburg, Va, on the 14th inst., after a protracted illness, Mrs. B. B. NORRIS (formerly of Baltimore) in her 74th year.

Died: Robert Waterman GRAY, departed this life April 22d 1876, ages 66 years.

Died: Near Millville on Tuesday, the 18th of April, Catharine WYNKOOP, the wife of William B. WYNKOOP, in the 64th year of her age. She had been for twelve months past in declining health, and on last Saturday evening fell, which caused her sudden death. Her funeral will be preached at North Fork Church, on 3d Sunday in May at 11 o'clock.

Mr. Jacob WENNER of this county died suddenly one day last week, at his home near Lovettsville.

Mr. John CLENDENNING died near Hillsborough, on Friday, April 21, in his 67th year. He was the oldest of the ten children of the late Wm. CLENDENNING, and the only one who has died.

Robt. W. GRAY, Esq. died at his home in this town, on Saturday morning last, in the 66th year of his age. He was a successful dry goods merchant in Leesburg. His funeral took place from St. James' Church on Monday morning.

Mr. Gustavus LERSNER died at the Reamer House, in this town, on Tuesday night last, in about the 55th year of his age. He was a native of Prussia, but had resided in this county the greater portion of his manhood. It was only last week that the Circuit Court of Fauquier issued an order directing Mr. LERSNER to be placed in possession of "Bollingbrook" a fine estate in that county worth at least $50,00, the ownership of which has been in litigation for the last eleven years.

Following the recent example of his elder brother, Mr. C. Boyd BARRETT, OF Washington, on Tuesday morning married Miss Mollie D. FADELY, youngest daughter of the late C. F. FADELY, of this town. Ceremony took place at 11½ o'clock.

Mrs. B. B. NORRIS, of Baltimore and formerly well known as the manufacturer of "Cedar Tar," died on Friday 14th instant at the house of Dr. Septimus SHUMAN, in Middleburg, in this county, in the 77d year of her age. She was a member of the Methodist Church. She was buried in Middleburg.

Mrs. Elizabeth Gilmore SWANN, wife of Hon. Thomas SWANN, died at her late residence in Baltimore on Tuesday morning in the 64th year of her age, after an illness of three weeks from bronchitis and typhoid fever.

Thursday, 4 May 1876   Vol. XX, No. 46

Dr. Bailey SHUMATE, who represented Fauquier in the Va Legislature, died at his residence in that county on the 25th.

Married: April 25th 1876, at the residence of the bride's mother, by Rev. John WOOLF, Mr. K. F. CUMMINS, to Miss Valinda CARLISLE, all of Loudoun.

Married: By Rev. Wm. M. SMOOT, Elder Primitive Baptist Church on April 20th, Mr. Henry W. KLIPSTINE to Miss Martha J. RIXEY, both of Fauquier.

Married: By Elder T. W. NEWMAN, at the residence, April 25th, Mr. Jeremiah HEFLIN, to Miss Emily KANE, all of Fauquier Co.

Married: On the 25th inst., at the residence of the bride's parents, by Rev. John S. LINDSAY, Dr. G. H. CHEWNING, of Fredericksburg, Va, and Miss Mary J., only daughter of Enoch K. JEFFRIES, of Fauquier County.

Died: At his home in Loudoun, near Mt. Gilead, Dr. Isaac EATON, in the 84th year of his age. Dr. EATON was a native of Chester county, Pennsylvania and came to Virginia when quite a young man, located in Mount Gilead.

Died: At her father's residence near Hamilton, on Friday, April 21st, Mary Clarke, infant daughter of L. C. and Mary A. HELM, aged 14 months.

Died: On the night of the 29th ult., After an illness of eight days, James Lupton, youngest child of Jefferson SPRING, aged 1y 10m.

Died: Mrs. M. M. DIXON, wife of J. W. DIXON, died on the 20th and was buried at Short Hill on the 22d.

Died: At the residence of John W. BEST, near Round Hill, on the 4th of February, 1876, Miss Amanda BEST. She had nearly completed her 65th year. Sister Amanda had been a member of the church for more than 30 years.

Thursday, 11 May 1876 Vol. XX, No. 47

Married: On the 27th of April 1876, at the bride's residence, near Edward's Ferry, by the Rev. Henry CLEMENT, Mr. Frank E. LUCKETT to Miss Alice V. MULLEN, all of Loudoun county.

Married: On the 26th ultimo, at the Hotel in Middletown, Md, by Rev. W. G. HERBERT, George F. GARROTT, to Miss Ella H., eldest daughter of Geo. W. ALEXANDER (formerly of Middletown), both of Loudoun county.

Died: Of pneumonia, near Mt. Gilead, at 7 o'clock Sunday evening, April 30th 1876, Sarah E. DAVIS, in her 43^{d} year, second daughter of Benj. DAVIS, Loudoun county.

Died: At the residence of Thomas HOUGH, near Newton, Iowa on the 29th of April 1876, Lida, daughter of Sarah A. and the late Jonas P. SCHOOLEY,

Died near Snickersville, May 4th 1876 of pneumonia, Thos. W. BEAVERS, in the 28th year of his age. He became a member of the Methodist Church at age 16 years.

County Ct.: Will of Gustavus LERSNER admitted to probate with H. G. LERSNER Executor. Will of John CLENDENNING admitted to probate, Wm. MATTHEW executor. Mason THROCMORTON qualified as guardian of Mary C. HUMPHREY and Americus J. SOUDER as Administrator of John SOUDER dec'd. Jos. FAWLEY guardian of John R., Minnie B., and Phillip H. HEATER, was allowed to remove funds of his wards to Ohio. Will of the late Robt. W. GRAY admitted to probate, Mrs. Mary E. GRAY Executrix.

Thursday, 18 May 1876 Vol. XX, No. 48

Married: May 10th 1876 in Harmony Church, Hamilton, by Rev. L. H. CRENSHAW, Mr. Wm. A. WILEY and Miss Annie D. FOSTER, both of Loudoun Co.

Married: At the residence of the bride's father, in Henderson, Texas, by Rev. J. S. MATHIS, on Wednesday, April 26, Mr. W. B. COOK to Miss Jane E. FRANCIS.

Married: By Elder T. W. NEWMAN at Elk Run, Fauquier county, May 4th, Mr. Elijah T. HANSBOROUGH to Miss Sallie E. REID, all of Fauquier county.

Died: On the 6th of April near Round Hill, Hattie V. HIGHMAN, daughter of Matthew and Elizabeth HIGHMAN, aged 2 years and 5 months.

Mr. Joseph THOMPSON died at his home in New Lisbon, Columbiana county, Ohio, on the 8th of May, in his 83d year. Born in Loudoun county, near a post town called Wheatland, on the 10th of Feb 1794, and moved to Ohio with his father, whose name was also Joseph. They arrived in Ohio in 1804, sometime in the month of December, being 21 days in reaching the Ohio river. In the year 1833 he was elected Sheriff of Columbiana county. In October 1835 he was elected to the State Senate and served another term of two years. In 1850 he was elected a member of the Constitutional convention from Starke County. About 1867, he was elected to the House of Representatives from Starke county and at the age of 74 or 75 served in the State Legislature for two years.

The death of Mrs. Pauline MOSBY, wife of Col. John S. MOSBY, occurred at her residence in Warrenton, Wednesday morning. Mrs. MOSBY was a daughter of Hon. Mr. CLARKE, formerly member of Congress from Kentucky. She leaves seven children, all quite young, the youngest only two months old.

On Friday night last, Sam. McPHERSON, a negro man belonging to Leesburg, got into a difficulty at the Point of Rocks with another negro, over some trivial matter, and in the melee Sam. received a lot of shot in the calf of his left leg. P. S. Sam died Wednesday afternoon.

Thursday, 25 May 1876   Vol. XX, No. 49

Died: At her residence in Purcellville, on the 4th instant, of dropsy, Mrs. Mary PURCELL, in the 76th year of her age.

Died: At Lincoln, Loudoun county, April 23, Mary Beaudric, infant daughter of John M. and Fannie L. HOWELL.

Died: On the 8th of April 1876, Beula Lee, infant daughter of J. C. and Martha J. MILBURN.

Died: At Shenandoah City, Jefferson county, on Thursday, April 27th, 1876, Mr. Philip DERRY, aged about 44 years.

Thursday, 1 June 1876   Vol. XX, No. 50

Married: In this county, May 18th, by Rev. J. F. CANNON, Mr. Thos. B. VIRTZ and Miss Delia BURCH, daughter of Thomas BURCH, Esq.

Married: On the 18th instant, at the Dill House, in Frederick city, Md., by Rev. Robert H. WILLIAMS, Columbus P. COOPER to Cornelia Y. ARNOLD, both of Loudoun Co.

Married: In Kalamazoo, Mich., in Tuesday evening, May 16th 1876, by Rev. M. C. HODGE, D.D., Mr. Anson PHILLIPS, of Grand Junction, Van Buren county, Michigan, to Miss Etta SMITH, of Lovettsville.

Thursday, 8 June 1876   Vol. XX, No. 51

Married: On the morning of June 1st, in Christ Episcopal Church, Winchester, by Rev. Dr. HUBARD, Alex. N. BRECKINRIDGE, Stewart of the Deaf, Dumb and Blind Institution at Staunton, Va. to Miss Bettie WRIGHT, daughter of the late Robert L. WRIGHT, of Loudoun county.

Died: At the residence of her son-in-law, Mr. R. C. McCARTY, near Mountsville, on Monday night last, of heart disease, Mrs. Mary A. MEGEATH, consort of the late Samuel MEGEATH, in about the 67th year of her age.

Died: In this town, on Tuesday morning last, after a somewhat protracted illness, Mr. Henry WOODARD, in the 24th year of his age.

Died: On June 7, Richard Thomas, child of Joseph and Mary ABBOTT, aged four months.

Died: Near Taylortown, on Thursday, 1st of June, Mrs. Susan GARRETT, in the 53d year of her age.

Last Saturday morning, Mr. Michael L. HUNTER, a thrifty farmer living near Morrisonville, in this county, took a load of wheat to Hamilton depot, driving his five horse team. Upon his returned in the afternoon he was overtaken by the severe storm that then raged, he was struck by lightning and himself and every horse attached to the wagon were instantly killed. He was about 40 years of age and leaves a wife and eight children.

Three men, William HORAN, James REARDON and Daniel LEARY, employees of the B. & O. R.R. Co., were struck by lightning and killed near Winchester, on Saturday afternoon last.

Thursday, 15 June 1876   Vol. XX, No. 52

Married: On June 5th, by the Rev. Henry CLEMENT, Mr. James OTTERBACH and Miss Frances A. RIDGEWAY, all of this county.

Married: In Richmond, Va, on Wednesday, June 6th, by the Rev. Dr. JETTER, at the residence of the bride's parents, Mr. David P. GULICK, of Loudoun county, to Mary Louisa TALMAN, daughter of Mr. John TALMAN, of that city.

Died: On the 19th of April 1876, at his residence in Washington City, D.C., A. Roszell JACOBS, in the 36th year of his age, son of Catharine and the late Wm. H. JACOBS, of Bolington.

Died: In Hillsborough on Friday, the 2d of June, 1878, Mrs. Jane JONES, widow of the late John JONES of this county, in the 73d year of her age.

Died: At his residence, near Hillsborough, on Sunday the 11th inst., Mr. Edward D. POTTS, in the 72d year of his age.

Died: At Round Hill, Thursday evening, June 8, 1876, at 4 o'clock, Julia Ida TOLSON, daughter of E. L. and Ada A. TOLSON, aged 1y 8m 5d.

County Ct.: R. S. CHINN appointed guardian of Anna and Rosa HOLLIDAY. B. P. NOLAND qualified as Admr. of the estate of W. A. WILSON. Will of Mary PURSELL admitted to probate with J. H. & E. R. PURSELL Executors. Will of Sarah P. VIRTS admitted to probate, Geo. HUNTER Admr. Will of Charles BLAKELY admitted to probate, with Lacey BLAKELY as Admr. Geo. HUNTER qualified as Admr. of Michael HUNTER dec'd. Dr. A. R. MOTT qualified as Guardian of Kate L. BENTLEY. Parmelia A. BEST qualified as Admx. of estate of late Enos T. BEST.

Thursday, 22 June 1876   Vol. XXI, No. 1

Married: In St. James' Church, Leesburg, on Tuesday morning, June 21, 1876, by Rev. R. T. DAVIS, Mr. Erastus C. BENEDICT, of New York, and Maria L., eldest daughter of the late R. Mont. BENTLEY, of Leesburg.

Married: In St. James' Church, Leesburg, on the 15th inst., by Rev. Theo. REED, assisted by Rev. R. T. DAVIS, Amelius Hunton MOREHEAD, formerly of Alexandria, Va, to Massie Rosa MACDANIEL, daughter of J. W. MACDANIEL, Esq. of Loudoun county.

Married: On June 15th at the M. E. Parsonage, Leesburg, by the Rev. H. CLEMENT, Richard W. FRY to Miss Nancy C. GREGG, all of Loudoun.

Married: At "White Hall," Loudoun county on the 15th instant, by Rev. Theodore REED, Mr. Benj. C. BARTON to Miss Sallie M. WRIGHT, all of Loudoun.

Married: In Brooklyn, June 1st, at the residence of the bride's uncle, by Rev. Mr. TALMAGE, Mr. Daingerfield LEWIS of King George county, Va, to Miss Sadid CHAPIN, only daughter of Dr. B. E. CHAPIN, formerly of Mobile, Alabama.

Married: On May 25th, 1876, at the residence of the bride's parents, near Hillsborough, by the Rev. Mr. JONES, Mr. Samuel E. NICHOLS and Miss Mollie E. STOCKS, daughter of Mahlon STOCKS, all of Loudoun county.

Died: Near St. John's Church, Prince William Co., Va, May 16th, 1876, Milton Ludwig, son of Mrs. Sarah E. PEUGH, widow of Dr. Wm. L. PEUGH, aged 14y 7m 11d.

Died: In Leesburg, on the 12th instant, George Lafayette, infant son of Henry A. and Susan FEASTER, aged 5m 15d.

Died: On Friday, June 16, 1876, at Kinlock, near the Plains in Fauquier Co. in the 65th year of his age, Mr. James SKINNER, eldest brother of N. J. SKINNER. the mother of Mr. SKINNER, aged 85, is yet living in good health.

Thursday, 29 June 1876   Vol. XXI, No. 2

Married: On Thursday, June 15, 1876, at Cerro Gordo, Prince William County, by Rev. John AMBLER, Col. Grayson TYLER and Miss Annie HUNTON, daughter of the late Charles H. HUNTON.

Married: In Zion Church, Charlestown, on the 14th of June, 1876, by Rev. Wm. H. MEADE, Lawrence WASHINGTON, of Fauquier county, and Miss Fannie LACKLAND, daughter of the late Thomas LACKLAND, of Jefferson county.

Married: In Charlestown, on June 14th, 1876, by Rev. Wm. H. MEADE, Jas. H. TIMBERLAKE and Miss Martha Virginia CRANE, daughter of Col. Joseph CRANE, all of Jefferson Co.

Married: In Jefferson county, June 17th 1876, by Rev. Wm. H. MEADE, Robert EARL, Esq., formerly of Washington city, to Miss H. Virginia, daughter of the late Roger CHEW, Esq., all of Jefferson county.

At Concord, Stafford county, Va., the residence of the bride's parents, June 21, 1876, by Rev. Joseph H. TEMPLE, W. W. GANTT, of Fairfax county, and Miss Helen W., daughter of John R. MacGREGOR, Esq., formerly of Prince George county, Md.

Died: At the residence of Joel L. NIXON, in Leesburg, on Saturday, June 24th, Miss Elizabeth SIMPSON, in about the 66th year of her age.

Died: At her residence, "The Grove," on Tuesday morning, June 27th, Helen E., relict of the late Thomas L. ELLZEY, in the 68th year of her age.

Died: On Saturday morning last, Ida Sophia, infant daughter of Thos. B. and Amanda NORRIS.

Died: At the residence of his grandfather in Hamilton on Sunday evening last, John, only child of John H. and Emma ALEXANDER, of this town, aged 7m 5d.

Died: On Saturday evening last, infant child of Wm. and Miranda GRIMES.
Died: On Sunday morning last, ___, youngest child of Albert and Katrina SHINER.
Died: On Tuesday morning, June 27th, infant child of Dr. Michael and Mary MORIARTY.

Thursday, 6 July 1876   Vol. XXI, No. 3

Died: Sunday evening, the 18th of June at 6 o'clock, Edmund C., infant son of Robert F. and Virginia HILLARD, aged 7 weeks.
Died: On the 13th of June, at the residence of her husband, Mr. Fenton FURR, near Bloomfield, Mrs. Susan E. FURR, in the 59th year of her age.
Died: At the residence of her son-in-law, Blanco BRAMHALL, on Wednesday June 28th 1876, Mrs. Elizabeth GRUBB, widow of the late John GRUBB, of Lovettsville District, aged 76y 9m.
Died: At home, of consumption, on 13th of June 1876, in the 59th year of her age, Mrs. Susan E. FURR, consort of Mr. Fenton FURR, and daughter of Mr. John GILL.

Thursday, 13 July 1876   Vol. XXI, No. 4

Married: On the 4th inst., at the Reform Church, Lovettsville, Va, by the Rev. H. St. J. RINKER, Mr. Samuel J. BECK to Miss Roselia SLATER, all of Loudoun.
Died: At the residence of his father, on Thursday night the 29th of June, Thomas Francis, son of Thomas G. and Mollie ELGIN, aged six months.
Died: June 8th, 1876, at his residence in this county, two miles below Gum Spring, David D. LANE, aged about 77 years. He had been confined to his bed for the last three years with paralysis.
July Ct.: Will of Miss Elizabeth SIMPSON admitted to probate. R. S. CHINN qualified as Admr. of Betsey FRY dec'd. Wm. GAINES qualified as Admr. of Mary A. MEGEATH dec'd. Joshua HATCHER qualified as guardian of Rosa M. and Laura K. CHAMBLIN.

Thursday, 20 July 1876   Vol. XXI, No. 5

Married: Near Hillsborough, at the residence of the bride's father, on the 13th of July by the Rev. L. R. JONES, assisted by the Rev. A. B. DOLLY, Mr. Alfred IRWIN, of Paris, Texas, to Miss Mollie T. LESLIE, of Loudoun Co.
Married: On Thursday, June 22d, 1876, at the residence of the bride's mother in Boonsboro, Md, by Elder Joseph FURR, of Loudoun Co., Robert Saunders HENRY, of Harford county, Md, to Miss Angie F. CRAMPTON.

Died: After a lingering illness, at N. H. MASSIE's in Charlottesville, on Saturday evening, July 8, Rev. William Meade NELSON, formerly assistant rector of the Episcopal Church in that place, in the 52d year of his age.

Rev. Chas. H. NOURSE died at his residence in Georgetown, on Wednesday last, after a brief illness. He was 60 years of age and was born in Washington City.

Mr. Carter ROLLISON, a son of Mr. Wm. ROLLISON, living about one mile from Leesburg, died very suddenly on Monday morning. Mr. R. was about 30 years of age.

Frank HOOE, a negro man living with Mr. Joseph D. TAYLOR in the lower part of Loudoun, had a sun stroke on Monday, the 10th of this month, from which he died on Wednesday.

Mr. Geo. W. SADLER of Charlestown, W. Va. died at the Sappington Hotel in that town last week, in the 57th year of his age. On Saturday afternoon when his funeral took place, all the principal business houses in town were closed.

Case of Burr POLLARD, negro, charged with rape. Given fifteen years in the penitentiary.

Thursday, 27 July 1876   Vol. XXI, No. 6

Ludwell LAKE Sr. of Fauquier County died at his home near Rector X Roads on Wednesday in the 70th year of his age.

Thursday, 3 August 1876   Vol. XXI, No. 7

Died: At Rectortown, Fauquier county, on the 15th of July, after a lingering illness, Captain John WEADON, in the 84th year of his age. A veteran of 1812, he was a native of Loudoun county.

Died: At the residence of his son, in Waterford, July 12th, Mr. John MOUNT, in the 78th year of his age.

Thursday, 10 August 1876   Vol. XXI, No. 8

Died: In Middleburg, August 4th, at the residence of E. C. BROWN, Mrs. Maria L. TEBBS, wife of the late Rev. F. C. TEBBS, after an illness of a few moments.

Died: In Warrenton, on Monday, the 31st ultimo, Ann Amelia, youngest daughter of James V. and Mary E. BROOKE.

Thursday, 17 August 1876   Vol. XXI, No. 9

Married: On the 3d instant, near Lovettsville, by the Rev. H. St. J. RINKER, Mr. David Eli AXLINE to Miss Martha E. GREEN, all of Loudoun.

Married: In Zion Church, Charlestown, on Wednesday evening, August 9th, 1876, by Rev. Wm. H. MEADE, Mr. John POTTERFIELD, Teller of Bank of Charlestown, to Miss Annie

L. GREEN, daughter of Judge Thomas C. GREEN, of the Supreme Court of Appeals, all of this town.

Died: In Middleburg, on Sunday afternoon, August 13th, 1876, in the 36th year of her age, Corrie H., wife of Major Burr P. NOLAND, and daughter of the late Burr W. HARRISON, of Leesburg.

Died: Sunday, Aug. 13, 1876, at 12 o'clock, m.. at Farmville, Loudoun county, Miss Lucretia Virginia BENJAMIN, in the 29th year of her age.

Died: At Lovettsville, August 4th, at the residence of her sister, Mrs. H. W. CLAPHAM, Miss Susan A. HODGE, in the 67th year of her age.

August Ct.: Wills of Jos. H. FRY, David T. LANE, John MOUNT, and Geo. PUSEY admitted to probate. Letters of Administration granted upon estates of Jacob W. ALLENDER and Philip DERRY. Estates of B. P. NICHOLS and John CLARE committed to the Sheriff.

Rev. Norvell WILSON, of the M. E. Church, South, and father of Rev. Alpheus WILSON, died at the residence of Mr. Jas. M. BROWN, near Charlestown, on Wednesday morning Aug. 2d, at an advanced age.

Thursday, 24 August 1876   Vol. XXI, No. 10

No marriage or deaths.

Thursday, 31 August 1876   Vol. XXI, No. 11

Died: In Leesburg on August 4, Bertha, youngest child of George and Kate E. JACOBS, aged 2y 11m.

Died: In Danville, Va, on the night of the 24th of August at the residence of her father, Jannie Sutherlin, beloved wife of Francis L. SMITH Jr. and the only child of Major W. T. and Jane B. SUTHERLIN.

Died: In Washington, D.C., August 7th in the 18th year of her age, Mary M., daughter of George H. and Ann KIDWELL, formerly of this county.

Died near Newton, Jasper county, Iowa, on the 29th of April 1876, Lidie, daughter of Sarah A. and the late Jonas P. SCHOOLEY, of Loudoun county.

Thursday, 6 September 1876   Vol. XXI, No. 12

Married: At the residence of the bride's father, in this county, on Tuesday morning, September 5, 1876, by Rev. L. H. CRENSHAW, Mr. John W. PIGGOTT, and Miss Bettie H., daughter of Mr. Fenton M. LOVE, all of this county.

Died: At the "College Farm," near Blacksburg, Va. on the 1st inst., Lavinia H. BERKELEY, wife of Colonel Norborne BERKELEY, and dau. of the late Dr. Edmond BERKELEY, of Staunton, Va.

Died: At the residence of his son-in-law, Gibson CATLETT, near Catlett's station, on Tuesday last, Stephen McCORMICK, of Auburn, Fauquier county, in the 93d year of his age.

Died: On the 25th ultimo, at Cherry Grove, Fauquier Co., Mrs. Nannie, wife of R. B. GAINES, in the 26th year of her age.

Died: In Leesburg, on Monday night, Sept. 4th, after one week's illness, Asa Jackson, son of James F. and Susan RINKER, aged 3y 5m 4d.

Died: In Leesburg on the 28th ultimo, Mary E. ATHEY, aged 18 months, infant daughter W. W. and Isabella ATHEY.

Died: In Louisa county, at the house of her son-in-law, J. V. L. McCREERY, Mrs. S. R. KEPLER, wife of Rev. Henry S. KEPLER, on Thursday morning, 31st of August.

Thursday, 14 September 1876   Vol. XXI, No. 13

Died: In Leesburg, August 9th at the residence of his grandfather F. J. CRISSEY, Frederic Archibald, infant son of Jennings and Mollie E. KITZMILLER, of Washington, aged 17m 11d.

Died: At her home near Hillsboro on the 11th inst., Margaret, beloved wife of Henry GAVER, aged about 62 years.

Thursday, 21 September 1876   Vol. XXI, No. 14

Died: On Saturday, Sept. 9th at the residence of Joseph THOMAS, near Upperville, Mrs. Sallie M. J. JACOBS, in about the 38th year of her age, and daughter of the late Abraham SMITH.

Died: In Leesburg, Sept. 9th, 1876, Janet Charlton, infant daughter of George W. and Alice M. SURVICK, aged 4m 21d.

Died: In Leesburg, on Saturday, Sept. 16th 1876, Julian, youngest child of Wm. D. and Mary E. EASTERDAY, in the 4th year of his age.

Died: At the residence of her uncle, in Leesburg, on Tuesday, Sept. 19, 1876, Nellie, youngest child of Lewis H. SAUNDERS, of Philadelphia, aged about 2 years and six months.

Mr. John BRENNER, who resided on Wolfe street, in this city, died quite suddenly from hemorrage of the lungs, at the residence of his son, in Middleburg, on Friday morning last. Mr. BRENNER was about 63 years of age, and leaves several grown sons most of whom reside here. His remains were brought to his late residence in this city, from which he was buried this morning. *Alex. Gazette of Monday.*

Thursday, 28 September 1876   Vol. XXI, No. 15

Married: In Frederick City, on Sept. 7th, by the Rev. C. ALLEN, Miss Gulielma BROWN to Mr. John J. CRIM, all of Loudoun.

Died: In Charlestown, W. Va. at half past eight o'clock on the morning of the 23d of September, 1876, Mary Nailor GREEN, daughter of Hon. Thomas C. GREEN of the Supreme Court of Appeals of that State, in the 16th year of her age.

Thursday, 5 October 1876   Vol. XXI, No. 16

Married: October 3rd, 1876, by Rev. L. H. CRENSHAW, Mr. James B. PEUGH and Miss Ella TAVENNER, only daughter of Mahlon TAVENNER, Esq., all of Loudoun county.

Died: At his residence, near Austin, Ark., Sept. 7th 1876, Abram YOUNG, formerly of Loudoun county, in his 69th year.

Died: L. D. WORLEY, departed this life July 28th in Martinsburg, Montgomery co., Md. Formerly a resident of Loudoun county.

Died: In Charlestown, on Thursday night, September 28, 1876, Mr. Nathaniel MYERS, in the 83d year of his age.

Mr. Silas SIMPSON, living about three miles east of Leesburg, died very suddenly on Sunday night. He was in about the 45th year of his age.

Mr. George NIXON, of this county and a soldier in the war of 1812, died at the residence of Mr. James W. CONNER, near Woodburn, on Saturday morning last, in the 88th year of his age. His remains were interred in the Presbyterian burying ground at Leesburg on Sunday.

Thursday, 12 October 1876   Vol. XXI, No. 17

Married: Oct. 10th in the Presbyterian Church of this town, by Rev. J. F. CANNON, Mr. Wm. T. TITUS and Miss E. Norah ANDERSON.

Married: In Leesburg, on Thursday, Oct 5th 1876, by Rev. J. S. GARDINER, Mr. George Y. DODD AND Mrs. M. Olivia MEGEATH, all of Loudoun.

Married: At the residence of Miss M. EBBERT, Loudoun county, on the 26th ult., by Rev. J. M. FRIDAY, Napoleon B. RILEY and Miss Annie M. C. EDWARDS.

Died: On Thursday, the 27th of September, at the residence of her husband, near Aldie, of typhoid fever, Mrs. Martha WARD, wife of Charles WARD.

Died: Suddenly, September 14th, of diphtheria, in Loudoun County, Monimia Fairfax, fourth daughter of Arthur and Alice HERBERT, aged 4y 7m 9d.

Mr. Webb DOWELL, youngest son of the late Col. C. R. DOWELL, of this county, died rather suddenly, on Sunday morning last, at the hotel of Mr. Frank SMITH, at Purcellville, where he had been staying for several days previous. His remains were taken to the residence of Mr. Maurice OSBURN, near Round Hill, from whence they were conveyed on Tuesday, and interred at Short Hill burying ground.

Mr. Franklin WILLIAMS of Point of Rocks, son of the late Henry S. WILLIAMS, of this county, met with a fatal accident while out hunting last Wednesday. He was attempting to cross a creek, slipped and shot himself through his head crown and his temple, tearing away part of his head.

J. Henry CLAPHAM qualified as Admr. of Susan A. HOGE dec'd.

Thursday, 19 October 1876   Vol. XXI, No. 18

Married: On the 27th ultimo, at the residence of the bride's parents, by Rev. Mr. MILLER, Cost J. CARMACK, of Maryland, to Miss Jennie HOUGH, OF Lovettsville.

Thursday, 26 October 1876   Vol. XXI, No. 19

Married: At Hamilton, October 19th 1876, by Rev. L. H. CRENSHAW, Mr. Bayless HOLLEY, of Kentucky and Miss Martha AMBLER, of Loudoun county.

Married: In the Episcopal church, Middleburg, on Wednesday, the 4th of October, 1876, by Rev. W. H. JOHNSON, Mr. R. S. OLDHAM, of Philadelphia and Miss Lavinia P. SHUMAN, daughter of Mr. George SHUMAN, of Middleburg.

Married: At the residence of the bride's parents, on Tuesday, October 17th, by Rev. Thomas E. CARSON, J. Carlin CREIGHTON, of Alexandria, and Miss M. Ella SMITH, daughter of A. G. SMITH, of Middleburg.

Married: On the 19th of October, by the same, Wm. LACKEY and Miss Sarah M. JACOBS, both of Loudoun county.

Married: On the 25th of October by the same, Mr. John GLASSCOCK and Miss F. May FRAZIER.

Married: On the 25th of October, by the same, Mr. Fenton T. ROSS and Miss Emma FRAZIER.

Died; At "Raspberry Plains," near Leesburg, on Sunday afternoon, Oct. 22d 1876, after a brief illness, Miss Sophia HOFFMAN.

Thursday, 2 November 1876   Vol. XXI, No. 20

Died: At her residence at Martinsburg, a few days since, Mrs. WITHEROW, widow of the late Dr. W. P. WITHEROW, deceased Dentist, aged about 50 years.

Death of John HOFFMAN – at his residence at "Raspberry Plains," about 3 miles from Leesburg on Monday afternoon in about his 74th year, making the third member of the family that has died during the past year and the second within the last fortnight. Vestryman of St. James' Church of Shelbourne Parish.

Thursday, 9 November 1876   Vol. XXI, No. 21

Married: On Wednesday morning November 8th 1876, at St. James Church, Leesburg by Rev. Theodore REED, R. Bently GRAY to Lilly, daughter of the late Joseph PANCOST, both of this county.

Married: On the 25th of October at the residence of the bride's father, near Taylortown, by Rev. S. A. BALL, Mr. Geo. Wm. MAGAHA and Miss Hannah E. WILLIAMS, both of Loudoun.

Married: On the 31st ult. at the residence of the bride's father, Bethel, Loudoun county, by the Rev. S. A. BALL, Mr. Jonas C. COMPHER and Miss Nettie HARPER, both of this county.

Married: In St. James' Church, Leesburg, October 30th, by Rev. Theodore REED, George Herbert DENNY, of Boon Co., Missouri, to Ella C. JARVIS, of this county.

Died: Monday morning, the 23d of October, between eight and nine o'clock, Willie A., the son of Christian and Kate CRIM, aged 5y 2d.

Died: At her residence in Grand Junction, Allegan County, Michigan, on the 25th October, 1876, Etta M, wife of Anson PHILLIPS and daughter of Mr. William SMITH, near Lovettsville, aged 27y 8m 16d.

Died: October 25th, 1876, after a brief illness of croup, little Willie, son of E. C. and Sarah C. PAXSON, aged 4 years.

Thursday, 16 November 1876   Vol. XXI, No. 22

Married: In Philadelphia, on Wednesday, Nov. 8th, 1876, by the Rev. F. A. KAHLER, Wm. H. CASSADAY Jr., of this county, and Fannie E., youngest daughter of S. R. BRICK, Esq., of Philadelphia, Pennsylvania.

Married: At Grace M. E. Church, Washington, DC, Nov. 9th by the Rev. G. W. HOBBS, Geo. T. GALLEHER, formerly of Leesburg, to Florence V., daughter of Wm. POPE, Esq. of Washington, DC.

Married: At Prospect Church, October 19, 1876, by the Rev. C. C. CRONIN, Caldwell A. JAMES, of Loudoun county, to Miss Sallie F. JAMES, of Frederick county, Md.

Married: October 31st by Rev. W. S. KERNS, Mr. George H. WORTMAN and Miss Elizabeth BLINCOR, all of Loudoun.

Died: In Leesburg, Tuesday, Nov. 7th, 1876, after a short illness, Sally Lee, daughter of the late Richard H. COCKERILLE, of Fairfax and granddaughter of the late Launcelot LEE of "Locust Grove," Jefferson county, Va.

County Ct.: Miss Bettie JANNEY's will admitted to probate. John MEAD qualified as Guardian of Eugenia D. LICKEY. Rev. Robt

R. ACRES licensed to celebrate rites of matrimony. Lucinda PALMER's estate committed to the Sheriff.

Thursday, 23 November 1876   Vol. XXI, No. 23

Died: November 6th, at his residence near Neersville, Mr. William SMALLWOOD, in the 86th year of his age.

Departed this life, October 11th, 1876, Corbin WYNKOOP, son of G. W. and J. E. WYNKOOP, aged 15y 6m 13d.

Died: In Hamilton on Sunday morning, November 12th, Jimmie E., son of John E. and Eliza BENEDUM, aged 5y 5m.

Married: November 16th at the residence of the bride's father, by Elder Benj. BRIDGES, Mr. C. F. LAYCOCK and Mollie, youngest daughter of Joseph DAVIS, of Loudoun.

Married: On the 8th of November, 1876, at the residence of Mr. Geo. L. MOORE, near Wheatland, by Rev. I. B. LAKE, Mr. Wm. S. BEATTY to Miss Lizzie MOORE.

Married: November 7, at "Welbourne," Loudoun county, by Rev. W. JOHNSON, Robert G. NEVILLE, of "Barrismore," Ireland to Mary, daughter of Col. R. H. DULANY.

Married: November 7th at the residence of the bride's parents, Loudoun county, by the Rev. J. M. FRIDAY, Mr. Jesse LEE and Miss Lucy PEYTON.

Sydney (New Guinea) Morning Herald of October 11th: Death of Dr. W. H. JAMES, son of the late Robt. JAMES, of this county. A short time ago we published a letter from him detailing his travels since leaving Leesburg a few years since. Letter dates 26 Sep 1876 from Somerset tells of his death on 23 August, of Dr. JAMES, late of Chevert of an attack by New Guinea men.

Thursday, 30 November 1876   Vol. XXI, No. 24

Married: On the 16th inst., at the residence of the bride's father, Mr. Alfred STANTON, of Loudoun county, to Mary, only daughter of Hon. S. ROSS, of Coudersport, Pa.

Married: At Bladensfield, Westmoreland county, on November 21st, by Rev. Wm. N. WARD, Dr. Pearson CHAPMAN, of Maryland, to Miss Eddie K. WARD, daughter of the officiating minister.

Married: At "Westwood Grove," Loudoun county, Thursday, November 16th 1876, by Rev. John McGILL, Dr. Rush W. CHANCELLOR, of Va, and Lily, daughter of the late Thos. L. ELLZEY, Esq.

Married: At Cave Hill, Rockingham county, on the morning of the 22d inst. by the Rev. Jacob HOPKINS, Miss Fannie HOPKINS, sister of officiating minister, to Henry W. CHAMBLIN, of Loudoun county.

Married: November 16th 1876, by Rev. Thomas E. CARSON, Mr. James H. SKINNER and Miss Rebecca Ellen COCHRAN, both of Fauquier county.

Died: In Sherman, Texas, on Nov. 24th 1876, Joseph C. MILLAN, eldest son of Dr. Lyle MILLAN, of Rappahannock County, in the 30th year of his age. A few years ago Mr. M. married the daughter of Mr. F. M. HENDERSON of Leesburg and with his bride repaired at once to Texas. The body was forwarded to Virginia for interment in its native soil.

Died: In Leesburg, on Saturday morning last, Charles Davis, youngest child of Joseph and Mary ABBOTT, aged 8y 4m.

Died: At the residence of her brother, Miss Kate V. STEWART.

Died: In Washington county, Md, November 10th, 1876, Henry Washington, infant son of Geo. W. and Lavinia BENJAMIN, aged 5m 4d.

Died: In Middleburg, on the morning of the 23d of August, Miss Susan CHINN. Member of M. E. Church, South.

Mr. James T. REED, of Harper's Ferry, W. Va, while returning from Loudoun county late last night met with a frightful accident which resulted in his death. His horse became frightened by a broken shaft, and REED was dragged with his foot entangled under the seat.

Thursday, 7 December 1876   Vol. XXI, No. 25

Married: At Atlanta, Ga., on the 29th of November 1876, at the residence of A. J. HULSEY, Esq., 49 Wheat street, by the Rev. R. C. FOUTE, Rector of St. Philip's Church, James W. MORTON, Esq. of Culpeper C. H., to Emily D., daughter of W. Walton HARPER, of that city.

Died: In Leesburg, November 19th 1876, Harry Linden, son of James A. J. and Mary E. COOPER, aged 6y 1m.

Died: Also, on Leesburg, November 13th, 1876, Hattie Eugene, eldest child of the same parents.

Died: At the residence of her son-in-law, C. W. JOHNSON, near Lovettsville, October 22d, '76, Mrs. Elizabeth CONARD, in 78th years of her age.

A colored boy, about 10 years old, named Joseph JACKSON, was killed at the depot in this town on Wednesday night, Nov. 29th by being run over by the cars.

Gen. Samuel COOPER died at his residence, "Cameron," Fairfax county, last week. He was a son of Gen. COOPER, of revolutionary memory, was born in New York in 1797 and graduated at West Point in 1815. ... He married a daughter of Gen. John MASON, of Clermont, Fairfax county, and was a brother-in-law of the late Hon. James M. MASON, for a long time a U.S. Senator.

Thursday, 14 December 1876   Vol. XXI, No. 26

Married: On the 30th ultimo, by the Rev. Hy. St. J. RINKER, Mr. Chas. AYERS to Miss Mary C. BAKER, all of Loudoun county.

Married: On the 8th of December, at Grace Church, Plains, Va, by Rev. W. H. H. POWERS, Wm. P. HERBERT, of Baltimore, to Rebecca, daughter of Robert BEVERLY, Esq., of Fauquier county.

Died: At the residence of her son, Thomas H. ATWELL, near Goersville [Goresville], Loudoun county, on the 18th of November, Mrs. Harriett H. ATWELL, in the 70th year of her age. Member of the Baptist Church.

Died: On Thursday morning, December 7th, 1876, of dropsy, at Oak Grove, near Leesburg (the residence of his brother, Mr. Robt. HARPER) Mr. Wells A. HARPER, for many years a prominent merchant in Alexandria.

Hannah STEPTOE, an aged and highly respected colored woman living near Coe's Mill, in this county, died on Sunday, the 3d of December. She formerly belonged to the SAUNDERS family, and is believed to have been at least 100 years old.

County Ct.: Will of Sue V. CHINN admitted to probate. Jonathan MATTHEW qualified as guardian of the infant children of Michael BEAMER dec'd.

Thursday, 21 December 1876   Vol. XXI, No. 27

Died: At Evergreen Mill, on the 10th of November of diptheria, Annie, daughter of Robt. and Sarah MILLS, in her 9th year.

We regret to hear of the death at her home in Hillsborough, Tuesday night, the 12th last, of Mrs. Lizzie MATTHEW, the wife of Mr. Wm. MATHEW, on of our representatives in the House of Delegates, of consumption.

Mr. Wm. CARUTHERS, of this county, died at his home near Lincoln, on the 13th inst., in the 60th year of his age.

Thursday, 28 December 1876   Vol. XXI, No. 28

Married: On November 19th 1876, by Rev. Louis R. JONES, Theodore F. WILT to Emma E. TALLY, both of Loudoun.

Married: At the M. E. Church Parsonage, Leesburg, on Wednesday evening, December 20th, by Rev. Henry CLEMENT, Albert G. JACKSON and Emma J. PORTER, all of Leesburg.

Married: December 20, 1876, near Upperville, by Rev. J. B. LAKE, Miss Virginia LANHAM to Mr. Robert STICKLE, all of Loudoun.

Married; On December 18, 1876, by Rev. Robert S. ROWE, Robert BROOKS, of Baltimore to Miss Mary S. TREHERN, of Virginia.

Died: Near Hillsborough, August 29th, 1876, Mr. John SCHAFFER, aged 81 years.

Died: Of consumption, December the 11th, 1876, Miss Martha C. ORRISON, in the 24th year of her age.

Died: At the residence of his mother, near Bloomfield, in this county, on Dec. 23d, 1876, A. Rush CHAMBLIN, in the 27th year of his age.

Death of Col. John West MINOR – died at his farm a few miles from Leesburg, on Saturday night, in the 72d year of his age. He once represented this county in the Legislature of Virginia and at time of his death was the door-keeper in the State Senate. A short time ago he connected himself with the Episcopal Church. On Christmas day his remains were conveyed to Falls Church and interred beside his ancestors in the old family burying ground.

Thursday, 4 January 1877   Vol. XXI, No. 29

Littleton S. HELM, a promising young lawyer of the Warrenton bar, and the law partner of General HUNTON, died in that town last week.

Married: December 17th in Loudoun county, by Rev. J. M. FRIDAY, Mr. Jos. E. B. PEYTON and Miss Ruth J. WEBB.

Married: On Thursday, Dec. 20th, at the residence of the bride's parents, in Waterford, by the Rev. S. A. BALL, Mr. James W. RUSSELL and Miss Alice RUSSELL, both of Loudoun county.

Married: On the 21st ult., at the Frederick City Hotel in that city, by the Rev. Dr. DIEHL, Frederick KIDWELLEN, of Jefferson County, Va, to Miss Florence M. HARVEY, of Loudoun county.

Married: At the Parsonage of M. E. Church, South, Leesburg, December 6, 1876, by Rev. J. S. GARDNER, Mr. L. M. STEVENS and Miss Sarah A. OTLEY, both of Loudoun county.

Died: December 11th, 1876, Mary Julia, infant daughter of W. A. and Laura P. BRAWNER.

Thursday, 11 January 1877   Vol. XXI, No. 30

Married: January 4th, 1877, at the residence of the bride's mother, by Rev. L. H. CRENSHAW, Mr. Burr ORRISON and Miss Mag. WYNKOOP, only daughter of Mrs. Mahala WYNKOOP, all of Loudoun county.

Married: At the residence of the bride, Wednesday, Dec. 20th, by the Rev. J. C. SMITH, E. M. HOUGH of Virginia, and Miss M. A. LONG of Washington, DC.

Died: In Washington City, December 28th, 1876, of pneumonia, John W., infant son of Fannie E. and Albert A. SHIPLEY, aged 5m 1d.

Died: In Loudoun county, December 21st, 1876, Mr. Adam S. EBBERT, aged 50y 1m 1d.

Died: At Mount Prominent, December 22d, Bertha Elgin, only child of Humphrey and Pasilia LYNN, aged 1y 3m 14d.

Mrs. E. S. HAMILTON, widow of the late John HAMILTON, of this county, met with a distressing death on Wednesday last, the 3d instant. Mrs. HAMILTON, who was somewhat advanced in years and blind, was living with her step-daughter, Miss Lizzie HAMILTON, near Morrisonville, and while moving about her room on the day named, in front of an open fire, her clothing took fire and she was badly burned, death ensued in a few hours. She was buried at Waterford on Saturday.

The Post yesterday contained a death notice of Mr. A. Rush CHAMBLIN, of Loudoun county. Mr. CHAMBLIN a few years ago engaged as a teacher by Mr. Wm. T. DAVIS, president of the Southern Female College.

County Ct.: Will of Wells A. HARPER admitted to probate, W. Walton HARPER Admr. wwa. Will of Wm. CARRUTHERS dec'd. admitted to probate with J. T. CARRUTHERS Exor. Administration granted Wm. SMITH on the estate of Mary A. BOGER.

Thursday, 18 January 1877   Vol. XXI, No. 31

Married: On the 4th of January 1877, in Boulder, Colorado, at the residence of Mrs. M. T. EVERITT, Mr. Thos. S. WORSLEY, formerly of this town, of St. Louis, Mo. to Miss Moselle DeLANNAY, of Columbus, Ga.

Married: In Middleburg, on Thursday morning, January 11th 1877, by Rev. Dr. HAYNES, Mr. William H. BROOKS, of the firm of Brooks & Son of Leesburg, and Miss Jennie, daughter of John W. PATTON, of the former place.

Married: In Baltimore, on the 7th of January, by Rev. John C. BACKUS, Donnell SWAN to Sidney S. TURNER, daughter of the late Wm. F. TURNER, of Jefferson county, West Va.

Married: At Warrenton on the 10th inst., by Father John DOHERTY, of the Roman Catholic Church, Mr. Edward P. FURLONG of Loudoun county, to Miss Isabella DOBSON, of Fairfax county.

A little three year old child of Mr. Hiram SMITH, living about two miles east of Leesburg, met with a sad death last week from scalding.

Thursday, 25 January 1877   Vol. XXI, No. 32

Married: At the residence of the bride's aunt at Taylorsville, on Tuesday, January 16, 1877, by Rev. J. B. HUTSON, Mr. W. B.

PETTIS, of Cairo, Ill., and Miss Lizzie E. COOKE, daughter of Dr. J. G. COOKE, of Fauquier county.

Married: At residence of the bride's brother Jno. O. BRADFIELD, near Delta, Louisiana, on Thursday, January 4th 1877, at 3:30 p.m. by the Rev. Bishop W. F. ADAMS, Miss Rosalie BRADFIELD, of that parish, to Mr. J. C. BEARD of Mississippi.

Married: By Rev. O. C. BEALL, January 10th 1877, at the residence of the bride's father, George W. LEE and Rebecca DONOHOE, all of Loudoun.

Married: By Rev. O. C. BEALL, January 11th, 1877, at Belmont Church, James T. DARNE to Catharine C. BAUCHMAN, all of Loudoun.

Married: In Alexandria, January 17th, by Rev. Dr. NORTON, Amos B. SLAYMAKER and S. Florence, daughter of the late B. C. MILBURN.

Married; On December 21st 1876, at the M. E. Parsonage, in Frederick city, by the Rev. A. H. AMES, Archilles WILLEY, of Loudoun county, to Miss Alice YOUNG, of Frederick county, Md.

Married: Thursday, 18th inst., by Rev. Jno. F. POULTON, at the residence of the bride's parents, Mr. James GRAY AND Miss Virginia GRAY, all of Fauquier county.

Died: On the 19th inst., at "Springdale," in this county, after a brief illness, Maria W., wife of Aquila JANNEY, in the 64th year of her age.

Died: At the residence of his uncle, Mr. Jos. L. HAWLING, on Saturday morning, Jan. 28th, 1877, of consumption, Mr. Edward C. ROGERS, son of Jas. H. ROGERS, of Fauquier, in about the 24th year of his age.

Died: Near Leesburg, Jan. 13th, Hermon Parker, son of Hiram R. and Philena E. SMITH, aged 2y 9m 13d.

Death of Mrs. Mary CLARKE occurred at the residence of her son-in-law, Mr. L. HELM, on Tuesday morning last. She had attained about the 70th year of her age.

The neighborhood of Pursellville, in this county, was shocked on Saturday last, by the announcement that Mr. Benj. CRAVEN, who, with his twin brother, Giles, resided on their farm about 1½ miles from Pursellville, had committed suicide. The two brothers being twins, quite large, and so much alike in appearance as to be hardly distinguishable one from the other. Neither was married, but lived together on the farm which they bought a few years ago from Mr. Bernard TAYLOR.

Thursday, 1 February 1877   Vol. XXI, No. 33

Married: On Wednesday morning, 31st January 1877, by the Rev. Theodore REED, Rector of Christ Church, at the residence of her parents, in Loudoun county, John M. ORR, of Leesburg, and Miss Orra Virginia PRESTON, eldest daughter of George W. PRESTON.

Married: on the 23d of January 1877, at the residence of Wm. GAINES, by Rev. John WOLF, Mr. Jno. F. MORRIS and Miss Virginia E. NICHOHS [NICHOLS?], all of Loudoun.

Married: On Thursday, January 17th 1877, at the residence of Adam A. CORDELL, near Taylortown, by Rev. S. A. BALL, Mr. George F. WILLIAMS and Miss Martha A. CORDELL, both of this county.

Married: At the residence of the bride's parents, Locust Grove, Loudoun county, November 21st 1876, by Rev. D. M. MUTESSBAUGH, Mr. Charles RADLEY, of Lewis county, N. Y. to Miss Anna E. WRIGHT.

Married: In Christ Church, Goresville, on the 18th inst., by Rev. Theodore REED, Mr. Chas. FRAME to Miss Julia V. DAVIS, both of Loudoun county.

Died: On Wednesday morning, January 27th, 1877, Willie Herbert, infant son of Thos. L. and Sue L. POTTERFIELD.

Died: At the residence of his sister, Mrs. FRY, near Lovettsville, on Monday the 15th instant, Edgar H. STONE, in his 24th year.

Died: At the residence of her husband, John BENJAMIN, at Frankville, Loudoun Co., Mrs. Harriet Ann BENJAMIN, in the fifty-three year of her age.

Died in Indianapolis, Indiana, on Sunday the 14th of January 1877, Mrs. Augusta T. CALDWELL, daughter of Col. H. B. TYLER, of Fairfax C. H., of consumption. Interred by the side of her late husband, in Fairfax Cemetery. Her husband, Jno. M. CALDWELL, Esq. died her a short time ago, of consumption.

Thursday, 8 February 1877   Vol. XXI, No. 34

Married: On Jan. 23d, by Rev. L. R. JONES, James W. VIRTS and Alverta V. CLENDENNING, daughter of Samuel CLENDENNING, Esq., near Hillsborough.

Married: January 20, 1878, at the parsonage of Ascension Church, by Rev. Dr. ELLIOTT, William GORDON and Susan M. STANLEY.

Mr. Joseph DAVIS, of this county, died at his home near "The Grove," on Tuesday night last at an advanced age.

Henry L. SIMPSON, a prominent citizen of Alexandria, died in that city on Tuesday, in the 72d year of his age.

Thursday, 15 February 1877   Vol. XXI, No. 35

Died: In this town, at 7 o'clock on Monday morning last, after several weeks confinement to his bed, Mr. Samuel C. JACKSON, in the 67th year of his age.

Died: In Leesburg, on Thursday night, February 8th, Mrs. Elizabeth LITTLETON, wife of Mr. Thomas LITTLETON, in her 74th year.

Died: At her residence, in Loudoun county, February 5, 1877, Mrs. Elizabeth TILLETT, of consumption, in the 53d year of her age.

Died: In this county, on the 11th inst., in the 72d year of her age, Mrs. Cassandra NIXON, widow of the late John NIXON. A few weeks before her death she made a profession of faith in Christ.

Mrs. Elizabeth LITTLETON, wife of Thos. LITTLETON and mother of Mr. Edgar LITTLETON, Clerk of the County Court, who died on Thursday night, in the 74th year of her age.

On Monday morning, Mr. Samuel C. JACKSON, breathed his last in the 67th year of his age.

Feb. Ct.: Powers of Henry W. GREGG as Executor of Emily J. GREGG revoked. Mary C. JAMES qualified as guardian of Thos. C. ARNOLD. Rodney C. HOUGH qualified as guardian of Chas. R. VIRTS, John W. S. VIRTS and David F. VIRTS. Chas. N. TAYLOR and G. G. CRAVEN qualified as Administrators of Benj. G. CRAVEN dec'd. Wills of John G. AYRE and Geo. NIXON admitted to probate. R. C. CHAMBLIN qualified as Admr. of Harriet A. ATTWELL. Estates of Sallie E. JACOBS, Philip HENSON, Thos. W. SHRIVER, and Eliz. CONARD committed to Sheriff.

Thursday, 22 February 1877   Vol. XXI, No. 36

Died: Near Leesburg, February 2, 1877, Leler Blanche, daughter of William and Susan BENJAMIN, aged 1y 15d.

Died: Clarence, infant son of William H. JACKSON, died Friday, January 12th, aged 2y 5m. Also Lizzie, Wednesday, the 17th, 8m 3d.

Died: On Monday evening, February 5th, in Louisville, Ky, Mr. Henry C. RINKER (formerly of Leesburg) in the 34th year of his age. The deceased is the son of Jno. L. RINKER, of this place.

Died: On the 6th inst., Joseph DAVIS, at his residence, near the Grove Church, in this county. Member of the Primitive Baptist Church.

Thursday, 1 March 1877   Vol. XXI, No. 37

Married: On Thursday, February 15th, 1877, at the residence of the bride's father, by Rev. G. STEPHENSON, assisted by Revs. Samuel ROGERS, and S. TOWNSHEND, Rev. J. Watt SHOAFF to Miss Jeannette R. FRAZIER, of Frederick county.

Married: February 8th, by Rev. T. W. NEWMAN, Mr. M. W. COURTNEY to Miss Susan A. BROWN, all of Fauquier county.

Married: By the same, at Morrisville, Fauquier county, February 11th, Mr. Thevn [Theron?] William NEWMAN to Miss Margaret Elizabeth NEWMAN, only daughter of officiating minister.

Married: By the same, February 15th, Mr. M. C. GREEN to Miss E. W. THORN, all of Fauquier county.

Died: At the residence of his son, Montgomery county, Md, February 19th, Thomas OXLEY Sr., aged 84y 11m 25d. An old defender of the war of 1812.

Thomas OXLEY Sr., one of the oldest citizens of this county, died at the residence of his son, in Montgomery county, Md, on the 19th of February. He was a soldier of the war of 1812.

Thursday, 8 March 1877   Vol. XXI, No. 38

Married: At his residence in Loudoun county, February 25th, by Rev J. M. FRIDAY, Henry JONES and Susan E. BARTLETT.

Married: At the Parsonage, Hamilton, Feb. 28th, 1877, by Rev. L. H. CRENSHAW, Mr. Charles F. SILCOTT and Miss Mary V. HUNT, both of Loudoun county.

Died: February 19th, 1877, at his old home, near Hillsborough, Eli PIERPOINT, in the 86th year of his age, after a protracted season of suffering.

Thursday, 15 March 1877   Vol. XXI, No. 39

Married: At Neersville, March 6, 1877, by Rev J. M. FRIDAY, Walter B. POTTS and Miss Annie M. SHRIVER.

Married: At the Parsonage, Hamilton, March 7th, 1877, by Rev. L. H. CRENSHAW, Mr. Jas. E. MOCK and Miss Sarah A. FULTON, daughter of Mr. John E. FULTON dec'd., all of Loudoun county.

Died: In Clarke county, on Wednesday, the 28th of February, 1877, Mrs. Sallie PENQUITE, in the 76th year of his age.

Died: At the residence of her son, Henry SAUNDERS Jr., near Leesburg, on Saturday morning, March 19th, 1877, Mrs. Susan SAUNDERS, widow of the late Everette SAUNDERS, in the 79th year of her age.

Died: On the 11th of March, at 11½ o'clock, Lafayette MUSE, youngest son of Thomas MUSE, aged 17y 4m 2.

Died: On the 8th inst., at the residence of his son, in Bloomfield, of pneumonia, John L. GILL. He was born in Prince William

County, Va, Sept. 8th, 1793, moved thence to Bloomfield in 1816. He was a soldier of the war of 1812.
March Ct.: Geo. H. NIXON qualified as Admr. of Elizabeth SIMPSON dec'd. Ebenezer J. CONARD qualified as Admr. of Thos. BATEMAN dec'd. Isaac VANDEVANTER qualified as Admr. of Mary CLARKE dec'd. Jas. E. CARRUTHERS qualified as Admr. of Mary HOUGH dec'd.

Thursday, 22 March 1877   Vol. XXI, No. 40

Married: At Andrew Chapel, on the 8th inst., by Elder Benjamin BRIDGES, Mr. Thomas L. POWELL, of Loudoun, and America, daughter of Charles ADAMS, of Fairfax county.

Married: On the 8th of March, 1877, at Bethel Church, Loudoun county, by Rev. P. H. MILLER, Mr. Charles F. McKIMMY and Miss Sarah A. EDWARDS, of Loudoun.

Married: March 6th, at the residence of the bride's parents, in Washington, DC, by Rev. Joseph WHELLER, Mr. Theodore F. GAVER, of Loudoun county, to Miss Mamie W. DANIEL, of Washington.

Died: At his residence in Madison county, Florida, on Friday, March 16th, 1877, William Archie HAMMERLY, in his 67th year. Native of Loudoun, and brother of Mr. John HAMMERLY, of this town, but had been residing in Florida for the last 35 years.

Died: On the 3d of March, after a lingering illness, at the residence of her parents, near Leesburg, Mattie I. WORKS, in the 31st year of her age.

Died: At the residence of his father, in this county, on the 13th inst., James W. BURGESS, second son of William and Martha BURGESS, aged 29y 4m 11d. He leaves a wife and one child.

From the *Marquette Michigan Journal* March 10th – Died at Stoneville on the morning of the 8th inst., of inflammation of the intestines, Celia V., the only child of Dr. and Mrs. Townsend HEATON. The funeral took place on Friday afternoon.

Mrs. Charlotte PALMER, mother of Mrs. John R. HART, died at the residence of her son-in-law, on Parker street, Mansfield, O., on Sabbath morning last of paralysis, after two days sickness in her 89th year. Born and raised in Loudoun Co., living there 58 years, when she came to Ohio, and lived until her deceased with her only daughter and only child, Mrs. John R. HART.

Thursday, 29 March 1877   Vol. XXI, No. 41

Died: At Liberty, Bedford county, on Sunday evening, March 25th, 1877, after an illness of but four days, Mr. Samuel P. NELMS, of Baltimore.

Died: In Brooklyn, New York, on Thursday, March 23d, 1877, on consumption, Mr. George MOORE, eldest son of Capt. John MOORE of Aldie, in the 49th year of his age.

Died: In Brooklyn, N.Y., on the 24th inst., Beverley Randolph, son of George and Laura F. LEE, aged 1y 3m.

Died: At his home, near Adamsville, Muskingum county, Ohio, on Friday morning, March 9th, 1877, Tholemiah COCHRAN, formerly of Loudoun county.

Died: Near Gumspring, Loudoun county, March 5th, 1877, Motta, youngest son of Charles L. and Lavinia MANKIN, aged 11 mos.

Died: At Redkey, Jay county, Indiana, on the 11th of March, of consumption, Miss Hattie E. GARNER, formerly of Leesburg, in the 21st year of her age.

Married: Feb. 25, 1877, at the residence of Mrs. WATERS, Loudoun county, by Rev. J. M. FRIDAY, Mr. Nathan E. CONARD and Miss Sarah V. SEXTON, both of Loudoun.

Married: March 18, 1877, at Harper's Ferry, by the same, Mr. Phillip H. DERRY, of Loudoun county, and Miss Florence V. HOBBS, of Harper's Ferry, W. Va.

Married: March 20, 1877, near Hillsborough, by the same, Mr. Eli A. MOORE and Miss Elizabeth MAUZY.

Married: March 15th, at Lovettsville, by Rev. P. H. MILLER, Mr. Stephen H. CONARD, of Jackson county, Md, and Miss Mary V. NICHOLS, of Loudoun.

Married: by the same at the same place, Mr. Edwin C. COMPHER and Miss Lydia A. WENNER, both of Loudoun.

Married: At St. Johns church, Washington City, March 20th, 1877, by the Rev. J. V. LEWIS, Dr. Edward A. BUTTS, of Washington, to Miss Sallie A. C. BARTLETT, eldest daughter of B. D. BARTLETT, formerly of Middleburg.

Married: On March 22, 1877, at St. Paul's church, Washington, DC, by the Rev. Dr. DOMAR, Louis M. MILLER, of Frederick county, Va, to Mary M, daughter of the late Ludwell LUCKETT, of Loudoun county.

Married: In the Presbyterian Church, Waterford, on March 27th by Rev. Henry BRANCH, Chas. Henry MINOR and Ellen GOVER, all of Loudoun county.

Thursday, 5 April 1877   Vol. XXI, No. 42

Married: On the 28th instant, at the residence of the bride's parents, near Hillsboro, by the Rev. S. A. BALL, Mr. Wm. H. CUMMINGS and Miss Sallie A. OGDEN, both of Loudoun.

Married: On the 18th of March, 1877, by Rev J. M. FRIDAY, in Harper's Ferry, Philip H. DERRY, of Loudoun county, and Miss Florence V. HOBBS, of Jefferson.

Died: In Waterford, on the 3rd day of the 4th month, 1877, Arthur H., son of J. W. and Eliza HUTCHINSON, aged 2 months.

Died: Of liver complaint, at his late residence, near Falls Church, Fairfax county, March 20, 1877, Mr. Richard S. BURKE, in the 49th year of his age.

Died: At her residence in Warrenton, on the 24th instant, Mrs. Matilda C. HUNTON (relict of the late James HUNTON) in the 47th year of her age.

Died: At his residence in Hillsboro in the 19th of March, Robert F. JONES, son of the late John JONES Sr., in his 37th year. At the beginning of the late war he offered his service as a private in the Loudoun Cavalry, was afterwards transferred to White's Battalion, and at a raid in Maryland, he was shot through the spine, and was never able to walk or use his limbs afterward.

Thursday, 12 April 1877   Vol. XXI, No. 43

Married: In Baltimore, March 5th, 1877, by the Rev. J. DOERSKEN, Mr. W. E. HOOVER to Miss Julia Gertrude HOUGH, both of Washington, DC.

Died: Near Gumspring, Loudoun county, March 31st 1877, Lucinda, wife of Melville HUTCHISON, Esq. in the 71st year of her age.

Miss Sallie MOORE, daughter of the late Cato MOORE, of Charlestown, died in that town on Sunday last, of Neuralgia of the heart, in the 61st year of her age. She was taken sick about four o'clock in the morning and by ten o'clock was a corpse.

April Ct.: Wm. H. GILL qualified as Admr. of John L. GILL dec'd. Chester C. GAVER qualified as Admr. of Eli PIERPOINT dec'd.

Thursday, 19 April 1877   Vol. XXI, No. 44

Died: Little Josie, daughter of E. E. and S. H. STICKELY (and granddaughter of Rev. Jos. HELM, of this county,) died at her parents residence of Woodstock, Va, April 3d, aged 4y 2m 27d.

Died: At his residence near Gum Spring, on the 25th day of March, 1877, on pneumonia, Mr. C. W. MAFFETT, in his 49th year.

Thursday, 26 April 1877   Vol. XXI, No. 45

Died: April 18th 1877, near Guilford, Loudoun county, of consumption, Mrs. Theresa MARTIN, in her 32d year.

Married: In the Friends' Meeting House, at Waterford, on Thursday, April 19th, 1877, by Friends' Ceremony, William WILLIAMS, President of the Mutual Fire Insurance Company of Loudoun, and Mary R. WALKER, both of this county.

Married: At the residence of her brother, near Guilford, on Tuesday morning, April 24th 1877, by Rev. Dr. HEAD, Rev. Oliver C.

BEALL, of the M. E. Church, South, and Miss S. Kate, youngest dau. of the late John I. COLEMAN, of this county.

Married: By Rev. T. W. NEWMAN, on the 5th inst., Robert O. ANDERSON and Miss Ellen F. HARDING, both of Fauquier.

Married: By Rev. J. K. BOOTEN, on the 8th instant, Jas. H. HANBACK and Mary KNIGHT, both of Fauquier.

Married: On the 10th instant, by Rev. J. H. DULANEY, James W. HAMPTON, of Memphis, and Miss Mildred E. ALLEN, of Fauquier.

Married: On the 11th instant, in the Methodist Church, by Rev. W. WOOD, Mr. Daniel P. WOOD and Sarah W. PARKINSON, of Warrenton.

Married: On the 8th inst., by the Rev. Jno. F. POULTON, Mr. Jas. W. BUTLER and Miss Mary A. DENNIS, both of Fauquier county.

Married: On the 17th inst., by the same, Arthur F. DAYMUDE and Miss Malvina POWELL, both of Fauquier county.

Thursday, 3 May 1877   Vol. XXI, No. 46

Died: At his residence, near Guilford Station, Loudoun county, on 8 April last, Mr. George W. PRESGRAVES, in his 60th year.

Died: At the residence of her son, in Essex county, Va, on the 13th of the 4th month, 1877, Phebe P. BAYNE, in the 78th year of her age, widow of the late Henry T. BAYNE, of Loudoun.

Thursday, 10 May 1877   Vol. XXI, No. 47

Married: In the M. E. Church, South, Leesburg, on Thursday morning, May 3d, 1877, by Rev. H. H. KENEDY, Mr. Richard S. BURKE and Miss Mary JOHNSON, all of this town.

Married: In Leesburg, on the 1st inst., by the Rev. Wm. H. FORSYTH, Mr. George W. VIRTS to Miss Ellen MOCK, both of this county.

Married: In Leesburg, Mary 3d, 1877, by the Rev. W. H. FORSYTH, Mr. Luther F. HARDING to Miss Martha DODSON, all of this county.

Died: March 18th, 1877, in Lafayette City, Mo., of pneumonia, Mrs. Fannie PEACOCK, wife of Milton PEACOCK, and daughter of Joseph and Elizabeth GARRETT, formerly of this county.

Died: March the ninth, at his residence, near Adamsville, Muskingum county, Ohio, Tholemiah COCHRAN, formerly of Loudoun county, in the 69th year of his age.

Died: On the 20th ulto, at her residence in Jefferson, Frederick county, Md, Miss Annie MARLOW, in the 71st year of her age.

Died: Near Unison, Loudoun county, on the 15th of April 1877, Patsey Violet, infant daughter of Turner H. and Jane D. GALLEHER, aged 5m 2d.

Thursday, 17 May 1877   Vol. XXI, No. 48
Married: In Baltimore, on the 28th of April, 1877, by Rev. A. M. RANDOLPH, rector of the Church of the Emanuel, C. D. MERVIN, of New York, and Mary THOMPSON, daughter of the late General, M. Jeff. THOMPSON, of New Orleans, La.

Married: On Thursday, May 3d, at St. George Church, Flushing, L.I., by the Rev. Francis E. LAWRENCE, A. Stephen DANDRIDGE, of Jefferson county, W. Va., to Caroline D. BEDINGER, daughter of the late Hon. Henry BEDINGER, and grand-daughter of Hon. John W. LAWRENCE, of Flushing, L. I.

Died: In Aldie, on Thursday, May 3d, 1877, Mrs. M. L. MOORE, wife of Capt. John MOORE, in the 73d year of her age.

Died: At his mother's residence, near Farmwell Station, Loudoun county, on the 17th of April, 1877, Alexander W. ROSE, with hemorrhage of the bowels, aged 24y 23d.

Died: On the 8th of May, 1877, at the residence of her brother, Mr. Samuel SHIPMAN, near Goresville, Etheless RUSSELL, in the 88th year of her age.

County Ct.: Adrain L. SWART qualified as Admr. of Elizabeth SWART dec'd. R. S. CHINN qualified as Admr. of Christina FREY dec'd. P. F. VANSICKLER qualified as Admr. of Joseph DAVIS dec'd. Silas A. HOUSEHOLDER qualified as Admr. of Eliza B. SCHOOLEY dec'd.

Thursday, 24 May 1877   Vol. XXI, No. 49
Married: At the Southern Methodist Parsonage, Leesburg, May 15th, 1877, by Rev. H. H. KENNEDY, Mr. Chas. H. HOUSE, to Miss Sarah R. PIERPOINT, both of this county.

Married: At the residence of the bride's parents, May 22nd, !877, by Rev. H. H. KENNEDY, Mr. Samuel W. COCKRELL to Miss Lizzie R. McCABE, all of Leesburg.

Died: From cancer, May 4th, 1877, near Falls Church, Fairfax county, George Smith MYERS, son of Charles W. MYERS and Sallie A. MYERS, aged 8y 6m 1d.

On Saturday morning last about 6 o'clock, Mary, a worthy and much respected colored woman, the wife of Charles CHANCELLOR, was so horribly burned by the explosion of a coal oil can, that death ensued in eight hours. On Sunday her remains were followed to the grave by the Sons and Daughter of the Samaritans, including a number of white citizens.

Thursday, 31 May 1877   Vol. XXI, No. 50
Married: In Bryan, Texas, on Wednesday, May 2d, 1877, at the Episcopal Church, by Rev. J. W. DOREMUS, Mr. George W.

SMITH, formerly of Loudoun county, and Mrs. Annie FOOTE, of Byran.

Thursday, 7 June 1877   Vol. XXI, No. 51

Mr. Clinton ADAMS, a farmer residing near Mt. Gilead, died on Sunday night. His death was sudden and sad. He was in Leesburg on Saturday, in the flush of health. It is supposed to have been caused by the excessive heat of the day, and died that night. He was about the 40th year of his age, and leaves a wife and several children.

Death of Asa M. JANNEY – died at his residence near Lincoln, on Thursday night last, in the 75th year of his age. He was a miller by trade, came to Richmond about the year 1832, and took charge of Rutherford's old mill on the canal two miles west of that city. ... Member of the Society of Friends.

Thursday, 14 June 1877   Vol. XXI, No. 52

Married: In Charlestown, June 5th, 1877, by Rev. W. H. MEADE, Mr. Miller B. ALLEN of Giles County, Va and Miss Mary V. AISQUITH, eldest dau. of R. M. AISQUITH, Esq. of that town.

Married: In Maryland, opposite Harper's Ferry, Thursday evening, May 31st, 1877, by Rev. J. M. FRIDAY, Mr. F. G. OTT, of Halltown, Jefferson county, to Miss Annie HOWARD, daughter of the late Grafton HOWARD, of Charlestown.

Married; At the residence of the bride's father, near Upperville, on the 7th of June, by Rev. J. B. LAKE, Miss Tacey GLASSCOCK, daughter of Thomas GLASSCOCK, to Mr. Robert FLETCHER.

Died: Suddenly of dropsy of the heart, Mrs. Susan WYNKOOP, wife of Philip Henry WYNKOOP, and daughter of George CORR, Esq. of Spotsylvania county, Va in her 39th year.

Mr. Joseph LODGE a citizen of this county, died at his home near Snickersville, Friday last in the 84th year of his age.

Major Chas. F. POWELL, the newly appointed Consul of Iquique, died suddenly at that place a few weeks ago. Maj. POWELL was a brother of Mrs. HENNAGE, of Washington City, a lady well known in this community.

Thursday, 21 June 1877   Vol. XXII, No. 1

Married: On the 13th inst., at the residence of the bride's father, by Rev. O. C. BEALL, Mr. Henry E. SKINNER, to Miss M. C. S. SHREVE, all of Loudoun.

Married: At the residence of the officiating minister, in Leesburg, on Wednesday, June 14th, 1877, by Rev. Dr. Nelson HEAD, Mr. George P. SLAUCK to Miss Edith TAVENNER, all of Loudoun.

Married: On the 7th inst., at the Lutheran Parsonage, by Dr. DIEHL, Albert MOCK to Miss Lizzie A. DAVIS, both of Loudoun county.

Married: At Emmanuel Church, Baltimore, Md, on the 14th instant, by the Rev. A. M. RANDOLPH, D.D., assisted by the Rev. George W. PETERKIN, the Rev. John S. LINDSAY, rector of St. James Church, Warrenton, and Miss Carrie W. SMITH, daughter of Mrs. Mary H. SMITH, of Baltimore.

Died: Near Lovettsville, on the morning of the 12th inst., Mrs. Caroline SMITH, the wife of Samuel SMITH, in her 53d year.

Died: In Alexandria, at the residence of his brother, U. M. MONROE, of Marysville, California, in the 41st year of his age. Mr. MONROE was a native of Loudoun county and migrated to California in 1859. He returned to his native state last October somewhat impaired in health and only, as it seems, to die.

Died: In Union, Loudoun county, on Sunday, June 17th, 1877, of brain fever, Lizzie Muse GREEN, infant daughter of Charles P. and Mollie E. GREEN, aged 8m 17d.

Thursday, 28 June 1877   Vol. XXII, No. 2

Married: June 25th, in Baltimore, by Rev. O. C. BEALL, B. A. SHREVE, of Loudoun, to Sallie NELSON, of Baltimore.

Married: On the 21st inst., at the residence of the bride's father, Upperville, Fauquier county, by Rev. Wm. H. JOHNSON, Mr. S. G. BOOKER of St. Louis, Mo., and Miss Mary G. STEPHENSON, of Fauquier.

Married: On the evening of 21st, in Hillsborough, by Rev. Theo. REED, Dr. A. P. SMITH, of Md, to Miss Amanda TAYLOR, of this county.

Died: In Louisville, Ky, on Thursday, 21st inst., at 6:20 p.m., Virginia F., wife of the Right Rev. Thomas U. DUDLEY, Bishop of Kentucky, and daughter of the late John H. ROWLAND, of Norfolk, Va.

Thursday, 5 July 1877   Vol. XXII, No. 3

Married: June 21st, 1877, at Lovettsville, by Rev. P. H. MILLER, Mr. Walter S. DONALDSON, and Miss Mary C. ARNOLD, all of Loudoun.

Died: On the 16th instant, at the residence of her brother, near Hughesville, Malinda FURR, in the 80th year of her age.

Thursday, 12 July 1877   Vol. XXII, No. 4

Died: At the residence of her husband, in Montgomery Co., Md, on Monday July 9th, after an illness of about one week, Mrs. Mary L., wife of Jas. M. ALLNUTT, and daughter of the late Geo. MARLOW, of this county.

Died: At his residence, near Arcola, Mr. John T. LIGHTFOOT, in about the 60th year of his age.

Died: At her residence, near Middleburg, on Sunday, 24th ult., Mrs. Huldah CRAIN, relict of Baily CRAIN, dec'd., in her 65th year.

Died: Of paralysis, at the residence of his son, A. J. MARTIN, in Moundsville, West Virginia, June 18th, 1877, Col. G. T. MARTIN, aged 74 years. Born in Loudoun county in 1802. He moved to and settled permanently in Marshall county, now West Va. Member of the Virginia Legislature of 1841. ...

James GARDNER and J. W. GROVE, who were arrested June 22d on suspicion of being the murders of Rev. J. M. FRIDAY, late pastor of the Lutheran Church at Hagerstown and Harper's Ferry, were committed to jail to await the action of the grandjury in November.

Thursday, 19 July 1877   Vol. XXII, No. 5

Died: At his residence in Richmond city, Va. on the 12th of July, 1877, Joseph L. VANDEVANTER, formerly of Loudoun county, in the 67th year of his age.

Died: At the residence of her husband, in this town on Tuesday night, July 17th, 1877, Mrs. Mary SAUNDERS, wife of Wm. H. SAUNDERS, in the 67th year of her age.

Died: At her mother's residence, near Leesburg, on Thursday, July 12th, 1877, Miss Lucy E. LAYCOCK, daughter of the late Samuel LAYCOCK, in the 25th year of her age.

Married: July 4th, 1877, in the English Lutheran Church at Omaha, by the pastor, Rev. W. A. LIPE, Mr. John W. TYLER, formerly of Philomont, and Miss Mattie JOHNSON, formerly of Michigan, now both of Sarpy county, Neb.

Married: On the 20th of June, at Christ Church, Millwood, by Rev. Joseph R. JONES, Percy W. CHARRINGTON, Esq., of London, England, to Mary Harrison, only daughter of Maj. Beverly RANDOLPH, of Clarke Co., Va.

Married: At the Monumental Church, Richmond, Va, by Rev. Dr. WOODBRIDGE, on the 28th of June, Lucy Minor, youngest daughter of the late Com. M. F. MAURY, and Meverell L. Van DOREN, of Blenheim, Albemarle Co.

Mr. Geo. BEAMER of this county, died at his residence near Hoysville, on Tuesday last. He had passed his 90th year. He was one of the wealthiest men in Loudoun.

Thursday, 26 July 1877   Vol. XXII, No. 6

Died: In Washington, on July 11, 1877, Thomas ALEXANDER, in the 51st year of his age. Birth place, Leesburg.

Died: Near Aldie, June 29, Charles RITICOR, after a short illness, in a few days of being 79 years old.

Died: At the residence of her father-in-law, in this county, on the morning of the 15th inst., Mrs. Clarissa M., wife of Luther MYERS, and daughter of Levi and Eliza HENDERSON, formerly of Madison county, Va, aged 22 years.

Mrs. Lilly KEITH, the young wife of Judge James KEITH, of this judicial circuit, died at her home, in Warrenton, yesterday, after a protracted illness. A daughter of Mr. Arthur MORSON, and grand-daughter of the late Judge SCOTT, of Fauquier.

Thursday, 2 August 1877   Vol. XXII, No. 7

Died: At Sycolin Mills, Tuesday morning, July 24th, 1877, Mary S., daughter of James H. and Bettie LAWSON, aged 10m 27d.

Died: In Leesburg, July 25, 1877, at the residence of its grandfather, W. W. DIVINE Sr., Willie, infant son of Henry and Sallie MORGAN, of Washington, DC, aged 10m 15d.

Died: Near Aldie, Prince William county, on the 16th of July, 1877, Mrs. Sallie GARDNER, in the 69th year of her age.

Died: On Bush Hill farm, Fairfax county, July 27, 1877, at 11 a.m., of bilious fever, Sarah E., beloved wife of John P. BRAWNER, Esq., late of Prince William county, aged 38.

Died: At his home, in Loudoun county, on July 16th, 1877, Wm. RILEY, in the 91st year of his age.

Thursday, 9 August 1877   Vol. XXII, No. 8

Married: At the residence of the bride's parents, August 1st, by Rev. Andrew P. KEATING, S. J., M. T. RUST, of Loudoun county, to Mary Estelle, daughter of James C. NEVETT, of Alexandria.

Died: Near Waterford, on Wednesday, July 4th, 1877, Mrs. Sallie A. STEAVENS, in the 31st year of her age.

Died: On Friday, July 27th, at the same place, Willie T. STEAVENS, aged 2 months.

Mr. Townsend McVEIGH, died at his home near Middleburg, on Saturday morning last, at an advanced age.

Thursday, 16 August 1877   Vol. XXII, No. 9

A telegram received her today announced the death at his residence near Shepherdstown, West Virginia, of Edmund I. LEE, Esq., formerly of this city, and the eldest brother of Mr. Cassius F. LEE of Seminary Hill. Mr. LEE was upward of 80 years of age, and the oldest member of that LEE family in the state. Much sympathy to Mr. C. F. LEE who in three days has lost his daughter, Mrs. PETERKIN, his relative and former partner, Mr. W. G. CAZENOVE, and now his oldest brother. (Edmund I. LEE was a brother, also of Maj. C. H. and Col. R. H. LEE, of the Loudoun bar.)

Died: In this town, on the 8th instant, of typhoid fever, in the 25th year of her age, Mrs. Emma Nora TITUS, daughter of James A. ANDERSON, and wife of Wm. TITUS. The deceased was for several years a member of Providence M. C. Church (South).

Died: On the 2d inst., in Lovettsville, Mrs. Martha A. COST, aged 76y 6m 26d. Member of the Reformed Church.

Died: Near Broad Run Bridge, on Sunday week, very suddenly, Mr. Jefferson HAVENNER, aged 50 years.

Died: Near Middleburg, of cholera infantum, Earnest Franklin, infant son of Benjamin and Annie E. DAVIS, aged 2m 21d.

At her home near Philomont, July 27th, 1877, Orra O. OTLEY, only daughter of James G. OTLEY, in the 20th year of her age.

Aug. Ct.: Will of Geo. BEAMER, Wm. RILEY, Frederick MILLER and Arminda SWARTS admitted to probate. Administrations granted on the estates of Barton RICHARDS, John FRY, Chas. RITICAR, and Elisha JANNEY. Estates of Martha NIXON and Jas. R. HUTCHISON committed to Sheriff.

Thursday, 23 August 1877   Vol. XXII, No. 10

Died: At her residence, in Mechanicstown, Md, on Tuesday, July 31st, 1877, Ginnie, wife of Cost CARMACK, and daughter of Charles and Ara Ann HOUGH, of Loudoun county.

Died: In Charlestown, on Saturday, August 11th, 1877, Mrs. Rachael A. EASTERDAY, wife of Mr. John S. EASTERDAY, and daughter of Judge Joseph EASTERDAY, of Frederick county, Md, in the 34th year of her age.

Isaac D. BUDD, a former resident of Loudoun county, and who since the war represented that county in the Legislature, died at his residence, in Richmond, yesterday afternoon, at 5 o'clock, after a short illness. He was a son-in-law of Mr. Townsend McVEIGH, who died about two weeks since.

Thursday, 30 August 1877   Vol. XXII, No. 11

Married: In Austin, Arkansas, on the 25th of July, 1877, by the Rev. Mr. McLAUCKLIN, Mr. T. M. YOUNG and Miss Mary Alice JACKSON.

Married: Near Purcellville, August 15, 1877, by the Rev. Samuel BROWN, Mr. Geo. H. BROWN and Miss Laura J. SEATON, all of Loudoun county.

Died: At the Rectory of St. James' Church, Leesburg, on Wednesday, August 22d, 1877, Richard Terrell, infant and only son of Rev. R. T. and Louisa T. DAVIS, aged 13 months.

Old Aunt Easter, a negro woman, formerly belonging to Mr. Maurice OSBURN, of this county, still lives near Purcellville and is said to be in her 106th year.

An accident occurred in the vicinity of Leesburg on Friday evening, which resulted in the death of Mr. Lewis DONOHOE, drowning by crossing a swollen Tuscarora where it cross the Ball's Mill road, one mile from town. Finally, around noon on Saturday, the water was drawn off of Hempstone's dam about 200 years from where he attempted to cross and body was discovered lodged in an eddie against the roots of a tree. In his 71st year. Leaves a wife and several grown children. On Sunday interred in Union Cemetery, Rev. R. T. DAVIS officiating.

Thursday, 6 September 1877   Vol. XXII, No. 12

Married: In the city of Wichita, Kansas, on the 18th of July, 1877, by the Rev. Father SCHNEZ, in the Catholic Church, T. C. MAJOR, formerly of Ohio, to Miss Lina A. A. LESLIE, formerly of Virginia and daughter of Col. John LESLIE dec'd.

Married: August 20th 1877, at Hamilton, Va, by Rev. L. H. CRENSHAW, Mr. Wm. EVERHART and Miss Malinda COX, both of Hamilton.

Married: On the 27th of August, near the Trappe, by the Rev. Frazier FURR, Mr. John LANHAM Jr., and Miss Margaret E. LANHAM.

Died: Near Goresville, on Thursday, August 16th, 1877, Henry, infant son of Henry B. and Louisa E. HIBLER, aged nine months.

Thursday, 13 September 1877   Vol. XXII, No. 13

A difficult occurred here Friday between James JOHNSON and Capt. John AVIS, of Charlestown, W. Va, during which JOHNSON was mortally wounded. He died yesterday morning, AVIS was arrested. He was an officer in the Virginia regiment in the Mexican war, and was also an officer in the Stonewall Brigade, Confederate army during the late war, and at the time of the surrender was provost marshal at Staunton. One of his sons is now a cadet at the West Point Military Academy.

County Ct.: Will of Thomas MONROE admitted to probate. Administrations were granted on the estate of Parmelia HAMILTON and Henry REED. Estate of Philip BOGER, Wm. SMALLWOOD, Edward D. POTTS, and John W. VIRTZ, committed to Sheriff.

The funeral of the late Wm. F. PHILLIPS, whose sudden and sad death was announced last week, took place on Thursday. He was in the 57th year of his age.

Died: In Washington on Sunday morning, at 2 o'clock, John BIRD, of Leesburg.

Thursday, 20 September 1877   Vol. XXII, No. 14

Married: On the 13th, by Rev. W. H. FORSYTH, Wm. H. HARDY to Miss Mary F. CRIDLER, all of Loudoun.

Married: On the 13th of September, 1877, at "Avon," the residence of the bride's father, in Fairfax county, by Rev. John McGILL, Mr. Lewis H. FREEMAN, of Loudoun county, and Miss Hattie L. COCKERILLE, second daughter of Hon. R. H. COCKERILLE.

Married: On the 13th instant, at St. James Church, Warrenton, by the Rev. J. S. LINDSAY, rector, Edward WADE, of Springfield, Fauquier county, third son of Colonel WADE, C. B. of Hauxwell Bedale, Yorkshire, England, to Evylyn, eldest daughter of Captain ASSHETON, of Rock Spring, Fauquier county, and of Walmersley, Lancashire, England.

Died: Near Austin, Lonoke county, Ark., August 31st, 1877, Thomas M. YOUNG, formerly of Loudoun, in his 24th year.

Mr. Frank H. CRAIGHILL was found dead in his barnyard, near Charlestown, West Virginia, on Tuesday evening last. He was subject to attacks of epilepsy or some similar affection and the supposition is that one of these caused his death.

Thursday, 27 September 1877   Vol. XXII, No. 15

Married: On September 12, at Saint Matthew's Church, Washington DC, by the Rev. Father REVEILLE, M. B. McABEE, of Baltimore, to Miss Nellie BENTLEY, of Leesburg.

On the 20th inst., at Meadland, the residence of the bride, in Culpeper county, by the Rev. C. Y. STEPTOE, R. O. GRAYSON to Mrs. Mary A. REAGAN, all of Culpeper.

Death of Rev. Dr. Jas. A. DUNCAN – Leesburg was one of the first if not the first charge assigned Dr. D, after entering the ministry, he having been stationed in this town as earl as 1852. He was buried in Hollywood Cemetery, Richmond, on Tuesday, Bishop DOGGETT delivering the funeral discourse.

Rev. James A. DUNCAN, President of Randolph-Macon College died in Ashland this morning at 4 a.m., or erysipelas. In his 47th year, son of Prof. David DUNCAN, of Wofford College, South Carolina, now in his 84th year. Prof. Wallace DUNCAN of the same college is his brother. He had been married twice. His first wife was Miss TWITTY of North Carolina and his second was Miss WADE, of West Virginia. Leaves a number of children. ...

Thursday, 4 October 1877   Vol. XXII, No. 16

Married: At 8 p.,., October 2nd, 1877, at St. James Church, Leesburg, by its Rector, Rev. R. T. DAVIS D.D., assisted by Rev. Theo C. REED, Emilie W. GRAY, fourth daughter of Mary

E. and late Robt. W. GRAY, to Jno. J. WILLIAMS, Esq., of Winchester, Va.

Married: According to the rites of the Episcopal Church, September 27th, 1877, at Dunbarton, Loudoun county, the residence of the bride's parents, George Harrison BURWELL, of Richmond, Va, and Laura Dunbar LEE, Rev. Wm. H. JOHNSON, assisted by Rev. R. T. DAVIS, D.D., officiating.

Married: In Washington, DC, at the residence of the bride's father, on Monday, Sept. 24th, 1877, by the Rev. Mr. WHEELER, Captain Will D. VINCEL, of Lovettsville, to Miss Alice M. HATTON, of that city.

Married: On the 20th of Sept. at the residence of Mr. LAYCOCK, by the Rev. John WOOLF, Mr. Jos. REED and Miss Maggie CANIFORD, all of Loudoun.

Married: At Morven, Fauquier, residence of the bride's parents, on the 29th September, by the Rev. Robb WHITE, assisted by the Rev. Jas. R. WINCHESTER, the Rev. H. B. LEE, formerly of Shepherdstown, to Lucy J., only daughter of J. KEITH and F. L. MARSHALL, all of Fauquier county.

Died: At "Roanoke" the residence of her son-in-law, A. J. BRENT, Esq., in Northumberland Co., on Tuesday the 11th of September 1877, Mrs. Sarah Barnes Hooe STITH, widow of Major John STITH, and only surviving child of George MASON, Esq., of "Lexington" who was eldest son of Colonel George MASON of "Gunston Hall" in Fairfax County, and of Elizabeth Mary Ann Barns HOOE, of "Barnesfield" in King George county, aged 83y 3m 15d.

Died: September 23d, Adie Gray, youngest child of Martha A. and James A. ROLLINS, aged 11m 3d.

The wedding at St. James' Church, on Tuesday evening, was a brilliant affair. The contracting parties were Jno. J. WILLIAMS, Esq., of Winchester and Miss Emilie W. GRAY, of this place. The rector, Rev. R. T. DAVIS, officiated assisted by Rev. Theo. REED.

Thursday, 11 October 1877   Vol. XXII, No. 17

Married: September 27th 1877, by Rev John WOOLF, at the residence of Mr. CREAL, Mr. R. W. WHITTINGDON, of Loudoun, to Miss Helen PAYNE, of Fauquier.

Married: At the Parsonage of the M. E. Church, Oct. 3d, 1877, by Rev. Wm. H. FORSYTH, Chas. C. BELL to Florence M. JACOBS, all of Loudoun county.

Married: In St. James' Church, Leesburg, on Wednesday, October 3d, 1877, by the Rev. R. T. DAVIS, D.D., Annie Farrand, second daughter of the late Prof. Wm. B. BENEDICT, U.S.N., to Walter J. HARRISON, both of Leesburg.

Married: October 4th, 1877, at the residence of the bride's father, by Rev. L. H. CRENSHAW, Mr. Wm. A. McFARLAND and Miss Ginnie HESS, daughter of L. Dow HESS, Esq., all of Loudoun county.

Married: Oct. 9th, 1877, by Rev. L. H. CRENSHAW, Mr. James LAYCOCK, of Loudoun county, to Miss Mary TORRISON, of Washington, DC.

Married: In St. James' Episcopal Church, Leesburg, on Wednesday morning, October 10th 1877, by Rev. R. T. DAVIS, D.D., Mr. Samuel S. LUTZ and Miss Ida FECHTIG, all of this county.

Died: In Alexandria, on October 6th, 1877, at the boarding house of Mrs. WILKINS, William O. HENDERSON, only son of F. M. HENDERSON, of Leesburg, in the 24th year of his age, from internal injuries received by a fall from the cars at the depot of the Virginia Midland Railroad, on the morning of the 4th.

Died: In Leesburg, on Tuesday afternoon, Oct. 9, 1877, Mrs. Catharine A. HAMMERLY, wife of Mr. John HAMMERLY, aged 56y 10m 15d.

Died: In Washington, on the morning of September 29, 1877, of chronic disease of the heart, Asatia C. GOVER, wife of A. J. MARTIN, after a long and protracted illness, in the 41st year of her age. Mrs. MARTIN was a daughter of the late Robert GOVER, of Leesburg.

Died: At the Louisa Home, Washington, DC, on the 3d of October, '77, Mrs. Margaret ESKRIDGE, widow of the late C. G. ESKRIDGE, of Leesburg, in the 74th year of her age.

County Ct.: P. D. COPELAND qualified as Admr. of Augustin S. EVERHART. Jno. W. GARRETT qualified as guardian of John E., John A. and John B. LESLIE. Thos. J. BROWN qualified as Admr. of Chas. W. SCOTT. Samuel DONOHOE qualified as Admr. of Lewis J. DONOHOE. Estates of Caroline COCKERILLE, Cassendra NIXON, John T. LIGHTFOOT and Wm. H. JAMES committed to Sheriff.

Death of William O. HENDERSON – an employee at the shops of the Va. Midland Railroad Company in Alexandria, was assisting in shifting a train of cars at the depot, fell and was passed over by the train. ... Mr. HENDERSON was born and reared in this town, he was in the 24th year of his age and the only son of Mr. F. M. HENDERSON. His remains were brought to Leesburg Saturday afternoon. and buried Sunday morning from St. James Church to his last resting place by his mother's side in Union Cemetery. Services conducted by Rev. R. T. DAVIS. Loudoun Lodge, I.O.O.F., of Leesburg of which he was a member participating.

Drowning of Mr. W. E. CARTER, of the firm of Kelly & Carter, Commission Merchants of Alexandria, Va. On Thursday morning while crossing the rain swollen Sycolin creek where it crosses Aldie Turnpike, just this side of Mr. Chas. POWELL's residence. His brother, Mr. Marshall CARTER landed in shallow water, while he was swept away. Mr. CARTER was raised in the neighborhood of Aldie, was about 30 years of age and leaves a wife and two children.

Thursday, 18 October 1877   Vol. XXII, No. 18

Married: On Thursday, the 11th inst., in the Presbyterian Church, Farmwell, by Rev. J. F. CANNON, Mr. William LEFEVRE to Miss Nellie BAUCHMAN, both of Loudoun.

Died: At the residence of her parents, in Leesburg, on the morning of the 11th of October, 1877, little Maud, only daughter of J. H. and C. E. MANNING, aged 16 months.

Died: At Washington city, at 12 o'clock., on the night of October 9th, 1877, of diphtheria, Albert N., and at 3 o'clock on the morning of the same night of the same disease, Nettie F., the only children of R. Neville and Emma V. SAUNDERS, formerly of this county, aged respectively six and seven years.
Thursday their remains were brought to Leesburg and at mid day, in Union Cemetery, two little coffins were lowered into a single grave.

Thursday, 25 October 1877   Vol. XXII, No. 19

Married: At the Rectory in Leesburg on the 13th day of August, 1877, by the Rev. R. T. DAVIS, Mr. T. W. FRANKLIN, to Miss Lucy J. KUHLMAN, all of Loudoun county.

Married: On the 20th of September 1877, at the bride's residence at Upperville, Fauquier, by the Rev. Thomas E. CARSON, Mr. William CHAMBLIN to Miss Olevia J. CALVERT.

A few weeks ago Mr. John ZELLERS and his wife, of Washington county, Md, left home to attend the funeral of his sister in Leesburg, leaving behind a little boy of eight years old. A few hours after the parents had started the child was missed. The search followed the direction of the parents and finally overtook him between Weverton and Pt. of Rocks, having traveled about 25 miles in nine hours.

Thursday, 1 November 1877   Vol. XXII, No. 20

Married: At Towsontown, Md, on July 5, by Rev. Mr. RICE, Dr. I. C. GORDON, of Baltimore, to Mary M., oldest daughter of C. D. BIRD, Esq., formerly of Leesburg.

Married: In Baltimore, on October 16th, at Christ Church, by Rev. A. M. RANDOLPH, Frank FISHER and Frances Virginia, daughter of the late Alfred POOR, all of Baltimore.

Thursday, 8 November 1877   Vol. XXII, No. 21

Married: On the 24th inst. at Lovettsville, Va, by Rev. P. H. MILLER, Wm. C. STONEBURNER and Miss Sallie E. SMITH, both of Loudoun county.

Married: On the 30th ultimo, near Lovettsville, by the Rev. H. St. J. RINKER, Mr. Thomas J. COOPER to Miss Virginia C. FRY, all of Loudoun county.

Married: At Locust Grove, the home of the bride's father, on Wednesday, October 31, 1877, by Rev. Henry E. BRANCH, Mr. G. W. BRADEN and Miss Corrie E., daughter of Mr. Washington VANDEVANTER, all of this county.

Married: At Belmont, near Alexandria, the residence of the bride's father, on the evening of the 24th ult., by Rev. Dr. BULLOCK, Dr. G. Wythe COOK, of Upperville, Fauquier county, and Miss Rebecca LLOYD, daughter of Richard LLOYD, Esq.

Married: At Ewell's chapel, Prince Wm. County, on Wednesday, November 3, 1877, by Rev. Mr. JOHNSON, Mr. Robert L. MOORE, of Aldie, and Miss Isabella TYLER, of Loudoun county.

Thursday, 15 November 1877   Vol. XXII, No. 22

Married: In the M. E. Church, South, on Tuesday morning, November 13th, 1877, by Rev. H. H. KENNEDY, Mr. Clement W. HOWARD, of Washington, DC, and Miss Addie M., only daughter of F. A. LUTZ, of Loudoun county.

Married: In the Presbyterian Church, Leesburg, on Wednesday morning, November 14th, 1877, by Rev. J. F. CANNON, Mr. Maurice J. ALDER, of Georgetown, DC, and Miss Gertrude H., eldest daughter of Robert HARPER, Esq., of Loudoun.

Married: At the Parsonage of the M. E. Church, South, on Tuesday, Nov. 14th, 1877, by Rev. H. H. KENNEDY, Mr. Edward AUSTIN, and Mrs. Elizabeth LEWIS, both of Hamilton.

Died: In Leesburg, on Sunday, Nov. 11th 1877, Mr. Charles A. JOHNSTON, in the 72d year of his age.

Mr. Chas. A. JOHNSTON of this town died on Sunday last, in the 72d year of his age. For many years Mr. J. was an active business man in this community.

County Ct.: Samuel W. CHINN qualified as Executor of Sue V. CHINN dec'd. Townsend McVEIGH's estate committed to Sheriff. P. W. CARPER qualified as Executor of Jane C. AUSTIN dec'd.

An unfortunate even occurred near Lovettsville on Friday night last. On Thursday last Mr. Joseph B. MANN was married in Frederick city and returned that evening with his bride, to his mother's residence about two miles from Lovettsville. The Rattle Band Club visited a brother of MANN and persuaded them to accompany them. The brother advised them that Joseph had advised them not to come but the paid no attention and chose on the way Mr. John BRISLAN as Captain. When they arrived at the house they were fired upon, BRISLAN was shot in the back of the neck and died about 8 o'clock Saturday morning. MANN fled but on Sunday evening surrendered himself.

Thursday, 22 November 1877   Vol. XXII, No. 23

Married: At the bride's residence in Gum Spring, Loudoun county, on Sunday morning, November 11th 1877, by the Rev. D. N. GILBERT, Rev. Augustus WATKINS, of the M. E. Church, to Miss Jennie McFARLAND, of the above named county. Bridesmaids and groomsmen: Mr. Alfred LEIGH and Miss Jannie F. FERGUSON, Mr. C. J. C. MAFFETT and Miss Mollie C. FERGUSON.

Died: November 23d, at the residence of her husband, James W. M. SMITH, Esq., near Georgetown, DC, Mrs. Ann Elizabeth, daughter of John and Elizabeth CURRY, of this county.

Several years ago, a Mrs. LONGACRE gave to John T. GRIMES her infant child, a little girl of two or three summers to raise. The contract was a verbal one and now the mother claims possession of the child. Court opinion that child be remanded to the custody of the mother, but appealed and child to remain with defendant for now.

Thursday, 29 November 1877   Vol. XXII, No. 24

Married: On the 4th inst., at Lovettsville, by Rev. P. H. MILLER, Mr. Mahlon EDWARDS and Miss Susan Virginia RILEY, all of Loudoun.

Married: In Leesburg, on the 22d of November 1877, by the Rev. R. T. DAVIS, at the residence of the bride's grandmother, Mrs. Rebecca WILDMAN, Mr. Samuel FRY and Miss Elizabeth E. MOSS.

Married: On the 15th inst., at the residence of the bride's father, by the Rev. Dr. HAYNES, Mr. Franklin P. TIFFANY and Miss Annie V. BALL, all of Loudoun.

Married: On Tuesday, the 22d inst., at the church of the Ascention, Baltimore, by the Rev. Campbell FAIR, William S. POWELL, formerly of Loudoun to Elizabeth B., daughter of the late Bowin SMITH, of Baltimore.

Thursday, 6 December 1877   Vol. XXII, No. 25

Departed this life on the morning of 19th instant, at her residence, Gum Spring, Loudoun county, Mrs. Mary Louisa LAMBERT, wife of Dr. Francis LAMBERT, in the 49th year of her age.

Died: Of consumption on the 20th of November, at the residence of his father, near Round Hill, Mr. Matson JAMES, son of Mr. Mason JAMES, in the 22d year of his age. He had just finished his education at Richmond College.

Married: November 28th, at Hill Dale, Fauquier county, by Rev. Mr. ALLEN, Mr. E. B. FADELY, of Washington, DC (formerly of Leesburg) to Miss M. A. FURR, daughter of M. B. FURR, Esq. of Fauquier county.

Married: At the Parsonage of the M. E. Church, Nov. 25th, by the Rev. W. H. FORSYTH, John M. RAWLINGS to Annie E CARTER, all of Loudoun county.

Married: Nov. 28th, 1877, at the residence of the bride's father, by Rev. L. H. CRENSHAW, Mr. Sydnor B. FRANCIS and Miss Ella McCRAY, daughter of Wm. McCRAY, all of Loudoun.

Thursday, 13 December 1877   Vol. XXII, No. 26

The bodies of the twin little children of Mr. John HOUSER, drowned during the late freshet, on Mason's Island, were found last week. That of the younger was picked up on the river bank near Edward's Ferry, on Thursday, and on Saturday, the eldest child was found, almost buried in the sand on a small island a few miles below Masons. The two were interred in Union Cemetery. Neither the bodies of Miss MILBOURN, nor those of the two negro men, who lost their lives in their heroic efforts to save those three unfortunate victims of the flood have yet been discovered. The body of the colored man has been found near Seneca.

County Ct.: Estate of Chas. TURNER committed to the Sheriff. Will of Susan ORANGE dec'd. admitted to probate.

Thursday, 20 December 1877   Vol. XXII, No. 27

Married: On the 13th inst., at the residence of the bride's father, by the Rev. I. B. LAKE, Mr. John A. LYNCH, and Miss Sallie C., daughter of Craven JAMES, of Loudoun Co.

Married: At the residence of the bride's parents, at Waterford, December 6th, 1877, by Rev. Wm. H. FORSYTH, John W. McKINNEY and Annie B. HOUGH, all of Loudoun County.

Died: In Leesburg, on Thursday, the 13th of December, 1877, after a protracted illness, Mr. A. D. ACHER, in his 35th year.

Died: In Leesburg, December 2d, 1877, Mrs. Susan ORANGE, in the 78th year of her age.

Died: At his residence near Mt. Gilead, in this county, December 11th, 1877, after a short but painful illness, Mr. John J. RUSK, in the 51st year of his age.

Mr. David ACHER died at his residence in this town, on Thursday evening last, in the 35th year of his age. During the late war Mr.

A. was a gallant member of Col. MOSBY's command. He was a member of the I.O.O. Fellows, the Good Templers, the Y.M.C.A. Association and the M. E. Church, South. Buried on Saturday afternoon. He leave a wife and three children.

Thursday, 27 December 1877   Vol. XXII, No. 28

Married: At Morrisonville, on the 16th instant, by the Rev. P. H. MILLER, Mr. Samuel CRIMM and Miss Ellen V. ADAMS, all of Loudoun.

Married: December 19th, 1877, by Rev. John WOOLF, Mr. Eli WALKER to Miss Sarah C. GARRISON, all of Loudoun.

Married: On the evening of the 13th of December, 1877, at the bride's residence, by the Rev. C. W. BALL, Mr. Israel VIRTS to Miss A. E. VIRTS, both of Loudoun

Married: On the 15th of November, 1877, by Elder Joseph FURR, at the residence of the bride's father, Mr. Geo. Henry FURR, of Loudoun county, to Miss Rosa, eldest daughter of Joseph WHITE, of Montgomery county, Md.

Married: On the 13th inst., at Mr. Ebin FURR's, by Rev. J. A. HAYNES, Mr. Albert CROUCH and Miss Mary Virginia TINSMAN.

Married: By Elder S. M. ATHEY, December 20th 1877, Mr. La Vega MOFFETT to Miss Mary A. ASHBY, both of Fauquier.

Married: By the same, on the same day, Mr. Thomas PAYNE to Miss Georgianna HARREL, both of Fauquier.

Married: by the same on the same day, Mr. Henry H. LUNSFORD to Miss Lizzie E. HALL, all of Fauquier.

Married: By the same, on the same day, Mr. Reuben F. HITT to Miss Alice E. HALL, all of Fauquier.

Married: In Washington, DC, December 18th, 1877, James W. SHIRLEY and Miss Nettie BRODIE, both of Fauquier.

Married: On Thursday, the 20th inst., at the residence of the bride's parents, by Rev. James S. HIGGINS, Robert A. COCKRILL and Miss Mary E. McCONCHIE, all of Fauquier.

Married: Dec. 26, 1877, at Washington HAINES,, Esq., by Rev. L. H. CRENSHAW, Mr. Frank L. TUGGLE and Miss Sallie L. NESMITH, of Loudoun.

Died: At her residence near Leesburg, on the morning of the 18th inst., Mrs. Caroline M. E. BARRETT, in the 68th year of her age.

Thursday, 3 January 1878   Vol. XXII, No. 29

Died: On Monday, Dec. 10, of spinal meningitis, Miss Willie C. FITZHUGH, at the residence of her mother, Mrs. M. W. FITZHUGH, "The Grove," in Loudoun county, near Upperville.

Died: In Staunton, suddenly of heart disease, on Monday, the 24th instant, Miss Margaret L. POLLARD, of Warrenton, aged about 50 years.

Died: Near Warrenton, on the 25th instant, Mr. Lewis SHUMATE, aged about 74 years.

Died: Near Middleburg, on the 17th of October, 1877, Bettie, wife of Milton BYRNE, Esq. and daughter of the late Thomas FRANCIS, aged 42 years.

Marriage of Mr. Elijah S. BEAVERS to Miss May MATSELL – took place at the residence of the bride's mother, #25 Fifth Avenue at half past eight o'clock last evening. The officiating clergyman, the Rev. Mr. SMITH of the First M. E. Church. ... *Leavenworth (Kansas) Times, Dec. 21.*

Thursday, 10 January 1878   Vol. XXII, No. 30

Married: At Lebanon, Mo., Wednesday, Dec. 26th, Geo. J. BRADFIELD and Miss Lucy HERNDON.

Married: At the M. E. Parsonage in Leesburg, on Dec. 19, 1877, by Rev. H. H. KENNEDY, Benton H. BALDWIN and Mrs. Annie CARTER, all of Loudoun.

Married: At the same place, by the same, on Jan. 3, 1878, Mr. John James LEE and Miss Lucinda R. MORAN, all of Loudoun.

Died: At the residence of her son, Mr. Samuel H. FRAZIER, on the 4th of January, 1878, Mrs. Mary A. FRAZIER, in her 71st year.

Death of Mrs. Geo. R. HEAD – from lock jaw on Friday night, in the 53d year of her age. On Sunday she was buried as she requested by the side of her father, the late Rev. Samuel GOVER, in the graveyard of the M. E. Church.

Thursday, 17 January 1878   Vol. XXII, No. 31

Married: At Ickesburg, Pa, on Dec. 27th, 1877, by Rev. CLEVER, assisted by Rev. J. L. KISTLER, Rev. Geo. W. CHRIST, Lutheran Minister at Harper's Ferry, W. Va, and Miss Annie B. ORR, of Ickesburg, Pa.

Married: Jan. 9th, 1878, by the Rev. S. M. ATHEY, at the residence of C. B. ADAMS, Esq., Mr. F. A ISH to Miss Alice L. ADAMS, all of Loudoun county.

Married: At Upperville, Va, January 18th, 1878, by Rev. J. B. LAKE, Miss Sarah F. DUNBAR to George W. COLBERT, of Jefferson Co., West Virginia.

Married: On January 15th, 1878, at the residence of the bride's mother, by Rev. L. H. CRENSHAW, Mr. Wentworth C. ZEVERLY and Miss Rachel H. BIRDSALL, daughter of Benjamin BIRDSALL deceased, all of Loudoun Co.

Died: On Friday, the 4th of January, 1878, at the residence of her son-in-law, C. W. BARTON, near Middleburg, after a lingering illness, Mrs. Elizabeth CRAIN, wife of John CRAIN and daughter of James WORNAL, in the 81st year of her age.

Mr. William T. TITUS, for several years a merchant in this town, died at the residence of his brother, near Taylortown, on Friday night last, of consumption in about the 35th year of his age. Mr. T. was a widower, and leaves a little boy about five years old. Mr. T. had his life insured for $2,000.

At Marquette, Michigan, on the 12th of January, while some hands were loading 4,800 lbs. of nitro-glycerine, the compound exploded, killing seven men and injuring five or six others. Among the killed was William SPILLMAN, a native of Va.

Jan. Ct.: John W. GARRETT appointed Guardian of Lula LAYCOCK and Edward LAYCOCK. Wm. F. BARRETT qualified as Exor. of Geo. BEAMER dec'd. Wm. F. GRAY qualified As Admr. of Willie C. FITZHUGH. A. P. HUMMER qualified as Admr. of John H. TIPPETT. T. H. CARTER qualified as Admr. of Geo. YOUNG dec'd.

Thursday, 24 January 1878   Vol. XXII, No. 32

Married: In Washington, DC, December 13th, 1877, at the parsonage of the N. C. Ave. M. P. Church, by the Rev. Jesse SHREEVE, Mr. Jno. E. GEORGE and Miss Orra B. VIRTS.

Married: On Tuesday, January 15, 1878, at the residence of the bride's parents, in Washington, by Rev. E. D. OWEN, pastor of Ryland M. E. Church, G. Newton WHITE, of Loudoun county, and Fannie Gertrude WALKER, of that city.

Married: On Thursday evening, January 17th, at the M. E. Church, by Rev. W. R. WEBB, George E. HEPBURN and Amanda E. KNIGHT, both of Washington city.

Died: At his residence, near Guilford, on the 12th of November, 1877, Mr. Thos. H. LYNE, from cancer in the stomach, in the 64th year of his age.

Died: At her residence near Leesburg, on Tuesday night, January 22, 1878, Mrs. Mary CURRY, in the 70th year of her age.

Thursday, 31 January 1878   Vol. XXII, No. 33

Married: On the 23d of January, by Rev. Thos. E. CARSON, Mr. Jas. M. REED and Miss Sallie A. DISHMAN, both of Loudoun.

Died: At Roseville, Loudoun Co., Jan. 9th, 1878, Miss Mary C. FERGUSON, daughter of Romulus and Catharine FERGUSON, in the 22d year of her age.

Died: At her residence in Alexandria, the 24th inst., Mrs. S. A. BARKER, wife of H. S. W. BARKER, in the 52d year of her age. Member of the Baptist Church for about ten years.

Daughter of the late Rev. Henry STEVENS, formerly of Loudoun county.

Some three years ago a Mrs. LONGACRE gave to John T. GRIMES of this county, one of her children, a girl then a year or two old, to raise as his own. The contract was a verbal one and a few months since the mother wanted the child back. Appeal decision reversed original decision and now leaves GRIMES in possession of the child.

Thursday, 7 February 1878 Vol. XXII, No. 34

Married: At the residence of Mason THROCKMORTON, near Snickersville, January 24th, 1878, by Rev. I. B. LAKE, Miss Virginia HUMPHREY to Volney OSBURN.

Married; At the residence of Thomas SMALLWOOD, Blue Ridge mountain, on the 24th inst. by Rev. J. E. EVANS, Thomas SMALLWOOD to Miss Caroline HARRIS, of Fauquier county.

Married: At the same time and place, by Rev. J. E. EVANS, Albin W. HARRIS, of Loudoun county to Miss Caroline SMALLWOOD, of Clarke county, Va.

Died: At her home in Philomont, January 17th, 1878, Mrs. Mary F. SAFFLE, in the 24th year of her age.

Died: At the boarding house of Miss OSBURN, in Leesburg, 2 o'clock on Friday morning, February 1st, 1878, Mrs. Delia North SAUNDERS, widow of the late Major Henry SAUNDERS, in the 77th year of her age.

Died: In Middleburg, on 24th January, 1878, Mrs. Elizabeth R., wife of Mr. Edward M. BAKER, in her 74th year. The deceased for 27 years was a member of the Methodist Church.

J. Hunter SMITH, oldest son of Col. Robert W. SMITH, of Alabama, and formerly of Fauquier county, was killed by a desperado named JOHNSON, last Saturday, while attending the wedding of a Mr. MURPHY near Choctow Bluff. The difficulty grew out of a toast given by a friend of SMITH's. SMITH knocked down JOHNSON and the groom interposed to separate the combatants received a fatal shot from SMITH's pistol aimed at JOHNSON. JOHNSON then shot SMITH in the head.

Thursday, 14 February 1878 Vol. XXII, No. 35

Died: At her residence in Leesburg, at 8 o'clock, on Friday evening, February 8th, 1878, Mrs. Emma HANVEY, daughter of Mr. Thomas LITTLETON, in about the 52d year of her age.

Died: In Winchester, Frederick county, on Tuesday, the 5th instant, at the residence of Mr. Charles R. HANCOCK, of typhoid fever, Lula A. SMITH, daughter of P. H. SMITH, of Loudoun county.

Died: At his residence, near Farmwell, on Friday the 25th of January, 1878, Mr. Daniel DIEDRICK, in his 87th year. He was born in Hanover, Germany, and emigrated to this country in 1837, and has been a resident of Loudoun ever since.
Died: At her home (below Aldie) on Wednesday the 9th ultimo, Mollie E. FERGUSON.
Married: In Barnesville, Montgomery county, Jan. 22d, by Rev. J. S. BIRCH, George W. DIEDRICK, of Loudoun, and Miss A. M. OFFUTT, of Montgomery county, Md.
Married: At the residence of the bride's father, Mr. Jackson MINOR, on the 31st of January, 1878, by Elder J. FURR, Mr. C. W. GRAY to Miss Mary W. MINOR, all of Loudoun.
Married: In this county, on the 6th inst., by Rev. J. F. CANNON, Mr. Joseph WYNKOOP and Miss Mary A. WORKS, both of Loudoun.
Married: At the residence of the bride's parents, in Loudoun Co., by Elder J. N. BADGER, Mr. W. W. HUMPHREY and Miss Rose B. MOORE, all of Loudoun Co.
Married: In the Presbyterian Church, Farmwell, on the 12th inst., by Rev. J. F. CANNON, assisted by Rev. L. B. TURNBULL, Mr. William E. DARNE and Miss Ellen A. BIGGS, both of Loudoun county.
We regret to learn that Mr. W. Scott DOWNEY, proprietor of the Taylortown Mills, in this county, died at his home on Monday night, from the effects of injuries inflicted on his head a few days previous, by the kick of a horse.
Feb. Ct.: N. B. PEACOCK qualified as guardian of Telulah DOWELL. Will of Delia North SAUNDERS admitted to probate. John S. MEAD qualified as Admr. of John T. RUSK dec'd. Stephen P. SHIPMAN qualified as Admr. of Etheless RUSSELL. Americus J. SOUDER qualified as Admr. of Mary A. FRASIER. Estate of Mary BEATTY committed to Sheriff. Authenticated copy of the will of Jennie C. AYRE dec'd. admitted to probate. Geo. W. DIEDRICK qualified as Admr. of Daniel DIEDRICKS dec'd.

Thursday, 21 February 1878   Vol. XXII, No. 36

Married: At "Mountain View," the residence of the bride's mother, on Wednesday, Feb. 13th, by the Rev. Chas. F. JAMES, assisted by Rev. J. B. LAKE, Octavius OSBORNE and Lizzie H. JAMES, daughter of the late Robt. JAMES, all of Loudoun.
Married: In this County, on the 19th inst., by Rev. J. F. CANNON, assisted by Rev. L. B. TURNBULL, Mr. P. L. BIGGS and Miss Sarah C. GREENLEASE, both of Loudoun.

Died: January 26th, 1878, Martha E., wife of Robt. W. ALEXANDER, in the 27th year of her age. Member of the Baptist Church at Mt. Hope.

Rev. Dabney BALL, of the M. E. Church, South, died in Baltimore last week, of heart disease. Born in Fairfax county in 1821 and was in his 57th year. During the late war he served on the staff of Gen. J. E. B. STUART with the rank of Major. He was presiding Elder of East Baltimore district at the time of his death.

Death of Mr. W. Scott DOWNEY – of Loudoun Mills, near Taylortown, met with a fearful accident on Sunday evening last. [gives details of the accident and his life]

Thursday, 28 February 1878 Vol. XXII, No. 37

Married: At "Locust Grove," near Purcellville, on Fourth day second month 20th 1878 Edward B. GREGG and Mary C. NICHOLS, both of Loudoun.

Married: In Waterford, February 26th, at the residence of Townsend ORRISON, Esq., by Rev. Henry BRANCH, Joel HAINES and Alice WRIGHT.

Died: February 15th, at his residence in Prince William Co., Rev. Dr. Thomas B. BALCH, in the 86th year of his age.

Died: At the Grove, in Loudoun County, on Tuesday, Feb. 15th, 1878, Mr. Richard WHITE, in the 78th year of his age.

Died: At his residence in Leesburg, on Wednesday of last week, Mr. James ORANGE, in the 65th year of his age.

Mr. Joseph CONRAD of Waters' Precinct, died at his residence on Friday, February 22d, 1878, in the 75th year of his age.

James C. JANNEY was the brother of the late John JANNEY, and father of our fellow townsman, Mr. C. P. JANNEY. He died at his residence in Hillsboro, after a long and painful illness, on 25th of February 1878. He was born in Alexandria in 1894, and was in the 74th year of his age. He moved, with his father, from Alexandria to Hillsboro shortly after his birth.

Holloway's Ointment.

Captain Ferdinand A. ROGERS died at his residence in this city at half past one o'clock this morning. He had only returned from a sojourn in San Antonio, Texas a few days. At the time of his death was sheriff of Cooper county. He was born in Belmont county, Ohio, in August 1833, but his parents removed in 1845 to Fauquier county, Va, where he resided till 1857, when he came to this county, and was in his forty fifth year when he died. In 1869 he married Miss Sallie LIONBERGER a daughter of the late Isaac LIONBERGER. His widow and three little girls survive him. *Booneville (Mo.) Advertiser.*

Thursday, 7 March 1878   Vol. XXII, No. 38

Married: On the 26th of February, 1878, near Lovettsville, by the Rev. H. St. J. RINKER, Mr. Robert B. CARTER to Miss Ann W. GREEN, all of Loudoun.

Married: March 5th, 1878, at the Parsonage, Hamilton, by Rev. L. H. CRENSHAW, Mr. P. Henry WYNKOOP and Miss Harriet A. HAISLOP, both of Loudoun Co.

Married: In Washington, Feb. 22d, in the Metropolitan M. E. Church, by the Rev. J. P. NEWMAN, Mr. Edward L. WREN, of Fairfax Co., to Miss Mary D. HOLLAND, of Leesburg.

Married: In this county, on the 5th inst., by Rev. J. F. CANNON, John W. McCLEAREN and Miss Caroline McKINNEY, both of Loudoun.

Died: In Brooklyn, at the residence of William COLES, Esq., on Thursday the 21st of February, Mrs. Mary E. EDWARDS.

Dr. J. D. HARMAN, for several years a prominent physician of this county, died at his residence in Hamilton on Friday morning last of consumption. His wife and four children, in a comparatively brief space of time preceded him to the grave. On Sunday his remains were brought to this town and interred in Union Cemetery, attended by his brethren of Hamilton Lodge, A. F. & A. Masons.

Death of Mrs. Mary L. EDWARDS – died in Brooklyn, New York, on the 21st of February at an advanced age.

Thursday, 14 March 1878   Vol. XXII, No. 39

Married: On February 27th, 1878, at the M. P. Parsonage, in Frederick city, by the Rev. J. Earle MALOY, James F. HESS to Miss Mattie D. GAVER, both of Loudoun County.

Died: January 24th, 1878, Francis CORNELL, youngest daughter of Thompson CORNELL, of Fairfax (formerly of Loudoun) in her 32nd year. Leaves an aged father and sisters and brothers.

Aylett NICOL, county Judge of Prince William county, died at Brentsville on Sunday.

Dr. Cornelius BOYLE died at his residence in Washington Monday last.

March Ct.: Will of Jno. D. HARMON admitted to probate. Will of Barbara STREAM admitted to probate. Estate of Thos. H. LYNN committed to Sheriff. Laura J. DOWNEY qualified as Admx of W. Scott DOWNEY. Daniel CARNES qualified as Admx [Admr.?] of John BRISLIN. Jas. E. CARUTHERS qualified as Admr. of Richard WHITE. John E. FRANCIS qualified as Admr. of Thos. HOGE. Wm. B. NOLAND appointed Guardian of Claud NOLAND.

Thursday, 21 March 1878   Vol. XXII, No. 40

Died: At the residence of her father, Wm. H. RUSSELL, near Waterford, on Thursday last, in her 23d year, Miss Kate RUSSELL, after painful illness of nervous irritation of the brain.

Died: At Revenswood, March 13th, of pneumonia, after a short but painful illness, Charles H. NICHOLS, aged 34y 4m 8d.

Died: At the residence of his father, in Waterford, Feb. 28th 1878, C. Willie HOUGH, son of Samuel and Mary HOUGH, aged 19y 4m.

Died: In New Orleans, March 11, 1878, John Sneden QUINBY, son of Dr. George A. and Mary G. QUINBY, aged 7 years. Interment in Greenwood Cemetery, New York. Dr. QUINBY and his family left their home in Loudoun about the first of January to spend the Winter in the South.

Died: At her home, near Lincoln, on March 5th, 1878, Lydia Alice CRAVEN, in the 59th year of her age.

Married: At the Lutheran Parsonage, Lovettsville, by Rev. P. H. MILLER, Mr. Aaron SWANK and Miss Mary E. SMITH, all of Loudoun.

Married: In Washington, on the 14th of March, 1878, by Rev. W. P. HARRISON, D.D., pastor of Mt. Vernon Place M. E. Church South, Chaplain House of Representatives, Mr. Oscar J. ORRISON, of Loudoun county, to Miss Rebecca SEBASTIAN, of that city.

At the residence of the bride's brother, near Hamilton, on Monday the 14th inst., by the Rev. Alfred ROGERS, Mr. J. W. DEAR, of New Red Cloud Agency, formerly of Loudoun, to Miss Mary A. ROGERS, daughter of the late Samuel ROGERS, of Loudoun.

Thursday, 28 March 1878   Vol. XXII, No. 41

Married: On the 5th instant, at St. Mark's P. E. Church, in Petersville, by Rev. W. L. BRADDOCK, assisted by Rev. Dr. Joseph TRAPNELL, James H. W. BLAKE to Miss Mollie, dau. of the late James GIDDINGS, of Middletown Valley, Md.

Married: In Hamilton, March 21st, 1878, by Rev. L. H. CRENSHAW, Mr. Joseph H. LOWE and Miss Virginia SILCOTT, dau. of Washington SILCOTT, Esq., all of Loudoun.

Died: In this town, at 3 o'clock on Tuesday afternoon, March 26th, 1878, in the 71st year of her age. Several months ago, Mr. SAUNDERS was stricken with paralysis and is to day an almost helpless invalid. They had been married more than half a century. The funeral will take place from her late residence at 10 o'clock Thursday morning.

Died: at the residence of her father, Mr. Wm. H. RUSSELL, near Waterford, on Wednesday March 13th, 1878, Miss Kate RUSSELL, aged 23y 5m 12d.

Died: Near Hillsborough, March 19th, 1878, Sarah, second daughter of Geo. A. RECTOR, Esq.

Oscar WILEY, a son of Mr. J. H. WILEY, of Hamilton, ages about eight years, died on Wednesday morning last, of consumption.

At a regular meeting of Martha Washington Lodge, I. O. G. T., Aldie, held March 23, 1878, a committee was appointed to draft resolutions of respect on the death of Sister Margaret GANT, a member of Martha Washington Lodge, who departed this life on the 20th of March, 1878.

Thursday, 4 April 1878   Vol. XXII, No. 42

Married: March 20th 1878, by Rev. John WOOLF, at his residence, Mr. Clinton TINSMAN to Miss Virginia HAWS, all of Loudoun.

Died: In Union, Mr. Samuel TORREYSON, in his 76th year. He was a great sufferer from the effects of paralysis, until the evening of the 22d of March, when he fell asleep in Jesus, having been a member of the M. E. Church for more than 45 years.

Died: March 30th 1878, near Leesburg, Mrs. Ann M., wife of H. M. HARDY, aged 64y 7m 15d. She was a great sufferer for 15 years. Poem by her children.

Thursday, 11 April 1878   Vol. XXII, No. 43

Married: On the 28th instant, at the Reformed Church, Lovettsville, by the Rev. H. St. J. RINKER, Mr. Chas. M. HAMMOND to Miss Kate W. WENNER, all of Loudoun.

Married: On the 27th of March, 1878, by Rev. Mr. BOYLE, of the M. E. Church, South, Mr. Chas. MANKIN to Miss Sadie E. BROWN, both of Alexandria, Va.

Died: At the residence of her husband, in Shelby county, Illinois, on Monday, the 1st of April, 1878, after a short illness, Mrs. Mary Catherine, wife of J. Wade BARRETT, formerly of this county, in the 43d year of her age.

Died: Near Middleburg, April 7, 1878, Alice, daughter of Thompson and Mary ASHLY, in the 22d year of her age.

April Ct.: Will of Lydia A. CRAVEN dec'd. admitted to probate. T. S. TITUS qualified as Admr. of Susan O. TITUS. Rodney C. HOUGH guardian of Charles R. VIRTS &c gave new bond.

Thursday, 18 April 1878   Vol. XXII, No. 44

Died: April 7th 1878, at his residence in Clarke Co., after a brief illness, John G. MORRIS, in his 63d year. A native of this county.

Died: In Alexandria, on Friday night, May 12th, Mrs. M. W. ATHEY, the venerable mother of Mr. W. W. ATHEY, of this town.

Died: In this town, at 3 o'clock on Sunday morning, April 14th 1878, Wilson Shepherd, the second son of L. W. S. and Lou HOUGH, aged 3y 6m 7d.

The recent death of Mr. Powell HARRISON calls to mind that fact that he is the twelfth member of that connexion who has died in Loudoun since the close of the war, thirteen years ago. During that time six member of his own immediate family, the father, three sons and two daughters, have heard the dread summons.

Three weeks ago yesterday, Mr. Joseph HAMMERLY bid adieu to his family and friends in Jackson, and started on a health seeking pilgrimage to Hot Springs, Ark. At a late hour on Wednesday evening, Dr. J. W. COLLINS dispatched to Mr. Henry HAMMERLY in Jackson that his father was dangerously sick at Little Rock. He was delayed in Memphis and while delayed he received a dispatch that his father was dead. *Jackson (Tenn.) Whig and Tribune.* [Native of Loudoun county, and a brother of Mr. John HAMMERLY, of this town. He was in about the 62d year of his age.]

Thursday, 25 April 1878   Vol. XXII, No. 45

Married: In the Presbyterian Church, Leesburg, on Wednesday morning, April 24th 1878, by Rev. J. F. CANNON, Mr. Nicholas D. OFFUTT, of Montgomery county, Md, and Miss Nettie G. EDWARDS, of Leesburg.

Married: On April 7th, 1878, by Rev. J. O. FIRERMAN, W. W. PEPPER and Miss Susan E. ROSS, eldest daughter of J. R. ROSS, formerly of Virginia.

Married: At the residence of the bride's father, April 18th, 1878, by Rev. L. H. CRENSHAW, Mr. R. French SIMPSON to Miss Mattie E. PALMER, daughter of D. T. PALMER, Esq., all of Loudoun.

Died: April 17th, 1878, at her residence at Union, Mrs. Charles MONROE. Member of the M. E. Church, South. She was united in marriage to Bro. Charles MONROE last November.

In Memoriam: The CLIPPER of the 12th inst., contained a brief notice of the death of Mrs. Cecelia McPHERSON, which occurred in Ralls county on the 11th. The deceased was 84y 6m old. Born in Loudoun county, August 3d, 1793, the oldest of a family of seven children of Wm. NEWLON and her childhood was spent in the wilderness of the western portion of that state. In 1808 she returned to the place of her birth and was married there April 1, 1810, to Stephen McPHERSON, whose faithful consort she was until his death in 1847, and who also was a native of Loudon county, Va. In 1835 she with her husband and children came to Missouri, landing at Hannibal, and shortly afterwards settled on the farm where she died, after a continued residence of 42 years. Mother of eleven children, eight of whom arrived at the age of maturity and became heads of families. She lived to see her descendants of the fourth generation, more than 80 of whom are still living and the dead her direct descendants number more than 125.

During the severe freshet in November last, it will be remembered that in attempting to rescue the family of Mr. HOWSER, living on Mason's Island, in the Potomac river, Mr. H's two children, his wife's sister, Miss Alice MILBURN, and two colored men who undertook their rescue were drowned. On Saturday morning last, as some colored men were at work on the Maryland side of the river opposite AULT's, some 3-4 miles from where the victims went down, and not more than 100 yards from where one of the children was found last fall, they discovered the remains of a human body. Papers in the pocket of the dress identified the remains as Miss MILBURN. They brought it to her father's home in Leesburg, from whence they were interred in Union Cemetery Sunday afternoon.

Thursday, 2 May 1878   Vol. XXII, No. 46

Married: On the 16th inst., by Elder Benjamin BRIDGES, Mr. Wm. A. OFFUTT, of Georgetown, DC, to Miss Mary, youngest daughter of Alfred LEIGH, Esq., of Fairfax Co.

Married: On the 23d ult, at the residence of the bride's father, Dr. F. LAMBERT, Gum Spring, by Rev. B. BUTLER, D.D., of M. P. church, Miss Florence F. LAMBERT to Mr. John M. RATRIE.

Circuit Ct.: Will of the late Powell HAR[R]ISON proved by B. P. NOLAND and A. J. BRADFIELD and ordered to be recorded, and certificate granted Janet Knox HARRISON the Executrix named.

Trial of Joseph B. MANN for the killing of John BRISLAIN – found guilty and sentenced to 18 years in penitentiary.

Thursday, 9 May 1878   Vol. XXII, No. 47

Died: In Waterford, May 2d, 1878, Lewis SHUEY, in his 78th year.

Thursday, 16 May 1878   Vol. XXII, No. 48

Married: At the residence of the bride's father, in Hamilton, on Thursday the 9th instant, by the Rev. L. H. CRENSHAW, Mr. Geo. H. NIXON, of Leesburg, to Miss Hattie MILBURN, daughter of Jefferson MILBURN, Esq.

Married: On the evening of May 8th, 1878, in the M. E. Church by Rev. M. V. B. EVANS, Mr. Edward LAMBERT and Miss Lucy DRUSE, all of Belpre, Ohio.

Married; At the parsonage of the M. E. Church, April 28th, by Rev. Wm. H. FORSYTH, Frederick SHELHORN, of Loudoun county, to Miss Eliza DIMER, of Germany.

Died: In Waterford, April 20th, 1878, Catherine A., wife of John E. STEWARD, in the 43d year of her age.

Died: Suddenly about 10½ o'clock, Thursday night, May 9th, 1878, at "Ivon," the residence of Capt. A. M. CHICHESTER, near Leesburg, Miss Lucy E. GRAY, daughter of the late Dr. Joseph GRAY, of this county, in the 43d year of her age.

Mr. John SMALE, of this town died on Friday afternoon after an illness of less than one week, in his 68th year. Leaves a wife and two young children. His funeral took place on Sunday afternoon, Rev. Messrs. FORSYTH and KENNEDY officiating. His remains were followed to the grave by members of the Loudoun Lodge, I.O.O.F. of which he was a member.

Thursday, 23 May 1878   Vol. XXII, No. 49

Married: On Tuesday evening, May 14th, in St. Stephen's Church, Culpeper, Va, by Rev. Dr. Chas. MINNIGERODE, of St. Paul's Church, Richmond, Va, assisted by Rt. Rev. George W. PETERKIN, D.D., Bishop elect of West Virginia, Rev. James G. MINNIGERODE, Rector of Calvary Church, Louisville, Ky, to Annie, daughter of George G. THOMPSON, of Culpeper.

Died: Near Gumspring, Loudoun County, May 10th, 1878, Mrs. Maria ORRISON, in the 36th year of her age.

Died: May 4th, 1878, at the residence of her son, Mr. James E. KIDWELL, near Red Hill school house, Mrs. Fannie E. KIDWELL, in the 76th year of her age.

Died: At the residence of his son, near Gumspring, in this county, on the evening of the 19th inst., Major Francis E. SHREVE, in his 65th year of age. He was a member of the M. E. Church.

On the 27th of April, while John S. UMBAUGH, 16 years of age, son of George and Catherine UMBAUGH, of this county, was fishing in Catoctin Creek, near Point of Rocks ferry, his foot slipped and he fell into the creek and was drowned before assistance could reach him, although his father and three brothers were within 30 yards of him when he fell.

Thursday, 30 May 1878   Vol. XXII, No. 50

Married: In St. James' church, Leesburg, on Wednesday evening, May 22d, 1878, by the Rev. R. T. DAVIS, D.D., William Gray BEVERLEY to Annie Lee, daughter of the late Robert HENDERSON, all of Loudoun.

Married: At the residence of the bride's father, May 22d, 1878, by the Rev. L. H. CRENSHAW, Mr. John T. CUMMINS and Mrs. L. Janie McFARLAND, daughter of Wm. EVERHART, Esq., all of Loudoun county.

Died: At her residence in Hamilton, at 1 o'clock Thursday night, May 23d, 1878, Mrs. Catharine HAINES, wife of Manly HAINES, in her 54th year. Mrs. HAINES had for years been in ill health, and about ten days since was attacked with pneumonia which caused her death.

Death of Beverley HUTCHISON, Esq. occurred at his home near Aldie, in this county, on Sunday afternoon. He was for many years a Justice of the Peace.

Thursday, 6 June 1878   Vol. XXII, No. 51

Died: In Middleburg on the evening of the 29th, Nannie Rogers FRED, only daughter of Frank L. FRED, in her 13th year.

Died: At the residence of her husband, near Leesburg, on the 24th of May 1878, Mrs. Ann Eliza WILLIAMS, wife of John H. WILLIAMS, in the 42d year of her age.

Thursday, 13 June 1878   Vol. XXII, No. 52

Married: Near Waterford on the 6th inst., by Rev. W. H. FORSYTH, Mr. Mahlon H. MYERS to Miss Mary J. COATES, all of Loudoun county.

Married: On Thursday evening, the 6th instant, at the house of the bride's parents, near New Hope, by Rev. Andrew ROBEY, A. T. FISHER to Miss Nannie Lee PIERCE, youngest daughter of Rev. A. E. PIERCE, all of Augusta County, Va.

Died: At Herndon, June 4th, Mrs. Maria Emma COCKRELL, in the 61st year of her age.

Died: At her residence near Snickersville, May 28, 1878, Mrs. Delilah, wife of Washington BEAVERS. Born in this county March 2, 1812, and continued to reside here until her death. Immediate cause was paralysis, the first attack of which occurred just two years and a half before her death. Member of the M. E. Church, South, on Loudoun Circuit.

Death of John S. EDWARDS – the eldest son of the late Gen. Samuel M. EDWARDS, died at the residence of Mr. John W. WOOD, in this town, on Thursday last, in the 67th year of his age. Born in Leesburg, where he passed the early years of his life. For a number of years he spent his time in various sections of the country. On Friday evening his remains were interred in Union Cemetery.

June Ct.: Jas. W. FOSTER qualified as Guardian of Minnie Bell YAKEY. John GRAY qualified as Admr. of Lucy E. GRAY.

Barckley LLOYD qualified as Guardian of Rebecca L. WALKER.

She didn't long survive him – Mrs. Minerva SHREVE, widow of the late Francis E. SHREVE, died on Tuesday last, in about the 62d year of her age. Mr. S. died just three weeks ago.

Thursday, 20 June 1878   Vol. XXIII, No. 1

Died: On the second of the present month, near Morrisonville, Mrs. Susannah CRIM, in the 89th year of her age.

Died: At the residence of her husband, in Warrenton, on the 3d instant, after a short illness, Mrs. Emma POWERS, wife of Samuel POWERS, and daughter of the late James SPINKS, of Alexandria, aged 38 years.

Died: At the residence of her son, in Loudoun county, June 14th 1878, Mrs. Elenor Louis STEVENS, relict of the late Amos FOUCHE, in the 70th year of her age.

Died: At his father's home, near Round Hill, on Monday, June 17th, 1878, Montgomery, only child of E. C. and Maria W. BENEDICT, aged 14 months.

Thursday, 27 June 1878   Vol. XXIII, No. 2

Died: At "Fruitland," near Leesburg, the residence of her husband, on Tuesday afternoon, June 25, 1878, Mrs. Sarah E. EDWARDS, wife of Mr. Thos. W. EDWARDS and daughter of the late Mason CHICHESTER, of this county, in her 59th year. For several months, she had been in declining health. [on next page] The funeral will take place from St. James' Episcopal Church, this (Thursday) morning, at 11 o'clock.

Mr. Thos. Martin WREN, for many years a Commission of the Revenue in this County, before the war, died at his home near Gumspring, on Monday last, in the 75th year of his age.

Thursday, 4 July 1878   Vol. XXIII, No. 3

Married: On the 25th of June, by the Rev. Wm. H. FORSYTH, Mr. Wm. L. BEEVERS to Miss Utoca CLARKSTON, all of Loudoun county.

Mr. Henry MILHOLLEN, a citizen of Loudoun, died at his home in Philomont, on Saturday, the 15th of June.

Thursday, 11 July 1878   Vol. XXIII, No. 4

Married: On Wednesday, June 24, 1878, at the chapel on Seminary Hill, by the Rev. George W. DAME, assisted by the Rev. W. W. WALKER, the Rev. Nelson P. DAME, of Blacksburg, Va. to Mary N. WALKER, daughter of the Rev. C. WALKER, D.D., of the Theological Seminary of Va.

Married: In Leesburg on 2nd inst., by Rev. J. F. CANNON assisted by Rev. L. B. TURNBULL, Mr. L. L. LEFEVRE and Miss Mary E. McPHERSON.

Married: On May 16th, at Bunker Hill, W. Va., in the M. E. Church, by Rev. George FIELDMIRE, Charles F. M. WOODARD to Miss Jennie E. ROBEY, fourth daughter of Cobert ROBEY, Esq., of West Virginia.

Died: On the 17th of June, 1878, in Harrisburg, Pa., Mrs. Mary M. CROUSE, aged 71y 24d. Born and raised in Leesburg, where she married and shortly after which she moved to Pennsylvania with her husband.

July Ct.: Wills of Beverley HUTCHISON dec'd., Susan CRIM dec'd. and Henry MILHOLLEN dec'd. admitted to probate. Estates of Peter STEPTOE, Thos. PARKER, Geo. W. HOUGH and John CRIDLER committed to Sheriff. Mary E. MINOR qualified as Admr. of B. S. MINOR. Winifred JAMES executed new bond as Exor. of Robt. JAMES dec'd. Rev. Geo. W. CRIST licensed to celebrate rite of matrimony.

Thursday, 18 July 1878   Vol. XXIII, No. 5

Died: On Friday, June 28th, 1878, at 9:15 p.m., in Washington city, Mrs. Annie HAVENNER, consort of John F. HAVENNER, aged 50y 20d.

Died: On June 29th, 1878, at her father's residence, Laura, daughter of Andrew J. and Jane BEACH, in the 16th year of her age.

Died: Near Unison, on the 18th of June, 1878, Michael Henry Plaster, infant son of William M. and Susan V. MONROE, aged 7m 9d.

Died: (*From the Henderson Texas Beacon of July 11th*) Mrs. Ann E. FRANCIS, the wife of Edward FRANCIS, died on Thursday night July the 4th. Born in Virginia in 1806, her maiden name was HAMILTON. Married Mr. FRANCIS on November 27th, 1828, and if she had lived until the 27th of next November they would have celebrated their golden wedding. [Mrs. FRANCIS was a younger sister of Mrs. Jane D. WILDMAN, of this town.]

Married: On the 11th inst., by Rev. J. E. EVANS, near Snickersville, Robert C. CARLISLE to Miss Elizabeth E. O'BANNON, all of Loudoun county.

Married: On Thursday, June 26th, Dr. Robert HENDERSON, of Leesburg, Va, to Minnie, daughter of John H. KINCADE, of Fort Wayne, Indiana.

Thursday, 25 July 1878   Vol. XXIII, No. 6

[no marriages or deaths]

Thursday, 1 August 1878   Vol. XXIII, No. 7

Married: On the 24th instant, at the Parsonage of the M. E. Church, by the Rev. Wm. H. FORSYTH, Mr. Jas. T. TRENARY, to Miss Annie C. JACKSON, all of Loudoun.

Married: At Norwood, Nelson county, Va, on Tuesday the 16th instant, by Rev. Edmund WITHERS, A. MOORE Jr., of Clarke county, Va, and Miss Annie B. CABELL, eldest daughter of Wm. D. CABELL, Esq.

Died: In Leesburg on Tuesday morning, July 30th, 1878, Mary, infant daughter of R. S. and Mary BURKE, aged 5m 12d.

Died: On the 22d inst., at the residence of the Misses DONOHOE, G. Washington ROSZEL, in the 77th year of his age.

Died: In Philomont, July 20th, Lelah Jane, infant daughter of Henry W. and the late Mary Fannie SAFFEL, aged 9m 2d.

Died: Near Silcott's Springs, on Sunday, 21st of July, Rodney, infant son of A. T. and Clementina HESSER, aged about 6 months.

Alfred PAINE, colored, convicted a short time ago of attempting to burn the jail of this county, and sentenced to one year in the penitentiary, left for his new quarters on Monday in charge of Deputy Sheriff, R. B. POULTON.

Thursday, 8 August 1878   Vol. XXIII, No. 8

Married: July 24th, 1878, at Clarksburg, West Va., by Rev. E. J. WILLIS, R. B. McCORMICK, of Loudoun Co., to Miss H. R. McVeigh, daughter of Thomas ROGERS dec'd.

Married: At the residence of the bride's parents, near Gum Spring, July 30, 1878, by the Rev. B. A. SHREVE, Mr. John H. CORNELL and Miss Laura C. GARRETT, all of Loudoun.

Married: At Mr. H. WILBURN's at 7½ o'clock, p.m., on Tuesday, July 23d, 1878, by Rev. St Geo. T. ABRAHAMS, Mr. Charles SING, son of Hong Wah SING, Esq., South Canton, China, to Miss Ida V. WILBURN, of Fauquier County.

Died: At Bloomfield, August 3d, Willie Strother, infant son of Wm. A. and Laura P. BRAWNER.

Died: On Friday morning the 26th inst., at the residence of his uncle, Logan OSBURN, at Kabletown, Jefferson county, W Va., Logan Osburn SMITH, Esq. of St. Mary's county, Maryland, aged 40 years. Mr. SMITH came on a visit to his relatives of Jefferson county, Dr. Abner and Logan OSBURN, about two weeks since in hope of improving his health. He leaves a wife and 4 children. His remains were sent on Friday evening last accompanied by Logan OSBURN Jr.

Wm. LIGHTFOOT, a driver in the employ of the Great Falls ice company, was almost instantly killed on Friday night last by being thrown from the rear of his wagon, the wheels passing over and dislocating his neck. He leaves a large family. Mr. LIGHTFOOT was a native of this county and son of Mr. John LIGHTFOOT, of Aldie. On Monday his remains reached Leesburg, under an escort of the Knights of Pythias, of which he was a member, and carried at once to Aldie for interment.

Thursday, 15 August 1878   Vol. XXIII, No. 9

Married: In the M. E. Church, Waterford, on the 10th inst. by Rev. J. F. CANNON, Mr. Chas. A. MICHENER, of Ohio, and Miss Anna E. DUTTON, of Waterford.

Died: On Thursday, Aug. 8th 1878, at her grandfather's, Mary, youngest child of W. N. and Ella WISE, aged 4m 5d.

August Ct.: W. Henry TAYLOR qualified as Admr. of Lydia B. TAYLOR dec'd. Albert J. BEST qualified as Admr. of Amanda M. BEST dec'd. W. W. PRESGRAVES qualified as Admr. of Thomas KEENE dec'd. Jas. A. DOWNING qualified as Admr. of Loura HARMON dec'd. Estate of Francis E. SHREVE dec'd. committed to Sheriff. Receipts of commissioners to assign dower to Ruth Ann HUNTER widow of M. L. HUNTER dec'd. confirmed. N. B. PEACOCK's powers as committee of Rachel BEAMER revoked. Thos. S. AVARD licensed to celebrate rites of matrimony.

Death of Mrs. Ann E. FRANCIS – wife of Edward FRANCIS, and for many years residence of Brandon, died at Henderson, Texas, on the 4th instant, aged 72 years. We knew Mrs. FRANCIS intimately from 1852 to the time she left here for Texas, some ten years ago. She was a member of the Baptist Church. *Brandon (Miss.) Republican.*

Thursday, 22 August 1878   Vol. XXIII, No. 10

Married: At the residence of the bride's father, by the Rev. Wm. DOBBINS, Beverly D. HUTCHISON, formerly of Loudoun county, to Miss Sadie J. SAWYER, both of Addison, Webster county, West Virginia.

Died: In Loudoun Valley, on Sunday evening, July 28th, Mrs. Sophie E. DEMORY, relict of the late Mahlon DEMORY, aged 70y, 2m 23d, was buried Tuesday morning at the Ebenezer Church. The deceased had been a consistent member of the M. E. Church for many years.

Died: August 1st, 1878, near Woodgrove, Mr. James M. HOWELL, aged 65y 6m 23d. He had been afflicted with disease of the kidneys for a number of years.

Thursday, 29 August 1878   Vol. XXIII, No. 11

Married: Near Guilford, Aug. 22d, 1878, by B. A. SHREVE, Samuel E. JENKINS, and Annie E. JENKINS, all of Loudoun.

Thursday, 5 September 1878   Vol. XXIII, No. 12
Died: On Saturday, August 24th 1878, at the residence of his daughter near North Fork, after a painful and lingering illness, departed this life, Mr. Benjamin SAUNDERS, aged 77y 2d.

Mr. John B. WEBSTER, died of paralysis in Alexandria, Va, on Monday. He was in his 82d years, and was the uncle of Mrs. SURRATT, who was executed with the Lincoln conspirators.

Thursday, 12 September 1878   Vol. XXIII, No. 13
Died: Of Yellow Fever, at Memphis, Tenn., William Temple POWELL, fourth son of the late Dr. William L. POWELL, of Alexandria, Va, in the 47th year of his age.

Death in Memphis, Tenn, a day or two ago, of Mr. Wm. T. POWELL, a native of this county, and brother of Capt. E. B. POWELL, of Leesburg. At the time the fever broke out Mr. P. was editor of a Catholic Magazine in the city of Memphis. Mr. POWELL was unmarried and in the 47th year of his age.

County Ct.: Wills of Benjamin SAUNDERS and Sophia E. DEMORY admitted to probate. Administration granted on the estates of Mahlon DEMORY dec'd., Sarah SYPHERD and Chas. A. JOHNSTON. Jas. M. HOGE qualified as Guardian of Malinda E. and Mary E. WARNER. Andrew TILLMAN, col'd, licensed to celebrate rites of matrimony.

Thursday, 19 September 1878   Vol. XXIII, No. 14
Married: On the 7th inst., at the parsonage of the M. E. Church, in Leesburg, by the Rev. Wm. H. FORSYTH, Mr. Jas. T. HORSMON, of Fairfax county, to Miss Lavinia DAWSON, of Loudoun county.

Married: At the residence of the bride's father, R. T. BARBER, Esq., on Monday, the 2d of September, 1878, by the Rev. Dr. BUNTING, Mr. J. T. WAMPLER, of Front Royal, Va, to Miss Carrie M. BARBER, of White Hall, St. Mary's county, Md.

Married: In Charlestown, W. Va. on Wednesday, Sept. 4th, 1878, by Rev. Wm. H. MEADE, Mr. T. M. CALDWELL, of Knoxville, Tenn, and Miss Jennie K. KEARSLEY, daughter of Maj. G. W. T. KEARSLEY.

Died: At Leesburg, on Friday morning, 13th of September, Preston ORR, infant son of John M. and Orra V. ORR.

Thursday, 26 September 1878   Vol. XXIII, No. 15
Married: On Tuesday, September 17, 1878, at Christ Church, Millwood, Clarke Co., Va, by the Rev. Wm. LEE, assisted by

the Rev. Jos. R. JONES, the Rev. Jas. R. WINCHESTER to
Eliza A., daughter of Col. R. H. LEE.

Married: At the Parsonage, Hamilton, Va, September 18th, 1878, by Rev. L. H. CRENSHAW, Mr. Geo. W. CURL to Miss Ginnie C. BALLENGER, both of Loudoun county.

Married: On the 27th ulto., at the residence of the bride's father, by Rev. H. BRANCH, Rebecca E., daughter of Mr. Samuel CROCKETT, to Geo. W. HOLMES.

Married: On the 19th inst., at the Parsonage of the M. E. Church, in Leesburg, by the Rev. Wm. H. FORSYTH, Mr. Jno. Oscar HANVY to Miss Mattie E. RINKER, both of Loudoun county.

Married: On the 11th inst., at North Fork Church, Loudoun county, by Rev. Dr. HAYNES, Mr. Edgar D. JONES, of Missouri, and Miss Eliza E. JONES, of Loudoun.

Died: Harry, son of Joseph and Mary VIRTS, Monday, August 26th, aged 8 years.

Thursday, 3 October 1878   Vol. XXIII, No. 16

Death of Dr. D. Preston PAYNE – this young gentleman came to his death by the careless handling of a pistol in his possession last Tuesday, near Delaplane Station. In leaning over to rein his horse the hammer struck the pommel, and the ball went crashing through the brain.

Married: At "Rose Valley," the residence of the bride's father, on Tuesday, September 24th, by Rev. J. S. HANCKEL, Walter D. DABNEY and Mary B., daughter of Arch. N. DOUGLAS, all of Albemarle.

Married: In Leesburg, October 1st, by Rev. J. F. CANNON, Mr. James L. GARDNER and Miss Martha A. LYONS, both of Loudoun county.

Died: At Middleburg, Sept. 11, 1878, at 5 o'clock a. m., Henry Van Dyke, third son of Helen Jane and the Rev. Arthur S. JOHNS, aged 4m 18d.

Mr. Enos B. CORDELL, a native of Leesburg, died in St. Louis on the 17th of September, at the age of 71 years.

Thursday, 10 October 1878   Vol. XXIII, No. 17

Died: In this town, on Friday, Sept. 27th, 1878, Mrs. Margaret WIGGINGTON, in the 91st year of her age.

Mr. J. F. MILBURN, of this town, died suddenly, on Wednesday morning, of heart disease. He was in about his 50th year.

Thursday, 17 October 1878   Vol. XXIII, No. 18

Married: In the Lutheran Church, Lovettsville, October 9th, by Rev. Theodore REED, Rev. Curtis GRUBB to Annetta F. SCHOOLEY, both of Loudoun county.

Married: Rev. Mr. GRUBB and Miss SCHOOLEY, of Waterford, were married today, and passed through here on their way to missionary work in Africa.

Married: At Christ church, Alexandria, on October 3d, by Rev. Mr. SUTER, John Lloyd STEARNS, to Ella, daughter of Cuthbert POWELL.

Died: At Middleburg, Sept. 14, 1878, at five o'clock a.m., Henry Van Dyke, third son of Helen Lane and the Rev. Arthur S. JOHNS, aged 4m 18d.

Died: On the 17th of August, Susan E. KEARNES, in the 30th year of her age.

County Ct: Administrations were granted on the estates of H. M. JONES, Wm. WIRTZ and John R. BRADFORD dec'd. John F. MILBOURN's will admitted to probate.

Thursday, 24 October 1878   Vol. XXIII, No. 19

Married: At "Cedar Grove," the residence of Dr. R. H. STUART, in King George Co., on 22d Oct. by the Rev. Melville BOYD, of Brooklyn, N.Y., Rev. Theodore REED, of Loudoun Co, to Kate R., second daughter of the late Dr. R. Stuart LOMAX, of King George county, Va.

Married: In this town, on the evening of 22d, at the residence of the bride's mother, by Rev. J. F. CANNON, Mr. John MORIARTY and Miss Sarah J. THOMPSON.

Married: Oct. 16th by Rev. W. H. WILSON, at the residence of the bride's mother, near Hillsborough, Samuel J. COE, of Ill., to Miss Mary M. GRUBB, daughter of late Wm. GRUBB, of Loudoun county.

Married: On the 17th instant, at the parsonage of the M. E. Church in Leesburg by the Rev. W. H. FORSYTH, Thomas L. M. STEPHENS to Miss Carrie MYERS, both of Loudoun county.

Married: On Wednesday the 2d of October, at the residence of the bride, by Elder Benjamin BRIDGES, Mr. Alpheus P. HUMMER to Mrs. M. B. THOMPSON, all of Loudoun.

Died: On the morning of the 10th instant, Marietta SIMPSON, wife of R. H. SIMPSON, and daughter of J. STEINER. She died at her residence in Alexandria.

Died: Very suddenly, near Morrisonville, in this county, on the morning of the 14th instant, Mrs. Mary Jane WENNER, the beloved wife of John WENNER, aged 51y 7d.

It is due to the memory of Henson SPENCE, who died in this town on the 4th inst., that those of his birth place should know of his deceased, in this his home since 1847. Born in Leesburg, 25 Dec. 1811 and with his twin brother, Vincent (now a reputable citizen of this place) learned his trade with James GARRISON. Funeral ceremony by Rev. F. A. BROWN, under supervision of

Order of I. O. O. F. He leaves a wife, three sons and five daughters. [McConnelsville, O., Oct. 14th, 1878]

Mrs. Virginia VANDEVANTER, wife of Mr. Chas. O. VANDEVANTER, of this county, died in Baltimore City, on Sunday last. Mrs. V. Had gone to Baltimore for the purpose of undergoing a delicate and painful surgical operation, which was performed on Thursday. But the shock to her system was more than she could endure and she died as stated on Sunday night. Her remains were brought to Leesburg on Tuesday. The funeral services were conducted in the Presbyterian church, by Revs. Messrs. CANNON, BRANCH and KENNEDY. She leaves an infant five months old.

Thursday, 31 October 1878   Vol. XXIII, No. 20

Married: At the Parsonage, Hamilton, October 24th, 1878, by Rev. L.. H. CRENSHAW, Mr. Benj. F. CUMMINS to Miss Lydia ALLDER, daughter of Jas. ALLDER, Esq., all of Loudoun co.

Married: On Wednesday, October 23, 1878, at Mount Vernon Place M. E. Church, Baltimore, Md., by the Rev. J. O. PECK, D.D., William MATTHEW, of Hillsborough, to Ella CALDWELL, of Baltimore, daughter of the late S. B. T. CALDWELL, of Loudoun.

Married: On Tuesday morning the 15th instant, in the Presbyterian Church at Collierstown, Rockbridge county, Mr. Salmon M. WITHERS, of Washington county, and Miss Lillias P. SMITH, eldest daughter of Rev. H. R. SMITH, the officiating minister.

Married: On Wednesday, the 23d inst., at the residence of the bride's father, by the Rev. W. H. WILSON, Mr. Luther L. COPELAND to Miss Mary E., daughter of Fenton and Sarah A. HAMPTON, all of Loudoun.

Married: On the 17th inst., at Lovettsville, by Rev. P. H. MILLER, Mr. Wm. S. GEORGE and Miss Florence M. COOPER, of Loudoun county.

Mrs. Sallie BURKE, wife of Mr. Wm. BURKE, of Washington city, and daughter of the late Wm. D. DRISH, of Leesburg, died at her home in Washington, on Monday afternoon.

Thursday, 7 November 1878   Vol. XXIII, No. 21

Married: At the Parsonage of the M. E. Church, South, in this place, on July 23d, 1878, by Rev. H. H. KENNEDY, Mr. Buchanan GRIMES to Miss Josephine TYLER, both of Loudoun county.

Mrs. Mary E. PEYTON, wife of Col. Henry E. PEYTON, and daughter of the late Noble S. BRADEN, of this county, died at the residence of her husband, near Waterford, on Thursday.

Thursday, 14 November 1878   Vol. XXIII, No. 22

Died: At Lovettsville, on the 23d ult., after a short illness, Mrs. Mary Catherine WILLIAMS, in the 52d year of her age.

Died: At Lovettsville, on the 31st ult., and very suddenly, Mrs. Catherine GRUBB, in the 62d year of her age.

Died: On Monday, the 4th inst., at the residence of Mr. Samuel SIMPSON, near North Fork, of typhoid fever, Martha A. JONES, in the 55th year of her age.

Died: At her residence in Waterford, Oct. 17th, 1878, Mrs. Elizabeth HANVY, consort of the late John HANVY, in the 63d year of her age.

Married: In Hamilton, Nov. 12th, 1878, by Rev. Henry BRANCH, James M. HOGE and Julia N. ARCHER, sister of the officiating clergyman.

Married: Nov. 12th, 1878, near Hillsborough, by Rev. W. H. WILSON, John CARLES, of Lebanon, Ohio, to Miss Alice J. UNDERWOOD, of Loudoun county.

Married: On same day, by the same, near Round Hill, Levi W. NIXON, to Miss Ruth, daughter of Mahlon THOMAS, Esq., all of Loudoun Co.

Married: October 30th, 1878, at Christ Episcopal Church, Winchester, Va. by Rev. Dr. J. R. HUBARD, P. Williams FAUNTLEROY, of St. Louis, Mo., and Miss Netta BATTLE, of Winchester.

Married: On Tuesday, November 5th, 1878, at the Short Hill Church, by the Rev. Mr. LAKE, Mr. Henry TAYLOR to Miss Dorcas TAYLOR, both of Loudoun county.

Married: At the residence of the bride's father, Nov. 6th, 1878, by Rev. L. H. CRENSHAW, Mr. John H. ORRISON to Miss Laura THOMAS, daughter of Robt. W. THOMAS, Esq., all of Loudoun county.

Married: November 7, near Neersville, at the residence of the bride's father, John GRUBB, Esq., by the Rev. W. H. WILSON, Wm. A. ABELL to Miss Annie M. GRUBB, all of Loudoun.

Married: Same day, by same, at Parsonage of the M. E. Church, South, Landon DAVIS to Fannie E. FIELDS.

Mr. Asa BOND, of this county, died at his home in Waterford, on Saturday last, in the 75th year of his age.

Capt. John MOORE, one of the oldest of Loudoun's citizens, died at his home in Aldie, on Tuesday night, in about his 76th year.

Nov. Ct.: Letters of administration granted on the estates of the late Thos. WHITE Sr., Martha A. JONES, Matson JAMES, Alfred MEGEATH, Jacob WENNER and John F. MILBOURN. Wills of Catherine GRUBB and John H. LOWE were admitted to probate. Revs. L. B. TURNBULL and George W. POPKINS and Elder E. V. WHITE were licenced to celebrate the rites of matrimony.

Thursday, 21 November 1878   Vol. XXIII, No. 25

Married: At Guilford Park, Nov. 13th 1878, by Rev. O. C. BEALL, George L. LAWSON, of Md., to Miss Ellen ASHTON, of Loudoun county.

Married: In Zion Church, Charlestown, W. Va. on Thursday morning, Nov. 14th, 1878, by Rev. W. H. MEADE, Bushrod Corbin WASHINGTON, Esq. of Jefferson county, and Miss Emma Edwards WILLIS, youngest daughter of Thomas H. WILLIS Esq. of Charlestown.

Married: On Thursday, October 14th, at the residence of Dr. James N. GARLICK, by the Rev. J. J. ANDERSON, Miss Sadie B. OSBORNE, to Judge B. W. LACY, all of New Kent county, Va.

Married: On the 12th instant, in St. James' Church, Warrenton, by the Rev. Philip SLAUGHTER, D.D, assisted by Rev. John S. LINDSAY, Kate Ramsay, daughter of John Murry FORBES, Esq., of Fauquier county to Mr. Otto WITTICHEN, of Prince William County.

Married: At "Smithfield," the residence of the bride's mother, Montgomery county, on the 14th day of November 1878, by Rev. Nelson P. DAME, Aubin L. BOULWARE, of Richmond, to Jane Grace, youngest daughter of the late Gov. W. Ballard PRESTON, all of Virginia.

We understand that diphtheria has made inroads upon the family of Mr. Geo. BOLLING, living near Hughesville. One child died on the 8th of November, another on the 15th, and a third was dangerously ill with the same disease.

Hannah, a colored woman, formerly owned by the late Richard ADAMS, of this county, died last week at her home near Mountain Gap, at the advance age of not less than 100 years.

Mr. Francis GARDNER, aged 93y 11m 8d, died at his home near Charlestown, Jefferson county, W. Va., on Monday last. He owned 1,700 acres of the best land in that fertile county. He leaves 1 son and 2 daughters.

Thursday, 28 November 1878   Vol. XXIII, No. 26

Married: In the M. E. Church, South, Leesburg, on Tuesday morning, Nov. 26th, 1878, by Rev. H. H. KENNEDY, Mr. Wm. H. VANDERHOOF and Miss Lilla GALLEHER, daughter of the late Jas. W. GALLEHER, all of Loudoun.

Married: In Leesburg, on Wednesday evening, Nov. 29th, 1878, by Rev. L. B. TURNBULL, Mr. Wm. W. WALLACE and Miss Lizzie McNEALY, all of Loudoun.

Married: On the 20th inst., at the M. E. Church, South, in Dranesville, by the Rev. ___, Mr. James O. HODGKIN, to Miss Roberta DAY, daughter of Dr. DAY, of Fairfax county.

Married: At the residence of the bride's father, in Waterford, on the 20th inst., by the Rev. Wm. SCHOOLEY, Mr. Flavius BEANS to Miss Rosa HOUGH, both of Waterford.

Married: At the residence of the bride's father, near Waterford, on the 14th inst., by the Rev. Henry BRANCH, Mr. Thos. CARR to Miss Mollie BENNETT, both of Loudoun county.

Died: At the residence in Aldie, on Thursday, November 14th, 1878, Mr. Sanford GULICK, aged 65 years.

Died: At her residence in Hamilton, on the night of the 20th inst., Mrs. Elizabeth PEUGH, in the 53rd year of her age.

Died: In Georgetown, on Monday, Nov. 18th 1878, at 9:30 a.m. of remolisment of brain, Emily Virginia, wife of Thos. D. DIVINE, in 49th year of her age.

Died: November 3d, at Memphis, Tenn. of yellow fever, Mrs. Jerry COCKRELL, formerly of S. Carolina, and a sister of Mr. S. W. COCKRELL and Mrs. C. A. ENGLISH, of this place. Two sons of the deceased had died of the same disease on October 15.

Thursday, 5 December 1878   Vol. XXIII, No. 27

Married: At the M. E. Church, Alexandria, Va, on the 27th of November, by the Rev. Mr. PEARCE, Mr. Charles N. NEWTON, of Leesburg, to Miss Wilhelmina PATTON, of Alexandria, Va.

Married: Dec. 3d at 7½ p.m. at the parsonage of the M. E. Church, South, in this place, by Rev. H. H. KENNEDY, Mr. Richard F. GREEN to Miss Jennie McDONOUGH, all of Leesburg.

Married: On the 28th inst., by Elder E. V. WHITE, Mr. George W. HEATER to Miss Julia E. CROSS, all of Loudoun county.

Married: On the 21st inst., by the same, Mr. Wm. H. ATHEY and Miss Sarah C. CROSS, all of Loudoun.

Married: On the 27th inst., at the Parsonage of the M. E. Church, in Leesburg, by the Rev. W. H. FORSYTH, Mr. John W. HARPER to Miss Nettie COMPHER, all of Loudoun.

Died: At the residence of his father near Unison, on the 21st of November, 1878, James MURPHY, son of Hiram MURPHY, in the 22d year of his age.

Died: On November 26th, of typhoid fever, Louisa, wife of E. Calvin WILLIAMS, and daughter of Hugh DOUGLAS, of Nashville, Tenn.

Died: Thursday, Nov. 21st at Whitehall, the residence of his mother, near Leesburg, J. William HAWLING, in the 41st year of his age.

Died: Nov. 30th, at 5:25 a.m. at the residence of his father, "Springwood," Loudoun county, Mr. John A. LUTZ, aged 32. An invalid for a year or more. He leaves a widow. Funeral services at the M. E. Church, South, of this place, on Monday last, and interment of the remains took place in the afternoon of the same day at Oak Hill Cemetery, Georgetown, DC.

Last Wednesday morning, on a pond near the residence of Mr. C. R. PAXTON, the dead body of a newly born negro infant was found.

A dispatch from New Orleans, dated December 2d, says Right Rev. J. B. P. WILMER, bishop of the disease of Louisiana, a native of Virginia, aged about 65 years, died suddenly at the St. Charles hotel, in this city, at 7 p.m. today of apoplexy.

New Orleans, Dec. 1 – steamer collision occurred at Bringler's Point, La, opposite Donaldsonville, La. between the Morgan and the Cotton Valley, of the Red River Transportation Company's line was sunk. Twenty lives were lost, among those Miss SANFORD of Alexandria, La. Miss SANFORD was a niece of Mr. Wm. L. SANFORD, of this county. Mr. SANFORD's wife and niece left here a few weeks ago for the purpose of visiting their old home in Louisiana, Mrs. SANFORD was among the rescued.

Thursday, 12 December 1878   Vol. XXIII, No. 28

Married: Nov. 28, 1878, near Upperville, by Rev. J. B. LAKE, Mr. Dallas P. GUNNELL, of Fairfax county, to Miss Blanche GIBSON, daughter of Mr. Joseph GIBSON.

Died: In Leesburg, of inflammatory croup, on Wednesday night at 12 o'clock, Charles P. JANNEY Jr., fourth child of Charles P. and Nannie L. JANNEY, aged 2y 9m.

Died: At her home, two miles north of Leesburg, on Friday night, Dec. 6th, 1878, of typhoid fever, Miss Catharine THOMAS, daughter of the late John THOMAS, in the 60th year of her age.

Death of Col. John P. DULANY – one of the oldest and wealthiest of Loudoun's citizens, died at his home in this county, on Tuesday the 3d of December, 1878, in his 93d year. Born at Shooter's Hill, near Alexandria, in 1786, but has resided in Loudoun since 1812. Descended from Daniel DULANY, celebrated in McMAHON's history of Maryland, as a distinguished patriot and lawyer before the Revolution. Member of M. E. Church and the M. E. Church, South, for more than 50 years.

Mrs. Elmina S. ROGERS, wife of the late Thos. ROGERS, of Loudoun, died at the residence of her son-in-law, Rev. Mr. WILLIS, in Clarksville, W. Va. on the 5th inst., in her 67th year. Her remains were brought to this county for interment and on

Friday were laid beside those of her husband in the burying ground at North Fork.

Death of James W. STEPHENSON – occurred at Greenville, Mississippi, on the 4th of November from yellow fever. He was a native of Loudoun, where for several years preceding the war he was engaged in the book and stationery trade. He leaves a wife in St. Louis, he was in the 40th year of his age.

Ct.: Letters of administration granted Harrison OSBURN on the estate of C. F. DOWELL dec'd.; J. B. THROCMORTON on the estate of J. B. SILCOTT dec'd.; James B. PEUGH on the estate of Elizabeth PEUGH dec'd.; Wm. SMITH on the estate of Mary C. WILLIAMS dec'd.; R. H. DULANY, Arthur HERBERT and John A. CARTER on the estate of John P. DULANY dec'd.; A. B. MOORE on the estate of John MOORE dec'd.; Sarah A. BOND on the estate of Asa M. BOND dec'd.

Thursday, 19 December 1878   Vol. XXIII, No. 29

Married: At the International Hotel, Helena, Montana, on Nov. 25th, 1878, by Gov. B. F. POTTS, Mr. Harvey L. KEENE, formerly of this county, to Miss Inez POWERS, of Maine.

Died: At the residence of her daughter, Mrs. Alfred POOR, in Baltimore, on Saturday, Dec. 14th, 1878, Mrs. Sallie A. E. Smith, widow of the late Benjamin P. SMITH, of Loudoun co.

Died: At the residence of her son, in Fairfax county, on December 3d, 1878, Mrs. Amassa C. HOGELAND, widow of the late John W. HOGELAND, in the 86th year of her age.

Died: In the city of Manchester, Va. at 3½ o'clock, a.m., December 14th, 1878, Martha M., wife of Joseph W. BRONAUGH Jr., in the 28th year of her age.

Thursday, 26 December 1878   Vol. XXIII, No. 30

Married: At the residence of the bride's father, near Hillsborough, by Rev. W. H. WILSON, Miss Emma J. POTTS, daughter of E. H. POTTS, Esq. and Mathias P. ZACHARIAS, of Frederick County, Md.

Died: In Leesburg, on Sunday night, Dec. 22d, 1878, after a protracted illness and great suffering, Mrs. Martha Ellen, wife of Benj. F. HEAD, in about the 42d year of her age.

Died: Near Woodgrove, on Saturday, Nov. 9th, of diphtheria, Mattie PALMER, daughter of S. E. and Alice PALMER, aged 6y 7m.

Died: At his residence near Hillsboro, on Thursday, December 5th, 1878, Bernard Turner CLENDENNING.

Died: In Washington city, on the 19th of December, 1878, of consumption, John W. DALTON, aged 21, son of Wm. H. DALTON.

Died: On Saturday morning, December 20th, 1878, at 5 o'clock, of consumption, Wm. H. DALTON, aged 51. [The above parties were father and son, who before their removal to Washington several years ago, were residents of this town.]

Died: At his residence near Hillsboro, after a short illness, December 22d, 1878, Edwin H. POTTS, in the 70th year of his age. Mr. POTTS belonged to one of the oldest and successful families in Loudoun.

Thursday, 2 January 1879   Vol. XXIII, No. 31

Married: December 17th, at the residence of the bride's father, in Upperville, by Rev. J. B. LAKE, Mr. Joseph PATTON, of Middleburg, and Miss Mary LUNCEFORD.

Married: On 24th December, by Rev. Dr. C. G. LINTHICUM, Benjamin THRIFT to Annie, daughter of the officiating minister.

Married: At the residence of the bride's father, on Wednesday, Dec. 11, 1878, by Rev. Frank PAGE, Philip W. CARPER and Minnnie, daughter of Mr. James COCKERILLE, all of Loudoun county.

Married: In the M. E. Church, South, Leesburg, on Tuesday morning, Dec. 31st, 1878, by Rev. H. H. KENNEDY, H. H. RUSSELL (Deputy Sheriff of Loudoun county) and Mary Alice, eldest daughter of Capt. Chas. P. McCABE, all of this county.

Death of William C. LYNCH – second son of Wm. B. LYNCH, editor of the *Washingtonian*, of this place. Had he lived until the 8th of March 1879, he would have been 22 years of age. ... Willie's remains enclosed in a metallic case left Lexington and were brought to Leesburg, interment at Union Cemetery.

Thursday, 9 January 1879   Vol. XXIII, No. 32

Married: Jan. 2nd, 1878 [1879] by Rev. W. H. WILSON, at residence of the bride's father, Joseph H. JENKINS to Miss Julia A. CONRAD, daughter of E. J. and Virginia CONRAD, all of Loudoun county.

Died: At her residence, near Waterford, on Saturday morning, Dec. 28th, Mrs. Ann Eliza BRADEN, widow of late Rodney BRADEN.

Died: In this town, on Friday night, January 3d, 1879, Mr. Fenelon SLACK, in the 66th year of his age.

Died: At her residence in Fauquier county, December 5, 1878, in the 81st year of her age, Mrs. Francis HARPER, widow of the late Joel Zane HARPER.

Joe WATSON, a well known old colored man of this town, was found dead in his room last Monday morning. He died at an advanced age, probably not far short of 90 years.

Thursday, 16 January 1879   Vol. XXIII, No. 33

Married: At Christ's Episcopal Church, near Goresville, on the morning of the 14th inst., by the Rev. R. T. DAVIS, Mr. Herbert OSBURN to Bettie, eldest daughter of Jno. H. WHITMORE, Esq., all of Loudoun

Married: January 7th 1879, at the residence of the bride's father, by Rev. L. H. CRENSHAW, Mr. George W. PRESGRAVES to Miss Louisa M. NIXON, daughter of Jonah NIXON, Esq., all of Loudoun county.

Married: In the M. E. Church, South, Hamilton, January 8th, 1879, Mr. Israel T. MYERS to Miss Ginnie HAWKINS, both of Loudoun county. Rev. L. H. CRENSHAW, officiating.

Married; By the same at the Parsonage of the M. E. Church, South, Hamilton, January 9th, 1879, Mr. Isaac BALLENGER to Miss Eliza HUNT, both of Purcellville.

Married: January 9th, 1879, at the residence of the bride's father, Mr. Wm. Nelson HICKSON to Ella LOVELESS, daughter of John W. LOVELESS, Esq., all of Loudoun. Rev. L. H. CRENSHAW, officiating.

Married: January 9th, at the residence of the bride's father, near Waterford, by the Rev. W. H. WILSON, James PEACOCK to Miss Mariah J. HOUGH, dau. of William HOUGH, Esq. of B.

Died: In Leesburg, Thursday, Dec. 26th, 1879, after a long and painful illness, of consumption, Laura Jane, daughter of John T. and Annie E. GANT, in the 26th year of her age.

Died: In Warrenton, on Monday the 7th of January, in the 79th year of her age, and the 58th year of her married life, Elizabeth Smith, daughter of James M. and Amelia BELL, and wife of Ex-Governor Wm. SMITH.

Mrs. Mary CROSS, widow of the late Dr. William CROSS, died on the afternoon of the 14th of January, in this place. Maiden name was JAMES, and relatives live near Snickersville, where she was born. For thirty years, or more, she has resided here.

Death of William BEVERLY – on Monday, 30th of December, He left Leesburg to visit his son in Fauquier. On Saturday afternoon he was seized with pneumonia and on one o'clock on Friday morning, January 10th he died in his 51st year.

County Ct.: Estates of Sarah OFFUTT, Wm. C. AMES and John BOGER committed to Sheriff. Wm. MOORE qualified as Guardian of Margaret E. and Catharine MOORE.

Thursday, 23 January 1879   Vol. XXIII, No. 34

Married: In St. James' Episcopal Church, Leesburg, at 12, on Tuesday, January 21st, 1879, by Rev. Dr. R. T. DAVIS, assisted by Rev. John ELLIOTT, of Ascension Church,

Washington, Dr. W. R. WINCHESTER, and Sallie, eldest daughter of the late Matthew HARRISON, Esq., all of this town.
Died: At his residence near Farmwell, in this county, on the 18th inst., John AKERS, in the 63d year of his age.
Died: At her residence in Hillsboro, on the night of the 16th inst., after a short but painful illness of 4 days, Mrs. Louisa HOUGH, wife of Mr. William HOUGH, aged 64y 2m 13d. She leaves a husband, 2 sons and 2 daughters.
Mrs. Nellie NETTLES, an old lady of Waterford, died suddenly at her residence in that town on Monday, of apoplexy. She got up in the morning as well as usual, and in a few minutes thereafter was a corpse.

Thursday, 30 January 1879   Vol. XXIII, No. 35

Married: January 21st, 1879, at the residence of the bride's parents, near Farmwell Station, by Rev. B. A. SHREVE, Allen S. DARNE and Sallie L. HAVENNER, both of Loudoun county.
Married: On the 21st inst., at the Reformed Church, Lovettsville, by the Rev. H. St. J. RINKER, Mr. James MOCK to Miss Laura V. DENT, all of Loudoun.
Married: On the 23d of January, 1879, at Louisville, Ohio, by Rev. John W. FORSYTH, Mr. Chas. G. STREAM, of Licking County, Ohio, to Miss Sallie SLATER, of Lovettsville.
Died: On Sunday, the 19th of January, 1879, at her residence near Ball's Bluff, Mrs. Margaret A. JACKSON, in her 60th year.
Died: At her residence, near Leesburg, on Saturday morning, January 25th 1879, Mrs. Jane MEAD, widow of the late Joseph MEAD, in her 66th year. Member of the Episcopal Church from which her funeral took place on Monday afternoon.

Thursday, 6 February 1879   Vol. XXIII, No. 36

Married: At the Aldie Church, on Wednesday morning, January 29, 1879, by Rev. Dr. J. A. HAYNES, Mr. Christian REAMER and Emma, daughter of the late Jonathan NIXON, all of Loudoun.
Died: Near Langley, Fairfax county, at 3:15 a.m., of heart disease, John P. SKINNER, in the 37th year of his age. He had suffered for a number of months with this afflication.
At meeting of Vestry of Christ Church held at Goresville, 25 Jan 1879, tribute for death of Vestryman Wm. BEVERLY. Born and reared an Episcopalian. Left widow and children.
Homer MURRAY, a colored man from Middleburg neighborhood, struck his brother George over the head with a billett of wood on the 4th of Jan and George died Sat. night. Homer committed to jail on Tuesday evening. Homer was confined last summer several weeks for cutting a white man near Leesburg with a razor.

Maj. B. P. NOLAND, grand-son of Burr POWELL, has put us in possession of a verified copy of the proceedings of a public meeting held in Leesburg on 14 Jun 1774. Original document was found among papers of Col. Leven POWELL, at one time member of Congress from this District, who died 1810. His son, Burr POWELL, forwarded a copy to R. H. LEE, Esq., who in 1826 was about to publish a second edition of his memoirs. [transcribes the document] Leven POWELL, William ELLZEY, John THORNTON, George JOHNSTON and Samuel LEVI chosen for a committee. Signed by John NORTON, Thos. RAY, Thomas DRAKE, William BOORAM, Benj. Isaac HUMPHREY, Samuel MILLS, Joshua SINGLETON, Jonathan DRAKE, Matthew RUST, Thomas WILLIAMS, James NOLAND, Samuel PEUGH, William WORNALL, Thos. LUTTRELL, James BRAIR, Poins AWSLEY, John KENDRICK, Edward O'NEAL, Barnet SIMS, John SIMS, Samuel BUTLER, Thomas CHINN, Apollos COOPER, Lima HANCOCK, John McVICKER, Simon TRIPLETT, Thos. AWSLEY, Isaac SANDERS, Thos. WILLIAMS, John WILLIAMS, Henry AWSLEY, Wm. FINNEKEN, Richard HANSON, John DUNKER, Jasper GRANT, Francis TRIPLETT, Joseph COMBS, Jno. Peyton HARRISON, Robert COMBS, Stephen COMBS, Samuel HENDERSON, Benjamin OVERFIELD, Adam SANGSTER, Bazzell ROADS, John WILDEY, James GRAYDEY, Joseph BAYLEY, John REARDON, Edward MILLER, Richard HIRST, James DAVIS. 11 Jan 1826 letter from B. P. in Middleburg. Burr POWELL wrote that in looking at the papers of his father, Leven POWELL, who died in 1810, found letter [above] Signers were mostly residence of the neighborhood in which Col. POWELL lived. Robert COMBS and Joshua SINGLETON, are now living, the first named about 4 miles from me.

Thursday, 13 February 1879   Vol. XXIII, No. 37

Married: In Baltimore, on 4th February 1879, by Rev. Robert PIGGOTT, D.D., C. Douglas GRAY to Sophie S., youngest daughter of the late Thomas PIGGOTT, all of that city.

Married: In Hamilton, February 5th, 1879, by Rev. L. H. CRENSHAW, Mr. Charles F. STANSBURY, of Alexandria, to Miss Laura C. WILEY, daughter of John H. WILEY, Esq., of Hamilton.

Married: January 30th 1879 near Morrisonville, by Rev. P. H. MILLER, Mr. Jesse E. TRIBBY and Miss Jane A. ADAMS.

Married: February 5th by the Rev. Wm. H. FORSYTH, Chas. E. FRITTS to Miss Ollie A. DERRY, both of Loudoun county.

Married: February 6th by the same, John E. STEWARD to Miss Rebecca VIRTZ, all of Loudoun county.

Married: Feb. 11th 1879, at the residence of the bride's mother, by Rev. L. H. CRENSHAW, Mr. Geo. Wm. JAMES, to Miss M. Ella FULTON, daughter of Mrs. Massey FULTON, all of Loudoun.

Died: Near Alexandria, January 28th, 1879, Samuel LAMB, formerly of Loudoun Co., in the 56th year of his age.

Departed this life, the 4th of April, 1878, near Aldie, Mildred SINCLAIR the wife of John SINCLAIR, dec'd., in her 87th year.

Died: On Saturday, Feb. 8th at the residence of his father, Mr. Levi W. NIXON, near Leesburg, Mr. Joseph NIXON, in the 26th year of his age. His funeral took place from the M. E. Church, South, of this place, on Tuesday last, and he was buried (with Masonic honors) in Union Cemetery.

Death of William JACKSON – at his home in Leesburg last Saturday morning, after a brief illness, in about the 60th year of his age. He was well known as an old driver in the days of stage coaching between Winchester and Washington. On Sunday afternoon his remains were placed in Union Cemetery.

Charles WILLIAMS had a difficulty with Beverly CLAGETT (both colored) on the farm of Mr. John ALDRIDGE, near Mt. Gilead, on the 28th of January, during which WILLIAMS struck CLAGETT over the head with a stick of wood, from which CLAGETT died on the 4 February. WILLIAMS was arrested.

Feb. Ct.: Wills of Wm. WENNER and Sarah NETTLES admitted to probate. Letter of administration granted on the estates of Matilda YOUNG, Edwin H. POTTS, Elizabeth A. BRADEN and Catherine GRUBB. Elizabeth R. GRAHAM qualified as Guardian of James E. GRAHAM.

Letter in Southern Churchman from Rev. C. C. PENICK, dated Capt. Mount, Liberia, West Africa, Dec. 23, 1878, announces the safe arrival at that point on the 11th of Dec. of Rev. Curtis GRUBB and his wife.

Howard HOLTZCLAW, telegraph operator and depot agent at Warrenton Junction, was shot and instantly killed last Thursday night, near the stile on the way from his office upon the premises of Mr. B. G. SHUMATE where the deceased boarded. It is believed he was killed for the money he was supposed to have. Richmond, a colored man engaged about the telegraph office, was missed last Friday morning when the body was found, traced to Montrose a few miles distant, where he was found with some of the articles stolen from Mr. HOLTZCLAW hidden in the lining of his coat.

Thursday, 20 February 1879   Vol. XXIII, No. 38

Married: On the 5th inst., near Lovettsville, by the Rev. H. St. J. RINKER, Mr. Thomas LEMON to Miss Mollie E. STOUTZENBERGER, all of this county.

Married: On the 6th inst., at the house of the bride's father, by the Rev. Dr. HAYNES, Harry HATCHER, Esq., and Miss Sophy DOWELL.

Married: On the same day, by the same, at Long Branch Church, Mr. Charles M. DOWNS and Miss Lucy M. FOSTER.

Married: At Thoroughfare, Va., Wednesday evening, February 5th, 1879, by Rev. John AMBLER, Mr. P. D. BRAWNER, of Fauquier co., to Miss C. E. MOUNT, of Prince William co.

Married: At the University of Virginia, on Thursday, February 13, 1879, by Rev. J. S. HANCKEL, D.D., James P. HARRISON, of Danville, and Mary Jane, eldest daughter of Prof. John S. DAVIS.

Died: On the 31st ulto., William WENNER Sr., in his 87th year.

Died: At Lovettsville, of diphtheria, on the evening of February 9th, 1879, Harriet Eliza, daughter of R. M. J. and Caroline ATWELL, aged 5y 7m.

Thursday, 27 February 1879   Vol. XXIII, No. 39

Died: At his new home in California, after a lingering illness, John MICHENER, father-in-law of Mrs. Anna MITCHENER, daughter of John B. DUTTON.

Died: At his late residence in Monroe township, on the 6th inst., of dropsy, Wm. McARTOR, aged 83 years. Mr. McARTOR moved from Loudoun County, to Perry county 40 years ago. He was buried in the Methodist cemetery at Whippstown. *New Lexington Herald.*

Died: At the residence of his son, Chas. A. SMITH, Middleburg, Loudoun county, Feb. 15th, 1879, Augustus G. SMITH, in the 72d year of his age.

Thursday, 6 March 1879   Vol. XXIII, No. 40

Married: Feb. 26th at the residence of the bride's father, by Rev. Wm. H. FORSYTH, Edgar N. BROWN to Miss Maggie J. ADLDER [ALLDER], all of Loudoun.

Married: By the Rev. G. W. POPKINS, on the 26th of Feb., Mr. Wm. S. JENKINS to Miss Orra L. DANIEL, at the bride's residence, near Mt. Gilead, all of Loudoun county.

Married: On the 26th of Feb., 1879, by the Rev. B. A. SHREVE, in the Methodist Church, Gum Spring, Mr. Edgar McFARLAND and Miss Lavinia G. WYCKOFF, all of Loudoun.

Died: Monday, Feb. 17th 1879, at the residence of her nephew, Leven OGDEN, Esq., near Hillsboro, Mrs. Nancy MORRIS, relict of the late Capt. MORRIS, in the 99th year of her age.

Died: Saturday, Feb. 15th, 1879, at the residence of his son, Charles A. SMITH, Esq., in Middleburg, Mr. Augustus G. SMITH, in the 72nd year of his age. Mr. SMITH was born in Frederick city, Md, came from there to Leesburg, when quite a young man, where he married. Became a citizen of Middleburg, in 1832.

Died: In Leesville, Ohio, February 17th, 1879, of typhoid fever, Thomas Arthur, son of Edmund and Martena K. BENEDUM (formerly of Leesburg) and grandson of the late S. M. BOSS, aged 23y 5m 27d.

Mr. Wm. C. BRONAUGH, an old resident of this county, died at his residence near Col. BERKELEY's in the upper part of this county on Wednesday last. Up to the commencement of the war he had for many years held a position in the Postoffice Department. At the time of his death he was about 85 years of age. *Manassas Gazette.* Mr. BRONAUGH was a brother of the late Dr. P. H. W. BRONAUGH, of this town.

Thursday, 13 March 1879   Vol. XXIII, No. 41

Married: At the Parsonage of the M. E. Church, in Leesburg, March 5th, 1879, by the Rev. W. H. FORSYTH, Mr. Isaac RIDGEWAY to Miss Elizabeth UTTERBACK.

Married: March 2d, 1879, in Davis County, Kansas, by the Rev. J. O. FOREMAN, of the M. E. Church, South, Thomas G. McKINLEY and Virginia G., third daughter of J. F. and M. J. ROSS, formerly of Loudoun county.

Died: On the 27th of February, of pneumonia, Benjamin NEWMAN Sr., in the 66th year of his age.

March Ct.: Wills of Joseph W. NIXON, A. G. SMITH and Ann MORRIS dec'd. admitted to probate. Administrations granted on the estates of Andrew HEFFNER, Peter FRY, William WENNER. Jonathan MATTHEW resigned as Guardian of G. H. T. BEAMER and others, children of Richard BEAMER. John MILTON appointed guardian of D. W. W. BEAMER, M. A. V. BEAMER, M. J. M. BEAMER and S. R. W. BEAMER.

Death of Mrs. Mary J. DAVIS – mother of Dr. J. Staige DAVIS and Capt. Eugene DAVIS, died at the residence of the latter on

Tuesday night last after an illness of some months duration. *Charlottesville Chronicle, of March 8th*. The deceased lady was also the mother of Rev. Dr. DAVIS, pastor of St. James church, Leesburg.

Thursday, 20 March 1879   Vol. XXIII, No. 42

Married: On Wednesday, March 12th, at First Presbyterian Church, by the Rev. Dr. W. T. HALL, Jas. M. BOOKER Jr. to Mazie Faulkner, daughter of Hon. Thos. S. BOCOCK, of Lynchburg.

Married: On the 19th of February, 1879, by the Rev. Dr. J. H. CUTHBERT, of the 13th Street Baptist Church, Barnard T. FELLOWS, of Essex county, Massachusetts, to Miss Ellen A. LUCKETT, youngest daughter of the late Ludwell LUCKETT, of Loudoun county.

Died: On Monday evening, March 3d, 1879, near Lovettsville, Robert W. GRAY, in the 23d year of his age.

Died: Near Mountsville, March 5, 1879, Oliver R., son of Cecelia and John RHODES, aged 6m 25d.

Died: At the residence of her parents, near Reiterstown, Md, on Sunday, March 9th, 1879, of consumption, Miss S. Annie, only daughter of C. and Sarah GINGRICH, aged 18y 3m 9d. She was the only sister of Dr. C. M. GINGRICH of this town.

Thursday, 27 March 1879   Vol. XXIII, No. 43

Married: On the 16th instant, at the residence of the bride's father, by the Rev. J. TURNER, Mr. Mahlon D. ARNOLD, of Loudoun county, to Miss Emma O. HUFFER, only daughter of David HUFFER, near Burkettsville, Frederick county, Md.

Died: In Baltimore, Md, on Thursday evening, 20th of March, 1879, of pneumonia, Lillian Julia, aged 7m 3w 1d, the youngest child of Edgar L. and Mamie E. BENTLEY and granddaughter of John T. and Julia McABEE.

Daniel PAYNE, a well known old colored man of this town, was stricken with appoplexy on Monday afternoon and died Tuesday night, never having recovered consciousness.

Thursday, 3 April 1879   Vol. XXIII, No. 44

Married: At the Parsonage of the M. E. Church, South, Hamilton, March 25th 1879, by Rev. A. A. P. NEAL, J. Wm. DILLON and Miss Lou L. GREGG, daughter of Harmon GREGG, Esq., all of Loudoun.

Died: John W. MOSBURG, at an advanced age, at the residence of Mrs. SAUNDERS, near Clark's Gap, on Friday, 20th inst.

Died: James M. FRAME, aged 72 years, died at his residence, near Hamilton, at 12 o'clock Wednesday night, March 26th.

Died: Mary Ann BOLYN died at her residence near Lincoln, last Sabbath morning, March 23d, at about 67 years of age.
Died: Susan HUNT died at the residence of B. F. TAYLOR, at Hughesville, on Wednesday the 26th inst.
Died: At Mealia, White Post, Clarke county, on the 27th instant, Miss Mary MEADE, sister of the late Bishop MEADE, aged 84.

Thursday, 10 April 1879   Vol. XXIII, No. 45

Clarke Courier: Mr. Bailey WYNDHAM died at his home in this county, last week, from the effects of a wound received in a finger by running a splinter into it some 8 or 10 days before his death.
Married: At the residence of the late Edwin POTTS, near Hillsboro, by Rev. W. H. WILSON, Samuel O. CLENDENING to Miss Laura A. POTTS, all of Loudoun county.
Married: At the residence of the bride's father, near Leesburg, April 2d, 1879, by Rev. B. A. SHREVE, Joseph H. COCKRILL and Elizabeth BENJAMIN, all of Loudoun.
Married: On the 8th inst., at Farmwell by Rev. L. B. TURNBULL, Miss Annie M. AKERS and Charles W. BEACH, all of Loudoun.
Died: In Brooklyn, L. I., on the 13th of March, 1879, Mrs. Charlotte A. SMART, widow of the late John P. SMART, of Leesburg, and daughter of the late James ORAM, of New York.
Died: In Alexandria, on Tuesday morning, April 8, 1879, of pneumonia, Mrs. Cornelia A. JANNEY, wife of Eli H. JANNEY, in the 46th year of her age.
Died: In Leesburg, on Monday morning, March 24th, William Albert, infant son of A. G. and Emma J. JACKSON, aged 1m 2w 2d.
Maj. A. E. RICHARDS, a native of Loudoun, and during the war a gallant member of Mosby's command, is now practising law in Louisville, Ky.

Thursday, 17 April 1879   Vol. XXIII, No. 46

Died: In Alexandria, on Monday morning, April 14th, 1879, at the residence of E. J. LLOYD, Sally LEE, daughter of the late Edmund I. LEE, of Alexandria.
Died: Of consumption, at the residence of his mother, near Bloomfield, Loudoun county, on Sunday night, April 6th, Thomas L. HESS, in the 19th year of his age.
Died: Near Farmwell, Thaddeus HOUGH, born July 1st, 1859, died October 6th, 1879.
Died: March 26th, 1879, at the residence of B. F. TAYLOR, Esq., near Hughesville, Susan HUNT, in the 58th year of her age.
Mr. Humphrey BEANS, a successful farmer, died at his home near Woodgrove, on the 8th inst., in the 50th year of his age.

April Ct.: Wills of James M. FRAME dec'd., Sarah M. BEAVERS dec'd. and Robt. MATHERS dec'd. admitted to probate. The powers of Edward and Jno. D. BROWN as Admrs. of David BROWN dec'd. revoked. W. H. WOOLF, of the M. E. Church, South, licensed to celebrate rites of matrimony.

On Sunday morning last, at the residence of Col. Hamilton ROGERS, near Middleburg, Catherine CAVENS departed this life in the 87th year of her age. She was a member of the M. E. Church, having joined the church in this town in 1815. The deceased had been an inmate of Col. ROGERS' family for more than sixty years. Her remains were brought to Leesburg on Monday and buried in Union Cemetery.

Thursday, 24 April 1879   Vol. XXIII, No. 47

Mrs. BROOKE, wife of Jas. V. BROOKE, Esq., of Warrenton, died Friday of pneumonia.

Married: Near Philomont, on Sunday, the 20th of April 1879, by Rev. Samuel SAUNDERS, Geo. W. WILLIAMS and Laura WILLIAMS, all of this county.

Died: On Friday evening April 11th, at the residence of her niece, Ann E. DONOHOE, Miss Nancy CROSS, in the 80th year of her age.

Died: April 7th, 1879, at Silcott's Springs, Mrs. Isabella JACOBS, wife of Herbert JACOBS, in the 36th year of her age.

Last Thursday, the 17th of April, 1879, Mr. Thos. LOVELESS died at the residence of his son-in-law, Mr. T. W. WEADON, near Woodburn. Mr. L. was born in 1789, and was in the 90th year of his age. He was a soldier in the war of 1812.

Thursday, 1 May 1879   Vol. XXIII, No. 48

Married: At Leesburg, on Thursday, April 24th, 1879, by Rev. Samuel SAUNDERS, Mr. R. H. HENDERSON and Miss Martha E. FRANKS, both of Loudoun county.

Mr. Frederick J. CRISSEY, of this town, died at his home in Leesburg on Tuesday night, after a few days illness in the 66th year of his age.

Thursday, 8 May 1879   Vol. XXIII, No. 49

Died: In Baltimore, on April 30, 1879, Amelia R., in the 24th? year of her age, wife of Henry S. DULANEY and daughter of W. W. KENNEDY. [Mrs. DULANEY was a sister of Rev. H. H. KENNEDY, of this town]

Died: In Leesburg, on the 29th ult., in the 66th year of his age, Mr. F. J. CRISSEY. Mr. CRISSEY was born in Berkley county, Va, and when quite a young boy was moved by his parents to

York, Penn., where he resided until manhood, when he came to Leesburg, married one in our midst and settled in our town.
Died: In Leesburg, at the residence of his mother, on Thursday, April 17th, 1879, Charles E. ROLLINS, in his 42d year.
Died: In Bellingham, Mass., April 23d, 1879, Mrs. Catharine P., wife of Rev. Joseph T. MASSEY, aged 63 years.

Thursday, 15 May 1879   Vol. XXIII, No. 50

Married: April 29th, by Rev. John WOOLF, at the residence of the bride's father, Mr. F. P. ASHBY, of Clarke, to Miss Maggie MERCER, of Loudoun.
Died: In Baltimore, on the 2d instant, Mrs. Louisa A. LUCKETT, wife of the late Horace LUCKETT, of this county, in the 85th year of her age.
Died: On May, 2d, 1879, in Hillsborough, at the residence of her brother-in-law, Mr. Thos. POTTS, of pneumonia, Miss Catherine Lucretia WALRAVEN, aged 59 years, dau. of the late Jonas and Lucretia WALRAVEN, of Jefferson co., W. Va.
May Ct.: T. W. WEADON qualified as committee of Elizabeth LOVELESS. Jas. S. HARRIS qualified as Admr. of F. J. CRISSEY.

Thursday, 22 May 1879   Vol. XXIII, No. 51

Married: On Tuesday last, in the Baptist Church at Alexandria, by the Rev. Mr. PENICK, Mr. C. Decatur HAMMERLY, of Leesburg to Miss Molly L. MURRAY, of Alexandria.
Married; May 13th, at Mt. Hope Church, by Rev. W. S. KERNE, Mr. A. E. ANKERS and Miss M. A. HIGDON, all of Loudoun co.
Married: On Thursday, the 15th of May, 1879, at the residence of the bride's parents, in Charlottesville, by Rev. Alpheus L. EDWARDS, Mr. J. Washington EDWARDS, son of the officiating minister, and Miss Emma W., daughter of Jesse W. JONES, Esq.
John SUTTLES, Wm. BOYD, Frank BOYD and Henry MALORY convicted in stoning of Rev. John H. RUSSELL, a colored preacher at Waterford, on the 28th of March.

Thursday, 29 May 1879   Vol. XXIII, No. 52

Married: In Zion Church, Fairfax C. H., on Monday night, May 20th, 1879, by Rev. Mr. PAGE, Mr. Maurice G. VANDEVANTER, of Washington city, and Miss Bessie, daughter of Albert T. WILLCOXEN, of Fairfax, and granddaughter of the late Chas. G. ESKRIDGE, of Loudoun.
Married: In Addison, W. Va. at the residence of the bride's father, April 8th, by Rev. D. SKIDMORE, Miss Lucy F. HUTCHINSON, formerly of Loudoun co., to Mr. Joseph BRADFIELD, of Texas.

Died: In Leesburg, on Friday, May 23, 1879, Mrs. Margaret M. ROLLINS, in about the 65th year of her age.

Died: At Fairfax C. H., on Thursday, the 23d inst., Virginia B. TYLER, daughter of Colonel Henry B. TYLER.

Dr. Robt. GORMAN, of this county, died at his home in Hamilton, on Tuesday afternoon.

Thursday, 5 June 1879   Vol. XXIII, No. 51

Died: George WERKING, on the 19th inst., at his residence in Lovettsville, on the 57th year of his age.

Died: In Columbus, Ohio, on the 26th of May, 1879, Mr. John WEADON, formerly of this county, in the 85th year of his age. His remains were brought to Loudoun and last Thursday interred in the cemetery at Middleburg.

Mr. Edward HAINES, an old citizen of this county, died at his home at Farmwell on Tuesday last, in the 81st year of his age. He was buried in the cemetery at Leesburg on Wednesday.

Thursday, 12 June 1879   Vol. XXIII, No. 52

Died: In Washington city, on Tuesday morning last, Minnie, infant dau. of R. N. and Emma V. SAUNDERS, formerly of this co.

June Ct.: Mrs. Sarah C. BEANS qualified as Executrix of A. Humphrey BEANS dec'd., and A. W. HOSKINSON as Admr. of Robert J. HOSKINSON dec'd., and Samuel W. GRUBB as Executor of Elizabeth MANN dec'd. Isaac YOUNG qualified as Guardian of Carrie HEFFNER.

Mr. N. W. MANNING, formerly a citizen of Jefferson County, W. Va. died suddenly in the King Street Presbyterian Church, Winchester, Va. Sunday evening last.

Thursday, 19 June 1879   Vol. XXIV, No. 1

Near Bealton, Fauquier Co, last week, three journeymen were seated in a blacksmith shop when lightning struck a tree near by, the belt glancing into the shop, instantly killing Edgar REESE.

Married: On June 4th, 1879, in Leesburg, by Rev. H. H. KENNEDY, Mr. Chas. E. SILCOTT to Miss Elizabeth W. GARRETT, both of Loudoun county.

Mr. John CUSACK, who has been residing in Leesburg for the past two or three years, left on Tuesday with his family for their home in old Ireland.

Miss Annie Maria WASHINGTON, a daughter of the late Thos. B. WASHINGTON, of Jefferson Co., W. Va. was married at the British Legation, Yeddo, Japan, May 14, to Mr. James Alfred EWING.

Thursday, 26 June 1879   Vol. XXIV, No. 2

[damaged] Married: June 15th near Ebenezer Church, Short Hill, by Rev. P. H. MILLER, Mr. Amos T. HUNT and Miss Elizabeth BAGENT.

Miss Sadie PAYNE, daughter of Gen. Wm. H. PAYNE, of Fauquier, died at her father's residence in Warrenton yesterday. The funeral took place today.

Thursday, 3 July 1879   Vol. XXIV, No. 3

The M. E. Church, South, Lovettsville, will be dedicated July 12th and 13th.

Last Thursday morning, Nancy JOHNSTON, a colored girl about 13 years of age, living with Mr. T. T. TITUS, near Goresville, met with a horrible death, from the explosion of a coal oil lamp. She died about day light Wednesday morning.

Thursday, 10 July 1879   Vol. XXIV, No. 4

Died: At the residence of her mother, at Silcott's Springs, on Thursday, the 19th of June, 1879, Harriet BARTLETT, in the 27th year of her age.

Thursday, 17 July 1879   Vol. XXIV, No. 5

Chillingworth KITZMILLER, son of the late A. M. KITZMILLER, of Harper's Ferry, died in Richmond, on the 28th of June, Mr. K. was born in Leesburg on the 26th of November, 1834.

Married: On July 6th, 1879, by Rev. John WOOLF, at his residence, Mr. John H. WILLIAMS to Miss Catherine ODEN, all of Loudoun.

Died: After an illness of seven months, on the firth day of July 1879, at his residence in Fauquier county, Thomas MARTIN, in the 82 year of his age.

Died: Mrs. Elizabeth MEGEATH, the widow of the late Jos. P. MEGEATH, departed this life, at the residence of her son-in-law, Samuel RODGERS, near Hamilton, on the 6th of July, 1879, in the 75th year of her age. Mother of ten children, eight of whom survive her. Born and reared in Loudoun county.

June Ct.: Fenton FURR qualified as Executor of Elizabeth MEGEATH dec'd.; Lee BRYANT qualified as Admr. of Gregg BRYANT dec'd.; and Joseph A. HUTCHISON qualified as Admr. of John BURSON dec'd.

Warrenton, July 11: first execution of criminals condemned to suffer capital punishment in Virginia since the passage of the law requiring the same be done in private occurred here this morning, the culprits being two negroes, John WILLIAMS, who murdered Howard HOLTZCLAW, acting railroad agent and telegraph operator at Warrenton Junction, on the Va Midland road, in Feb last, and Winter PAYNE, for killing an old negro names James ADAMS, near Salem, Fauquier Co, in April. The executions took place in the yard of the Fauquier co jail. Both were hung. ... First execution in this county since 1839.

Thursday, 24 July 1879   Vol. XXIV, No. 6

Mrs. Imogene BOLLING, wife of Mr. Charles C. BOLLING, died Friday afternoon, in Richmond. But a few weeks since the sister of Mr. BOLLING was burned to death.

Married: On Thursday, July 17, 1879,, by Rev. W. S. PENICK, John HUNTER, of Washington, D.C. to Miss Lula M. BEACH, daughter of Presley BEACH, formerly of Loudoun.

Died: On Friday, July 11th, 1879, in Leesburg, after a long and painful illness, Miss Susanna SEIBER, in her 53d year.

Died: At her home, in Prince William County on Friday the 11th inst., Mary A. E., beloved wife of Robert L. LYNN, in her 36th year. Daughter of the late Col. Wm. FULTON, of this county.

Died: Near Hamilton, July 16th, 1879, Willie E., son of T. W. and Lucy FRANKLIN, aged 10m 10d.

Garland Davis FRANKLIN, an infant son of J. B. FRANKLIN, formerly agent of the W. & O. R. R. at Hamilton, died at Conway, Arkansas, on the 7th inst.

Thursday, 31 July 1879   Vol. XXIV, No. 7

Died: At Brightside, Lake Rowland, near Baltimore, on July 19, 1879, William Sothoron POWELL, infant son of William S. and Lily B. POWELL, and grandson of Capt. E. B. POWELL, of Leesburg.

Died: At Westwood Grove, Loudoun county, on the 17th of July, 1879, Stuart JORDAN, second son of J. O. and Alice E. JORDAN, aged 10m 18d.

Thursday, 7 August 1879   Vol. XXIV, No. 8

Married: At the Reamer Hotel, Leesburg, July 31st, by Rev. H. H. KENNEDY, Mr. Kemp B. FURR to Miss Margaret M. MILEY, both of Loudoun county.

Married: At the same place and time, by the same, Mr. Philip A. HUTCHISON to Miss Susan J. FURR, both of Loudoun county.

Married: In the Calvary Baptist Church at Farmwell on the 30th of July, by the Rev. G. W. POPKINS, Mr. S. E. HORSMAN to Mrs. Josephine BURGESS, all of Loudoun.

Married: In Philadelphia, on the 16th of July, 1879, by the Rev. C. P. CROUTH, D.D., L. L. D., Charles H. GROSS to Mrs. Josephine C. FRY, only daughter of W. H. CASSADAY, Esq., formerly of this county.

Died: July 23, 1879, Albert Lewis, infant son of Edward L. and
Mary D. WREN, of Fairfax county, aged 6m 3d.
Died: At her residence, a few miles south of Leesburg, on Monday,
the 21st of July 1879, Mrs. Margaret A. ELGIN, widow of the
late Ignatius ELGIN, in the 68th year of her age.
Last week the family of Capt. Daniel DODSON, of Petersburg,
consisting of himself, wife and five daughter, partook of ice
cream, prepared by the family, all of who were poisoned by its
use. Mr. DODSON died two days after, and two of the
daughters, at last accounts, were still quite ill.

Thursday, 14 August 1879   Vol. XXIV, No. 9

Married: On the 1st of August, 1879, at the residence of Mr. Wm.
BARTON, near Unison, by Rev. J. B. LAKE, Miss Amanda A.
MOORE to John A. HESS.
Married: August 6th, at the Parsonage of the M. E. Church,
Leesburg, by the Rev. Wm. H. FORSYTH, Millard M.
ATTWELL to Miss M. E. MILLER, all of Loudoun.
Died: At the residence of her Aunt, in St. Louis, Mo., Friday the 8th
instant, Rosalie, daughter of R. B. McCORMICK. Buried at
Middleburg, Va. Aug. 13th.
Died: On the 25th of July, at Langley, Fairfax county, in the 24th
year of his age, after a protracted illness, of consumption,
Chas. L. SKINNER, recently of Loudoun county.
Died: At the residence of her father, William HORSEMAN, near
Farmwell, on the 4th of August 1879, Miss Sarah E.
HORSEMAN, in the 20th year of her age.
Mr. Beverly SANDERS, son of Maj. William C. SANDERS, died at
his father's residence near Goresville, on Saturday last, and
was buried in Union Cemetery, Leesburg on Monday. Mr. S.
have been living in Missouri for a number of years but owing to
ill health returned to his father's house about one month prior
to his death.
August Ct.: Wills of Lydia UNDERWOOD and Wm. TRIPLETT
admitted to probate. Administration granted G. P. HUNTER on
estate of Geo. WERKING.

Thursday, 21 August 1879   Vol. XXIV, No. 10

A gentleman from Philadelphia informs me that a granddaughter of
the late Hamilton McVEIGH, of Loudoun county, whose father
resides in Philadelphia, was thrown from a carriage in that city
a day or two ago and was killed. *Cor. Alexandria Gazette.*
Married: At the Parsonage of the M. E. Church, South, Leesburg,
Aug. 7, 1879, by Rev. H. H. KENNEDY, Mr. Thaddeus T.
PRESTON and Miss Ida C. MILBOURN, both of Loudoun.

Died: At his father's residence, Maj. Wilson C. SANDERS, Aug. 9th, Beverly SANDERS, in the 33d year of his age. The subject of this notice left home 12 years past, and after exploring the West to its fartherest boundaries, returned to Callaway county, Mo, where he became the Agent of the C. & A. Railroad at McCredie. *Fulton (Mo.) Telegraph* please copy.

Thursday, 28 August 1879   Vol. XXIV, No. 11

Died: At her residence near Philomont, August 4th, 1879, Mrs. Phoebe EWERS, in the 82nd year of her age.

Died: In this town, on the 16th inst., of cholera infantum, Annie Beulah RYON, daughter of Theodore and Annie B. RYON, aged 1y 10m 10d.

Abraham LAYMAN, a bachelor, aged 77 years, and Miss Ann LAYMAN, aged 13 years, both of Rockingham Co, Va were married on the bridge at Harper's Ferry, recently.

Thursday, 4 September 1879   Vol. XXIV, No. 12

Married: On Wednesday, July 30th 1879, at the Bingham House, Philadelphia, by the Rev. J. Richard BOYLE, pastor of Christ M. E. Church, James M. MOUNT, of Mountsville, Loudoun county, and Ann W., daughter of the late Samuel J. DOWNING, of Downingtown, Chester county, Pa.

Married: At "The Grove" near Farmwell on Tuesday morning, Sept. 2d, 1879, by Rev. R. T. DAVIS, Mr. Lyman W. SHEPHERD and Miss Mary, daughter of the late Thos. L. ELLZEY, all of Loudoun County.

Died: At Lincoln, in Loudoun County, Richard H. Corbin, son of Mahlon H. and Willie H. JANNEY, aged 7m 5d.

Died: Suddenly of heart disease at his residence near Middleburg, August 19th 1879, Benjamin DAVIS, in the 70th year of his age. May his large family of children and widow be comforted.

Mr. E. C. BROUN, for many years a leading merchant of this county, died at his home in Middleburg on Friday after a long and painful illness. Active member of the M. E. Church.

Died at Purcellville, on Tuesday afternoon, the 2d of September, 1879, Smith GREGG, one of the oldest citizens of Loudoun county. Mr. GREGG was born 26th of July 1798. He died at the ripe old age of 81y 38d. The grandfather of Smith GREGG, whose name was Stephen GREGG, moved with his family to Virginia from Chester or Bucks County, Pennsylvania, in November, 1770, and settled on the farm at the south end of Short Hill, where Harrison OSBURN now resides. He died in the year 1795 and was followed by son Thomas GREGG, the father of Smith, who lived for many years on the same farm, and raised a family of ten children, and on the night of the 26th of September 1826, both father and mother died, and were buried in the same grave at Goose Creek. Now another aged member of the family has gone, leaving only three living of the ten brothers and sister of Thomas GREGG's family.

Death of Edmond C. COLEMAN – a native of Leesburg, and a son of the late Ed. COLEMAN, but for many years a residence of Chicago, died at the boarding house of Mrs. Eugenia HOUGH, in this town, on Friday night, August 29th, 1879, of Bright's disease, in the 44th year of his age. Dying in the full communion of Catholic Church, his funeral took place from the Chapel in Leesburg on Sunday morning, Rev. Father LYNCH officiating. He leaves a widow and four children. His remains were interred in Union Cemetery.

Mr. Daniel G. SMITH, of this county, died at his residence near Charlottesville, on Tuesday morning last. The funeral services were held at the Methodist Episcopal church, in this place, on Wednesday at 10 a.m. He was the father of Professor Francis H. SMITH, of the U. of Va., Prof. E. B. SMITH, of Richmond College, and J. Howard SMITH, late representative of this county in the House of Delegates of Va. *Charlottesville Chronicle.* For many years an active citizen of Leesburg. He left here in 1853 for his new home in Albemarle, where he died on Tuesday the 26th inst., in the 79th year of his age.

Thursday, 11 September 1879   Vol. XXIV, No. 13

Married: At the Lutheran Parsonage, Lovettsville, September 2d, by Rev. P. H. MILLER, Mr. Samuel COOPER to Miss Barbara LEWIS.

Ct.: Wills of Edwin C. BROWN dec'd. Smith GREGG dec'd. were admitted to probate. Administration granted on the estates of Wm. S. OTLEY dec'd. and Sarah A. STEPHENS dec'd. Isaac W. BOBST, Minister of the Southern Church, licensed to celebrate rites of matrimony.

Chas. JEWETT son of Present JEWETT, of the Erie railway, died at Denver, Colorado, on Saturday last. The body was sent to Ohio. The deceased was a nephew of Mr. Joseph H. JEWETT, of Lincoln, in this county.

Sheriff CARRUTHERS received a dispatch from the authorities in Coshocton Co Ohio requesting him to look out for and arrest Chas. E. SMITH. The arrest was made on Wed. evening, near Lovettsville. About 15 years ago, Mr. Jas. W. SMITH removed from Loudoun and settled in Coshocton Co Ohio where he purchased a small farm, married a wife, and had five children, the eldest of whom is now 12 and the youngest 3 years old. A little more than a year ago, his brother, Chas. E. SMITH, also left Loudoun and removed to Coshocton, where he was employed by his brother James and lived in his family. On 10 Aug. last James took ill, dying within a day or two and was buried. A few days after his burial suspicions of foul play arouse, and his widow, Mary E. SMITH, and brother, Chas. E., were arrested, charged with having administered poison. Body was exhumed, but bore no outward signs of any wrong-doing, no post mortem exam was made. Charles left for Loudoun, but the grave was again opened and chemical analysis done. Mary was re-arrested. Charles says his brother died of typhoid fever.

Thursday, 18 September 1879   Vol. XXIV, No. 14

Mrs. Mary Louisa APPLE, died at the residence of her husband, Thomas APPLE, at the Limestone Mill, Loudoun county, on Thursday, the 28th of August, in the 57th year of her age.

Died: On the 3d of February, 1879, in San Buena Ventura, Mexico, Dr. Francis L. BRONAUGH, in his 42d year. He was a son of Dr. J. W. BRONAUGH, of Manchester, and was a native of Loudoun county, but had resided for many years in Mexico.

Died: On Saturday, Sept. 13th 1879, Lilly, daughter of George and Rosabell FRY, aged 3y 2m 21d.

Thursday, 25 September 1879   Vol. XXIV, No. 15

Married: On the 11th inst., in the Reformed church, at Lovettsville, by the Rev. H. St. J. RINKER, Mr. Samuel SMITH, to Miss Susan, dau. of the late Jacob WENNER, all of Loudoun co.

Married: On the 16th instant, on the bride at Harper's Ferry by Rev. J. A. McFADEN, T. H. EVERHART, to Miss Ida L. RITCHIE, both of Loudoun county.

Thursday, 2 October 1879   Vol. XXIV, No. 16

[no marriages or deaths]

Thursday, 9 October 1879   Vol. XXIV, No. 17

Married: At the Parsonage of the M. E. Church, South, Leesburg, on Tuesday morning, Oct. 7, 1879, by Rev. H. H. KENNEDY, Mr. Thos. H. NICHOLS and Miss Ruth H. NICHOLS, all of Loudoun.

Married: By Rev. J. A. HAYNES, in Middleburg, on the 30th ulto., Mr. Richard B. TANNER and Miss Mollie M. BEALES, both of Loudoun.

Married: At Grace Church, Berryville, on Thursday the 25th of September 1879, by the Rev. P. P. PHILLIPS, assisted by the Rev. Arthur P. GRAY, Rev. Wm. B. LEE, Rector of Emanuel church, Rapidan, Culpeper county, and Miss S. Jannie B.

KOWNSLAR, eldest daughter of the late Dr. Randolph and Mrs. E. S. KOWNSLAR, of Clarke county.

Died: On the 3rd inst., at the residence of her dau., Mrs. KLINE, near Snickersville, Sarah W. HUDSPETH, in her 84th year.

Died at "Resting," Loudoun county, Sunday Sep. 28th, 1879, in the 41st year of her age, Mrs. Eliza JOHNSON, wife of Col. V. M. JOHNSON, and daughter of L. A. BOGGS, Esq. of Spottsylvania.

Died: At his residence near Lincoln, on the 5th of Sept. 1879, Wm. S. OTLEY, in the 63d year of his age.

Mr. John J. CHANCELLOR, cattle dealer of Baltimore, formerly of Middleburg, died Saturday at the Eutaw House. He was unmarried. He was a cousin of Dr. C. W. CHANCELLOR, present of the second branch city council.

Thursday, 16 October 1879   Vol. XXIV, No. 18

Rev. Samuel CORNELIUS, at one time pastor of the old M. E. Church, in Leesburg, died at his home in Baltimore last Thursday.

County Ct.: Administration granted on estates of Ignatius ELGIN dec'd., Mary A. ELGIN dec'd., Phineas OSBURN dec'd., Martin H. SWART dec'd., Wm. GREGG dec'd., Phebe EWEN dec'd. Will of John H. CRIM dec'd. admitted to probate.

We learn of a serious misfortune that befell Mr. Daniel FOUSCHE (a brother-in-law of Mr. L. W. S. HOUGH) formerly of this county, but now living on his farm about 10 miles from Petersburg Illinois. On Sunday 5th of Oct his house cause fire and was entirely consumed. There was nobody at home except Mrs. FOUSCHE and her mother, Mrs. HOUGH, the latter now 84 and confined to her bed quite sick. They both got out. In the excitement Mr. FOUSCHE fell and broke his leg.

In Cincinnati, Ohio, Oct. 8, at St. John's Protestant Episcopal Church, by Bishop JAGGAR, the Rev. J. G. KINSOLVING, rector of the church, to Miss Grace JAGGAR, sister of Bishop JAGGER. ...

Died: Near Unison, on the 4th of October 1879, after a short illness, Mattie V. HAWS, daughter of Turner H. and Maria C. GALLEHER, aged 23 years.

Thursday, 23 October 1879   Vol. XXIV, No. 19

Married: Oct. 15, 1879, in the Methodist Episcopal Church in Warrenton, by Rev. W. G. HAMMOND, Mr. Samuel S. SHAFER, formerly of Leesburg and Miss Cordelia B. PATTIE, of Warrenton, daughter of Wm. A. PATTIE, Esq.

Married: At the residence of the bride's father on the 15th of October, 1879, by Rev. T. B. SHEPHERD, Mr. James W.

ROGERS, of Missouri, formerly of Loudoun county, and Miss Georgie M. COLSTON, daughter of Robert A. COLSTON, Esq. of Clarke county, Va.

Died: At his residence near Bolington, on Sunday, October 5th, 1879, after a protracted and painful illness of many months, John H. CRIM, Esq. in the 64th year of his age.

Death of John L. RINKER – at his home in Leesburg on Saturday last, October 18th, in his 71st year. On Sunday afternoon his remains were laid away in Union Cemetery. On yesterday evening, just as twilight was fading into starry night, the wedding of Mr. Samuel SHAFER and Miss Delia PATTIE, dau. of Wm. A. PATTIE, Esq., was celebrated at the Methodist Episcopal church, Rev. Dr. HAMMOND officiating. *Warrenton Solid South, 16th*.

Thursday, 30 October 1879   Vol. XXIV, No. 20

Married: In St. James' Episcopal Church, Leesburg, on Wednesday morning, Oct. 29th, 1879, by Rev. Dr. R. T. DAVIS, Mr. Robert S. VANDEVANTER and Miss Laura B., daughter of Dr. R. H. EDWARDS, all of Loudoun county.

Married: At. 10 o'clock a.m. on Tuesday, October 21, 1879, at the residence of Lewis HAWLING, Esq., Loudoun county, by the Rev. R. T. DAVIS, Silas SHELBURNE to Emily BALMER, daughter of Thomas BALMER, of Powhatan county, Va.

Married: On the 22d inst., at the Episcopal Church in Gordonsville, Va, by Rev. Arthur JOHNS, assisted by the Rev. Mr. JOYCE, C. Powell NOLAND, of Middleburg, to Rosalie, youngest daughter of R. Barton HAXALL, Esq.

Married: At 10 a.m., October 22d, 1879, at the residence of the bride's father, by Rev. H. H. KENNEDY, Mr. J. Beverly CRISSEY and Miss Bertie A. SILCOTT, all of Loudoun.

Married: At Bethel Evangelical Lutheran Church, Tankerfield, Oct. 9th, 1879, by Rev. P. H. MILLER, Mr. Burr F. SNOOTS to Miss Sarah A. MOCK.

Married: By the same at Lovettsville, Oct. 15th, 1879, Mr. Charles J. TURNER, of Mo. and Miss Rosa M. GARDNER, of Loudoun county.

Married: On the 7th, near Ebenezer church, by Rev. Wm. H. FORSYTH, Daniel L. BAGENT to Miss E. M. RILEY, all of Loudoun county.

Married: By the same, on the 16th inst., at Bolington, at the residence of the bride's father, Mr. Silas WOOLFORD to Miss Dora D. KALB, of Loudoun county.

Died: At the residence of his parents, near Leesburg, Oct. 12th, 1879, Legrand, infant son of Benjamin D. and Sallie SURVICK, aged 1 week.

Died: On Thursday, 23d inst., Mrs. Susan A. COMPHER, daughter of Henry and Christina FAWLY, and wife of John COMPHER, dec'd., aged 69y 28d. Rev. P. H. MILLER preacher her funeral service Friday afternoon. Her remains were laid in the Lutheran burying ground at Lovettsville.

Last Thursday, Samuel J. ROBINSON, colored, was committed to jail of this county charged with having shot another colored man, Edward THOMAS, on Wednesday. The shooting took place near Lincoln. ... P. S. THOMAS has since died.

Near Barbee's Cross Roads, in Fauquier Co, last Sat., Jacob STRIBLING, colored, killed Nelson PRIEST, colored, by striking him on the head with a wagon standard. STRIBLING is in jail at Warrenton. Judge KEITH adjourned his Court last Thursday and repaired to the death bed of a favorite nephew, Wm. Steptoe KEITH, who died at the home of his parents in Warrenton, of Bright's disease, on Friday last, in his 24th year. Mr. KEITH was a graduate of the Va. Military Institute and for a time teacher at Bethel Academy and deputy in the office of the Clerk of the Circuit Court of Fauquier. Judge KEITH returned to Leesburg on Tuesday and resumed his Court.

Last Monday night Flavius LEVENBURG, a young colored man living with his father, Elwood LEVENBERG, at Hamilton, returned home at a rather late hour, when some angry words ensued between the father and son resulting in a slith scuffle. The old man gasping for breath, died. The cause of death was natural causes, probably from disease of the heart.

Thursday, 6 November 1879   Vol. XXIV, No. 21

Married: In San Antonio, Texas, by Rev. T. J. JOHNSTON, October 27, 1869, Lt. J. T. MARSTELLER, U.S. Army, son of the late Dr. C. C. MARSTELLER, of Virginia, to Susie ORD, niece of General ORD, U.S. Army and daughter of the late Major ORD, U.S. Army.

Died: At "Ivon," near Leesburg, Monday Nov. 3, 1879, Bowie, youngest child of A. M. and Mary CHICHESTER, aged about three years.

Died: Near Ripon, in Jefferson county, on Tuesday morning, October 28th, Mrs. Martha E. WHITMORE, wife of Samuel R. WHITMORE, aged about 26 years.

Mrs. Mary HAVENNER, wife of R. H. HAVENNER, Esq., died at his residence on Prince street today. Mr. H. had been ill for several months. *Alex. Gazette.* The remains of Mrs. HAVENNER were brought to Farmwell Station, where they were interred on Friday last. Native of this county.

Thursday, 13 November 1879   Vol. XXIV, No. 22

Married: At Upperville, Nov. 5th, 1879, by Rev. L. H. CRENSHAW, Mr. Christian N. SAUNDERS to Miss Annie B. MYERS, daughter of William MYERS, Esq., all of Loudoun County.

Married: At Trinity Church, Baltimore, Nov. 6th, by Rev. George A. LEAKIN, Mr. Chas. T. BIRKBY, of Leesburg, to Miss Mary E., daughter of Mr. Thomas SHAFFAR, of Baltimore City.

Mr. Aaron DAILY, whose fall from a horse we noticed last week, died on Sunday, never having entirely recovered consciousness. Mr. D. was in about the 74th year of his age. He was buried in Union Cemetery on Tuesday.

County Ct.: Wills of John W. WENNER dec'd., Lydia J. HOLLINGSWORTH dec'd., Sarah W. HUDSPETH dec'd., John L. RINKER dec'd., and Aaron DALEY dec'd. were admitted to probate. Estate of Ellwood LEVENBURY committed to Sheriff. Olevia J. SMALE appointed guardian of Emma C. and Mary M. SMALE. Benj. BRIDGES Jr. appointed guardian of Wm. A. HAVENNER.

Thursday, 20 November 1879   Vol. XXIV, No. 23

Married: Nov. 12, 1879, at Parsonage M. E. Church, South, in Leesburg, by Rev. H. H. KENNEDY, Mr. Peter SMITH and Miss Eliza CORNEL, both of Loudoun county.

Married: Nov. 12, 1879, at parsonage M. E. Church, South, in Leesburg, by Rev. H. H. KENNEDY, Mr. Jos. Edwin BROWN and Miss Gertrude A. TILLETT, both of Loudoun county.

Married: On the 4th inst., at the residence of Mr. SWANK, near Berlin, by the Rev. E. SMITH, John W. SWANK, of Maryland, to Miss Elizabeth V. SHAFER, of Loudoun county.

Married: On the 5th inst., 1879, at the Methodist Protestant Parsonage, in Frederick, by Rev. J. Earle MALOY, Chas. H. BELL [BALL] to Miss Jane KEYS, both of Loudoun county.

Died: In New York City, at 7 o'clock on the morning of Monday, November 17th, 1879, of cancer, Mrs. Jane A. BUSSARD, wife of Mr. O. M. BUSSARD, of this county, in her 40th year.

Capt. Ellis L. PRICE died at his residence on Prince St, near St. Asaph St, about 9 o'clock last night. He was about 67 years of age. He was the father of Capt. Mark L. PRICE, of the W & O RR, and Mr. E. F. PRICE, Deputy Tax Collector. *Alex. Gazette of Saturday.*

Thursday, 27 November 1879   Vol. XXIV, No. 24

Married: At the residence of the bride's father, Nov. 18th, by Rev. John WOOLF, Miss Lucy R. HIBBS and Mr. Wm. E. BROUN, all of Loudoun.

Married: At the residence of the bride's mother, Nov. 19th, 1879, by Rev J. WILLIS, Mr. J. N. KALB, of Washington D.C, and Miss Bettie A. BUHRMAN, of Frederick Co., Va.

Married: By Rev. J. A. HAYNES, on the 20th instant, at the residence of the bride's mother, Mr. Preston M. BROWNING, of Loudoun co., to Miss Tacey L. FLETCHER, of Fauquier co.

Died: At Woodgrove, in this county, on Thursday night, Nov. 25th, 1879, after a long and painful illness, Mrs. Eliza R. BEARD, widow of Lewis BEARD dec'd., and daughter of the late Dr. Jonathan HEATON, in her 64th year. Interment in Union Cemetery, Leesburg today (Thursday) at about one o'clock.

Died: In Leesburg, on Tuesday night, Nov. 25th, 1879, after an illness of several months, Mrs. Elizabeth McCABE, wife of Mr. John McCABE, in the 75th year of her age.

Died: Wednesday, Nov. 19, 1879, at the residence of her husband, three miles west of Leesburg, after a protracted and painful illness, Mrs. Laura E. T. Carr, consort of Col. Wm. F. PHILLIPS, Sixth Auditor to the U. S. Treasury.

Died: At the residence of his father, near Leesburg, on Thursday night last, John Z. AULT, in the 12th year of his age, eldest son of John W. AULT.

Mrs. Elizabeth McCABE, mother of C. P. McCABE, late member of the House of Delegates, died in this town on Tuesday night, at the advance age of 75 years.

Thursday, 4 December 1879   Vol. XXIV, No. 25

Married: Nov. 27, 1879, at the residence of the bride's father, Loudoun Co., by Rev. H. H. KENNEDY, Mr. William W. ORRISON, and Miss Lilla SWART, both of Loudoun county.

Married: At the residence of the bride's father, November 26th, 1879, by Rev. L. H. CRENSHAW, Mr. Oscar F. LITTLETON to Miss Mary GAVER, daughter of John C. GAVER, Esq., all of Loudoun County.

Married: Mr. Richard JAMES and Miss Laura EWERS were married on Tuesday evening, Nov. 25th, at White's Ferry, by the Rev. Mr. FORSYTHE.

Married: At the residence of the bride's father, Nov. 18th, by Rev. John WOOLF, Miss Lucy H. HIBBS and Mr. Wm. E. BROUN, all of Loudoun.

Married: by Rev. J. A. HAYNES, on the 20th instant, at the residence of the bride's mother, Mr. Preston M. BROWNING, of Loudoun co., to Miss Tacey L. FLETCHER, of Fauquier co.

Married: On Tuesday, November 25th, 1879, at St. Paul's Church, Woodville, Virginia, by Rev. E. W. HUBARD, Frank Patterson BERKLEY, of Fairfax, to Mamie Lewis, daughter of J. W. GEORGE, Esq., of Rappahannock.

Thursday, 11 December 1879   Vol. XXIV, No. 26

Married: At the residence of the bride's parents, Dec. 1st, 1879, by Rev. E. J. TRUSSEL, of Washington, John T. PALMER, of Loudoun county, to Miss Sarah E. WENZEL, of Alexandria, Va.

Died: At "Boxwood," October 22nd, 1879, Mrs. Sarah CRUZEN, widow of the late Jacob CRUZEN, aged 76 years.

County Ct.: J. P. HICKMAN qualified as Admr. of estate of Susan COMPHER dec'd. Estates of Abram YOUNG, Chas. OFFUTT and Fenton M. OFFUTT committed to the Sheriff. Will of Mrs. Eliza R. BEARD dec'd. admitted to probate.

Thursday, 18 December 1879   Vol. XXIV, No. 27

Death of George C. SANFORD – Monday morning train brought remains of Geo. C. SANFORD, son of Wm. L. SANFORD, Esq., of this county, who died at the University of Virginia on Saturday in his 19th year. Third son that the bereaved father has lost while off at College. The remains were brought to Leesburg, taken to the Episcopal Church, and laid to rest at Union Cemetery.

U. of Virginia, Dec. 13 – George Compton SANFORD, a student from Loudoun County, died at the infirmary this morning at 11 o'clock from inflammation of the stomach. His brother is a student.

Married: At Christ Church, near Goresville, on Wednesday morning, Dec. 17th, 1879, by Rev. S. S. WARE, Mr. George M. GRAYSON and Miss Bessie, daughter of Dr. N. G. WEST, all of Loudoun.

Married: At Glen Welby, Fauquier county, the resident of the bride's father, Wednesday Dec. 10th, 1879, by the Rev. John MAGILL, Robert BEVERLY Jr. to Richardetta E., daughter of Major R. H. CARTER.

Married: At half past one o'clock, on Thursday morning, Dec. 12th 1879, at Goff's Hotel, Frederick City, Md, by Rev. Dr. LEECH, Mr. Harry WHITZELL and Miss Hattie, second daughter of Mr. Chas. P. McCABE, all of Leesburg.

Married: In the Church of the Holy Trinity, Philadelphia, on Tuesday, the 9th instant, by the Right Rev. G. W. PETERKIN, D.D., of West Virginia, assisted by the Rev. Francis D. LEE, Dr. Edmund I. LEE to Mary, daughter of Chas. SMITH, Esq. of that city.

Married: In Baltimore, on the 9th instant, at the residence of the bride's father, by the Rev. J. C. BACKUS, D.D., and Rev. F. H. KERFOOT, Chester Backus TURNBULL and Annie Stewart, daughter of Edward T. NORRIS.

Married: At the residence of the bride's mother, Richmond, Va., on Wednesday, Nov. 19th, by Rev. H. S. KEPLER, D.D., W. Benton WILMARTH, of Loudoun county, and Ella May VANDEVANTER.

Married: Dec. 9th 1879 at half past four o'clock, p.m., at the residence of Mr. E. M. SPILMAN, by the Rev. Father DONAHUE, Mr. Robt. R. CAMPBELL and Miss May V. MOSBY, eldest daughter of Col. John S. MOSBY.

Married: At "Mount Beulah," the residence of the bride's parents, Dec. 9th, 1879, by the Rev. S. M. ATHEY, Mr. William F. WHALEY, of Fairfax county, to Miss Orra V., eldest daughter of Mr. J. S. PALMER, near Aldie.

Married: December 11, near Hillsboro, by Rev. W. H. WILSON, Wm. VIRTZ to Miss Elizabeth HOWSER, all of Loudoun co.

Married: Same day, by the same at the residence of bride's mother, Jonathan COGAL to Miss Lucy E. DERRY, both of Loudoun county.

Died: Mrs. Annie STONE, at her residence near Lovettsville, on Wednesday, Dec. 3d, 1879, in the 47th year of her age.

Thursday, 25 December 1879   Vol. XXIV, No. 28

Col. H. B. TYLER died at his residence at Fairfax Court House, Va, Wednesday night, of general debility. The Colonel was about 82 years of age. He was the brother of the late Judge John Webb TYLER, and was for years major of the U.S. Marine Corps. He leaves a widow and nine children.

Married: At St. James' Church, Leesburg, by Rev. R. T. DAVIS, D.D., on Thursday, Dec. 18th, Mr. J. H. HOFFECKER Jr. of Wilmington, Del., and Miss Bettie W. MEAD.

Married: Dec. 18, 1879, by Rev. W. H. WILSON at the residence of the bride's father, in Clarke Co., Mr. Chas. W. MILLER, of Loudoun Co., to Miss Amelia BRABHAM, of Clarke Co.

Married: At the residence of the bride's father, near Philomont, on the 16th inst., according to the Friends ceremony, W. Henry BROWN to Maria P. T. NICHOLS.

Married: At the M. E. Parsonage in Hamilton on Tuesday, Dec. 16th by the Rev. A. A. P. NEAL, Mr. Thos. T. TAYLOR to Miss Adelaide HALEY, both of Loudoun.

Married: On Tuesday, 16th inst., at the residence of the bride's father near the Grove, Mr. Samuel C. PRESGRAVES to Miss Annie M. NIXON, Rev. A. A. P. NEAL officiating.

Married: Dec. 16th, 1879 at Exeter, the residence of the bride's parents, by the Rev. S. S. WARE, Mr. Charles TITUS to Miss Ginnie, daughter of Thomas BURCH, Esq., all of Loudoun.

Married: Dec. 17th at the Parsonage of the M. E. Church in Leesburg, by Rev. Wm. H. FORSYTH, Mr. Samuel H. LIGHTFOOT to Miss Mollie R. NELSON, both of Loudoun.

Married: In Leesburg, December 18th, 1879, by Rev. J. F. CANNON, Mr. William CROSS and Miss Annie V. RYON.

Married: At Bethel, on the 10th inst., by Rev. Wm. H. FORSYTH, Randolph E. BARNHOUSE to Miss Lillie E. FRY, all of Loudoun.

Married: At Christ Church, near Goresville, at 3 o'clock on Tuesday afternoon, December 23d, 1879, by Rev. S. S. WARE, J. W. BOWIE and Mamie, second daughter of Dr. N. G. WEST, all of this county.

Mrs. Eliza WEST, wife of Dr. George WEST of Petersburg, Md [mother of Dr. N. G. WEST, of Loudoun county] died at her home on Friday of last week at the advanced age of 73 years.

St. James' Episcopal Church presented a beautiful appearance last Thursday morning of the marriage of Mr. J. H. HOFFECKER Jr., a young lawyer of Wilmington, Delaware, and Miss Bettie W. MEAD, of Leesburg. At 11 o'clock the bridal party entered the building in order: Miss Lizzie WORSLEY and Mr. H. Clay CHAMBLIN; Miss Alice HARRISON and Mr. __ STAPLER, of New York; Miss Mollie HOUGH and Dr. W. V. GIDDINGS; Miss __ GIDDINGS and Mr. Henry HARRISON; Miss Lizzie CROSS and Mr. Frank HOFFECKER, of Wilmington, Del.; Miss Florence HOFFECKER and Mr. Henry J. MEAD, followed by the bride and groom. The ceremony was conducted by Rev. Dr. DAVIS.

INDEX

ABBOTT
  Charles D., 251
  Joseph, 240, 251
  Mary, 240, 251
  Richard T., 240
ABEL
  Christopher, 16
  Geo., 16
ABELL
  Wm. A., 298
ACHER
  A. D., 276
  David, 276
ACHERS
  A. D., 195
  Ella R., 195
  Frank, 195
ACLEBERGER
  Mary E., 182
ACRES
  Robt. R., 250
ADAMS
  A. S., 165, 187
  Alice L., 278
  America, 259
  Amos S., 195
  B. F., 87
  Benjamin F., 129
  C. B., 278
  Charles, 259
  Clinton, 264
  Dorcas, 43
  Ellen V., 277
  Frank, 231
  Geo. W., 155, 192
  Hattie R., 195
  James, 51, 59, 316
  Jane, 51
  Jane A., 306
  Jno. A., 187
  Maria V., 87
  Mary E., 105
  Mary L., 187
  Richard, 57, 299
  Samuel R., 57
  W. H., 25
  Wm. F., 56
ADIE
  Gustavia B., 224
  Julia H., 224
  Lewis, 75
  Mary, 56
ADRAIN
  John M., 82
AISQUITH
  Edward, 75
  Mary V., 264
  R. M., 264
AKERS
  Annie M., 311
  John, 305
ALDER
  Elizabeth, 66
  James, 27
  John I., 27
  Johnny, 26
  Latimer, 186
  Mary J., 27
  Maurice J., 274
  Nathan N., 66
  Rosanna A., 66
  Sally, 27
ALDRIDGE
  Andrew, 211
  Ellen, 146
  Harriet W., 211
  J. West, 183
  John, 146, 233, 307
  John., 232
  Mary E., 232, 233
ALEXANDER
  Bettie M., 5
  Charlton, 113
  Daniel G., 89
  Ella H., 238
  Emma, 242
  Geo. W., 238
  I. T., 122
  John, 242
  John H., 192, 242
  Martha E., 282
  Noah S., 113
  Robt. W., 282
  Sarah C., 122
  Thomas, 266
  W. F., 48
ALFRED
  Aaron E., 192
ALLDER
  Abraham, 7
  George F., 7
  George H., 7
  Jane A., 7
  Jas., 297
  John E., 7
  Lydia, 297
  Maggie J., 308
  Nathan, 7
  Rosannah, 7
ALLEN
  Edward C., 188
  Emma H., 196
  Geo. H., 133
  Geo. Henry, 1
  Israel, 87
  Jacob, 188
  John F., 121, 132
  Martha, 47
  Mildred E., 262
  Miller B., 264
  Samuel C., 8
  Susan, 188
  Tiphen W., 95
  Virginia, 87
  Wyatt, 206
ALLENDER
  Jacob W., 245
  John, 66
ALLISON
  Aramanta, 219
  Frances, 176
  Margaret R., 220
ALLMOND
  Mary G., 135
  Phebe H., 135
  Thomas W., 135
ALLNUT
  Rebecca D., 33
ALLNUTT
  B. A., 232
  James A., 169
  James N., 232
  Jas. M., 265
  Mary L., 265
  Robt. G., 10
ALSTON
  M. S., 228
AMBLER
  Charles E., 37
  Chas. E., 227

INDEX

Martha, 248
Susan E., 45
Thomas, 217
AMES
  Will C., 54
  Wm. C., 304
ANDERSON
  Annie E., 214
  Chas., 178
  E. Norah, 247
  Emily, 64
  James A., 268
  Lavinia P., 8
  Mary, 139
  Robert O., 262
ANKERS
  A. E., 313
ANSLEY
  J. A., 189
  Lou S., 189
APPEL
  Elizabeth C., 125
  Mary, 116
  Mary A., 116
  Thomas, 116
APPELL
  Mason, 133
  Matilda A., 80
  Sophia, 80
APPLE
  Mary L., 320
  Thomas, 320
APSEY
  Virginia, 167
ARCHER
  Julia N., 298
ARMISTEAD
  Cecelia, 202
  Lewis, 202
ARNETT
  Ann, 201
  C. Elizabeth, 66
  Eliza M., 80
  Frank, 201
  Louisa C., 101
  Samuel, 201
  Theodore J., 199
  William, 168
  Wm., 101
ARNOLD
  Anna M., 231
  Annie, 148

Cornelia Y., 240
Emma, 39
Mahlon D., 310
Martha J., 61
Mary C., 60, 265
Thos. C., 257
ARTHER
  Lewis, 74
ARUNDEL
  Joseph, 138
ARUNDLE
  Honor, 126
  Jno. W., 141
  Joseph, 126, 161
  Sarah A., 161
ASH
  Martha S., 10
ASHBY
  A. M., 102
  Austin O., 99
  Blanche, 170
  F. P., 313
  Geo., 195
  John J., 229
  Mary A., 277
  Nimrod T., 208
  Presley, 219
  Sam., 208
  Samuel T., 170
  Turner, 57
  Turner M., 102
ASHFORD
  F. A., 143
  Julia, 120
ASHLY
  Alice, 285
  Mary, 285
  Thompson, 285
ASHTON
  Ann A., 231
  Ellen, 299
ASHWORTH
  Elizabeth, 39
  Granville H., 39
ASSHETON
  Evylyn, 270
ATHEY
  Alice, 194
  Benedict W., 84
  Elizabeth M., 140
  Isabella, 94, 246
  J. M., 123

John M., 123, 194
Lucy A., 208
M. W., 286
Mary E., 194, 246
Mollie A., 123
S. M., 189
Thomas W., 94
W. W., 246, 286
William W., 94
Wm. H., 300
ATKINSON
  James W., 217
ATTWELL
  Ewell, 36
  Harriet A., 257
  Hattie R., 195
  Mary, 165, 187, 195
  Millard M., 317
  Ratie J., 115
ATWELL
  Caroline, 308
  Carrie V., 148
  Harriet E., 308
  Harriett H., 252
  Hattie R., 165
  John Y., 148
  R. M. J., 148, 308
  Sarah E., 45
  Thomas H., 252
AULT
  John W., 325
  John Z., 325
  Mary J., 68
AUSTIN
  Edward, 274
  Georgeanna, 68
  Jane C., 274
AVARD
  Thos. S., 293
AVIS
  John, 17, 269
  Martha E., 44
  Sarah E., 17
  William, 44
AWSLEY
  Henry, 306
  Poins, 306
  Thos., 306
AXLINE
  David E., 244
AYERS
  Chas., 252

John G., 153
Sue, 196
AYRE
　Geo. H., 158
　Geo. S., 147, 155
　Jennie C., 281
　John G., 257
　Mary V., 216
　Thos., 147, 155
　Thos. E., 187
　Wm., 191
AYRES
　C. R., 31
　Laura, 30
　Martha C., 84
　Mary, 75
　Massie V., 195
　T. S., 30
　William H., 76

BACKHOUSE
　Catharine M., 178
　George, 46, 178
　Sarah, 46
BAGBY
　George, 94
　Lewis C., 94
BAGENT
　Daniel L., 322
　Elizabeth, 315
BAILY
　Bettie A., 232
BAIN
　Wm. I., 130
BAKER
　Beatrice, 118
　Carl, 200
　Charles W., 217
　Edward M., 280
　Elizabeth, 280
　Emma, 183
　Geo. H., 194
　George W., 65
　Henry M., 118, 198
　John, 23, 57
　John C., 87
　John S., 200
　John W., 223
　Margaret E., 228
　Mary C., 252
　Mary R., 235
　R. L., 57, 74

Sarah, 200
Sarah J., 112
Sarah R., 74
T. Richard, 132
William H., 4
Wm. A., 26
Wm. B., 183
BALCH
　Thomas B., 282
BALDWIN
　Benton H., 278
　Cornelius, 74
　Julia, 200
　M. H., 57
BALENGER
　Sallie, 87
BALES
　David, 61
　Hannah E., 61
　Josephene E., 146
　Mary, 127
　Mortimore, 61
　Sarah E., 61
　William, 171
　Wm., 222
BALL
　A. M., 49
　Albert, 92
　Annie V., 275
　Charles, 231
　Charles H., 324
　Chas. H., 77
　Dabney, 282
　Elizabeth, 39
　George W., 58, 60
　Henrietta, 39
　Henry, 200
　Henry A., 39, 80, 121
　John L., 220
　John T., 107
　Kate E., 121
　Lucy C., 102
　M. Dulany, 40
　Margaret A., 74
　S. A., 182
　Susan, 200
　Susan A., 121
　Warring, 220
　William, 220
　William E., 233
BALLARD
　J. N., 191

John M., 201
Laura, 201
BALLENGER
　Carrie B., 217
　Edgar, 146
　Frances A., 68
　Ginnie C., 295
　Isaac, 304
　Martha, 83
　Martha E., 226
　Mary E., 160
　Troy, 18
BALMER
　Emily, 322
　Thomas, 322
BALTHIS
　Mollie, 168
BANCROFT
　? W., 126
　Carrie D., 126
BANEY
　John J., 115
BANTZ
　Fannie M., 96
BARBEE
　George T., 216
BARBER
　Andrew J., 96
　Carrie M., 294
　Mary A., 96
　R. T., 294
BARBOUR
　John S., 62
　Susan, 215
BARKER
　Louise, 22
　M. M., 85
　Rebecca A., 130
　S. A., 279
　S. B., 130
　S. W., 279
　Willie M., 4
BARNES
　Lizzie G., 37
BARNEY
　Mariah, 24
BARNHOUSE
　Randolph E., 328
BARR
　Adam, 47
　George W., 30
　Mary J., 47

BARRETT
  Boyd, 237
  C. Boyd, 236
  Caroline M. E., 277
  J. Wade, 285
  John W., 183
  Mary C., 183, 285
  Nannie O., 125
  Rosalie A., 183
  W. F., 200
  Wm. F., 128, 234, 235
  Wm., F., 279
BARTLETT
  B. D., 260
  Harriet, 315
  J. E., 57
  John, 20
  John W., 30
  Joseph C., 34
  Sallie A. C., 260
  Sarah, 20
  Susan E., 258
BARTON
  Bailey R., 120
  Benj. C., 241
  C. Marshall, 22
  C. W., 279
  Charles W., 68
  Mary V., 82
  Sarah, 120
  Wm., 317
BASCUE
  Eliza, 61
  Virginia, 169
BASHAW
  Sallie, 153
BASS
  Margaret E., 34
BASSETT
  Ella M., 41
  Geo.W., 41
BATEMAN
  Thos., 259
BATTLE
  Netta, 298
BAUCHMAN
  Catharine C., 255
  Nellie, 273
BAUCKMAN
  Aquilla, 91
  Laura J., 205

BAUKMAN
  Susan A., 151
BAUMBACK
  Joseph, 133
BAYLEY
  Joseph, 306
BAYLISS
  Buckner, 186
  John H., 135
BAYLOR
  J. C., 172
  Kate K., 75
  R. W., 75
BAYLY
  Albert, 198
  John, 95
  M.Buckner, 83
  Robert, 203
BAYNE
  Henry T., 204, 262
  Phebe P., 262
BEACH
  Andrew J., 291
  Cath., 49
  Charles W., 311
  J. W., 70
  Jane, 291
  Jas. D., 232
  John G., 4
  Laura, 291
  Lula M., 316
  Mary B., 67
  Mason B., 101
  Mattie A., 235
  Presley, 316
  Sarah, 11
  Sarah J., 194
  Silas W., 230
BEACHAM
  Elizabeth M., 3
BEALE
  M. Kate, 25
BEALES
  Annie, 194
  Catharine E., 70
  Ernest E., 194
  Mattie E., 137
  Mollie M., 320
  R. D., 194
  Richard, 193
BEALL
  David, 205

  Maggie A., 205
  Mrs., 91
  Oliver C., 262
  Thomas P., 10
BEAMER
  D. W. W., 309
  G. H. T., 309
  Geo., 266, 268, 279
  Isabella, 170
  M. A. V., 309
  M. J. M., 309
  Michael, 220, 252
  Nelson, 178
  Rachel, 293
  Richard, 309
  S. R. W., 309
BEANS
  A. H., 29
  A. Humphrey, 314
  Aaron T., 176
  Amos, 142
  Ed. H., 203
  Elizabeth, 62
  Flavius, 80, 300
  Humphrey, 311
  Isaiah B., 62, 99
  Levi, 234
  Mahlon, 215
  Mary, 12
  Mary J., 88
  R. Albert, 99
  Sarah C., 314
  Uriah, 12
  William, 59
  Wm. H. H., 76
BEARD
  Amelia H., 34
  Eliza R., 325, 326
  J. C., 255
  Lawson G., 151, 152
  Lewis, 25, 325
BEATTY
  Albert, 224
  E., 15
  Mary, 281
  Wm. S., 250
BEATY
  Emma E., 210
  John, 148, 210
BEAUFORD
  Charles B., 219
  Fannie C., 219

The Mirror
INDEX
333

BEAVERS
  Delilah, 289
  Elijah S., 278
  G. H. M., 92
  Mrs., 112
  Sarah M., 312
  Thos. W., 105, 238
  Washington, 289
BECK
  Samuel J., 243
BECKTOL
  Mary L., 144
BEDINGER
  Caroline D., 263
  E. W., 236
  Henry, 2, 6, 83, 111, 263
  Mary, 111
  Virginia, 83, 190, 236
BEETLE
  Walter T., 150
BEEVERS
  Wm. L., 290
BEIMENDERFER
  Elizabeth, 209
BELL
  Amelia, 304
  Ann, 14
  Chas. C., 271
  Elizabeth S., 304
  Harriet, 14
  Henry, 27
  J. W., 97
  James, 108
  James M., 304
  James W., 87
  Lucinda, 44
  Mary, 14
  Mary E., 71
  Matilda, 14
  Theophilus, 66
BELT
  A. E., 220
  Alfred, 135, 220
  John L., 140
  John W., 100
  Maria, 147
  Maria L., 4
  Townsend, 193
BENEDICT
  Annie F., 271
  E. C., 290

  Erastus C., 241
  Maria W., 290
  Montgomery, 290
  Wm. B., 271
BENEDUM
  Charles E., 65
  Edmund, 309
  Eliza, 250
  Jas. H., 116
  Jimmie E., 250
  John E., 250
  Martena K., 65, 309
  Sarah E., 116
  Thomas A., 309
BENFORD
  Julian, 143
BENJAMIN
  Elizabeth, 311
  Geo. W., 251
  Harriet A., 256
  Henry W., 251
  John, 256
  Lavinia, 251
  Leler B., 257
  Lucretia V., 245
  Susan, 257
  William, 257
BENNET
  Sydnor, 181
BENNETT
  Elizabeth A., 234
  Hannah A., 81
  John H., 81
  Lizzie A., 235
  Mollie, 300
  Sydney, 60
  Sydnor, 81, 159, 234, 235
BENTLEY
  E. L., 80, 221
  Edgar L., 165, 310
  Helen, 165
  Kate L., 241
  Lillian J., 310
  Mamie E., 310
  Maria L., 241
  Nellie, 270
  R. M., 132, 134
  R. Mont., 241
  Robert, 138, 174
  Robt., 139
  Thomas, 19

BENTLY
  E. L., 215
  Edgar L., 210
  R. M., 34
BENTON
  Emma V., 229
  J. G., 19
BERKELEY
  Charles F., 59, 117
  Chas. F., 132
  Edmond, 246
  Edmund, 132
  Lavinia H., 246
  Norborne, 246
  Wm. N., 58
BERKER
  Samuel B., 128
BERKLEY
  Frank P., 325
BERNARD
  Alice M., 101
BERNAUGH
  J. W., 59
BERRY
  Arthur H., 193
  Emma J., 64
  George, 64
  Mary, 16
  R. T., 193
  Sandy, 9
BEST
  Albert J., 293
  Amanda, 238
  Amanda M., 293
  E. T., 233
  Enos T., 241
  James, 151
  Jane E., 107
  John W., 238
  Lydia R., 236
  Parmelia A., 241
  William, 121
BETHUNE
  J. B., 228
  Jenny, 228
BEUCHLER
  John R., 83
BEVERLEY
  Maria, 101
  Robert, 101
  William G., 288
BEVERLY

The Mirror
INDEX

Rebecca, 252
Robert, 158, 252, 326
Virginia, 158
William, 86, 98, 304
Wm., 183, 305
BEYER
  Sadie B., 130
BICKSLER
  John W., 99
  Mary C., 108
BIEBELHEISER
  B. C., 201
Biedler & Barrett, 236
BIGGS
  Ellen A., 281
  P. L., 281
BIGHAM
  Marshall M., 62
BINNS
  Chas., 180
  Elizabeth D., 17
BIRCH
  John, 120
BIRD
  Alexander, 155
  C. D., 273
  Charles D., 52
  Charles W., 52
  John, 52, 269
  John W., 83, 155
  Mary E., 52
  Mary M., 273
  Susan, 83
  Susan V., 155
  Willy, 83
BIRDSALL
  Benj., 57, 152
  Benjamin, 147, 278
  Eli W., 152
  Elizabeth, 57
  Mrs., 162
  Nathan J., 170
  Rachel H., 278
  Wm. G., 152, 220
BIRKBY
  Annie S., 13
  Chas. T., 175, 324
  Henry C., 64
  John M., 64
  Susan, 13
  Thomas W., 13
BIRKETT

William, 213
BIRKIT
  John, 112
  Mary, 112
  Mary C. A., 26
BITZER
  Catherine F., 97
  Geo. L., 118
  George L., 119
  Harmon, 97, 118
  Harry, 94
  John W., 224
BLACK
  George J., 7
  Lewis W., 22
  Sarah M., 7
BLACKWELL
  Elizabeth C., 6
  Jas., 6
BLAKE
  James H. W., 284
  John A., 36
BLAKELEY
  Eliza P., 65
BLAKELY
  Charles, 241
  Lacey, 241
BLAKEY
  Harriet, 85
  R. O., 85
BLANDHEIM
  John R., 135
BLINCOE
  John T., 101
BLINCOR
  Elizabeth, 249
BLONDEL
  Elizabeth R., 102
BLUNDELL
  Daniel W., 46
BLUNDON
  John F., 77
BOBST
  Isaac W., 319
BOCOCK
  Mazie F., 310
  Thos. S., 310
BOGER
  Ella V., 116, 175
  Jacob, 110
  John, 304
  Mary A., 254

Philip, 269
BOGGS
  Eliza, 321
  L. A., 321
BOGUE
  William L., 21
BOLAND
  Daniel, 185
  John, 59
  Sophia, 185
  William, 59
BOLEN
  Ezra, 55
BOLEY
  Sarah J., 215
BOLLING
  Charles C., 316
  Geo., 299
  Imogene, 316
BOLYN
  Bushrod T., 206
  Mary A., 311
  Summerfield, 105, 130
  T. M., 205
BOND
  Asa, 298
  Asa M., 302
  Sarah A., 302
  Thomas M., 149
BONHAM
  A. M., 16
BONNYCASTLE
  Ann M., 160
  Chas., 160
BOOKER
  Jas. M., 310
  S. G., 265
BOORAM
  William, 306
BOOTH
  M. C., 19
  Robert, 39
  Sarah E., 165
BORCHFORD
  Catherine, 22
BOREN
  Elizabeth, 5
BOSS
  Elizabeth, 65
  Elizabeth F., 9, 184, 185

The Mirror
INDEX
335

Elizabeth J., 9
Julia W., 145
Martena, 65
S. M., 9, 65, 145, 309
Samuel M., 184
BOTELER
 Alexander R., 39, 74
 Angelica, 39
 Helen M., 74
BOUGHIE
 Eliza, 60
BOULWARE
 Aubin L., 299
BOUYER
 Jacob E., 154
BOWEN
 Maranda, 14
 Martha C., 14
BOWERS
 Isabelle, 86
 John H., 128
BOWIE
 J. W., 328
 L. V., 225
 Mary Oden, 153
 Robert G., 59
 Wm. D., 153
BOWMAN
 J. B., 140
 Libbie, 140
 Robert, 191
 Robt. C., 192
BOYD
 Frank, 313
 Wm., 313
BOYE
 John, 57
BOYER
 Constace, 114
 Jacob E., 92
 John, 152
 Mollie J., 144
 Phillip, 57
 W. H., 152
BOYLE
 Cornelius, 228, 283
 Thos. M., 139
BOZZAL
 Geo. H., 100
 Virginia T., 100
BRABHAM
 Amelia, 327

Wm., 44
BRADEN
 Ann E., 303
 Elizabeth A., 307
 G. W., 274
 John A., 36
 Joseph A., 12
 Mary A., 70
 Mary E., 14, 297
 Noble S., 14, 70, 111, 113, 297
 Oscar, 59
 R. C., 36
 Rodney, 303
BRADFIELD
 A. J., 212, 287
 Abraham N., 7
 Ann, 7
 Bushrod O., 7
 Elizabeth, 15
 Francis M., 15
 Franklin, 7
 Geo. J., 278
 Geo. W., 35
 Jno. O., 255
 John, 7
 John K., 15
 John W., 7
 Joseph, 313
 Lewis K., 35
 M. E., 35
 Mary M., 115
 Nathan, 7
 Rosalie, 255
 Thomas D., 7
 William I., 222
BRADFORD
 Howard, 192
 John R., 296
 Lydia J., 106
BRADLEY
 Anon H., 71
 Henry, 192
 Sallie M., 71
BRADSHAW
 Lewis N., 37
 Thatcher S., 148
 Walter R., 101
BRADY
 Catharine, 112
 Robert A., 196
BRAIR

James, 306
BRAMHALL
 Blanco, 243
 Blanco W., 5
BRAMWELL
 Emma F., 148
BRANCH
 Henry, 186
 Melissa M., 186
BRAWNER
 Elizabeth, 18
 John E., 87
 John P., 267
 Laura P., 253, 292
 Mary J., 253
 P. D., 308
 Sarah E., 267
 W. A., 253
 Willie S., 292
 Wm. A., 292
 Wm. B., 21
BRECKENRIDGE
 Alexander P., 164
 Emily V., 30
 Nancy, 30
 Samuel, 30
BRECKINRIDGE
 Alex.N., 240
 Alexander P., 7
BREMERMAN
 Annie E., 79
BRENNER
 Fannie C., 159
 J. E., 159, 189
 John, 246
 John E., 54
BRENT
 A. J., 271
 George W., 230
 Lucy, 230
BREWER
 Robert H., 10
 William G., 132
BRICK
 Fannie E., 249
 S. R., 249
BRIDGES
 Benj., 172, 324
BRIGGS
 C. Cullin, 187
BRISCOE
 David S., 145

The Mirror
INDEX

BRISLAIN
  John, 287
BRISLAN
  John, 275
BRISLIN
  John, 283
BRISLINE
  Wm., 62
BRITTON
  J. Blodget, 191
BRODDUS
  Amanda, 32
  Wm. F., 32
BRODIE
  Nettie, 277
BRONAUGH
  Anne S., 226
  Francis L., 320
  J. W., 226, 320
  John C., 224
  John T., 31
  Joseph W., 302
  Martha M., 302
  P. H. W., 309
  S. M., 221
  Sallie, 104
  Sally, 130
  Wm. C., 309
BROOK
  James V., 98
BROOKE
  Ann A., 244
  James V., 244
  Jas. V., 312
  Mary E., 244
  William, 108
BROOKENS
  Jim, 54
BROOKS
  Ann E., 58
  Annie E., 179
  David, 149, 150, 152
  Earnest L., 58
  George W., 232
  Harriet, 149
  James, 160
  Philip, 75, 179
  Phillip, 58
  Robert, 252
  Rosabel, 182
  Rosie L., 179
  William H., 254
  Wm., 182
  Wm. H., 152
  Brooks & Son, 254
BROUN
  E. C., 19, 318
  Emma W., 36
  George, 36
  J. Conway, 15
  Wm. E., 324, 325
BROWN
  Albert O., 82, 136
  Aurelius P., 14
  B. Peyton, 106
  Benj., 17, 197
  Benjamin, 157, 172
  Ceretta J., 211
  David, 65, 312
  E. C., 244
  Ed. L., 232
  Edgar N., 308
  Edward, 312
  Edwin C., 319
  Ella, 172
  Fannie A., 66
  Fielding, 54
  Geo., 66
  Geo. H., 268
  Geo. W., 232
  Gerard C., 126
  Gulielma, 247
  J. W., 187
  James, 158
  James W., 13
  Jas., 176
  Jas. M., 245
  Jno., 141
  Jno. D., 312
  John, 134
  John H., 198, 200
  John J., 74
  John V., 98
  Jos. E., 324
  Jos. G., 99
  Joseph, 76
  Joseph W., 7
  M., 141
  Margaret, 76
  Maria, 176
  Martha S., 134
  Mary A., 119
  Mary H., 67
  Richard, 106
  Sadie E., 285
  Samuel N., 13, 119, 166
  Sarah A., 130
  Sarah E., 106, 157
  Sarah J., 158
  Susan A., 258
  Thomas J., 31
  Thos. J., 272
  Virginia, 124
  W. D., 124
  W. Henry, 327
  W. L., 155
  William, 76
  Wm., 65, 232
BROWNER
  Harrison, 50
BROWNING
  Preston M., 325
BRUBAKER
  Zechariah T., 227
BRUCE
  Wm. B., 174
BRYAN
  Charles A., 108
BRYANT
  Gregg, 315
  Lee, 315
  Wm. C., 179
BRYDO
  Robert, 141
BRYNE
  John M., 225
BUCHANAN
  Charles, 171
  Florence, 141
  James, 180
BUCKNER
  Ariss, 14
  B. H., 14
  Daniel H., 14
  Eliza A., 101
  Richard B., 101
BUDD
  Isaac D., 268
  J. D., 98
BUGGY
  Robt. E., 148
BUHRMAN
  Bettie A., 325
BUNDLE
  Thos., 216

BURCH
  Delia, 240
  Edgar F., 175
  Florence M., 95
  Ginnie, 327
  Jane, 25
  John L., 33
  Lewis D., 231
  Mary, 231
  Mary A., 128
  Thomas, 128, 240, 327
  Thomas F., 126
BURGESS
  B. F., 187
  Charles, 174
  Charles F., 131
  James W., 259
  Josephine, 316
  Margaret A., 84
  Martha, 259
  Mary E., 174
  William, 259
  Willie L., 174
BURGORYE
  John, 174
BURKE
  Benjamin, 15
  Florence J., 31
  Hattie C., 42
  J. D., 31
  Lucinda, 31
  Mary, 292
  Mary S., 229
  Mildred, 15
  R. S., 292
  Richard S., 261, 262
  Robert G., 167
  Sallie, 297
  Sallie C., 42
  William, 42
  Wm., 297
BURKET
  William E., 133
BURNS
  Caleb, 69
  Jane A., 69
  John, 198
  Nettie, 198
BURR
  Alverd, 222
  Charles N., 131

John R., 212
BURSON
  John, 315
  Mary, 205
BURTON
  Eugenie H., 157
  James H., 16, 157
  Virginia M., 157
BURWELL
  George H., 271
BUSKIRK
  Orra M., 91
  Wm. V., 91
BUSSARD
  Jane A., 324
  Martena W., 133
  O. M., 324
BUSSEY
  James H., 124
BUTLER
  Charles T., 31
  Jas. W., 262
  John H., 64
  Samuel, 306
BUTTS
  Calvin, 150
  Charles W., 170
  Edward A., 260
  Mary E., 170
  William, 120
BUXTON
  Juliann, 32
BYRD
  Courtney B., 38
  John W., 38
BYRNE
  A. C., 134
  Bettie, 278
  Jane E., 212
  Milton, 278

CABELL
  Annie B., 292
  Elizabeth C., 174
  P. Henry, 174
  Virginia L., 31
  Wm. D., 292
CABLE
  Jno. W., 89
CALDWELL
  Augusta T., 256
  Carrie L., 62

David, 6
Ella, 297
Jno. M., 256
Judge, 84
Mary G., 228
Mollie, 121
S. B. T., 72, 210, 297
T. M., 294
CALHOUN
  William, 15
CALLAHAN
  Eugene, 90
  George, 46
CALVERT
  George, 115
  J. S., 115
  Olevia J., 273
CAMERON
  Mary E., 5
  Samuel, 5
CAMP
  Ada B., 117
  E. C., 102
  Johnnie, 174
  Mary J., 116, 117, 174
  Mollie G., 116
  Thomas E., 116, 117, 174
CAMPBELL
  Alice C., 214
  Annabell, 160
  Antoinette A., 196
  James, 186
  James W., 12
  Jane C., 12
  John, 30, 48
  Mary E., 118
  Matha E., 118
  Michael, 58
  Robt. R., 327
  Samuel, 196
CANBY
  Samuel T., 142
  William H., 106
CANIFORD
  Maggie, 271
CANTWELL
  America I., 158
  Joseph T., 158
CAPERION
  Eliza J., 137

The Mirror
INDEX

Hugh, 137
Jennie, 137
CAPERTON
  Eliza J., 157
  Hugh, 157
CARLES
  John, 298
CARLISLE
  Albert, 44
  David, 128, 130
  James, 143
  Jas., 130
  Matilda, 99
  Robert C., 291
  Valinda, 237
  Wm., 113
CARLTON
  Ambrose, 79
  Helen F., 79
CARMACK
  Cost, 268
  Cost J., 248
  Ginnie, 268
CARMICHAEL
  John, 126
  William, 41
CARN
  Catharine M., 40
CARNES
  Daniel, 283
CARPENTER
  Marshall, 24
  Marshall W., 61
  Milton, 24
CARPER
  Ellen, 232, 233
  P. W., 274
  Philip, 303
  Philip W., 68
CARR
  Amanda V. L., 54
  Annie, 67
  David, 45, 149
  Isaac, 60
  John, 97
  Joseph, 57
  Josephus, 67
  Lewis N., 200
  Mary E., 97
  P. H., 215, 235
  Sallie, 54
  Thomas E., 98

Thos., 300
Thos. E., 57
CARRAWAY
  J. P., 172
CARRELL
  William C., 70
CARRICO
  Laura V., 173
CARRINGTON
  Helen M., 161
CARROLL
  John W., 195
  Miriam E., 7
  Patrick, 1
  Thomas W., 7
CARRUTHERS
  J. T., 254
  Jas. E., 229, 259
  John E., 70
  Sheriff, 319
  Thos. N., 70
  Wm., 254
CARSON
  Catharine, 79
  James H., 79
  William, 79
CARTER
  Annie, 278
  Annie E., 276
  B. G., 171, 211
  B. M., 228
  Chas. L., 4
  Edward L., 114
  Eli, 3
  Elizabeth, 57
  F. M., 57, 215
  Franklin, 36, 50
  Geo. F., 184
  George W., 21
  Hannah, 9
  James L., 38
  Jim, 9
  John, 190, 215
  John A., 302
  Judith A., 46
  Landon E., 184
  Lewis C., 38
  M. E., 215
  M. M., 229
  Maggie, 21
  Margaret A., 215
  Margaret E., 148

Marshall, 273
Martha E., 160
Mary E., 38
Mary J., 69, 89
Mary W., 183
Nick, 57
R. H., 326
R. Welby, 78
Richardetta E., 326
Robert B., 283
Rose M., 184
S. Rolberta, 50
Sarah J., 29
Sophia D., 78
Steuart, 46
T. H., 279
W. E., 272
Wm. W., 160
CARUTHERS
  Jas. E., 283
  Wm., 252
CARVER
  James, 124
CASSADAY
  Josephine C., 316
  W. H., 316
  Wm. H., 249
CASTLE
  Annie B., 16
  E. S., 1, 16
  Roena, 16
  Roena E., 1
  Rowena, 87
  Virginia B., 1
CASTLEMAN
  Alfred, 42
  Charles M., 32
  Henry W., 29, 30, 188
  Jane, 36
  John R., 117
  Mary, 29
  Mary E., 30, 42, 188
  Stephen D., 36
CATHER
  Ann Virginia, 153
CATLETT
  Esther A., 135
  Fairfax, 135
  Gibson, 246
  Jas. M., 131
CAUFMAN

INDEX

E. G., 230
E. Grey, 14
Joel F., 99
CAVENS
Catherine, 312
CAWOOD
Mary J., 220
Steven, 220
CAYLE
Sallie J., 176
CAYLOR
Annie G., 131
Laura L., 167
CAZENOVE
W. G., 267
CHAMBERLIN
S. E., 95
CHAMBERS
Anthony S., 39
Geo. W., 150
CHAMBLIN
A. Rush, 253, 254
Albert G., 139
Alice, 167
Annie, 98
Aseneth, 190
Charles I., 11
Charles T., 77, 122
Clay, 328
Deuana, 11
H. C., 212
H. W., 149
Hebe, 149
Helen, 173
Henry W., 187, 250
James H., 122
Jas. H., 122, 173
Jno. M., 175
Laura K., 243
Mary, 21
Mason, 11, 211, 212
Norval, 171
Noval, 17
Payton W., 26
R. C., 257
Richard, 105
Richard C., 45
Robt. C. L., 226
Rosa M., 243
Sarah T., 171
T. H. H., 171
Thomas S., 118

William, 190, 273
Wm., 98
CHANCELLOR
C. W., 321
Charles, 263
John J., 321
L., 213
Lorman, 124
Rush W., 250
Chancellor & Bro, 75
CHANDLER
Catharine, 37
Marie C., 37
William, 37
CHAPALEAR
G. W., 125
CHAPIN
B. E., 241
Sadid, 241
CHAPMAN
Mary L., 196
Pearson, 250
CHAPPELEAR
Adeline, 103
CHAPPELLEAR
Emily A., 211
CHARLTON
Alice M., 85
CHARRINGTON
Percy W., 266
CHAYTOR
Edmund C., 56
George H., 56
CHEW
H. Virginia, 242
Mollie B., 142
R. P., 113
Roger, 142, 242
CHEWNING
G. H., 237
CHICHESTER
A. M., 137, 144, 288, 323
Arthur L., 59
Bowie, 323
Mary, 137, 139, 144, 323
Mason, 137
Richard M., 236
Sarah E., 290
CHILTON
J. M., 23

Jeannie B., 98
Samuel, 98
CHINN
Eliza McH., 159
Frank, 119
Mrs., 119
R. H., 159
R. S., 139, 183, 241, 243, 263
Rebecca, 47
Sallie, 139
Samuel W., 274
Sarah M., 139
Sue V., 252, 274
Susan, 251
Thomas, 306
CHISWELL
Maggie, 173
CHRISMAN
Harriet A., 74
CHRIST
Geo. W., 278
CHRISTIAN
Bolivar, 211
Boliver, 211
CHURCH
Samuel, 22
Church Dedication
M. E. Church, South, 315
CISSELL
Humphrey, 194
CLABAUGH
Emma F., 43
N. N., 43
CLAGETT
Beverly, 307
Elizabeth A., 73
Fannie C., 10
Helen, 75
Henry, 73
Mary E., 228
Thomas, 75, 228
William B., 170
CLAGGETT
Julia, 3
Thomas H., 3
CLAPHAM
H. W., 245
J. Henry, 248
Josias H., 26
CLARE

The Mirror
INDEX

John, 245
CLARK
 Archibald, 59
 Carrie, 178
 Emma, 4
 Isaac, 59
 Wade N., 190
CLARKE
 George, 101
 James F., 140
 Margaret, 2
 Marie B., 101
 Mary, 255, 259
 Pauline, 239
 Wm. C., 2
CLARKSON
 Caroline, 112
 Geo., 112
 Harriet, 140
 Mary, 112
 Thos., 112
CLARKSTON
 Utoca, 290
CLAYTON
 Phebe, 35
CLEGGETT
 Henry C., 59
CLEMENS
 Wm. B., 118
CLENDENING
 Ruth, 135
 Samuel O., 311
 William, 135
CLENDENNING
 Alverta V., 256
 Bernard T., 302
 John, 236, 238
 Samuel, 168, 172, 175, 217, 256
 Wm., 236
CLEVENGER
 Alfred, 106
CLINE
 Alfred, 156
 Annie, 156
 John T., 85
 Mary, 214
 Wm., 185
CLIPP
 James B., 169
CLOE
 Charles W., 108

CLOWE
 Charles A., 33
 Henry W., 33, 105
 Laura B., 105
CLOWES
 Ella M., 143
 Martha, 29
 Thomas, 29
COATES
 Mary J., 289
 Thomas, 123
COATS
 Andrew, 144
COCHERELL
 John, 129
COCHLAND
 Michael, 19
COCHRAN
 Fanny B., 17
 Rebecca E., 251
 Tholemiah, 260, 262
 Wm. B., 17, 62
COCKEREL
 Mary E., 108
COCKERELL
 Richard, 147
COCKERELLE
 Thomas S., 29
COCKERILL
 Edgar, 110
 Elisha, 110
 Samantha, 110
COCKERILLE
 Alice, 50
 Annie E., 61
 Caroline, 272
 Florida R., 135, 136
 Hattie L., 270
 James, 303
 John W., 71
 Joseph R., 226
 Martha, 50
 Mary B., 146
 Minnie, 303
 Nannie, 236
 R. H., 135, 146, 236, 270
 Richard H., 50, 136, 249
 Sally L., 249
COCKRAN
 M. F., 92

William T., 92
Wm. J., 92
COCKRELL
 Annie M., 3
 Jerry, 300
 Katie A., 144
 Maria E., 289
 S. W., 300
 Samuel W., 263
 Wm., 3
COCKRILL
 Jonathan, 29
 Joseph H., 311
 Robert A., 277
COCKS
 Alice L., 100
COE
 Aurelius, 4, 235
 David J., 47
 Elizabeth, 106
 Maria L., 235
 Norman, 235
 Samuel J., 296
COGAL
 Jonathan, 327
COGSILL
 H. L., 139
COLBERT
 Ellen C., 29
 George W., 278
 Jesse, 172
 John M., 172
 Sarah M., 172
COLCLAZER
 Sarah E., 58
 Zachary T., 58
COLE
 Hannah, 133
 K. B., 151
 Peter, 91
 Sarah E., 91
COLEMAN
 Ed., 319
 Edmond C., 319
 Elizabeth, 169
 J. C., 215
 James, 45
 Jas. R., 232
 John I., 169, 262
 S. Kate, 262
 Sallie L., 170
COLES

William, 283
COLLIER
  Jane A., 7
  Oliver P., 7
COLLINS
  J. W., 286
  Laura B., 149
  Laura J., 213
COLSTON
  Georgie M., 322
  Raleigh T., 43
  Robert A., 322
COLVIN
  Calhoun, 144
  Wm. R., 173
COMBS
  Joseph, 306
  Robert, 306
  Seth R., 168
  Stephen, 306
COMES
  Samuel L., 86
  Silas C., 86
COMET
  Sarah J., 80
COMPHER
  Catherine, 21
  Chas. L., 177
  Edwin C., 260
  Elizabeth, 20
  Elizabeth A., 20
  Hannah A., 20
  J. Franklin, 175
  J. J., 227
  Jacob F., 177
  John, 20, 200, 323
  John H. W., 20, 31
  John W., 86
  Jonas, 20
  Jonas C., 20, 249
  Joseph, 20
  Marietta, 20
  Mary C., 20
  Mary M., 95
  Nettie, 300
  Peter, 5, 19, 21
  Samuel, 20, 90, 143
  Sarah C., 20
  Sarah C. E., 90
  Susan, 20, 326
  Susan A., 323
  Wm. F., 20

CONARD
  Abner, 91
  Abner W. M., 199
  Ebenezer J., 259
  Eliz., 257
  Elizabeth, 251
  J. P. M., 206
  Mary, 214
  Mary B. M., 91
  Nathan E., 260
  Rosia M., 231
  Stephen H., 260
CONNELLY
  Clara, 92
  Thos. C., 92
CONNER
  James W., 247
  Jas. W., 220
  John T., 67
  Joseph, 80
  Mary E., 63
  William, 221
CONRAD
  Abner, 89, 143
  Betty W., 136
  David, 109
  E. J., 303
  Elizabeth, 38
  Elizabeth W., 136
  Joseph, 282
  Julia A., 303
  Mary E., 38
  R. Y., 74, 136
  Robert Y., 136
  Robt. Y., 210
  Sallie H., 74
  Virginia, 303
COOK
  G. Wythe, 274
  Henry, 124
  W. B., 239
COOKE
  Edward E., 18, 162
  J. G., 255
  Lizzie E., 255
  Maria C., 18
  Maria P., 23
  Philip P., 23
COOKENDORFER
  Thomas, 36
COOKSEY
  Alberta, 182

William T., 170
COOMBS
  J. N., 199
  Jno. N., 200
COOPER
  Adam, 87
  Apollos, 306
  Bettie A., 153
  Columbus P., 240
  Florence M., 297
  G. W., 141
  Hannah A., 9
  Harry L., 251
  Hattie E., 251
  James A. J., 251
  John W., 153
  Margaret A., 64
  Marry E., 251
  Mary E., 194
  Matilda J., 31
  Mollie, 143
  Mollie E., 141
  Rachel A., 198
  Robert H., 64
  Samuel, 59, 166, 251, 319
  Sarah R., 86
  Thomas J., 274
  Tilghman, 72
  Virginia M., 166
COPELAND
  Harmon, 128
  Luther L., 297
  Mary J., 203
  Nathan H., 37
  P. D., 272
  Richard, 12
  Sarah J., 66
CORBIN
  Jas., 201
CORDELL
  Adam A., 256
  Enos B., 295
  Henrietta, 91
  Martha A., 256
CORDER
  Mary J., 25
  Wm. G., 25
CORNEL
  Eliza, 324
CORNELIUS
  Samuel, 321

INDEX

CORNELL
  Francis, 283
  James, 50, 51
  John H., 292
  Thompson, 283
CORNWELL
  Abner, 133
  Geo. M., 170
CORR
  George, 264
  Susan, 264
CORRUTHERS
  Joel, 127
CORSE
  Mary W., 220
  W. D., 220
CORUM
  Enoch, 110, 113
COST
  chas. F., 160
  Jacob, 57, 160
  Martha A., 268
  Mary Ann, 57
  Peter, 61, 69
  Thomas J., 39
  Thos. J., 195
COSTELLO
  Mary C., 146
COURTNEY
  M. W., 258
COX
  Armstead M., 182
  Hannah, 179
  James W., 152
  John F., 194
  John W., 167
  Malinda, 269
  Samuel, 152
  Samuel L., 94
CRAIG
  Ann R., 8
  Emily J., 127
  Francis T., 127
  Geo. W., 127
  Martha J., 30
CRAIGHEDS
  T. G., 142
CRAIGHILL
  Frank H., 270
CRAIN
  Baily, 266
  Elizabeth, 279
  Huldah, 266
  James, 9
  John, 279
CRAMP
  Mary E., 169
CRAMPTON
  Angie F., 243
CRANBECKER
  Samuel, 58
CRANE
  James, 156
  Joseph, 242
  Martha V., 242
CRAVEN
  Albinah, 36
  Benj., 255
  Benj. G., 257
  G. G., 257
  Giles, 255
  Guilford, 227
  Guilford G., 87
  James F., 73
  John R., 145
  Jno. R., 206
  Joel, 36, 100
  John R., 203
  Lydia A., 284, 285
CREAL
  Appa H., 92
  Mr., 271
CREIGHTON
  J.Carlin, 248
CRIDDER
  Roberta V., 201
CRIDER
  Charles A., 24
  Frederick, 24
  J. H., 24
  John H., 24
  Lemuel, 24
  Mary, 24
  Matilda A., 24
  William H., 24
CRIDLER
  Charles C., 219
  John, 291
  Mary F., 270
  Mary V., 107
CRIM
  Armistead M., 148
  Christian, 249
  Florence, 234
  John H., 321, 322
  John J., 247
  John W., 40
  Kate, 249
  Peter, 152
  Sarah C., 86
  Susan, 291
  Susannah, 290
  Willie A., 249
CRIMM
  Samuel, 277
CRISSEY
  F. J., 159, 246, 312, 313
  Fannie, 159
  Fannie C., 54
  Frederick J., 312
  J. Beverly, 322
  Mary E., 159
CRIST
  Geo. W., 291
CRITTENDEN
  T. T., 170
CROCKETT
  Lizzie A., 68
  Rebecca E., 295
  Samuel, 68, 295
CROCKFORD
  Wm. H., 68
CRONK
  Greenberry M., 196
CROOK
  Samuel, 117
CROSS
  B. R., 229
  Elizabeth W., 189
  Emily A., 189
  Emily E., 31
  Geo. L., 208
  Harrison, 130
  Julia E., 300
  Lewis, 200
  Lizzie, 328
  Mary, 212, 304
  Nancy, 312
  Sarah C., 300
  William, 210, 304, 328
  Wm., 212
  Wm. G., 31, 48, 161
CROUCH
  Albert, 277

Jno. W., 154
CROUSE
  Mary M., 291
CROW
  Hyland, 104
CROWL
  Mrs., 81
CROWN
  John O., 165
CRUMMITT
  Winter W., 188
CRUSON
  Jacob, 89
  Nathaniel M., 89
CRUZEN
  Jacob, 326
  Sarah, 326
CULLEN
  Dr., 161
  Jennie T., 201
  John, 219
  Thomas, 201
CUMMINGS
  Eliza A., 2
  Wm. H., 260
CUMMINS
  Benj. F., 297
  Jane V., 4
  John T., 289
  K. F., 237
  Martha A., 86
CUMPSTON
  Edward, 165
CUNNINGHAM
  Margaret E., 102
  Robert H., 198
  Robt., 198
CURL
  Geo. W., 295
CURRELL
  John, 212
  Pamelia, 212
CURRY
  Robert, 64
CURRY
  Ann, 206
  Ann E., 275
  Annie, 206
  Annie E., 44
  David H., 123
  Elizabeth, 275
  John, 206, 275

Mary, 279
CUSACK
  John, 314

DABER
  Frederick, 78
DABNEY
  R. Heath, 134
  Virginia, 134
  Virginius, 94
  Walter D., 295
D'ACCEGLIO
  Louis T., 181
DADE
  Lee M., 72
  Mr., 150
DAILEY
  Aaron, 12
  Francis A., 12
  Hannah, 12
  Hattie E., 25
  Mary J., 82
DAILY
  Aaron, 324
  Rebecca V., 122
  Samuel, 34
DAINGERFIELD
  Foxhall A., 117
DALEY
  Aaron, 324
DALGARN
  John W., 126
  Mildred E., 126
  Nancy, 126
DALGERN
  John W., 183
DALTON
  Emma E., 119
  John W., 302
  Wm. H., 302, 303
DAME
  Ellen P., 141
  Nelson P., 290
DANDRIDGE
  A. Stephen, 263
DANGERFIELD
  Henry, 62
  Susan S., 62
DANIEL
  Althea, 67
  David, 17, 77
  Edmonia, 102

Elizabeth, 17
J. W., 66
Lemuel, 67
Mamie W., 259
Orra L., 308
DANIELS
  Frances, 208
  James E., 121
  John T., 27
DARBY
  Alice, 112
  Upton, 112
DARNE
  Allen S., 305
  Annie E., 93
  James T., 118, 255
  Mary J., 118
  William E., 281
DARNES
  Barbary, 127
DARR
  John P., 219
  Mary, 93
  Samuel D., 9
DARRELL
  Florence E., 16
  William S., 16
DAUGHTRY
  Mrs., 152
DAVIS
  ___, 104
  Albert, 45
  Annie E., 268
  Benj., 61, 238
  Benjamin, 268, 318
  Carrie, 101
  Charlotte, 90
  Earnest F., 268
  Edward H., 148
  Eugene, 309
  Gideon, 88
  Harriet, 6
  J. R., 6
  J. Staige, 309
  James, 6, 306
  James S., 151
  John, 101
  John S., 308
  Joseph, 160, 250,
    256, 257, 263
  Joseph L., 32
  Joseph M., 98

344 The Mirror
INDEX

Josephine A., 107
Julia V., 256
L., 6
Landon, 298
Lizzie A., 265
Louisa T., 268
M. A., 76
Mamie, 151
Martin V. B., 10
Mary F., 224
Mary J., 308, 309
Mary L., 26
Mollie, 250
Peyton H., 227
R. S., 6
R. T., 268
Rev. Dr., 310
Richard T., 104, 268
Sarah E., 238
Sarah P., 33
Susan, 90
Susan H., 61
Wm. T., 254
DAVISSON
  Frederick A., 47
  Rose D., 107
  Sophia A., 47
  Theodore N., 14
DAWSON
  Charles, 59
  Lavinia, 294
  Nicholas, 59, 166
DAY
  Annie D., 199
  Roberta, 300
  Sarah W., 146
  Wm. B., 199
DAYMUDE
  Alfred G., 52
  Arthur F., 262
de BURGHEIM
  Philip F., 10
DEAN
  John, 196
DEAR
  J. W., 284
  Jennie M., 189
DeBOW
  Christian, 38
  Christopher, 50
  Elizabeth, 50
  Mary, 50

DeBUTTS
  J. P., 63
  Jno. P., 162
DELANEY
  Thomas J., 121
DeLANNAY
  Moselle, 254
DELANY
  S. L., 152
DELONY
  Robert J., 144
DEMARY
  John, 65
DEMORY
  C., 54
  John W., 28, 186
  Mahlon, 293, 294
  Margaret E., 186
  Sarah, 207
  Sophia E., 294
  Sophie E., 293
  Wm. H., 167
DENHAM
  L. J., 56
DENNIS
  Frances C., 23
  Mary A., 262
  Mary F., 87
  Olivia J., 194
  William A., 44, 45
  Wm. A., 125
DENNY
  George H., 249
DENT
  Laura V., 305
DERRY
  Elizabeth E., 200
  John P., 11
  L. W., 113
  Lucy E., 327
  Martha A., 232
  Ollie A., 306
  Peter, 48, 114
  Philip, 239, 245
  Philip H., 260
  Phillip H., 260
DIBBREL
  Agnes, 191
  Anthony, 191
  Charlie, 191
DIBBRELL
  Anthony, 224

DICKEY
  William T., 2
DIDIER
  Henry A., 39
DIEDRICK
  Daniel, 281
  Geo. W., 281
  George W., 281
DIEDRICKS
  Daniel, 281
DILLON
  Anne, 57
  J. Wm., 310
  John J., 57
  Joseph W., 174
DIMER
  Eliza, 288
DINGES
  Wm. E., 149
DINKLE
  Lewis, 31
DISHMAN
  Adelia, 16
  James W., 229
  Sallie A., 279
DISMUKES
  M. L., 176
DIVINE
  Alice, 132
  Alonzo, 115
  Betsy, 181
  Elizabeth, 104
  Emily V., 300
  F. Alonzo, 138
  Frank P., 32
  H. Elizabeth, 32
  J. Mortimer, 26
  Jacob, 181
  James F., 32, 97
  Jas. F., 32, 104
  John A., 104
  John S., 201
  Julia A., 94
  Kate M., 97
  Martha, 104
  Mary A., 43
  Robert E., 75
  Robert W., 138
  Thos. D., 300
  W. W., 267
  William, 104, 112
  William B., 104

INDEX

Willie M., 138
DIXON
  J. W., 233, 238
  James W., 115
  John, 91
  M. M., 233, 238
  Orra M., 91
DOBSON
  Isabella, 254
DODD
  Amanda, 219
  Elizabeth, 88
  Emma A. V., 127
  George Y., 247
  Jas. H., 219, 224
  Saml., 189
DODSON
  Daniel, 317
  Martha, 262
DOGGETT
  Annie M., 118
  D. N. S., 118
  George F., 20
  M. A., 118
DONALDSON
  Walter S., 265
DONOHOE
  Ann E., 312
  C. J., 113
  Lewis, 269
  Lewis J., 272
  Margaret M., 92
  Miss, 292
  Rebecca, 255
  S. Roszel, 225
  Samuel, 128, 272
  Sarah J., 151
DORRELL
  George W., 122
  James, 67
  Susan M., 122
DORSEY
  R., 24
DOUGHTY
  James, 205
DOUGLAS
  Ann, 70
  Arch. N., 129, 130, 295
  Charles, 70, 129
  Chas., 130
  Eliza, 232

Hugh, 300
J. E., 208
James, 232
Louisa, 300
Mary B., 295
R. Stuart, 232
Rosa L., 208
DOUGLASS
  Ann B., 70
  Charles, 70
  J. E., 163, 221
  Margaret F., 163
DOVE
  Carrie E., 150
  Jilson J., 16
  Maggie J., 180
  Matilda, 228
  Sallie, 180
  Thomas, 180
  Wm., 131
DOWDELL
  Annie A., 118
  C. F., 130
  Charles F., 143
  Jas G., 212
  Louisa P., 143
  Mary E., 130
  Sarah, 212
  Thos. G., 123
  William F., 67
DOWELL
  C. C., 232
  C. F., 302
  C. R., 200, 222, 247
  Conrad R., 135
  Jennie E., 232
  John T., 154
  Laura E., 222
  Malinda, 135
  Sophy, 308
  Telulah, 281
  Webb, 247
DOWNES
  Chas., 219
DOWNEY
  Laura J., 283
  Scott, 213
  W. Scott, 281, 282, 283
  Wm. B., 127, 152
DOWNING
  Ann W., 318

Jas. A., 293
Samuel J., 318
DOWNS
  C. L., 43
  Charles M., 308
  Cicero, 83
  Hugh H., 40
  James W., 6
  Sarah E., 93
DRAKE
  Jonathan, 306
  Mary A., 213
  Thomas, 306
DRANE
  Peter A., 66
  Robert J., 77
DRISH
  Edwin, 8
  Harriet, 40
  John H., 217
  Phebe A., 217
  Sallie, 297
  William D., 40
  Wilson J., 42
  Wm. D., 79, 297
DROOP
  Edwin, 191
  Sophie, 191
DRUSE
  Lucy, 288
DUDLEY
  Fanny B., 62
  Thomas U., 62, 265
  Thomas W., 17
  Virginia F., 265
DUFFEY
  John H., 30
DUKE
  Thomas H., 28
DULANEY
  Amelia R., 312
  Henry S., 312
DULANY
  Ann, 179
  Dan. F., 162
  Daniel, 301
  Daniel F., 44, 63
  French, 179
  Henry S., 5
  John P., 162, 301, 302
  Mary, 250

The Mirror
INDEX

Nannie, 63
R. H., 250, 302
Tingey A., 44
DULIN
  Alfred, 72
  Geo. C., 113, 116
  Samuel G., 113
DUNBAR
  Sarah F., 278
  Sophie, 209
DUNCAN
  David, 270
  James A., 270
  Jas. A., 270
  Sarah C., 37
  W. W., 47
  Wallace, 270
DUNKER
  John, 306
DUNLOP
  Helen, 75
  Henry, 75
DUNOTT
  Thomas J., 76
DURBURROW
  Mary E., 22
DUST
  Isaac, 55
DUTTON
  Anna E., 293
  Emma E., 90
  John B., 90, 308
  Warren B., 188
DUVAL
  Eli, 75
  Harvie S., 41
  Lucien S., 22
DUVALS
  Mrs., 130

EAMICH
  Frederick, 119
  Kate E., 119
EARL
  Robert, 242
EASTER
  Albert, 18
EASTERDAY
  John S., 91, 268
  Joseph, 91, 268
  Julian, 246
  Mary E., 103, 246
  Rachael A., 91, 268
  Thomas M., 103
  W. D., 128
  Wm. D., 103, 116
  Wm..D., 246
EASTON
  Geo. S., 169
  Isaac, 15, 237
  Isaac N. F., 15
  Malinda, 15
  W. B., 66
EBBERT
  Adam S., 254
  M., 247
EBBUT
  Elizabeth R., 227
EDD
  John, 104
EDELIN
  Maria S., 217
EDWARDS
  Abner, 91
  Alpheus L., 6, 41, 234
  Annie M. C., 247
  Catharine S., 144
  Charles G., 145, 197
  Chas. G., 221
  Hattie G., 221
  Isa A., 197, 221
  J. Washington, 313
  Jane E., 11
  John S., 289
  Laura B., 322
  Lizzie, 89
  Lucy, 226
  Lydia D., 45
  Mahlon, 275
  Marcellus, 226
  Mary E., 283
  Mary L., 283
  Mary M., 11
  Mary S., 6
  Matilda, 234
  Nettie G., 286
  R. H., 84, 322
  S. H., 114
  Samuel M., 27, 289
  Sarah A., 259
  Sarah E., 290
  Thomas J., 75
  Thomas W., 58, 60, 89
  Thos. W., 153, 290
  Edwards & Hutchison, 154
EGGLESTON
  Herbert A., 36
  Horatio N., 36
  Mary L., 36
  W. G., 203
EGLIN
  Benjamin, 146
EIDSON
  Joseph, 57
  W. H., 57
ELDRIDGE
  John, 58
ELGIN
  Alexander, 130
  Angeline D., 83
  Ann E., 94
  Charles F., 94
  Charles M., 11
  Charles R., 88
  David A., 83
  Edward B., 97
  Francis, 101
  George R., 93
  Gustavus, 35
  Ignatius, 317, 321
  James B., 41, 97
  John F., 76, 235
  Lloyd G., 83
  Margaret A., 317
  Margaret E., 212, 215
  Mary A., 321
  Mary J., 26
  Mollie, 243
  Pauline, 94
  Rebecca, 47
  Robert, 14, 212
  Robt., 215
  Rosalia S., 168
  Sarah, 97
  Simon, 170
  Thomas F., 243
  Thomas G., 243
  Walter, 47
ELIASON
  Mary M., 5
ELLIOTT
  Hanson, 113

INDEX

ELLMORE
  Charles, 199
  George M., 66
  James R., 161
  John, 199
  John R., 62
  Mary L., 199
  Samuel, 108
ELLZEY
  Alice, 166
  Helen E., 242
  Lily, 250
  Lucy E., 35
  Mary, 318
  Thomas, 166
  Thomas L., 242
  Thos. L., 171, 250, 318
  William, 35, 306
ELMORE
  Jennie, 114
EMANUEL
  Victor, 181
EMBREY
  Sarah E., 125
  Staunton G., 125
  Wilford S., 125
EMERSON
  Judson, 168
ENGLISH
  C. A., 300
  Chas. A., 144
  Inez, 132
  Inez J., 106
  J. A., 106
ERWIN
  W. S., 114
ESKRIDGE
  C. G., 272
  Charles G., 60
  Chas. G., 313
  Louisa L., 130
  Margaret, 272
ETHERINGTON
  E. H., 185
  Violet, 185
EUBANK
  C. H., 225
  Joseph C., 225
  Otis, 225
EVANS
  Asbury, 148
  Gen., 51
  John P., 87
  Mary E., 228
  Sophia C., 209
EVERHART
  Annie, 82
  Augustin S., 272
  Jennie, 178
  John, 152
  John B., 9
  T. H., 320
  Tilghman, 28
  William N., 82
  Wm., 269, 289
EVERHEART
  John, 150
EVERITT
  M. T., 254
EWART
  David, 222
  Sophia S., 222
EWEN
  Phebe, 321
EWERS
  Eliza, 100
  Emma F., 100
  Emma J., 203
  Jonathan, 161
  L. G., 153
  Lauck, 203
  Laura, 325
  Nancy, 161
  Phoebe, 318
  William, 47, 100
EWING
  James A., 314
EYSTER
  G. H., 106

FADELEY
  C. F., 133
  C. Fenton, 54
  Chas. F., 133
  Elizabeth, 21
  Hattie, 54
  Thomas, 21
FADELY
  C. F., 237
  Charles F., 134, 236
  Chas. W., 134
  E. B., 276
  Mollie D., 236, 237
FADLEY
  John M., 124
FAIR
  William H., 42
FAIRFAX
  Ann, 6
  John W., 58, 111
  Mary J., 111
FANT
  Fannie F., 172
  J. M., 172
  John L., 184
FARE
  Margaret, 3
FARNHAM
  Robert, 222
FAUNTLEROY
  A. M., 74
  Chas. M., 104
  P. Williams, 298
FAWLEY
  Elizabeth, 20
  Henry, 35
  Jeremiah, 125
  Jos., 238
  Laura, 169
  Margaret A. A., 100
  William, 20
  Wm., 169
FAWLY
  Christina, 323
  Henry, 323
  Susan A., 323
FEAGANS
  C. H., 115
  Rebecca, 115
FEAGINS
  Alvina, 177
FEASTER
  Fannie, 229
  George L., 242
  Henry A., 151, 242
  Herod, 23
  Susan, 242
FECHTIG
  Alice, 204
  Isa, 272
FELLOWS
  Barnard T., 310
FERGUSON
  Catharine, 192, 279
  Jannie F., 275

The Mirror
INDEX

Mary C., 279
Mollie C., 275
Mollie E., 281
Romulus, 192, 279
Thomas B., 97
Walter R., 192
FERROL
  Nelson, 210
FEWELL
  Ethelred, 187
  Fannie S., 186
  Rhoda, 140
FIELDS
  Fannie E., 298
FILLER
  ___, 18
  A. T. M., 22
  Elizabeth, 87
  John M., 185
  Lizzie A., 125
  Lydia M., 22
FINDLAY
  James, 50
FINKS
  Fielding, 184
  John W., 126
FINNEKEN
  Wm., 306
FISHER
  A. T., 289
  Edward L., 68
  Frank, 273
  Georgianne, 68
  Julia A., 139
  Minnie B., 139
  Thomas, 137
  Thomas N., 139
FITZHUGH
  Augustine, 211
  Cook, 66
  Henry, 91
  Jane E., 91
  Lollie, 144
  M. W., 277
  N., 144
  Peregrine A., 25
  William D., 117
  Willie C., 277, 279
FLAGG
  Thomas G., 78
  Virginia, 78
FLATHER
  Henry, 19
FLEMING
  A. J., 221
  Mrs., 67
  Thomas W., 214
FLETCHER
  Albert, 126
  Amanda, 217
  Benjamin C., 135
  Ellen, 51
  Isaac, 42
  Joshua, 51
  Joshua C., 135
  Lizzie, 51
  Maggie B., 135
  Robert, 264
  Susan A., 181, 224
  T. N., 149
  Tacey L., 325
  Tacie G., 64
  Wm., 123, 144
FLING
  Annie E., 198
  Charles E., 161
  William H., 199
  Wm. T., 169
FLINN
  James T., 6
  Malinda, 92
  Rachel, 92
FLOOD
  Wm., 185
FLOWERS
  Catharine, 48
  Levinia, 38
  Sarah F., 23
FLOYD
  Mary E., 46
FOLEY
  Alice S., 174
  Annie M., 121
  Benjamin F., 182
  Fannie E., 195
  James, 139
  Maggie A., 182
  Mary T., 182
  Sallie J., 182
FOLK
  Annie E., 215
  John, 215
FOLLIN
  John N., 72
Laurena, 140
Samuel, 140
FONTAINE
  Lucy N., 175
FOOTE
  Annie, 264
  Richard H., 21
FORBES
  John M., 55, 299
  Kate R., 299
  Mary E., 55
  Murray, 226
  Sophia S., 55
FORD
  C. F., 177
  Chas. F., 39
  Mary R., 39
  Wm. E., 98
FOREMAN
  Kate M., 52
  Mary C., 2
FORREST
  A. M., 230
  David, 228
  Elizabeth D., 230
FORSYTH
  Henrietta, 103
  James H., 196
  Jno., 205
  Maggie, 135
  Sarah E. G. O., 137
  W. H., 205
FORTNEY
  G. W., 2
  Geo. S., 2
  Mary E., 2
FOSTER
  Annie D., 238
  J. W., 110
  Jas. W., 289
  Lucy M., 308
  Mary A., 71
  Thomas, 71
FOUCHE
  Amos, 290
  George W., 118
  Sidney, 204
FOUSCHE
  Daniel, 321
FOUT
  Grafton, 210
  Isadora V., 210

The Mirror
INDEX

Lillie, 170
FOWLE
 William, 27
FOWLER
 Mary E., 8
FOX
 Ada L., 64
 Addison C., 189
 Alice C., 64
 Amanda O., 8
 Annie M., 104
 BradenE., 161
 Bush, 150
 Bushrod L., 38, 151
 Bushrod W., 64
 C. Osborn, 149
 Charles E., 226
 Geo. K., 104, 217
 Geo. W., 114
 George K., 25, 56, 99, 145
 James W., 29
 Joseph B., 8
 Mary J., 6
 Newman T., 102
 Roland B., 38
 Sallie A., 114
 Thomas J. E., 79
 Virginia, 38, 64
 William H., 123
FRAME
 Chas., 256
 James M., 310, 312
FRANCIS
 Ann E., 291, 293
 Bettie, 278
 Edward, 291, 293
 Independence C., 57
 Jane E., 239
 John, 4, 19
 John E., 37, 283
 Laura, 117
 Lucinda, 43
 Minnie, 32
 Olivia, 170
 Sydnor B., 276
 Thomas, 170, 278
 Wm. H., 57, 117, 162
FRANKLIN
 Eliza, 109
 Garland D., 316
 J. B., 109, 316

Lucy, 316
 Martha J., 84
 Mary M., 118
 Mattie, 109
 T. W., 273, 316
 Willie E., 316
 Wm. H., 167
FRANKS
 Aarean E., 3
 Addison, 60
 Benjamin, 3
 C. F., 100
 Martha E., 312
 Nancy E., 3
FRANNIE
 Mary A., 104
FRASIER
 Mary A., 281
FRAZIER
 Emma, 248
 F. May, 248
 J. H. T., 211
 Jeannette R., 258
 Jno. A., 149
 Mary A., 278
 Samuel H., 278
 Thomas, 198
FRED
 Burr P., 90
 Frank L., 289
 Nannie R., 289
FREEMAN
 Annie E., 234
 Lewis H., 270
FREEMEN
 Annie, 232
FRENCH
 Annie, 101
 Mary E., 72
FRERE
 Carrie C., 56
 Elizabeth, 180
FREY
 Christina, 263
 John, 171
FRIBBY
 James, 86
FRIDAY
 J. M., 266
 Jno. M., 178
FRIDELL
 Emma, 116

John, 116
 Maudie, 116
FRISTOLE
 Eugenia D., 78
FRITTS
 Ann E., 116
 Chas. E., 306
 Elizabeth, 39
 Frederick H., 123
 John, 91, 219
 Robert, 119
 Sallie A., 91
FRITZ
 Sally, 34
FROST
 Louise T., 104
FRY
 Barbara E. B., 24
 Betsey, 243
 Charles W., 96, 143
 Daniel J. H., 90
 David E., 75
 David W., 100
 George, 128, 320
 George M., 3
 Hannah A., 47
 Isaac W., 228
 Jacob, 94
 John, 24, 268
 John D., 47
 John W., 90, 220
 Jos. H., 245
 Joseph, 62, 98, 220
 Joseph H., 80
 Josephine C., 316
 Julia A., 87
 Lillie E., 328
 Lilly, 320
 Margaret A., 20
 Martha E., 210
 Mary R., 178
 Mrs., 256
 Peter, 309
 Peter W., 99
 Richard W., 241
 Rosabell, 320
 Samuel, 85, 86, 207, 275
 Sarah C., 223
 Sarah E., 75
 Virginia C., 274
FULLER

The Mirror
INDEX

Amanda, 44
FULTON
  Charles E., 171
  Jane, 37
  John, 37
  John E., 258
  M. Ella, 307
  Massey, 307
  Sarah A., 258
  William, 26
  Wm., 316
FULWILER
  Robt. W., 108
FURLONG
  Edward P., 254
  John, 161
  Mary A., 161
FURR
  Annie, 81
  Ebin, 277
  Ellen, 41
  Emsey, 160
  Ephraim, 44
  Evelina, 93
  Fenton, 14, 24, 88, 118, 243, 315
  Geo. H., 277
  Hannah C., 88
  Kemp B., 316
  M. A., 276
  M. B., 276
  Malinda, 265
  Mary I., 118
  Mary V., 28
  Matilda, 56, 60
  Minor, 93
  Octavia, 28
  Richard E., 28, 56, 60
  Susan E., 243
  Susan J., 316
  Wm., 41, 160
  Wm.G., 81

GABRET
  Ann, 125
GAINES
  Annie E., 10
  John, 63
  Martha E., 63
  Nannie, 246
  R. B., 246
  Thos. B., 10
  Virginia, 227
  Wm., 243, 256
GALLAHER
  B. Frank, 101
  Belle W., 159
  Cornelia A., 159
  Eliza A., 101
  W. W. B., 159
GALLEHER
  Bryon L., 10
  Geo. T., 249
  J. W., 26
  James H., 119
  Jane D., 235, 262
  Jas. W., 299
  Lilla, 299
  Maria C., 321
  Patsey V., 262
  Rosalie B., 235
  T. L., 36, 66
  Thos. W., 13
  Turner H., 33, 235, 262, 321
  V. A., 26
  W. W. B., 97
  Willis B., 26
GALLOWAY
  Charles F., 85
GANT
  Annie E., 304
  Charles, 18
  Elizabeth H., 121
  John T., 304
  Laura J., 304
  Margaret, 285
GANTT
  Anna B., 29
  Annie E., 206
  Ella J., 206
  John F., 29
  W. W., 242
GARDINER
  William H., 32
GARDNER
  Amelia F., 165
  Francis, 299
  James, 266
  James L., 25, 295
  Presley G., 93
  Rosa M., 322
  Sallie, 267
GARLICK

  James N., 299
GARNER
  Amanda M., 154
  Annie L., 154
  Hattie E., 260
  Hezekiah, 154
  Laura L., 111
  Martha E., 43
GARNETT
  M. R. H., 35
GARRET
  Alcinda, 147
  Burr W., 43
GARRETT
  Albert T., 100
  Elizabeth, 147, 207, 262
  Elizabeth W., 314
  Enoch, 74, 125
  J. W., 220
  Jno. W., 192, 272
  John W., 125, 200, 279
  Joseph, 147, 207, 262
  Laura C., 292
  Mary E., 41
  Mary F., 207
  Susan, 240
  W. E., 51
GARRISON
  James, 41, 132, 134, 296
  Jas., 132, 180, 200
  Lillie L., 187
  Mary A., 132
  Mary Ann, 200
  Sarah C., 277
  Sarah J., 41
  Thos. W., 146
GARROTT
  George F., 238
GASKINS
  Ella D., 201
  Hannah G. B., 231
  Samuel A., 77
  Samuel S., 73
  Sarah, 51
  Wm. E., 231
GASSAWAY
  Catherine, 105
  Charles, 105

INDEX

Frank H., 147
Henrietta, 42
Henry N., 170
Thomas, 42
GATTON
　Harriet A., 101
　James H., 69
GAVER
　C. C., 219
　Chester C., 90, 261
　Henry, 246
　John C., 325
　Margaret, 246
　Mary, 325
　Mattie D., 283
　Theodore F., 259
GAY
　M. A., 221
GAYNOR
　Patrick, 199
GEARY
　John W., 4
GEASLAN
　Georgeanna, 23
GEE
　Joseph C., 29
GELKINSON
　M. R., 121
GENTLE
　David, 68
GEORGE
　Annabelle, 149
　Ashland C., 208
　Isaac, 42
　J. W., 325
　James W., 231
　Jno. E., 279
　John, 35, 59
　Laura G., 205
　Mamie L., 325
　Olevia E., 89
　Robert L., 155
　Samuel W., 87
　Wm. S., 297
GHANT
　Alice, 114
GIBBONS
　Geo. A., 159
　Jane, 60
　Stephen H., 1
GIBSON
　Blanche, 301

Douglass, 63
Ensebia E., 30
Gilbert B., 215
Henry C., 146
Jas. D., 67
John M., 5
Joseph, 301
Joshua, 181
Laura V., 133
M. A., 181
Nelson, 133
Robert A., 143
Seldon M., 22
GIDDINGS
　Charles J., 59
　James, 284
　Kate G., 183
　L., 183
　Miss, 328
　Mollie, 284
　W. V., 328
　William, 128
GILCHRIST
　Thos. M., 210
GILKESON
　J. Smith, 31
GILL
　John, 243
　John L., 258, 261
　Susan E., 243
　William, 24
　Wm. H., 261
GILMOR
　Harry, 88
GILMOUR
　Matthew, 225
GINGRICH
　C., 310
　C. M., 310
　S. Annie, 310
　Sarah, 310
GINN
　G. W., 154
　Jennie, 154
GIST
　Henry C., 52
　Lizzie G., 52
　Nettie, 52
GLASCOCK
　Aquilla, 65
　Ellen, 65
　George, 65

Sallie E., 98
GLASSCOCK
　Alfred, 54, 134
　Annie, 144
　Belle, 124
　Fred, 136
　John, 248
　Mahlon J., 125
　Tacey, 264
　Thomas, 264
GOCHNAUER
　P. S., 205
GOECHNEUER
　Elizabeth J., 208
　Frances, 208
GOLDEN
　John W., 187
GOODHART
　Annie, 230
　Charles W., 31
　J. W., 177, 210
　John, 205, 206
　Lucinda, 205
　Sophie, 177
GOODIN
　John J., 194
GOODING
　Margaret A., 65
GOODRICK
　J. T., 195
GOODWIN
　James W., 4
　John H., 165
　John W., 115
　Rachel, 165
　Willie E., 165
GORDON
　George M., 3
　I. C., 273
　William, 256
GORE
　Enos, 8
　Jane E., 8
　John G., 130
　Jonathan, 45
　Sarah, 8
　Susan V., 14
　T. H., 153
　Thomas, 173
　Tilghman, 14
GORMAN
　Joseph, 2

Patrick, 179
Robt., 314
Susan M., 179
GORRELL
  Elenora S., 168
  Reazina S., 168
GORU
  Bushrod T., 215
GOSHORN
  Delia A., 92
  Wm. A., 92
GOSSUM
  Roxey, 6
GOTT
  Richard T., 168
GOUGH
  Isabella, 229
GOVER
  Asatia C., 272
  Ellen, 260
  John, 178
  John W., 128
  Robert, 272
  Robert W., 33
  Samuel, 213, 214, 278
  Samuel S., 23
  Sarah Y., 128
  Virginia, 128
GRACE
  John, 156
GRADY
  E. B., 162
  Edward T., 21
  Frank, 205
  Frank T., 39
  Jane P., 94
  Sarah, 162, 163
GRAHAM
  Elizabeth R., 307
  Gertrude, 40
  James E., 307
  John W., 40
GRANBERRY
  J. C., 6
GRANT
  James H., 124
  Jasper, 306
  John N., 124
  Kate, 124
GRAY
  Algernon S., 117

C. W., 281
Douglas, 306
Emilie W., 270, 271
Hattie, 53
James, 255
John, 289
John T., 220
Joseph, 98, 288
Lucy E., 288, 289
Mary E., 238, 271
Minnie V., 98
Nathaniel E., 73
Orra H., 117
Phoebe, 103
R. Bently, 249
Robert W., 236, 310
Robt W., 237, 238
Robt. W., 53, 271
Samuel J., 210
Sarah E., 30
Virginia, 255
Virginia M., 158
William H., 59
Wm. E., 42
Wm. F., 279
Wm. S., 217
GRAYDEY
  James, 306
GRAYSON
  Alexander, 224
  Benjamin, 4
  Bettie C., 117
  Elizabeth L., 223
  Geo. M., 224
  Geo. W., 149
  George M., 326
  George. M., 223
  John B., 117
  R. O., 270
GRAZIER
  Catharine, 5
GREEN
  Ann W., 283
  Annie L., 245
  Charles P., 165, 265
  Charles T., 176
  Lizzie M., 265
  M. C., 258
  Martha E., 244
  Mary N., 247
  Mollie E., 265
  Richard F., 300

Thomas C., 245, 247
William T., 146
GREENLEASE
  Mary E., 82
  Sarah C., 281
GREENWELLE
  M. E., 20
  Margaret M., 20
GREGG
  Anna A., 86
  Annie M., 142
  Betsey, 42
  Bettie A., 66
  Edward B., 282
  Elisha, 84
  Emily J., 257
  Fannie J., 174
  Gibson, 86, 151
  Guilford, 166
  H. H., 183
  Harmon, 310
  Henry W., 257
  Lou L., 310
  Mary, 166
  Mary S., 174
  Nancy C., 241
  Nathan, 59
  Samuel, 92, 99
  Smith, 318, 319
  Stephen, 318
  Thomas, 1, 169, 174, 318
  Thos., 172
  Wm., 125, 321
GREGORY
  D. S., 166
  Mary C., 226
  Wm., 226
GRETTER
  George W., 127
  Maria E., 127
GREYSON
  George W., 187
GRIFFITH
  Charles, 194
  James F., 175
  Julia, 194
  Wm. S., 65
GRIGGS
  Fanny J., 62
  George R., 195
  James, 62

GRIGSBY
  J. Randolph, 5
GRIMES
  Buchanan, 297
  Daniel T., 27
  Geo.W., 207
  Henry, 127
  John T., 68, 103, 275, 280
  Mary E., 103
  Mary J., 120
  Miranda, 243
  Mrs., 112
  Richard H., 97
  Sallie, 127
  Sarah E., 103
  Sarah T., 82
  Wm., 243
GROSS
  Charles H., 316
  Elizabeth S., 3
  Flora L., 231
GROVE
  J. W., 266
GRUBB
  Annie M., 298
  Benj., 57
  Catherine, 298, 307
  Curtis, 169, 295, 307
  Ebenezer, 173, 197, 200
  Elizabeth, 26, 243
  George, 223
  James, 186
  James W., 106
  Jane A., 223
  Jas. W., 215
  Jno. E., 146
  John, 5, 85, 207, 212, 243, 298
  John T., 199
  Jos., 175
  Joseph P., 24
  Lydia E., 26
  Mary, 212
  Mary E., 57
  Mary L., 119
  Mary M., 296
  Mr., 296
  Nellie, 223
  Rachel, 183
  Rebecca J., 5
  Rebecca S., 169
  Rosana M., 150
  S. Lewis, 20
  Sallie, 199
  Samuel W., 314
  Susannah, 85
  William, 183
  Wm., 57, 150, 186, 296
GRUBBS
  James T., 214
  Wm., 2
GRYMES
  George, 14
GULICK
  Ann V., 168
  David P., 241
  Fannie A., 92
  Francis, 200
  Henry H., 168
  Ida R., 200
  Isabel L., 125
  James H., 168
  Jas. W., 132
  Nancy, 200
  Sanford, 300
GUNNEL
  Martha, 24
GUNNELL
  Ada B., 176
  Dallas P., 301
  W. P., 176
GUSTIN
  Emma, 4
  Robert, 4

HACKLEY
  Josephine, 204
  Sopha, 173
HAGAN
  Patrick, 150
HAGON
  Hugh, 173
HAINES
  Catharine, 289
  Dora W., 108
  Edward, 314
  Ellen, 23
  Franceria, 67
  Joel, 282
  Manly, 289
  Nathan, 23
  Portia, 23
  Reuben, 23
  Washington, 277
HAISLOP
  Harriet A., 283
HALEY
  Adelaide, 327
  Franklin, 17
  R. D., 114
  Sarah E., 17
HALL
  Alfred, 44
  Alice E., 277
  Andrew J., 201
  Eliza A., 55
  Ella L., 170
  Isabella M., 85
  James D., 170
  Lizzie E., 277
  Mary C., 8
  Snowden C., 139
  William, 55
HAMILTON
  Ann E., 291
  E. J., 35
  E. S., 254
  Edward F., 45, 209
  James, 156, 189
  James W., 10, 45
  John, 24, 45, 209, 217, 254
  Lizzie, 254
  Lydia V. H., 35
  Parmelia, 269
  Sarah, 95
  Thos. J., 24
HAMMAT
  Alice, 162
  Giles, 162
  John W., 132, 162
  Mary R., 132
HAMMATT
  Giles, 28
HAMMERLY
  C. Decatur, 313
  Catharine A., 272
  Helen A., 126
  Henry, 286
  Jno. W., 126
  John, 217, 259, 272, 286
  John W., 116

INDEX

Joseph, 286
Lizzie, 116
William A., 259
HAMMOND
  Chas. M., 285
HAMNER
  J. C., 126
HAMPTON
  James W., 262
  Mary E., 297
  Sarah A., 297
  Sarah E., 89
  William F., 24
HANBACK
  Jas. H., 262
HANCOCK
  C. F., 159
  Charles R., 280
  Corbin F., 128
  J. W., 183
  Jane T. L., 183
  Lima, 306
  Samuel G., 43
HANES
  G. B., 187
  Margaret H., 47
  Sarah E., 16
  Thadeus W., 4
HANSBOROUGH
  Elijah T., 239
HANSON
  Richard, 306
HANVEY
  Anna, 101
  Emma, 280
HANVY
  Elizabeth, 298
  Jno. O., 295
  John, 298
HARDING
  Edward, 168, 172, 175
  Ellen F., 262
  Garah, 76
  H. C., 229
  Henry C., 75
  John, 114
  Luther F., 262
  Mabyl, 229
  Margaret J., 28
  Nettie B., 229
  Samuel D., 80, 175

HARDY
  Ann M., 285
  Georgianna, 56
  H. M., 285
  Henson, 124
  Howard, 135
  Virginia F., 124
  Wm. H., 270
HARMAN
  Eva, 230
  J. D., 163, 230, 283
  Laura, 163
  Winton, 163
HARMON
  J. D., 222
  Jno. D., 283
  John D., 200
  Laura E., 222
  Loura, 293
HARPER
  Alice E., 142
  Charles, 176
  Eliza, 176
  Emily D., 251
  Francis, 303
  Frank, 188
  George W., 70
  Gertrude H., 274
  J. N., 71
  Joel Z., 303
  John, 188
  John W., 300
  Mary L., 71
  Nettie, 249
  Robert, 142, 204, 274
  Robert G., 63
  Robt., 252
  W. Walton, 142, 254
  Walton, 251
  Washington T., 20
  Wells A., 252, 254
  William H., 95
HARREL
  Georgianna, 277
HARRIS
  Albin W., 280
  Caroline, 280
  Geo. W., 82
  George W., 214
  Henry T., 20
  J. W., 224
  Jas. S., 313

John T., 46
William J., 204
HARRISON
  Alice, 328
  Anne H., 37
  Burr, 212
  Burr W., 60, 161, 177, 201, 245
  Corie C., 177
  Corrie H., 245
  Elizabeth L., 223
  Fannie W., 139
  George W., 29
  H. T., 223
  Harriotte J., 203
  Henry, 328
  Henry T., 37, 191
  James P., 308
  Janet, 161
  Janet K., 287
  Jno. P., 306
  John M., 231, 232
  M., 212
  Mary E., 191
  Mary L. C., 233
  Matthew, 58, 201, 203, 305
  P. L., 96
  Powell, 104, 161, 212, 229, 286, 287
  Sallie, 305
  Shep., 180
  Susan E., 231, 232
  Thomas, 233
  Walter J., 139, 271
  William E., 89
  Wm. E., 153
HARROVER
  Frances, 196
HART
  Edward, 12
  Eliza, 12
  Georgianna, 12
  John R., 259
  Jonathan, 18
  Joseph S., 24
  Rachel A., 24
HARTMAN
  Laura B., 199
HARVEY
  Florence M., 253
HATCHER

Adalaide, 205
Elizabeth, 179
Elizabeth H., 98
Ellwood, 98
Elwood, 179
Frank, 205
Harry, 308
Joshua, 243
Lindley, 206
Lucy, 206
Mahlon G., 68, 205
R. G., 147
Rodney, 145
T. W., 206
HATTON
  Alice M., 271
HAVENER
  Ada J., 195
  Annie E., 195
  Beverly T., 122
  Edgar B., 140, 195
  Michael, 46
  Wm. H., 128
HAVENNER
  Annie, 291
  Emily T., 89
  Jefferson, 268
  John F., 291
  Jos. K., 116
  Joseph R., 89
  Linnie E., 100
  Lucinda C., 79
  Martha J., 101
  Mary, 323
  Mary E., 87
  R. H., 323
  Rosa Ellen, 89
  Sallie L., 305
  Wm. A., 45, 324
  Wm. D., 66
HAVENNOR
  T. A., 127
HAWES
  James E., 180
  Lydia E., 105
  Susan, 106
HAWKINS
  Ginnie, 304
HAWLEY
  Andrew, 22
  Artemus, 22
  Catherine, 22
  Lamech, 22
  Louise, 22
  Richard, 22
  Roseline, 22
HAWLING
  Charles, 140
  J. Lewis, 206
  J. William, 300
  Jennie, 206
  John S., 192
  Jos. L., 255
  Lewis, 140, 322
  Martha, 206
HAWS
  Annie, 160
  Emma, 128
  Isaac F., 67
  Mary E., 135
  Mattie V., 321
  Sallie, 147
  Virginia, 285
  W. G., 130
HAXALL
  Barton, 41
  Bolling W., 192
  Hattie, 41
  R. Barton, 322
  Rosalie, 322
HAYES
  Nathaniel, 106
  Winifred A., 106
HAYMAKER
  Chas., 2
HAYNE
  Jas. T., 159
HAYS
  Wm. H. B., 10
HEAD
  Annie M., 214
  Benj. F., 302
  Clarence G., 213
  Geo. R., 278
  George R., 58, 59
  John W., 70, 89
  Martha E., 302
  Mary, 18
  Mary N., 42
  William, 18
HEATER
  Ebin, 149
  George W., 300
  Jno., 175
  John, 173
  John R., 238
  Minnie B., 238
  P. H., 133
  Phillips H., 238
  Richard, 80
  Rich'd., 175
  Sally, 149
  Sarah J., 218
HEATH
  Alfred, 22
  Charles H., 22
  Frances A., 22
  Gustavus, 22
  John, 22
  Richard, 22
  Shelton, 22
  William, 22
HEATON
  Celia V., 259
  Decatur, 11
  Eliza R., 25, 325
  Harriet M., 110
  Henry, 229
  James D., 11
  Jonathan, 325
  Lucy C., 86
  Lydia V., 35
  Townsend, 166, 259
HEBRON
  J. S., 112
HEDGES
  Irianna K., 2
  Lucy G., 142
  W. L., 132
  Wm. L., 2, 142
HEFFNER
  Andrew, 309
  Carrie, 314
  Elizabeth, 175
  Mr., 199
  Stephen, 58
HEFLEBOWER
  Samuel, 231
HEFLIN
  Jeremiah, 237
  Louisa, 233
HEISKELL
  Esther F., 160
  J. Monroe, 94, 160
HELM
  Frank, 129

The Mirror
INDEX

Jos., 261
Joseph, 76
L., 255
L. C., 238
Littleton S., 253
Mary A., 238
Mary C., 238
Mary T., 76
William T., 36
HEMPSTON
Anna M., 70
Christian, 70
HEMPSTONE
Cephas, 69, 185, 195
Christian, 150
Lina, 194
Mary E., 69
Vernon, 219
W. D., 190
HENDERSON
___, 9
Alexander, 14
Anne M. C., 9
Annie L., 288
Annie T., 163
Arch'd., 63
Archibald, 9
Charles, 152
Charles A., 63
Clarissa M., 267
Eliza, 267
Ellen V., 169
F. M., 251, 272
Fenton M., 163
Geo. W., 203
James L., 225
Jane H., 203
Jennett S., 38
John, 192
Levi, 267
Margaret, 14
Maria E., 12
Marie E., 159
Mary B., 5
Mary E., 131
Mrs., 4
R. H., 122, 312
Rebecca, 152
Richard, 9, 38
Richard H., 14
Robert, 288, 291
Samuel, 306

William O., 272
HENDRICK
Wm. R., 53
HENDRICKS
Daniel W., 147
HENING
Julia E., 14
Wm. H., 14
HENNAGE
Mrs., 264
HENRY
Edward, 95
James B., 18
Robert S., 243
HENSEY
Mary J., 29
HENSHAW
J. J., 75
HENSON
Philip, 257
HEPBRON
Edgar, 197
HEPBURN
George E., 279
HERBERT
Alice, 247
Arthur, 247, 302
Jno. T., 223
Monimia F., 247
Wm. P., 252
HERNDON
John G., 72
Louisa A., 229
Lucy, 278
HESKELL
William A., 91
HESKETT
Susannah, 217
HESS
Dow, 272
Ginnie, 272
James F., 283
John A., 317
L. Dow, 107
Nancy W., 99
Thomas L., 311
HESSER
A. T., 292
Clementina, 292
Jacob P., 165
James E., 16
Mary D., 94

Rodney, 292
HEWETT
Judith, 79
Lydia, 79
Maria, 79
HEWITT
Abraham, 23
Charles A., 171
Isabella, 23
Oscar G., 171
HIBBS
Henry, 92
Jos. L., 168
Lucy H., 325
Lucy R., 324
Melinda Emma, 120
Wm. H., 31
HIBLER
Emma T., 169
Geo. M., 113, 169, 192
Henry, 269
Henry B., 269
Louisa E., 269
Theresa R., 169
HICKMAN
Caroline R., 81
Geo. S., 99
George, 43, 81
George H. C., 103
J. P., 326
Kate, 43
Kertis, 231
Luther W., 231
Mary C., 31
Mary S., 99
William S., 206, 207
HICKS
Anna M., 43
Annie E., 119
Kimball G., 134
HICKSON
Wm. N., 304
HICOTT
Susie W., 142
Wm., 142
HIGDON
James, 56
M. A., 313
HIGGINS
Hugh, 175
HIGHMAN

INDEX

Elizabeth, 239
Hattie V., 239
Matthew, 239
HILL
  Elizabeth, 109
  Joseph R., 68
  Laban L., 27
  Mary, 29
  Mary S., 86
  Volney P., 157
  William, 86
HILLARD
  Edmund C., 243
  Robert F., 243
  Virginia, 243
HILLEARY
  H. C., 215
  Hugh C., 198
HILLERY
  John, 38
HINDMAN
  Jas., 176
HINDS
  M. A., 138
HIRST
  Elizabeth J., 9
  Hester, 161
  John T., 161
  Richard, 306
  S. N., 9
  Saml. S., 161
  Samuel N., 9
  Thompson M., 193, 194
HITAFFER
  Roberta, 207
  Wm. H., 205, 207
HITT
  Reuben F., 277
HIXON
  Tracy H., 176, 177
HIXSON
  David, 15, 22, 43
  Isabella S., 129
  Sarah J., 151
HILLERY
  Henry C., 90
HOBBS
  Florence V., 260
HOCKENSMITH
  Sarah S., 19
HODGE

Susan A., 245
HODGKIN
  James O., 300
HODSON
  Julia V., 157
HOFFECKER
  Florence, 328
  Frank, 328
  J. H., 327, 328
HOFFMAN
  Jacob, 225
  John, 248
  Mary E., 225
  Phebe, 35
  Sallie, 159
  Sophia, 248
HOGE
  Anna, 212
  Daniel J., 42
  Eli J., 212
  Emma, 140
  Henrietta, 119
  Isaac, 105, 196, 212
  James M., 298
  Jas. M., 294
  Jesse, 119
  John B., 228
  Lewis N., 87
  Mary, 140
  Mary E., 37
  Rachel, 195
  Rachel N., 196
  Rachel W., 105
  Solomon, 153
  Susan A., 248
  Thomas, 140
  Thos., 284
  Wm. S., 174
HOGELAND
  Amassa C., 302
  John J., 195
  John W., 302
HOLE
  Elias, 16
  Mary, 107
HOLLADAY
  Patsey L., 22
  Waller L., 5
  William H., 22
HOLLAND
  Mary D., 283
HOLLEY

Bayless, 248
HOLLIDAY
  Anna, 241
  Caldwell, 183
  Caroline C., 142
  F. W. D., 142
  Margaret B., 7
  R. J. McK., 7
  Rosa, 241
  W. F. M., 116
HOLLINGSWORTH
  Chas. L., 116
  Lewis D., 142
  Lydia J., 324
  Robt. I., 115
  Robt. J., 116
HOLLINSWORTH
  Chas. L., 155
HOLLIS
  Edward G., 124
HOLLYDAY
  Richard C., 6
HOLMES
  Eiza T., 159
  Elijah, 102
  Elisha, 154
  Geo. W., 295
  Sarah, 105
  William, 105, 159
HOLT
  Henry, 229
HOLTZCLAW
  Alex M., 28
  Howard, 307, 315
  Jas., 132
  Martha V., 132
HONLEY
  Richard, 181
HOOD
  Jonah, 109
HOOE
  Catharine, 18
  Catherine E., 15
  Elizabeth M. A. B., 271
  Frank, 244
  Henry D., 15
  Howison, 18
  Mary A., 15
HOOK
  Mary E., 31
HOOVER

The Mirror
INDEX

W. E., 261
HOPE
  C. Ellen, 171
  Madison, 26
HOPKINS
  Fannie, 250
  Josephine H., 105
  Lewis, 105
  Philip, 158
  Richard E., 198
HORAN
  William, 240
HORNER
  Anna M., 160
  Eliza B., 123
  Fanny B., 191
  Inman, 160
  Joseph, 156
  Moses, 31
  Nathalie, 156
HORSEMAN
  Sarah E., 317
  William, 317
HORSMAN
  S. E., 316
HORSMON
  Jas. T., 294
HOSKINSON
  A. W., 314
  Robert, 223
  Robert J., 314
  Thos. L., 223
  Wm. D., 209
HOSPITAL
  Josephus, 146
HOUGH
  Amelia A., 195
  Amosa, 45
  Ann E., 45
  Annie B., 276
  Annie M., 143
  Aran Ann, 268
  B., 304
  B. W., 201
  Benj. F., 73, 77
  Bernard, 72, 210
  C. K., 194
  C. Willie, 284
  Charles, 1, 268
  E. M., 253
  E. T., 152
  Elizabeth M., 45

Estell, 223
Eugene, 105
Eugenia, 319
Fanny A., 9
Florida S., 208
G., 179
Geo. W., 291
Ginnie, 268
H. Isabella, 60
Henrietta, 83
Henry, 56
Henry H., 89
James T., 60
Jane, 32
Jennie, 248
Jno., 11
Jos., 152
Joseph F., 13
Julia G., 261
L. W. S., 1, 34, 134, 286, 321
Leven, 34
Lou, 286
Louisa, 305
Mariah J., 304
Mary, 259, 284
Mollie, 328
Nancy C., 100
Phebe E., 142
Pleasants, 11
Roberta, 180
Robt. D., 152
Rodney C., 198, 257, 285
Rosa, 300
Samuel, 284
Sarah, 1, 34
Setha, 169
Thaddeus, 311
Thomas, 60, 238
Thomas E., 212
Thos. W., 208
William, 32, 304, 305
Wilson S., 286
Wm., 179, 223
HOUSE
  Chas. H., 263
  Eli C. H., 19
HOUSEHOLDER
  Adam, 65
  Catharine, 19
  Catherine, 21

George W., 10
Gideon, 10
Jacob, 19, 21, 86, 87, 88
S. A., 181
Sarah C., 87
Silas A., 263
Valeria, 86
Virginia C., 88
HOUSER
  Chas. W., 224
  Christopher, 126
  John, 276
  Margaret A., 4
  Martha V., 148
  Rosanna, 126
HOUSHOLDER
  Columbus, 45
  Gideon, 45
  Hamilton, 45
  Julia, 45
  William O., 89
HOWARD
  Annie, 264
  Clement W., 274
  Grafton, 264
  Norman DeV., 180
  William G., 230
HOWELL
  Amanda, 166
  Amy W., 176
  Charles E., 109
  Craven, 176
  David, 109
  Emily R., 127
  Fannie L., 239
  Geneva, 166
  Gennetta, 166
  Hannah, 72
  James M., 293
  John M., 127, 179, 239
  Jos. W., 166
  Joseph, 177
  Joseph M., 176
  Mary B., 239
  Rodney C., 176
  Samuel, 3
HOWSER
  Christopher, 92
  Elizabeth, 327
  Harriet R., 66

John H., 96
John W., 51
Mary E., 66
Mr., 287
Wm. C., 100
HUDNELL
　Roberta, 90
HUDSON
　Leo, 157
　Wm. A., 210
HUDSPETH
　Sarah W., 321, 324
HUFFER
　David, 310
　Emma O., 310
HUGES
　Ada L., 73
　Jno. H., 73
HUGHES
　David L., 44, 57
　Edmund B., 20
　Edward, 164
　Emma J., 192
　Fanny L., 181
　Frances, 181
　John, 36, 181
　Margaret F., 44, 57
　Martha, 36
　Oliver, 181
　Thomas, 44
　Virginia S. F., 20
HULSEY
　A. J., 251
　Augustus J., 142
HUMMER
　A. P., 279
　Adelaide D., 145
　Alpheus P., 296
　Braden E., 37, 233
　Branden E., 197
　Geo. W., 161, 206
　John, 91, 209
　L. M., 155
　Laura T., 197
　Mary E., 91
　Richard E., 155
　Washington, 55
HUMPHREY
　Abner G., 232
　Annie, 195
　Isaac, 306
　John G., 133

Ketmah, 98
Mary C., 232, 238
Phoeba, 230
Phoebe, 231
Thomas O., 98
Virginia, 280
W. W., 281
HUMPHREYS
　David, 4
HUNNICUTT
　G. T. S., 111
HUNT
　Amos T., 9, 315
　Eliza, 304
　James, 80
　Lewis, 228, 229
　Mary V., 258
　Susan, 311
　William, 158
　Wm. H., 160
HUNTER
　Edith, 63
　G. P., 317
　Geo., 241
　Geo. P., 96
　George W., 163
　John, 316
　M. L., 293
　Michael, 241
　Michael L., 96, 240
　Ruth A., 293
HUNTON
　Annie, 242
　Charles H., 242
　Elizabeth M., 71
　Eppa, 71, 191, 204
　General, 253
　James, 261
　Jas., 204
　Matilda C., 261
HURLEY
　Reuben, 4, 5
HURST
　Benj. F., 92
　James G., 27
　Jennie A., 23
　Kate D., 27
　Thompson M., 196
　William, 23
HURT
　Joseph, 59
HURXTHAL

Geo. A., 156
HURXTHALL
　Wm. Edmond, 98
HUTCHINSON
　Arthur H., 261
　Eliza, 261
　J. W., 261
　John, 94
　John W., 90
　Lucy F., 313
　Ludwell, 99
　Martha R., 183
　Mary C., 44
　Thomas H., 66
　Virginia, 95
　Wm. N., 183
HUTCHISON
　Annie, 61
　Beverley, 289, 291
　Beverly, 61
　Beverly D., 293
　Eli, 189
　Elizabeth, 221, 224
　F. P., 187
　George H., 75
　Jas. R., 268
　Joseph A., 315
　Julian A., 154
　Leah, 4
　Lucinda, 261
　Mary, 146
　Mary C., 123
　Mary V., 107
　Melville, 261
　Philip A., 316
　Sampson, 221
　T. B., 61
　Thomas, 216
　Thos., 146
　William A., 131
　William N., 118
　William P., 59
　Wm. A., 189
　Wm. D., 107

IDEN
　Jno., 128
　John, 223
　John T., 224
　Virginia, 224
INGIN
　Thomas, 101

The Mirror
INDEX

INGRAM
　S. L., 48
　Thos. J., 207
IRWIN
　Alfred, 243
ISETT
　George, 40
　John J., 138
ISH
　Ed., 172
　Edgar, 151
　F. A., 278
　George, 52
　Jacob, 218
　Mary, 218
　Robt., 218
　Robt. A., 58
ISLER
　Abraham, 37, 38
　Charles H., 74
　George, 37
　Sarah W., 38

JACKSON
　A. G., 311
　Albert G., 252
　Alice, 197
　Anna, 76
　Annie C., 292
　Asa, 78, 128
　Clara M., 136
　Clarence, 257
　Emma J., 311
　Giles, 204
　H. Melville, 214
　Harry M. M., 160
　Henry W., 214
　Isaac, 192
　John T., 204
　Joseph, 251
　Julia, 182
　Lizzie, 257
　Lucinda, 136
　Margare A., 305
　Mary A., 268
　Mildred, 175
　Pamela, 154
　Rebecca L., 214
　S. F., 175
　S. K., 118
　Samuel C., 256, 257
　Sarah A. T., 123

　Sophonia, 204
　Susan J., 128
　Susannah M., 116
　Thomas H., 136
　William, 307
　William A., 33, 311
　William H., 257
　Wm., 182
　Wm. B., 76, 197
JACOBS
　A. R., 134
　A. Roszell, 241
　Alcinda E., 224
　Bertha, 245
　Catharine, 241
　Charles W., 33
　Elam, 46
　Elizabeth, 153
　Florence M., 271
　Geo., 235
　George, 153, 245
　George L., 153
　Harvey, 235
　Herbert, 312
　Isabella, 312
　Jane D., 33
　Kate E., 235, 245
　Louisa R., 134
　R. P., 33
　Rosalie S., 176, 177
　Rynord, 34
　Sallie E., 257
　Sallie M. J., 246
　Sarah M., 248
　Wm. A., 20
　Wm. H., 20, 241
JAGGAR
　Grace, 321
JAMES
　Abel, 22
　C. F., 167
　Caldwell A., 249
　Craven, 276
　Eliza E., 206
　Fannie, 212
　Geo. Wm., 307
　John E., 180
　Jos., 212
　Lizzie H., 281
　Mahlon, 206
　Mary, 212, 304
　Mary A., 47

　Mary C., 257
　Mary E., 143
　Mason, 208, 276
　Matson, 276, 298
　Richard, 57, 60, 235, 325
　robt, 107
　Robt, 107
　Robt., 250, 281, 291
　Sallie C., 276
　Sallie F., 249
　Sally, 22
　Thomas B., 65
　Thos. H., 218
　W. H., 250
　Winifred, 291
　Wm. A., 119
　Wm. H., 272
JANNEY
　Alice S., 129
　Amos, 172
　Aquila, 255
　Aquilla, 24
　Asa M., 76, 264
　Asbury, 79
　Becky, 222
　Bettie, 249
　C. P., 145, 282
　Charles P., 301
　Chas. P., 154, 188, 222
　Cornelia, 194
　Cornelia A., 311
　Cornelia G., 24
　Corrie, 194
　Edgar, 234
　Eli, 194
　Eli H., 311
　Elisha, 122, 268
　Elizabeth V., 129
　Emily, 21
　Florence, 166
　Frank H., 21
　G. W., 166
　Geo. W., 108
　George W., 166
　Hugh S., 106
　James C., 282
　James W., 193
　John, 122, 129, 282
　Joseph, 83
　Joseph T., 63

INDEX

Lydia N., 76
Mahlon H., 318
Maria W., 255
Mary M., 21
Mollie S., 153
N. H., 153
Nannie, 108
Nannie L., 301
Phineas, 92
Richard H. C., 318
Samuel, 83
W., 167
Walter, 71
Willie H., 318
Janney & Hoge, 193
JAQUES
  Joseph, 196
JARVIS
  Edgar, 125
  Edgar J., 126
  Ella C., 249
  Louisa, 13
  Louisa A., 126
  Washington, 13, 126, 128
JAVINS
  Mary E., 207
JEFFRIES
  Enoch K., 237
  J. W., 114
  Mary J., 237
  Mattie, 109
  Mattie D., 81
JENKINGS
  Samuel, 108
JENKINS
  Adolphus J., 228
  Annie, 141, 143
  Annie E., 293
  Charles, 88
  George F., 102
  James, 141
  Jas., 143
  Joseph H., 303
  Owen, 199
  Sallie, 80
  Samuel, 31
  Samuel E., 293
  Sarah Jane, 44
  Wesley, 142
  Wm. S., 308
JENNINGS

Ada C., 5
Frank W., 209
Mary E., 175
William H., 5
JEWETT
  Chas., 319
  Joseph H., 319
  Present, 319
JOHNS
  Arthur S., 295, 296
  Bishop, 2
  Helen J., 295
  Helen L., 296
  Henry V., 295, 296
  Kersey, 2
JOHNSON
)___, 280
  Annie, 122
  Baker W., 5
  C. P., 172
  C. W., 251
  Catharine, 123
  Chas. W., 152, 181
  Eliza, 321
  Ella C., 208
  Fanny E., 89
  Flora L., 202
  Francis E., 56
  Geo., 169
  Hattie B., 167
  Henry A., 30
  Horace, 175
  James, 269
  James A., 79
  John Y., 196
  Lawson E., 95
  Lizzie A., 70
  Lydia J., 30
  Malinda, 16
  Malinda B., 92
  Margaret, 46
  Mary, 262
  Mary J., 174
  Mary P., 19
  Mattie, 266
  Melvin, 174
  Peter W., 167
  Reuben, 149
  Richard M., 49
  Robert, 16
  Robt., 150, 152, 181
  Robt. W., 172

Thomas, 89
V. M., 321
W. H., 223
William, 202
William H., 23
William W., 56
Wm., 202
Wm. H., 56
JOHNSTON
  Charles A., 274
  Chas. A., 274, 294
  George, 306
  James W., 32
  Margaret, 134
  Nancy, 315
JOLLIFE
  Susan B., 87
JOLLY
  Bushrod, 140
  Jacob, 140
JONES
  Amanda, 189
  Anna M., 74
  Arthur L., 178
  Edgar D., 295
  Edward, 216
  Eliza E., 295
  Emeline B., 147
  Emma W., 313
  Francis A., 27
  Frank F., 25
  H. M., 296
  Henrietta, 178
  Henry, 258
  Henry A. W., 27
  J. H., 123
  James F., 83
  James H., 27, 118
  Jane, 241
  Jas. H., 178
  Jesse W., 313
  Jno., 180
  John, 14, 241, 261
  John W., 178
  Jos. R., 38
  L. T., 218
  Lewin T., 183, 190
  M. Patterson, 73
  Maggie A., 84, 85
  Marshall J., 74
  Martha, 1
  Martha A., 298

The Mirror
INDEX

Mary, 203, 205
Mary J., 85
Mattie, 124
Paul, 81
Philip A. C., 183
Philip DeC., 190
Richard, 29
Richard H., 147
Robert F., 261
Roger, 183
Susan, 146
Thomas A. C., 73, 183
Victoria M., 227, 228
Walter, 191, 201
William T., 85
Wm., 204
Wm. R., 66
JORDAN
  Alice E., 316
  J. O., 316
  John O., 166
  Mr., 127
  Stuart, 316
JORDON
  Hattie L., 209
  John L., 209
JOYNER
  John R., 148
JUNKIN
  Evelyn, 235

KAIGHN
  Philip T., 27
KALB
  A. J., 155
  Absalom, 155
  Dora D., 322
  J. N., 325
  Maggie M., 206, 207
  Susannah, 155
KANE
  Elizabeth, 233
  Emily, 237
KAYLOR
  Samuel H., 235
KEARNES
  Susan E., 296
KEARSLEY
  Annie H., 179
  G. W. T., 179, 294
  Jennie K., 294

KEEN
  Alfred D., 52
  Amanda, 32
  Charles R., 81
  Elizabeth, 81
  John, 32
  Sallie E., 81
KEENE
  Alfred S., 18
  Arthelia, 5, 18
  Benjamin B., 141
  Charles F., 202
  Elizabeth, 202, 205
  Erville E., 5
  Geo., 153
  George, 24
  Harvey L., 302
  J. W., 18
  James W., 5
  Richard, 120
  Thomas, 293
KEEYS
  Mary V., 130
KEFAUVRE
  Charles N., 186
  Lizzie, 186
KEITH
  J., 271
  J. G., 183
  James, 159, 267
  Judge, 323
  Lilly, 267
  Lucy J., 271
  Wm. S., 323
KELBER
  ___, 73
KELCHNER
  John H., 43
KELLEY
  Belle, 143
  Maggie A., 31
  Moses, 144
KELLY
  Eliza, 34
  John W., 62, 83
  Mary E., 44
  Kelly & Carter, 272
KEMPER
  J. Adeline, 188
KENDELL
  Eoline V., 181
KENDRICK

  John, 306
  Martha A., 176
KENNEDY
  Amelia R., 312
  Andrew E., 23, 71
  H. H., 312
  Henry S., 312
  Mary E., 40
  William, 71
KENNERLY
  Caleb B. R., 46
KENT
  Chas. O., 42
  Margaret, 46
KEPHART
  Martha, 79
  Miss, 170
  W. F., 80
KEPLER
  Henry S., 246
  Mary, 76
  S. R., 246
  Samuel, 48
KERBY
  F. A., 199
KERCHEVAL
  Kate, 56
KERFOOT
  Daniel S., 93
  John D., 97
  Josephine, 93
KERICK
  Matthew, 225
KERN
  Elizabeth H., 30
  Jane H., 180
  Margaret, 20
  William, 20
KERNS
  Catharine A., 172
  John N., 176
  Martha, 176
KERSEY
  Capt., 131
KESSLER
  A. M., 127
  Edward M., 177
  Martha E., 218
KETTLE
  James M., 151
  Nancy, 60
KEYES

Daniel H., 39
H., 37
Susan W., 37
William S., 7, 75
KEYS
  Hannah, 175
  Isaiah, 188
  Jane, 324
KIDWELL
  Alfred, 30
  Amanda E., 223
  Ann, 245
  Bessie V., 183
  Eliza, 46
  Fannie E., 288
  George H., 245
  George R., 164
  Henson, 180
  James E., 44, 183, 288
  Jas. E., 182
  Martha V., 186
  Mary E., 183
  Mary M., 245
  Sarah W., 170
  Wm. H., 46
KIDWELLEN
  Frederick, 253
KILGOUR
  Alexander, 219
  Charlotte, 164
  Chas. J., 219
  Eppie, 192
  Gennie, 219
  James M., 192
  Jas. M., 164
  William, 4
KIMMA
  Mary, 66
KINCADE
  John H., 291
  Minnie, 291
KINCHELOE
  Annie, 61
  Elisha D., 211
KINNER
  Elvira F., 116
KINSOLVING
  J. G., 321
  O. A., 18
KIRBY
  Ann V., 201

Jane E., 10
John, 201
Meshick, 10
KIRK.
  Anne E., 27
KIRKBY
  Joshua, 201
KITSEN
  Samuel, 196
KITTLE
  Mary E., 139
KITZMILLER
  A. M., 315
  Chillingworth, 315
  Frederic A., 246
  Jennings, 246
  Mollie E., 246
KLINE
  Mrs., 321
  Sarah E., 32
KLIPSTINE
  Henry W., 237
KNAPP
  Carrie F., 148
KNIGHT
  Amanda E., 279
  Cornelia, 44
  Mary, 262
  Mary E., 195
KNOONCE
  Alice R., 127
  George, 127
KNOTTS
  Annie E., 171
  Katie B., 171
KNOWLS
  Carr, 168
KNOX
  Janet, 104
  John S., 2
  Thos. P., 145
KNOXVILL
  Robert, 148
KOWNSLAR
  E. S., 321
  Randolph, 46, 321
  S. Jannie B., 321
KUHLMAN
  Lucy J., 273
KUHLMANN
  Justus, 195
KYLE

David W., 55
Sophia S., 55
LACEY
  Benj. C., 139
  Joseph, 139
  Laura E., 29
LACKEY
  Leila L., 222
  Robert J., 222
  Wm., 248
LACKLAND
  Fannie, 242
  Lt. Col., 51
  Thomas, 242
LACOCK
  Jacob, 188
  James W., 45
  Mary E., 197
  Matilda, 45
  Sallie M., 227
  Samuel, 45, 227
LACY
  B. W., 299
LAFITTE
  Fannie S., 179
LAGLE
  George V., 232
LAKE
  Balis, 63
  Ludwell, 96, 244
  Mary A., 96
  Sarah E., 55
  T. Sherman, 34
LALEY
  John J., 20
LAMAR
  J. T., 215
LAMB
  Samuel, 307
LAMBERT
  Edward, 288
  F., 287
  Florence F., 287
  Francis, 275
  Lee J., 218
  Louisa, 275
  Mary, 218
  Maurice W., 170
LAMBRIGHT
  George W., 178
LAMDEN

Charles, 40
Ellen, 40
Geo. T., 40
LANDERS
  Edward, 232
LANE
  Benedict M., 215
  David D., 243
  David T., 245
  Susan, 215
LANGHORNE
  Thomas N., 117
LANHAM
  John, 269
  Margaret E., 269
  Virginia, 252
LANKAM
  Lewellen, 27
LANMAN
  Mary J., 195
LARERTY
  Esther A., 135
  Henry, 135
LATHAM
  Geo. W., 149
  Georgia O., 149
LAWRENCE
  John W., 263
LAWS
  John T., 96
  Laura, 220
  T. L., 199
LAWSON
  Annie E., 98
  Bettie, 267
  George L., 299
  James H., 267
  John W., 172
  Mary S., 267
  Wm. L., 98
LAYCOCK
  C. F., 250
  Edward, 279
  James, 272
  Jas., 213
  Lucy E., 266
  Lula, 279
  Mary A., 213
  Mr., 271
  Samuel, 266
  Samuel A., 172
  Virginia E., 60

LAYMAN
  Abraham, 318
  Ann, 318
LEADBEATER
  Anna, 85
  E. S., 85
  Lizzie J., 214
  Thos., 214
LEARNED
  Geo. F., 196
LEARY
  Daniel, 240
LEAVELL
  Julia Y., 105
LEE
  A. D., 27
  Alex. H., 159
  Alice, 27
  Beverley R., 260
  C. H., 134, 144, 267
  Cassius F., 156, 267
  David J., 128, 159
  Dodridge, 121
  Edmund I., 38, 267, 311, 326
  Edmund L., 218
  Eliza A., 295
  Eliza M., 202
  Emily L., 130
  Evelyn B., 121
  George, 34, 121, 206, 260
  George W., 106, 255
  H. B., 271
  Ida, 38
  James, 166
  Jesse, 250
  John B., 119, 130
  John J., 278
  Launcelot, 249
  Laura D., 271
  Laura F., 260
  Ludwell, 202
  Margaret G., 76
  Martha M., 97
  Mary G., 121
  Mary R., 69
  Matthew, 216
  Matthew P., 75
  Orra, 206
  Philip L., 202
  R. H., 267, 295, 306

Richard H., 202
Robert E., 76
S. M., 206
Sallie L., 219
Sally, 311
Sally M., 164
William, 21
William W., 74
Wm. B., 320
LEFEVER
  Mary Francis, 82
LEFEVERS
  Sarah, 137
LEFEVRE
  L. L., 291
  William, 273
LEG
  Margaret A., 21
LEIGH
  Alfred, 275, 287
  Mary, 287
  Rebecca, 35
  Thos., 35
  William, 43
LEITH
  Mary F., 105
  Nellie E., 156
  R. H., 161
  Theoderic, 24
  Theodorick B., 86
  Wm. G., 161
LEMON
  Thomas, 308
LENT
  Franklin, 222
  Samuel E., 203
LENT
  Lafayette, 203
LEOPOLD
  Geo. W., 110
LERSNER
  Gustavus, 237, 238
  H. B., 238
LESLIE
  Benjamin, 151, 170
  Elizabeth, 192
  Jno., 212
  Jno. A., 192
  John, 77, 184, 185, 269
  John A., 272
  John B., 192, 272

The Mirror
INDEX

John E., 272
Julia B., 192
Kate M., 151
Lina A. A., 269
Mollie T., 243
Samuel D., 88
Sarah A., 67
LEVENBERG
  Elwood, 323
LEVENBURG
  Flavius, 323
LEVENBURY
  Ellwood, 324
LEVI
  Samuel, 306
LEWEN
  Nicholas, 163
LEWIS
  Ann, 215
  B. F., 132
  Barbara, 319
  Daingerfield, 241
  Elizabeth, 274
  Ellen J., 210
  James, 214
  Jas., 210, 215
  John H. B., 40
  Martha J., 163
  Wm. H., 129, 173
LICKEY
  ___, 57
  E., 35
  Elizabeth, 71
  Eugenia D., 249
  G. W., 35
  George, 154
  Julia A., 87
  Sampson, 71
  Wm., 57
  Wm. B., 35
LICKY
  Martha A., 121
  Sampson, 121
LIEUTY
  Burton, 32
LIGGETT
  Catharine, 30
  S. W., 30
  Samuel W., 30
LIGHTFOOT
  Catharine E., 107
  John, 168, 293

John T., 266, 272
Samuel H., 328
W., 107
Wm., 292
LIKENS
  Kate K., 75
  Thomas J., 75
LIMERICK
  Sidney, 175
LINDSAY
  John S., 265
LINDSEY
  Jos. B., 8
  Susan, 37
LINE
  John D., 71
  Mary C., 71
LINFIELD
  Mary J., 186
LINK
  Daniel, 7
LINKINS
  Henry B., 101
LINN
  Pamelia C., 14
LINTHICUM
  Annie, 303
LIONBERGER
  Isaac, 283
  Sallie, 283
LIPSCOMB
  Bettie, 68
  Helen A., 17
  M. J. C., 17
  W. C., 17
LITTLE
  Joseph, 55
LITTLETON
  Charles M., 29
  Edgar, 196, 257
  Elizabeth, 257
  Emma, 280
  Fielding, 43
  George, 222
  John, 12
  Martha J., 34
  Mary C., 14
  Nannie F., 118
  Oscar, 101
  Oscar F., 325
  Thomas, 12, 257, 280

Thos., 223, 257
LLOYD
  Andrew J., 3
  Annie, 127
  Barckley, 290
  Charles E., 75, 127
  E. J., 311
  Emily E., 127
  Fred'k., 204
  James W., 33
  John J., 160
  Lucy L., 204
  Mary, 156
  Rebecca, 160, 274
  Richard, 156, 274
LOCK
  Amelia E., 216
  Franck, 216
  Jane A., 69
  Lucie M., 172
  Rachel, 71
  Sue R., 70
  William F., 69, 70
  Wm. French, 172
LOCKE
  Bettie C., 71
  John M., 71
  Lizzie M., 71
LOCKER
  Eliza V., 66
  Jarod, 195
  Sophia C., 90
LOCKHART
  John B., 75
LOCKWOOD
  B. A., 197
LODGE
  Alice A., 136
  Benjamin, 117
  Harman, 26
  Harmon, 136
  John, 151
  Joseph, 264
  Marcia A., 26
  Samuel, 28
  Sarah E., 68
LOGAN
  Mrs., 208
  Parmelia A., 72
LOMAX
  Kate R., 296
  L. L., 151

INDEX

R. Stuart, 296
LONG
  Burgess B., 161
  M. A., 253
  Mrs., 234
  Sallie, 137
  Sarah J., 23
LONGACRE
  Mrs., 275, 280
LONGBRAKE
  Geo. F., 121
LORMAN
  Alexander, 124
LOTT
  Betsy, 234
  Elizabeth A., 38
  Parkinson L., 59
LOUGHBOROUGH
  Anna H., 200
  Nathan, 200
LOVE
  Bettie H., 245
  Cecelia, 202
  Eliza M., 202
  Elizabeth R., 10
  Fenton M., 245
  Flora L., 202
  James M., 180
  John, 202
  Ludwell, 202
  Richard, 202
  Richard H., 202
  Samuel P., 80
  Susannah, 104
  Thomas, 202
LOVELESS
  Alcinda C., 169
  Elizabeth, 313
  Ella, 304
  John W., 169, 304
  Lizzie, 163
  Mason, 70
  Thos., 312
  William T., 169
LOVETT
  Catharine, 100
LOVETTE
  Mort. C., 110
LOWE
  Emily, 203
  George W., 67
  John H., 298
  Joseph, 203, 213
  Joseph H., 284
LOWNDS
  Jas. A., 56
LOWRY
  Emma J., 222
  Hannah, 111
  Peter, 111
  Wm., 222
LOY
  Adam, 179, 214
  Adam F., 47
  George H., 91
  John W., 107
  Mary E., 99
  Richard F., 236
  Virginia E., 214
LUCAS
  Wm., 190, 236
LUCK
  Jno. M., 19
  William J., 105
LUCKETT
  Annie F., 164
  Arabella, 77
  C. D., 212
  Ellen A., 310
  Francis, 212
  Francis L., 4
  Francis W., 222
  Frank E., 238
  Henrietta, 4
  Horace, 55, 313
  John R., 33
  L. H., 212
  L. Henry, 4
  Louisa A., 313
  Ludwell, 25, 211, 212, 260, 310
  Margaret, 150
  Mary B., 95
  Mary M., 260
  Robert, 78
  S. C., 66
  Sallie A., 222
  Sallie J., 25
  Samuel C., 57, 95, 156
  Sarah J., 156
  Sarah S., 224
  Virginia, 150
  William C., 145
  William F., 115
  Wm. H., 156
LUMM
  Martha E., 3
LUNCEFORD
  Mary, 303
  William A., 24
LUNSFORD
  Evan O., 100
  Harriet A., 175
  Henry H., 277
  Wm. A., 130
LUPTON
  Jonah J., 13
  Mary E., 13
  Wm. M., 93
LUSBY
  Wilhimah M., 115
  Wm. H., 115
LUTTRELL
  Thos., 306
LUTZ
  Addie M., 221, 274
  F. A., 151, 274
  John A., 301
  Mamie, 151
  Samuel S., 272
LYBRAND
  Geo. H., 195
LYNCH
  Burr C., 50
  Charles, 117
  Eliza H., 47
  Jane D., 117
  John A., 276
  Laura R., 50
  W. B., 50
  William B., 59
  William C., 303
  Wm. B., 65, 117, 303
LYND
  John, 5
LYNE
  Thos. H., 279
LYNN
  Augusta, 136
  Bertha E., 254
  Elizabeth, 110
  Frances, 172
  Gertrude, 172
  Humphrey, 254
  Jno. T., 136

INDEX

John, 128, 151
John F., 143
John H., 110
John T., 138, 139
Luther, 144
Luther L., 136
Mary A. E., 316
Mary C., 2
Pasilia, 254
Permelia C., 151
Robert L., 316
Thos. H., 283
William M., 129
Wm. H., 81
LYON
  Isabella, 180
  Virginia C., 160
LYONS
  Martha A., 295
LYTH
  Cecelia S., 215
  Hannah T., 215
  Isaac P., 215
  Sallie Q., 215
LYTTON
  Lyda, 64

MACDANIEL
  J. W., 241
  Massie R., 241
MacFARLANE
  Virginia, 221
MacGREGOR
  Helen W., 242
  John R., 242
MADDEN
  Luranah, 227
  William, 227
MADDOX
  Alice G., 155
  Florence, 179
  James D., 155
  R. E., 179
MAFFETT
  C. J. C., 275
  C. W., 261
MAGAHA
  Geo. Wm., 249
  John, 127
MAGEATH
  James T., 170
MAGILL

Ann, 200
Chas. W., 23
MAJOR
  Elizabeth H., 174
  Eliz'h. H., 175
  Laura, 63
  T. C., 269
MALORY
  Henry, 313
MANCHE
  John, 91
MANINGLY
  Orlando F., 143
MANKIN
  Charles L., 260
  Chas., 285
  Chas. L., 57
  Christiana M., 73
  G. W. F., 44
  James W., 73
  Lavinia, 260
  Lewis F., 57
  Motta, 260
MANN
  Charity, 24
  Elizabeth, 314
  John, 89
  John S., 24, 110
  Joseph B., 274, 287
  Mary C., 47
  Sarah V., 89
  Wm., 24
MANNING
  C. E., 112, 273
  E., 20
  G. Upshur, 74
  Harry, 210
  J. H., 112, 210, 273
  Jacob H., 59
  Lucy E., 193
  Margaret, 20
  Maud, 273
  N. W., 193, 314
  Uphemia, 33
MANSFIELD
  Alferando, 127
  David, 118
  Margaret, 127
  Samuel, 127
MANTOR
  E. B., 2
MANUEL

Lucien M., 92
Mary S., 92
MARA
  P. H., 233
MARCH
  H. L. E., 17
  James H., 17, 21
  Laura A., 17
  Mary J., 21
MARCHE
  Frances, 24
  Frances E., 24
  Thomas B., 24
  Thos. B., 19
MARLOW
  Annie, 262
  Draco, 22
  E. G., 104
  Edmonia, 226
  Elijah, 162
  Ellen, 44
  Geo., 265
  George, 106, 226
  Jane E., 27
  John, 59
  John S., 22
  Louisa, 22
  Martha E., 44
  Mary L., 265
  Mary W., 106
  Millie L., 169
  Olivia, 22
  Parmenio, 22
  Richard, 59
  Robert, 22
  Sarah, 22
  Thomas, 22, 44
  Thomas J., 22
  Tuisce, 22
  Wm. G., 22
MARMADUKE
  Kate V., 52
  Lucie, 26
  Presley, 52
  Silas, 26
MARSHALL
  Ellen H., 22
  F. L., 271
  Hester M., 220
  Jacob, 21
  James M., 146
  James P., 220

The Mirror
INDEX

Jaquline A., 22
Lemuel, 113
Rhuel, 138
Susan, 86
W. B., 113
MARSTELLER
  C. C., 323
  J. T., 323
  Korenore A., 131
  L. A., 227
  S. A., 131
MARTIN
  A. J., 266, 272
  Alfred, 162
  Alice J., 124
  Asatia C., 272
  G. T., 266
  Hannah, 103
  Hattie R., 46
  James L., 129
  John S., 177
  John W., 100
  Mary E., 100
  Phillip D., 30
  Sarah, 187
  Theresa, 261
  Thomas, 315
  Thos., 190
  Wm. A., 103
MARTS
  Anna, 223
  Samuel, 223
MASON
  Adam, 190
  Augustine S., 5
  B. C., 156
  Charles C., 82
  Elizabeth M. A. B. H., 271
  Francis, 59
  G. F., 7
  George, 271
  James M., 251
  John, 251
  N. Carrol, 152
  Sarah B. H., 271
  Temple, 152
MASSEY
  Catharine P., 313
  Joseph T., 313
  Virginia, 6
MASSIE

  N. H., 244
MATHERS
  George, 86
  Mary, 59
  Robt., 312
  William, 84
MATHEW
  Wm., 252
MATHEWS
  Catharine, 104
  James M., 104
  William, 104
MATHIOT
  George, 157
MATSELL
  May, 278
MATTHEW
  George W., 47
  Jonathan, 252, 309
  Lizzie, 252
  William, 297
  Wm., 238
MATTHEWS
  C. B., 207
  Chas. B., 168
  Dennis M., 211
  Edith D., 95
  Edward Y., 95
  Eliza F., 128
  Elizabeth, 71
  Ella F., 167
  John, 57
  John H., 56
  Johnathan, 88
  Lizzie F., 207
  Rose, 207
  Sarah J., 95
  Squire, 111
  Squire E., 128
  William, 167
MAULSBY
  Benj., 43
  Benjamin, 82
  Charlotte, 82
MAURAN
  Joseph, 209
MAURY
  John W., 166
  Lucy F., 166
  Lucy M., 266
  M. F., 266
MAUZY

  Elizabeth, 260
  Eugenia H., 16
  Geo., 16
  Ginnie, 176
MAVIN
  Anna B., 144
MAXWELL
  Jno. T., 133
  William E., 78
McABEE
  John T., 310
  Julia, 310
  M. B., 270
  Mamie E., 221
McARTHUR
  E. S., 224
  Mamie, 224
McARTOR
  Wm., 308
McAUTHER
  Samuel, 177
McBLAIR
  Charles, 162
McCABE
  Annie, 128
  C. P., 325
  Chas. P., 303, 326
  Earnest L., 128
  Elizabeth, 325
  Hattie, 326
  Isabella S., 52
  John, 325
  John C., 52
  Lizzie R., 263
  Mary A., 303
  T. A., 128
McCANCE
  Ellen, 87
  Thomas W., 87
McCARTY
  Billington, 232
  Daniel, 125
  Dennis, 117
  Eliza, 117
  Ella C., 106
  Frances, 144
  Geo. B., 219
  Geo. W., 40, 219
  Margaret E., 232
  Page, 161
  R. C., 212, 240
  R. Chichester, 206

The Mirror
INDEX
369

Richard C., 96
Sarah R., 40
Susan F., 232
Wm. T., 185
McCLANAHAM
Mary M., 33
McCLANAHAN
___, 40
M. C., 24
Sarah J., 24
McCLEAREN
John W., 283
McCONCHIE
Eugenia L., 173
Mary E., 277
McCORMICK
Ann E., 69
Ann J., 8
Ann R., 15
Charles, 30
Charles F., 181
James M., 134
Mary E., 8
Ottoway, 8
Province, 30
R. B., 292, 317
Rosalie, 317
Stephen, 246
McCOY
C. F., 155
John, 144
Lizzie, 144
Mr., 149
McCRAY
Edgar, 200
Ellan, 276
Wm., 147, 200, 276
McCREA
Wm., 97
McCREARY
James, 164
Lucy, 164
McCREERY
J. V., 62
J. V. L., 246
Nannie, 62
McCRON
John, 22
McCURDY
Charles H., 111
McDANIEL
Albina A., 30

Archibald, 53
Henrietta, 133
James, 67, 81
James W., 66
Sarah C., 95
Turner, 58
McDONALD
Edward H., 105
Elizabeth V., 81
Fannie B., 137
John B., 160
Kate S., 137
Martha A., 141
Wm. N., 137
McDONOUGH
Charles, 54
James W., 69
Jennie, 300
McDUELL
R., 120
McENDREE
John H., 23
Louisa T., 23
Sallie, 63
McFARLAND
Alexander, 107
Alice S., 125
Annie K., 107
Carrie, 159
Edgar, 308
James L., 137, 159
James N., 184
Jas., 178
Jas. M., 185
Jennie, 275
Jos., 187, 189
L. Janie, 289
Mary, 93
Mary A., 137
Mary E., 49, 235
Morris W., 125
Virginia P., 137
W. A., 185
W. Y., 33
Wilson E., 49
Wm. A., 272
McGILL
Arabella W., 157
Edward W., 157
John, 158
McGINN
John B., 72

Robert C., 11
McGINNIS
J. W., 45
McGLAUGHLIN
Wm. J., 125
McGUIRE
Bettie C., 166
E. R., 116
Edward, 235
Gettie, 135
Robert L., 235
Wm. D., 135
Wm. P., 109
McILHANY
Hugh M., 124
J. W., 185
James K., 185
Mortimer, 41, 185
McILLHANEY
James, 193
Lizzie, 193
McINTOSH
Annie, 61
Frances O., 189
Jesse, 69
Job P., 52
Martha F., 101
Mary, 189
Walter, 189
Wm., 189
McINTYRE
Ellen, 173, 177
Patrick, 173
McKENZIE
Alex., 154
Henson, 213
McKILRICK
Mary, 24
Wm. H., 24
McKIM
Elizabeth, 22
Jane, 22
John, 22
Joseph M., 22
Mary, 22
Robert W., 22
S. H., 22
Samuel H., 22
Sarah E., 1
William A., 22
William M., 22
McKIMMEY

Wm. F., 170
McKIMMY
 Charles F., 259
 John, 41
 Mary C., 125
McKINLEY
 Thomas G., 309
McKINNEY
 Caroline, 283
 Cornelia J., 45
 James H., 45
 John W., 276
 Sarah, 28
McKNEW
 Wm. F., 63
McLEAN
 Elvira, 38
 Hector D., 38
McLEAREN
 Mary M., 177
 T. C., 177
McMURRAN
 Chas. H., 49
 Robert L., 15
McNEALY
 Lizzie, 299
McNELEA
 John R., 84
 William H., 28
McPHERSON
 Cecelia, 286
 Mary, 234
 Mary E., 291
 Nancy A., 103
 Sam, 239
 Samuel, 171
 Stephen, 286
 Virginia, 32
 W. S., 103
 Wesley, 113
McVEIGH
 Elizabeth, 136
 H. R., 73
 H. T., 181
 Hamilton, 317
 Hamilton T., 167
 Harvey, 120
 James, 136
 James H., 179
 Job G., 221
 K. Blanche, 98
 Kernon H., 50

Norman, 73
R. N., 209
Sallie A., 181
T., 220
T. J., 220
Townsend, 50, 98, 167, 267, 268, 274
Wm. H., 47, 73
McVICKER
 John, 306
MEAD
 Bettie, 328
 Bettie W., 327
 Fannie, 83
 Geo., 199
 Henry J., 328
 Jane, 83, 305
 John, 128, 249
 John S., 281
 Joseph, 83, 305
 Lavinia, 87
MEADE
 Bishop, 311
 Cornelia F., 90
 Joseph, 7
 Mary, 311
 Mary E., 7
 William, 90
MEADOR
 C. C., 118
MEGAHA
 David A., 206
MEGEATH
 Alfred, 298
 Elizabeth, 14, 15, 315
 J. T., 205
 James G., 14, 82, 133
 James T., 204
 Jos. P., 315
 Joseph M., 15
 Joseph P., 14
 Judie, 133
 Lizzie E., 209
 M. Olivia, 247
 Marrietta, 14
 Martha E., 15, 96
 Mary A., 240, 243
 S. D., 56
 Saml. A., 133
 Samuel, 15, 236, 240
 Stephen D., 15

Tholemiah, 15
Virginia, 14
MELVILLE
 Andrew, 218
MELVIN
 Wm. B., 173
MENEFEE
 A. F., 86
 James A., 220
MERCER
 Charles F., 114
 Maggie, 313
 Mollie E., 165
 Washington, 79
MERCHANT
 James, 17
 James T., 95
 Landon O., 106
 Margaret, 106
MERCIER
 Charles C., 121
 Gaither, 220
 Martha, 220
 S. B., 205
 Washington, 220
MERRIMAN
 Franklin A. T., 165
MERVIN
 C. D., 263
MICHAEL
 Samuel, 99
MICHENER
 Chas. A., 293
 John, 308
MICHIE
 Henry T., 83
MIDDLEKAUF
 Mary E., 39
MIDDLETON
 Benj., 163
MILBOURN
 Cecelia A., 21
 Ida C., 317
 John F., 21, 296, 298
 Malinda A., 96
 Miss, 276
MILBURN
 Alice, 287
 B. C., 255
 Beula L., 239
 Ethelbert, 131
 Hattie, 287

INDEX

J. C., 239
J. F., 295
Jefferson, 287
Martha J., 239
S. Florence, 255
MILEY
  Julia, 95
  Margaret M., 316
MILHOLLEN
  Henry, 14, 290, 291
  Mary E., 226
MILLAN
  Joseph C., 163, 251
  Lyle, 251
MILLARD
  Charles H., 84
  Chas. H., 85
MILLER
  Arthur, 94
  Charles M., 38
  Chas. W., 327
  Edward, 306
  Elizabeth, 131
  Frederick, 268
  George R., 134
  Jacob, 207
  Job M., 89
  John T., 2
  Louis M., 260
  M. E., 317
  Mary S., 94
  Robt. H., 178
  S. A., 144
  Sallie C., 195
  Sallie E., 207
  Thomas, 85, 134, 164
MILLS
  Annie, 252
  Harvey O., 46
  James L., 165
  John W., 147
  Lizabeth, 27
  Mary A., 147
  Robt., 252
  Samuel, 306
  Sarah, 252
  Sarah R., 81
  Susan R., 172
MILTON
  John, 309
  T. D., 165

Minister
ABRAHAMS, St.
  Geo. T., 292
ADAMS, W. F., 255
ADDISON, ___, 153, 180
ADDISON, T. G., 166
ADDISON, Thomas G., 150
ALLEN, ___, 276
ALLEN, C., 247
AMBLER, C. E., 178
AMBLER, Charles E., 18
AMBLER, John, 159, 242, 308
AMES, A. H., 255
AMES, Alfred, 141
AMOS, John E., 48
ANDERSON, J. J., 299
ANDREWS, ___, 38
ANDREWS, C. W., 21
ANDREWS, Charles W., 38, 39, 74
ANDREWS, Robert H., 71
ANTHONY, J. B., 5, 9, 20
ARMSTRONG, J., 69
ARMSTRONG, J. E., 95, 124
ATHENS, ___, 234
ATHEY, S. M., 277, 278, 327
AVIRETT, J. B., 74
BACKUS, J. C., 326
BACKUS, John C., 254
BADGER, J. N., 281
BAIER, Leo., 221
BAILY, J. C., 34
BAIRD, W. S., 3
BAIRD, Wm. S., 1, 6, 9, 10, 11
BALL, ___, 194, 225
BALL, C. W., 277
BALL, Dabney, 170
BALL, S. A., 148, 150, 196, 201, 218, 219, 227, 233, 249, 253, 256, 260
BALL, Samuel A., 125, 147, 180
BANKS, A. R., 176
BARTEN, ___, 65
BARTLEY, D., 200
BAYTON, T. J., 24
BEACH, Chas., 112
BEALL, ___, 187
BEALL, O. C., 201, 255, 264, 265, 299
BEDINGER, E. W., 190
BELL, Robert, 61
BENDER, A. J., 127
BENNETT, W. W., 6
BERKLEY, E., 4
BERRY R. T., 62, 193
BILLINGS, Silas, 45
BIRCH, J. S., 204, 281
BITTENGER, B. F., 184
BITTINGER, ___, 194
BITTINGS, ___, 65
BLACKWELL, ___, 100
BLACKWELL, J. D., 78
BLAKE, S. V., 2
BLUNT, Wm. C., 30
BOON, ___, 70
BOOTEN, J. K., 262
BOTCLER, J. W., 159
BOURBMAN, ___, 155
BOYD, Melville, 296
BOYDEN, ___, 122
BOYLE, ___, 16, 285
BOYLE, J. Richard, 318
BRADDOCK, ___, 226
BRADDOCK, W. L., 284
BRANCH, ___, 153, 297

The Mirror
INDEX

BRANCH, H., 171, 204, 295
BRANCH, Henry, 147, 151, 159, 260, 282, 298, 300
BRANCH, Henry E., 274
BRANDSTETER, ___, 201
BRANHAN, Frank, 224
BRANNIE, Jas. F., 173
BRIDGES, Beal, 233
BRIDGES, Benjamin, 141, 143, 207, 228, 250, 259, 287, 296
BROADDUS, A., 41
BROOKs, G. G., 37
BROWN, ___, 3, 4, 90, 98
BROWN, B. Peyton, 200
BROWN, F. A., 296
BROWN, G. L., 125
BROWN, Peyton, 197
BROWN, R. T., 40, 176
BROWN, Samuel, 215, 268
BRUCE, Silas, 194
BRUN, Thomas W., 222
BRURY, W., 10
BRYAN, Jas. L., 146
BUHRMAN, A., 148, 149, 167, 169, 170, 177, 193, 194, 198, 206
BULLOCK, ___, 274
BULLOCK, J. D., 165
BULLOCK, J. J., 70
BULLOCK, Jos., 170
BUNTING, ___, 294
BUSEY, ___, 140
BUSEY, E. F., 131
BUTLER, ___, 35
BUTLER, B., 287
BUTLER, C. M., 20
BUTLER, J. G., 216

CALLAWAY, C. M., 144
CAMPBELL, ___, 194
CAMPBELL, C. N., 167
CAMPBELL, J. F., 81
CAMPBELL, W. W., 164
CANNON, ___, 213, 297
CANNON, J. F., 169, 170, 198, 210, 214, 215, 230, 232, 234, 240, 247, 273, 274, 281, 283, 286, 291, 295, 296, 328
CAREY, Green, 6
CAROTHERS, Andrew G., 2, 11
CARROL, John L., 209
CARROLL, J. C., 124
CARROLL, J. L., 149, 175
CARROLL, John L., 123, 229
CARSON, Theodore, 104
CARSON, Thomas E., 32, 219, 224, 225, 229, 248, 251, 273, 279
CARTEIR, ___, 209
CAST, C., 5
CHAMPION, Wm., 43
CHEATHAM, Henry C., 39, 42
CLARK, ___, 58
CLARK, John, 33, 193, 194
CLEMENT, ___, 223
CLEMENT, H., 214, 219, 228, 229, 241
CLEMENT, Henry, 226, 238, 240, 252
CLEMENTS, Henry, 186
CLEMMENTS, ___, 213

CLEVELAND, H. A., 158
CLEVER, ___, 278
COE, W. G., 40
COE, Wm. G., 25
COLL, P. C., 62
COMPTON, A., 6, 10
CONOVER, R., 171
CORNELIUS, Samuel, 49
CORRAWAY, ___, 41
COSBY, John, 53
CREIGHTON, William, 19
CRENSHAW, L. H., 104, 106, 117, 140, 170, 201, 209, 218, 220, 225, 226, 227, 228, 238, 245, 247, 248, 253, 258, 269, 272, 276, 277, 278, 283, 284, 286, 287, 289, 295, 297, 298, 304, 306, 307, 324, 325
CRONIN, C. C., 249
CROUTH, C. P., 316
CROWN, R. T., 117
CUMPSTON, E. H., 165
CURNS, James, 89
CURTIS, ___, 75
CUTHBERT, J. H., 310
CUTTER, ___, 68
DALBY, ___, 6
DAME, George W., 141, 290
DAME, Nelson P., 299
DAME, William M., 141, 192
DAME, Wm. M., 227
DAVIS, ___, 210
DAVIS, James N., 69
DAVIS, R. T., 104, 120, 128, 163, 166, 169, 173, 177, 192, 196,

The Mirror
INDEX
373

204, 211, 218, 226, 232, 241, 269, 270, 271, 272, 273, 275, 288, 304, 318, 322, 327
DAVIS, T. R., 145
DEALE, ___, 10
DEIHL, ___, 96, 209
DESHIELD, John H., 123
DEWITT, W. R., 4
DICE, J. C., 142, 155, 163, 166, 172, 178, 181, 202
DICE, J. M., 158
DIEHL, ___, 54, 105, 112, 157, 165, 253, 265
DIEHL, G., 55, 82
DIEHL, George, 55, 66, 69
DINWIDDIE, ___, 226
DINWIDDIE, William, 204
DOBBINS, Wm., 293
DODGE, H. W., 21
DOERSKEN, J., 261
DOGE, H. W., 110
DOGGETT, ___, 270
DOHERTY, ___, 143
DOHERTY, John, 254
DOLLEY, ___, 155
DOLLY, ___, 171, 199
DOLLY, A. B., 199, 209, 243
DOMAR, ___, 260
DONAHUE, ___, 327
DOREMUS, J. W., 263
DOSH, T. W., 87, 118
DOUGHERTY, ___, 4, 25
DOWNING, ___, 20
DULANEY, J. H., 262
DULIN, B. F., 118

DULIN, B. P., 106, 122, 128, 172, 191, 224
DUNAWAY, Thos. S., 177
DUNCAN, J. A., 170
DUTTON, ___, 23, 27, 31
DUTTON, W. B., 4, 38
EAKIN, J. T., 2
EDWARDS, ___, 23
EDWARDS, Alpheus L., 313
EDWARDS, Henry, 157
EDWARDS, Wm. B., 79
EGGLESTON, W. C., 106
EGGLESTON, W. G., 4
EGGLESTON, Wm., 82
ELIOT, W. G., 131
ELLIOTT, ___, 194, 220, 256
ELLIOTT, John, 304
ENGEL, A., 125
ENGLE, E. H., 221
ENGLE, Osburn, 114
ERVING, D. B., 11
ESCHBACH, E. R., 206
ETCHISON, J. P., 28, 30
EVANS, J. E., 280, 291
EVANS, M. V. B., 288
EWING, D. B., 5
FAIR, Campbell, 275
FERGUSON, S. G., 201
FIELDMMIRE, George, 291
FINLEY, ___, 105
FIRERMAN, J. O., 286
FLEWERS, B. C., 64
FLOURNEY, Parke P., 236

FLOWERS, B. C., 58
FOLLANSBEE, ___, 202
FOLLANSBEE, J. M., 169, 173, 205
FOLLANSBEE, James M., 164, 165, 167, 171
FOLLINSBEE, J. M., 177
FOREMAN, J. O., 309
FORREST, Douglas F., 134
FORSYTH, ___, 202, 288
FORSYTH, J. H., 207
FORSYTH, John W., 305
FORSYTH, W. H., 152, 160, 165, 182, 198, 207, 262, 270, 276, 289, 296, 300, 309
FORSYTH, Wm. H., 137, 143, 160, 173, 178, 184, 194, 262, 271, 276, 288, 290, 292, 294, 295, 306, 308, 317, 322, 328
FORSYTHE, ___, 325
FOSTER, ___, 143
FOULK, S. S., 39
FOUTE, R. C., 251
FRANCIS, A. B., 163
FRAUNING, Jas. F., 196
FRIDAY, J. M., 199, 203, 218, 229, 232, 247, 250, 253, 258, 260, 264
FRIDAY, S. M., 199
FULTON, ___, 131
FUR, Joseph, 85
FURR, ___, 3
FURR, Armstead, 135
FURR, Frazier, 269

INDEX

FURR, J., 127, 148, 199, 281
FURR, Joseph, 76, 93, 98, 118, 130, 143, 173, 175, 208, 227, 243, 277
GARDINER, ___, 213
GARDINER, J. S., 247
GARDNER, ___, 228, 229
GARDNER, J. S., 217, 222, 229, 253
GIBBONS, ___, 142
GIBSON, A. E., 205
GIBSON, Churchill J., 143
GILBERT, D. M., 183
GILBERT, D. N., 275
GILLMORE, William, 30
GILLMORE, Wm., 25
GILMORE, W., 43
GILMORE, Wm., 28, 33
GOVER, S., 2, 3, 6, 23, 27, 28, 39, 43, 47, 50, 57, 61, 62, 63, 65, 67, 68, 71, 74, 76, 85, 100, 107, 120, 140, 141, 147, 160, 180
GOVER, Samuel, 2, 4, 7, 8, 13, 16, 18, 21, 28, 29, 40, 63, 69, 70, 73, 80, 81, 83, 84, 87, 89, 91, 94, 95, 99, 101, 106, 146, 188
GRAHAM, J. R., 74
GRAHAM, James R., 3
GRANBERRY, J. C., 134
GRAY, Arthur P., 320
GREENAWAY, N. S., 42
GRIMSLEY, ___, 210
GRIMSLEY, A. M., 187
GRIMSLEY, B., 8
GURLEY, R. R., 5
H. R., 66
HACKEL, J. S., 308
HAINES, ___, 94, 120, 167
HAL, Charles H., 11
HALL, W. T., 310
HAMILTON, ___, 38
HAMILTON, J. H., 219
HAMMOND, ___, 322
HAMMOND, Goheen, 37
HAMMOND, W. G., 44, 321
HAMMOND, Wesley, 146
HAMMOND, Wm. G., 218
HAMMOND, Wm. S., 1, 10
HANCKEL, J. S., 295
HANES, ___, 70
HANK, J. D., 225
HARDY, A. S. M., 48
HARISCOCK, S. W., 139
HARRIS, ___, 97
HARRIS, G. W., 45
HARRIS, George W., 30, 41, 42, 48, 84, 85, 86, 88, 93
HARRISON, ___, 5
HARRISON, W., 61
HARRISON, W. H., 96
HARRISON, W. P., 284
HARTMAN, Daniel, 130
HAYNE, ___, 308
HAYNES, ___, 81, 106, 254, 275, 295
HAYNES, J. A., 61, 96, 98, 100, 107, 120, 125, 127, 134, 146, 151, 154, 174, 193, 199, 277, 305, 320, 325
HAYNES, J. H., 99
HAYNES, J. S., 123
HEAD, ___, 105, 116, 141, 145, 167, 168, 215, 224, 229, 235, 261
HEAD, Nelson, 42, 104, 115, 119, 144, 236, 264
HEBORN, ___, 165
HELM, 50
HELM, Joseph, 61, 63, 67, 68, 70, 71, 76, 83, 88, 98, 197
HENDERSON, James S., 152
HENNING, J. G., 195
HENRDON, Thad., 233
HENRY, E. B., 125
HENRY, E. H., 124, 199
HENRY. E. H., 196
HEPBRON, ___, 121, 133
HEPBRON, S., 197
HEPBRON, S. S., 137, 156, 169, 170
HERBERT, W. G., 238
HERNDON, ___, 56
HERNDON, J., 25
HERNDON, T., 28, 64, 89, 121, 122, 195, 214
HERNDON, Thaddeus, 37, 47, 71, 72, 86, 87, 229
HERNDON, Thadeus, 67
HERRON, L. D., 44
HIGGINS, James S., 277
HILE, ___, 8
HILLCRUP, John K., 201
HOBBS, G. W., 249
HODGE, M. C., 240
HODGES, ___, 228
HOFF, ___, 190
HOFFMAN, J., 67
HOGE, M. D., 120
HOLMEAD, ___, 124

HOPKINS, A. C., 142, 176, 198
HOPKINS, Jacob, 250
HOUGH, ___, 151
HOUGH, Robert R. S., 133
HOYLE, S. V., 4, 16
HUBARD, ___, 240
HUBARD, E. W., 325
HUBARD, J. R., 78, 298
HUETT, ___, 23
HUGHES, ___, 78
HUMMER, J. C., 84, 89, 93
HUTSON, J. B., 254
JAGGAR, ___, 321
JAMES, Chas. F., 281
JENNINGS, ___, 7
JETTER, ___, 241
JOHNS, ___, 42, 126
JOHNS, Arthur, 166, 322
JOHNS, Bishop, 2
JOHNS, Henry V. D., 6
JOHNSON, ___, 274
JOHNSON, H. E., 124, 125, 129, 144, 222
JOHNSON, W., 250
JOHNSON, W. H., 248
JOHNSON, Wm. H., 265, 271
JOHNSTON, James T., 5
JOHNSTON, T. J., 323
JONES, ___, 23, 223, 242
JONES, Edw. V., 144
JONES, John W., 52, 67, 82
JONES, Joseph R., 266, 295
JONES, L. R., 243, 256
JONES, Louis R., 252

JONES, Wm. D., 94
JOYCE, ___, 322
JOYNER, J. E., 20
JUDKINS, Wm. E., 24
JUNKIN, Wm. F., 235
JUTTEN, D. B., 131
KAHLER, F. A., 249
KAIN, J. J., 102, 169
KEANE, ___, 147
KEATING, Andrew P., 267
KEMIE, H. C., 43
KENEDY, H. H., 262
KENNEDY, ___, 288, 297
KENNEDY, G. W., 40
KENNEDY, H. H., 176, 177, 263, 274, 278, 297, 299, 300, 303, 314, 316, 317, 320, 322, 324, 325
KEPLER, H. S., 62, 327
KERFOOT, F. H., 326
KERNE, W. S., 313
KERNS, W. S., 189, 249
KIDWELL, ___, 6
KIDWELL, Lloyd, 46
KILGOUR, Chas., 219
KING, Charles, 116, 119, 123
KINGSOLVING, O. A., 94
KINSOLVING, ___, 6
KINSOLVING, O. A., 3, 5, 7, 17, 29, 34, 41
KISTLER, J. L., 278
KREMER, A. R., 115
LADD, ___, 220
LAKE, ___, 166, 211, 298
LAKE, I. B., 250, 276, 280
LAKE, J. B., 154, 163, 181, 184, 225, 227, 252,

264, 278, 281, 301, 303, 317
LAKE, J. H., 195
LAKE, T. B., 211
LANDSTREET, ___, 63, 65
LANDSTREET, John, 16, 23, 25, 26, 27, 31, 33, 38, 63, 85, 86, 88, 94, 95, 98, 99, 100, 101, 106, 107, 108, 109, 115, 121, 123, 127, 133, 144, 146, 148, 150, 151, 176
LATANE, James A., 99
LaTOURRETTE, James A. M., 10
LAWRENCE, Francis E., 263
LEA, John W., 188
LEAKIN, George A., 324
LEAVELL, ___, 29, 160
LEAVELL, W. T., 105
LEE, Francis D., 326
LEE, H. B., 218
LEE, John, 163
LEE, Wm., 294
LEECH, ___, 326
LEECH, S. V., 141
LEFTWICH, J. T., 66, 85
LEMON, S. H. M., 39
LEWIS, J. V., 260
LEYBURN G. L., 183
LINDSAY, J. S., 172, 270
LINDSAY, John S., 159, 170, 187, 191, 208, 217, 220, 226, 237, 299
LINDSEY, John S., 156
LINTHICUM, ___, 175
LINTHICUM, C. G., 196, 201, 211, 227
LINTHICUM, G., 228

LIPE, W. A., 266
LITTLETON, ___, 178
LUPTON, ___, 109
LUPTON, J. W., 107, 109, 116, 118, 120, 121, 122, 123, 126, 128, 129, 130, 131
LYDA, W. B., 142
LYNCH, ___, 319
MAGILL, John, 326
MAGUIRE, ___, 94
MAHAN, ___, 97
MALOY, J. Earle, 283, 324
MAN, Ambrois M., 207
MANN, ___, 108
MANN, A. L., 166
MANN, L. A., 139
MARCH, J. H., 70, 198
MARKHAM, Geo. C., 82
MARTIN, ___, 156
MARTIN, G. H., 9, 19, 23, 26, 28, 31, 40, 60, 64
MARTIN, George H., 39
MARTIN, John S., 46
MARTIN, T. F., 135, 165, 172
MATHIS, J. S., 239
MAURY, Magrude, 192
MAXWELL, A., 78
MAXWELL, T., 97
McALISTER, F. M., 174
McCABE, ___, 6, 165
McCABE, Jas. D., 168
McCARTHY, F., 56
McCAULEY, ___, 43
McDANIEL, H. C., 85
McDONOUGH, James, 96, 100, 116
McFADEN, J. A., 176, 320

McGILL, ___, 236
McGILL, John, 146, 172, 189, 250, 270
McGUIRE, ___, 115
McGUIRE, Wm., 166
McKIM, ___, 121
McKIM, R. H., 131, 158, 160, 193
McLAUCKLIN, ___, 268
McMURRAN, John W., 15
McPHERSON, Steven M., 220
McVEIGH, T. J., 92, 98
MEAD, W. H., 178
MEADE, ___, 156
MEADE, W. H., 142, 179, 211, 230, 264, 299
MEADE, William H., 113, 145, 242, 244, 294
MEADOR, C. C., 186
MEREDITH, W. C., 74
MILLER, ___, 248
MILLER, L. C., 177, 188
MILLER, P. H., 259, 260, 265, 274, 275, 277, 284, 297, 306, 315, 319, 322, 323
MINNEGERODE, Chas., 87, 146
MINNIGERODE, ___, 78
MINNIGERODE, Chas., 288
MISKIMON, H. E., 115, 135
MISXIMON, H. F., 127
MITCHELL, ___, 103, 222
MORRISON, ___, 161
MOTZER, Daniel, 4
MULLALLY, F. P., 190

MUTESSBAUGH, D. M., 256
MYERS, A. J., 11
NADAL, ___, 8
NEAL, A. A. P., 157, 310, 327
NELSON, ___, 170
NELSON, Kinloch, 151
NEWMAN, J. P., 283
NEWMAN, T. W., 10, 11, 92, 101, 102, 237, 239, 258, 262
NICE, Henry, 54
NIXDORFF, G. A., 32
NIXON, L. D., 123, 124, 125, 127, 131, 137, 138, 140, 141, 145, 151, 160, 161, 165, 166, 172, 193, 195, 199
NIXON, Lorenzo D., 121, 122
NIXSON, L. D., 122
NORTH, ___, 175
NORTH, J. B., 212
NORTH, N. G., 34
NORTON, ___, 143, 220, 255
NORTON, G. H., 68
NOURSE, C. H., 20, 49, 58, 112
NULLEY, George W., 41
NURSE, Charles H., 105
ODENHEIMER, W. H., 35
O'KANE, D., 176
OLIN, ___, 146
OWEN, E. D., 7, 22, 28, 36, 279
PACKARD, ___, 207
PAGE, ___, 313
PAGE, Frank, 303
PALMER, W. S., 135
PEARCE, ___, 300
PECK, J. O., 297
PEET, ___, 224
PELCE, A. J., 119
PENICK, ___, 313

INDEX

PENICK, W. S., 316
PERKINS, E. T., 83, 89, 98, 145, 196
PERKINS, T. T., 95
PERRY, Wm. J., 36
PETERKIN, G. W., 326
PETERKIN, George W., 265, 288
PETERS, J. A., 231
PETERSON, P. A., 101
PETTY, J. Spilman, 155
PHELPS, E. P., 135
PHILIPS, J. W., 123
PHILIPS, R. H., 124
PHILLIPS, ___, 32
PHILLIPS, P. P., 320
PICKETT, John, 49
PIGGOTT, Robert, 306
PINCKNEY, ___, 19
PINCKNEY, Wm., 194
PINDELL, A. T., 190
PINKNEY, ___, 85
POINDEXTER, J. E., 105
POLK, Leonidas, 15
POLLOCK, ___, 66
POLLOCK, A. D., 41, 123, 225
POPKINS, G. W., 308, 316
PORTER, Jesse, 33, 34, 44, 46, 99
POULTON, J. F., 98, 171, 204, 205, 220, 233
POULTON, John F., 47, 226, 255, 262
POWELL, J. D., 108
POWERS, W. H. H., 180, 183, 252
PRATT, J. W., 109, 126
PRICE, J. A., 133, 143
PROCTOR, Jos. A., 14, 16, 19, 48
PROCTOR, Joseph A., 10
PUGH, J. W., 68
PUGH, John W., 98
PURINGTON, Joseph L., 176
PURRINGTON, ___, 146
RANDOLPH, A. M., 263, 265, 273
READ, C. H., 143
REED, ___, 213
REED, Theo C., 270
REED, Theodore, 197, 221, 241, 249, 255, 256, 265, 295
REED, W. H., 124
REESE, W. W., 187
REVEILLE, ___, 270
RICE, ___, 273
RICHARDSON, X. J., 34, 47, 60, 65, 72, 75, 80, 86, 87, 89, 91, 93, 94, 95, 96, 99, 100, 101, 102, 107, 119, 123, 128, 134, 206, 207, 213
RICHEY, F. H., 19, 27, 45, 80, 86, 88
RICHEY, Francis H., 85
RIDDICK, C. B., 52
RIDDLE, D. H., 207
RINGGOLD, Samuel, 80
RINKER, ___, 230
RINKER, H. St. John, 208, 223, 233, 243, 244, 252, 274, 283, 285, 305, 308, 320
RITCHIE, ___, 64
ROBERTS, J. L., 114
ROBEY, A., 21, 45
ROBEY, Andrew, 3, 13, 26, 27, 28, 29, 32, 33, 35, 44, 60, 68, 108, 111, 114, 144, 148, 168, 182, 184, 186, 189, 207, 232, 235, 289
ROBY, Andrew, 153
RODGERS, Samuel, 68, 71, 72, 79, 82, 83, 84, 87, 92, 96, 100
RODGERS, Samuel H., 97
ROGERS, ___, 209
ROGERS, Alfred, 284
ROGERS, S. H., 4
ROGERS, Samuel, 258
ROSZEL, S. S., 41, 44, 62
ROSZELL, S. S., 26
ROWE, Robert S., 252
ROYLE, ___, 101
RYLAND, C. H., 174
SAMSON, ___, 65
SAUNDERS, Samuel, 312
SCHNEZ, ___, 269
SCHOOLEY, W. T., 212
SCHOOLEY, Wm., 300
SCOTT, ___, 88
SCOTT, J. A., 211
SCRUGG, ___, 18
SEWELL, Thomas, 1
SEYMOUR, Chas., 26
SHACKELFORD, J. A., 27
SHAND, P. J., 148
SHARP, ___, 47
SHAULL, H., 45
SHEPHERD, P. B., 136
SHEPHERD, T. B., 126, 192, 228, 233, 321
SHEPHERD, T. R., 90
SHIELD, C. H., 22
SHIP, E. G., 20
SHIPLEY, ___, 94
SHOAFF, ___, 102

The Mirror
INDEX

SHOAFF, D., 105, 107, 108
SHOAFF, David, 103, 106
SHREEVE, Jesse, 279
SHREVE, B. A., 292, 293, 305, 308, 311
SHUFORD, M. L., 129
SKIDMORE, D., 313
SKYLES, N. H., 231
SLAUGHTER, Philip, 299
SMELTZER, ___, 7
SMELTZER, J. P., 19
SMITH, 47
SMITH, ___, 63, 278
SMITH, E., 324
SMITH, G. G., 127
SMITH, H. R., 1, 13, 25, 28, 30, 41, 42, 44, 45, 47, 48, 52, 54, 59, 61, 66, 68, 72, 77, 79, 80, 82, 88, 89, 93, 95
SMITH, J. C., 92, 253
SMITH, J. W., 103
SMITH, Joseph E., 105
SMITH, Robert, 91
SMOOT, Wm. M., 237
SOUDER, J. M., 208
SOUTHGATE, ___, 183
SPARROW, Wm., 18, 159
SPILLMAN, A. H., 44
SPILMAN, A. H., 29
SPRIGG, D. F., 217
STARR, ___, 195, 221
STATZMAN, C., 231
STEARN, C. T., 167
STEPHENSON, G., 258
STEPHENSON, Josias, 92
STEPTOE, C. Y., 270
STEVENSON, G., 175, 215

STEVENSON, G. W., 97
STONESTREET, ___, 194
STORK, ___, 64
STROBLE, ___, 92
STRYKER, A. P., 219
SUNDERLAND, ___, 48
SUTER, ___, 296
SUTER, H., 15, 42, 68, 81
SUTHERLAND, B., 30
TALMAGE, ___, 241
TAYLOR, A. A., 77
TEMPLE, Joseph H., 242
TILLINGHAST, ___, 70
TOMPKINS, S. T., 167
TONGUE, J. W., 172
TOWELS, ___, 198
TOWLES, John, 219
TOWNSHEND, S., 258
TRAPNALL, Joseph, 91
TRAPNELL, ___, 73, 211
TRAPNELL, Joseph, 226, 284
TRONE, John, 173
TRUSSEL, E. J., 326
TUDOR, W. V., 109
TURNBULL, L. B., 281, 291, 299, 311
TURNER, J., 310
TYLER, George T., 212
VALIANT, ___, 150
VAUGHAN, E. H., 231
VERBOUTSRAETEN, ___, 10
WADDELL, A. W., 117
WADE, W. A., 132, 172, 213
WAGNER, ___, 230
WALKER, C., 7

WALKER, C. C., 31
WALKER, W. W., 290
WALL, Henry, 91
WARD, ___, 36
WARD, Wm. N., 250
WARE, ___, 25
WARE, S. S., 326, 327, 328
WARE, T. A., 11, 14
WARE, Thomas, 3
WATTS, R. W., 34, 45, 50, 85
WATTS, Robert W., 31
WAUGH, ___, 63
WAUGH, Hoffman, 68
WAUGH, J. H., 2, 37, 46
WAUGH, J. Hoffman, 66
WEBB, ___, 176
WEBB, W. R., 279
WHEAT, J. C., 124
WHEELER, ___, 271
WHELLER, Joseph, 259
WHITE, ___, 34
WHITE, C., 52
WHITE, Charles, 16, 5, 75
WHITE, E. V., 300
WHITE, Robb, 271
WHITE, S. R., 212
WHITTLE, F. M., 168, 229
WIDEMAN, L. T., 114
WILHELM, W. F., 170
WILLIAMS, G. H., 167, 196
WILLIAMS, G. W., 5
WILLIAMS, Geo. H., 120, 177
WILLIAMS, John A., 132
WILLIAMS, Robert H., 240
WILLIAMS, W. W., 26, 54, 56, 139, 222

The Mirror
INDEX

WILLIAMS, Walter, 70
WILLIAMS, Walter W., 25, 37, 48, 65, 72
WILLIAMS, William J., 103
WILLIS, E. J., 153, 292
WILLIS, J., 325
WILLS, D. P., 10
WILSON, ___, 188
WILSON, J., 105
WILSON, J. O., 101
WILSON, Joseph R., 189
WILSON, L. F., 63
WILSON, N., 97
WILSON, Norval, 21
WILSON, W. H., 296, 297, 298, 302, 303, 304, 311, 327
WINCHESTER, Jas. R., 271
WING, ___, 15
WIRE, W. C., 143
WISLER, H., 71
WISSLAR, H., 96
WISSLER, H., 112, 121, 123, 125
WITHERS, Edmund, 292
WOLF, John, 65, 95, 143, 148, 199, 256
WOLFF, James H., 173
WOLFF, Jas. H., 108
WOOD, Aaron, 180
WOOD, W., 262
WOODBRIDGE, ___, 124, 266
WOODBRIDGE, George, 41
WOOF, John, 95
WOOLF, Jas. H., 106
WOOLF, John, 63, 87, 91, 99, 101, 109, 130, 135, 168, 195, 237, 271, 277, 285, 313, 315, 324, 325

WYER, H. H., 126, 172, 173, 175, 200, 201, 229
WYNN, L. B., 223
YATES, ___, 199
YATES, P. W., 86
YATES, Paul, 100
YORK, ___, 140
ZACHARIAS, ___, 54, 66, 76, 90, 101, 137
ZACHARIAS, D., 27
ZACHERIAS, ___, 61
MINNICK
 Mary E., 97
MINNIGERODE
 James G., 288
MINOR
 Ann E., 4
 Ann Maria, 4
 B. S., 291
 Catharine A., 163
 Chas. H., 260
 Essie F., 94
 Jackson, 281
 John W., 17, 59, 94, 160, 163, 253
 Louisa F., 160
 Mary E., 291
 Mary W., 281
 Wm., 17, 163
MISKEL
 George W., 31
MITCHEL
 Susan R., 99
MITCHELL
 Charlotte, 227
 Emma S., 113
 James, 113
 John F. B., 111
 Lydia A., 92
MITCHENER
 Anna, 308
MOBBERLY
 Emily R., 108
MOCK
 Albert, 265
 Eliza L., 82
 Ellen, 262
 Emma J., 100
 James, 305
 Jas. E., 258

 Joseph, 155
 Orra, 155
 Sarah A., 322
MOCKE
 John C., 8
MOFFATT
 Harriet A., 27
MOFFETT
 Charles T., 67
 La Vega, 277
 Laura M., 224
 Thomas D., 126
 Wm. H., 67
MOLER
 Frances, 189
 Jacob H., 91
 Lydia E., 91
 Milton, 189
MONCASTLE
 B. A., 56
MONDAY
 Aaron W., 146
 Elizabeth, 8
 Ellen, 70
 George, 43
 John R., 134
 Mary, 16
 Robt., 149
 Samuel E., 217
 Virginia, 99
MONEY
 Albert, 228
 Geo. W., 149
 Nancy, 147
 Nicholas, 147
MONROE
 Charles, 286
 James H., 95
 Kate, 178
 Katie, 179
 Michael H. P., 291
 Susan V., 291
 Thomas, 269
 U. M., 265
 Ulysses M., 24
 Washington, 177
 William M., 291
MOODEY
 Kate, 127
MOORE
 A., 292
 A. B., 302

Albert J., 55
Amanda A., 317
Bessie, 188
Catharine, 304
Cato, 261
Eli A., 260
Erasmus D., 188
G. W., 123
Geo. L., 116, 250
George, 260
Henry, 67
J. H., 190, 236
J. Hamilton, 221
Jane C., 12
Jno., 208
John, 163, 223, 260, 263, 298, 302
Julia A., 123
Kate, 225
L. T., 224
Leanna C., 7
Lizzie, 250
M. L., 263
Margaret E., 304
Margaret S., 188
Maria E., 116
Mary B., 123
Mary G., 7
Mary L., 229
Nancy T., 217
Presley, 225
Robert L., 274
Rose B., 281
Sallie, 261
Sallie A., 68
Sarah, 116
Sarah A., 217
Susan E., 196
Thomas A., 12
Thos. R., 173
Virginia, 148, 236
Wm., 304
Wm. H., 34, 80
MORALLEE
  Thomas C., 12
MORAN
  Catharie B., 127
  Elizabeth, 19, 69
  Gustavia E., 166
  J. L., 48
  J. M., 19
  J. W., 4

Lucinda R., 278
Martha J., 141
Orlinda, 141
Richard Y., 166
MORDECAI
  John B., 161
MOREHEAD
  Amelius H., 241
  James M., 71
MORELAND
  George J., 26
  Rachel C., 203, 204
  Sallie, 95
  William T., 203
  Wm. H., 203, 204
  Wm.T., 204
MORGAN
  Benj., 42, 68, 172
  Benjamin F., 25
  Cecelia, 42
  Ella C., 172
  Eveline, 112
  Henro, 112
  Henry, 161, 267
  John, 81
  Mary C., 196
  Mattie E., 68
  Mollie J., 177
  Sallie, 112, 161, 267
  Willie, 267
MORIARTY
  John, 296
  Mary, 243
  Michael, 243
  Mollie, 223
MORRIS
  Ann, 309
  Governeur, 144
  Jno. F., 256
  John G., 285
  Nancy, 309
MORRISON
  Edward, 24, 25
  Edward H., 24
  Eliza J., 24
  Frances E., 19, 24
  Frances M., 24
  James A., 129
  Joseph E., 24
  William W., 129
MORROW
  Mr., 79

MORSON
  Arthur, 267
  Arthur A., 159
  Lilias G., 159
  Lilly, 267
MORTON
  Amanda, 176
  J. W., 176
  James, 108
  James W., 251
  Lucy H., 108
  Margaret N., 108
MOSBURG
  John W., 310
MOSBY
  Alfred D., 84
  Jno. S., 186
  John S., 84, 239, 327
  May V., 327
  Pauline, 186, 239
  Prestiss, 186
  Victoria C., 84
MOSS
  Blanche, 133, 163
  Elizabeth, 62
  Elizabeth E., 275
  Mary R., 163
  Thomas, 62, 71, 121
  Townsend M., 133
  Vincent, 38
  William V., 98, 133, 163
MOSSBURY
  John W., 109
MOTT
  A. R., 59, 138, 139, 241
MOUNT
  Bettie, 79
  C. E., 308
  Ella, 221
  James, 48, 225, 226, 229
  James M., 318
  John, 36, 244, 245
  John E., 229
  John T., 79
  Wm. T., 79, 221
MOUNTJOY
  John, 188
  Sallie M., 188
MOXLEY

The Mirror   381
INDEX

James A., 8
MUDGE
 D. C., 167
 Lillie E., 167
MUGANT
 James, 34
MULL
 James M., 82
MULLEN
 Alice V., 238
 Chas., 223
 Jane, 43
 Lydia, 231
 Michael, 43
 Rodger M., 231
 Samuel H., 231
MUNCASTER
 Otho M., 105
MUNDAY
 Susannah, 95
MUNDY
 Margaret A., 61
MUNROE
 Washington, 175
MURPHY
 Bridgett, 96
 Hiram, 300
 James, 300
 Jas. T., 82
 John, 178
 Mr., 280
 S. W., 117
MURRAY
 George, 305
 Harriet, 43
 Homer, 305
 John, 43
 Josiah, 43
 Lucie T., 98
 Molly L., 313
 Ralph, 43
 Samuel, 43
 Sarah A. B., 129
 Stirling, 85
 William, 140
MUSE
 Ann Eliza, 1
 Eliza R., 22
 James, 1
 James H., 31, 44, 50, 166
 Lafayette, 258

Mary E., 50
Mary S., 166
Mollie E., 165
Nancy E., 165
Owen C., 1
Rebecca J., 50
Susan E., 25
Thomas, 258
Thomas W., 165
Virginia C., 44
MYERS
 Amey A., 50
 Annie B., 324
 Carrie, 296
 Charles L., 118
 Charles W., 11, 263
 Clarissa M., 267
 Edward F., 205
 Frank M., 110
 George N., 50
 George S., 263
 Gracie T., 157
 Isaac B., 111
 Israel, 182, 183, 193
 Israel T., 304
 James W., 87
 John H., 138
 John T., 60
 Jonathan, 225
 Joseph, 64, 73
 Luther, 267
 Mahlon H., 289
 Mary A., 173
 Mary E., 44
 Mr., 214
 Nathaniel, 247
 Peter C., 16, 95, 107
 Sallie A., 263
 Samuel B., 182
 Susan, 2
 William, 324
 Wm., 57
NAGLE
 Samuel, 156
NALLS
 Jos., 120
 Margaret, 100
NEAR
 Geo., 146
 Margaretta, 146
NEER

D. C., 169
Edward H., 164, 169
Eliza, 164
Florence, 155
Nathan, 63
Susan A., 9
Negro
 Alfred, 57
 Charles, 19
 Clara, 57, 216
 Easter, 268
 Edgar, 19
 Hannah, 299
 Jennie, 180
 Marietta, 4
 Mary, 263
 Richmond, 307
 Tom, 4, 5
NEILL
 Fauntleroy, 104
 George W., 45
NELMNS
 Samuel, 200
 Susan, 200
NELMS
 Samuel P., 121, 204, 259
NELSON
 Emma, 39
 Hugh, 80
 Julia C., 80
 Mollie R., 328
 Nancy C., 74
 Pattie B., 101
 Philip, 39
 Rose, 80
 Sallie, 265
 William M., 244
NESMITH
 Sallie L., 277
NETTLES
 Nellie, 305
 Sarah, 307
NEVETT
 James C., 267
 Mary E., 267
NEVILLE
 Robert G., 250
NEVITT
 R. G., 121
NEWLON
 Cecelia, 286

INDEX

Jno. F., 192
Rosalie S., 227
Samuel E., 227
Wm., 286
NEWMAN
  Benjamin, 309
  Jacob F., 234
  Margaret E., 258
  Theron W., 258
NEWTON
  Alexander, 218
  Amelia V., 173
  Charles, 127
  Charles N., 300
  Martha J., 207
  Mary, 218
  Mary E., 19
  Nelly S., 22
  Sinah A., 111
  William, 17
  Wm., 111
NICEWANER
  Christian, 137
NICHOLS
  Annie, 79
  B. P., 245
  Burr P., 138
  Catharine, 43
  Charles H., 284
  Charles L., 101
  Ed., 212
  Eli J., 105
  Elizabeth, 46
  F. J., 154
  G., 141
  James W., 72
  Jno., 155
  Jno. A., 226
  Joseph, 193
  Joshua, 13
  Lucy, 193
  Maria P. T., 327
  Mariam G., 13
  Mary A., 13
  Mary C., 282
  Mary J., 43
  Mary V., 260
  Nathan, 7
  Rebecca, 166
  Ruth H., 320
  Samuel, 154
  Samuel E., 155, 242

  Samuel T., 24
  Sarah, 209
  Stacy M., 9
  Thomas, 46, 79
  Thos. H., 320
  Thos. J., 57, 155
  Virginia E., 256
  William, 43
  Wm., 147
NICHOLSON
  Joseph H., 18
  Mary H., 18
NICOL
  Aylett, 283
NISEWANNER
  Christian, 30
NIXON
  Anne M., 26
  Annie M., 327
  Asbury M., 144
  Benj., 144
  Cassandra, 257
  Cassendra, 272
  Eliza N., 203
  Emma, 305
  Geo., 257
  Geo. H., 287
  Geo.H., 259
  George, 219, 247
  Joel L., 242
  John, 257
  Johnathan W., 82, 96
  Jonah, 219, 304
  Jonathan, 194, 305
  Joseph, 307
  Joseph W., 309
  L. D., 203
  Laura J., 96
  Levi, 63
  Levi W., 298, 307
  Lorenzo D., 202
  Louisa M., 304
  Martha, 268
  Martha V. G., 21
NOLAND
  Anna W., 94
  B. P., 7, 8, 94, 192,
    230, 241, 287, 306
  Burr P., 58, 128, 177,
    245
  C. Powell, 322
  Claud, 284

  Corrie, 245
  Euphemia A., 96
  Fannie F., 77
  Frank M., 147
  G. W., 163
  Geo. W., 96
  George W., 64, 91
  James, 306
  Lena A., 192
  Lizzie R., 163
  Lloyd, 7, 17, 221
  Noble B., 7, 17
  R. W. N., 147, 221
  Ruth H., 64, 96
  S. T., 180
  Samuel C., 91
  Susan W., 128
  Thomas E., 64
  Wm. B., 284
NORMAN
  Andrew, 200
NORRIS
  Amanda, 242
  Annie S., 326
  B. B., 236, 237
  Charles N., 50
  Edward T., 326
  George W., 94, 187
  Henry DeB., 187
  Ida S., 242
  John, 141
  Mollie, 222
  Sophia E., 141
  Thomas, 110
  Thomas B., 54
  Thos. B., 242
  Wm. O., 142
NORTH
  Emily K., 226
  Jas.H., 226
  Jos. B., 154
  Robert W., 176
  Wm., 230
NORTHEY
  George E., 125
NORTON
  John, 306
NOURSE
  Chas. H., 112, 244
NURSE
  Mary R., 105
NUTT

The Mirror
INDEX

Alice E., 5
William D., 5
O'BANNON
  A. J., 36
  Elizabeth E., 291
  Mollie E., 194
  Mollie R., 215
  Susan J., 168
  Wm. A., 81
ODAIR
  Samuel C., 130
ODELL
  Euphemia A., 96
  James, 96
  Jno. C., 163
  John C., 96
ODEN
  Catherine, 315
  Sarah E., 199
OFFATT
  Henry, 104
OFFUTT
  A. M., 281
  Alice, 198
  Chas., 326
  Fenton M., 326
  Nicholas D., 286
  Sarah, 304
  Wm. A., 287
OGDEN
  Elizabeth, 224
  Leven, 309
  Sallie A., 260
O'HARRO
  Maria, 72
OLDHAM
  R. S., 248
OLIVER
  James, 196
OMEAR
  Albert B., 172
O'NEAL
  Edward, 306
ONLY
  Edwin R., 58
ORAM
  James, 311
ORANGE
  . James, 282
  Susan, 276
ORD

Susie, 323
OREAR
  Bettie, 86
  Enock, 2, 86
  Hattie N., 2
OREM
  Nathanniel P., 134
ORME
  Marietta, 93
  Robert S., 93
  Sallie S., 148
  Virginia, 168
ORR
  Annie B., 278
  Hannah V., 26
  John M., 58, 206, 256, 294
  Orra L., 206
  Orra V., 294
  Preston, 294
ORRISON
  Burr, 253
  Catharine, 156
  Chas. W., 137
  Cumberland G., 50
  Ellen E., 233
  George, 50
  George W., 81
  Hannah B., 93
  Jane E., 233
  Jno. W., 93
  John H., 298
  Joseph, 188, 233
  Laney, 103
  Lavenia, 154
  Lilian, 137
  Lizzie, 137
  Maria, 288
  Martha C., 253
  Oscar J., 284
  Samuel, 75, 103
  Townsend, 139, 282
  William W., 325
OSBORN
  Logan, 163
OSBORNE
  Ann E. J., 122
  Octavius, 281
  Sadie B., 299
OSBOURN
  Mary A., 69
OSBURN

Abner, 292
Amanda C., 3, 190
Bushrod, 79, 132
Dorcas A., 119, 190
Emily, 52
Fayette, 20
Flavius, 52
Frances, 189
Harrison, 215, 302, 318
Herbert, 304
Joel, 9, 52, 189
Joseph C., 98
Logan, 188, 292
Mary C., 163
Massey, 189
Maurice, 248, 268
Maurice G., 145
Miss, 280
Nicholas, 3
Patsy, 213, 215
Phineas, 148, 321
Pleasant, 171
Richard, 213
T. M., 158
T. V. B., 132
Tarleton V. B., 79
Tarlton V. B., 79
Thompson, 171
Volney, 280
Walter C., 132, 211
OSBURNE
  Armistead F., 24
  Maria B., 7
OTLEY
  Alice, 217
  Arthur, 217
  Emma R., 217
  James G., 268
  John J., 67, 122
  Mary, 217
  Orra O., 268
  Sarah A., 253
  Wm., 67
  Wm. H., 63
  Wm. S., 319, 321
OTT
  F. G., 264
OTTERBACH
  James, 240
OTTWUNDER
  Geo., 3

OVERFIELD
  Benjamin, 306
  Marshall, 171
  W. O., 165
OXLEY
  Bushrod, 67
  Thomas, 258
PAGE
  John E., 39
PAINE
  Alfred, 292
PAINTER
  Addison T., 167
PALMER
  Alice, 302
  Alphonzo, 198
  Annie, 225
  Cecilia L., 75
  Charlotte, 259
  D. T., 286
  J. S., 327
  Jennie, 146
  John T., 326
  Joseph M., 178
  Leah F., 106
  Lucinda, 212, 250
  Mattie, 302
  Mattie E., 286
  Orra V., 327
  Richard H., 122
  Robbie, 225
  S. E., 302
  Thomas, 225
  Wm. C., 212
PANCOAST
  Bertie M., 145
  Jane E., 231
  Joshua, 48
PANCOST
  Joseph, 249
  Lilly, 249
PARKER
  Edgar M., 150
  John W. B., 23
  Lafayette, 207
  Mr., 79
  Nellie E., 150
  R. W., 217
  Thos., 291
PARKINSON
  ___, 162

  Sarah W., 262
PARKS
  Marshall, 118
PARRAN
  Lillie, 21
  Richard, 21
PARROTT
  John H., 204
  Roberta W., 204
PASCHAL
  Bessie, 147
  Geo. W., 147
PATTEN
  John W., 200, 201
PATTERSON
  Julia B., 77
  M. E., 141
  Mary B., 95
PATTIE
  Alice E., 188
  Cordelia B., 321
  D. M., 201
  Delia, 322
  Wm. A., 188, 321, 322
PATTON
  Jennie, 254
  John, 18
  John M., 6
  John W., 14, 18, 254
  Joseph, 303
  Mary, 18
  Wilhelmina, 300
PAXSON
  C. W., 73, 75
  E. C., 249
  Edward B., 122
  J. W., 54
  John C., 168
  M. C., 59
  Mr., 110
  Samuel B., 98
  Sarah C., 249
  Willie, 249
PAXTON
  C. R., 301
  Charles R., 211
  Margaret, 211
  Margarett, 211
  R. C., 211
PAYNE
  Alban S., 151

  Bettie W., 151
  D. Preston, 295
  Daniel, 310
  Helen, 271
  J. B., 187
  Jas. S., 207
  Jno. S., 11
  John D., 204
  Lavinia E., 193
  Lilly W., 217
  Livinia E., 194
  Minnie W., 204
  Richards, 217
  Sadie, 315
  Thomas, 277
  William E., 106
  Winter, 316
  Wm. F., 73
  Wm. H., 315
  Wm. W., 189
PEACH
  M. S., 64
PEACHER
  Lydia A., 10
PEACOCK
  Angelina, 228
  Ann, 30
  Fannie, 262
  James, 304
  James W., 141
  Licinda, 10
  Lucinda, 11
  Milton, 262
  N. B., 172, 215, 220, 281, 293
  Naaman, 207
  Nancy C., 10
  Nannie, 228
  Narcissa, 228
  Noble B., 10, 11, 110, 186
  Thomas J., 228
  Thos. J., 228
  Winfield S., 11
PEARCE
  Hector, 57
PEARSON
  Wm., 64
PECK
  Amanda C., 221
  Charles T., 79
  Julius L., 221

PEMBERTON
  John C., 172
  Pattie, 172
PENDALL
  Arthur, 195
PENDLETON
  Dudley D., 74
PENICK
  C. C., 307
PENQUITE
  Sallie, 258
PEPPER
  W. W., 286
PEREGOY
  Nora E., 22
PERKINS
  E. T., 221
  Ida, 145
  Isa A., 145
PERRY
  C. W., 175
  John T., 36, 122
  Mary, 36
  Theodore I., 36
  Wm. J., 46
PETER
  George, 40
  J. P. C., 49
  Jane, 49
  Jas. H., 40
  Jno. P. C., 40
PETERKIN
  Mrs., 267
PETERMAN
  Allie M., 170
PETTET
  Jemima, 28
PETTIS
  W. B., 255
PEUGH
  Elizabeth, 300, 302
  James B., 247, 302
  Jas., 110
  Leonidas, 110
  Milton L., 242
  Samuel, 306
  Sarah E., 242
  Wm. L., 242
PEYTON
  Ann E., 136
  Henry B., 36
  Henry E., 14, 36, 297

Jos. E. B., 253
Joseph E. B., 199
Lucy, 250
Mary E., 36, 297
Townsend, 136
PHELPS
  E. P., 76
  Mary W., 76
PHILIPS
  ___, 31
  Alex. K., 29
  Baily T., 186
PHILLIPS
  Anson, 240, 249
  Broadus M., 211
  Emma, 198
  Etta M., 249
  Laura E. T. C., 325
  S. Gustavus F., 109
  Wm. F., 109, 269
  Wm. F., 325
  Wm. H., 198
PICKETT
  Dodridge, 121
  Elizabeth, 153
  Sanford W., 153
  Susan F., 64
  William S., 75
PIDGSON
  E. J. W., 49
PIERCE
  A. E., 289
  Eli M., 174
  Nannie L., 289
  Oscar F., 176
  Perry B., 146
  Zachariah T., 118
PIERPOINT
  Eli, 258, 261
  John W., 27
  Martha E., 73
  Mary J., 19
  Sarah R., 263
PIGGOTT
  Jno. W., 195
  John W., 245
  Rebecca, 192
  Ruth H., 195
  Sophie S., 306
  Thomas, 306
PILCHER
  James V. B., 1

PILES
  Joseph, 129
PIPER
  A. M., 15
  John, 182
  Mary C., 15
PITMAN
  Vincent, 173
PLASTER
  Geo. D., 211
  Geo. E., 156, 158, 203
  Henry, 203
  Michael, 105
  Sallie T., 203
POINDEXTER
  Alice B., 146
POINTS
  Alexander G., 205
POLAND
  Alex., 216
  Alexander, 57, 167, 197, 216
  George W., 167
  James E., 57
  Luther L., 196
  Margaret, 167
  Richard F., 148
  Susan E., 69
  Virginia T., 199
POLLARD
  Burr, 244
  Margaret L., 278
POLLOCK
  A. D., 188
  Roberta, 225
POMEROY
  Rachel A., 85
POOLE
  Allie, 168
  Geo. W., 228
  Lizzie, 219
  Thos. H., 219
POOR
  Alfred, 153, 273, 302
  Frances V., 273
POPE
  Florence V., 249
  John, 176
  Wm., 249
POPKINS
  George W., 22, 298

James P., 22
Jno. T., 101
Richard, 22
Thomas, 22
PORTER
  Emma J., 252
  H. Clay, 232
POSEY
  Elizabeth A., 163
  John F., 163
Post Offices
  Hoysville, 54
  Taylortown, 54
POSTON
  Benj. F., 155
  Wm. W., 155
POTTERFIELD
  John, 244
  Joseph, 20
  Luther H., 119
  Mary E., 20
  Sue L., 256
  Thos. L., 256
  Willie H., 256
POTTS
  Ann E., 171
  B. F., 302
  David, 14
  E. F., 167
  E. H., 302
  Edward D., 88, 165, 241, 269
  Edwin, 311
  Edwin H., 303, 307
  Eliza, 165
  Emma J., 302
  Ezekiel, 14
  James T., 61
  Jennie F., 167
  Jonas, 14
  Jonas W., 165
  Joshua O., 209
  Laura A., 311
  Martha A., 88
  Mary E., 67
  Sarah, 135
  Thomas W., 21
  Thompson, 149
  Thos., 313
  Walter B., 258
POULTON
  Alfred, 193
  J. F., 107
  Lydia L., 193
  R. B., 292
  Reed, 131, 132
  Rose D., 107
POWELL
  Alfred H., 131
  Annie, 167
  Burr, 306
  Catharine, 124
  Charles E., 43
  Chas., 213, 273
  Chas. F., 264
  Chas. L., 112
  Cuthbert, 124, 296
  D. Lee, 18, 108, 111
  E. B., 294, 316
  E. O., 167
  Elizabeth W., 136
  Ella, 296
  F. W., 41, 197
  Fannie W., 139
  Florence, 108
  Grafton, 8
  H. B., 6
  H. P., 13
  Harriet H., 41
  Hugh L., 99
  Humphrey, 136
  Hunter H., 183
  Jno. H., 35
  John L., 162
  Leven, 306
  Lily B., 316
  Lucy L., 204
  Lucy P., 18
  Malvina, 262
  Maria L., 18, 163
  Marietta F., 6
  Marion S., 25
  Mary, 55, 56
  Mrs., 208
  R. C., 226
  Robert T., 218
  S. Indiana, 8
  Selina, 112
  Thomas L., 259
  Thomas S., 15
  Thos., 61
  W. A., 25, 111
  William L., 294
  William S., 275, 316
  William T., 294
  Wm. A., 55, 204
  Wm. L., 139
  Wm. T., 294
POWER
  Annie Jennet, 57
  Joseph T., 166
  Margaret A., 57
  Robert, 57
POWERS
  Emma, 290
  Inez, 302
  Samuel, 290
PRESGRAVE
  Prudence V., 93
PRESGRAVES
  Burr W., 89
  George W., 262, 304
  Samuel C., 327
  W. W., 293
PRESTON
  A. A., 144
  George W., 256
  Jane G., 299
  Massie A., 232
  Orra V., 256
  Thaddeus T., 317
  W. Ballard, 299
PRICE
  Bailey, 155
  E. F., 324
  Ellis L., 324
  Joseph, 69
  Mark L., 324
  Mary E., 215
  R. F., 62
PRIDE
  Charles, 15
PRIEST
  James G., 124
  John H., 119
  Nelson, 323
PROCTOR
  J. A., 52
PROSSER
  Mary, 218
PUGH
  John W., 5
PULLER
  Parmelia M., 6
  Rebecca J., 26
  Samuel, 6, 26

INDEX

Sarah, 26
PURCELL
  E. R., 110
  John B., 142
  Mary, 239
  Mollie, 225
  Nancy, 141
  Thomas, 141
  Volney, 114
PURSEL
  Jonah, 61
  Samuel, 3
  Volney, 132
PURSELL
  E. R., 241
  Franklin, 86
  J. H., 241
  John, 236
  Mary, 241
PUSEY
  Geo., 245
PUSSEY
  George, 85

QUEEN
  Rose, 4
QUINBY
  George A., 284
  John S., 284
  Mary G., 284

RADCLIFF
  Alice, 92
  Emily, 92
  William, 92
RADCLIFFE
  Daniel, 179
RADER
  W. H., 208
RADLEY
  Charles, 256
RAMEY
  Elizabeth, 104
  John, 104
  Sanford I., 58
RAMSAY
  Anna B., 165
  G. W. D., 165
RAMSEY
  Amanda, 80
  Charlotte C., 120
  Laura E., 219

Samuel C. E., 94
RAND
  Sarah J., 5
RANDALL
  Mary M., 108
RANDOLPH
  Beverly, 266
  Mary H., 266
  William F., 18
RANSON
  J. Frank, 79
RATHIE
  Benjamin D., 13
  Jos. L., 233, 234
  Lizzie, 69
  Mary E., 233, 234
RATRIE
  Henry H., 174
  John M., 287
RAUM
  Joseph A., 37
RAWLINGS
  James W., 106
  John M., 276
  John W., 116
RAWLINS
  Dolphin T., 74
RAY
  Thos., 306
REAGAN
  Mary A., 270
REAMER
  Christian, 305
  James, 154
REARDON
  James, 240
  John, 306
REAVES
  Julia A., 28
RECTOR
  Ann F., 106
  Asa H., 106
  Bettie, 105
  Elizabeth, 81
  Geo. A., 285
  George, 81
  H. N., 161
  Howard, 105
  Isa F., 210
  Maria F., 28
  Mary F., 106
  Robert, 186

Samuel, 210
Sarah, 285
Thomas A., 186
REED
  Charles E., 101
  Gertrude, 96
  Henry, 269
  James S., 201
  James T., 251
  Jas. M., 279
  Jas. R., 229
  John, 96, 114
  John W., 142
  Jos., 271
  Laura, 96
  Maria, 66
  Theo., 192, 271
  Theodore, 296
  Thomas, 192
  Virginia, 96
REEDER
  Gourley, 217
  William A., 88
  Wm. A., 217
REESE
  Edgar, 314
REEVES
  John, 165
  John F., 82
  Wm. W., 178
REID
  Harmon, 112
  John, 167
  Sallie E., 239
REILY
  ___, 190
  Louisa, 190
  Wm., 190
Residences
  Arcadia, 69
  Aron, 50, 146
  Aspen Hill, 210
  Aspin Hill, 27
  Avon, 270
  Avon View, 163
  Ayreshire, 147
  Barrymore, 187
  Bedford, 38
  Bellmont, 160
  Belmont, 79, 202
  Beveridge House, 44
  Beverly, 198

The Mirror
INDEX

Big Spring Farm, 58
Blakeley, 113
Bollingbrook, 237
Boxwood, 326
Braden Farm, 59
Brightside, 316
Cameron, 251
Cassilis, 71
Cedar Grove, 116, 296
Chelsea, 100
Clarenton, 234
Clifton, 196
Contest, 151
Cottage Grove, 120
Cottage Hill, 60
Darby's Delight, 206
Dunbarton, 144
Easternview, 66
Edge Hill, 63
Ellerslie, 38
Eudora, 70
Eudora Manse, 186
Exeter, 41, 119, 128
Fair View, 172
Fontanville, 39
Forrest Mills, 76
Fruitland, 153, 290
Glebeland, 232
Glen Burnie, 235
Glen Owen, 174
Glen Welby, 183, 326
Glenn Welby, 78
Graseland, 170
Grassland, 8
Greenway, 160
Groveton, 215
Hayfield, 169
Hazle Hill, 194
Huntley, 157
Ivon, 288, 323
Killmane, 94
Langolan, 158
Locust Grove, 147, 249, 282
Locust Thicket, 38
Mary Hill, 175
Meadland, 270
Meadow Hill, 192
Meadows, 6
Mealia, 311
Media, 105

Montpelier, 211
Morven, 271
Mount Beulah, 327
Mount Prominent, 254
Mountain Dell, 212
Mountain Farm, 78
Mountain Home, 76
Mountain View, 193, 281
Mt. Easton, 217
Mt. Ephraim, 15
Mt. Prominent, 151
Nesting, 225
Oak Grove, 252
Oak Hill, 83, 152
Oak Level, 185
Oakfield, 162
Oakham, 29
Oakley, 36
Oakwood, 41, 76
Orksey, 14
Otterbourne, 75
Parnwillallice, 5
Peachgrove, 212
Pickett House, 70
Pleasant Valley, 196
Raspberry Plains, 159, 225, 248
Resting, 321
Revenswood, 284
Risteau's Fancy, 48
Rock Spring, 230
Rockland, 218
Rose Valley, 295
Rosemont, 139
Salentium, 212
Salentum, 224
Salisbury, 184
Selma, 86, 98
Sharon, 73
Sherwood Forest, 91
Smithfield, 299
Soldier's Rest, 92
Springdale, 255
Springsbury, 114
Springwood, 301
Strawberry Vale, 29
Sunny Bank, 203
Temple Hall, 39, 121
The Cottage, 133

The Grove, 242, 256, 277, 282, 318
The Neck, 112
The Shelter, 117
Valley View, 98
Vineyard, 23
Walnut Hill, 9
Waveland, 40
Way Side, 172
Welbourn, 228
Welbourne, 250
Westly Farm, 59
Westwood Grove, 250, 316
White Hall, 241
Whitehall, 300
Windsor, 232
Woodbine, 183
Woodland, 114
Woorull, 59
REVENCOMB
  Carrie H., 175
REYNOLDS
  E. J., 110
  Mary J., 225
RHODERICK
  Julia A., 54
RHODES
  Annie, 58
  Cecelia, 310
  Ellen, 168
  George, 58, 93
  H. H., 4, 41
  John, 310
  Jos., 185
  Jos. R., 185
  Joseph, 168, 185
  Mary A., 168, 185
  Mary C., 94
  Nannie S., 4
  Oliver R., 310
  Virginia A., 71
RHOE
  Rachel, 207
RICE
  Mary V., 152
  Medora, 47
  Mollie, 212
  Wm. H., 152
RICH
  Mrs., 85
  Thomas, 217

The Mirror
INDEX
389

RICHARD
 Mary C., 89
 William, 89
RICHARDS
 A. E., 311
 Amanda, 98
 Barton, 268
 Burr H., 14, 15
 Josephine, 15
 Sarah, 205
RICHARDSON
 Junius, 96
 Mary, 120
RICHERSON
 Sallie B., 177
RICKETTS
 Adam G., 154
RIDGEWAY
 Alverna D., 168
 Benjamin D., 2
 Frances A., 240
 Isaac, 309
 Joseph M., 112
RIELY
 James P., 3, 19
 Virginia, 3
RILEY
 Cornelia A., 91
 E. M., 322
 Geo. W., 9
 Margaret E., 106
 Margaret G., 143
 Napoleon B., 247
 Susan V., 275
 Wm., 267, 268
RINKER
 Angelina, 39
 Asa J., 246
 Charles R., 101
 Henry C., 257
 James F., 128, 246
 Jas. F., 152
 Jno. L., 257
 John L., 83, 322, 324
 Mary V., 83
 Mattie E., 295
 Susan, 246
 Virginia, 7
RIPLEY
 Dwight, 159
RISTEAU
 Kate V., 48

RITCHIE
 Geo. M., 175
 Ida L., 320
 Mary E., 103
RITICAR
 Chas., 268
RITICOR
 Charles, 266
 Charles A., 152
 Elijah V., 195
RIVES
 James H., 41
RIXEY
 Martha J., 237
ROACH
 Catharine A., 134
 Ed. N., 134
ROADS
 Bazzell, 306
ROBBINS
 Frank G., 10
 Isaac H., 20, 53
ROBERTS
 Carrie B., 230
 John D., 123
 Lorenzo D., 75
 Mary V., 153
 Ruth H., 96
ROBERTSON
 Norvelle R., 230
ROBEY
 A., 1
 Andrew, 24, 116
 Cobert, 291
 Francis E., 63
 Jennie E., 291
 Martha E., 1
 Sarah E., 121, 163
 William, 180
 William H., 1
ROBINSON
 A. M., 160
 Conway, 43
 James T., 68
 John, 26
 John G., 123
 John S., 6
 Lydia A., 196
 Samuel J., 323
RODEFFER
 Mark M., 71
RODGERS

Arthur L., 58
Samuel, 315
ROE
 T., 7
ROGERS
 A. H., 7, 192
 A. L., 125
 Alexander H., 3, 181
 Alexandria H., 36
 Anne D., 29
 Arthur L., 6, 115
 Asa, 18, 34, 115
 Charlotte A., 125
 Cuthbert B., 61
 Edward C., 255
 Ella V., 47
 Elmina S., 301
 Farley C., 52
 Ferdinand A., 282
 H. R. McV., 292
 Hamilton, 29, 312
 Helen J., 63
 James S., 153
 James W., 322
 Jane E., 177, 178
 Jas. H., 255
 John D., 52
 Julia H., 36, 181
 Juliet L., 153
 Laura F., 34
 Lucy L., 18
 M. M., 221
 Margaret E., 94
 Mary A., 284
 Mollie M., 233
 Parke F., 52
 Pendleton, 87
 Rebecca J., 90
 Richard, 136
 Richard H., 67
 Richard L., 94
 S. E., 209
 Sallie, 282
 Saml. H., 22
 Samuel, 177, 284
 Thomas, 47, 233, 292
 Thomas C., 36
 Thos., 301
 W. W., 63
 William, 199
 Willie C., 181

The Mirror
INDEX

ROLLER
  Frederick, 206
ROLLINS
  Adie G., 271
  Airy A., 88
  Ary A., 130
  Ary Ann, 154
  Charles E., 50, 88, 130, 313
  Charles W., 88
  Chas., 154
  Hattie W., 218
  James A., 271
  Jane, 218
  Jas. A., 191
  Lewis, 218
  Lorenzo D., 130
  Maggie E., 213
  Margaret M., 314
  Martha A., 271
ROLLISON
  Carter, 244
  W. H., 140
  Wm., 244
RONALD
  F. S., 21
  M. A. B., 21
ROPER
  James, 99
ROPP
  Nicholas, 15
ROSE
  Alexander W., 263
  Charlotte F., 191
  Frances M., 200, 201
  Henry B., 144
  Virginia, 144
ROSS
  Amelia, 80
  Emiline A., 80
  Fenton T., 248
  J. F., 309
  J. R., 286
  John, 230, 231, 232
  John A., 80
  John T., 159, 212, 215, 231
  Lizzie, 207
  M. J., 309
  Mary, 250
  S., 250
  Susan E., 286
  Virginia G., 309
ROSSEAU
  Catharine, 52
ROSSITER
  Charlotte E., 224
  Thomas P., 224
ROSZEL
  Addie V., 169
  G. Washington, 292
  Mary L., 41
  S. G., 169
  Stephen A., 41
  Stephen G., 213
ROSZELL
  Samuel, 63
ROUSE
  Milton, 163
ROUSER
  Henry, 76
  Maggie, 76
ROWE
  Edward S., 109
ROWLAND
  Hannah F., 15
  John H., 265
ROWLETT
  James W., 18
ROYALL
  J. J., 15
  Mary A., 15
RUNNELLS
  Louisa H., 173
RURTON
  Mary S., 85
RUSE
  Agnes J., 62
  Anna R., 193
  Edward L., 61, 62
  Frank M., 61
  John, 89
RUSK
  John J., 276
  John T., 281
  Manly W., 26
  Violinda H., 126
RUSSEL
  Robert E., 41
RUSSELL
  Alice, 159, 253
  Catharine, 213
  Etheless, 263, 281
  Eugenia H., 159
  H. H., 303
  Henry R., 159
  James W., 75, 253
  John H., 313
  Kate, 284, 285
  Mahlon H., 157
  Miss, 216
  Wm. G., 159
  Wm. H., 284, 285
RUST
  A. T. M., 189, 218
  Armistead T., 59
  Armistead T. M., 38
  Charlotte, 6
  Fleet, 38
  Fleet G., 38
  Frederick G., 189
  George, 6, 59
  George T., 23
  Lawrence, 235
  M. T., 267
  Maggie A., 36
  Maria, 38
  Matthew, 306
  Rebecca, 218
  Rebecca L., 189
  Vincent R., 43
RUTHERFORD
  Richard D., 230
RUTTER
  Catherine E., 33
  Eliza, 148
  Sarah E., 27
RYAN
  Alonzo T., 118
  James H., 84
  James W., 69
  Jno. F., 189
  John A., 114
  Jos. F., 8
  William H., 214
RYON
  Annie B., 318
  Annie V., 328
  Beulah, 318
  Frances, 226
  John H., 226
  Mollie, 196
  Theodore, 160, 318

SADLER
  Geo. W., 244

The Mirror INDEX 391

Leonard, 51
SAFFEL
  Henry W., 292
  Lelah J., 292
  Mary F., 292
SAFFER
  Benjamin F., 59
  H. F., 152
  Susan, 75
  W. M., 58
SAFFLE
  Mary F., 280
SAGLE
  Catharine, 148
  Samuel R., 91
SAMPSELL
  A. J., 39
  Henry G., 35
  Sarah M., 39
SAMPSON
  Mrs., 161
SANBOWER
  Mollie S., 121
SANDERS
  Beverly, 317, 318
  Fanny, 94
  Isaac, 306
  Larkin N., 94
  Medora L., 72
  William C., 317
  Wilson C., 9, 72, 318
SANDS
  Sarah, 44
SANFORD
  George C., 326
  Miss, 301
  Wm. L., 224, 301, 326
SANGSTER
  Adam, 306
SANTMYERS
  John B., 101
SAPPINGTON
  George W., 60
SAUNDERS
  ___, 252
  Aaron R., 50
  Albert L., 137
  Albert N., 273
  Ann, 133
  Ann E., 186

Benjamin, 45, 90, 294
Catharine, 48
Chas., 174
Christian N., 324
Cyrus G., 102
Delia N., 280, 281
Emily A., 48
Emma V., 273, 314
Everette, 258
George, 155
George H., 34
George W., 212
Henderson, 140
Henry, 57, 230, 232, 258, 280
Jno. W., 175
Jourdan M., 206
Lewis H., 105, 186, 246
Martha, 102
Mary, 12, 90, 266
Minnie, 314
Mr., 284
Mrs., 310
Nellie, 246
Nettie F., 273
R. G., 57
R. N., 314
R. Neville, 273
Susan, 258
Susan A., 45
Thomas, 12, 102
William E., 188
Wm. H., 3, 266
SAVAGE
  George D., 226
SAWYER
  Sadie J., 293
SCHAEFFER
  Thos. H., 94
SCHAFER
  Susannah, 30
SCHAFFER
  Jacob, 171
  John, 253
SCHELHORN
  Anton, 157
SCHLEIF
  John V., 116
SCHLEY
  Frederick, 11

SCHOOLEY
  Annetta F., 295
  Eli L., 128
  Eliza B., 263
  Emily, 32
  J. P., 22, 57, 181
  Jonah P., 238
  Jonas P., 60, 208, 245
  Jonathan, 32
  Lida, 238
  Lidie, 245
  Mahlon, 174
  Mary E., 60
  Milton, 229
  Miss, 296
  Sarah A., 238, 245
  William T., 94
  Wm. H., 162
SCHRIVES
  Daniel, 59
SCOTT
  Charles W., 198
  Chas. W., 272
  Eliza G., 41
  Emma S., 113
  Heningham L., 208
  John, 76, 143
  Judge, 267
  Lizzie C., 143
  Margaret G., 76
  Richard C., 143
  Robert E., 41, 208
  Thomas F., 23
SCRIVENER
  Mary A., 8
SEATON
  James W., 106
  L. B., 210
  Laura J., 268
  P. W., 121
  Samuel R., 30
  Townsend D., 19
SEBASTIAN
  Rebecca, 284
SEDWICK
  Charles Z., 177
SEEDERS
  Sarah S., 72
  Susan B., 7
  Wm., 72
SEIBER

Eleanor, 43
Sarah J., 116
Susanna, 316
SEITZ
  Andrew, 39, 114
  Sallie A., 233
  Winfield S., 193
SELLMAN
  ___, 218
  A. E., 220
  H. C., 210
  J. J. M., 220
  John P., 70
SELSAM
  Emma, 115
SETTLE
  John H., 61
  Kate M., 61
SEWELL
  Charles I., 135
  Margaret, 68
  Rachel, 135
  Thomas, 135
  Willie, 162
SEXTON
  Elizabeth, 89
  John W., 67
  Sarah V., 260
  Thomas F., 141
SHACKELFORD
  Margaret, 57
SHAFER
  Daniel, 106
  Elizabeth V., 324
  Ella, 204
  Portia, 28
  Samuel, 322
  Samuel S., 321
SHAFFAR
  Mary E., 324
  Thomas, 324
SHAFFER
  L., 199
SHAFFNER
  Harriet, 235
SHALL
  Thomas M., 118
SHAULL
  Bartholomew, 45
  Rosanna E., 45
  Sally, 45
SHAW

  F. C., 160
  Frederick C., 97
  Jackson N., 204
  John D., 160
  Kate M., 160
  Lanie K., 136
  Marshal G., 136
SHAWEN
  Cornelius C., 166
  W. C., 113, 224
SHEARER
  L. V., 129
SHEETZ
  Adaline M., 63
  Catharine C., 111
  Daniel M., 63, 125
  Margaret, 34
  Michael, 34, 111
SHEID
  Catharine K., 2
SHELBURNE
  Silas, 322
SHELHORN
  Antoine, 191
  Catherine, 190
  Frederick, 288
  Godfrey, 190
SHELL
  Alfred, 123
  Craven, 44
  Elizabeth T., 2
SHELLHORN
  Catherine, 160
SHELTON
  Susan F., 108
SHEPARD
  Elizabeth W., 45
SHEPHERD
  Ellen, 173
  George C., 172
  Humphrey, 18, 173, 176
  Joseph H., 68
  Lyman W., 318
  Margaret, 18
  Mary C., 207
  Thomas B., 47
SHERMAN
  Abram B., 226
  Lucinda A., 226
  Mary C., 48
SHERRARD

  Joseph H., 37
  Robert B., 37
SHERZER
  John, 25
SHIFFET
  James, 20
  Mildred A., 20
SHINER
  Albert, 160, 190, 243
  Catherine, 190
  Katrina, 243
SHIPLEY
  Albert A., 253
  Fannie E., 253
  John W., 253
SHIPMAN
  Ann M., 198
  Ellen L., 65
  Etheless, 263
  John M., 65
  Samuel, 263
  Stephen P., 281
SHIRLEY
  James W., 277
  John G., 41
SHOAFF
  D., 175
  J. Watt, 258
  Nannie E., 175
SHOEMAKER
  Naylor, 130
  Susanna, 148
SHORT
  Jacob, 217
  Rosanna, 123
  Wm., 217
SHREVE
  Ann O., 3
  Arthur B., 4
  B. A., 265
  Barbara, 218
  Benjamin, 4, 51
  Benjamin F., 3
  Charles, 3
  Charles W., 3
  Daniel, 3
  Daniel T., 137, 193
  Emma, 137
  Francis B., 106
  Francis E., 106, 288, 290, 293
  M. C. S., 264

INDEX

Margaret R., 137
Mary E., 3
Minerva, 290
Minerva A., 106
Thomas J., 3
William, 3
Wm., 218
SHRIGLEY
　Mary E., 27
SHRIVER
　Amelia F., 90
　Annie M., 258
　David, 90
　Thos. W., 257
SHROFF
　P. F., 141
SHRY
　Mary, 230, 231
　Sarah E., 89
SHRYOCK
　Elizabeth, 172
　John F., 122
SHRYOCKE
　Samuel, 27
SHUEY
　Lewis, 287
SHUGARS
　George M., 28
SHUGART
　Jno. Z., 108
SHUGARTS
　Sarah J., 182
SHUMAKER
　Rosa, 201
SHUMAN
　George, 248
　Lavinia P., 248
　S. T., 236
　Septimus, 237
SHUMATE
　B. G., 307
　Bailey, 237
　Lewis, 76, 278
SHUSTER
　Mellville C., 220
SIBBS
　Chas. F., 58
SIDEBOTTOM
　Elizabeth, 24
SIEBER
　John, 53
SILCOTT

Albert, 93, 228
Anna, 178
Bertie A., 322
Charles F., 258
Chas. E., 314
J. B., 302
J. W., 136
James, 225
James B., 178
James E., 228
Jas., 224
Mary C., 228
Virginia, 284
Virginia C., 224
Washington, 284
SIMMONS
　Ann Virginia, 175
　Henry A., 194
　Jas., 175
SIMPSON
　Alcinda, 25
　Burr W., 3
　Elizabeth, 181, 200, 242, 243, 259
　French, 218
　Henry L., 256
　Henson, 205, 208
　J. W., 142
　Jas. E., 51
　Jno., 134
　John F., 42, 58
　John T., 66
　John W., 142, 197, 228
　Laura, 228
　Marietta, 296
　Mary A., 197
　R. French, 286
　R. H., 296
　Robt. I., 39
　Samuel, 298
　Samuel L., 134
　Silas, 247
　Thomas, 143
　Virginia F., 218
　Wm. F., 64
SIMS
　Barnet, 306
　John, 306
SINCLAIR
　George B., 92
　Jas., 29, 30

John, 307
Mary, 29
Mary E., 30
Mildred, 307
SING
　Charles, 292
　Hong Wah, 292
SINGLETON
　A. J., 125
　Albert N., 125
　E. M., 125
　Joshua, 306
SKILLMAN
　Allison F., 181
　Anna, 105
　Elizabeth, 43
　Lucinda, 181
　Wm. F., 89
SKILMAN
　___, 8
SKINKER
　Anna H., 180
　James K., 180
SKINNER
　Albert T., 71
　Alex. G., 57
　Benj. F., 19
　Calvin, 186
　Charles G., 172
　Chas. L., 317
　Elizabeth E., 157
　Fannie M., 123
　Fanny R., 99
　Henry E., 264
　James, 242
　James H., 251
　James T., 19
　Jas. K., 157
　John P., 305
　John R., 215
　M. Annie, 125
　Mary J., 57
　N. J., 242
　Peter, 183
　Rose, 65
　Samuel R., 183
　Sarah E., 148
　Thos., 148
　William W., 40
SLACK
　Charles, 110
　Fenelon, 303

INDEX

James H., 73
John T., 122
Mahala J., 92
Olevia J., 184
Sarah V., 229
SLATER
  George, 65
  George E., 86
  James M., 93
  Roselia, 243
  Sallie, 305
  Samuel, 87
  Samuel W., 54, 155
SLAUCK
  George P., 264
SLAYMAKER
  A. H., 214
  Amos B., 206, 255
  Harry C., 85
  Lizzie J., 206, 214
SLAYMAN
  Susan, 78
SMALE
  Betsy, 234
  Elizabeth, 233
  Elizabeth F., 36
  Emma C., 324
  Frances, 109
  John, 36, 61, 109, 184, 288
  Mary M., 324
  Olevia J., 324
  Simon, 233
SMALL
  Levi H., 184
SMALLWOOD
  Caroline, 280
  George, 195
  L., 225
  L. W., 201
  Thomas, 280
  William, 250
  Wm., 269
SMARR
  Susan F., 232
SMART
  Charlotte A., 311
  Eliza, 48
  John P., 4, 48, 55, 311
SMILEY
  Matilda C., 41

SMITH
  A. G., 164, 235, 248, 309
  A. P., 265
  Abraham, 246
  Agnes C., 171
  Albert G., 6
  Alex. G., 136
  Alice C., 143
  Ann V., 103, 129
  Annie A., 96
  Augustus G., 308, 309
  Benjamin P., 302
  Bowin, 275
  Carl, 216
  Caroline, 265
  Carrie W., 265
  Channing M., 100
  Charles A., 163, 170, 198, 203, 216, 309
  Chas., 326
  Chas. A., 161, 308
  Chas. E., 319
  Clara, 61
  Courtland H., 224
  Daniel G., 319
  Daniel L., 7
  E. B., 319
  Edgar L., 173, 174
  Edmonia E., 185
  Edward A., 85
  Edward J., 159
  Elizabeth, 213
  Elizabeth B., 275
  Etta, 240
  Etta M., 249
  Francis H., 319
  Francis L., 119, 143, 245
  Frank, 247
  Geo. D., 112
  George D., 173, 174
  George W., 264
  Gunnell, 63
  H. R., 297
  H. S., 130
  Harriet N., 126
  Henry G., 44, 78
  Henry H., 55
  Hermon P., 255
  Hiram, 254

Hiram R., 255
Hugh, 37, 213
Hugh M., 194
J. Howard, 319
J. Hunter, 280
J. Rice, 71
James, 120
James P., 121
James W. M., 275
James W. N., 44
Jannie S., 245
Jas., 58
Jas. E., 235
Jas. M., 208
Jas. W., 319
Jesse, 224
Job, 113, 229
John L., 149
Lillias P., 297
Logan O., 292
Lucie D., 100
Lula A., 280
Lydia K., 5
M. Ella, 248
Margaret, 136
Martha L., 112
Martha V., 129
Mary, 326
Mary E., 103, 284, 320
Mary F., 65, 231
Mary H., 265
Mary J., 182
Mary V., 229
Matilda L., 121
Olive, 198
Olive P., 216
Olivia M., 203
P. H., 185, 280
Peter, 114, 324
Philena E., 255
Rachel, 42
Rice, 230
Robert W., 280
Sadie J., 165
Sallie A. E., 302
Sallie E., 274
Sallie M. J., 246
Samuel, 265, 320
Sarah V., 87
Scott B., 37
Sidney W., 42

Sue, 129
Susannah F., 87
Thomas, 157
Thos. R., 23
Tingey A., 44
Treadwll, 165
W., 24
W. D., 150
William, 100, 129, 231, 249
William J., 158
William P., 103, 129
Wm., 152, 198, 254, 302, 304
Wm. D., 149, 152, 155
Wm. G., 46
Wm. J., 23, 159
Wm. R., 1
SMOOT
  John T., 124
  W. A., 166
SNAUFFER
  Archibald F., 33
SNEDEKER
  Samuel W., 49
SNELL
  Thos., 12
SNOOTS
  Burr F., 322
  Elizabeth, 28
  George H., 86
  Henry S., 149
  John, 1, 23
  Mary A., 177
  Mary J., 1
  William, 61
SNOOTZ
  Amanrella V., 226
SNOWDEN
  Harold, 222
SNYDER
  Joseph A., 87
SOLLERS
  Wm. A., 101
SOLOMON
  Carrie, 70
  Isaac, 70
SOMMERVILLE
  James, 2
  M. C., 2
  William G., 2

SOUDER
  Americus J., 238, 281
  Eliza, 27
  John, 234, 238
  Mary K., 71
  Philip H., 169
SOUDOR
  Geo. P., 130
  Susan, 130
SOWERS
  Brooks, 72
  Daniel H., 2
  Daniel W., 21
  David A., 68
  Lucy E., 21
  Martha L., 209
  R., 65
  Ruth, 72
  Sue Ida, 68
  Virginia, 2
  Wm. D., 87, 129
SPATES
  Thomas, 168
SPAULDING
  George, 130
SPEARS
  Ed. F., 192
  Henry, 18
SPECHER
  Columbus, 45
  Martha, 45
SPEGER
  Louisa, 190
SPEIDEN
  A. C., 184
  Edgar, 184
SPENCE
  Henson, 296
  Vincent, 296
SPILLMAN
  William, 279
  William M., 208
SPILMAN
  E. M., 327
SPINKS
  Alex., 173
  Christie V., 230
  Emma, 290
  J. Thomas, 59
  James, 290
  Jas., 173
SPRING

  Casper, 100
  Henrietta, 143
  James L., 238
  James W., 26
  Jefferson, 238
  Jonas S., 112
  Lydia A., 20
  Margaret A., 31
  William, 20
SPROUSE
  Richard A., 168
SQUIRES
  Amanda V., 44
  Mary F., 201
SRY
  William, 75
STAATS
  A. C., 140
STABLER
  Edward, 84
  Mary, 84
  Rebecca, 84
  Robert M., 8
STALEY
  Ann C., 120
STALLINGS
  James R., 93
STANDIFORD
  Arthur, 230
  John, 230
  Josephine, 230
STANLEY
  Susan M., 256
  Susannah M., 200
STANSBURY
  Charles F., 306
  Daniel E., 29
  Theo. S. B., 195
STANTON
  Alfred, 250
STAPLER
  Mr., 328
STAUB
  Bettie P., 34, 48
  J. H. T., 34
  John F., 48
  John H., 34
  Ludwig H., 5
  R. P. H., 92
STEADMAN
  Carrie H., 198
  David W., 206

Emily, 216
Frank M., 157
Henry C., 141
J. P., 219
J. T., 216
James W., 32, 95, 157
John A., 219
M. B., 216
Rosa B., 152
Sallie A., 157
Sarah, 216
Sarah E., 62
Susan F., 198
Thomas F., 216
Thomas J., 71, 131
Virginia W., 216
STEARNS
  John, 174
  John L., 296
  May B., 174
STEAVENS
  Sallie A., 267
  Willie T., 267
STEELE
  Joseph I., 135
STEER
  James M., 196
  Lewis W., 45
  Lydia A., 196
  Samuel M., 198
  Wm., 229
STEINER
  J., 296
  Marietta, 296
STEPHENS
  M. Virginia, 109
  Nancy, 141
  Sarah A., 319
  Thomas, 141
  Thomas L. M., 296
  William J., 22
STEPHENSON
  James, 190
  James A., 131
  James W., 302
  Kenner, 132
  Mary G., 265
  Wm. H., 190
STEPTOE
  Hannah, 252
  Peter, 291

STERNWELL
  Mary E., 188
STERRETT
  Lydia H., 186
STEVENS
  E. A., 35
  Elenor L., 290
  Henry, 280
  John, 4
  John W., 44
  L. M., 253
  Martha A., 4
  Mary C., 84
  Mary P., 35
  Mr., 130
  Roxanna, 4
  S. A., 280
STEWARD
  Catherine A., 288
  John E., 288, 307
STEWART
  Charles H., 84
  Emma P., 146
  Fannie A., 42
  George W., 51
  Gustie, 134
  John T., 146
  Kate M., 12
  Kate V., 251
  Septimus H., 70
  T. B., 90
STICKELY
  E. E., 261
  Josie, 261
  S. H., 261
STICKLE
  Robert, 252
  Sophia, 27
STICKLES
  Sarah J., 3
STILLIONS
  Eliza A., 13
STIMMEL
  Joana, 157
STITH
  John, 271
  Sarah B. H., 271
STOCKS
  Mahlon, 114, 242
  Mary E., 128
  Mollie E., 242
  Sarah J., 102

Stephen S., 162
Wm., 114, 166
STOCKTON
  Eliza, 215
STONE
  Annie, 327
  Courtney S., 8
  Edgar H., 256
  Elizabeth S., 155
  George B., 204
  Nancy, 127
  Samuel, 8
  William, 99
STONEBURNER
  Catharine, 20
  Charles, 24
  Charlotte, 10
  Emily F., 24
  Flora V., 10
  J. C., 10
  Peter, 20
  Samuel G., 21
  Wm. C., 274
STONESTREET
  James E., 207
STORK
  Wm. L., 64
STORM
  Dora, 232
  Mrs., 135
STOUT
  Elenor, 3
  John L., 3
STOUTZENBERGER
  Mollie E., 308
  William F., 54
STOVER
  Edwin A., 128
  Elizabeth, 128
  John, 58
STRAITH
  Alexander, 34
  Amelia, 34
  Ella, 145
  John J. H., 145
STRATHER
  Wm., 25
STREAM
  Barbara, 283
  Chas. G., 305
STRIBLING
  Ellen M., 99

Francis T., 99
Jacob, 323
STRICKLY
　E. E., 172
STRINGFELLOW
　Robert, 196
STRONG
　Jasper, 88
　William E., 143
STROTHER
　Alpheus W., 171
　Frank A., 170
　J. F., 10
　James F., 38
　Kate, 16
　Maria B., 197
　Martha S., 84
　Mary E., 16
STUART
　Alex. H. H., 143
　C. C., 2
　Caroline C., 116, 142
　J. E. B., 282
　Julia C., 142
　Laura, 2
　R. H., 142, 296
　Richard H., 116
　Susan B., 143
SUDDITH
　Amelia, 21
　Arebella, 20
　Henry C., 21
　Inman H., 40
　Wm. A., 21
SUGAR
　Joseph, 59
SULLIVAN
　Annie B., 109
SUMMERS
　Daniel, 208
　Lydia A., 95
　Mary E., 49
　Rebecca, 34
　Richard H., 34, 208
　S. H., 84
　Sallie J., 84
　Samuel, 49
　W. S., 208
　William, 146
　Wm. S., 229
SUNDERLIN
　Henrietta, 189

SURGHNOR
　John, 33
SURRATT
　Mrs., 294
SURVICK
　Alice M., 246
　Benj. D., 229
　Benjamin D., 322
　George W., 85, 246
　Janet C., 246
　Legrand, 322
　Sallie, 322
SUTHERLIN
　Jane B., 245
　Jannie, 245
　Jannie L., 119
　W. T., 119, 245
SUTHRON
　Susan, 55
SUTTLES
　John, 313
SWAIN
　Wm. H., 184
SWAN
　Donnell, 254
SWANK
　Aaron, 284
　Anna J., 147
　John W., 324
　Mary M., 194
　Mr., 324
　Samuel F., 123
SWANN
　Elizabeth G., 237
　Henrietta, 66
　Jennie B., 97
　Thomas, 97, 237
SWART
　Adrain L., 263
　Elizabeth, 263
　James, 154
　James H., 36
　Lilla, 325
　Martin H., 321
SWARTS
　Arminda, 268
SWARTZ
　Charles J., 102
　Edmund P., 105
SWEEDY
　Ann E., 140
SWEENEY

A. R., 132
SWEET
　Wm. T., 158
SWENEY
　John, 21
SYMONS
　Jacob W., 121
SYPHERD
　Sarah, 294

TALBOTT
　H. M., 200
　Lillie, 165
TALIAFERRO
　J. M., 14
　James M., 158
　Marion L., 14
　Mrs., 104
　Sally M., 158
TALLIAFERRO
　Mattie C., 211
TALLMAN
　Cynthia A., 7
TALLMAN
　Emma, 199
TALLY
　Emma E., 252
TALMAN
　John, 241
　Mary L., 241
TANNER
　Richard B., 320
TARLTON
　Mary, 134
TAVENER
　Geo. A., 191
　Hannah, 128
　Howard F., 90
　James E., 90
　Mahlon, 128
　Mary J., 90
　Pleasant, 78
　Sarah J., 191
　Stacy J., 78
TAVENNER
　Alpheus, 199
　Caroline V., 40
　Charles H., 184
　Edith, 264
　Edward, 109
　Elizabeth, 179
　Ella, 247

The Mirror
INDEX

Fielden, 178
Fielding, 40
Hannah, 40, 178
Hiram, 109, 179
John V., 66
Jonathan, 16
Katie, 109
Lanea, 40
Lott, 67
Maalon T., 98
Mahlon, 37, 247
Maria, 67
Mary, 57
Mary E., 13
Nimrod, 88
Pleasant, 13
Robert, 223
Stacy J., 13, 69
Veline, 85
TAYLOE
John, 91
TAYLOR
___, 216
Agnes, 163
Alexander, 6
Alfred, 3
Alice, 39
Amanda, 265
Annie M., 235
Armstead, 151
B. F., 41, 57, 311
B. Fenelon, 48
Benjamin F., 39
Bernard, 145, 255
Bushrod J., 116
Charles, 228
Charles E., 120
Chas. N., 257
Cornelius S., 17
Dorcas, 298
E. S., 34
Eliza R., 48
Elizabeth, 149
Euphema, 57
Geo. W., 155, 217
George P., 221
Hannah, 227
Hannah B., 8
Henry, 57, 298
Henry H., 224
Henry S., 73
J. W., 137, 155, 174

James W., 47
John, 97
Jonathan, 118
Joseph D., 244
Josiah B., 11
Josiah R., 174
Julia A., 28
K., 173
Laura, 155
Lawrence B., 134
Lewis, 10
Lydia B., 118, 293
Margaret, 133
Margaret V., 199
Mary, 24
Mary L., 11
Rebecca, 145
Rosalie A., 134
Sallie L., 6
Sarah, 41
Sarah E., 42
Susan C., 45
T., 48
Thomas C., 117
Thos. T., 327
Timothy, 227
Virginia, 137, 221
W. H., 224
W. Henry, 293
William, 166
William H., 235
Willie Annie, 235
TEBBS
A. Sidney, 68, 138
Caroline M., 32
Charles, 136
Charles B., 22
Clement K., 68
Cornelia C., 22
F. C., 232, 244
Hannah, 8
Hattie, 68
John W., 183
Maria L., 244
Samuel J., 8, 22
Thomas F., 32
THACHER
George A., 96
THARPE
Narcissa, 92
THOMAS
A. C., 217

Albert C., 116
Amelia, 12, 30
Ann C., 121
Catharine, 301
Cecelia H., 156
Edward, 323
Elizabeth, 22
Elizabeth H., 217
Evelina, 92
G. E., 121
George T., 12
H. W., 146
Henry W., 36
Herod, 85, 158, 159
J. M., 36
Jacob D., 140
James, 66, 171
John, 301
John H., 3, 74
John W., 80
Joseph, 159, 246
Julia B., 171
Kate S., 36
Laura, 298
Maggie A., 220
Mahlon, 220, 298
Margaret, 80
Margaret E., 66
Martha A., 25
Martha R., 118
Martha T., 159
Mary A., 6, 85
N., 184
Nannie, 146
Nathaniel, 151, 212, 215
Otho, 67
Owen, 156
Robt. W., 298
Ruth, 298
Ruth H., 156
S. V., 217
Sarah T., 127
William E., 74
Wilson, 217
Wm. P., 92
THOMPSON
___, 59
Albert, 28
Annie, 288
Dorcas O., 146
Edward, 207

The Mirror   399
INDEX

Elizabeth C., 152
Frank A., 172
Geoerge G., 288
John, 146
John A., 81
John M., 161
Joseph, 239
Lucinda, 64
Lucy, 81
M. A. B., 21
M. B., 296
M. Jeff., 263
M. T., 21
Maggie J., 108
Mary, 263
Mary E., 193
Mortimer, 182
Pembroke, 193
Randolph S., 125
Saml. P., 152
Samuel, 108, 130
Samuel P., 32
Sarah C., 154
Sarah J., 196, 296
Susan E., 191
Thos. N., 161
Wilson H., 172
Wm., 106
Wm. H., 135
THOMSON
  James, 74
  John A., 74
  Orrel, 163
THORN
  E. W., 258
THORNE
  Alice, 124
THORNTON
  Anna, 85
  Caroline M., 32
  John, 306
  Stuart, 32
THRASHER
  Luther, 88
  Sarah E., 116
  Susan A., 88
THRESHER
  Archibald, 186
THRIFT
  Annie, 193
  Benjamin, 303
  Francis E., 106, 178

James, 191
Lizzie, 191
Mary V., 11
Sanderson, 59, 60
Wm., 88
THROCKMORTON
  J. B., 219
  Lucinda, 22
  Mason, 195, 280
  Sarah M. C., 219
  Thomas R., 22
THROCMORTON
  J. B., 302
  Mason, 238
TIBBS
  Chas. F., 58
  Charles T., 59
  Thomas F., 59
TIFFANY
  Franklin P., 275
  Wm. S., 176, 177
TILLET
  Annie L., 120
TILLETT
  Edward, 51, 209
  Elizabeth, 209, 257
  Gertrude A., 324
  Giles E., 182
  Harriet B., 233
  John, 212
  Samuel, 203
  Samuel A., 214
TILLMAN
  Andrew, 294
TIMBERLAKE
  Jas. H., 242
  Thomas W., 62
TIMS
  Mary E., 13
TINSMAN
  Clinton, 285
  Mary V., 277
TIPPETT
  John H., 279
  Wm. H., 39
TITLOW
  Clara, 197
TITUS
  Burr T., 148
  Charles, 327
  Edward L., 125
  Emma N., 268

Joseph P., 230
Susan O., 210, 285
T. S., 285
T. T., 315
William T., 279
Wm., 268
Wm. T., 210, 247
TODD
  John R., 217
TOLSON
  Ada A., 241
  E. L., 241
  Julia I., 241
TOMPKINS
  Robert, 162
TONGUE
  Virginia, 24
TORREYSON
  G. L., 43
  Lucelia E., 88
  Samuel, 88, 285
TORRISON
  Catherine A., 4
  Mary, 272
  William, 25
TOTTEN
  Lucy E., 70
TOWNER
  Cora, 101
  Charles J., 9
  Eva, 11
  John L., 70
  Victoria, 98
TRAMMELL
  Milley, 181
TRAPNELL
  Joseph, 187
  Richard, 226
  William, 187
TRASSELL
  James M., 67
TRAVERS
  John A., 137
TREHEARN
  Richard, 110
TREHERN
  Mary S., 252
TRENARY
  ___, 110
  Jas. T., 292
TRIBBEY
  Charles, 197

INDEX

Gordon H., 187
John T., 187
Sallie A., 187
TRIBBY
  James, 86
  Jesse E., 306
  William F., 100
TRILBY
  Sarah Margaret, 137
TRIMBLE
  Henry W., 181
TRIMMER
  James E., 186
TRIPLETT
  Arthur W., 201
  Francis, 306
  Samuel, 98
  Simon, 306
  Wm., 317
TRITAPOE
  Elizabeth A., 20
  George C., 20
TRITIPOE
  Philip B., 89
TRONE
  John T., 22
TROUNCER
  Ann D., 52
TROUT
  Mattie C., 124
  N. K., 124
TRUNDLE
  Abner C., 41
  Christiana, 162
  H. L., 80
  H. Lewis, 162
  Hezekiah, 162
  Lizzie A., 41
  Sallie, 41
  Sallie E., 80
  Sarah F., 73
TRUSSELL
  Julia A., 157
  Thomas, 28
TRUXTON
  Commodore, 225
TUCKER
  Alfred B., 114
  Ann, 200
  Beverley D., 160
  Eliza T., 114
  J. R., 200

J. Randolph, 109, 126
Nannie H., 109
Robert W., 118
Virginia B., 126
William T., 114
TUGGLE
  Frank L., 277
TURLEY
  Charles F., 59
TURNBULL
  Chester B., 326
  L. B., 298
TURNER
  Anne E., 65
  Beverly, 65
  C., 79
  Charles J., 322
  Chas., 276
  Duane M., 68
  Henry, 65
  Richard H., 65, 205
  Robert F., 220
  Samuel, 42
  Sidney S., 254
  Stonewall J., 79
  Wm. F., 142, 254
TUTWILER
  Idela, 38
  Jacob, 38
TWITTY
  Miss, 270
TYLER
  Augusta, 256
  Grafton, 221
  Grayson, 242
  H. B., 256, 327
  Henry B., 11, 314
  Isabella, 274
  John W., 102, 266, 327
  Josephine, 297
  Lyttleton, 102
  Mr., 110
  Virginia B., 314
  William, 221

UMBAUGH
  Catherine, 288
  George, 288
  John S., 288
UNDERWOOD

Alice J., 298
Betty, 100
Bushrod, 61
Lydia, 317
Mary P., 80
UNGER
  Joseph F., 143
UPDIKE
  J. Byrd, 155
UPDYKE
  F. M., 57
UPSHUR
  John N., 168
UTTERBACK
  Addison W., 24
  Elizabeth, 309
  Lucinda, 35
  W. H., 75

Van BENNETT
  Capt., 120
Van BUREN
  F. B., 116
Van DOREN
  Meverell L., 266
VANDERHOOF
  Wm. H., 299
VANDEVANTER
  A. M. T., 57
  Chas. O., 219, 297
  Corrie E., 274
  Eliza, 204
  Ella, 147
  Ella M., 327
  Gabriel, 164
  Henry, 204
  Isaac, 259
  Joseph L., 266
  Lillie, 165
  Maurice G., 313
  Robert S., 322
  Townsend H., 108
  Virginia, 297
  Washington, 147, 204, 274
  William, 90
VANDEVENTER
  C., 42
  C. Means, 5
  Mary E., 5
  Mrs., 140
  Sarah J., 5

INDEX

W. H., 81
VANHORN
  B. F., 100
  Decatur, 136
  Edward O., 116
  Frank, 136
  W. Decatur, 227
VANMETRE
  A.Morgan, 207
VANSICKLER
  Emanuel, 154
  John, 57
  Margaret, 154
  P. F., 263
  Philip F., 33
  Rosa B., 128
VANVACTOR
  Charity, 39
  Elizabeth, 39
  Solomon, 39
VEALE
  Florence J., 201
VERMILLION
  Charles, 151
  Lewis, 161
  Nancy, 236
VICKERS
  John T., 123
  Susan, 66
VILLARD
  Andrew J., 222
  Sophia DeM., 222
  Thos. J., 152
VINCEL
  Alice L., 139
  Anson B., 102
  Louisa, 28
  Will D., 271
VINCENT
  Ann E., 136
  Thos., 136
  Wm. B., 136
VINSEL
  Alcey V., 149
VINSON
  Edgar D., 152
VIRTS
  A. E., 277
  Annie R., 80
  Charles R., 285
  Chas. R., 257
  Clara H. A., 229

David F., 257
Elizabeth, 65, 138
George W., 33, 262
Harry, 295
Henry, 51
Henry J. T., 229
Israel, 277
Jacob, 51
James W., 256
Jane P., 28
Jeannie E., 211
John M., 198
John W., 83, 138, 233
John W. S., 257
Jonas S., 16
Joseph, 295
Martha, 33
Mary, 295
Mary C., 62
Orra B., 279
Peter, 33
Peter S., 19
Rosella V., 229
Sally A., 11
Sarah P., 241
Virginia, 80
Virginia E., 76
William H., 93
Wm. H., 148, 198
VIRTZ
  George W., 168
  J., 23
  John W., 269
  Lydia C., 165
  Mary A., 9
  Rebecca, 307
  Thos. B., 240
  Wm., 327

WADDELL
  Dr., 126
WADE
  Edward, 270
  Mary E., 169
  Miss, 270
  Rachel A., 123
  Susan, 123
WAESCHE
  John F., 75
WAKE
  Herewaldo R., 119

WALDRON
  Hiram C., 203
WALKER
  C., 290
  Chas. C., 93
  Eli, 277
  Fannie G., 279
  Isaac, 130, 208
  J. Ed., 132
  J. M., 132
  Jacob R., 121
  James M., 146
  Jas. M., 198
  Mary N., 290
  Mary R., 261
  Rebecca L., 290
  Sarah E., 31
  Susan, 130, 132, 146
WALL
  Mary A., 7
  Nicholas, 8
  Wm., 7
Wall, Stephens & Co., 8
WALLACE
  Almeda, 89
  Edwin, 63
  H. Clay, 103
  James M., 63
  James W., 75
  Jas. M., 59
  Jennie, 118
  Margaret H., 13
  Michael, 14
  William, 23
  Wm. W., 299
WALRAVEN
  Catherine L., 313
  John, 178
  Jonas, 313
  Lucretia, 313
WALTER
  Columbus, 28
WALTMAN
  Emanuel, 88
  V. B., 88
WALTON
  Florence, 144
WAMPLER
  J. T., 294
WARD
  Charles, 247
  Eddie K., 250

John, 220
Martah, 247
Mary A., 220
WARING
  Cora H., 131
  Moses, 131
WARNER
  Alcinda, 163
  Charles G., 40
  Clintonia W., 64
  Gabriel V., 102
  Geo., 205
  George, 163
  James E., 203
  James H., 64
  Jas. E., 203
  Malinda E., 294
  Malinda P., 7
  Mary E., 294
WASHBURNE
  Sarah A., 177
WASHINGTON
  Anna M., 160
  Annie M., 314
  Bushrod C., 299
  Eleanor L., 40
  Florence, 11
  Geo., 41
  John, 234
  John A., 40, 113, 160
  Lawrence, 242
  Lewis W., 41, 115
  Louisa F., 113
  R. C., 11
  Richard B., 113
  Thos. B., 314
WATERMAN
  Ann B., 70
  Asher, 70
WATERS
  George S., 108
  John F., 129, 152
  Levi, 129
  Mary, 59
  Mrs., 260
WATKINS
  Augustus, 275
  Lucy A., 158
  Mary E., 176
WATSON
  ___, 158
  Joe, 303

Joseph H., 205
Lemuel, 215
Mary E., 205
Mary J., 205
Moses P., 14
T. B. S., 161
Taylor, 210
WATTS
  J. G., 134
  Mary L., 134
WAUGH
  A. P., 108
  Rachel, 108
WAY
  Charles C., 211
WEADON
  Amanda, 50
  Ashford, 50, 215
  Charles, 195
  Fanny, 204
  Hariet, 46
  James, 85
  John, 46, 244, 314
  Louisa A., 67
  Lydia, 172
  Margaret V., 27
  Mary, 195
  Ruth E., 195
  T. W., 312, 313
  Thomas M., 68
WEANING
  John O., 27
WEAVER
  Ann E., 187
  Charles, 180
  Maria, 180
  R. A., 13
WEBB
  C. Louisa, 19
  J. Watson, 19
  John E., 170
  Ruth J., 253
  Thomas W., 143
WEBSTER
  John B., 294
WEEDEN
  Sanford J., 227, 228
WEEDON
  Lucetta J. W., 33
  Mary M., 33
  Thomas, 33
  Thos., 33

WEELAND
  William, 191
WEIGLE
  Albert J., 197
  Maria B., 197
WELCH
  Gertrude V., 194
  James S., 194
WELLFORD
  Dr., 115
WELLS
  James A., 181
  Susan, 181
WELSH
  B. W., 195
  Benjamin W., 196
  Franklin D., 56
  Joseph S., 100
WENNER
  Catharine, 73
  Charles F., 137
  Emanuel, 73
  Emeline A., 9
  Geo. H., 217
  Jacob, 236, 298, 320
  John, 296
  John W., 324
  Kate W., 285
  Laninia C., 137
  Lydia A., 260
  Mary E., 206
  Mary J., 296
  Susan, 320
  William, 28, 308, 309
  Willie, 137
  Wm., 307
  Wm. W., 30
WENZEL
  Sarah E., 326
WERKING
  Geo., 317
  George, 314
WERTENBAKER
  Vernon D., 184
  Virginia, 151
  Wm., 151
WEST
  Bessie, 326
  Eliza, 328
  George, 328
  Mamie, 328
  N. G., 326, 328

WHALEY
  James H., 75
  James W., 105
  Jas. H., 152
  Laura, 159
  Laura T., 37
  Lillie B., 105
  Mary, 105
  William F., 327
WHARLEY
  Martha A., 131
WHIP
  Cornelia C., 82
WHITACRE
  Amos, 48
  Bettie J., 48
  Robert, 144
WHITE
  Adelaide, 209
  Agnes, 224
  Agnes P., 212
  Albina, 57
  Annie, 135
  Arabella, 78
  B. R., 167
  B. S., 74, 83
  Ben S., 132
  Benj. S., 7
  Carrie B., 106
  Cecilia, 38
  Charles W., 61
  Crawford K., 66
  Daniel, 73, 236
  Daniel T., 169
  E. V., 119, 299
  Elizabeth, 57
  Elizabeth R., 111, 113
  G. Newton, 279
  George W., 61
  Hannah, 70
  Ida, 132
  James B., 224
  John H., 135
  John J., 15, 212
  John R., 38, 135, 144
  Joseph, 277
  Josiah, 58
  Josiah T., 110, 113, 222
  Leah E., 10
  Levi, 7
  Lizzie, 119
  Mary B., 222
  Mary C., 212
  Mary E., 83
  Mary J., 110, 222
  Nathan, 106, 129
  Nathaniel, 198
  Rebecca J., 88
  Richard, 157, 282, 283
  Robert, 78
  Robt., 113
  Robt. J. T., 11
  Rosa, 277
  Samuel C., 173
  Sarah E., 157
  T. W., 57
  Thomas, 58
  Thomas W., 110
  Thos., 298
  Virginia E., 70
  William, 129
WHITEMAN
  James, 59
  John, 167
WHITLOCK
  Sarah, 104
WHITMAN
  James, 58
  Joseph, 58
WHITMORE
  Bettie, 304
  Hattie, 61
  Jno. H., 304
  Martha E., 323
  Phoebe E., 193
  Samuel P., 193
  Samuel R., 323
WHITOCK
  John, 137
WHITTINGDON
  R. W., 271
WHITTINGTON
  Alberta, 103
  Emma, 225
  Joseph T., 103
WHITTLE
  F. M., 168
  Lucy P., 168
WHITZELL
  Harry, 326
WIARD
  J. S., 179
WICKERSHAM
  M. D., 78
  Mary, 181
  Morris S., 181
WICKS
  Mary L., 144
  Wm., 144
WIGGINGTON
  Margaret, 295
WIGGINTON
  John, 107
WILBURN
  H., 292
  Ida V., 292
WILDER
  Henry C., 179
WILDEY
  John, 306
WILDMAN
  Anna S., 32
  Burr M., 163
  C. B., 181
  Emily, 70
  J., 95
  James, 71
  Jane D., 32, 65, 291
  Jane H., 32
  John W., 32
  Rebecca, 275
  William, 218
WILEY
  Adeline V., 6
  J. H., 285
  James F., 99
  John H., 306
  Julia A., 52
  Laura C., 306
  Mary, 195
  Nancy, 28
  Oscar, 285
  Susan M., 28
  Thomas, 229
  Wm. A., 238
WILKENSON
  Mary A., 63
WILKINS
  Mrs., 272
WILKINSON
  Bushrod E., 28
WILKLOW
  John H., 123

INDEX

WILL
  Anna E., 105
  John G., 105
WILLARD
  Gertrude E., 12
WILLCOXEN
  Albert, 313
  Bessie, 313
WILLEY
  Archilles, 255
WILLIAMS
  Ann E., 289
  Charles, 3, 31, 307
  Charles T., 233
  E. Calvin, 300
  Edward, 82
  Ellis, 35
  Franklin, 248
  Geo. W., 312
  George F., 256
  Gertrude, 84
  Gustavus B., 32
  Hannah E., 249
  Henry S., 155, 159, 248
  Isreal W., 64
  Jacob, 133
  Jno., 192
  Jno. J., 271
  John, 24, 184, 189, 306, 315
  John H., 129, 164, 218, 289, 315
  Jos., 164
  Laura, 312
  Levi, 24
  Louisa, 300
  Magdalena, 35
  Margaret E., 30
  Mary, 31
  Mary C., 298, 302
  Mary E., 208
  Mary J., 196
  Ormemelia, 189
  Rebecca K., 154
  Sam, 219
  Sarah E., 98
  Sarah M., 122
  Theodrick, 84
  Thomas, 306
  Thos., 306
  Walter B., 84
  William, 208, 261
WILLIAMSON
  Annie, 1
  Carlene B., 1
  Geo. D., 1
  Olympa, 142
  Thos. H., 142
WILLIS
  Clara H., 201
  E. J., 233
  Emma E., 299
  Mr., 301
  Peyton E., 233
  Thomas H., 299
WILMARTH
  W. Benton, 327
WILMER
  J. B. P., 301
WILS
  Mary, 43
WILSON
  Alpheus, 245
  Alpheus W., 149
  Anna B., 29
  Belle, 97
  Charlotte, 29
  Charlotte F., 191
  Cora E., 200
  Corushia S., 184
  Elizabeth, 125
  Elizabeth N., 182
  Enoch, 100
  James W., 123
  Moses, 87
  N., 97
  Norval, 159
  Norvell, 245
  Ophelia F., 63
  Robert, 120
  T. R., 215
  W. A., 241
  Wm., 125, 182
  Wm. A., 230
WILT
  Frank, 219
  Margaret A., 219
  Theodore F., 252
WINCHESTER
  Jacob, 185
  Jas. R., 295
  W. R., 185, 305
WINE
  Daniel T., 100
  Jacob, 119
  Louis D., 164
  Thomas D., 57
WINEGERD
  E. F., 167
  J. P., 167
WINN
  Cora F., 170
WINSTON
  Edmund, 18
  John J., 189
WINTERSMITH
  Charles G., 38
WIRE
  Kate M., 143
  Lizzie E., 149
WIRTZ
  Wm., 296
WISE
  Ella, 293
  Frank A., 146
  Geo. P., 111
  Henry A., 41
  Mary, 293
  Peter, 5
  Sinah A., 111
  W. N., 293
  William N., 147
WITHEROW
  W. P., 151, 248
WITHERS
  J. Betty, 180
  James O., 235
  Jenneta, 124
  Margaret H., 235
  R. W., 124
  S. Melvin, 180
  Sallie A., 126
  Salmon M., 297
  T. T., 235
WITTICHEN
  Otto, 299
WOLF
  William, 89
WOLFE
  Alfred, 198
  SallieC., 198
WOLFORD
  Charles, 210
  Chas., 210
  George W., 212

INDEX

John W., 210
WOOD
  Ann S., 144
  Daniel P., 262
  Daniel T., 13
  David F., 46
  Eleanor H., 155
  G. B., 16
  Geo. M., 155
  John W., 289
  Thos. B., 192
  William S., 214
WOODALL
  James, 69
WOODARD
  Charles F. M., 291
  Henry, 240
WOODDY
  Amanda E., 77
  Dolly, 82
  Jno. W., 77
  John W., 82
  Mary A., 77, 82
WOODS
  G. M., 229
  Geo. M., 154
  Jacob E., 91
  Margaret C., 155
  Nannie, 229
WOODWARD
  Ann, 76
  Jabez T., 46
  William H., 76
WOODY
  Ellen A., 126
  John W., 126, 131
  Mary, 126
  Mary A., 126
  Rebecca, 58
  Samuel H., 234
  Stephen A. D., 126
WOODYARD
  Nancy A., 10
WOOLF
  W. H., 312
WOOLFORD
  Silas, 322
WOOTTEN
  Edward, 86
WORFORD
  Abraham, 1, 192
  Elizabeth, 1

Margaret J., 1
WORKING
  Jacob, 7
  Lucretia N., 167
WORKS
  Mary A., 281
  Mattie I., 259
WORLEY
  B. Elma, 170
  L. D., 247
WORNAL
  Elizabeth, 279
  James, 279
WORNALL
  William, 306
WORSLEY
  Lizzie, 328
  Thos. S., 254
WORTHAM
  John B., 74
WORTHINGTON
  Eleanor A., 34
  L. W., 1
  Landon W., 1
  Louisa, 1
  Robert, 34
  Sarah, 20
  William B., 1
WORTMAN
  Geo. H., 25
  George H., 249
WREEN
  James O., 140
WREN
  Albert L., 317
  Edward L., 283, 317
  Mary D., 317
  Thos. M., 290
WRENN
  James M., 70
  James O., 114
  Leah H., 70
  Lulu, 140
  Wm., 70
WRIGHT
  Alfred, 217, 227, 229
  Alice, 282
  Ann C., 72
  Anna E., 256
  Bettie, 240
  Edward S., 43
  Geo., 98

Geo. S., 233
Geo. W., 210
George T., 120
Henrietta, 55
John E., 55
Lizzie, 11
Mary E., 55
Robert, 11
Robert L., 55, 240
Robt. L., 57
Sallie E., 139
Sallie M., 241
Sallie U., 40
Samuel P., 100
Silas W., 145
Tenie, 236
Victoria V., 70
W. H., 205
WYATT
  Joshua G., 27
WYCKOFF
  Lavinia G., 308
WYNDHAM
  Bailey, 311
WYNKOOP
  Albert J., 127
  Alfred, 10
  Ann C., 109
  Annie C., 50
  Catharine, 236
  Catherine E., 91
  Charles W., 95
  Chas. W., 230
  Corbin, 250
  Decatur, 181
  Elizabeth, 131
  Flora, 230
  G. W., 250
  Garret A. E., 28
  Geo. W., 25
  George W., 45
  J. E., 250
  James W., 225
  Joseph, 131, 281
  Mag., 253
  Maggie, 181
  Mahala, 253
  Mary E., 28
  Mary V., 175
  MaryE., 164
  P. Henry, 283
  Philip H., 264

Richard, 91
Samuel T., 91
Susan, 264
Thos., 227
William B., 236
William C., 164
William H., 172
YAKEY
  Jane A., 39
  Jno., 48
  Martin, 39
  Minnie B., 289
  Thos. S., 206
YEAKY
  John, 87
  John W., 75
  Mary M., 75
  Virginia, 87
YELLETT
  John, 23
  Rebecca C., 23
YELLOTT
  Coleman, 19
  Emily, 190
  Georgietta, 19
  John, 190
  M. Virginia, 19
YOUNG
  Abram, 247, 326
  Alice, 255
  Bettie, 94
  David, 94
  Deborah M., 93
  Geo., 279
  George, 124
  Georgie, 131
  Henrietta, 122
  Howard H., 16
  Isaac, 314
  J. Edwin, 34
  John, 131
  Joseph, 6
  Lewis F., 179
  Mary E., 34
  Matilda, 307
  S. W., 176
  Susan M., 176, 179
  T. M., 268
  Thomas M., 270
  William, 71
ZACHARIAS
  Lizzie, 76
  Mathias P., 302
  Rev. Dr., 76
ZELLERS
  John, 273
ZEVERLY
  Wentworth C., 278
ZIMMERMAN
  Milton, 219

Other Heritage Books by Patricia B. Duncan:

1850 Fairfax County and Loudoun County, Virginia Slave Schedule

1850 Fauquier County, Virginia Slave Schedule

1860 Loudoun County, Virginia Slave Schedule

Clarke County, Virginia Will Book Abstracts: Books A-I (1836-1904) and 1A-3C (1841-1913)

Fauquier County, Virginia, Birth Register, 1853-1880

Fauquier County, Virginia, Birth Register, 1881-1896

Fauquier County, Virginia, Marriage Register, 1854-1882

Fauquier County, Virginia, Marriage Register, 1883-1906

Fauquier County, Virginia Death Register, 1853-1896

Hunterdon County, New Jersey 1895 State Census, Part I: Alexandria-Junction

Hunterdon County, New Jersey 1895 State Census, Part II: Kingwood-West Amwell

Genealogical Abstracts from The Lambertville Press, *Lambertville, New Jersey: 4 November 1858 (Vol. 1, Number 1) to 30 October 1861 (Vol. 3, Number 155)*

Genealogical Abstracts from The Democratic Mirror *and* The Mirror, *1857-1879, Loudoun County, Virginia*

Genealogical Abstracts from The Mirror, *1880-1890, Loudoun County, Virginia*

Genealogical Abstracts from The Mirror, *1891-1899, Loudoun County, Virginia*

Genealogical Abstracts from The Mirror, *1900-1919, Loudoun County, Virginia*

Jefferson County, Virginia/West Virginia Death Records, 1853-1880

Jefferson County, West Virginia Death Records, 1881-1903

Jefferson County, Virginia 1802-1813 Personal Property Tax Lists

Jefferson County, Virginia 1814-1824 Personal Property Tax Lists

Jefferson County, Virginia 1825-1841 Personal Property Tax Lists

1810-1840 Loudoun County, Virginia Federal Population Census Index

1860 Loudoun County, Virginia Federal Population Census Index

1870 Loudoun County, Virginia Federal Population Census Index

Abstracts from Loudoun County, Virginia Guardian Accounts: Books A-H, 1759-1904

Abstracts of Loudoun County, Virginia Register of Free Negroes, 1844-1861

Index to Loudoun County, Virginia Land Deed Books A-Z, 1757-1800

Index to Loudoun County, Virginia Land Deed Books 2A-2M, 1800-1810

Index to Loudoun County, Virginia Land Deed Books 2N-2U, 1811-1817

Index to Loudoun County, Virginia Land Deed Books 2V-3D, 1817-1822

Index to Loudoun County, Virginia Land Deed Books 3E-3M, 1822-1826

Index to Loudoun County, Virginia Land Deed Books 3N-3V, 1826-1831

Index to Loudoun County, Virginia Land Deed Books 3W-4D, 1831-1835

Index to Loudoun County, Virginia Land Deed Books 4E-4N, 1835-1840

Index to Loudoun County, Virginia Land Deed Books 4O-4V, 1840-1846

Loudoun County, Virginia Birth Register, 1853-1879

Loudoun County, Virginia Birth Register, 1880-1896

Loudoun County, Virginia Clerks Probate Records Book 1 (1904-1921) and Book 2 (1922-1938)

(With Elizabeth R. Frain) *Loudoun County, Virginia Marriages after 1850, Volume 1, 1851-1880*

Loudoun County, Virginia 1800-1810 Personal Property Taxes

Loudoun County, Virginia 1826-1834 Personal Property Taxes

Loudoun County, Virginia Will Book Abstracts, Books A-Z, Dec. 1757-Jun. 1841

Loudoun County, Virginia Will Book Abstracts, Books 2A-3C, Jun. 1841-Dec. 1879 and Superior Court Books A and B, 1810-1888

Loudoun County, Virginia Will Book Index, 1757-1946

Genealogical Abstracts from The Brunswick Herald, *Brunswick, Maryland: Mar. 6 1891-Dec. 28 1894*

Genealogical Abstracts from The Brunswick Herald, *Brunswick, Maryland: Jan. 4 1895-Dec. 30 1898*

Genealogical Abstracts from The Brunswick Herald, *Brunswick, Maryland: Jan. 6 1899-Dec. 26 1902*

Genealogical Abstracts from The Brunswick Herald, *Brunswick, Maryland: Jan. 2 1903-June 29 1906*

Genealogical Abstracts from The Brunswick Herald, *Brunswick, Maryland: July 6 1906-Feb. 25 1910*

CD: *Loudoun County, Virginia Personal Property Tax List, 1782-1850*

www.ingramcontent.com/pod-product-compliance
Lightning Source LLC
Chambersburg PA
CBHW050832230426
43667CB00012B/1972